Designing and Managing Organizations

The Irwin Series in Management and The Behavioral Sciences

L. L. Cummings and E. Kirby Warren *Consulting Editors*
John F. Mee *Advisory Editor*

Designing and Managing Organizations

Stephen L. Fink
R. Stephen Jenks
Robin D. Willits

1983　RICHARD D. IRWIN, INC.　Homewood, Illinois　60430

© RICHARD D. IRWIN, INC., 1983

All rights reserved. No part of this publication may be reproduced, stored in a retrieval system, or transmitted, in any form or by any means, electronic, mechanical, photocopying, recording, or otherwise, without the prior written permission of the publisher.

ISBN 0-256-02628-9

Library of Congress Catalog Card No. 82–83831

Printed in the United States of America

1 2 3 4 5 6 7 8 9 0 MP 0 9 8 7 6 5 4 3

We wish to dedicate this book to our families and friends, who struggled with us through the sturm and drang of its conception and who can now join us in the excitement of its birth.

PREFACE

IN WRITING THIS BOOK we had to make some difficult choices. Should we cover all topics micro and macro, including individual, interpersonal, small group, and leadership, as well as such strictly macro topics as goals, control systems, and the environment? Should we orient it towards the traditional organization theory market, which we see as strongly research-oriented? Should we make it another principles of management text, with a strictly managerial emphasis?

We decided to write a book that would not only provide a framework for *understanding* the organization as a social system but also translate that understanding into its implications for the practice of management. Thus, it is primarily a macro book that contains some concepts that might be found in a principles of management book. We have sought to provide a framework for viewing, understanding, and managing the various activities that constitute organizational life, with an emphasis on the thought processes behind the dimensions and models discussed. That framework views organizations as holistic entities with their various dimensions (goals, structure, etc.) representing different cuts at the one being. It stresses the fact (especially in the last two chapters) that organizations grow, develop, and respond to the outside world in a *total* sense, along all the dimensions simultaneously. While the chapters present topics that are covered in most books on organization and management, they also present various "windows" through which one can view any organization. Each window provides a different perspective, but the scene inside is all of a piece.

The book introduces organizational concepts by way of a set of questions that everyone entering or working in an organization should ask. These questions set the stage for all the chapters in the book, since each pertains to an important dimension of organizational life. Furthermore, the book anchors most of the concepts to experiences familiar to students, as well as to examples of actual organizational life. In this way, even if you have had limited experience in work settings, you can still appreciate the practical value of good theory in a personal and immediate way.

Insofar as possible, the writing style is conversational and organized in a way that makes it easy for you to grasp the concepts and see their application to designing and managing an organization. Thus, the flow of ideas is not constantly interrupted by reference upon reference to various theories and alternative ways of viewing organizations, as are many textbooks in the field. However, additional academic or scholarly material is introduced through an annotated bibliography at the end of each chapter and by means of boxes set apart throughout the chapters; the boxes are used to present material that requires more elaboration or detail than is possible in an annotated bibliographic item.

To use this book to its best advantage, it is important to appreciate the selection of cases. They represent a wide range of contexts: industrial, service, public, private, small, large, high-tech, traditional, innovative, typical, and unique. Some were based on student experiences, others on the authors' consulting work, and many were selected from other sources (International Case Clearing House, other books, etc.) to ensure a balance and rich variety. Some, intended to pose a challenge to one's analytical skills, are lengthy and complex; others serve mainly to illustrate the ways in which the various dimensions of organizational life appear in a particular setting. For those whose organizational experience has been limited in time or narrow in range, the cases can serve as an introduction to a rich variety of settings, with all their inherent problems and dilemmas.

As authors we like to think of this book as a journey into the world of management and organizational life. As with most journeys, it is important to have a map; the theories, concepts, and models offered throughout the book are intended to serve as that map. It is also important to have stopping places, to take the time necessary to appreciate the journey and to identify what can be learned from it; the chapters and sections within the chapters provide those stopping places. Your instructor will be your guide and will help you to know when to stop and when to move on.

Your most important responsibility is to take in and make personally relevant the ideas and insights afforded by those who have preceded you on this same journey. Don't just read the ideas and commit them to memory; apply them to the cases and to your own experience, and think of them as tools for understanding future experiences. By so doing you can become a better manager, both inside and outside an organizational setting.

Stephen L. Fink
R. Stephen Jenks
Robin D. Willits

ACKNOWLEDGMENTS

THIS BOOK has been more than four years in the making. We wish we could attribute that exclusively to the time and care that went into testing the material in the classroom and on different audiences. That was one major part of our efforts, but not the whole picture. The other side of the story really could serve as an additional case study in management, especially the management of time and the management of the enormous number of distractions and diversions that inevitably occur as one pushes forth on a hoped-for straight line to the finish. In other words, the writing of this book represented many aspects of the topics about which we were writing. We had our goals, division of labor, rewards (yet to come!), controls (in the form of deadlines), decision problems, performance evaluations (manuscript reviews), and problems with the external environment (you name it!). It is easier to write about organization and management than it is to organize and manage one's own life.

But we got there, and feel pleased with the result. We feel a stronger identification with those who manage in organizations—as well as a little compassion. We also wish to thank the many managers who, in taking our courses and seminars over the years, provided insightful and constructive feedback on the several drafts of the manuscript. Even though the book is intended for an undergraduate audience, we found the reactions and suggestions of practicing managers to be of enormous value in our attempts to make the material readable and practical.

In the actual preparation of the manuscript, a number of graduate students provided hours and hours of help, ideas, and just plain grunt labor. For their efforts we wish to thank Cynthia Easterling, Lindsay Schuyler, Tom Law, Hilary O'Donnell, and Harry Nelson.

Over the several drafts of the book we were very fortunate to have the critical, helpful, and sometimes painful comments of R. D. Irwin's consulting editors, Larry Cummings and Kirby Warren. As in previous projects with Irwin, we found Larry's and Kirby's efforts to be most constructive. Similarly, we benefitted from the comments of Allen Bluedorn, at the University of Missouri, and Jack Wimer, of Baylor University, both of whom offered extensive and thorough reviews of every chapter. They were direct and constructive at every point, even though at times our own choices did not follow their suggestions. We thank them for the time and effort they gave us.

One of the most important developments in writing technology is word processing. We don't know who invented it, but thank you! And we thank most deeply the people who provided the typing support—both on and off the word processor—including Madeline Piper, Janice Bourque, Debbie Sayers, Pamela Dyson, and Mildred Prussing. But the person who deserves a gold medal for her efforts is Jane Gaskell, who came through with draft after draft of chapter after chapter. We can never really repay the kind of help and commitment she provided, especially during times when her normal work load was heavy. We can credit her for the fact that we did meet our final deadline.

It is also important that we thank the Whittemore School at the University of New Hampshire for providing the support and resources that made completion of the book possible. Dean Dwight Ladd and his assistant, Wayne Burton, were enormously supportive.

S.L.F.
R.S.J.
R.D.W.

CONTENTS

1. Dimensions of Organizational Life **3**

Introduction, 4
1. Goals, 6
2. Structure, 6
3. Climate, 7
4. Reward Systems, 8
5. Controls and Control Systems, 9
6. Decision Making, 9
7. Human Resources Development, 11
8. External Influences, 11

The Special Role of Chapter 9 on External Influences, 12
Related Theory and Research, 13

2. Organizational Goals **15**

Introduction, 16
How We Are Using the Term Goals, 16
The Importance of Goals to an Organization, 16
Superordinate Goals and Values, 17
Overarching Social Values, 19
The Means-End Chain of Goals, 22
Goal Categories, 24
    The Categories as an Aid to Diagnosis, 27
Some Basic Dimensions of Goals, 31
1. General versus Specific Goals, 31
2. Long-Term versus Short-Term Goals, 34
3. Total-System versus Sub-System Goals, 34
4. High-Priority versus Low-Priority Goals, 36
5. Explicit versus Implicit Goals, 38

Overview of Goal Dimensions, 39

3. Organizational Structure **45**

Introduction, 46
    The Example of a Large Orchestra, 47

xiii

Classical Forms of Organization, 48
The Bureaucratic Model, 50
    1. Responsibility and Authority, 52
    2. Span of Control, 53
    3. Line and Staff Functions, 55
    4. Vertical and Horizontal Divisions of Labor, 57
    5. Departmentation, 58
    Implications for Goals, 60
Formal and Informal Structures, 61
    Formalizing the Informal, 62
The Emergence of Modern Structures, 62
    Matching Goals and Resources, 65
    Variables Relevant to Organization Structure, 66
An Overview, 75

4. Organizational Climate 91

Introduction, 92
Climate Defined, 92
Understanding Organizational Climate, 92
    Goals, 92
    Structure, 95
    Rewards, 95
    Size, 96
    Geographic Location, 97
    Physical Setting, 97
    Norms, 98
    Communications (Open and Closed Environments), 100
Dimensions of Climate, 101
Diagnosing Organizational Climate, 103
Consequences of Climate, 105
Changing Organization Climate, 106

5. Reward Systems 113

Introduction, 114
Purposes Served by a Reward System, 114
    1. Attracting and Holding People in the Organization, 115
    2. Guaranteeing At Least Minimal Dependable Performance on the Job, 115
    3. Encouraging Performance beyond the Minimum, 115
    4. Encouraging Initiative and Creativity in Members of the Organization, 115
    5. Promoting Collaborative Behavior, 115
Human Motivation, 117
    What We Seem to Know about Human Needs, 117

Maslow's Hierarchy of Needs, 118
Significance of Maslow's Hierarchy, 123
Herzberg's Two-Factor Theory, 124
Comparison of Maslow and Herzberg, 125

The Nature of Rewards, 126
1. Rule Compliance, 127
2. General System Rewards, 128
3. Individual Rewards, 129
4. Intrinsic Satisfactions, 130
5. Internalized Organizational Values, 131
6. Social Satisfaction, 132

The Entrepreneur—A Special Case, 133

Overview, 134

Rewards and the Individual, 135
Determinants of Effort and Performance: Attraction and Expectancy, 136

Determinants of Attraction and Expectancy, 138
Organizational Context, 140
An Imaginary Experience with a Reward System, 144

Design of a Reward System, 146
1. Organizational Goals and Related Behavior, 146
2. Nature of the Employee Group, 147
3. Long-Run Development, 148

6. Control Systems 157

Introduction, 158
What Is Control? 158
  The Bank Line Example, 159
What Is a Control System? 160
Timing of Controls: Pre, Concurrent, and Post, 160
  Postcontrol Consequences, 161
Purposes of Control Systems, 161
1. Required Task Roles, 162
2. Organizations as Institutions, 164
3. Deviations from Standards, 166

Sources of Control, 178
1. Supervisory Control, 179
2. Self-Control, 180
3. Social Control, 182
4. System Control, 183

Assessing and Designing a Control System, 187

7. Decision Making 197

Introduction, 198

Phases of Decision Making, 200
    A. Problem Discovery, 202
    B. Problem Definition, 203
    C. Goal Setting, 204
    D. Developing Solutions, 207
    E. Evaluating Solutions, 207
    F. Choice, 208
    G. and H. Implementation: Planning and Execution, 210
    I. Outcome and Process Evaluation, 211
    Data Gathering as a Repeated Step, 211
Applicability of the Rational Approach, 212
Behavioral and Emotional Aspects of Decision Making, 214
    Behavioral Barriers, 214
    Emotional Barriers, 217
Dealing with Indecision and Barriers to Decision Making, 218
    Developing Scenarios, 219
    Exaggerating the Issues, 219
Individual versus Group Decision Making, 220
Group as Decision Maker, 224
Organization as Decision Maker, 226

8. Human Resources Development 237

Introduction, 238
Human Resources Planning, 238
    1. Strategic Planning, 240
    2. Work Force Planning (Structure), 243
    3. Job Planning, 245
Individual Responsibility and Development, 246
Recruiting, Selecting, and Hiring, 247
    Goals, 248
    Structure, 249
    Climate, 249
    Rewards, 249
    Controls, 250
    Decision Making, 250
Training and Development, 251
    Career Paths, 253
    Nonprogrammatic Methods: Mentoring, 254
Management Succession Planning, 254
Performance Appraisal, 255
    Specific Purposes of Performance Appraisal, 256
    Performance Appraisal Process, 259

9. The Organization and Its Environment 267

Introduction, 268
   Your Personal System, 270
Multiple Environments, 270
   Economic Environment, 271
   Technological Environment, 272
   Political/Legal Environment, 273
   Social/Cultural Environment, 275
   External Physical Environment, 276
Static versus Dynamic Attributes of the Environment, 278
Static Attributes, 278
   Environmental Complexity, 278
   Environmental Routineness, 279
   Environmental Interconnectedness, 280
   Environmental Remoteness, 281
Dynamic Attributes, 283
   Rate of Change, 283
   Predictability of Change, 283
Impact of External Attributes on Internal Operations, 284
   Static Attributes, 284
   Dynamic Attributes, 288
Planning for the Future, 290
   Desirable versus Undesirable Aspects of the Environment, 290
   Open Systems Planning, 291

CASES 302

Adirondack Preservation Council, 332
An Administrative Decision, 304
Associated Insurance Services, Inc., 306
Blair, Inc. (1), 315
The Case of the Missing Time, 326
Chris Hammond (A), 338
Chris Hammond (B), 348
Conference at Miniatronics, 359
Conflict at a Research and Development Laboratory, 376
Decision at Zenith Life, 383
Design and Delivery: The Dilemma at Eleanor Roosevelt, 412
The Devon School Case, 430
Dominion Acceptance Company Limited, 443
The Eunice MacGillicudy/Marcus Warren Case, 451
Evolution in the Mailroom, 454

The Fate of the Underwriters, 458
Fujiyama Trading Co., Ltd., 464
GenRad, Inc., 473
The Hampton Shipyard, 489
Highland College (Student Affairs Division), 498
The Hillcrest Commercial Bank (A), 508
Hovey and Beard Company, 519
Introducing a New Appliance Model, 524
Is There a Better Way, 527
Lewis Equipment Company, 529
Mailorder Merchandise, Inc., 544
The Mayfield Medical Center, 545
Merger Talks at Canal and Lake, 548
McMaster-Barry Communications, Inc. (MBCI), 558
The Montville Hospital Dietary Department, 568
Omega Aerospace Corporation, 576
Opportunities at Mid-State U., 588
A Promotion in Sri Lanka, 590
The Seacoast Mutual Insurance Co., 597
Southeast Municipal Association, 603
Techni-Cal, Inc., 608
Why Play Football? 616
Working for the Old Alma Mater, 624
Williston University, 632

INDEX 643

Designing
and
Managing
Organizations

CHAPTER 1

Dimensions of Organizational Life

INTRODUCTION

THIS BOOK IS INTENDED to help you think as a manager might think. It is written not only to you as a student but also to you as a future manager. In understanding and managing organizations, there are no absolutes, no surefire methods, no best ways to do things for all situations. It is similar to understanding and managing your own life; different circumstances call for different insights and different ways of coping. What we wish to do is to increase your awareness and provide you with concepts and tools that will help you think more systematically and clearly about the problems and complexities of organizing and managing. If you're looking for easy answers, you won't find them. But if you want to build on and improve what you already know, this book is designed with that in mind.

Although you may think organizing and managing are activities that take place in business, industry, hospitals, and other organizations, people engage in these activities all the time. Such basic things as planning meals for a family, delegating chores around the house, organizing social events, and engaging in community activities all require planning, deciding who should do each task, coordinating the different tasks, monitoring progress and making sure people do what is expected of them, as well as recognizing and rewarding people's efforts. In other words, a great deal of what you normally associate with formal organizations may, in fact, be what you are doing (obviously on a much smaller scale) in your everyday life. By using your own experience as a reference point and by relating what we describe about organizations to that reference point, what you learn will stay with you in a more personal way.

One objective in writing this book is to help you use what you learn as a basis for making better choices about the organization for which you work or will work. Many, if not most, of you are nearing a time when you will make an important decision about a career and the setting in which you will begin that career. Some of you may even have made the initial employment decision and be considering whether to stay with your employer or shift to a different organization. In deciding whether or not a particular organization is the place for you, you might want to consider the following questions:

1. What are the goals and objectives of the organization?
2. What kinds of jobs and tasks are there?
3. What is the atmosphere like?
4. What do people get in return for their efforts in the organization?
5. Are people watched closely or given some freedom in their jobs?
6. How are decisions made and carried out? Individually? In groups? From the top down?

7. How do people find out how they are doing? Are they given guidance when they are not doing well? Are there opportunities to learn and grow? How does the organization go about hiring, firing, and promoting its employees?
8. What is the future of this organization in our changing world? Can I count on its ability to remain solid and secure? What is its place in the overall economy?

These are only a few of the questions you might ask. We have written this book in a way that will help you answer these questions for any organization and, thereby, understand that system a little better before you make your decision about it.

The book is structured so that each chapter addresses concepts pertaining to one of these eight questions. We have not yet used any formal academic language, but if you look carefully at the questions, you will find that they pertain to the following eight topics:

1. Organizational goals and objectives.
2. Structure and division of labor.
3. Organizational climate.
4. Reward systems.
5. Control systems.
6. Decision making.
7. Human resources planning and development.
8. External influences (environment).

In essence, we have an outline for a text on designing and managing organizations. These are all topics you will find in any standard text on the subject (sometimes under the heading of "organization theory"), but they are not as abstract or difficult to understand as the formal language might convey. They are really everyday ideas backed up by years of research, practical experience, and systematic thought.

We have also tried to arrange the chapters (topics) in a way that reflects the order in which the questions would strike you as a new member of an organization. Obviously, your personal concerns and needs will dictate the sequence of questions, but we adopted a general view in our approach here. Whether or not your sequence and ours match will not make any significant difference in how you learn the contents of this book. What *will* make a difference is your ability and willingness to make connections between the concepts and *your* own experience. The rest of this chapter gives an overview of the eight topics and our orientation to them. You will get an idea of the territory to be covered in the rest of the book as well as some of the key building blocks in creating your own theory of organization.

1. Goals

Goals normally are essential in doing a job. You need to have some idea of what you are trying to accomplish. Going on a picnic, putting on a play, and building a house are familiar activities with visible outcomes. In such instances, the goals are relatively clear-cut; the steps toward these goals are also clear and measurable, so you can evaluate your progress as you go. It is not nearly so simple in an organization, but the process is the same. Learning how to articulate goals and keep employees oriented toward them is what management is all about. You may be good at doing that now in your activities, but managing multiple (and often conflicting) goals in a large organization will really stretch your imagination—and your patience.

Most of you who are reading this book have, or will receive, a college degree with a major in some special area (most likely related to management or administration) and will seek employment in a setting that matches your background. You have your own goals, objectives, dreams, and perhaps even a mission in life. The first thing you want to determine is the goals of an organization. Do they match yours? For example, do you want to work for a manufacturer, a service agency, a medical organization, a school system, a consulting firm, or the government? Knowing the *raison d'etre* of the organization is the initial step in your choice to enter or go somewhere else.

Look at some of the organizations of which you have been or are a member. What are their goals, purposes, reasons for existence? Undoubtedly there is a fit between these and your own goals. If there is not, you might ask what you are doing there. Being in school might be a mismatch for some people. Perhaps you are in college only because your parents demand it. It reflects *their* goals, not yours. It is not very different from holding the wrong job but not having any other options. In both cases, motivation is usually low—perhaps no more than what it takes just to "get by." *There can be many reasons for poor motivation, but one very important one is a mismatch between your own goals and those of the organization of which you are a member.*

2. Structure

If you think about the various organizations of which you have been a member, you can probably conjure up pictures of the arrangements of people in them. Where did you fit into these pictures? How did you feel about your place in the system? When you take a job in an organization, these could be the next critical questions to ask.

We are talking about something more than just the job or task to which you are assigned; we are referring to where that job fits into the overall scheme of things, which could be just as important to your success and satisfaction as the work itself.

In its simplest definition, *organizational structure* refers to the arrangement of people established to get the work done. Structure enables people to know where they fit relative to others. A family has a structure, and there are tasks and roles associated with each position in the family. In traditional societies, the family structure with its associated functions and roles is fairly clear-cut and hierarchical. This arrangement reflects who has what authority and responsibility and also provides a natural way to assign chores and duties. Modern families may also have structures, but these are not always so easy to discern. Roles, functions, and decisions tend to be more shared, or sometimes more ambiguous, and often lead to tensions and conflicts.

Organizations have all sorts of possible structural arrangements for getting tasks accomplished. Each possible arrangement has its own strengths and weaknesses. Often the structure of an organization develops over time in a way that may not fit well with some of its goals. The guiding principle in building an effective organizational structure for a family, a church, or a multinational corporation is that *form should follow function*. When this is observed, structure can be invented or changed to suit the changing roles and functions of those who live and work in the organization.

3. Climate

Once you know the goals of the organization and the formal arrangement of its people, how do you understand things that are not prescribed by the rules and job assignments? What is atmosphere of the place? How does it *feel* there? Some settings make you feel welcome and supported, some tense and fearful, some excited and challenged. The goals may match yours and your assigned position relative to others may meet your desires, but you may or may not be comfortable in the climate that pervades the organization. Perhaps it is too stuffy, or too loose, or even a bit paranoid. What you seek is a setting that does indeed "feel right."

One of the most visible aspects of organizational climate is the physical setting—the arrangement of architecture, interior space, furnishings, and decoration. Some settings are inviting, whereas others are foreboding. Look around the setting you are in right now and try to determine what you find inviting and what you find unpleasant. Often we don't pay enough attention to physical settings and the effects they have on overall climate.

In any event, do not underestimate the potential impact of organizational climate on your success and happiness in a job. Sometimes an unpleasant environment can eat away at you in subtle ways; by contrast, a supportive atmosphere can stimulate you to greater creativity and keep you going even in the face of heavy work demands. Next time you go into a company, a hospital, or any large organization, pay particular attention to the "feel" of the place. You can pick up the cues by listening to the levels and kinds of noise or watching the movement patterns and the pace of people. If you are considering working there, try to match your own needs to the setting; that is, determine how you *feel* in that environment.

4. Reward Systems

A *reward* is the payment you get for your efforts; a *reward system* is the whole complex set of rewards that an organization offers its members. We don't need to comment on the importance of a reward system for you when you take a job, but we urge you to examine carefully all its dimensions and complexities. It's easy to find out how much you will get paid, but much more difficult to get a clear picture of other aspects of the reward system, such as recognition, opportunities for advancement, available career paths, and social satisfaction.

People want a variety of rewards in order to enjoy and feel fulfilled by their work. The mix of rewards needed at any particular time in your life may vary. Think, for example, of the reward represented by a good grade in school. It probably has more meaning to you today than it would 20 years from now. Recognition of your accomplishments is an example of an extrinsic reward. The good feelings you have when you achieve a goal is an intrinsic reward. All of us need both extrinsic and intrinsic rewards. Organizations must be able to provide a wide range of extrinsic rewards to respond to the differing needs of their members. It might be useful for you to write down all the different sources of reward that pertain to you. As these sources become more explicit, you may find it easier to match your reward system with that of a potential employer.

Remember, *you* will grow and change and, therefore, may find different things rewarding tomorrow than are relevant today. For example, when you first become a member of the organization, you may feel some strong social needs to get connected with your co-workers. Does the setting encourage or even allow the kinds of interactions that will meet those needs? Or perhaps you think about the long-term security issues that might pertain to a benefits package. Some people find it rewarding just to be associated with a particular organization, perhaps because of its mission or image or reputation. In short, you will want to consider intangible rewards, such as recognition, tangible rewards, such as pay, and the organization's potential to keep on meeting your needs as you grow and develop.

5. Controls and Control Systems

Ideally, a system of controls in an organization should guide or steer the organization along its path, just as you steer a car along a highway. In your family, for example, you can probably think of many activities that were fun and interesting and that your parents did not have to force you to do. Your parents may have exercised control in the form of guidance and planning—for example, on a camping trip or picnic—but there was probably little need for them to nag or cajole you to do your part.

As long as you feel motivated in a task, you are likely to serve as your own control. Certainly most people need a pull from outside once in a while to help along the push from inside, even in those tasks for which they feel the strongest motivation. But the important thing with respect to an organization is the *basis* of its control system—that is, internal or external.

If you tend to prefer external controls to keep you at a job, you may want to find a work setting that provides that type of control. You might find it useful to examine your own needs and try to figure out what kind of job or career would tap into your *internal* reward system. Personal *commitment* to a job generally has a much more sustaining effect than *compliance* to external demands, even though both can lead to productive behavior.

There is another area for which an organization provides a control system; that is in regard to the rules of conduct or social behavior (e.g., dress code, treatment of employees, relations with clients or customers). Some of these rules are spelled out in written policy and others are reflected in the norms of the system. Can you think of the rules of conduct that characterize your family, your social group, the place you work? What about your college or university? You undoubtedly have a copy of students' rights and rules, and you must know what you can and cannot do in the classroom, the cafeteria, the residence hall, or on campus. All these can serve as contexts for you to learn about yourself in relation to an organization's control system. What you learn there can be transferred to other settings, and you can make a better choice about the kind of control system you can accept, thrive under, or simply tolerate.

Control systems, like the steering wheel on a car, must *monitor progress*, *assess results*, and *initiate corrective action*. Too much control permits little forward motion or progress; too little control leads to haphazard movement in unproductive directions.

6. Decision Making

Let's assume that you have finally settled into your job. You have a basic picture of the purpose of your job, where it fits into the total scheme, the overall feel of the place, the rewards you will receive, and the rules you have to follow. Perhaps the next issue you will face pertains to who makes the decisions about your work. Do you direct your own activities? Does someone else (your boss, most likely) do some or all of that for you? Or is it done jointly and collaboratively with your boss or others?

The answers to these questions can have a major impact on your motivation and thus your productivity, satisfaction, and own development. If you prefer to have personal responsibility for decision making, then you will not be happy in a strict hierarchy where decisions come from the top down, with little room for self-direction. On the other hand, if you prefer and work best when others do most of the decision making, then a loose, informal system with a great deal of individual autonomy will be difficult for you.

Perhaps the most useful way to look at this issue is to think of it developmentally. You may need and want little individual responsibility at first, but you may wish to move toward more and more as your competencies and knowledge develop. This philosophy suggests that you look at the organization in terms of opportunities for growth and career development.

In most academic programs, for example, the introductory courses tend to be structured in a way that gives students little freedom or responsibility for making decisions about what to study or how to learn. During the upper-class years, students usually take courses that require more self-management. They can then make decisions for which the previous years of experience and increased knowledge have prepared them.

Similarly, most organizations have ways of making decisions that are consistent with the levels of competence and experience of the employees. Relative newcomers are usually given little responsibility or authority for decisions, which may be appropriate and comfortable for all concerned. In effective organizations, as people develop and demonstrate their skills and knowledge, they are given concomitant freedom and responsibility for making decisions, at least those decisions that most directly affect their work.

There are always exceptions to this scenario, since many newcomers bring with them expertise that enables them to assume more decision-making power than is typical. You may be one of those exceptions. Given all the possible and unpredictable circumstances most organizations face, they need to be prepared to make decisions in a variety of ways, sometimes from the top (an executive decision) and sometimes with participation. You may need to learn to live with that variety, whatever your personal preferences may be.

7. Human Resources Development

When you apply for a job, chances are you will be interviewed by someone in a personnel department. That person's job is concerned with one aspect of human resources development—that is, matching the needs and requirements of the organization to the talents and abilities of people. It's like casting a play or interviewing college applicants; you try to make the best match to produce future success. No doubt you've been through this kind of process, but have you ever had the responsibility of making the decisions? If you have, then you know something of what it's like to carry out a personnel or human resources development function.

Very often it isn't possible to make a perfect match between the task requirements and an individual's abilities. Sometimes specific *training* is needed. The director of a play needs to work with the actors and help them develop their roles; there are very few "stars" who make the parts into themselves. Training, then, is another very important aspect of the human resources development function.

There may be no more familiar activity to you than *performance evaluation*. (Even the most idealistic student is grade conscious to some degree.) Everything else in the organization could suit you fine, but if the system of performance evaluation is weak or unfair or divisive, then you could end up being dissatisfied with your job.

Few people like to be evaluated and not many like to evaluate others, but people do it all the time in one form or another. Unfortunately, the forms are usually vague, ineffective, based on poor data, full of preconceived ideas, and badly managed. What kind of performance system could you live with comfortably? Our guess is that it would have to be one with few surprises, clear acceptable criteria, and a way of allowing (even encouraging) people to *learn and grow* from the process. When you choose to work for an organization, you would do well to learn as much as you can about its approach to performance evaluation. Everything else you do can be colored by the impact of that approach.

Modern organizations view human resources development in the context of long-range planning. Therefore, we will discuss specific activities like recruiting, selection, training, and performance evaluation as part of the overall business and work force plans required to attain the organization's long-range mission. Chapter 9 expands the concept of long-range planning by exploring the organization's relationship with its external environment. It will be important for you to appreciate this relationship.

8. External Influences

What you become as a person depends on both your internal makeup (heredity, temperament, abilities) and your external environment (experiences, parents, teachers, economic factors). It is the same with an organization; its successes or failures, growth or decline, depend on both its internal resources and the environment in which it exists. Radio was in its heyday and loaded with talent when television came along. The speed of air transportation turned the successful railroads into a dying industry.

Would you join a club, fraternity, sorority, or any group that had a poor reputation and was not likely to survive for very long? By the same token, would you want to work for an organization that was on the verge of bankruptcy or had little growth potential? Although we raise these questions toward the end of the book, it may be important for you to think about them before you even join an organization. Your own success and happiness as an employee can be affected by your organization's place in the world. Some organizations are deeply embedded in the surrounding society, such as a bank, a hospital, or the principal employer in a town. These often have a long history shared by several generations of people living in the same geographic area. Some organizations are direct products of new technologies. They grow rapidly and may either become established enterprises or die as rapidly as they grew. Computer companies are examples.

The choices you make about a career and about employers reflect your needs, abilities, values, and the opportunities available to you. If you consider working for an organization, learn as much as you can about both its inside workings and its outside environment. What might appear to be a healthy, exciting internal setting could be badly matched to the world around it and might never survive in that world unless it has the ability to adapt and change.

In thinking about the attributes of an organization, you may find many aspects of a large (or even small) organization too constraining for you, especially if you have an entrepreneurial spirit. Consequently, you might at some time wish to start your own venture. Even though the material in this book is most obviously related to management in relatively large organizations, even the most entrepreneurially minded individual needs to understand the workings of any setting that brings people together for the purpose of achieving a common goal.

THE SPECIAL ROLE OF CHAPTER 9

The last chapter of the book (Chapter 9) integrates all the chapters that precede it. It looks at the impact of external influences on each dimension of organizational life—goals, structure, climate, rewards, controls, decision making, and human resources development. That chapter helps to fit together all the pieces that make up this book; in effect it brings you back to the questions and issues introduced in this chapter. We suggest, in fact, that you read Chapter 9 *before* going on to Chapters 2–8. Starting out with an integrated perspective can help to keep you aware of the forest even as you examine the individual trees.

RELATED THEORY AND RESEARCH

We chose to write this book with application in mind. Insofar as possible, all concepts and theoretical material are linked by example to the real world of the manager. The effective application of sound theory helps to build effective organizations; as the title of this book implies, this is our overall objective.

We also recognize, however, that important research and theory deserve explicit attention, particularly for readers who wish to pursue individual topics in some depth. Although our presentation style is informal and our orientation is applied, we have chosen to introduce a variety of important contributions to the organizational literature by means of two techniques:

1. An annotated bibliography at the end of each chapter.
2. Boxes that describe key research or theory related to a given topic.

These methods are supplemented by a list of suggested readings at the end of each chapter. While we do not suggest that this text provides a comprehensive review of organizational theory and research, we have attempted to provide enough information to get you started in the pursuit of a wide variety of topics that might interest you.

CHAPTER 2

Organizational Goals

INTRODUCTION

EVERYTHING IN AN ORGANIZATION takes on meaning in relation to its goals. Without goals, managers would have little sense of direction, no solid basis for making and evaluating decisions, and no way to plan and organize human resources over time. In fact, organizations are created to attain goals that could not otherwise be reached. It is the job of a manager to make sure that the collective efforts of the organization's members fit together in ways that ensure goal achievement.

In this chapter we will introduce you to organizational life by defining the concept of goals and discussing why goals are important to an organization and its members and how goals get translated into specific activities. We will show you how complicated the task of management is with the multiplicity of goals and their inherent conflicts in an age of change and uncertainty. Then we will present a way of categorizing goals that we have found helpful in understanding and solving problems. Finally, we will discuss some basic characteristics of goals that can aid you as a manager of a complex organization.

HOW WE ARE USING THE TERM GOALS

Organizational literature contains many terms that are sometimes interchangeable and sometimes used differently. In the context of this chapter, we could generate a list of terms—like *goals, objectives, needs, purposes, aims, targets,* and *motives*—and attach specific meanings to each. However, we do not think that is either necessary or important; therefore, we will limit ourselves to the term *goals,* adding to it such qualifiers as *general, specific, short-term, long-term,* and *sub-* and *superordinate,* as they are needed to convey special meaning. We may use another term to avoid the monotony of word repetition; however, it can always be assumed that we are referring to the same concept.

By the term goal, *we are referring to a future state, condition, or outcome toward which an individual or social system is striving.* It is through the attainment of goals that individuals and organizations achieve their sense of success—a fact that attests to their importance.

THE IMPORTANCE OF GOALS TO AN ORGANIZATION

Contrast the times in your life when you've had a clear sense of direction with those when you have not; think about what gives you a sense of identity or purpose, what provides a common bond with other people; and consider how you want to be judged relative to your accomplishments. These kinds of questions illustrate the importance of goals in a person's life; it is really no different for an organization.

Goals are important to an organization because:

1. They represent the basic ideas for what the organization is all about; that is, they define its *mission.* In this way, goals help to give the organization an identity, thus linking it to those people whose lives it affects, and vice versa.
2. They provide the basis for *direction,* for guiding the organization, and for giving its members outcomes toward which they can aspire.
3. Individuals and groups can coalesce around goals; that is, they provide a source of *cohesiveness.*
4. Goals provide bases for measuring progress, establishing standards, and building controls; that is, they provide the means for *evaluation* of the organization's effectiveness and efficiency (see Box 2–1).

As we look at the concept of goals and related issues in detail, keep these fundamental purposes in mind. Such issues as; how specific the goals ought to be, how measurable, over what span of time, in what order of priority, how many, and so forth ultimately can be judged in relation to one or more of these considerations—*mission, direction, cohesiveness,* and *evaluation.*

As a prospective or new employee in an organization, you must ascertain its goals. It could make a difference in your initial decision to join that organization, and it certainly will be important in guiding your own choices as well as understanding the choices of others.

BOX 2–1

EFFECTIVENESS AND EFFICIENCY

Many writers have pointed out the distinction between organizational effectiveness and organizational efficiency.

Effectiveness: Success in moving toward and reaching the organization's goals.

Efficiency: The relative amount of resources consumed in pursuing those goals.

Ideally, an organization would be both effective and efficient, but too often organizations fall short on one or the other. Thus, an organization can be effective yet very wasteful in its use of resources (inefficient), consuming an inordinate amount of raw material and even "grinding up" its people emotionally. Such an organization is similar to a secondhand car that faithfully gets you to school each day but burns a quart of oil every 500 miles and gets only 12 miles per gallon of gasoline.

Similarly, an organization could be efficient yet not effective. If it produced products efficiently so that the cost was low, but failed to provide a product that met customers' needs and quality expectations, it could lose sales. Before long, its goals of profit, growth, and even survival might be threatened. This is analogous to a car that gets 50 miles per gallon of gasoline but is always in the repair shop.

In evaluating an organization's overall performance, both its effectiveness and its efficiency should be considered.

SUPERORDINATE GOALS AND VALUES

Since organizations are created by people, they possess human characteristics. People seek to survive; therefore, they work to attain the necessary economic means to guarantee their survival. It is the same with an organization: it seeks to survive, so it establishes goals (profit, public support, grants, etc.) to meet that purpose.

Survival is an example of what is sometimes called a *superordinate goal*—that is, a goal that supersedes all other goals and serves as an index of the ultimate success or effectiveness of the organization. Other superordinate goals might be to foster a better standard of living for organization members, promote social good [e.g., the role of the American Civil Liberties Union (ACLU) in the civil rights movement], or improve the state of society's knowledge (e.g., the purpose of a university).

Often the superordinate goals of an organization include more than management might orginally have intended. They are determined by members of the organization and by external influences. Whatever their sources, they all are important to the life of the organization.

You are probably familiar with businesses and industries that have become social institutions in their geographic regions. A town grows up around the local mill, or a huge metropolitan district with interrelated spin-off businesses develops from the growth of a single corporation. Such an organization takes on (often unknowingly or involuntarily) superordinate goals that reflect the external environment as much as the original intent of the owners or managers. The decision to establish an organization (whatever its stated purpose) has consequences that affect the lives of many people both directly and indirectly. And every major decision that follows can be understood and judged in relation to its effects on those same people. Whether intended or not, an organization's goals are ultimately shaped by the goals of the people who work for it and the people whose lives are affected by it. By the time the March of Dimes had achieved its ultimate goal of eliminating polio, it had become an established organization that was serving internal members' needs and was part of our society. Whereas a superordinate goal of survival might not have been intended by the founders, it had emerged over time and became the force that moved the organization to adopt a new immediate goal—reducing birth defects.

Unfortunately, not all organizations choose goals that serve the public welfare. Too often, in the name of survival, a company may choose the most expedient goal, with little consideration of values. A company that prides itself on the *quality* of its merchandise or service may sustain quality as its most important goal, perhaps even at the risk of survival. A decision to sacrifice quality for the sake of faster production and greater profit would be a shift in (or violation of) the company's values.

Since values are judgments of what is right or wrong, good or bad, they vary from person to person and social system to social system. It is not our intent here to dictate any particular set of values, only to make you conscious of the connection between goal choices and values. Boxes 2–2 and 2–3 show some ways in which values have been studied in connection with organizational life in this country. Use these schemes as a basis for examining your own values; they can aid choices in your own work life and career.

OVERARCHING SOCIAL VALUES

In Western society we have come to prize three important values: *freedom, distributive justice,*[1] and *security-survival*. (For a comprehensive discussion of how Western society has struggled with these values in relation to population control, see Daniel Callahan's article in the February 2, 1972, issue of *Science*.) While one might argue what priority should be given to each, it is safe to say that they tend to be universal goals of people in our society. As such, they inevitably creep into the goals of any organization. If they are deliberately considered in long-range planning, then the organization is likely to manage them more effectively than if they are considered only when violated. When you join an organization as an employee, you may be trading off one of the three values (freedom, distributive justice, or security-survival) for the sake of another. For example, you take a job to earn a living. Your employer usually sets your working hours, the nature of the work, the pay, and other conditions. You, in effect, trade certain freedoms in order to feel more secure, which, as it turns out, normally gives you some other freedoms (e.g., to buy things you want). If you get paid less than someone else who does the same work, then you might feel unfairly treated and take action to correct the injustice, but only if such an action doesn't threaten your own security (or maybe even if it does, depending on which value is more important to you at the time).

Many large organizations genuinely attempt to maximize these three values, but usually security-survival takes precedence over the other two. Participative management, self-controlled working hours, and other freedoms are generally not seen in companies that are struggling to survive, even though these approaches or philosophies might be the

---

[1] By *distributive justice* we mean the principle that guides people's judgments regarding the fair distribution of the goods and services of society; that is, "to each his fair share."

BOX 2-2

Robin M. Williams singled out the following as "major value orientations in America":

1. Achievement and success—The value we place on achievement is particularly related to "occupational secular achievement" and a tendency to equate "standards of personal excellence with competitive occupational achievement."
2. Activity and work—Our emphasis is on action, on doing.
3. Moral orientation—Americans tend to see the world in moral terms—i.e., in terms of right and wrong, good or bad, ethical or unethical.
4. Humanitarian mores—While often violated, the proverbial generosity of Americans toward other societies facing mass disaster (flood, earthquake) demonstrates its existence as a major value in this society.
5. Efficiency and practicality—*Inefficient* and *useless* are epithets in the United States.
6. Progress—Similarly, *outmoded, stagnant*, and *backward* are epithets that emphasize our concern for progress.
7. Material comfort.
8. Equality.
9. Freedom—Freedom and equality are two values that often conflict. If people are free to pursue individual advantage, over time the equality of condition will disappear.
10. External conformity—Williams says that we tend to define tolerance for nonconformity largely in terms of sanctioning technological and economic innovation. In the field of so-called personal morals, the culture is one in which there is a tendency to legislate conformity—a tendency acted out again and again, from early "blue laws" to Prohibition and the Hays office—making it possible to continue the society in spite of clashes of interests and basic values.
11. Science and secular rationality.
12. Nationalism and patriotism.
13. Democracy.
14. Individual personality—We place a high value on the development of the individual personality and on the individual's independence and self-respect.
15. Racism and related group/superiority themes—Racism has not been confined to the black-white separation. We've always tended to attach value and grant privileges on the basis of race, ethnic group membership, or economic class.

Source: Robin M. Williams, Jr., *American Society: A Sociological Interpretation*, 3d ed. (New York: Alfred A. Knopf, 1970), pp. 452–502.

BOX 2-3

In 1957, C. L. Shartle tentatively identified the following 11 "organizational value dimensions":

1. Size—Bigger is better.
2. Achievement—Accomplishment or at least showing progress is best.
3. Rate—It is better to be fast than slow.
4. Quality—High quality is better than lower quality (even though the lower quality may not be "bad" quality).
5. Effort—Effort for its own sake is good; it is good to try.
6. Satisfaction—It is better to be happy than unhappy.
7. Efficiency—It is better to be efficient.
8. Security—A secure existence is best.
9. Newness—New ideas and things are better than older ones.
10. Changefulness—Frequent change is better than infrequent change.
11. Independence—It is better to be self-sufficient and independent than dependent.

We want to add a few items to this list that we see as common in the business world—namely:

1. Rationality—Being unemotional, logical, objective, and under control emotionally in dealing with problems and people while at work.
2. Status and prestige—Having a position that is respected and admired relative to others.
3. Power—Having and exercising power as a means of getting things done and exerting influence on your environment.
4. Justice and fair play—Being treated equally with others is often more important than the actual way one is treated.
5. Property rights—Respecting the physical well-being of another's possessions and his/her right to their exclusive use.

Source: C. L. Sharlte, "Value Dimensions and Situational Dimensions in Organizational Behavior," *Proceedings of the Tenth Annual Meeting, Industrial Relations Research Association*, 1957.

very key to their ultimate survival.[2] Unfortunately, when people feel threatened, they tend to behave in ways that curtail, not facilitate, the freedom of others. In general, organizations must often make the same kinds of trade-offs that individuals do, since it is rare that all three values can be maximized at one time. This problem also extends to society at large.

What happens, for example, when the freedom of an organization to act in its own self-interest conflicts with the values of the general

---

[2] Recent events in the auto industry reflect possible changes in this direction.

public—that is, threatens the security of large numbers of people? (Note what happens when a company wants to build a plant in a highly populated nonindustrialized area!) The company wants to protect its freedom of choice, but where should the line be drawn between one's own free choice and the consequences for others? Does the government have the right to restrict the free choice of some to protect the welfare of others? Obviously there are no simple answers, but it is also obvious that such value questions cannot be avoided in determining organizational goals.

To understand the significance of superordinate goals and values to the *operations* of an organization, it is necessary to look at the total picture of goals and sub-goals. The relationship between ultimate goals and sub-goals, whether looked at over time or in relation to the structure of the organization, is sometimes called a *means-end chain*. In the next section, we will see how this concept can provide a perspective for viewing the interconnections among the goals and sub-goals of an organization.

THE MEANS-END CHAIN OF GOALS

Whatever the organization's ultimate goals, there are a number of means of pursuing each of them. A goal of profit can be served by an efficient manufacturing activity and a creative marketing program. A goal of safe working conditions can be promoted through equipment design that has built-in safety features and a training program that encourages employees to follow safe operating practices.

Two characteristics of such means to a final goal are noteworthy. The means themselves constitute ends (goals). First, efficient manufacturing does not just happen; it is a goal, or more properly a *sub-goal*, that organizations strive to obtain. It is a sub-goal that itself can be pursued through a variety of means, and these means constitute *sub-sub-goals*. Thus, each major goal of an organization is the beginning of a chain of goals and sub-goals, in which each sub-goal is a means to a larger goal. Second, each sub-goal tends to be a more concrete and tangible objective than the related goal. The goal of efficient manufacturing is more concrete, in the sense that it is a more definitive guide for decision making, than is the goal of profit. As one moves along the means-end chain, the sub-goals tend to become ever more "operational."

Thus, one way to visualize an organization is as a tree-shaped structure of goals, with a means-end chain fanning out from each major goal to more operational goals.

Not only are the goals that are located farther down on the tree (hierarchy) more operational, but they are also less easily related to the ultimate goal to which they supposedly contribute. For example, the sub-sub-goal of conducting quality control inspection and testing, as depicted in Figure 2–1, is designed to contribute ultimately to the organization's survival and profitability, yet it is very difficult to determine the relationship between the amount of money spent to conduct such tests and their contribution to profits and survival. It is equally difficult to determine how stringent the testing ought to be to promote these distant objectives.

Finally, it is common practice to assign responsibility for one or more sub-goals to different individuals and departments within an organization. The individual responsible for carrying out the activities involved in testing may be different from the individual who designed the product and established the specifications against which the product is

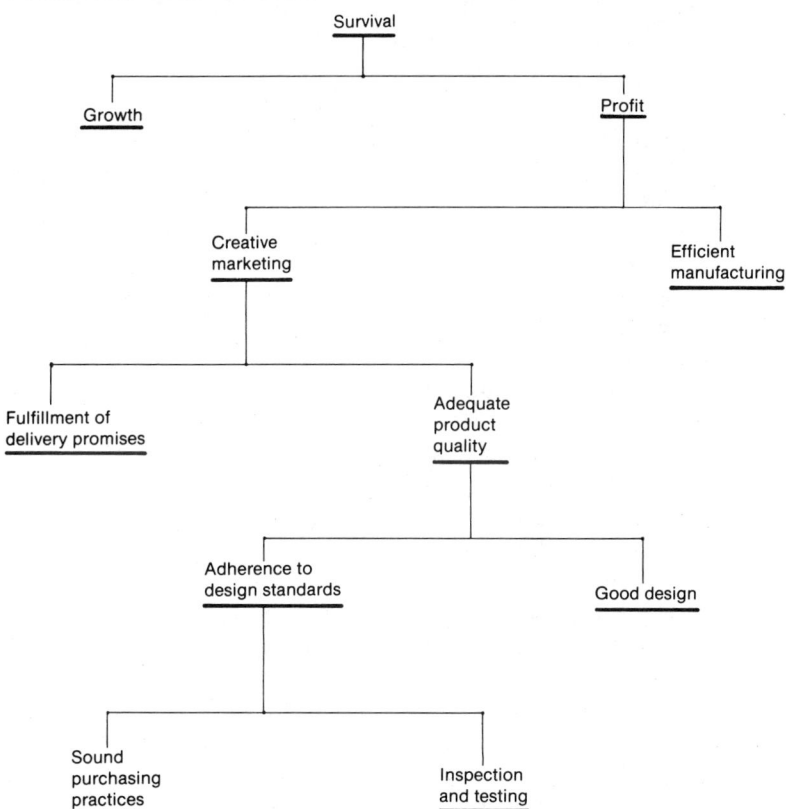

**FIGURE 2–1
Means-Ends Chain of Goals**

to be tested. And neither of these individuals necessarily reports to the person who is primarily responsible for pursuing the goal of a creative marketing program. In a typical industrial organization, the designer would be in an engineering department, the supervisor of testing in a manufacturing department, and neither in the marketing department. In Chapter 3 on structure, you will see where there are certain parallels between the means-end chain (as a goals structure) and an organization's division of labor and also where, as the above example reflects, the parallel disappears.

GOAL CATEGORIES

In this section, we will present a set of categories that will help you diagnose and handle more effectively some of the problems and conflicts of goal management. Like a physician, you cannot effectively deal with a long list of symptoms until you've found a way to organize them. Once the issues are organized in some systematic way, it becomes easier to see the factors beneath the surface and to trace the sources of the problems.

There are a number of descriptive ways of categorizing goals that are useful for creating order out of possible chaos. For example, obvious goal categories for a manufacturing firm are:

1. Financial goals.
2. Marketing goals.
3. Production goals.
4. Quality goals.
5. Technological goals.
6. Growth goals.

A health organization might have a list more like the following:

1. Medical service goals.
2. Health education goals.
3. Research goals.
4. Social goals.

You could probably construct categories like these for all different kinds of organizations and even for a specific setting. Such lists help managers check the degree to which an organization has in fact spelled out its full range of goals. Perrow's scheme, described in Box 2–4, is broader than the ones shown here but is primarily a descriptive classification.

A classification scheme that we think offers a relatively simple but *diagnostically useful* way of grouping goals is based on the work of

BOX 2-4

> Charles Perrow (1970) offered a very general set of categories that, when loosely defined, can apply to most organizations. He suggested the following:
>
> 1. *Societal goals*—These refer to the overall goods and services demanded of any organization of its kind in a given society.
> 2. *Output goals*—These pertain directly to the organization's market and what that demands in goods and services.
> 3. *System goals*—These goals are related to the effectiveness and efficiency of the organization itself, how it desires to operate and govern itself.
> 4. *Product goals*—These define the desired quantity, quality, uniqueness, availability, etc., of the organization's products or services.
> 5. *Derived goals*—These goals are related to the political or social aims of the organization, its relationship to its surrounding community, and how it chooses to deal with that relationship. These differ from the societal goals in that they may not necessarily pertain directly to the products or services of the organization.
>
> A newspaper is a familiar example of an organization that necessarily deals with goals in all five of Perrow's categories. There are certain things that society demands of *any* newspaper (societal goals)—for example, that it provide up-to-date information in a wide variety of areas. A particular newspaper must provide for the interests of its *own* readers (output goals). It needs to manage data gathering, writing, editing, production, and distribution in the most effective and efficient manner (system goals). It must define how its articles, features, special services, etc., will be more attractive than those of its competitors, or at least capable of retaining its readers (product goals). And it must determine its role within the social fabric of the surrounding community (derived goal); for example, does it have some responsibility for the welfare of people affected by its reporting?
>
> If you have ever worked on a school newspaper, you are probably familiar with these goals and might be able to think of areas in which the organization failed to achieve its goals—perhaps failed even to establish adequate goals. This can be a problem for any organization. Perrow's scheme offers a way of checking the adequacy of the range of goals in an organization.

Source: Charles Perrow, *Organizational Analysis; A Sociological View* (Belmont, Calif.: Brooks/Cole, 1970).

Richard Scott,[3] who identifies the following three perspectives on organizational goal setting:

1. A *rational* model in which one specifies the goods, services, activities, and productivity levels in very logical terms, as derived from the organization's self-definition.
2. A *natural* model in which one views the organization as a social system with many unspecified and emergent goals, reflecting the human needs of the system members at all levels.

---

[3] In P. S. Goodman and J. M. Pennings, eds., *New Perspectives on Organizational Effectiveness* (San Francisco: Jossey-Bass, 1977), chap. 4.

3. An *open system* model that recognizes the interdependency of the organization with its surrounding environment, consequently demanding change, adaptation, and flexibility in the exchange of resources.

In using this threefold categorization of goals, we want to point out that the labels (rational, natural, and open system) refer to the *sources* of the goals. A given goal might be rooted in any one or a combination of the sources. When management establishes the official goals of the organization, for example, the list might include goals that serve multiple aims related to all three sources. The goals of a school system would inevitably cut across all three, especially a goal such as providing quality education for the children of a given region (a rational goal), which obviously fits with the needs of teachers (a natural goal) and suits the demands of the people whose children attend the school (an open system goal).

We can neither understand nor evaluate the management of a firm without considering the influences of the surrounding environment—economic, social and political, immediate and remote. (Chapter 9 is devoted to this topic; it might be useful to preview that chapter now.)

Until it happened, most people would not have imagined that the actions of Middle East oil countries could affect the curriculum and course offerings at a university. Yet many colleges and universities, especially in northern states, were forced to cut expenses, limit growth, and even modify calendars as a result of the energy problems. The net result in many cases was limitations on teaching resources, colder classrooms, and inconveniences that inevitably affected the quality of learning that goes on. The espoused institutional goal of quality education could not help but be affected. You could probably list a number of your personal goals that were affected by the energy crisis.

Certainly it was not all negative; our increased awareness of the issue of energy conservation has led to new career paths, new courses concerned with energy uses, and a greater sensitivity to the interdependence of people in the world—and, more specifically, the interdependence of their goals, both organizational and personal.

When you enter an organization as an employee, your perspective will tend to be closely identified with the natural goals of the system. You will see things mostly from the perspective of your own goals (money, achievement, recognition, etc.) and those of your immediate co-workers, superiors, and subordinates. You may be aware of the organization's self-defined goals, but they will take on personal meaning for you only insofar as they match or conflict with your own. As you take on more and more responsibility and, in a hierarchical system, move into higher managerial ranks, you are likely to become more closely identified with the corporate-level rational goals. Unfortunately, many managers, as they advance to the top, lose the perspective of the natural goals, at least those related to the needs and values of the total membership.

To the extent that you can retain a sense of all the sources of organizational goals, which incidentally means keeping yourself well informed on social, economic, and political developments in the surrounding environment, you will find yourself in a stronger position to understand and manage the organizational goals that affect your role as a manager.

The Categories as an Aid to Diagnosis

Managing organizational goals involves dealing with goal conflicts, which generally stem from two sources: (1) *inherent differences* in the nature of the goals and (2) *competition for scarce resources* among departments associated with different goals. An example of an inherent conflict might be a hospital's goal of moving patients through as rapidly as possible, in contrast to that of maximizing the benefits of medical care for each patient; one goal would tend to speed up the discharge rate, while the other would tend to slow it down. Competition for scarce resources occurs frequently in a university setting, where financial constraints might cause one academic department to press its goal of adding faculty at the expense of the goals of other departments. Whichever type of conflict one is dealing with, the goals involved can have their roots in any category of sources. Some conflicts involve goals from more than one source, while others involve only goals within the same category. The difference, as you will see, is important.

Since rational goals are established as a necessary consequence of the organization's self-definition, goal conflicts *within* this category can usually be handled directly by the organization's top management (often at a corporate level in very large systems). For example, a frequent conflict occurs in a manufacturing firm when the goals of *quantity* and *quality* exist side by side. To the extent that management sets priorities for the two or, even better, preestablishes a priority scheme that also includes its other goals, the conflict can be resolved in favor of the higher-order goal. For a company whose products are not intended to last very long, quantity might take priority; for a company whose sales depend on the quality of its products, the reverse would probably hold.

As long as it is clear in management's eyes that the conflict lies *within* a category, the means of dealing with it can be direct and less complicated compared with the case of conflicting goals with sources from different categories. Returning to the above example, suppose the natural goals of the production people stress quality more than quantity, perhaps because of their background and values. And suppose the marketing people want to sell in large numbers, possibly because they work on commission. Now the conflict between quantity and quality is a more complicated issue. It is *diagnostically* important for management to recognize this complication if it hopes to resolve the conflict successfully. In this case, it means involving members of the organization (from production and marketing) in the process of resolving the problem. In short, the strategies for dealing with goal conflicts vary as a function of the kinds of goals (relative to their sources) that are in conflict.

It follows that goal conflicts can be most difficult to resolve when the open system sources are added to the other sources. Consider the preceding example and think of some open system goals or sources related to the same goals (quantity and quality) that might enter the picture. Then think of ways to approach the problem given the additional complications. Consider, for example, what goals might be introduced by consumer advocacy groups or from the influence of the Better Business Bureau.

An interesting example of how the goal of profit can be related to natural sources and *not* be an official goal occurred in a university. The student union, as a part of the total university, was established to serve the personal and social needs of the students apart from their more academic pursuits. Since many students enjoyed drinking beer and since the drinking age in the state was 18, the officials of the university decided to create a pub in the student union. There was no intention of making a profit from the sale of beer and food, simply to provide a socially attractive environment on campus, particularly for the beer drinkers, most of whom normally gravitated to the pubs in town.

It was inevitable that the students and university staff responsible for the management of the pub would become concerned about its cost of operation. Was it paying for itself? After all, the university was already struggling with inadequate funding; why should it subsidize the cost of the drinking needs of students? And the more enterprising students found the idea of making a profit a naturally attractive goal. It gave them a target to shoot at and a basis for evaluating their success. It seemed to have more appeal than just breaking even.

The influence of the surrounding environment—namely, the local pub owners—affected both the goals of the university and the natural goals of the student union pub. Given only the university's goals, it was possible to cover some losses if sales of beer were lower than the break-even point. However, local owners would resent this, because they did not have the luxury of operating at a loss. The competition would be unfair to them. This pressure tended to keep beer prices at the student union close to those at the local taverns.

However, the student pub managers were concerned that they might find it difficult to attract the students away from the town and onto the campus without offering lower prices. Should that happen, the university's objective of having students meet their social needs on the campus would be defeated. In other words, the three sets of goals—the official *rational* university goals, the *natural* student goals (in this case, the emergent desire to make a profit), and the *environmentally determined* goals (coming from the relationship between the student pub and the town pubs)—were not readily compatible.

What would you recommend be done in this situation? How would you go about resolving the goal conflicts? What other probable goals in each category ought to be considered? For example, what other official university goals might affect the situation? What other student needs might come into play? What other outside groups or individuals might have something to say about the problem?

A situation that starts out with a simple obvious set of objectives often becomes complicated by the personal needs of people and the influences of the surrounding social environment. When you, as a manager, establish organizational goals that make sense given the kind of system you are managing, do not forget that the members of your organization bring to their work all kinds of goals that are just as real as your official goals, and that your organization is part of the larger fabric of society, which will also have a lot to say about what goals you pursue.

Our observations and experiences with a variety of organizations suggest the following propositions:

1. *The greater the uncertainty about rational goals, the greater the tendency for behavior to be determined by natural goals.*

2. *When unresolved conflict occurs between open system goals and rational goals, the organization will tend to be dominated by the natural goals.*

The ideal situation is when there is congruence among the three kinds of goals. Take the following example: (1) Government policy on pollution imposes a goal (*open system*) of minimizing air-polluting factors in car engines; (2) people (including employees in the car industry) identify with the goal of having clean air for their own safety and survival (*natural* goal); and (3) the organization adopts the official (*rational*) goal of marketing the desirability of owning a nonpolluting automobile.

Congruence leads to maximum commitment. If either the rational or natural goals of the organization remain in conflict with the open system goals, then compliance is the best you can expect, failure to attain goals is the next best, and outright refusal to act is the worst outcome.

An effective manager will want to generate *commitment* to the task as much as possible, will settle for *compliance* under certain circumstances, but will never find *refusal* to act an acceptable outcome. Therefore, an effective manager will strive to establish congruence among the three kinds of goals and learn to recognize and cope with situations where goal congruence is not possible.

Figure 2–2 shows how the classification model can be used to sort out goals in three different settings: a manufacturing firm, a hospital, and a university. As you look across the rows for each type of organization, you can see where some of the goals in different cells seem to be naturally congruent (e.g., making a profit and providing financial security for employees; advancing medical knowledge and enhancing the status of doctors; serving the surrounding community and offering evening degree programs), whereas others suggest possible inherent conflicts (e.g., create career ladders and increase the number of women in the work force; provide medical care and provide recreation for patients; cater to the prestige needs of faculty and adapt entrance requirements to problems of social deprivation). Also, within a given

FIGURE 2–2
Examples of Different Kinds of Goals in Various Types of Organizations

	Goals		
Type of Organization	*Rational*	*Natural*	*Open System*
Manufacturing	Produce products. Make a profit. Expand markets. Establish and maintain a reputation for quality products.	Provide financial security for employees. Create career ladders. Provide jobs for relatives.	Reduce pollution. Increase number of women in work force. Reduce level of unemployment in community.
Hospital	Provide medical care to public. Advance medical knowledge. Educate medical students.	Provide recreation for patients. Enhance status of doctors. Increase responsibility of lower-level employees.	Expand outpatient services. Permit husbands in delivery room. Provide transportation for minority group employees.
University	Educate young people. Advance knowledge. Serve surrounding community.	Cater to prestige needs of faculty. Offer educational benefits to families of employees. Let students share in decisions.	Offer evening degree programs. Adapt entrance requirements to problems of social deprivation. Increase number of women faculty.

cell you can identify areas of natural congruence versus potential conflict.

The principal benefit of using this procedure is that it helps a manager to identify the constituencies or stakeholders that affect or are affected by the particular goals being examined. This, in turn, helps to make clear who should be involved in any efforts to increase commitment to goals or to resolve conflicts.

At a personal level, it might be useful for you to see how your goals relate to the examples shown and perhaps to add additional examples in any of the cells or to create an additional row of cells reflecting the type of organization in which you expect to work. Furthermore, it could be extremely valuable for you to gather some information about the goals of an organization that interests you, making sure you include data that are relevant to all three categories. This could provide you with an interesting picture of how your personal goals fit with those of the organization and how they relate to each source.

SOME BASIC DIMENSIONS OF GOALS

Organizations normally are not faced with just a few goals to manage; they must deal with an enormous number and variety of goals. It is natural to encounter many problems, inconsistencies, conflicts, and confusions in the process of goal management. Therefore, it is imperative that managers have some way to sort out the multiple goals and establish priorities and time sequencing, so that the goals serve as both incentives to action and bases for evaluating progress.

In this section, we will look at some basic dimensions and characteristics of goals that help to provide a framework for effective management. We will examine the following concepts:

1. General versus specific goals.
2. Long-term versus short-term goals.
3. Total-system versus sub-system goals.
4. High-priority versus low-priority goals.
5. Explicit versus implicit goals.

1. General versus Specific Goals

Goals can range from very general, diffuse kinds of things, e.g., "becoming one of the five leading minicomputer manufacturers" to very specific, concrete purposes, e.g., "raising $1 million for heart research". Sometimes the situation, the economy, the nature of the product or service, and other factors dictate the degree of specificity goals can have and still be realistic. Within those limits, you will still have some choice about the degree to which you want your organizational goals to be specific or general. In making decisions of this kind, it is important to keep in mind the advantages of specific as opposed to general goals (obviously recognizing that it is not black and white but, rather, a continuum).

What we consider general relative to specific can vary depending on the context and how we want to use the terms. For example, in a given sporting event, the team's general goal is to win the game, while the specific goal at any given time is to score points or to prevent the opponent from scoring. In a broader context, the general goal is to have a winning season, in which case the act of winning a single game is considered a specific goal. On an even broader level, the general goal is to have one of the best teams in the division; then having a winning season is a more specific goal. Where does one draw the line between general and specific? There is no clear answer, and it probably doesn't matter as long as we understand their *relative* meanings in a given context.

Box 2–5 presents in some detail the advantages and disadvantages of specific and general goals. Essentially, the more specific the goal, the more readily it can be used as a target, as a means of defining tasks and roles, as a basis for planning, and as a way of measuring progress. The more general the goal, the more it permits flexibility and initiative, maintains a total perspective, and provides a broad base for judging progress.

On the other hand, specific goals tend to sharpen differentiation among individuals and groups in the organization, thereby making it more difficult to integrate sub-goals and ultimate goals. General goals often have the disadvantage of being so vague as to defy attainment, remain open to misinterpretation, and, consequently, reduce the commitment of organizational members.

Organizations operate with both kinds of goals, but a critical task managers face is to maintain the *connections* between the general and the specific. The means-end chain model reflects the kinds of connections we're talking about; the sub-goals in the chain are relatively specific and ultimately must link with the final, more general goals. Serious problems can occur when specific goals become disconnected from general goals. Let's look at an example.

In a large midwestern city, an agency whose purpose was to provide vocational counseling services to the blind had established a general goal of serving all the unemployed blind persons in its metropolitan area. In line with this goal, the agency established a sub-goal for a given year of doubling the number of clients placed in jobs over the previous year. Indeed it was more than successful in reaching its sub-goal, at least according to the measure used. However, upon closer examination it was discovered that many of the clients had been placed in jobs several

BOX 2-5

SPECIFIC VERSUS GENERAL GOALS

Advantages of specific goals:
1. Provide clear targets for direction and easy benchmarks for evaluation.
2. Are intrinsically credible, since they can be closely tied to performance.
3. Facilitate the planning of time, manpower, and physical resources.
4. Translate readily into task requirements and role expectations.
5. Are readily prioritized and sequenced over time.
6. Can be translated into operational costs.
7. Provide a degree of certainty that helps minimize disruptive tensions.

Advantages of general goals:
1. Allow flexibility in work methods, particularly as circumstances change.
2. Encourage initiative and creativity in members of the organization.
3. Keep people from getting locked into specific outcomes and behavior that block seeing the broader perspective.
4. Help keep the evaluation of effectiveness measured in the aggregate sense, not in relation to only a few specific goals.

Disadvantages of specific goals:
1. They tend to close off options when options are needed.
2. They can easily be identified with the actions of specific individuals, thus running the risk of investing those individuals with inordinate power or control. Imagine, for example, the degree of control possible for someone whose job is to locate defects in a product but who never has any sense of the total picture of the goals, only one of which may be quality control.
3. They lend themselves to easy closure, thus encouraging people to maintain a sense of completion and satisfaction relative to a sub-part of a larger task. Too often one finds it easy to sit back and assume "my job is done," only to block the completion of the total job.
4. They can become so specific and concrete that they no longer fit together congruently relative to the whole.

Disadvantages of general goals:
1. Members of the organization may never know when these goals have been attained.
2. It is often difficult to enlist and maintain commitment to them.
3. They can be interpreted in so many different ways that members of the organization can operate at cross purposes and *think* they are working toward the same goal. One example of this might be where the goal of a university is "to bring quality higher education to the greatest number of people possible." The goal is general and vague enough to allow for differing interpretations and, consequently, different specific goals.

times in the same year, thus distorting what seemed to be a fairly straightforward method of measuring progress toward the general goal.

Translating general goals into specific sub-goals is not always simple. Goals can be attained by many routes. Any single objective represents only one route. The agency described above needed to look more closely at what it really means to "serve" its clients. It needed to broaden its sub-goals to cover quality of counseling, fit between client and job, satisfaction of client and employer, and so forth. In this way it could have effectively achieved the general goal.

At times, it may seem impossible for a manager to determine what degree of specificity to use in defining organizational goals. Fortunately, however, some of the other dimensions provide a basis for dealing with this dilemma. General goals also tend to be long term and related to the total organization, whereas specific goals tend more to be short term and related to sub-parts of the overall system.

2. Long-Term versus Short-Term Goals

Most people, when they take a long automobile trip, have a destination (long-term goal) but instinctively look for signs that they are making progress in the right direction (short-term goal). Without these checkpoints, they might become uneasy about the trip, especially if they have a great investment in getting to their final destination. But there is one assurance; chances are their destination will not move somewhere else before they get there.

For many organizations the environment is relatively stable, thereby allowing long-term goals to be relatively certain, maybe even quite specific. But for many others, perhaps an increasing number in this day of changing technology and changing world events, the best a manager can hope for is a very broad set of long-term goals, many of which may become obsolete before they are achieved.

Organizations normally need to have long-term goals for which more specific short-term goals can be developed. The short-term goals serve as concrete incentives to performance and provide criteria for the evaluation of effectiveness. As long as these remain consistent with and connected to the long-term goals, then the attainment of short-term goals moves the system toward its ultimate aims and purposes.

3. Total-System versus Sub-System Goals

Because large organizations are divided into smaller, more workable units (departments, divisions, groups, etc.), and because the goals of the organization get translated into sub-goals that are associated with these various sub-divisions, it is very easy for a group (task force, department, committee) to become strongly identified with its own objectives (i.e., *personalize* them) and lose sight of its relationship to other groups in the system and to the organization as a whole.[4] Each group has its own job of translating long-range into short-term goals, and each group struggles with the related issue of specificity. A key job of a manager is to maintain links with all parts of the system so that the goal-setting process begins and ends with *common* rather than conflicting goals.

The means-end chain model depicts the *structural* relationship between total system and sub-system goals, in addition to the relationship between general versus specific and long-term versus short-term goals. The model implies a *hierarchy* of goals (usually tied to the hierarchy of roles, responsibilities, and authority) that can serve as a framework for integrating the total array of goals. In particular, it is important for a manager to prevent sub-goals (or sub-system goals) from dominating the broader objectives.

Losing sight of the larger picture has serious consequences for any organization. For one thing, departments often begin to compete for scarce resources rather than find ways to make the best joint use of them; their commitment tends to become focused narrowly and without consideration for parts of the organization not directly seen; and goals easily become personalized to the point where judgments are made about people ("good guy" or "bad guy") on the basis of their association with specific goals. To some extent, problems of this sort are inevitable, but a manager cannot afford to let them pass lightly.

One example of a goal conflict that seems to be inherent in the nature of the goals themselves occurs in manufacturing firms where the goals of marketing are not easily reconciled with those of production. The latter often strives for routinization of the manufacturing process, whereas the former may strive for customizing products to customer needs. Neither by itself is "right" necessarily; a balance is most often appropriate. Imagine how the conflict can be intensified if *values* get into it; production people might feel that routine is "good," while marketing people might strongly disagree.

To establish common total system goals, most organizations begin at the top and work down; this is more appropriate for organizations whose missions have been defined by top management in the first place. The managment by objectives (MBO) approach (see Box 2–6) works in this way and normally results in communicating official goals downward in such a way that each level of the organization can translate them into specific operational objectives.

One problem with this approach is that it may not create opportunities for groups and individuals to take responsibility for setting goals that also reflect their own needs and preferences. There may be

---

[4] The term *suboptimization* is used to refer to this phenomenon.

> **BOX 2-6**
>
> ### MANAGEMENT BY OBJECTIVES
>
> One very important and rapidly growing approach to goal management is called management by objectives, which is built around the idea of translating general long-term organizational goals into specific short-term objectives using collaborative methods that involve managers, supervisors, and employees at all levels of the organization. The philosophy behind management by objectives (MBO) was developed by Peter Drucker.* It says, in essence, that commitment to organizational goals can best be achieved by allowing and encouraging members of the organization to play an active role in setting their own work objectives. Through a collaborative process in which superiors and subordinates jointly articulate work objectives, with targets and timetables mutually agreed upon, this approach to management keeps all members focused on the achievement of specific outcomes, which converge over time toward general goals and purposes. The method sets organizational direction as well as generates clear standards for measuring one's own performance.
>
> Since Drucker first proposed his philosophy, there have been thousands of applications as well as hundreds of research studies that examined its effectiveness. It has met with both success and failure, but the key element related to its success seems to be the *internalization of the philosophy*, as opposed to the mere implementation of procedures. (For those interested, there are some key references to MBO at the end of this chapter.)
>
> *Peter Drucker, *The Practice of Management* (New York: Harper & Row, 1954).

cohesion around a common imposed goal but not the same kind of cohesion that occurs when the common goal has emerged from within.

Voluntary organizations offer a good example of total system goals that develop from individuals' common concerns. The specific objectives of the parts of such an organization are, by their very nature, likely to dovetail into the total system goals and therefore require less watchdogging by managers.

4. High-Priority versus Low-Priority Goals

A small manufacturing firm in England faced a goal dilemma in the late 1960s when its main product line, mining machinery, failed to provide adequate income. To survive, the company was forced to expand its product lines into areas unrelated to mining. In doing so, the top management group felt that it was sacrificing, or at least jeopardizing, the company's identity. For many years it had managed to achieve the goals of making a profit and maintaining a reputation as one of the leading manufacturers of mining equipment. Now management had to decide which goal was more important. Since reputation would be meaningless if the company failed, they decided to expand the product line and modify the goals accordingly.

In this example the goal conflict was resolved because the two goals had an implicit relative priority. Profit (which determined survival) necessarily took precedence over image. The example illustrates how the concept of goal priorities can be extremely important in managing multiple goals, with all the potential conflicts.

In many situations, the resolution of a goal conflict is not so easy. Think of some situations in which you could not decide which was more important to you at the time. Suppose, for example, one of your goals was to get a good grade on an exam the next day and another was to spend more time with friends who had asked you to join them in some social activity. If the pulls were equal, then you might feel immobilized. Being out with friends meets one goal but threatens the other, and vice versa. By deciding which goal is more important to you—that is, where these goals lie in your personal priority system—you might find a ready resolution. But not always.

It is the same for a manager, who often must make decisions that serve one goal (or set of goals) and conflict with others. A set of organizational goal priorities is useful, especially if it is understood and supported by the members of the organization. When there is confusion about priorities, some management decisions appear unexplainable or inconsistent with some other decisions. In the earlier example, many employees who did not fully understand the survival issue faced by the company were puzzled by the decision to, as they saw it, become a manufacturer of many products unrelated to mining. What happened to the goal of reputation? Eventually, when they saw the goals in perspective—that is, relative to each other—they could accept and support the decision.

Some aspects of an organization's goal priorities tend to be determined by the natural order of things; goals that meet the survival needs of members often take priority over other goals. Most goals, however, must have priorities set by management and organization members. They reflect values, needs, and capabilities of the organization, as well as external demands and influences.

Effective planning requires setting goal priorities in order to *sequence* the work activities over time. How often have you been so overwhelmed with all the things you need to do that you can't even decide where to start? By establishing your priorities, you can sequence your activities. This does not mean that you necessarily start with the most important thing, although that is often wisest. At times you may need to get the minor things out of the way first to free your mind and energy to work best on the most important things. Priorities do not dictate sequencing; they only provide a framework for it. Their most important function is to keep your perspective focused on the most important matters; in addition, they provide a structure that prevents you from becoming immobilized by imagined chaos.

Because many organizations are hierarchically structured, it is easy to equate goal priorities with levels in the structure. In fact, one trap for managers is to assume that what they are working on is necessarily more important than what their subordinates are doing. They interrupt their subordinates thoughtlessly and thereby disrupt the workers' efforts to manage their time efficiently. Although the goals of top management may appear to take priority over those of middle or lower management, the issue may lie more in the *translation* of goals downward. *The high-priority goals of an organization should be reflected in activities at all levels of the structure; that is, the organizational goal priorities should cut across structure and be congruent at all levels to be effective.* What should be may not be what is, however. Because of the multiplicity of goals, personal needs, group needs, and even extraneous factors often distort the organization's priorities. What seems to be most important to the boss might be less related to organizational goals than to personal ones. Also, since the perspective is different at each level—greater generality, increasing vagueness, and wider time horizons in goals as one moves toward the top—the task of maintaining a consistent pattern of priorities is very difficult.

Even though it might be desirable to maximize the attainment of one's goals, much of the time it seems necessary to settle for something less—namely, the attainment of a given goal only to the point where it does not interfere with the attainment of other important goals. A company that seeks to maximize its profits might find it difficult also to maintain a credible image in the public eye. Reducing its profits might enable that company to achieve both goals. Relative to one goal, this choice often amounts to a *trade-off* for the sake of attaining another important goal. A union might accept a slightly lower wage settlement to gain other benefits or guarantees.[5] Such trade-offs and bargains are an everyday part of organizational life as well as personal life. Can you think of some examples in your own experience? Undoubtedly you have known people who settled for incomes that were less than ideal to remain in a given geographic region. Unfortunately, some managers have never realized that success may not necessarily be equated with individual or departmental goal maximization and, in fact, might even be contrary to it.

5. Explicit versus Implicit Goals

Many organizational goals are stated explicitly; others remain unstated; that is, they are implied by the behavior of people in the organization. Sometimes it seems like the *real* goals of an organization are not the

---

[5] Recent revisions in auto manufacturer contracts with the United Auto Workers Union (UAW) reflect this.

stated goals but the ones you have to infer from what actually goes on. Chances are the real goals are in part the stated ones and in part the implicit ones. When an organization is not fully aware of all its goals, the behavior of the organization is more likely to make the goals that are stated look suspect.

You've probably experienced this same problem in your relationships with others. If a person has blind spots in his or her behavior, they can easily lead to apparent contradictions between expressed intent (explicit goals) and actual outcomes (implicit goals). When this happens, it makes it difficult for people to trust the person who behaves in this way. It may not, in fact, be true that the person's "real" purpose lies in the behavior alone and that the stated purpose is phony. Very often both goals are real but represent conflicting needs of which the individual is not fully aware.

We already know that organizations deal with a multitude of goals, probably many more than any one person ever deals with. Indeed, as some people do, organizations may deliberately state one set of objectives for public consumption and another behind closed doors. In this case, we would have to agree that the real goals are not the stated ones. It can be vital for you, as a member of an organization (especially as a newcomer), to learn how to "read between the lines," to identify the implicit goals. They may become important determinants of your personal success and happiness in that organization.

In general, it might be most effective for an organization to make its goals fairly explicit, but there are times when it is more functional for management to keep its options open by not committing itself to definite goals. Given environmental uncertainties, it can be important for an organization to let some of its means (sub-goals) remain unstated until the moment of action, as long as it retains a clear picture of its ultimate goal.

Overview of Goal Dimensions

We want to emphasize again that these dimensions and characteristics are not independent of one another. In most organizations, top management is most directly in touch with the general, long-range goals, which also tend to be related to the total system and are viewed as highest priority. While not always the case, these highest-level goals are usually made explicit (official) and are used by management as relatively unchanging standards against which sub-goal modifications are evaluated. For example, a company might be willing to revise its sales objectives on the basis of market data, but it would not revise its goal to capture a given share of the market over the long run.

As long as you, as a manager, use these dimensions and characteristics as guides to evaluating your decisions about goals, not as absolute rules that always hold true, then you will find that the multiplicity of goals (and potential conflicts) poses a challenge rather than causes confusion.

One final point we want to make is that the five goal dimensions can be applied to any category of goals—rational, natural, or open system. In fact, while managers tend to be quite deliberate in applying these dimensions to rational goals, the natural and open system goals are frequently treated less thoughtfully. With respect to priorities, for example, rational goals are often *automatically* given highest priority, when, in fact, the highest-priority goals might appropriately encompass all three sources.

Each category of goals includes a *range* of sub-goals, from general to specific, long-term to short-term, related to different levels of the organization, having varying degrees of importance, and being more or less explicitly stated. In the process of sorting out organizational goals using the means-end chain model, it is important to check out goal and sub-goal compatibilities and potential conflicts at all levels within and across categories. It is not unusual to find that a specific short-term goal in one category conflicts with a long-term general goal in another category. For example, a hospital might, because of external pressures to increase bed space, establish a specific goal of cutting the average hospitalization period by 20 percent, only to find that it has violated its highest-priority general goal of quality service. In short, we suggest that by viewing the total array of organizational goals and sub-goals along their various dimensions and across the three categories, a manager is in a better position to understand and manage—and perhaps even anticipate—many of the problems and conflicts that inevitably occur.

SUMMARY

Organizations exist for a purpose. Whether the ultimate (*superordinate*) goal of an organization reflects the desires of the owners, top management, employees, surrounding community, society at large, or some combination of these, that ultimate goal represents the apex of a *means-end chain* of goals and sub-goals. Any one of the organization's goals or sub-goals may develop from the stated mission of the organization (*rational goals*), from the needs of system members (*natural goals*), or as a result of demands imposed from the external environment (*open system goals*).

Whatever may be the sources of the goals and sub-goals in the means-end chain, the goals may be *specific or general, short term or long term,* related to the *total system* or to just a *sub-system, high or low priority,* and *explicit or implicit* in nature. All goals are subject to conflict, some for inherent reasons and others because of competition for scarce resources. Because goals or sub-goals are often associated with particular subsystems of an organization, they are readily subject to inappropriate emphasis by organizational groups (e.g., departments) that lose sight of total system goals.

It is management's job to maintain the connections between general and specific, long-term and short-term, and total system and sub-system goals. Furthermore, it is management's job to establish priorities among the various goals and to determine their appropriate degree of clarity (implicit or explicit), keeping in mind issues related to basic underlying values.

It will be your job as a manager to identify and understand organizational goals accurately and thoroughly, so that you can contribute to their effectiveness in the organization. And it will be your job as an individual to make sure that the organization's goals and values are compatible with yours so that you can be both effective and satisfied—not compromised.

ANNOTATED BIBLIOGRAPHY

Georgion, P. "The Goal Paradigm and Notes towards a Counter Paradigm." *Administrative Science Quarterly* 18 (1973), p. 291.

> Author compares different goal paradigms (goal theories). He contrasts stated goals, systematic goals, and operative goals. Incentive analysis, the potential of an arbitrary focus, replaceability, and dispensability within the context of an organization's goals are also considered. The author concludes that the "emergence of organizations, their structure of roles, division of labor and distribution of power" make up the essential thrust of the counterparadigm concerning "the complex exchanges between individuals pursuing a diversity of goals."

Goodpaster, K. E., and J. B. Matthews, Jr. "Can a Corporation Have a Conscience?" *Harvard Business Review*, January–February 1982, pp. 132–41.

> Borrowing concepts and insights from moral philosophy, the authors attempt to present a perspective to see how to make ethical conflict within an organization manageable. Because the decision-making process concerning ethical issues usually attempts to involve many individuals with disparate backgrounds, the authors suggest that the organization, as the decision maker, exhibits a conscience.

Latham, G. P., and S. B. Kinne "Improving Job Performance through Training in Goal Setting." *Journal of Applied Psychology* 59 (1974), pp. 187–91.

> A study on 20 pulpwood-logging operations conducted by the authors yielded results showing that training in goal setting can lead to an increase in production and a decrease in absenteeism. The authors believe that the worker must be instructed in setting objectives and should be given performance feedback. In the authors' words, "goal setting led to effective performance, effective performance led to job satisfaction, and job satisfaction led to a reduction in absenteeism."

Latham, G. P., and E. A. Locke "Goal Setting—A Motivational Technique That Works." *Organizational Dynamics*, Autumn 1979, pp. 68–80.

The authors discuss the results and implications of a 14-year research project on the effectiveness of goal setting. The research, conducted both in the field and in the laboratory, shows that goal setting significantly increases production and reduces absenteeism and job-related injuries. In establishing goals to effectively motivate employees, the authors contend that they must be specific, challenging yet reachable, and perceived as fair and reasonable. The authors warn that goal setting is no panacea; used incorrectly, goal setting has the potential to add to the problems it attempts to resolve.

Levinson, H. "Management by Whose Objectives." *Harvard Business Review,* July 1970, p. 125.

Levinson argues that the MBO "technique can be improved by examining the underlying assumptions about motivation, by taking group action, and by considering the individual's personal goals first." He asserts that "the typical MBO effort perpetuates and intensifies hostility, resentment, and distrust between a manager and subordinates." The article includes analysis of the major problems in implementing MBO techniques and suggests improvements concerning motivational assessment, group goal setting, task description and appraisal, as well as "appraisal of appraisals."

Mohr, L. B. "The Concept of Organizational Goal." *American Political Science Review* 67 (1973), p. 470.

This article concerns Mohr's belief that the concept of organizational goals is important in the study of political science. He considers several organizational behavior lists and suggests that political scientists be aware that a whole host of goals is involved in a political group. Mohr discusses the intent of individual goals and group goals, different types of goals, and predictable outcomes.

Myers, B. S. "Conditions for Manager Motivation." *Harvard Business Review,* January 1966, p. 58.

This article analyzes both the human and management systems factors that affect levels of motivation. Factors such as interpersonal competence, style of supervision, and meaningful goals are considered. Administrative climate, status, and the delegation process are discussed. This analysis is based on a survey of managers at Texas Instruments. The motivation factors are identified in their goal-setting model, planning operation, and performance review. Projects on work simplification and inventory control are also considered.

Perrow, C. "The Analysis of Goals in Complex Organizations." *American Sociological Review* 26 (1961), p. 854.

Perrow argues that the most relevant type of goal in understanding organizational behavior is the operational goal rather than the official goal. Perrow considers a task-authority-goal sequence. He uses this analysis technique in determining the operational goals of four different hospital organizations. Perrow also contrasts voluntary and nonvoluntary service organizations.

Simon, H. A. "On the Concept of Organizational Goal." *Administrative Science Quarterly* 9 (1964), p. 1.

This article involves defining "organizational goal" in an entirely operational manner. Simon considers the multiple criteria found in an organization and how motivation for goals affects role behavior. Interpersonal differences and the organizational decision-making system are also discussed. Simon concludes that an analysis of the decision-making mechanism greatly contributes to an accurate prediction of the "extent overall goals . . . help to determine the actual courses of action chosen."

Wall, R. H. "Reconciling Organization and Personal Goals." *Personnel Journal,* January 1970, p. 41.

Wall asserts that organizations are becoming increasingly complex, creating growing demand for interaction between organizational functions. Employees are experiencing demands from a growing number of sources while employee loyalty to the company is diminishing. Wall argues that the organization must therefore accept the task of improving motivation, communication, and psychological closeness with its employees. He suggests that determining the employee's personal goals is an important first step in accomplishing these tasks.

SUGGESTED READINGS

Barrett, Jon H. *Individual Goals and Organizational Objectives: A Study of Integration Mechanisms.* Ann Arbor, Mich.: Institute for Social Research, 1970.

Campbell, John P. "On the Nature of Effectiveness." In *New Perspectives on Organizational Effectiveness,* ed. P.S. Goodman, J. M. Pennings, and Associates. San Francisco: Jossey-Bass, 1977, pp. 13–55.

Carroll, Stephen J., and Henry L. Tosi *Management by Objectives: Application and Research.* New York: Macmillan, 1973.

Cummings, Larry L. "Emergence of the Instrumental Organization." In *New Perspectives in Organizational Effectiveness,* ed. P.S. Goodman and J. M. Pennings, and Associates. San Francisco: Jossey-Bass, 1977, pp. 56–62.

Drucker, Peter *The Practice of Management.* New York: Harper & Row, 1954.

Hage, Jerald T., and Michael Aiken "Routine Technology, Social Structure, and Organizational Goals." *Administrative Science Quarterly* 14 (1969), pp. 366–77.

Ivancevich, John M. "A longitudinal assessment of management by objectives." *Administrative Science Quarterly* 17 (1972), pp. 126–38.

Mohr, Lawrence B. "The concept of organizational goal." *American Political Science Review* 67 (1973), pp. 470–81.

Mott, Paul E. *The Characteristics of Effective Organizations.* New York: Harper & Row, 1972.

Odiorne, George S. *Management by Objectives: A System of Managerial Leadership.* New York: Pitman, 1965.

Raia, Anthony P. "A second look at goals and controls." *California Management Review* 8 (1966), pp. 49–58.

Raia, A. P. *Managing by Objectives.* Glenview, Ill.: Scott, Foresman, 1974.

Simon, Herbert A. "On the concept of organizational goal." *Administrative Science Quarterly* 9 (1964), pp. 1–22.

Warner, W. Keith, and A. Eugene Havens "Goal displacement and the intangibility of organizational goals." *Administrative Science Quarterly* 12 (1968), pp. 539–55.

CHAPTER 3

Organizational Structure

INTRODUCTION

PEOPLE HAVE a natural inclination to impose order on the world. They tend to classify experiences into categories, to view others as "types," to plan events, and, in general, to organize or *structure* their lives. Similarly, people impose order on many activities by dividing tasks into sub-tasks, usually to make the work easier. If one of your chores is to wash and dry the dishes, chances are you will rinse and stack them first, then dry them, and finally put them away. By the same token, if several people set out to wash a large number of dishes, probably one will wash, several dry, and one put away, thus adopting a division of labor that parallels the division of the overall task into sub-tasks. This arrangement is undoubtedly more efficient and effective than if everyone simultaneously tried to do the complete job of washing, rinsing, drying, and putting away individual dishes. Finally, in doing each sub-task, each person will probably develop a routine way of doing it and use that method each time the task is repeated; for example, in drying dishes, the person might develop a habit of drying the outside of a soup bowl first and then the inside.

The structure of an organization involves a similar procedure. It creates a way of dividing tasks into sub-tasks (division of labor), assigning responsibility for these sub-tasks to different individuals (specialization), and carrying out those tasks in a consistent manner (standard operating procedures).

As an organization grows to need more than one person to do a particular sub-task, the tasks will likely be grouped into clusters (departments). Since the sub-tasks often need to be coordinated, it is common for another pattern to emerge—namely, a further division of labor between the doers and those who coordinate or supervise. From this pattern has grown the familiar pyramidal arrangement (structure) that is typical of modern organizations, where tasks are clustered into departments, each with its supervisor, and departments in turn are clustered into larger groupings headed by higher-level supervisors (managers).

In short, *organizational structure may be defined as the arrangement of people and tasks designed to accomplish the goals of the organization.* It includes the individual job descriptions, the clustering of those jobs into related and combined tasks, the assignments of responsibility and authority to manage the tasks, and general guidelines that link the structure (division of labor) to the organizational goals. A useful way to look at organizational structure is in terms of two fundamental processes: *differentiation* and *integration*. The first refers to the process of breaking down the task into sub-tasks; the second refers to the process of pulling all the pieces together to accomplish overall goals. Box 3–1

BOX 3-1

DIFFERENTIATION AND INTEGRATION AS BASIC ORGANIZATIONAL PROCESSES:
THE WORK OF PAUL LAWRENCE AND JAY LORSCH

In every complex organization, it appears to be necessary to *differentiate* tasks, roles, relationships, and organizational structure. It is generally taken for granted that subdividing tasks is more efficient than having everyone trying to do the same thing. However, since an organization exists to achieve overall goals, it is necessary to pull the differentiated pieces together—that is, to *integrate* them—which usually is much more difficult than differentiating them.

In their studies of problems related to differentiation and integration, Lawrence and Lorsch discovered that some of the major barriers to organizational effectiveness stem from the consequences of differentiation. These include:

1. Differences in backgrounds and interests of people in various departments or professions.
2. Minimal communication across differentiated groupings.
3. Tendencies of people to stereotype across group boundaries.
4. Differences in reward structures and organizational goals of various units.
5. Tendencies of units to give higher-order priority to their own roles than to those of others or the total system.

The process of integration represents attempts to overcome the barriers generated by differentiation. Some common approaches are:

a. Liaison or integrator roles.
b. Required interactions across groupings.
c. Joint responsibilities for common goals.
d. Task forces or committees with joint memberships.
e. Direct meetings to foster familiarity with each others' areas.

In many organizations, the system as differentiated is very nearly a given, while the tasks related to integration are constant and never ending. It is easier for an orchestra conductor to rehearse each instrumental section than to create a perfect blend of all the sections. And the conductor, unlike the manager, can at least hear the total system at one time.

Source: "Differentiation and Integration in Complex Organizations," *Administrative Science Quarterly*, June 1967; also *Organization and Environment* (Homewood, Ill.: Richard D. Irwin, 1969).

summarizes this concept as developed by Paul Lawrence and Jay Lorsch from Harvard University.

The Example of a Large Orchestra

Did you ever watch how an orchestra conductor works? Imagine you are watching Leonard Bernstein conduct the New York Philharmonic. He doesn't just stand there waving a baton and keeping time. He pays careful attention to the balance of sounds, signaling one or another section to play more softly, pick up the tempo, or emphasize certain notes. For him to communicate with the various instruments, it is necessary for the orchestra to be structured in a certain manner—strings in one place, woodwinds in another, and so forth.

Imagine what would happen if Bernstein tried to conduct 50 or 60 players scattered randomly across a stage—brass, percussion, strings, all mixed together. The sounds wouldn't blend and each player would find it almost impossible to coordinate his or her playing with that of others playing the same instruments. The conductor would be left with a very limited role, waving his baton and keeping time.

The structure of an orchestra is like that of any organization; it makes it possible to carry out its function or purpose. With an orchestra, however, it is relatively easy to "measure" its effectiveness. You can *hear* it directly and, consequently, you can correct and improve the performance without elaborate methods of feedback. Every once in a while, an orchestra plays a composition that deviates enough from the normal pattern that a change in the physical arrangement of players becomes necessary. This is an example of a structural adaptation in response to a new purpose.

Organizations are much more complicated to "conduct" than symphony orchestras. For one thing, the operations of an organization take place over an extended time. Thus, the task of conducting or managing these operations—for example, coordinating them, pushing one department faster, redirecting the performance of another—becomes more complex. As a manager, you cannot be aware of the performance of your total "orchestra" at a given time. For another thing, you cannot easily "go back to the top" and repeat the performance until it's right. However, the structure of your organization plays a critical role in determining your effectiveness as a manager and the effectiveness of the total system and its sub-parts.

As managers of our personal worlds, we create structures that help hold things together, that facilitate the task of organizing and carrying out everyday activities. Because professional managers have a similar task, it is quite natural for them to adopt organizational structures that give them a sense of control over organizational activities.

For as long as organized human activity has existed, the hierarchical arrangement of people—with control beginning at the top—has been an almost instinctive structure.[1] It fits together in an orderly way and thus provides the sense of control normally sought by a manager. And in fact, this classical organizational structure has worked effectively for

---

[1] Think about the typical structures of families, tribes, communities, and nations.

centuries. We will look at why it has been effective and what place it has in today's scheme of things.

An organizational structure does not exist for its own sake. It is there to provide a framework for the functions and activities of the system. And it is only as good as its ability to *facilitate* those functions and activities, not impede them. As you might guess, many organized activities do not work very well through a hierarchy of people. Often some other arrangement is more appropriate, and that arrangement needs to be one that is dictated by the functions it serves, not the other way around.

After looking at the pyramid type of organization, we will explore some alternate forms, some of which are minor modifications of and some major departures from the classical model. We will also show how the variations, while more logically related to the functions, may not be as "comfortable" to people, in part because they are unfamiliar, but also because they go against our instinctive sense of order and control. In other words, some of the organizational arrangements required by the complex tasks faced by modern organizations may, out of necessity, force us to move away from the apparent comfort of the more familiar, traditional forms of organization.

CLASSICAL FORMS OF ORGANIZATION

The familiar organizational hierarchy (or chain of command), though considered obsolete in many instances, is a viable form even today. It is important to understand its roots and to recognize that the conditions under which it developed still apply in one way or another to present-day organizational life.

When people lived in small tribes in scattered villages, there was little need for very formal, let alone complex, organizations other than the organization of the tribe or village itself. But as populations increased and formed large collections of people, the classical form we now call bureaucracy emerged. The earliest organizations to use this type of structure were military armies, the Roman Catholic Church, and the pharaohs of Egypt in constructing the pyramids. In fact, the military and church organizations were the models for early industrial organizations. With the Industrial Revolution at the turn of this century, new means of production made it possible to employ vast numbers of people, making it necessary to design ways of organizing people effectively and efficiently—that is, by creating *a clearly defined division of labor*.

The specific problems faced by industrial organizational managers included:

1. Defining the specific jobs to be done.
2. Assigning people to do those jobs.
3. Maintaining control over the work flow.
4. Minimizing work errors.
5. Meeting deadlines.
6. Minimizing idle time.
7. Maximizing output.

All these matters related directly to the production of goods. Industry had the means to mass-produce consumer goods at a low price, which meant that the more it produced, the more it sold and the more profit it made. Furthermore, it could provide employment for large numbers of people who were not only the producers of the goods but also the consumers.

The managers of these large enterprises were primarily concerned about production and assumed that people could take care of themselves. Around this time (1910), the concept of *scientific management* was introduced by Frederick Taylor in the United States (see Box 3–2). Not too long after that (around 1920), the ideas of Max Weber appeared in Europe (see Box 3–3). Even though Weber's writings were not published in English in this country until the late 1940s, his ideas reflected the thought of the earlier period and, interestingly enough, complemented Taylorism. The idea of scientific management made inherent sense to a world already excited about new discoveries in the physical sciences. The enlightened hopes of the future for a life of abundance for everyone seemed to lie in the sciences. The leaders of industry and business readily latched on to Taylor's proposals and embraced bureaucracy as the ideal way to establish and maintain rational control over their organizations.

Scientific management fits with Weber's model very nicely. In essence, Taylor's approach to management begins with breaking down complex tasks into relatively simple ones, training workers to perform these simple tasks (in the same way a machine might), and then assigning them to carry out the tasks under supervision. Presuming that every job can be scientifically analyzed and broken down in this fashion, Taylor's model assumes that the result is predictable and controllable. Human errors can be minimized through careful training.

This approach has had obvious appeal to the management of large industry. Combine bureaucracy with scientific management and one has maximum control over the production process. Managerial jobs (offices) have clearly defined roles and responsibilities; workers have clearly defined tasks to perform—with very little responsibility.

3 / Organizational Structure

BOX 3-2

TAYLOR'S SCIENTIFIC MANAGEMENT

Frederick Taylor built his concept of scientific management upon the concepts of *research, standards, planning, control,* and *cooperation.* These formed the basis for the following principles of management:

First: Develop a science for each element of a man's work, which replaces the standard rule-of-thumb method.

Second: Scientifically select and then train, teach, and develop the workman, whereas in the past he chose his own work and trained himself as best he could.

Third: Heartily cooperate with the men so as to ensure all the work being done in accordance with the principles of the science that has been developed.

Fourth: There is an almost equal division of the work and the responsibility between the management and the workman. The management takes over all work for which they are better fitted than the workmen, while in the past almost all the work and the greater part of the responsibility were thrown upon the man.

Source: Frederick Taylor, *Principles of Management* (New York: Harper & Row, 1911).

BOX 3-3

MAX WEBER'S IDEAL BUREAUCRACY

According to Weber, the ideal bureaucracy has the following characteristics:

1. Limited areas of command and responsibility attached to each position within the organization.
2. Hierarchial authority structure with control and responsibility concentrated at the top of the hierarchy.
3. Central system of file collections summarizing the activities of the organization.
4. High degree of specialization based on expert training.
5. Activity that demands the full working capacity of the member—that is, full-time staff and the job as a "career."
6. Definite outlined rules of procedure for rational coordination of activities.
7. Impersonality of relationships among the organizational members.
8. Recruitment of officials on the basis of ability and technical knowledge.
9. Distinct separation of private and public lives and positions of members.
10. Promotion by seniority.

Source: Rolf Roger's summary in chapter 1 of *Organizational Theory* (Boston: Allyn & Bacon, 1975).

THE BUREAUCRATIC MODEL

A bureaucracy is a hierarchical arrangement of offices (used in a very general sense), each with specific tasks, roles, and responsibilities. A given office has a reporting relationship to other offices; it normally reports upward to a higher (superior) office and has a responsibility downward to lower (subordinate) offices that report to it. The functions of a given office are carefully prescribed (usually in writing) and exist apart from any individual who might occupy the office. In this way the formal rules and regulations of the organization are presumed to provide all the control necessary to see to it that work is carried out properly. As long as the occupants of the offices exercise their required responsibilities, the system takes care of itself.

The underlying assumption of this organizational form is that by dividing up the tasks into specialties, by assigning individuals authority over clusters of activities, and by spelling out in advance who is to do what and how, the organization can accomplish its task most efficiently and effectively. This form also has the collateral advantage of giving the top a way to exert control over the organization and its members. In this section we will look at some important aspects of bureaucracy that enable it to serve organizational objectives. We will cover the following issues:

1. Responsibility and authority.
2. Span of control.
3. Line and staff functions.
4. Vertical and horizontal divisions of labor.
5. Departmentation.

Then we will discuss briefly the implications of these factors for organizational goals.

1. Responsibility and Authority

Historically, a basic tenet of management was that responsibility should equal authority. In general, it is very difficult to carry out a responsibility unless you do have matching authority. Where your work is defined and closely supervised by another person, you have little responsibility and consequently need little authority. As you are given increasing responsibility, you need to exercise more of your own judgment—that is, authority. Can you think of work experiences in which you have been given responsibility but not the freedom to exercise your own judgment? It can be very frustrating and might even lead to your doing the job badly, or to quitting!

One interesting dilemma of a bureaucracy pertains to the ways in which responsibility and authority are managed. It *seems* very straightforward: As you go up the hierarchy, each office carries with it a higher level of responsibility and a concomitantly higher level of authority. However, the needs of high-level managers for control can make it difficult for them to relinquish as much authority as might be needed by subordinates for them to do their jobs well, especially since the managers themselves are held accountable for subordinates' performance. It appears that responsibility is readily acknowledged as something that goes along with the job (i.e., the office), whereas authority can only be delegated from the top and must be earned. You can see the dilemma this can pose, especially when the boss is reluctant to delegate authority but expects you to carry out your responsibilities anyway. This is not easy to resolve and you may face it in your managerial career.

2. Span of Control

In Chapter 6 we will discuss in detail the various kinds of control systems that organizations use. However, in discussing organizational structure, it is impossible not to refer to the issue of control, since the structure of an organization is itself a form of control as well as a reflection of management's *assumptions* about control.

The bureaucratic model is based on a very formal approach to controlling the behavior of people in an organization. The tasks, offices, roles, and responsibilities are carefully defined to prevent people from departing very far from the assigned jobs. The lines of authority are depicted in the formal organization chart (see Figure 3–1).

In such a model management does not leave much work control to the discretion of the individual or group. Control is vested in the formal lines of authority, with a limited amount assigned to each successive level of the structure. For example, in the typical industrial firm, the line workers are supervised by foremen, who are in turn supervised by first-line managers, then middle managers, and so on up to the executives of the company.

It is important to recognize that the formality of control in a bureaucracy is not necessarily inappropriate nor does it produce totally negative attitudes. On the contrary, it creates important boundaries and guidelines by which employees can do their jobs and meet clearly defined expectations. For many functions (e.g., materials control and financial management) such an arrangement is valuable and helps people get their jobs done.

The purest form of this type of organization is found where technology and methods of managing tend to remain relatively stable over time—for example, in religious institutions, some health professions (like nursing), and many parts of the military. In fact, the concept of "chain of command," which is a way of describing this model, was borrowed directly from the military form of organization.

Since the common underlying issue for all these organizations is control, the immediate problem in setting up a hierarchical organization is the *span of control—that is, how many people, workers, units, etc., it is possible for any one supervisor or manager to control effectively and efficiently at any one time.*

**FIGURE 3–1
Classical Heirarchy***

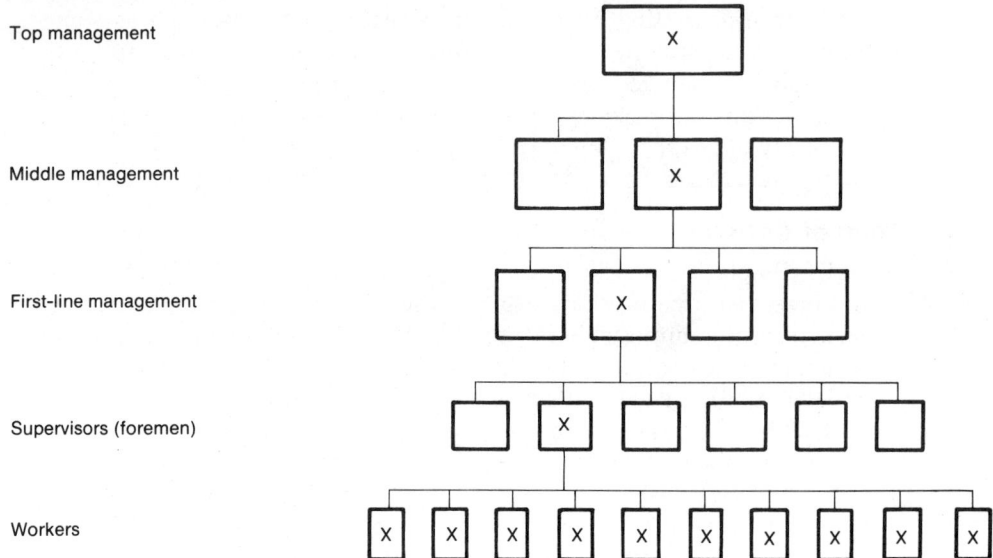

Top management

Middle management

First-line management

Supervisors (foremen)

Workers

*Space limitations permit us to show only one link between each level. In reality, each box (office) at any level may have one or more boxes (offices) at the next level that report to it.

Clearly, there is no rule-of-thumb answer to this question, although some research suggests that *seven* is an optimum number. The answer always depends on such factors as:

1. The type of work being done—whether it is routine, complex, frequently changing, highly interdependent with other tasks, and so on.
2. The competence and expertise of the person doing the job—whether he or she is a highly trained specialist or minimally trained, personally dedicated or indifferent to the work, and so on.
3. The competence and expertise of the person supervising or managing—whether he or she possesses the technical and managerial skills that are congruent with the higher-level role.
4. The relationship between the supervisor and supervisees—such matters as respect, willingness to listen and learn, and legitimacy of the supervisor in the eyes of those supervised.
5. The environmental pressures on the organization to maximize

production, service, or quality over and above all other considerations.

For example, the supervisor of a typing pool that handles repetitive material can normally oversee more than seven typists, since productivity and quality can be monitored easily. If nonroutine, more complex jobs come in, such as ones that go beyond the normal typing skills of the workers, the amount of control required by the supervisor would increase and consequently the appropriate span of control might have to decrease. This would be further affected by the attitudes of the typists; if they resented the extra work or if they did not respect the supervisor, then even more control (smaller span) might be needed to get the work out. These kinds of issues will be covered in great detail in Chapter 6, which is devoted to control systems.

3. Line and Staff Functions

The classical model as discussed so far, with its chain of command, spans of control, formal lines of authority, and clearly defined roles and responsibilities, has been used in relation to the *line* operations of the organization—that is, its direct production and service activities. The history of the classical model, however, has included some important and interesting variations on the basic theme, one of which is the so-called *staff* organization, which runs parallel to and complements the line organization. Originally, staff served in a supportive role relative to the line organization.

Imagine yourself managing a business, with all your time spent on matters directly concerning the task. How would you manage, in addition to all this, the problems of hiring, training, keeping abreast of the latest technology, establishing benefit plans, negotiating with a union, and so on? You couldn't. And neither could the line managers of any of the large organizations, especially with all the changing technological, social, economic, and political forces impinging on them. Managers had to create resources just to manage these additional functions, some of which started out as advisory to management (e.g., market research, technical research and development, personnel), later to become integral parts of the line organization. Even those that remained staff often developed levels of authority that equaled (and often exceeded) those of comparable line positions.

Did you know, for example, that a personnel department was not a normal part of an organization in the early 1900s? People performed the personnel functions—recruiting, hiring, orienting and training, disciplining, advising, etc.—but they were line managers who performed these other functions over and above their regularly assigned duties. In some instances, foremen did their own hiring, and there were obvious advantages to this arrangement. You were likely to be hired, trained, and supervised by the same person, which made it easier to know what was expected of you.

However, as various specialized areas that did not fall directly "in line" with the normal operations of the organization became more and more important to these operations, it became necessary to create staff departments. Members of staff departments played key roles and had major organizational responsibilities but normally did not fall directly into the chain of command and, consequently, did not have the same base of authority as line managers, even though they may have had a high degree of influence.

During the last 30 or so years, with all the advancements in technology and the increasing professionalization of management functions, the distinction between line and staff has become blurred. Personnel departments, for example, are now more a part of the line organization; research and development people carry more and more weight in matters pertaining directly to production methods; and one is likely to find top management teams that include such specialized areas as inventory control (once a purely staff function).

Along with this blurring of the difference, there has been a change in the bases of influence (power and control) associated with positions in the hierarchy. In a pure line organization, position defines authority, which determines degree of influence. An officer in the army is treated in a prescribed way by subordinates, irrespective of his experience, age, or competence. The power of a staff member in an organization tends to be based on the expertise associated with the position and how critical that expertise is to the organization as a whole, or at least to the key executives. Sometimes a staff person can carry what seems to line managers to be undue influence in the organization, because he or she has some special knowledge or ability that few others possess.

Some problems associated with the inevitable crossing of boundaries between line and staff are:

1. Uncertainty about one's own role and authority.
2. Confusion in reporting relationships.
3. Undermining of people's roles and their ability to carry out responsibilities.
4. Political game playing on the part of line managers trying to woo the favors of influential staff people.
5. Some uncertainty about who is running the show.

As long as an organization tries to maintain a distinction that is becoming obsolete, it will only perpetuate the uncertainty and confusion that have developed. This is not to say that the line/staff distinction is obsolete for all organizations; we are only suggesting that the increasing complexities of modern organizational life make it more and more difficult to retain this simple notion. As we explore alternative organizational forms, you will see the wide range of options available to managers.

A Hospital as a Case in Reverse Traditionally, hospitals were staffed, managed, and controlled by members of the medical profession. At one time there was no such position as a hospital administrator who was not also a physician. To make things work effectively, a voice of authority was needed at the top; only a physician could carry that authority with other physicians.

An interesting (at least in the present context) aspect of this situation is the fact that the hierarchy of a hospital was referred to as the medical *staff*. Its parallel in industry was the *line*. In other words, it was the staff of the hospital that carried out the principal operations related to patient care, service, research, and education.

As cost control and other such "business" matters became increasingly important, hospitals employed nonmedical people as professional administrators and thus began to face the dilemma of parallel structures with different, and often conflicting, bases of influence and control. Again, confusion and uncertainty developed about who was running the show, who *really* had the expertise to manage a hospital, and how much authority could legitimately be handed over to nonmedical people, whatever their expertise and competence. The issue (in some cases the conflict) still exists in many institutions across the country, and it may not be resolved until it changes from a power struggle to a common mission.

4. Vertical and Horizontal Divisions of Labor

As an organization grows larger, it tends to grow taller and wider. It is up to management to decide just how tall (i.e., how many levels) and how wide (i.e., how many individuals and groups at a given level) the organization should be. That decision is very complicated and depends on:

1. The issues related to span of control (see the earlier section).
2. The number of different departments, functions, and product lines (or service lines).
3. The mix (number and type) of professions and occupations that make up the organization.
4. The status needs of members.

In some professions, the nature of the work and associated expertise do not provide easy differentiation into levels beyond a certain point. The nursing field, for example, distinguishes among nurses' aides, licensed practical nurses (LPNs), and registered nurses (RNs). In addition, RNs have varying specialties (operating room, pediatrics, etc.) and, in some cases, advanced training and degrees (e.g., nurse practitioner). However, if you were to study the structure of a typical nursing department in a large hospital, you would find a great many levels (usually with numbers that identify them) that indicate *status* apart from function or degree. The hierarchy seems to be related as much to the recognition of experience (i.e., number of years) as to the different levels of expertise (even though experience can increase expertise). One of the authors had an occasion to discuss the nursing profession with a nurse in England. She stated that the government defined 16 levels of professional nurses. She also mentioned that in her particular setting (a very large one) *all* 16 levels existed. Can you image what that kind of structure can do to your aspiration and motivation as a nurse entering the system from the bottom?

Modern organizations, particularly manufacturing firms, seem to respond to current technological changes, market changes, and increased competition by diversifying—that is, expanding their range of product lines and services. (This will be explored further in Chapter 9.) Consequently, they tend to grow horizontally more than vertically. The number of vice presidents, for example, in a functionally organized company (production, marketing, finance, etc.) is likely to be smaller than in a company organized around product lines. The latter is usually structured to facilitate expansion. However, the horizontal growth often has the effect of requiring more vertical integration, usually for purposes of long-range planning. Consequently, new positions (e.g., executive vice president or regional product line manager) are introduced into the vertical dimension of the organization.

5. Departmentation

The major sub-divisions of an organization are created to accomplish work relative to the following:

1. *Specific functions* (sales, manufacturing, personnel, etc.).
2. *Products and/or services* (television sets, razors, repair, complaints, etc.).
3. *Clientele* (government, schools, discount outlets, geriatric patients, etc.).
4. *Geographic region* (Midwest, East Coast, Latin America, Far East, etc.).

The process of creating these subdivisions is called *departmentation*. It is evident in looking at the four categories, however, that the first two refer to the deployment of *internal* resources, while the latter two refer to the *external* context in which the resources are deployed. An organization that serves a limited clientele in a single locale tends to have greater choice about internal departmentation. The wider the range of clientele served or the greater the number of geographic locations served, the more likely is the organization to use some combination of functional and product/service departmentation.

Internal Departmentation Sub-division by function results in such departments as marketing, production, personnel, research and development, nursing, psychiatry, and social service, each of which is normally associated with some area of training and expertise and also tends to be made up of people with common interests and abilities. This structure is likely to be most evident in an organization that has a limited product or service line, as might be the case for a smaller, more local company or agency.

Sub-division by product or service is reflected in departments such as sporting goods, housewares, furniture, and clothing in a large store; outpatient, emergency, and maternity in a hospital; and farm machinery, trucking equipment, and automotive parts in a manufacturing firm. These are sometimes referred to as service or product lines. Examples of some companies that are organized by product line are General Electric, IBM, and many highly technical manufacturers.

Most *large* complex organizations are departmentalized along both dimensions: products/services *and* functions. This is because any given product or service is likely to require the expertise of several different functional areas. For example, if Digital Equipment Corporation decides to add a new product line, it must design, develop, manufacture, and market that line. Therefore, the sub-organization related to the new product line will include the departments that provide the necessary functions to get the job done.

External Context Two important contexts in which combined departmentation is necessary are sub-units that serve a particular *customer or clientele* and sub-units that serve a geographic *locale*. In both instances, there is likely to be a need for varied expertise as well as a variety of products or services.

Department stores, for example, often place branches in many locales; major manufacturers find it convenient to duplicate some of their operations (with a mixture of products and functions) in geographically remote places; and some corporations establish separate organizational units to serve the government as a principal customer or client.

Serving a single customer or region can provide a common focus for the members of an organizational unit and thus another basis for maintaining cohesiveness. At the same time, however, it is important for members of that unit to see themselves as part of a larger organization with greater resources than any local unit could possess.

A critical issue to consider in determining the appropriate form of departmentation is the efficient use of resources. How useful it turns out to be to have every functional area "at the scene" may depend in part on the nature of the products/services and the technology needed. Some functions might best be managed more centrally, especially ones that depend on very expensive equipment. Financial operations, for example, might depend so heavily on computer data that the cost of using a separate computer system in a remote geographic region or for a single customer/client might be prohibitive. Medical complexes that set up remote units to make their services more accessible often require expensive procedures (x-ray, lab work, etc.) to be carried out at a central location. There are obviously many options for combining resources in a given department. Weighing both the managerial and technological advantages and disadvantages of these alternatives is difficult but often worth the effort if one hopes to maximize the delivery of products or services as well as make the best use of talent in functional areas.

Implications for Goals

In Chapter 2 we discussed the problem of keeping sub-goals integrated and related to total system goals. Structure plays a key role in that problem. Sharp structural separations may keep people "out of each others' way," but they also can block communication. It is very easy to experience closure on a job that begins and ends with you alone. But how many tasks in an organization fit that picture? Very few. Closure on any one part of an interdependent task tends to prevent the successful completion of the whole task. This is one way in which organizational goal attainment is directly affected by the structure of the organization. We started this book with the concept of goals first and structure next in part because a manager's thinking must follow that same order, so that structure follows function, not the other way around.

When you add to the goals picture the problems associated with departmentation, authority, loyalty, and distribution of resources, you can see how a straightforward simple hierarchy may fall far short of being the best structure for all systems.

In this chapter, you will see how the management of large, complex, and ever-changing organizations generated structures to deal with these kinds of problems. The structures that have emerged over the years involve such crossings of groups and lines of authority that the problems we have just discussed relative to mixed departmentation seem minor. The classical organization of the early 1900s was never designed to handle this degree of complexity. But one should not make the mistake of throwing out the baby with the bath water; the problems for which the classical model was designed continue in modern organizations and thus maintain some relevance of that model even today.

In the next section, we will discuss how matters that were not handled in the formal organizational structure were initially managed through informal systems, which later became legitimized and formalized through the creation of a variety of structures found in modern complex organizations.

FORMAL AND INFORMAL STRUCTURES

Imagine yourself in a job where you must pay attention to the task only, are never to speak with the person(s) working near you, can obtain information or help only from your immediate supervisor (who is not always available), must produce at a prescribed rate, are held accountable for the quality of your work, need the job, and are only moderately interested in the work itself. How do you think you would behave over the long run? Would you stick to the rules and the formal structure? Or would you find a way to bypass them? What kinds of things would lead you to try to get around the system as it is prescribed?

The effective formal organization depends on the ability to predict and control factors and events both inside and outside the organization. However, as more and more managers are discovering, many factors and events are simply not predictable or controllable. Consequently, they are faced with increasing uncertainty for which no preestablished formal structure can be prepared. As we will see in discussing alternative organizational forms, some degree of flexibility (often a great deal) is required to respond to and manage these uncertainties. In a traditional structure, it tends to be the *informal* system that does this.

Furthermore, there are individual needs and goals that the formal structure fails to accomodate. We talked about rational goals as distinguished from natural goals. Now we can see how a formal structure tends to be related to the rational goals of the organization and may provide little room for meeting natural goals. At least this seems to be the case with classical organizations.

Because natural goals exert a strong influence in every organization, it seems inevitable that some structure must develop to provide for them. When the formal structure fails to do so, or even blocks those goals, then an informal structure will emerge to serve them. This is as predictable as the existence of the goals themselves.

An interesting exercise is to construct the informal structure of an organization. Your first clue lies in finding out who talks to whom and about what. Often a manager, in referring to the formal chart, may say, "That isn't *really* how things get done around here." Finding out "how things really get done" is equivalent to constructing a picture of the informal system. If you get an opportunity to visit an organization, especially if you are considering going to work there, make it your business to find out as much as possible about its informal structure.

Your position in the formal structure dictates only part of the roles and responsibilities you will have and how difficult or easy it will be to carry them out.

If, when you are trying to do your job, the person next to you can provide necessary information that you need, then you will be likely to seek it directly, rather than adhere rigidly to the rules and wait for a supervisor to appear. You may feel like you are bypassing the proper channels, but it often facilitates getting the job done. Similarly, if there is some slack time in your work, it will be natural for you to talk to people around you; social needs are not left at home.

To the extent that an organization permits—or even encourages—the informal structure to complement the formal one, it can increase its effectiveness. To the extent that its policies tend to be rigid and fail to legitimize the informal structure, it will pay the price associated with employee resistance, indifference, game playing, and even sabotage. Managers who have learned to understand, respect, and use the informal structure of their organizations are in better positions to know what is going on, to make more informed decisions, and to enhance their own bases of influence and respect. After all, what is more critical to effective management than being well informed?

Formalizing the Informal

The history of modern organizational structures has, in effect, amounted to a process of formalizing in systematic ways the various informal structures that have emerged in the more traditional organizations over time. Such problems as crossing the lines of authority or bypassing the rules, once thought to be akin to criminal acts, began to be recognized as useful ways to get information quickly to the scene of action or to get a decision made rapidly by the appropriate combination of resources. In other words, some of the so-called violations of the formal system stemmed from the legitimate needs and goals of individuals, some from the functions required of groups, and others from the requirement for varied expertise not normally built into the formal structure.

In the final section of this chapter, we will review organizational structures that have developed in relation to each of the three objectives —individual, group, and system—and offer some guidelines for matching structures with functions and purposes.

THE EMERGENCE OF MODERN STRUCTURES

It may be that a picture is worth a thousand words, but it should never be confused with reality. Organization charts are pictures or maps that are representations of what an organization is supposed to look like—obviously oversimplified. Unfortunately, the picture is just a picture, even though many managers may think otherwise.

One of the authors once consulted with the employment services division of a state government. In trying to set up a training program, the consultant was meeting with one of the administrators responsible for programs in the given area. The administrator required approval for his actions from someone in higher authority but always had to go through several other people first. In explaining this procedure to the consultant, the administrator pulled out the division's organization chart and pointed out the lines (channels) he was required to follow. The absurdity in the situation was that the two people (offices) he had to go through had no relevance to or interest in the program under consideration. Furthermore, they were in another area of the building, whereas the superior who did have final relevant power of approval was right across the hall! The chart had become internalized by the members of the system as the *only* appropriate way to get things done. You can imagine how *long* it took to get things done!

Earlier in this chapter we discussed how people naturally impose structure on their worlds and we suggested that the process of management requires that people structure things to accomplish tasks. So far we have shown how organization structure provides managers with conceptual frameworks that facilitate the attainment of goals, but only indirectly have we shown how these same structures can block goal attainment.

One way in which structure can impede function is when it creates intellectual rigidity. When you enter a situation with preconceived ideas, you tend to be selective about what you see and hear. If you happen to bring with you ideas and mental models that are suited to the situation, you will be effective in your actions and decisions. If not, you will tend to distort the problem or situation to fit your thinking. This is what happened in the example just described.

It may feel comfortable to rely on familiar ideas and methods, especially if you have been reasonably successful with them. It is much more difficult to discard or modify your ideas and enter a more uncertain world. But the nature of organizations today demands it.

Try the following exercise:

1. Draw a hierarchical form of organization with the usual lines connecting positions.
2. Write down whatever that chart communicates to you about the appropriate behavior of people.
3. Draw another chart identical to the first but with no connecting lines.

4. Now draw a circle around each manager and his or her subordinates. Note that each manager is enclosed in *two* circles, one as boss and one as subordinate with his or her peers.
5. Again, write down what *this* picture communicates about the appropriate behavior of people.
6. Contrast your two descriptions.

The first diagram is likely to communicate the formal lines of authority and responsibility that characterize a manager's job; the second diagram tends to reflect the group and interpersonal roles that a manager plays, as a member of a group for which he or she has responsibility and one in which he or she has peer membership and a subordinate relationship to its leader. Notice that the hierarchy in each case is the same; only the ways of connecting are different.

If you, as a manager, can keep in mind that your ways of *thinking* about structure can make a great difference in how you manage the tasks within that structure, then you will give yourself the flexibility necessary to cope with square pegs that don't fit into round holes.

During the past 30 or 40 years, organization theorists and managers developed important variations on the basic hierarchical form, variations that take into account the increasing number of roles that have come to characterize management. Most of these roles were not anticipated by the designs of the early large systems, but neither could they have anticipated the changing forces and values in society. The increasing social consciousness of the 1930s, the growth of the human relations movement in the 1950s and 1960s, along with the powerful influence of the social sciences on managerial education, all made it inevitable that organizational forms and practices would change (see Box 3–4).

We do not plan to review all the developments of the past 40 years. For those interested, the references at the end of this chapter include the key contributions to this growth. (In particular, note the work of Likert, Thompson, Woodward, Burns and Stalker, and Lawrence and Lorsch.) Our focus will remain on the *issues* pertaining to structure and on the different organizational designs and concepts intended to deal with those issues. It should be obvious by now that no one type of structure can serve every type of organization effectively. In her landmark research, Joan Woodward[2] looked at the *amount* of structure required by organizations and discovered that highly structured organizations worked best for routine and repetitive operations, whereas less structured organizations were more effective for nonrepetitive operations where products or services were limited in number. In the next section

---

[2] *Industrial Organization: Theory and Practice* (New York: Oxford University Press, 1965).

BOX 3-4

THE HUMAN RELATIONS MOVEMENT

The human relations movement began in the 1930s with the famous Hawthorne studies of Elton Mayo, which were a series of projects designed to study the effects of working conditions on worker productivity at the Hawthorne plant of Western Electric. The intent was technological, but the most important findings were social and psychological. Some of the results were:

1. Whenever changes in working conditions were made, both good and bad, output increased.
2. In every department, the supervisor played a different role.
3. A number of employees expressed a dislike for close, controlling supervision.

The most important outcome was the discovery of the importance and power of groups and group dynamics in the management of organizations. It was, in effect, the discovery of the *informal social system*.

Source: The most complete documentation of this research appears in *Management and the Worker*, by Fritz J. Roethlisberger and W. J. Dickson (Boston: Harvard University Press, 1939).

we will discuss the factors that should be considered in determining the particular form an organization might adopt.

Matching Goals and Resources

Different organizational goals require different combinations of human and technical resources. *The appropriate structure (i.e., arrangement of people and technology) for a given goal or set of goals is the one that most directly brings to the task the required resources.* You can undoubtedly think of examples of important decisions getting stuck in "red tape" or having to "go through channels" when immediate action was imperative. You can probably imagine ways in which the informal organization may attempt to get around such a problem. This kind of situation often occurs when organizational structure is no longer serving function but instead is creating barriers to it.

Jay Galbraith[3] views the flow of *information* as a basic variable in determining structure. He defines the issue as *minimizing uncertainty at the scene of action;* he defines *uncertainty* as the *discrepancy between information needed and information available.* For example, to forecast the future sales of a given product (an uncertain task to begin with), it can be vital to have information about previous sales. Not having that

---

[3] *Organization Design* (Reading, Mass.: Addison-Wesley Publishing, 1977).

information increases the uncertainty; an organizational structure that makes it difficult for the key people to have access to the information contributes to that uncertainty. The task of designing the appropriate structure, in Galbraith's terms, is a matter of making certain that management provides for a flow of relevant information to the people and functions where it is needed.

We agree with Galbraith's basic premise but wish to expand on the idea. Uncertainty can be related to many factors in addition to the availability of information itself. The necessary expertise to *use* that information, for example, is a vital factor in reducing uncertainty, as is the credibility of the sources of information, the degree of task differentiation or integration, and many other less obvious factors. Much has been written in this regard, and it will not be possible to cover the rich body of research and theory that has emerged in the last 10 years. Instead, we will present a list of eight variables that seem to be most critical in determining effective organizational structures. We will give examples of how these variables relate to managerial choices but leave you with the responsibility for constructing various combinations and alternative designs. Keep in mind that the purpose of an organizational structure is to provide the best vehicle for matching organizational goals with organizational resources.

Variables Relevant to Organization Structure

The eight factors that are important to determining the appropriate structure for an organization are:

1. The number of information sources required for the tasks.
2. The mix of information sources required for the tasks.
3. The levels of expertise involved.
4. The life of the tasks.
5. The degree of differentiation/integration involved.
6. The nature of the external demands on the organization.
7. The culture of the organization itself.
8. The influences of the surrounding culture.

These are not the only factors to be considered, but they represent issues that have cropped up repeatedly in organizational literature and in the experiences of people directly involved in organizational life. These eight are not presented in any particular order of importance, nor are they all necessarily pertinent to a given situation. It is also important to note that they are not completely independent of one another; some may vary predictably relative to others. For example, as a task calls for a greater mix of human and technical resources, it is also likely to involve more varied levels of expertise as well as more differentiation and integration.

1. Number of Information Sources Required Imagine yourself working for a large construction company that is building some expensively designed condominiums. Your job is to supervise the framing of one of the buildings, and you have a standard set of blueprints to work from. However, the blueprints fail to provide complete information on plumbing, heating ducts, electrical circuits, and air conditioning, all of which must be considered in framing. Assuming that you are an experienced and responsible person, the ideal arrangement (at least the most efficient) would be for you to go directly to the plumbing, heating, electrical, and air-conditioning contractors to obtain the information you need to get on with your job. They are the *sources* of your information, and there are *several* sources, not just one.

If the organizational structure were such that you had to work through your boss to obtain the information you needed, your workers might have a lot of idle time on their hands. Since the sources of information are multiple and varied, direct access tends to be the most effective and efficient way to obtain information.

At a very simple level, as just given, the manager himself can serve as liaison, information monitor, controller, and integrator. Sometimes, however, it is necessary for these different roles to be delegated, particularly when a manager is needed in two or more places at one time. In the preceding example, there may be occasions when one of the carpenters is assigned the task of checking out the locations of drain pipes or the positioning of electrical outlets. The important thing is that the information that is needed be made available *when* it is needed and from the *appropriate sources.*

In large complex systems, we find committees, task forces, and liaison groups being set up just to make sure that all the sources of information are pulled together and fed to the places where they are needed.

It may be stated generally, then, that *the greater the number of information sources required to carry out a given task, the more important it becomes to create organizational structures that provide for face-to-face exchange of information.* With the aid of computers and sophisticated management methods, organizations are learning to design sub-structures whose special job is to move information to and from relevant places in the system. When one is dealing with only a few easily accessible sources, then information flow can be managed directly by those carrying out the tasks.

2. Mix of Information Sources Required This is a *qualitative* variable, in contrast with the previous one, which is quantitative. Returning to the earlier example, chances are that you, as a supervisor, know enough about construction to use intelligently the information from the different sources. However, because you are dealing with *heterogeneous* sources of information, there may be times when you will need to bring those sources together directly at the scene of action. Suppose, for example, the plumbing lines require more space than anticipated and some of that space is occupied by the heating ducts. You may not have at your fingertips the information necessary to reroute plumbing or heating lines. You could run back and forth until you worked out the decision, or you could bring the relevant people together to sort out the options.

In general, *the more heterogeneous the sources of information related to a task, the more necessary it is to create structures that permit direct exchange of that information.* Since time and logistics often mitigate against bringing sources together directly, again we find complex organizations dealing with the issue by creating auxiliary sub-structures (as mentioned in the previous section), but paying particular attention to the *composition* of those sub-structures.

The first two variables, then, dictate the degree to which an organization needs to design into its overall structure different sub-structures to manage information flow and the degree of heterogeneity of those sub-structures. *To the extent that related information sources have easy access to one another, the need for auxiliary structures is reduced.*

3. Levels of Expertise Involved Again returning to the construction example, suppose one feature of the condominiums is energy efficiency, and suppose the company has hired a specialist in this field to advise you on various related aspects of construction. You, as a supervisor, would be hard put to make on-the-spot decisions that might affect energy consumption unless you happened to have that expertise. Therefore, the direct availability of the energy specialist could at times be important to the progress of the work.

What happens in large complex organizations that possess many different areas of expertise, the substance of which cannot be easily passed through nonexpert "channels"? What are the options for pulling those information sources together where and when they are needed?

Organizations that involve sophisticated research, highly technical operations, the invention or creation of new ideas or products, or the challenge of constant environmental change almost always face the problem of integrating the efforts of people with high levels of expertise. Given the nature of the tasks in such settings, traditional organizational hierarchies are not well suited to bringing together related information from multiple expert sources.

In general, *the greater the specialized expertise involved in tasks, the more appropriate it becomes to create organizational structures that bring them into direct contact, and the less appropriate it is to use intermediary channels.* Task forces, special teams, or temporary problem-centered groups may be established in advance to meet this requirement. However, in many organizations, the idea of *free access as circumstances dictate* may be the best way to operate. It is, in effect, a *free-form structure or colleague model*, which permits interactions and exchanges of information among any possible combination of people related to a task. (See Box 3–5 for an example of a free-form structure.)

4. Life of the Task   The classical model of organization is based on the premise that the system is relatively permanent, at least long standing. Modern organizations deal not only with permanent tasks but also with short-lived ones, many of which have a special character that does not readily fall into a traditional category. For example, a manufacturing firm might want to experiment with a new product, to try it out for a short time before deciding whether or not to make it part of the regular line. To test the product, the company might need to create a sub-company (i.e., a *temporary system*) with all the necessary ingredients to carry the process through from beginning to end. The sub-company would need marketing people, development resources, production people, and others, all devoted, for the time being, to the new product. To create such a sub-system would mean pulling people out of the "normal" structure and into a temporary separate structure. This, in fact, does go on in organizations, and appropriately so.

In general, *to the extent that an organization deals with tasks that have varying life spans, it needs to create structural arrangements that depart from the basic organizational structure with life spans that match those of the tasks to which they are related.* This means that you, as a member of such a setting, might operate in different work groupings at different times, perhaps several at one time, and be responsible to different bosses or for different personnel in each context.

Some organizations (for example, ones that operate from government

BOX 3–5

A FREE-FORM STRUCTURE

"No ranks, no titles, nothing but profits. W. L. Gore and Associates has an unusual approach to management structure—none at all." This unusual approach is described in an article in the August 1982 issue of *Inc.* magazine. The subject of the article, Bill Gore, refers to his system of "un-management" as a "lattice organization." In Gore's company, the manufacturer of products made of Gore-tex, "every individual within it deals directly with every other, one on one, in relationships best described as a cross-hatching of horizontal and vertical lines." There are "no titles, no orders, and no bosses." Gore encourages people to manage themselves; he builds on voluntary commitment, as opposed to command. It is important to note that Gore has some 2,000 employees in 20 plants around the world. He does not allow any plant to employ over 200 people, a figure he feels is an absolute maximum for successful lattice management. And successful indeed is Mr. Gore.

BOX 3-6

THE CONCEPT OF SOCIOTECHNICAL SYSTEMS (STS)

Every organization is both a social system and a technical system; the latter refers to the requirements of the task and the former to the possible arrangements of people to carry out those tasks. An effective organizational structure is one "that is responsive to the task requirements of the technology and the social and psychological needs of employees." The concept orginated in England at the Tavistock Institute of Human Relations, where research was conducted beginning in the late 1940s and continuing to the present day on the most effective ways to integrate social and technical systems. It has evolved over the years into much broader concerns that are reflected in the quality of work life movement, which views an organization in terms of its total impact on employees' lives, not just in relation to the required tasks.

STS theory suggests the following criteria for the design or structuring of jobs:

1. Optimum variety of tasks.
2. A meaningful pattern and wholeness of tasks.
3. Optimum length of work cycle.
4. Opportunity to set standards of quantity and quality, with suitable feedback of results.
5. Inclusion in the job of some auxiliary and preparatory tasks (e.g., taking care of equipment, setting up and planning a job).
6. Inclusion in the job of elements that engender recognition and respect from others.
7. Some connection of the job to the overall value of the product or service to the consumer.

If you are interested in pursuing the topic of quality of work life, we suggest the following sources:

L. Davis, "Enhancing the Quality of Work Life: Developments in the United States," *International Labour Review* 116 (1977), pp. 53–65.

A. Wilson, "Quality of Working Life: An Introductory Overview," in *The Quality of Working Life in Western and Eastern Europe*, ed. G. Cooper and E. Mumford (Westport, Conn.: Greenwood Press, 1979).

Source: Tom Cummings, "Self-Regulating Work Groups: A Socio-Technical Synthesis," *Academy of Management Review*, July 1978, pp. 625–34. List adapted from Doc Thorsrud, "Socio-Technical Approach to Job Design and Organizational Development," *Management International Review* 8 (1968), pp. 120–31.

---

grants) are themselves temporary systems. They are project related and, presumably, exist only as long as the project is funded. However, most organizations deal with a mixture of task life spans and, consequently, need to have structures to deal with that mixture. The so-called *matrix organization,* which we will describe later, uses a basic departmentation model, with temporary tasks managed by pulling various personnel out of their "home bases" for short times.

One of the authors consulted with an organization that was totally related to time-bound projects but wished to establish itself as a more permanent system. The task was to identify the common dimensions and functions of the temporary projects, determining which had the greatest prospects for self-support, and then begin to build a group of personnel to form the nucleus of the permanent system. It was a difficult "chicken and egg" problem because the wrong choice of permanent human resources could make it impossible for the organization to manage future projects effectively, but failure to establish the nucleus of resources could make it impossible to attract the projects and contracts that the organization needed to survive.

This example is a reversal of the situation faced by most established organizations that are attempting to adapt their structures to temporary endeavors. Perhaps the big difference is that the task of changing from a temporary to a permanent system is fundamentally a struggle for survival; the opposite is not.

5. Degree of Task Differentiation/Integration Let's return to the construction company. A team of carpenters framing and setting up walls needs to work together in a coordinated fashion, but the separate tasks are not highly differentiated. If you consider various sub-contractors and the differentiation among them is greater this places a greater burden on the construction supervisor to make sure that the work gets *integrated*—that is, that the separate pieces ultimately fit together.

Where differentiation is low, the task of integration is relatively simple; where differentiation is high, the task of integration may be either simple or complex, depending on the nature of the task itself. An assembly line sharply differentiates each job from its preceding and succeeding jobs, but the system is carefully designed so that all the jobs (errors notwithstanding) eventually fit together in a predictable way. Integration is provided for in advance by the technology and planning.

In contrast, the medical services on a hospital ward are highly differentiated, but because of the unique aspects of each patient, the variety of services involved, the different levels of expertise, and the unpredictable events that characterize any serious illness, the task of integration cannot be handled by technology or planning. Integration in this instance is a complicated procedure that requires full-time attention and great expertise. In fact, in many hospitals this task is no longer left to any one person, since no one can be expected to have the range of expertise required. The concept of the medical *team*, made up of the appropriate resources and trained *to work as a team*, has emerged as one viable method of integrating medical services. For such a team to be effective, its members often need to remove their "professional hats" —that is, ignore the *status* differences that might otherwise apply. The integrative process works best when it is determined by the functions being served, not by the organizational hierarchy from which the resources are selected. Imagine the effects on a patient of organizational politics that prevent medical specialists from working together.

In general, *when the levels of differentiation and integration in a task are high, it is important to create organizational structures that directly maximize integration.* Again, depending on the levels of expertise and the complexities of the task, these structures can range from liaison people or groups to task teams composed of individuals whose functions must remain integrated at all times (as in the medical team).

You ought to be able to see by now that as you add together the factors discussed so far, the case for designing modern organizations that have flexible arrangements of people and technology, in addition to existing departments and hierarchies, becomes stronger and stronger. Tasks that depend on multiple and heterogeneous sources of information, varied levels of expertise, both permanent and temporary operations, and high levels of differentiation and integration call for interactions of people and exchanges of information that cut across every direction of the organization's structure—vertical, lateral, diagonal, and a mixture of all three. (See Box 3-6 on a related matter.)

The variables discussed so far are *directly* related to the tasks of the organization. The last three variables we will discuss are tangentially related to the tasks and, though not less important than the first five, are less directly under the control of management.

6. Nature of External Demands on the Organization Some organizations describe themselves as *market or client oriented,* as opposed to *product or service oriented.* Apart from the form of departmentation in the organization, its orientation is often dictated by the *external* demands made on it. If, for example, the continued success of the organization depends on its ability to respond to changing customer or client demands, its structure must be such that resources can be readily shifted and adapted to those demands. Manufacturers of products that have fairly constant, predictable markets (e.g., food, clothing, appliances) need not worry as much about this problem, especially if they have long-established reputations. But those that are breaking new ground or moving into untouched geographic regions require the flexibility to respond to changing external circumstances, many of which cannot be anticipated or are the result of instability in the environment.

A major oil company, which had operated quite successfully with a traditional structure (i.e., chain of command) relative to its normal markets, found that it had to make some structural changes as part of its expansion into foreign countries. Since the expansion involved a broad range of petroleum and chemical products in highly competitive markets, the company needed to provide both expertise and decision-making authority geographically close to those markets. The creation of a self-contained branch—a kind of total company in miniature—proved to be the most effective way to deal with the situation. Unfortunately, there were many occasions when the chain of command of the total company refused to give the sub-system the necessary autonomy to act with dispatch when needed. The irony was that the company had developed a new structure well suited to the external demands but then canceled its effectiveness by letting the old structure, which was not suited to those demands, get in the way.

In general, *the more unstable the external demands made upon an organization or parts of it, the more necessary it becomes to create structures that directly combine the relevant resources close to the scene of action.* Compare, for example, the structure of the emergency division of a metropolitan hospital with that of an extended-care facility in a rural area. The differences can be attributed to many factors, but the most important are related to the external demands made upon each. Imagine what each would be like if it had to operate with the other's structure. Not many emergency patients would survive the time delays to get the necessary treatment, and the patients in the extended-care facility might find the crisis atmosphere confusing, if not frightening.

7. Culture of the Organization In Chapter 4 we will discuss organizational climate, which is determined in part by the norms and customs that characterize an organization. We sometimes refer to these aspects of an organization as its *culture*. In this section, we will pay some attention to the importance of an organization's culture in relation to its structure. In the next section, we will expand our points by looking at the broader cultural setting in which the organization exists.

A well-known pharmaceutical company has all employees report for work at 7:30 A.M., irrespective of their jobs or their level in the hierarchy. This custom was the habit of the company's founder, and he expected *every* employee to follow his example. In its more than 80 years of existence that custom was never challenged, at least to the point where changing it was seriously considered. Despite changes in technology, work patterns, market demands, and employee preferences, it persisted. It was part of the company's history; even more, it was part of its *heritage*. Also part of its heritage were many aspects of its structure, which happened to be, as you might expect, *very* traditional.

From the perspective of the distribution and movement of resources, the company's structure often created obstacles. However, somehow the informal system managed to compensate for these obstacles. Management was fearful that structural changes would violate the culture and might destroy the *image* of the corporation, which was attractive to present and prospective employees.

In general, *to the extent that an organization's structure is embedded in its internal culture, departures are best kept to a minimum.* Temporary systems are often acceptable and useful as long as they are closely linked to the ongoing system, but substantial rearrangements of people tend to be perceived as equivalent to destruction of the system.

8. Influences of the Surrounding Culture This factor has become increasingly important with the expansion of multinational corporations. High-technology firms face seemingly impossible dilemmas as they attempt to reconcile the management approaches dictated by the internal requirements of the organization with those characteristic of institutions in the surrounding environment. Long traditions of family-owned and -operated businesses, patriarchal forms of governance, and culture-bound social status systems exert powerful influences on the possible organizational arrangements in any foreign country.

The computer industry, whose markets have expanded more rapidly than those of almost any other industry in history, is a glaring case in point. The nature of that industry dictates organizational structures that are flexible, often temporary, and able to respond rapidly as information and decisions move in many directions simultaneously. What happens when such an industry runs up against a culture that is bound in traditions of hierarchy, class distinctions, educational privileges, family domination, and so on? Obviously no one company is going to change the surrounding culture, but to what extent can it afford to modify the structures and methods dictated by its own internal requirements to accommodate the customs of the host country? That is a basic dilemma of American companies expanding into foreign, non-Western cultures. Over the long run, change tends to take place on both sides; that is, the host culture begins to learn and modify some of its ways as it absorbs the people and ideas brought in from outside, and the company learns to be creative in implementing its customary management approaches in the foreign country. (Incidentally, this dilemma occurs even *within* our own borders—for example, when a normally urban operation expands into a rural setting.)

In general, *the greater the discrepancy between the organizational structure required by the internal nature of the system and that dictated by the external environment, the more important it becomes to invent structural forms that are compatible with both sets of demands.* To this principle, we add the following emphasis: *To the extent that the structures characteristic of the surrounding environment are historically embedded in its culture, the greater is the adaptation it becomes appropriate for the alien company to make.* For example, a research laboratory in the United States typically allows the individual researcher a lot of freedom in how he does his job. He is usually not closely supervised. While there is a hierarchy of authority, it does not receive constant emphasis. In walking through such a laboratory, it might be difficult to distinguish the boss from the subordinate. Such a relaxed situation seems to work best in the United States, but the system is not so likely to work in many less-developed nations where status is considered very important and deference toward someone of higher status is expected. A U.S. company opening a research laboratory in such a country would probably be ill advised to adopt the same relaxed approach as at home. Local researchers might easily misinterpret a deemphasis on the hierarchy as evidence that the boss is less than competent, and they might even resent the company's efforts to democratize. Instead, the company would need to operate its foreign research laboratory more like a factory at home, with clearer status symbols and at least the appearance of closer control by management. Many organizations fail to heed these principles, and consequently suffer the fate of "the ugly American."

This issue should make one stop and consider the whole question of the relationship between management methods and organizational effectiveness. We do not know how generalizable, for example, are the propositions we have stated relative to organizational structure. They may be very applicable to organizations in our own country, less applicable to some other Western nations, and only marginally useful in non-Western settings. Japan has certainly done very well in its competition for worldwide markets in the most sophisticated industries. Although somewhat westernized, Japan still carries many of its old customs into its modern organizations.

Our point here is that, as you evaluate the various structural forms and apply the concepts, keep in mind that they have limits relative to the context in which they are applied.

An Overview

The eight factors' influence on organizational structure can lead to what has been called an "organic" organization or to what has been called a "mechanistic" organization. (see Box 3–7.) In the former the structure *grows out of* the functions; in the latter the structure is *imposed upon* the functions. The use of the term *organic*, in fact, is intended to convey the idea of a living system in contrast to a mechanical one (machinelike). One interesting thing about the human body, for example, is that its structures and sub-structures (circulatory system, respiratory system, musculature, and so forth) serve their related functions very well. The theory of evolution poses that relationship as the key to understanding the form in which human structure has developed.

If you look at the history of organizations, you can see how the human relations movement of the 1930s, 1940s, and 1950s came as a rebellion against mechanistic organizational structures—that is, ones that treated people as machines, literally dehumanizing them. Modern structures attempt to retain the strengths of what became mechanistic, but integrate them with the organic forces that appropriately are

> **BOX 3–7**
>
> ### MECHANISTIC VERSUS ORGANIC ORGANIZATIONS: THE CONTRIBUTION OF BURNS AND STALKER
>
> From their extensive research on Scottish and English organizations, Tom Burns and G. M. Stalker differentiated two very general approaches to management:
>
> 1. *Mechanistic,* which appeared to work best for organizations operating under stable conditions, where tasks can be broken down into specialties, methods and duties can be clearly defined, unity of command can be adhered to, information can be effectively managed vertically, and control can be exercised from the top down.
>
> 2. *Organic,* which appeared to work best for organizations faced with constant change, where tasks are not easily broken down but tend to overlap, job definitions often change, frequent interactions with others are required, information needs to flow vertically, horizontally, and sometimes laterally, and control often needs to be exercised directly by individuals at the scene of action.
>
> The differences in these two systems of management are reflected in (a) the kinds of relationships that prevail among members of the organization and (b) the kinds of behavior that are considered appropriate and acceptable. Mechanistic organizations tend to encourage formal, distant, and exclusively task-related interactions and behavior; organic organizations tend to foster informal, close, and often socially related along with task-related interactions and behavior.

Source: T. Burns and G. M. Stalker, *The Management of Innovation.* (London: Tavistock Publications, 1961).

shaping today's complex organizations. We will devote the final section of this chapter to an examination of a few organizational forms that have been developed and found useful for matching organizational goals and organizational resources, taking into account the eight variables just covered. We will discuss the following four models:[4]

1. Linking pin.
2. Project team.
3. Collegial.
4. Matrix.

Take a look at pictorial representations of all four models shown in Figures 3–2, 3–3, 3–4, 3–5A and 3–5B. Without much elaboration, you can see what each suggests visually about the operations of its

---

[4] The selection of these four was influenced by a very clear and concise presentation by Ray Miles in his book, *Theories of Management* (New York: McGraw-Hill, 1975).

**FIGURE 3-2
Linking Pin**

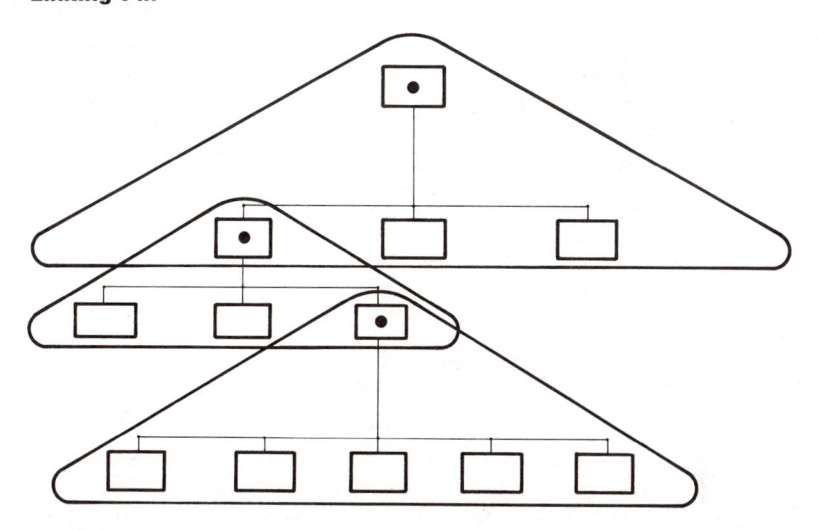

Rensis Likert proposed that organizations be viewed as a set of interrelated *groupings* of people, arranged in a hierarchy with managers serving as link-pins connecting the groups. A given manager, according to this conception, is both a member of a peer group of managers with comparable responsibilities and a leader-member of his or her own department or group. His role typically involves leading his staff in *group discussions and decision making,* and then *representing* his group's needs and views in meetings of the higher (peer manager) group—which is also oriented to reach decisions through group discussion and consensus.

related organization. With the exception of the collegial model, the traditional hierarchy is retained in each, with the linking-pin model representing the least departure from the classical form. (Refer back to the exercise in which we asked you to connect elements of a hierarchy by overlapping circles in contrast to lines.) The project team approach retains a simple relationship between a managerial group, which serves to integrate or coordinate different projects, and the members of the various project teams. The collegial form is likely to apply to very small sub-structures only, where it is possible to combine a number of resources without making a status distinction at all. *Within* project teams or managerial groups, for example, this structure is likely to be appropriate. The matrix model, as you can see, combines the features of the other three in a complex way, and has emerged in recent

**FIGURE 3-3
Project Team**

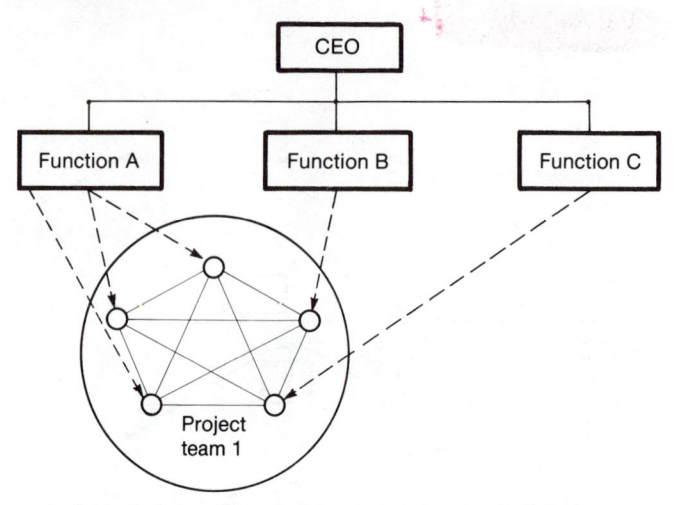

Individuals from different departments (such as electrical engineering, mechanical engineering and chemical engineering; or manufacturing, marketing and design engineering) are assigned to a project team with one individual named as team coordinator. The project is the responsibility of the team, but team members remain under the long-term supervision of their departmental managers. Several teams may exist at the same time.

**FIGURE 3-4
Collegial structure**

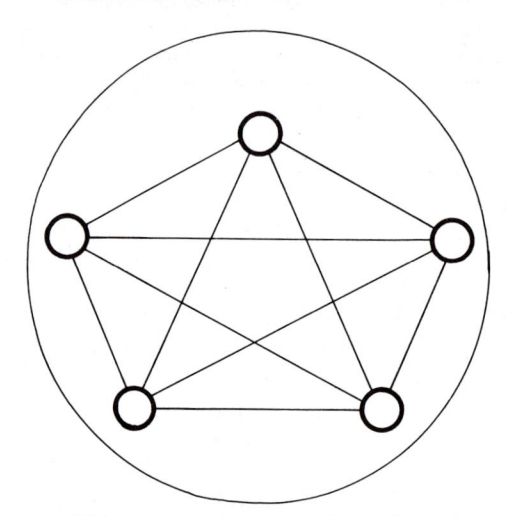

This structure is characteristic of a self-regulating group. There is no formally designated supervisor or chairman. Status and influence are emergent, with particpation and joint decision making assumed.

**FIGURE 3-5A
Matrix (1)**

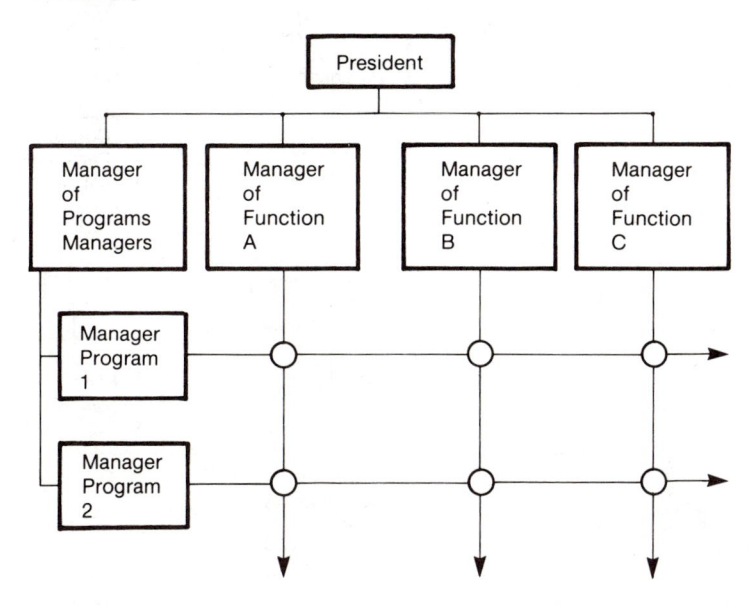

```
                           President
         ┌─────────────┬──────┴──────┬─────────────┐
    Manager         Manager       Manager       Manager
       of             of            of            of
    Programs       Function      Function      Function
    Managers          A             B             C
         │            │             │             │
    ┌────┴────┐       │             │             │
    │ Manager │       │             │             │
    │ Program ├───────○─────────────○─────────────○────▶
    │    1    │       │             │             │
    └─────────┘       │             │             │
    ┌─────────┐       │             │             │
    │ Manager │       │             │             │
    │ Program ├───────○─────────────○─────────────○────▶
    │    2    │       │             │             │
    └─────────┘       ▼             ▼             ▼
```

Managers of each functional department "look vertically" and concentrate on obtaining functional effectiveness (e.g., efficient production). Program managers "look horizontally" and concentrate on seeing that program needs are met (program effectiveness). Operating individuals, as represented by the circles, are subject to the direction of both managers—they have two bosses.

years as a viable structure for high technology organizations, as well as for those whose functions and goals cannot be served by simpler forms.

The linking-pin model stresses the importance of managerial and member roles both vertically and horizontally, as representatives of subordinates, superiors, and colleagues alike and as part of work *groups* that overlap. The project team model conveys the task-group identity that differentiates sub-systems, the frequently *temporary* nature of the structures (i.e., relative to the life of the task), and the need for integration through the use of a coordinating body composed of representatives from each project. The collegial structure points up the inherently interdependent nature of complex tasks, where information sharing and collaborative decision making are vital.

Whether or not the future will generate any more sophisticated organizational model than the matrix is hard to predict. It seems to address the basic issue we started with in this section—namely, match-

**FIGURE 3–5B
Matrix (2)**

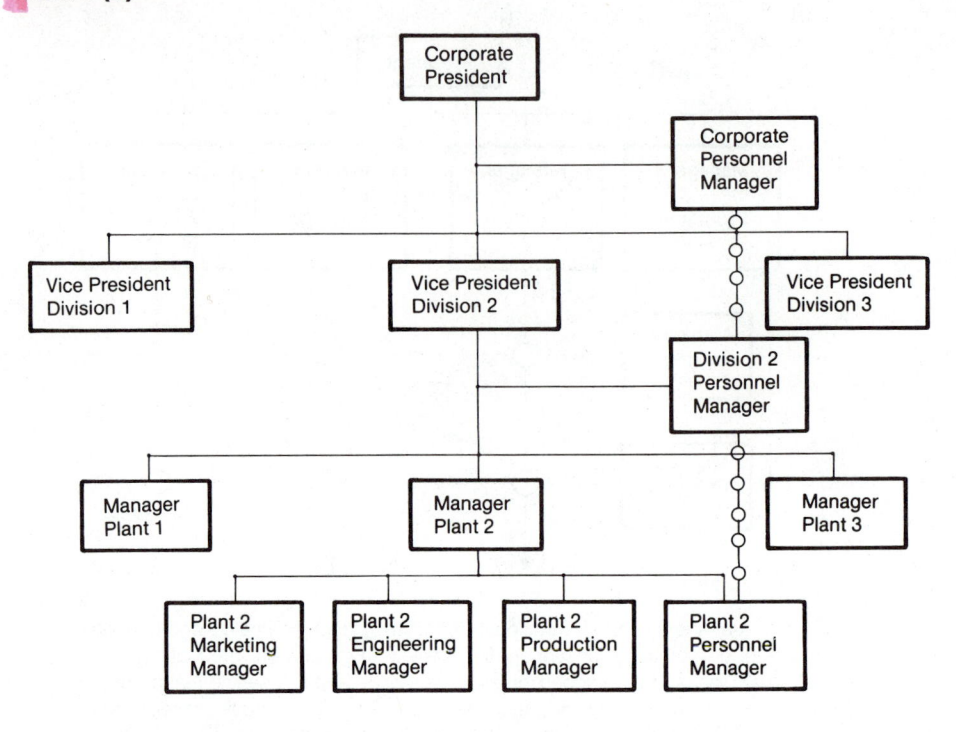

```
                          Corporate
                          President
                                            Corporate
                                            Personnel
                                            Manager
   Vice President     Vice President     Vice President
   Division 1         Division 2         Division 3
                                 Division 2
                                 Personnel
                                 Manager
        Manager          Manager             Manager
        Plant 1          Plant 2             Plant 3
              Plant 2   Plant 2     Plant 2    Plant 2
              Marketing Engineering Production Personnel
              Manager   Manager     Manager    Manager
```

The plant 2 personnel manager reports to the plant 2 manager on day-to-day operating matters, but also reports to the division 2 personnel manager on questions of division personnel policy. Both the plant 2 manager and the division 2 personnel manager give directives to the plant 2 personnel manager and evaluate his/her performance; however, the division personnel manager takes responsibility for the plant personnel manager's career development. A similar dual reporting relationship might exist for a plant controller, plant marketing manager, or other functional specialist.

ing organizational goals and resources effectively and efficiently.

However, a structure is only as good as the ability of managers to understand and use it. Simply fitting people into the slots and roles designated by a matrix (or any other) model will not guarantee that the structure will serve the functions. Our own experience suggests that the matrix type of organization requires a kind of *thinking* that many managers are not used to or may even resist, since it requires that some traditional assumptions about position and authority be tossed aside

BOX 3–8

MATRIX: "IF YOU DO NOT REALLY NEED IT, LEAVE IT ALONE"

Davis and Lawrence define matrix as "any organization that employs a *multiple command system* that includes not only a multiple command structure but also related support mechanisms and an associated culture and behavior patterns."

Their definition and the quotation from their book reflect a key point: To operate a matrix successfully, an organization must not just change its form (structure), it must also develop appropriate methods for operating in that structure.

For a matrix structure to be effective, people at all levels must work together, collaboratively blending the dictates of sub-goals and total system goals. Decisions must be based more on expertise, persuasion, and logic than on hierarchical position and formal role. Misunderstanding, disagreements, and conflicts must be dealt with primarily through confrontation and efforts to solve problems rather than through appeals to higher authority, win/lose domination, avoidance, or the "papering over" of differences. The general atmosphere must emphasize task contribution and accomplishment rather than personal status and rank.

These operating characteristics require that managers, staff specialists, engineers, and other personnel have certain capabilities and skills. They must:

1. Have good interpersonal skills and be able to communicate with others with minimal distortion and misunderstanding. They must be able to develop good relationships.
2. Be able to tolerate the ambiguity of unclear lines of authority, overlapping responsibilities, and unpredictable changes in requirements and circumstances.
3. Have the capacity to live with, and even thrive in, an atmosphere characterized by disagreements over task, conflicting demands on time and actions, and contradictory orders from "two bosses" (multiple command structures).
4. Be able to exert influence through personal persuasiveness and reliance on respect and trust rather than through the exercise of formal authority.
5. Be able to work in groups (meetings and more meetings) and tolerate joint decision making and the need to coordinate their activities with others.
6. Have a clearer sense of, and inner commitment to, total system goals and strategy than has traditionally been necessary.

The organization must also have other characteristics if the matrix structure is to be effective, such as clear goals and a reward system that encourages rather than discourages cooperation. It is truly a structural form that is not to be adopted hastily.

Source: Stanley Davis and Paul Lawrence, *Matrix* (Reading, Mass.; Addison-Wesley Publishing, 1977), p. 3.

(see Box 3–8). New structures often feel as risky as the tasks whose uncertainty they are intended to reduce.

For more extensive discussion of these and other organizational forms, we refer you to the suggested readings at the end of this chapter. Our purpose has been to introduce you to the *thought process* behind organizational structure and to help you to develop some criteria or guidelines for evaluating both the appropriateness and the effectiveness of *any* arrangement you encounter.

SUMMARY

Organizational structures reflect a natural human tendency to impose order on the world. The structure of any organization constitutes the arrangement of people and tasks that is intended to accomplish the organization's goals. In general, the effectiveness of a structure can be measured in terms of its ability to facilitate the goal-related activities of the system.

Classical (or traditional) organizations tend to be hierarchical and governed by relatively formal requirements, job descriptions, and patterns of interaction, with decisions flowing down from the top. They emphasize authority, responsibility, and control; they distinguish between line and staff functions; and they depend on the process of departmentation to manage: (1) different functions, (2) different products or services, (3) different clienteles, and (4) different geographic regions. Because such formalized systems have not been ideal to cope effectively with all the changes and uncertainties characteristic of modern environments, they gradually changed and adopted more flexible forms. The change was initially reflected in the ways the informal organization complemented the formal one; that is, members of the organization took the initiative to get a job done even if it meant "going around" the formal structure. Eventually organizations legitimized these departures and created structures that have been more responsive to changing demands and uncertainties.

An effective structure brings the required resources and information to any given task, thereby minimizing the uncertainty at the scene of action. Eight factors are proposed as important for determining an appropriate organizational structure:

1. The number of information sources required.
2. The mix of information sources.
3. The levels of expertise involved.
4. The life span of the tasks.
5. The degree of differentiation/integration involved.
6. The nature of external demands.
7. The organization's culture.
8. The surrounding culture.

The appropriate use of these criteria can lead to the development of organic (adaptable, flexible, growing) organizations as opposed to mechanistic (fixed, rigid, unchanging) organizations.

Although the hierarchical form has survived and continues to characterize most large organizations, several variations and modifications have reduced the mechanistic aspects of the classical form without actually eliminating it. These variations include the linking pin, project team, and matrix forms of organization. While the essential character of the classical form continues to serve many organizational functions (the more stable, predictable ones) very well, the modifications and variations have provided the vehicles for managing an equally important set of activities (ones related to change and turbulent environmental demands).

Finally, we emphasized the importance of the *thought process* behind organizational structure rather than exploring any specific form in depth. When it comes right down to it, organizational realities lie in the *activities* of the members, not in the abstract arrangement of these activities. The arrangement only provides boundaries, identifies points of interdependence, and reduces the chaos of organizational life. Structure is the map, not the road itself.

ANNOTATED BIBLIOGRAPHY

Aldrich, E. "Technology and Organizational Structure: A Reexamination of the Findings of the Aston Group." *Administrative Science Quarterly*, March 1972, pp. 26–43.

> The author investigates the importance of technology to organizational behavior, giving special attention to whether it should be treated as a dependent or independent variable in organizational theory. The question was examined by reanalyzing data collected from a study carried out at the University of Aston in Birmingham, England. A theory that treats technology as an independent variable is developed and a complex model of organizational structure is reconstructed from the Aston group's data. Both of these efforts support the importance of technology as an independent variable in organizational theory analysis.

Avots, I. "Why Does Project Management Fail?" *California Management Review*, Fall 1969, p. 77.

> Avots asserts that "the many instances where project management fails overshadow the stories of successful projects." He then considers why companies continue to use project management. Reasons for failure are analyzed in detail. Avots offered 10 "lessons for management" which should increase the likelihood of success.

Child, J. "Organizational Structure and Strategies of Control: A Replication of the Aston Study." *Adminstrative Science Quarterly*, June 1972, p. 163.

> Child discusses Max Weber's analysis of bureaucracy, the Aston study of organization structure, and current research. The replication highlights two problems in the Aston study involving the analysis of centralization. The replication, however, also "confirms the tight nexus between specialization, standardization of procedures, paperwork, and vertical span expressed by the concept 'structuring of activities'."

Child, J. "Predicting and Understanding Organization Structure." *Administrative Science Quarterly,* June 1973, p. 168.

"Size is examined as a predictor of organizational structure with data from a British sample of business organizations, supplemented by findings from British labor unions, engineering firms, and the Aston sample of varied work organizations. . . . It is concluded that, in organizations studied, complexity cannot be satisfactorily predicted or fully understood without reference to the economies of scale, but that it is neither theoretically convincing nor statistically demonstrable that size in itself is the major determinant of formalization."

Dewar, R., and J. Hage "Size, Technology, Complexity, and Structural Differentiation: Toward a Theoretical Synthesis." *Administrative Science Quarterly,* March 1978, pp. 111–36.

This article proposes a theoretical synthesis of the concepts of size, technology, complexity, and structural differentiation. The study suggests and finds that the most important determinant of differentiation in the division of labor is the scope of the organization's task, a technological dimension, and not organizational size.

Duncan, R. "Multiple Decision-Making Structures in Adapting to Environmental Uncertainty: The Impact on Organizational Effectiveness." *Human Relations* 26 (1973), p. 273.

The article details research that "will provide a framework for focusing on those factors within the organization which facilitate its ability to gather and process information about the uncertainty in the environment." The author studied 22 decision groups in order to identify "the types of structural modification decision units implemented in making decisions under uncertainty and the relationship of these structural modifications with organizational effectiveness." Duncan concludes that the research data not only confirm the contingency theories of organization but also go beyond the theories by indicating "that the *same* decision unit implemented different organizational structures and these differences . . . related to the decision unit's effectiveness."

Fouraker, L., and S. Stopford "Organizational Structure and the Multinational Strategy." *Administrative Science Quarterly,* June 1968, p. 47.

The authors discuss the proposition found in *Strategy and Structure* by H. D. Chandler. They then determine whether "Chandler's proposition is useful in examining recent organizational changes in the international field." The authors conclude that international divisions of companies may repeat the three stages of evolution of the organization as outlined by Chandler.

Hage, S.; M. Aiken; and C. Marrett "Organizational Structure and Communications." *American Sociological Review,* October 1971, p. 860.

"A theoretical model is developed in which organizational structure is related to the type of coordination in the organization. . . . Hypotheses are developed relating the variables of complexity, formalization and centralization to communication rates." The authors test their hypotheses in a study of 16 health and welfare organizations. They conclude that "as organizations become more diversified, more specialized and more differentiated, they have to rely less on a system of programmed interactions . . . and more on a system of reciprocal information flows to achieve co-ordination."

Lorsch, J., and P. Lawrence "Organizing for Product Innovation." *Harvard Business*

Review, January–February 1965, p. 109.

This article concerns the problems managers face in organizing for product innovation. Two plastics companies are studied to determine how companies innovate. Required collaboration, dimensions of specialization, coordination of departments, and decision authority are examples of organizational aspects the authors consider. The article concludes that "there is, indeed, a relationship between innovative performance and the internal organizational factors."

Marsh, R., and H. Mannari "Technology and Size as Determinants of the Organizational Structure of Japanese Factories." *Administrative Science Quarterly,* March 1981, pp. 33–57.

This article presents the results of a study examining the relative importance of size (number of personnel) and technology (means of production, i.e., job shop, automated, etc.) in determining organizational structure. These effects were examined in regard to their impact on 50 Japanese industrial manufacturing organizations. Results of the study indicate that labor inputs, cybernetic complexity, costs and wages, management/ownership differentiation, span of chief executive officer (CEO) control, and union recognition tend to vary more with technology than size. The authors consider cultural effects on organizations, concluding that these effects are relatively minor.

Oldham, G., and J. Hackman "Relationships between Organizational Structure and Employee Reactions: Comparing Alternative Frameworks." *Adminstrative Science Quarterly,* March 1981, pp. 66–83.

The authors studied two often-neglected frameworks in examining how organizational structure influences employee reaction/motivation to their jobs. The authors looked at attraction-selection (certain structural properties attract and/or select employees with certain personal attributes which, in turn, are associated with employee reactions) and at job motivation (structural properties influence employees by shaping the characteristics of their jobs). Research was carried out in 36 organizations on 2,960 employees. Results indicate that the job-modification framework better explains the relationship between structure and employee reaction. The authors contend, however, that a framework combining both factors is more effective.

Pugh, D.; D. Hickson; C. Hinings; and B. Turner "Dimensions of Organization Structure." *Administrative Science Quarterly,* 13 (1968), p. 65.

"This paper reports attempts to investigate and measure structural differences systematically across a large number of diverse work organizations, using scalable variables for multi-dimensional analysis." Fifty-two different English work organizations were studied. The article discusses the primary dimensions of structure and the intercorrelation of structural variables. The authors conclude that "the establishment of these scales and dimensions makes it possible to compile profiles characteristic of particular organizations. . . ."

Udell, J. "An Empirical Test of Hypotheses Relating to Span of Control." *Administrative Science Quarterly,* December 1967, p. 420.

Udell investigates hypothesized relationships between span of control and nine variables. Examples of variables are similarity of functions supervised, managerial assistance to the manager, and need for coordination of subordinates. Sixty-seven randomly selected chief executives in marketing and sales were studied. Linear correlations, multiple regression, and chi-square analysis were used to evaluate the results. The article contains the numerical results and interpretations.

Van de Ven, A., and A. Delbecq   "A Task Contingent Model of Work-Unit Structure." *Administrative Science Quarterly,* June 1974, p. 183.

"A model for explaining structural variations between work units within the complex organization is presented. Based upon an analysis of the impact of task difficulty and task variability on intra-organizational structure, a taxonomy of alternative work unit structures is derived. The taxonomy suggests that work units within a complex organization can be classified into three basic structural modes: (1) a systemized mode, (2) a service mode, and (3) a group mode, with variations in each mode." The authors detail research methodology, which largely verifies the taxonomy.

Walker, A., and J. Lorsh   "Organizational Choice: Product vs. Function." *Harvard Business Review,* November–December 1968, p. 129.

The authors discuss the choices of corporate structure by studying two plants, "one organized by product, the other by function." Differentiation, integration, organizational formality, performance, and attitudes are considered. The authors conclude that "the functional organization seems to lead to better results in a situation where stable performance of a routine task is desired, while the product organization leads to better results in situations where the task is less predictable and requires innovative problem solving." Suggestions for managers are included.

SUGGESTED READINGS

Aiken, Michael, and Jerald Hage   "The Organic Organization and Innovation." *Sociology* 5 (1971), pp. 63–82.

Aldrich, Howard, and Diane Herker   "Boundary Spanning Roles and Organization Structure." *Academy of Management Review* 2 (1977), pp. 217–30.

Barkdull, C. W.   Span of Control—A method of evaluation. *Michigan Business Review,* May 1963, pp. 25–32.

Bennis, Warren G.   "Beyond Bureaucracy." In *American Bureaucracy,* ed. Warren G. Bennis. Chicago: Aldine Publishing, 1970, pp. 3–16.

Blau, Peter M., and Marshall Meyer   *Bureaucracy in Modern Society,* 2d ed. New York: Random House, 1971.

Burns, T. and G. M. Stalker   *The Management of Innovation.* London: Tavistock Publications, 1961.

Carey, Alex   "The Hawthorne Studies: A Radical Criticism." *American Sociological Review* 33 (1968), pp. 403–16.

Carzo, R., and J. N. Yanouzas   "Effects of Flat and Tall Organization Structures." *Administrative Science Quarterly* 14 (1969), pp. 178–91.

Child, John   "Predicting and Understanding Organization Structure." *Administrative Science Quarterly* 18 (1973), pp. 168–85.

Copely, Frank Barkley   *Frederick W. Taylor: Father of Scientific Management.* Vol 1. New York: Harper & Row, 1923.

Dalton, D.; W. Todor; M. Spendolini; G. Fielding; and L. Porter "Organization Structure and Performance: A Critical Review." *Academy of Management Review* 5 (1980), pp. 49–64.

Davis, Stanley M., and Paul R. Lawrence *Matrix*. Reading, Mass.: Addison-Wesley Publishing, 1977.

Emery, Fred E "Bureaucracy and Beyond." *Organizational Dynamics* 2 (1974), pp. 3–13.

Etzioni, Amitai *A Comparative Analysis of Complex Organizations*. Rev. ed. New York: Free Press, 1975.

Ford, J. D., and J. W. Slocum "Size, Technology, Environment, and the Structure of Organizations." *Academy of Management Review* 2 (1977), pp. 561–75.

Franke, Richard H., and James D. Kaub "The Hawthorne Experiments: First Statistical Interpretation." *American Sociological Review* 43 (1978), pp. 623–43.

Galbraith, Jay R. *Designing Complex Organizations*. Reading, Mass.: Addison-Wesley Publishing, 1973.

Gouldner, Alvin W. *Patterns of Industrial Bureaucracy*. New York: Free Press, 1954.

Hall, Richard H *Organizations: Structure and Process*. 2d ed. Englewood Cliffs, N.J.: Prentice-Hall, 1977.

Harvey, Edward "Technology and the Structure of Organizations." *American Sociological Review* 33 (1968), pp. 247–59.

Ivancevich, John M., and James H. Donnelly Jr. "Relation of Organizational Structure to Job Satisfaction, Anxiety-Stress, and Performance." *Administrative Science Quarterly* 20 (1975), pp. 272–80.

Kimberly, J. R. "Organizational Size and the Structuralist Perspective: A Review, Critique and Proposal." *Administrative Science Quarterly* 21 (1976), pp. 571–97.

Kingdon, Donald R. *Matrix Organization: Managing Information Technologies*. London: Tavistock Publications. 1973.

Lawrence, Paul R., and Jay W. Lorsch "Differentiation and Integration in Complex Organizations." *Administrative Science Quarterly* 12 (1967), pp. 1–47.

Lawrence, Paul R., and Jay W. Lorsch *Organization and Environment: Managing Differentiation and Integration*. Boston: Division of Research, Harvard University Graduate School of Business Administration, 1967.

Likert, Rensis *New Patterns of Management*. New York: McGraw-Hill, 1961.

Likert, Rensis *The Human Organization: Its Management and Value*. New York: McGraw-Hill, 1967.

Lorsch, Jay W "Introduction to the Structural Design of Organizations." In *Organizational Behavior and Industrial Psychology,* ed. K. N. Wexley and G. A. Yukl. New York: Oxford University Press, 1975, pp. 256–67.

Mayo, Elton "Hawthorne and the Western Electric Company." In *Organization Theory,* ed. D. S. Pugh. Middlesex, England: Penguin Books Ltd., 1971, pp. 215–29.

Merton, Robert K. "Bureaucratic Structure and Personality." *Social Forces* 18 (1940), pp. 560–68.

Mohr, L. B. "Organizational Technology and Organizational Structure." *Administrative Science Quarterly* 16 (1971), pp. 444–59.

Parsons, Talcott *Structure and Process in Modern Societies*. New York: Free Press, 1960.

Parsons, Talcott, ed *Max Weber, the Theory of Social and Economic Organization*. Trans. A. Henderson and T. Parsons. New York: Free Press, 1947.

Pennings, Johannes M. "The Relevance of the Structural-Contingency Model for Organizational Effectiveness." *Administrative Science Quarterly* 20 (1975), pp. 393–410.

Porter, Lyman W., and Edward E. Lawler, III "Properties of Organizational Structure in Relation to Job Attitudes and Job Behavior." *Psychological Bulletin* 64 (1965), pp. 23–51.

Richetto, Gary M. "Organizations Circa 1990: Demise of the Pyramid." *Personnel Journal* 49 (1970), pp. 598–603.

Sayles, Leonard R. "Matrix Management: The Structure with a Future." *Organizational Dynamics,* Autumn 1976, pp. 2–17.

Tannenbaum, Arnold S; Bogdan Kavčič; Menachem Rosner; Mino Vianello and Georg Wieser *Hierarchy in Organizations.* San Francisco: Jossey-Bass, 1974.

Taylor, Frederick W. "The Principles of Scientific Management." In *Classics in Management,* ed. H. F. Merrill. New York: American Management Association, 1960, pp. 82–113.

Thompson, James D. *Organizations in Action.* New York: McGraw-Hill, 1967.

Thompson, Victor A. *Bureaucracy and Innovation.* University, Ala.: University of Alabama Press, 1969.

Udell, Jon G. "An Empirical Test of Hypotheses Relating to Span of Control." *Administrative Science Quarterly* 12 (1967), pp. 420–39.

Walker, Arthur H., and Jay W. Lorsch "Organizational Choice: Product versus Function." *Harvard Business Review* 46 (1968), pp. 129–38.

Weber, Max *The Theory of Social and Economic Organization,* trans. A. Henderson and T. Parsons. New York: Free Press, 1964.

Woodward, Joan. *Industrial Organization: Theory and practice.* London: Oxford University Press, 1965.

CHAPTER 4

Organizational Climate

INTRODUCTION

WHEN YOU WALK into a bank, restaurant, or classroom, you form an impression of the place. It may strike you as warm and inviting or as cold and forbidding. Have you ever stopped to think about what creates your impression? In this chapter, we will look at some things that make up what is called the "climate" of an organization, how climate develops, and some ways of changing it.

CLIMATE DEFINED

Organizational climate is the overall "feel" of an organization, the characteristic atmosphere in the system. Some elements that affect the climate of an organization are its *goals, structure, rewards, size, geographic location, physical setting, norms,* and *communications.* (Some definitions of climate are given in Box 4–1.) We will examine each of these elements to understand its impact on climate.

It is also important to point out that organizational climate is influenced by a number of *external* factors, including:

- The wider cultural environment in which the organization exists.
- The general economic conditions at any time.
- The actions of other organizations (for example, competitors, customers, suppliers).
- Outside intervention from government regulatory agencies, the courts, the Internal Revenue Service (IRS), consumer groups, and others.

We will not describe each of these external influences on climate in this chapter other than to note their importance and impact on internal climate. In Chapter 9 on the external environment, we will discuss how these factors affect all dimensions of organizational life, including climate.

[margin note: Summarizes chapter well]

UNDERSTANDING ORGANIZATIONAL CLIMATE

Goals

Suppose you were going to start an organization. First you would have to decide on the purpose of that organization. That decision begins the process of forming a climate. Imagine, for example, that you decided to start an organization with a mission of protecting and enhancing wilderness spaces, such as the Appalachian Mountain Club or the Sierra Club.

BOX 4-1

DEFINITIONS OF CLIMATE

1. Garlie A. Forehand and B. von Haller Gilmer, "Environmental Variation and Studies of Organizational Behavior," *Psychological Bulletin* 62, no. 6 (December 1964), pp. 361–82.

   "The set of enduring characteristics that describe an organization, distinguish it from other organizations, and influence the behavior of the people in the organization."

2. George H. Litwin and Robert A. Stringer, Jr., *Motivation and Organizational Climate* (Boston: Division of Research, Graduate School of Business Administration, Harvard University, 1968), p. 5.

   "The perceived, subjective effects of the formal system, the information 'style' of managers, and other important environmental factors on the attitudes, beliefs, values, and motivation of people who work in a particular organization."

3. L. K. Waters, Darrell Roach, and Nick Battis, "Organizational Climate Dimensions and Job-Related Attitudes," *Personnel Psychology* 27 (1974), pp. 465–76.

   These researchers identified five climate factors:

   1. Effective organizational structure—formalization, structure, adequacy of planning.
   2. Work autonomy—responsibility, hindrance.
   3. Close, impersonal supervision—production emphasis, aloofness.
   4. Open, challenging environment—conflict, openness, risk.
   5. Employee-centered orientation—warmth, consideration, tolerance of error, reward.

4. Fritz Steele and Stephen Jenks, *The Feel of the Work Place: Understanding and Improving Organization Climate* (Reading, Mass.: Addison-Wesley Publishing, 1977), p. 3.

   "The climate of an organization is the characteristic weather in that system or its parts (there may be different climates in different regions of the system). This is basically a property of the system, not just of the persons involved, although they are major contributors to the climate. The key dimensions of climate are:

   1. The amount of total energy people have available to them.
   2. How that energy is distributed or used.
   3. The amount of pleasure people get from being in the environment.
   4. How much people grow and develop within the system."

The organization's mission affects the type of people attracted to work there, the type of rewards available, and the organizational structure that would develop. These factors, in turn, influence the emergent climate. For example, it is likely that Sierra Club members would have a high commitment to the goals of the organization and experience rewards through identification with organizational goals and interest in the work itself. Consequently, it would be unlikely to have a sharp division of labor with tight supervision and control; instead, there would be a more informal structure with considerable reliance on self-control. There undoubtedly would be a high level of loyalty to the organization and perhaps even a willingness to make personal sacrifices for its well-being. Given the probable wide dispersion of the organization's activities, the structure might consist of a number of semiautonomous chapters. In contrast to a more centralized and tightly controlled organization, the result would be small working units with a face-to-face, "know everybody" atmosphere and a sense of common purpose (mission).

By way of contrast, suppose you decided to start a lumberyard. Your goals would be to make a profit, to give good service, and to have a wide range of products available. There undoubtedly would be an emphasis on efficiency and some degree of specialization and structuring along functional lines (retail sales, wholesale sales, inventory control and purchasing, recordkeeping, and accounting). The employees probably would not identify with company goals to the same extent as members of the Sierra Club (although many might identify with home carpentry and do-it-yourself projects). Consequently, supervision might be closer, pressure for productivity greater, security measures in clearer evidence, and working hours more regulated. Working at the lumberyard would feel quite different from working at a Sierra Club-type organization.

In general, then, the *goals* of an organization strongly determine the climate that will develop, even though they may tend to be a subtle influence. In sports, for example, a team's situational goals can have a powerful effect on the atmosphere among the players. The climate is quite different in each of the following three situations: (1) a team that is in first place and has the goal of staying there, (2) a team that is working toward the goal of having its first winning season, and (3) a team that is struggling to meet the goal of "staying alive" in its league. The confidence, spirit, and level of tension are likely to be very different for each situation. An organization that is struggling to stay "in the market" will have a more tense atmosphere than one that is growing rapidly in a market in which it is a dominant force. It is worth looking at an organization's basic goals, mission, and purpose at a given time to see what impact they might have on its climate.

Structure

The structures of our two organizations also contribute to different climates. In the conservation organization, the structure would be a small central staff of paid professionals flanked by a large number of volunteers with members organized into chapters scattered geographically. In contrast, the lumberyard would probably be in one location and structured for maximum efficiency, very likely on a functional basis. People with different interests and skills would be associated with each department, and consequently each department would tend to develop its own norms and distinctive operating style. When an organization has essentially the same structure repeated in different geographic settings, there tends to be a lot of similarity in the climate from one location to the next. But when an organization is structured functionally, each part of the organization—i.e., each function—has its own distinctive climate. For example, in a large organization, the climate or overall feel of a manufacturing department is likely to be very different from that of the same company's sales department. In fact, the climate of a manufacturing department of one company may be more similar to the climates of the manufacturing departments of other companies than it is to those of other departments within its own organization. The reason for the similarity is that the *goals* and *structure* of the manufacturing departments, as well as the type of people attracted there for employment, are likely to be fairly similar; consequently, the climates of the two manufacturing departments tend to be similar.

In general, the more formal the structure, the more formal the climate will tend to be. A formal organizational structure is one that has clear, singular lines of authority (chain of command) with few overlapping relationships. Such systems tend to emphasize rank, seniority, formal authority, and strict lines of communication. Some other organizations manage to be remarkably informal despite a rather rigid structure, but, as a rule, they tend to be much more formal than organizations with less rigid structures.

Rewards

Similarly, our two organizations' reward systems affect their climates. In our hypothetical conservation organization, the rewards are largely psychic; that is, people *feel* good working for and with the organization in achieving its goals. The feeling of sharing with others tends to be its own reward. In the lumberyard example, rewards are likely to be more of the kind typically associated with a profit-making organization. People are rewarded with pay, increased responsibility, more power, and promotions. Each different kind of reward is associated with a different attitude or feeling about the workplace. Students may notice the contrast between working for a grade in a course and working for pleasure in a campus social organization. Some reward systems focus on individual effort and frequently do little to encourage cooperation among individuals and, in fact, may actively encourage competitiveness. Such reward systems foster a less cooperative, "we work together" climate than one that rewards joint effort and uses group incentive payments.

Different kinds of rewards associated with different situations create different climates. It is not that any given set of rewards and related climate is inherently good or bad. They often are inevitable elements of a given type of organization. There is no way, for example, for a large bank, which needs to convey an image of stability and tradition, to have an entrepreneurial atmosphere and retain its image.

Size

Organizational size has a major effect on climate. Most people think of small organizations (or bounded sub-units of large organizations) as more friendly and intimate than large organizations. In fact, organizations do tend to become less personal as they become larger, in part because with larger numbers, people are less likely to know everyone and often have to work with others who are relative strangers. They may even do business with individuals they have never met but just talked to on the telephone. Similarly, large size often requires the introduction of various efficiency measures, such as computers, to say nothing about more formalized policies, procedures, and standard operating practices. In a small organization, paychecks are handed out on payday by the owner. As the organization grows, a payroll clerk or even a computer may make deposits into a bank account directly.

In our conservation club example, increasing size may not have such negative effects. As more members join, the club may be able to adopt some efficiency measures, such as computerized mailing lists, but the fundamental character of the organization won't be affected adversely. More chapters in more local areas may be added, but each is likely to retain the same face-to-face familiarity as was the case when there were fewer chapters. The climate of a *given* chapter is not likely to change much because of the addition of new chapters. The lumberyard, on the other hand, is likely to have a different climate associated with an increase in size. There will be further specialization of functions by department, more employees, and more complex administrative systems. Inevitably, these size-related changes cause substantial differences in the feel of the place. As it grows, an organization can seem more impersonally efficient, feel like a colder and less friendly place to work, appear more rigid and rule-bound, and even seem more dominating and beyond influence. In short, the larger an organization becomes, the more bureaucratic it becomes. Certain increased services and efficiencies of scale accompany increases in size but usually at the cost of the "personal touch" and informality.

Geographic Location

The geographic setting of an organization contributes to its internal climate. The same small shop located in a bustling metropolis as opposed to a remote little village is not the same small shop! Although both shops may be the same size, sell the same product, and be operated similarly, they will be quite different from each other simply on the basis of *location* or *geographic setting*. A shop in an urban location is likely to be one of a number of similar shops and, therefore, be faced with greater competition than the shop in the rural location. This, in turn, may cause the urban shop to specialize for a particular segment of the overall market. Suppose both shops are bookstores. The urban bookstore may decide to specialize in cookbooks, something the rural bookstore could not do without a much larger customer base. The urban shop will have many more people passing by each day. It also is likely to have more sources of supply, higher rent, and a greater chance of being robbed, all of which means it must do a larger gross business to return the same net profit as the rural shop. Consequently, the urban shop will be more active, busier, and more hurried than a similar shop in a rural location. Much of the difference between the two shops is attributable solely to their different locations.

Physical Setting

If you attended a variety of different schools during your childhood, think back to the differences in those schools from a physical standpoint and the different feeling imparted by each. Open space in a building gives a different feeling than does confined space. The amount of openness also has an impact. Too large a space may feel majestic and imposing rather than open and free. Enclosed space often feels cozy, whereas inadequate space feels cramped. All of us have had experience with different kinds and sizes of space, and we may react similarly or differently to those experiences. Look around the space you are in as you read this chapter and list your reactions to that space. How does it feel to you? What physical characteristics of the place make you react as you do? Are you aware of the kinds of physical settings that make you most comfortable? Most happy? Most peaceful? Most productive? What are the characteristics of those settings?

Many people are not aware (at least consciously) of the effect of physical setting on organizational climate or, for that matter, on their own moods and feelings. Yet, as we said at the start of this chapter, whenever you walk into a bank, restaurant, or classroom, you form an impression about the feel of the place. This *initial* reaction is almost solely based on the physical setting: size and shape of the space, effects of lighting and decor, colors, furnishings, and so on. In work situations, whether in a factory or an office, the physical setting has an impact on the organization's climate. At worst, it can detract from all positive influences on climate and convey a sense of depression to everyone who works there. At best, it can enhance productivity because of the sense of invigoration or excitement it creates. Some people are keenly aware of physical settings because of the kind of work they do. For example, orchestra musicians and opera singers are very sensitive to the acoustics and other characteristics of performance halls, which can affect the quality of their work enormously. Artists are acutely aware of the light in their studios and writers of the amount of noise. Most of us are somewhere between a relative lack of awareness of our physical surroundings and a strong sensitivity to those surroundings. In any case, the physical characteristics of an organization do play a significant role in the resulting climate of the organization and, consequently, have a powerful influence on one's behavior.

Norms

Probably the most important factor that affects an organization's climate is the norms of that organization. Norms are the "unwritten rules that are felt to govern what people should or should not do (in behavior) or be (in attitudes) in order to be acceptable members in good standing of a particular social system" (Steele & Jenks, 1977, p. 41). They are the informal "rules of the road" that people are expected to follow in the organization; that is, norms define what is acceptable behavior and set boundaries or limits within which people are expected to behave. While we often associate norms with small face-to-face groups, larger clusters of people and organizations also develop norms governing the behavior of their members. Norms give an organization some degree of stability, because they help to make people's behavior more predictable. Norms affect every individual's behavior to some degree in every organization. Those who break the norms are punished by others, usually by joking or other forms of sarcastic humor. For example, in an organization with rather formal dress requirements, a person who arrives in casual attire is often asked questions such as: "Are you on vacation?" or "Trying to start a new trend around here?" The message is that the person has broken the norm about proper dress and has been noticed in doing so. Sometimes norms become formalized into policies, and the related sanctions become very formal. During the 1960s, many high schools established elaborate dress codes (including standards for acceptable length of hair) when the unwritten norms were no longer sufficient to control students' behavior. In addition to restricting one's behavior, norms sometimes urge people into new previously untried behaviors. For example, many fraternities have a social service norm. People who join the fraternity may never before have participated in a Red Cross blood drive or a walkathon for a charity, but it is expected that they will do so in service to their fraternity. In this case, the person is pushed into new behavior because of a norm.

You might ask where norms came from. How do they develop? Many norms develop over time; that is, they evolve with the organization. Most organizations have traditions ("It's *always* been done this way") and rituals, which must be honored because they have become norms of the system. Another source of norms is precedent-setting events—that is, incidents that tend to determine a new course of action. For example, if a person sets a new standard of achievement, it may develop into a norm that others try to meet to be members in good standing. Breaking the four-minute-mile mark was just such a precedent-setting event, and it became a norm that all milers had to be members of the four-minute-mile club to be taken seriously.

The most important source of norms is power figures. Those at the top of any organization have a lot to say about the norms that get established for the group. This is true whether the organization is a street corner gang or a multinational corporation. The people in positions of power and influence either establish or condone a variety of behaviors that are subsequently adopted throughout the system.

When Jimmy Carter was president he issued a federal edict that required the temperatures of air-conditioning systems in large buildings to be set no lower than 78°. During the hottest part of the summer, one major corporation in New York City sent a memo to all managers that they could remove their suit jackets during working hours. The managers happily did so, but the practice lasted only one week. The chief officers of the company chose to wear their jackets at all times; their behavior had a much more powerful effect on what was acceptable than did the more official memo. Never underestimate the power of norms, even when the official word is different.

Norms also can be established (or altered) by conscious actions or decisions. People can *decide* to set a new or different norm, and then do so. This method of establishing norms is seldom used, because most people are unaware of where norms come from, or they feel powerless to change them. Norms are treated like the weather—something that's there to talk about or complain about, but not something one can *do* much about. In most groups and organizations, however, norms can be altered by individual action on the part of those at the top or by group decision and action on the part of a number of members.

How Norms Determine Climate   A look at the two organizations we have been using as examples will help clarify how norms affect climate. In the lumberyard, the founder or original entrepreneur probably had tremendous influence in setting the norms that established the climate of the place. If that person was informal and easy-going, the resulting climate would support friendly cooperation and banter among employees. If the founder was a stern, serious taskmaster, then the norms and consequent climate would be similarly serious and impersonal.

On the other hand, in our conservation club, norms would most likely have developed *from* the membership; that is, people would join the organization because they identified with its goals or because they wanted to affiliate with people whose interests were similar to their own. The climate of the organization would then grow out of the norms governing the association of members with one another. This could be a conscious and explicit process or a subtle and implicit process, depending on members' awareness of and concern about climate. Consequently, the climate of the organization would reflect the emergent *member* norms, rather than the influence of a power figure.

Communications (open and closed environments)

Communication patterns also affect the climate in an organization. Steele, in his book *The Open Organization* (1975), distinguished between high-disclosing (Hi D) and low-disclosing (Low D) organizations. High-disclosing organizations are characterized by openness, trust, and mutual understanding among members. These characteristics do not just happen magically; they are the result of high disclosure—that is, a great deal of communication. On the other hand, low-disclosing organizations are characterized by distrust, suspicion, and secrecy. The lack of communication and openness leads to speculation and rumor. In addition to the norms that exist, such organizations are characteristically low-disclosing environments as well, which leads to a climate of fear.

Often communicating with others in an organization seems to be a burden with little payoff, so it is easier not to bother. The consequence is a low-disclosure climate, which eventually will lower the organization's effectiveness. Communication *must* take place at a variety of levels if a healthy, high-disclosure climate is to be maintained. The most important form of communication is face to face. This means that people must move about the organization, see one another, spend time talking together. It also may mean, especially in large or geographically dispersed organizations, time spent talking on the telephone. Finally, it means time spent in meetings. Frequently, these kinds of activities can appear to be enormous wastes of time, which could better be spent "getting the job done." People often become frustrated with the amount of time and energy they spend in meetings, and they wish for more efficient forms of communication. Meetings can be run with varying degrees of efficiency and satisfaction, but many meetings also serve the important function of face-to-face communication, and there is nosubstitute for that, especially in the development of a healthy climate.

Other forms of communication that add to a high-disclosure environment are newsletters, written memoranda, formal reports (written and verbal), and norms that encourage people to be curious about what's going on, to ask questions, and to seek the information they need to do their jobs well.

In large organizations, cross-function or cross-departmental communication is of particular importance if there is going to be cooperation and coordination. It is amazing how often these kinds of communication lines are weak or altogether nonexistent. When organizations are in trouble, people in the organization frequently blame lack of communication, and usually they are right. Louis Allen of the Massachusetts Institute of Technology has found, for example, that people in the same office building whose work stations are more than 100 feet apart are no more likely to communicate with each other than if they were separated by several hundred miles!

Organizations that invest time and energy in good-quality, face-to-face communication and high disclosure backed up by good written communication mechanisms generally have much more invigorating climates than organizations with poor communications mechanisms and low disclosure. Communication patterns contribute heavily to peoples' sense of satisfaction and productivity at work.

Figure 4-1 summarizes the overall comparison between the conservation club and the lumberyard in all the factors that affect climate.

DIMENSIONS OF CLIMATE

There are many scales along which you can characterize the climate of an organization. Figure 4-2 lists some of these.

Any organization's climate is composed of some mixture of these dimensions. In some cases, the climate can exhibit a model characteristic or overall "tone." One such tone can have to do with fear versus excitement. For example, one organization's climate might be characterized by *tension and fear*, with people feeling constrained, where punishment for deviating from the straight and narrow is felt to be swift and severe. Another's might be characterized by *excitement*, with people feeling challenged, free to experiment and grow, where risk taking is

FIGURE 4–1

	Conservation Club	*Lumberyard Customer Service*
Goals	Conservation Ecology Protection of wilderness	Profit Customer service
Structure	Small headquarters Professional Many volunteer chapters organized by geography	Organized by: Function Wholesale Distribution Administration
Rewards	Fellowship Psychic rewards of goal achievement	Profit Pay Promotion Power
Size	Very small to very large Little impact on climate	Very small to very large Large impact on climate
Physical setting	Clubhouse Rural, outdoors wilderness, camps	Lumberyard Suburban, urban bustle, traffic
Physical characteristics	Old house taken over as office space	Several barns and sheds scattered about a central courtyard with the office tucked in one corner
Norms	Emergent norms based on association of members in club with one another Can be conscious or unconscious	Friendly and affable or stern and businesslike based on style of owner-founder
Communications	Newletters Social gatherings Business meetings	Face-to-face at work Formal written memos Business meetings—if large

encouraged. Most organizations fall between the extremes and have elements of both. Organizations that are toward the fear end of the scale have more predictable climates. Events in those organizations occur in relatively predictable patterns or cycles. As a consequence, people's behavior tends to be predictable. As the amount of freedom increases in the climate, there tends to be more variability; things become less predictable but often more exciting as well.

Two other factors influence the dimensions of climate at any particu-

FIGURE 4–2 *Good*
Dimensions along Which Organizational Climates May Vary

Conflicted	Cooperative
Slow	Fast, hurried
Relaxed	Tense, pressured
Apathetic	Excited
Ordinary	Special, unique
Fearful, suspicious	Trusting, comfortable
Open, disclosing	Secretive, suspicious
Considerate	Brusque
Cautious, conservative	Brave, risk taking
Warm, friendly, intimate	Cold, impersonal
Formal	Informal
Controlling	Free
Overpowering	Influenceable
Rigid	Flexible
Unpredictable	Predictable
Unsure	Confident

lar time and add to the amount of fear or excitement that exists. One is the *developmental stage* of the organization. The other is the *rate of change or growth* the organization is experiencing. Earlier stages of development tend to be characterized by high levels of excitement, often related to "newness," whereas later stages may be more serene and secure. During periods of rapid growth, things tend to be chaotic, unpredictable, and (sometimes) rather exciting. People feel challenged as their jobs grow and change. Change that is too rapid causes fear. People wonder whether they can keep up with their rapidly expanding responsibilities or worry about whether they will get caught by the Peter Principle, which says that people get promoted just to their level of incompetence. An organization that is losing market share or is otherwise in financial trouble may be changing (shrinking) so rapidly that fear sets in as employees worry about losing their jobs.

DIAGNOSING ORGANIZATIONAL CLIMATE

If you are interested in learning what kind of climate is satisfying for you, or if you want to know how to change a climate to make it more satisfying, you first must be able to diagnose the climate. Diagnosis is the most important step toward achieving either objective, just as it is in medicine. Without an accurate diagnosis, it is impossible to determine the degree of sickness or health of the patient or to prescribe a treatment to improve things. Also, the diagnosis itself frequently suggests possible directions for improvement.

One of the best ways to diagnose an organization's climate is through a simple device called a *norms census* (Steele & Jenks, 1977, p. 64). A norms census is a process of writing down and analyzing the norms that are operating in a group at a given time. Members are asked to list all the existing norms (dos and don'ts) they can think of. Then the lists are examined to identify those that are helpful and those that are hindering the organization and the people in it with respect to meeting their goals.

Another tool to help you diagnose an organization's climate is to look at the characteristic *style of communication*. The easiest to see is face-to-face communication. Do people call each other by first names? Do they address each other as Mr. Jones or Miss Clark? Do they refer to one another by title ("The sales manager wants information on our second-quarter projections")? In the U.S. Supreme Court (a rather formal organization), employees address the justices by title when speaking to them: "Yes, Mr. Justice, I have the file completed."

Another aspect of face-to-face communication that is easily observed is *body language;* is it open and full of movement, or closed and controlled (sitting behind a desk with a suit jacket on and hands folded on top of the desk)? *Dress* can also be a clue to climate by the degree of informality people express in the clothes they wear. Written communication can best be examined through an organization's *memos.* Internal memos reveal a great deal about an organization's climate through their style (formal or informal), tone (serious, punitive, questioning, etc.), length, clarity, and distribution (to whom are they sent—a long mailing list, a select mailing list, an individual). Procter & Gamble has some explicit standards for internal memos, and people spend enormous amounts of time being sure their writing style measures up.

Meetings also demonstrate the typical communication styles in an organization. A well-run meeting has an agenda and moves efficiently from topic to topic as each subject is discussed openly and a conclusion reached. It requires a skilled leader to conduct a good meeting; many meetings are monuments to wasted time, miscommunication, and nondecision. The success of a meeting is partially dependent on the quality of interpersonal communication, and that quality (or lack thereof) gives a clue to the wider organization climate. Skills most often missing are active listening skills, time management skills, and decision-making skills.

An obvious diagnostic tool for organizational climate is your eyes. If you look carefully at aspects of the *physical setting,* you can learn a lot about the overall climate. Some climates are busier than others. This is often indicated by the extent to which people move about in the organization. Is there a lot of traffic, or are people behind their desks most of the time? How is the physical space used? Organizations that want to emphasize the status hierarchy have the most important people on the top floor, in the most central location, or in the largest offices. Organizations that want to deemphasize the status hierarchy go to great lengths to treat people more equally; they give everyone similar sized offices and everyone (or no one) gets carpeting and windows. Even a quick tour of an organization's physical setting will give strong indications of its climate and its self-image.

Employee demeanor, reflecting attitudes and morale, gives an indication of the climate. Do people seem to enjoy their work? To get satisfaction from their work? Their co-workers? Or do they seem merely to be complying with the rules? Even in a place as standardized as McDonald's, differences in whether people seem to enjoy their jobs can be seen from one restaurant to another. Answers to these questions may reveal symptoms of poor climate, which can be a sign that changes are needed. Two things often affect whether or not people enjoy their work: one is the intrinsic satisfaction a person gets from the work itself, and the other is the satisfaction one gets from good interpersonal relationships with one's co-workers. Neither of these kinds of rewards is dependent on the pay system the organization uses to reward its members. A climate of indifference and low morale can be a signal to management that the rewards of the work are not meeting the needs of employees.

CONSEQUENCES OF CLIMATE

So far we have talked about the characteristics of an organization's climate, the sources of that climate, and some ways of diagnosing climate. We are now ready to consider how climate is important to you as a potential employee and a prospective manager in an organization.

Climate is important to you as both employee and manager because climate affects:

1. Member development.
2. Member productivity.
3. Member satisfaction.

As a potential employee, you should ask yourself; in what climate will I be most satisfied and most productive? Different kinds of people are attracted to different kinds of climate. Some people prefer a climate that is structured, well controlled, very predictable and where they know exactly what is expected of them. They find any other kind of climate ambiguous at best and, more likely, threatening. Others are nearly the opposite. Such people prefer a climate that is unstructured, variable and where they are expected to take risks and initiate actions. They find any other kind of climate constraining, confining, and stifling. No one kind of organizational climate is universally most satisfying; rather, different climates are satisfying to different kinds of people. Therefore, a satisfying climate for any given individual is one in which there is a good match between the person's preferences and the climate that actually exists in his or her organization. For example, if you like a fast-paced environment with a fair amount of variability and unpredictability as well as some chance for risk taking, then a small entrepreneurial type of organization would be a good place to look for work. If you like a slower work pace, clear lines of authority and responsibility, a lot of predictability, and reasonable performance standards, then a larger, more established organization may be a better place for you to look for work. The important point is to know something about the kind of environment in which *you* can thrive and something about how to determine what kind of climate exists in potential places of employment. When there is a good match between the style and needs of the person and the climate of the organization, both benefit; if there is a mismatch, both suffer, but the individual usually suffers more than the organization.

As a manager, you should ask yourself: What behavior does the climate encourage or discourage and how does this influence overall effectiveness and efficiency? Are the resulting behaviors compatible with the goals and needs of the organization?

A climate that discourages risk taking may be appropriate for a savings and loan association but inappropriate for a fashion-oriented retail clothing store. A climate that encourages people to think in visionary and creative ways can reinforce other factors that can make an entrepreneurial organization successful. A thoughtful analysis of what would constitute an appropriate climate can facilitate establishing the right climate in a new organization. An accurate diagnosis of the existing climate may suggest valuable changes.

CHANGING ORGANIZATIONAL CLIMATE

Suppose you are in an organization and find that the climate is unhealthy and needs to be changed. How do you go about creating the necessary changes?

It is very hard to change organizational climate unless there is a *felt need* for change. If people are unhappy or unproductive, it may be due to the climate. The only way to find out is to have free and open discussion about those aspects of the climate that people find troublesome. The discussion can be aided by an accurate description of the existing climate. From this description, a diagnosis can be made.

The description and diagnosis can be made through a data-based research approach, such as an attitude or morale survey or structured interviews with a carefully selected sample of employees; or they can be made through an informal approach such as "sensing"[1] meetings with employees or "what's on your mind" sessions. In either case, the objective is to learn what the people who live in the system perceive the climate to be. Some typical indicators of an *unhealthy* work climate are:

> People feel either frustrated through insufficient responsibility or threatened by too much.
>
> People are reluctant to admit responsibility for errors, try to cover up their mistakes, or blame someone else.
>
> People try to attribute the causes of problems to others or to outside influences beyond their control.

Some typical indicators of a *healthy* climate are:

> People feel free to discuss their performance frankly with others and to seek constructive help when they need it.
>
> People feel free to take risks to extend themselves and build new skills and experience.
>
> Mistakes are freely admitted and effort is expended to learn from them.
>
> People feel challenged by their jobs and responsibilities.

Once the extent to which the climate is unhealthy has been determined, a plan should be developed to create a more healthy environment. Since often it is impractical or impossible to change things like the size of an organization or its geographic location, change efforts usually focus on the organization's structure, norms, and reward system. Sometimes, changes in these dimensions are accompanied by changes in policies and procedures as well. In recent years, a great deal of attention has been paid to the way the Japanese manage their organizations and the kind of climate they strive for within them. Similar concentrated attention to rewarding the behaviors that are

---

[1] "Sensing" is a form of group interview, in which a small group of individuals is asked to respond to questions about their perceptions of the organization.

sought and the norms that support those behaviors would noticeably improve organizational climate in this country's workplaces as well.

Changes in reward systems to reduce the focus on individual accomplishment and increase the emphasis on teamwork can make a much more collaborative work climate. Changes in norms can help to redefine what is acceptable and expected behavior in the workplace and, therefore, help to emphasize teamwork, collaboration, experimentation, and learning new skills. These kinds of changes can be accomplished when there is support for new norms from those in positions of power in the organization. The best way to show that support is by example. Therefore, if the top person in the organization or any of its sub-units engages in teamwork and collaborative behavior while also stating that he or she thinks such behavior will make the organization more effective, such behavior is likely to become institutionalized by others throughout the system. If the reward system(s) are changed to support the desired behavior, there will be additional impetus for change.

Changing the organizational climate involves changing the values, attitudes, and behaviors of the organization's members. But the leverage points for making such changes lie in the basic dimensions of the organization—that is, its goals, structure, rewards, and controls, to name just a few.

SUMMARY

Organizational climate refers to the overall atmosphere of a setting, the so-called feel of the environment. Some organizations have a warm, inviting, supportive climate; others are more tense and forbidding. Although the effects of climate are difficult to measure directly, they are often very powerful.

The organizational elements that determine climate include:

1. Goals.
2. Structure.
3. Rewards.
4. Size.
5. Geographic location.
6. Physical setting.
7. Norms.
8. Communications.

These factors affect climate in both obvious and subtle ways, which can be assessed along a number of dimensions (see Figure 4–2). In the aggregate, the effects tend to occur along the very general dimensions of *tension* (or fear) at one end and *excitement* (enthusiasm) at the other.

There are several methods of measuring (diagnosing) organizational climate:

1. Conducting a norms census.
2. Examining communication skills.
3. Observing behavior, dress, and other factors.
4. Evaluating the quality of meetings.
5. Observing aspects of the physical setting.
6. Assessing employee attitudes.

Once climate is understood, it is important to evaluate its consequences with respect to employee productivity, satisfaction, and development. Then it is possible to decide which aspects of the existing climate are fostering desirable versus undesirable outcomes. In the final analysis, changing organizational climate for the better requires some form of intervention into one or more of the basic dimensions of the system (e.g., goals, structure, rewards).

ANNOTATED BIBLIOGRAPHY

Dieterly, D. L., and B. Schneider   "The Effect of Organizational Environment on Perceived Power and Climate: A Laboratory Study." *Organizational Behavior and Human Performance* 11 (1974), pp. 316–37.

>   The behavior of individuals in organizations was conceptualized as a function of two perceptions: the climate existing in an organization and the power individuals perceive themselves to have. It is suggested that the process by which the larger organizational environment becomes translated into individual behavior is a function of these two variables.

Friedlander, F., and N. Margulies   "Multiple Impacts of Organizational Climate and Individual Value Systems upon Job Satisfaction." *Personnel Psychology* 22 (1969), pp. 171–83.

>   The impact of organizational climate and individual job values on workers' satisfactions was explored. "Data gathered from 95 employees of a research and development organization indicated that maximal satisfaction with different areas of one's work demands different mixes of climate components." It was found that combinations of different climate components that maximize work satisfaction are moderated by values held by employees.

Guion, R. M.   "A Note on Organizational Climate." *Organizational Behavior and Human Performance* 9 (1973), pp. 120–25.

>   Organizational climate appears to refer to an attribute or set of attributes of the work environment. The concept of "perceived organizational climate" seems ambiguous; it is not clear whether it implies an attribute of the organization or the perceiving individual. "If it refers to the organization, then measures of perceived organizational climate should be evaluated in terms of accuracy of the perceptions. If it refers to the individual, then perceived organizational climate may simply be a different name for job satisfaction or employee attitudes."

Hellriegel, D., and J. W. Slocum Jr.   "Organizational Climate: Measures, Research and Contingencies." *Academy of Management Journal*, June 1974, p. 255.

"This paper critically reviews one of the most important but least understood concepts in management—organizational climate. A contingency approach is proposed, various measures are discussed, and the studies are reviewed. Recommendations for future research are enumerated based on an analysis of the existing literature."

Johanneson, R. E. "Some Problems in the Measurement of Organizational Climate." *Organizational Behavior and Human Performance,* 10 (1973), pp. 118–44.

"Much research effort has recently been expended in assessing a construct known as organizational climate. The present paper, through literature review and logical argument, questions the independence of climate factors from those identified in research on work attitudes. Assessing climate via perceptual self-report measures may result in the replication of the work attitude literature."

Kaczka, E. E., and R. V. Kirk "Managerial Climate, Work Groups, and Organizational Performance." *Administrative Science Quarterly* 12 (1968) p. 252.

"A large-scale computer model was developed which integrated an empirically based model of work groups and foremen with a behavioral theory of the firm." This model was then used to study the effects of managerial climate on organizational performance. The results indicate that "under certain conditions of managerial climate, work groups can have marked effects on organizational performance."

Lawler, E. E. III. D. T. Hall. and G. R. Oldham "Organizational Climate: Relationship to Organizational Structure, Process, and Performance." *Organizational Behavior and Human Performance* 11 (1974), pp. 139–55.

"The present study was designed to test the view that organization structure and process are related to organizational climate which in turn is related to organization performance and employee job satisfaction. Results showed that several organizational process variables (but no structural variables) were significantly related to the climate of the organization as perceived by scientists." Perceived climate was shown to be significantly related to measures of performance and job satisfaction.

Lyon, H. L., and J. M. Ivancevich "An Exploratory Investigation of Organizational Climate and Job Satisfaction in a Hospital." *Academy of Management Journal,* December 1974, pp. 635–48.

The organizational climate of a hospital was investigated and its impact on job satisfaction analyzed for nurses and administrators. Different climate dimensions were found to influence individual job satisfaction facets, and the impact of organizational climate on satisfaction varied with the climate dimension and the type of satisfaction.

Pritchard, R. D., and B. W. Karasick "The Effects of Organizational Climate on Managerial Job Performance and Job Satisfaction." *Organizational Behavior and Human Performance* 9 (1973), pp. 126–46.

"The effects of organizational climate on job performance and satisfaction as well as the effects of interactions between climate and individual needs on performance and satisfaction were examined for 76 managers from two organizations. It was found that climate was influenced by both the overall organization and by subunits within the organization." It was also found that climate affected both sub-unit performance and worker job satisfaction.

Waters, L. K.; W. Batlis; and D. Roach "Organizational Climate Dimensions and Job-Related Attitudes." *Personnel Psychology* 27 (1974), pp. 465–76.

"The purpose of the present study was to factor analyze 22 perceptually based organization climate scales from three climate questionnaires on which some validity data have been published and to relate the dimensions found in the factor analysis to employees' subjective reports of satisfaction, involvement, intrinsic motivation, effort, and performance."

SUGGESTED READINGS

Jackson, Jay M. "Structural Characteristics of Norms." In *Role Theory: Concepts and Research,* ed. B. J. Biddle and E. J. Thomas. New York: John Wiley & Sons, 1966.

Main, J. "Westinghouse's Cultural Revolution." *Fortune,* June 1981, p. 74.

Marrow, Alfred J.; David G. Bowers; and Stanley E. Seashore *Management by Participation: Creating a Climate for Personal and Organizational Development.* New York: Harper & Row, 1967.

Maslow, Abraham H., and N. L. Mintz "Effects of Esthetic Surroundings: I. Initial Short-Term Effects of Three Esthetic Conditions upon Perceiving "Energy" and "Well-being" in Faces." In *People and Buildings,* ed. R. Gutman. New York: Basic Books, 1972, pp. 212–19.

Proshansky, Harold M.; William H. Ittelson; and Leanne G. Rivlin "The Influence of the Physical Environment on Behavior: Some Basic Assumptions." In *Environmental Psychology,* ed. Harold M. Proshansky, William H. Ittelson, and Leanne G. Rivlin. New York: Holt, Rinehart & Winston, 1970, pp. 27–37.

Steele, Fred I. "The Top-Down Society: Spatial Decisions in the Organizational World." *Environment Planning and Design* 1 (1971), pp. 24–30.

Steele, Fred I. *Physical Settings and Organizational Development.* Reading, Mass.: Addison-Wesley, 1973.

Steele, Fred I. *The Open Organization.* Reading, Mass.: Addison-Wesley Publishing, 1975.

Steele, Fritz, and Stephen Jenks *The Feel of the Work Place: Understanding and Improving Organization Climate.* Reading, Mass.: Addison-Wesley Publishing, 1977.

Tagiuri, R., and G. Litwin *Organizational Climate: Explorations of a Concept.* Boston: Division of Research, Harvard Business School, 1968.

CHAPTER 5

Reward Systems

INTRODUCTION

REWARDS are what you receive or experience for your efforts. They might include money, recognition, satisfaction from a job well done, promotion, or social approval. An organization's reward *system* is the total array of rewards available from that organization for the various individual and collective efforts of its members. To be effective, a reward system must be comprehensive and varied enough to provide inducements to a great variety of individuals. It is the reward system that reinforces performance relative to organizational goals; consequently, it is the key to the organization's ultimate success.

When we talk about an organization's reward system, we refer to all the rewards available to its membership regardless of whether or not they are consciously provided by management action, including, for example, the social satisfaction gained from working with others. While management can and does concern itself with the type of people it employs, it cannot directly give or withhold social satisfaction from an employee as it can a pay raise. So, in your thinking, be open to all rewards regardless of their source and regardless of whether management has direct control over them.

In this chapter, we will examine the essential ingredients of an effective reward system, the factors that influence the nature of a reward system, and how it affects the performance of individuals and groups in the organization. We will pay particular attention to the role of human needs as they affect performance. First we need to look at the *purposes* of a reward system.

PURPOSES SERVED BY A REWARD SYSTEM

Why do you take a job in the first place? What keeps you working at that job? What makes you exert at least a minimum effort, and what induces you to go beyond that minimum, to use your initiative, to be inventive? What makes you try to work with others collaboratively? Most of you have had to deal with questions of this sort at one time or another; you certainly will have to in the future. Furthermore, these same questions apply to your efforts in college and even to your present behavior in this course.

All these questions are related to rewards. Their answers describe the consequences of those rewards for your behavior. They also pertain to organizations and, in effect, describe the purposes that organizational reward systems serve. Using a modification of a list suggested by Jay Galbraith, we view a reward system as serving the following five purposes.[1]

---

[1] From chapter 16 in *Organizational Design* (Reading, Mass.: Addison-Wesley Publishing, 1977).

1. Attracting and Holding People in the Organization

It doesn't do a manager much good to worry about performance levels if he or she cannot even attract the right people and hold on to them. Attempting to pursue organizational goals with unqualified personnel is likely to inhibit effectiveness and reduce efficiency. Failing to hold on to good people (high turnover) is at best costly and at worst disruptive and a source of confusion.

2. Guaranteeing At Least Minimal Dependable Performance on the Job

For some kinds of work, this may be enough. Assembly line work that remains the same over time normally doesn't require more than a basic minimum effort; the problem is to keep performance from dropping *below* that level in terms of both quantity (output) and quality.

3. Encouraging Performance beyond the Minimum

Compared with the first two purposes, this one can be difficult to achieve because it requires a supervisor or manager to address the issue of *individual differences* in needs and abilities, not just the question of what attracts, holds, and guarantees minimal performance from *most* people.

4. Encouraging Initiative and Creativity in Members of the Organization

Again, the design of a reward system becomes even more complex with this added purpose. Initiative and creativity cannot be imposed from outside the individual; they come from *inside*. The most one can do from the outside is provide the right kind of stimulation. It is for this reason that one needs to consider the effects of the organization's structure and climate (especially norms) as they support or discourage individual initiative and creativity.

5. Promoting Collaborative Behavior

This should be done in those organizations or around those tasks that are interdependent and require the joint efforts of people with different knowledge and ability. As in the previous purpose, this one is strongly affected by an organization's goals, structure, and climate, as well as the needs and abilities of individuals. Even employees who are eager to work together can do so only to the extent that they are accessible to one another (structure) and the norms support such behavior (climate).

As we examine the different kinds of rewards, we will show how some rewards tend to serve certain purposes better than others and how some rewards can be relevant to all five purposes. In the early days of bureaucracy and scientific management, most large organizations paid particular attention to rewards that attracted and held people in the organization and also guaranteed minimal dependable performance. But as the economy grew, as organizational life became more complex, as our society became more affluent and workers demanded more, and as our knowledge of human behavior increased, it became more important for managers to pay attention to rewards that encouraged performance beyond the minimum, supported initiative and creativity, and promoted collaboration among people in interdependent roles.

As we examine the nature of reward systems, we emphasize the importance of looking at rewards as only one part of a complex network of factors that determine human performance. We also want to stress the importance of assessing the effectiveness of a reward system in terms of organizational *goal* attainment. Figure 5–1 shows in a simple way the connection between performance and goals as affected by motivation (needs) and rewards in a given organizational context.

For now we will pay special attention to *human needs* and *organizational rewards* as determinants of individual performance. Then we will introduce a number of modifying variables that make things more complex and tend to tax the imagination and patience of most managers. Knowing the common needs of people and the rewards of the system helps to give you *general* insights into job performance; understanding

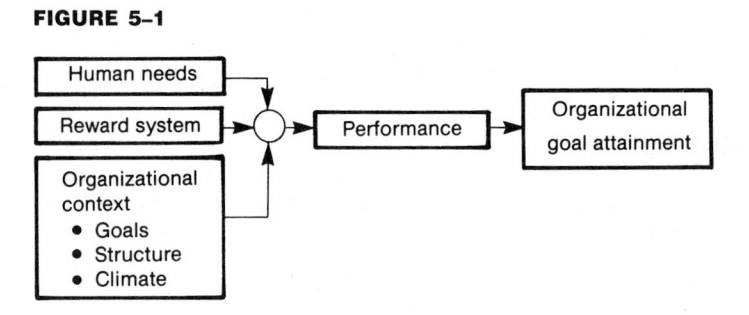

FIGURE 5–1

and predicting the *individual* case require a more careful analysis of an individual's own perceptions, experiences, place in the system, and other characteristics.

HUMAN MOTIVATION

Rewards exist in the environment or in a given situation or activity; needs exist inside people. Therefore, when we talk about linking an organization's reward system to human needs, we are talking about the links between external rewards and internal needs.

Human motivation is perhaps the most studied area of psychology. There are many theories, models, assumptions, hypotheses, and educated guesses about the nature of human needs; there are only a few reasonably established facts. We will start by listing some of the facts about motivation and then discuss several theories that have proved useful for understanding and managing people in organizations. These theories were selected because they seem particularly relevant to the reward system issues covered in this chapter.

What We Seem to Know about Human Needs

Although the idea of a "fact" tends to be resisted by many social scientists, the following statements are generally considered valid:

1. Human behavior is motivated by a variety of needs.
2. Human needs are physical, psychological, and social.
3. Some needs are met in relatively universal ways and some in ways relatively unique to the individual.
4. The physical needs tend to be met in universal ways and are often related to survival.
5. The psychological and social needs tend to be met in ways that are less universal and more subject to environmental influences.
6. The more that needs are related to survival, the less delayed gratification they will tolerate. Psychosocial needs can tolerate greater delayed gratification than physical or survival-related needs.

In addition to these six assumptions, there is a wide variety of theories and models of human motivations, all intended to provide ways of understanding and predicting behavior. The usefulness of each depends on the context in which it is applied.

In selecting the motivational theories most pertinent to the present discussion, we used three criteria:

1. The theory (or model) must provide a direct and useful way of organizing the wide range of human needs into a few simple and understandable categories.
2. It should have a history of useful application to problems of human motivation in organizations.
3. It should have fairly obvious relevance to the reward systems framework presented later in the chapter.

The two major theories of motivation that meet these criteria and also have had a major impact on management practices are Maslow's Hierarchy of Needs and Herzberg's Two-Factor Theory.

Maslow's Hierarchy of Needs

Perhaps the most influential motivational theory, at least with respect to organizational literature, was originally formulated in 1945 by Abraham Maslow, a distinguished psychologist who taught for many years at Brandeis University until his death in 1972. His theory is uniquely simple and elegant, yet it penetrates deeply into our understanding of human behavior. In some ways it was more of a discovery than an invention, since it was one of those ideas that had been "in the air" but never explicitly stated.

Maslow's formulation begins with the assumption that human needs exist in a *hierarchy*, that the hierarchy is determined by the successive *emergence* of different needs beginning at birth, and that the subsequent degrees of satisfaction or frustration of those needs determine the degree and kind of influence they will have on future behavior. His model classifies needs into five categories as follows:

1. Physiological needs.
2. Safety needs.
3. Love and belongingness needs.
4. Esteem needs.
5. Self-actualization needs.

These five are presented in their order of emergence according to the theory and thus constitute a hierarchy. The significance of this hierarchy is emphasized in Maslow's assertion that the emergence of a set of needs beyond the basic physiological level depends on some minimal degree of satisfaction of the previous level. In other words, the emergence (or expression) of safety needs occurs only after there is some degree of need satisfaction at the physiological level, and so on for each successive level. Maslow used the term *prepotency* to describe this relationship between levels.

Furthermore, he suggested that prepotency accounts for a person's tendency to withdraw attention from higher-level needs when lower-level ones are strongly frustrated or threatened. In general, a starving person will pay little attention to anything except obtaining food as soon as possible. Similarly, many organizations in the United States have found their employees expecting, even demanding, more interesting and less regimented work as their income levels have increased beyond the subsistence level and as they have come to feel less threat of an economic depression. There are obvious exceptions to the general principle (e.g., a person willing to die for a cause or someone so totally absorbed in some project that he or she neglects personal health), but it probably applies to most people in most circumstances. Let us examine each of these need levels and then return to a more general consideration of how the overall theory satisfies our three criteria.

1. Physiological Needs Although most of you who are anticipating or seeking employment will pay attention to other needs than just physiological ones, the satisfaction of some of your physiological needs is likely to play an important role, both directly and indirectly, in your overall job satisfaction. A physically uncomfortable work environment can produce prolonged discomfort that sooner or later begins to have detrimental effects on your productivity. Since physical comfort is a basic need in the hierarchy, you cannot afford to ignore it as an important aspect of your work environment. Think about the times when a classroom was too hot or too cold or too noisy. An exciting lecture or discussion can sometimes draw your attention away from the discomfort, but usually for only a short time. Imagine a steady diet of discomfort in a job!

In an indirect way, physiological needs are *always* a factor in determining your behavior. You work, in part, to keep yourself alive, to obtain adequate food and shelter to maintain your physical health and stamina. In developed societies like ours, most people perceive only a remote connection between working and eating (i.e., an economic link in the form of money), but even in America there are many pockets of poverty where physiological survival is directly connected to work behavior. For many people, basic survival is a way of life; higher-order needs may never enter the picture. In some sense, the concept of an *underdeveloped* country reflects not only its economic status but also the need levels that characterize it—that is, primarily concerned with basic survival (physiological and safety) issues.

2. Safety Needs In a physical sense, safety refers to protection from potential harm in the environment; in an economic sense, it refers to the assurance that one will not lack the wherewithal to provide for adequate shelter, clothing, and comfort; and in a psychological sense, it refers to a feeling of security and well-being as a member of society.

Working is a fundamental means of meeting safety needs. Therefore, most people have little choice (with obvious exceptions) about doing some kind of work to establish a secure place in society. Since organizations are the principal context in which people work, they are a primary vehicle for meeting these needs. If you were to list the reasons why you sought to work for a particular employer, some would undoubtedly be related to economic and personal security. Once you've established that kind of a base, you feel freer to devote your energies to meeting other needs that are more related to growth and development.

Certainly some people are more concerned about job security than others, depending on their previous experiences and current pressures. It may be that at this stage in your life, you are thinking more about other needs—social, career, creative—than job security. It may be that you have confidence in your ability to survive and, consequently, pay more attention to your other needs and goals. However, large organizations are populated with people whose principal concerns and efforts are aimed at establishing a safe, secure, and stable world for themselves and their families. For this reason, as you will see when we discuss the nature of reward systems, most organizations pay the greatest attention to rewards that address the survival needs of their employees. They are the most general and their means of satisfaction (the rewards) tend to be the most universal.

3. Love and Belongingness Needs This set of needs sounds like an unusual matter for an organization to be concerned about. We usually think of business, industry, and other institutions as relatively impersonal, task-oriented environments, certainly not worried about people feeling loved or having a sense of belonging. This might have been true at one time for all organizations and it is still true of many, but modern enlightened management recognizes and actively accepts the idea that people—*even on the job*—have interpersonal and social needs, want to be cared about, and want membership in their work environments.

Some people's needs of this type are much stronger than other people's, possibly even to the point where they impede a person's productivity. At the other extreme, there are individuals whose desire to be liked or to relate closely to others is relatively low—at least within the context of their work setting. Therefore, they do not seek or provide for others very much personal attention unrelated to task.

In recent years a great deal of attention has been given to efforts such as task-group development, shared decision making, and work teams. Although the primary reason for these efforts has pertained to maximizing and integrating resources, one important benefit has been to build a kind of camaraderie and support base from which members of an organization can build a greater sense of commitment. These experiences help people to meet many of their interpersonal and social needs in ways that are an integral part of the work itself, not an afterthought tacked on to "keep people happy."

As a social system, an organization cannot afford to write off needs in this category as "out of place" in the work setting. Attempts to do so are likely to result in an informal social system that can undermine the formal one. The challenge is to design reward systems that help to make the inevitable behavior of people support the goals of the organization. Social behavior can be considered inevitable when you bring people together for almost any purpose.

4. Esteem Needs At some level every individual needs to be appreciated, valued, and respected by others; that is, he or she needs to feel a sense of *esteem*. Different people have different ways of meeting esteem needs—through achievement, recognition, status, the respect of others, and so on. Such needs play a vital role in people's work behavior and careers. Few individuals are satisfied just to bring home a paycheck; they seek something more. One's personal sense of worth depends not on receiving the blanket rewards handed out to everyone, but rather on being singled out and valued for one's efforts, both in one's own eyes and in the eyes of others.

While the satisfaction of basic physiological, safety, and love needs provides a foundation for a person's survival and comfort in the world, it is the satisfaction of esteem and self-actualization needs that provides *growth* for an individual. Although some societies or cultures offer limited opportunities for meeting higher-level needs, these needs usually find their way into most people's lives, perhaps within only a limited context, such as a family.

Most organizations provide ways for members to meet esteem needs. They recognize the vital importance of giving people responsibility and ownership over some portions of their work. This is more easily done with managers, particularly at upper levels of an organization; it is often more difficult or even impossible to find ways to achieve such purposes at the lower, more routinized levels. Nonetheless, janitors and custodians can take pride in doing their jobs well and appreciate having their efforts recognized. Furthermore, even with such lower, more routinized jobs, creative managers have achieved some success. The work teams at Volvo and Saab are obvious examples. In those companies, individual team members are given the opportunity to control and master the more complex aspects of the work as well as to develop a greater sense of ownership of the product. The feeling of self-esteem that resulted for each worker was astounding, something a paycheck and fringe benefits could never accomplish.

If you think about your needs as a student, you can see how your sense of esteem plays a dominant role in your behavior. The grades you receive, the attention you receive from instructors, the respect you get from fellow students, and the sense of accomplishment you feel when you do a good job on a paper all build up—or tear down, when you fail—your feelings of worth and esteem. This, in turn, affects how you approach each successive assignment or task—namely, with a sense of either high expectation or despair.

If and when you ultimately find your way into a position of managerial responsibility, keep in mind that esteem needs are a part of all people: the person on the assembly line or sweeping the hall, as well as the hotshot sales manager who seeks prestige and recognition in obvious ways. Also keep in mind that there are many ways in which esteem needs can be met, unlike the more universal ways for survival needs.

5. Self-Actualization Needs There are things a person does to fulfill some inner capacity for its own sake. It may be an activity that produces sheer enjoyment apart from any outcomes or reactions from others—playing a musical instrument, building furniture, raising flowers, flying a glider, sailing, and the endless list of things that people seem to do almost because they cannot *not* do them. Even everyday activities like reading, walking, and watching the waves roll across a beach can fall into this category.

According to Maslow, something (perhaps many things) in each of us strives for fulfillment, gives each of us a sense of greater identity. The needs that fall into this category he identifies with *self-actualization,* which essentially amounts to the realization of one's inner potential. Environments and experiences can kill that potential or fail to provide the resources for people to meet such needs. When they go unmet, people may go through life relatively unfulfilled as human beings. This is not uncommon, as you might know.

Most societies reflect the needs of their members. Those that are struggling with survival or are in a stage of rapid development might have some distance to go before the self-actualization needs of their members will be fulfilled. However, organizations in modern Western society can be—and perhaps are now—more aware of and responsive to the highest and most individualistic needs of people. Because of the unique ways in which people strive for self-actualization, no organization can easily or inexpensively provide the means for meeting such needs. But there is no doubt that the increasing complexities and uncertainties of today's organizational life demand the creativity and imagination that are very often expressed in self-actualizing behavior. Tapping into that creativity can serve both the organization's goals and the individual's needs. (See Box 5–1 on other higher order needs.)

Box 5-1

ACHIEVEMENT, AFFILIATION, AND POWER NEEDS:
THE CONTRIBUTIONS OF DAVID MCCLELLAND

David McClelland's book *The Achieving Society* (New York: Van Nostrand Reinhold, 1961) was a landmark contribution to our knowledge of motivation in work environments. McClelland's research on *achievement* and *affiliation* needs throughout the 1960s provided valuable insights into the behavior of individuals as well as the growth of industrial societies. His work on entrepreneurship is critical to our understanding of successful businessmen.

McClelland's more recent research has been related to the need for *power* and has contributed to our knowledge of the behavior of leaders and their impact on society. His distinction between *personalized power* and *socialized power* may be critical in removing the usual negative connotation of the term *power*. McClelland's book *Power: The Inner Experience* (New York: Irvington Publishers, 1975) is his major work on this topic.

Significance of Maslow's Hierarchy

Whether or not human needs exist in a hierarchy, as Maslow proposes, or exert influence independent of one another seems to be a matter of some dispute. Some people find the concept of a hierarchy very helpful in explaining behavior, and some who accept the categories insist that the hierarchical order is irrelevant or even confusing. Since there is no absolute proof for either position, you may need to decide for yourself which position seems most valid.

In any event, the theory does satisfy our criteria; it provides a few simple, direct, and useful categories for sorting out a wide range of specific needs, it has an established history of application to organizations, and, as you will see, it provides a basis for judging the effectiveness of a reward system.

One implication of Maslow's theory is that the hierarchy of needs may be parallel to the organization's structural hierarchy; that is, people at the lower levels of an organization tend to be motivated by lower-level needs and people at higher levels by higher-level needs. Although there is some evidence to support this, there are too many exceptions to consider it completely valid. The relationship depends to a great extent on the nature of the organization, its sociocultural setting, its history, the labor market, the numbers of people, and other factors.

When it comes down to basics, *most* people in our society have needs at many (if not all) levels of the hierarchy. Whether you are a mechanic at the bottom of the organization or an executive at the top, you have a need for self-esteem. The *means* of meeting that need might vary for each person or might even be very much the same (e.g., seeking the respect of relevant colleagues or co-workers), but the satisfaction of that need may be equally important to both individuals.

As you evaluate any organizational reward system, you can use the need hierarchy as a framework for judging the degree to which the organization is addressing the *full range* of human motivation that affects performance at work. Obviously, a work environment is normally not intended to meet all of a person's needs; many needs are met at home through family, friends, recreation, or hobbies. However, you will probably find (or may have already) that a work environment that meets a wide range of human needs is likely to generate a high level of commitment and make it less necessary for employees to look for "escape" to other settings for need satisfaction.

Herzberg's Two-Factor Theory

An organizational psychologist named Frederick Herzberg identified needs related to survival and needs related to growth. The former he called *hygiene factors* and the latter *motivators*. Unlike Maslow, however, Herzberg described each set of needs as existing on an independent continuum, not in a hierarchical relationship. The distinction is significant because it stresses the importance of paying attention to both simultaneously, and furthermore it emphasizes the differences in the means by which these needs are met.

In Herzberg's model, hygiene factors tend to be evident when there is some *deficiency* related to them. You tend to pay attention to your physical comfort when you become uncomfortable, you worry about health benefits when you are afraid you don't have enough protection, you pay attention to your wages or salary when you find that the cost of living has increased again, and so on. In short, when there is some discrepancy between what you need and what you have, then the need prompts you to action to correct the deficiency. Once corrected, behavior related to the needs tends to desist.

What Herzberg calls motivators seem to operate differently; they have their own motivating force that affects people's behavior independent of the environment. Their satisfaction tends to result in an *increase* in behavior related to them, suggesting that there is never complete satisfaction.

Herzberg's research showed a significant relationship between job satisfaction and the two kinds of needs. Specifically, he found that dissatisfaction (complaints, negative feelings) tended to be associated with hygiene factors, while satisfaction (successes, positive feelings) tended to be associated with motivators. The importance of this finding lies in its implications for the degree to which managers pay attention to different sets of needs of employees. You can often reduce complaints through salary increases, benefits, and physical improvements, but you may not get *motivated* workers. To get motivated workers, you need to find ways to increase recognition, responsibility, self-determination, and achievement. The Herzberg approach to worker motivation does not suggest ignoring hygiene factors; it simply points out that attention to these factors is not enough. He suggests approaches like job enrichment and job enlargement for dealing with motivators, thus rounding out the picture with attention to factors that are more likely to have self-sustaining effects.

Comparison of Maslow and Herzberg

The similarities and differences between Maslow's and Herzberg's theories are both striking and important. The theories reinforce each other in their recognition of different levels of needs as well as the existence of a wide range of needs. Furthermore, despite differences in the labels, both models consider survival (hygiene) and growth (motivators) to be important elements of human motivation, and both approaches, when applied to organizational life, encourage managers to pay attention not only to what motivates most people but also to the individual ways in which people seek satisfaction and development.

One important difference between the theories pertains to prepotency versus independence. If you were to take Maslow's model literally, you might assume that the lower-level needs should be given primary attention—either sequentially or relative to one another at a given time—before worrying about the higher-level needs. For example, in building an organization following the prepotency principle, you might assume that your reward system should first be concerned with the survival needs of the members and then (even later in time) the growth needs. In some ways, this assumption makes inherent sense and probably is valid for many people.

Herzberg's model, by way of contrast, would push you to pay attention to hygiene factors and motivators simultaneously, recognizing that you are dealing with two different and independent issues. He does not assume that deficiencies in hygiene factors have any effect on motivators. Quite the contrary; Herzberg would insist that the two operate along separate continua.

Another important difference, especially as it affects the concept of a reward system, is the consequences of need satisfaction as implied in each theory. Maslow's hierarchy explicitly describes need satisfaction as leading to a freeing of energy for other purposes. It also explicitly states that unfulfilled or frustrated needs at lower (more basic) levels tend to pull energy from higher-level pursuits. In some sense, therefore, all needs in Maslow's scheme are affected by deficiencies, and the satisfaction of needs results in the withdrawal of continued investment in those needs until a deficiency is again experienced.

In Herzberg's theory, these principles would apply to only the hygiene factors, not the motivators. Motivators, in his theory, *increase* their influence on behavior as a consequence of satisfaction; that is, the satisfaction of higher-level needs leads to an increase in the activity related to them. This thesis is, in fact, consistent with what we know about learned behavior—namely, that we tend to do more of what leads to desired rewards.

There has been a long history of debate on the validity of the two views of motivation. The research is inconclusive and the arguments on both sides have merits. Perhaps both concepts (hierarchy and independent factors) have some validity, and circumstances and people in a given context may make one or the other more useful. For example, during a recession, management might appropriately emphasize rewards that satisfy lower-level needs and then, with a return to better times, refocus its attention on higher-level needs, but management should not be surprised if people seek more than hygiene factors even during bad times. You may have to discover for yourself which approach works best for you from a managerial standpoint.

We want to emphasize that, despite the differences, both theories provide a simple and yet comprehensive way of sorting out human needs, and they reinforce each other in identifying the kinds of needs that are relevant in an organizational setting. For these reasons, we feel that they serve well as a backdrop for evaluating a reward system. As we discuss the nature of reward systems, we will repeatedly refer back to the organizational purposes they serve and to the human needs they are intended to meet as criteria for judging their effectiveness.

THE NATURE OF REWARDS

Given the range of needs that people have and the multiple purposes of a reward system, such a system must be broad and inclusive. The model we found to be ideally suited to the situation was originally developed by Daniel Katz in 1964[2] and since incorporated into a number of writings on reward systems, most notably and recently by Jay Galbraith in 1977.[3]

The framework presented by Katz divides rewards into six very broad categories related to the following:

---

[2] D. Katz, "The Motivational Basis of Organizational Behavior," *Behavioral Science* 9 (1964), pp. 131–46.

[3] J. Galbraith, *Organization Design* (Reading, Mass.: Addison-Wesley Publishing, 1977).

1. Compliance with the rules and norms of the organization.
2. General rewards or benefits provided to all members of the organization.
3. Individual rewards based on merit, effort, and performance.
4. Intrinsic satisfactions accruing from task or role performance.
5. Internalized values congruent with the organization's mission and identity.
6. Social satisfactions stemming from interpersonal and group relationships.

Let's look at each of these categories and see how it relates to the purposes and needs already discussed.

1. Rule Compliance

For rule compliance to be a reward, organizational members must be *willing* to accept the idea that their behavior, within limits, is governed by others in authority. For some members of an organization, rule compliance often relieves fears about making "wrong" choices, thus satisfying a need for security or stability, especially in a new situation. For others, rule compliance is a way of living up to one's values about proper behavior or reinforcing one's self-concept as a responsible person.

Rule compliance is effective as a reward only insofar as those in authority communicate clear expectations and those who comply do so willingly, even to the point of suspending personal judgment. In the absence of compliance, there is no authority relationship at all, and when compliance is not the individual's willing choice, it no longer serves as a reward.

Where the norms of the organization support the rules, then those in authority have the legitimacy needed to enforce those rules. In other words, rule compliance is equivalent to norm compliance, further reinforcing the behavior of the individual as a "member in good standing" of the organization, both formally and informally.

Much of your behavior as a student is governed by rule compliance. However, whether or not you personally experience compliance as *rewarding* depends on your value system, your need for guidance from authority, the degree to which you feel some choice in the matter (as opposed to coercion), and the behavior of other students in treating the rules as legitimate or not. However, for many students, the idea of rule compliance automatically sets up resistance, if not open antagonism, often to the point where rule *defiance* is viewed as a reward.

Some organizations, especially long-established institutions like the church, the military, and many medical schools, depend on rule compliance as a necessary part of their reward systems. In many instances the rules embody the essence of the organization and, consequently, play a dominant role in determining membership.

Unfortunately, some people find following the rules so rewarding that they ignore other considerations. The stereotypic bureaucrat has totally suspended judgment and plugs questions and problems into predetermined categories, letting "the rules" make the decisions. Such behavior finds its reward in the act of compliance, all too often to the detriment of those affected by the behavior. In today's organizations, too many situations arise that require some exception be made to the rules to allow behavior of this kind to predominate. Consequently, rule compliance as a reward will very likely come to play a less and less important role in the future.

Relative to Maslow's hierarchy, rule compliance seems to satisfy security, belongingness, and some esteem needs, or a combination of these, in different people. However, rule compliance itself is normally not enough of a reward system to sustain the adequate performance of organizational members over a long time. It does not adequately tap into motivators (in Herzberg's terms), which tend to require rewards more suited to the uniqueness of the individual.

With respect to the purposes of a reward system, rule compliance can at best attract people who seek orderliness and clear expectations and can even guarantee some minimal level of performance from them, but it is rarely sufficient to inspire outstanding performance, creativity, or collaboration. Any organization that depends heavily on compliance to rules as its main basis of rewarding behavior risks limiting its appeal to a relatively small number of people—at least in the long run.

2. General System Rewards

Modern organizations have paid considerable attention to system-wide rewards, especially with the demands generated by unions and collective bargaining. These rewards take the form of wage and salary scales, health benefits, retirement plans, safe working conditions, and discounts on products of the organization. These are all rewards that accrue with membership in the system; that is, they don't have to be earned by the individual, since they apply to *all* members.

Broad-based rewards generally address the kinds of needs that all people have and that can be met in similar ways for most. In Maslow's model, these are the physiological and safety needs; in Herzberg's terms, these are the hygiene factors. Job security, for example, is a very pervasive concern to people; therefore, organizations that expressly provide some job security are building an important element into their reward systems. The same is true for health benefits and cost-of-living increases. In many respects, these rewards are the easiest to determine and satisfy, because they address the most basic and general human needs. No organization can afford to ignore the rewards that pertain to the most general human concerns and that, consequently, ought to accompany membership in the system. However, as we examine the other categories of rewards, you will see that broad-based rewards are not sufficient in themselves as a complete reward system. They go a long way to attract and hold people in the system, and they normally guarantee at least minimal performance from employees. However, system rewards seem to require frequent tending and periodic revision to motivate exceptional effort. An improvement produces an initial positive effect, but performance usually levels off or drops if no more self-sustaining rewards are offered. Only rarely do such general rewards encourage creativity or collaborative efforts.

3. Individual Rewards

Individual rewards are received as a result of individual performance. They take the form of incentive pay systems (e.g., piecework or commissions), merit raises, bonuses, promotions, special privileges, educational opportunities, recognition, and status. Though available to many members of the organization, they are administered individually and thus reinforce the personal efforts of employees independent of the performance levels of their co-workers.

Esteem and self-actualization needs in Maslow's hierarchy (motivators in Herzberg's theory) are met by an organization's individually oriented rewards. It is comparatively easy for an organization to establish a reward system for the more general common needs; it is much more difficult to design a system that can appeal to a great variety of personal preferences.

The kinds of opportunities you seek in a job, the responsibilities you anticipate, your personal career ambitions, the degree of autonomy you prefer, and the challenges that interest you all influence how the reward system will fit your individual constellation of needs, which is different from anyone else's. This means that individual rewards in an organization must be wide-ranging and flexible to meet the wide-ranging needs of the members. Furthermore, they must be realistic (within the reach of individuals seeking to attain them, assuming appropriate effort, of course).

Rewards in this category serve almost all, if not all, the purposes of a reward system. They attract and hold people; they guarantee not only minimal performance but usually performance well beyond that; and they encourage initiative but usually do not promote collaboration. You might ask: If individual rewards do all that, then why bother with any of the other categories? The fact is that individual rewards—which, as you know, relate to higher-level needs—are not necessarily relevant to all people. Large numbers of people work for a paycheck and the security it buys, finding means outside of work to meet other needs. Furthermore, many jobs do not easily lend themselves to individualization; attempts to individualize the rewards might be unrealistic, or very costly.

The important point is that to the extent that you want performance to go beyond the minimum, you need to introduce rewards that encourage it. How varied and complex those rewards need to be depends on how far and in what ways you want that effort to go beyond the minimum.

4. Intrinsic Satisfactions

Undoubtedly, there have been times when you have become completely absorbed in a project, when the process of doing the work was its own reward. Many vocations have this characteristic; unfortunately, not nearly enough provide this intrinsic satisfaction. Work that has its own built-in reward energizes a person, keeps that person motivated to do more, to go further. Perhaps you've taken a course in which you enjoyed the reading, thinking, writing, and discussion even to the point where a grade was almost irrelevant. That kind of experience may provide you with an important clue about an appropriate career.

To the extent that an organization can match people to jobs that are intrinsically satisfying or enrich jobs so that they become so, then the organization will bring out some of its most self-sustaining talents and resources. Again, certain kinds of settings impose severe constraints on such rewards, because of the nature of the work, the economic state of the organization, and other factors. However, many managers have made the mistake of assuming that unskilled workers do not have higher-level needs; these managers often have failed to seek ways to build intrinsic satisfactions into the work environment.

With respect to the purposes of a reward system, intrinsic satisfactions probably have little to do with attracting people to the organization in the first place, with the exception of individuals whose primary job focus is the reward derived from the work itself (e.g., research scientists). Usually people develop intrinsic satisfaction as they involve themselves in the work. Intrinsic rewards certainly sustain effort at a level well beyond the minimum and also promote initiative and creativity. Whether or not collaboration is affected by them depends on the nature of the work. Where joint effort is an intrinsic part of the work, then the satisfaction is built in. Where it is not a part of the work, then the intrinsic reward is not likely to promote collaboration; it could even work against it, as with highly individual research activities.

5. Internalized Organizational Values

If your personal values fit those of an organization as reflected in its identity or mission, then being a part of that organization serves as a reward. It helps to affirm you as an individual. Throughout their lives people join clubs, social organizations, churches, the Boy Scouts or Girl Scouts, campaign drives, and other groups, because they *identify* with these organizations. Sometimes there is no other reward attached to the time and effort one puts into such a setting apart from the personal fulfillment of one's values.

It is probably rare for employees in a manufacturing company to identify with the mission of the company, unless the product happens to benefit society. Identification of this sort is more likely to occur in organizations that provide a service, especially when that service directly addresses important social needs and values. Educational institutions, health care settings, and perhaps even hotel and recreation industries are examples of contexts that tend to attract people who identify with the *raison d'etre* of the organization. Perhaps you have found even menial tasks to be rewarding when they were in the service of a cause or goal with which you strongly identify. When a person chooses a professional career, that choice often reflects personal identity and mission. To the extent that the organization of which the person is a member reflects that same identity and mission, then membership in that organization is its own reward. Even where the primary goal of a company is profit, some employees might identify with its product or service because of their own personal interests (e.g., an amateur photographer working for Polaroid or Eastman Kodak).

Although it is difficult to link internalized organizational values with any one category of needs, since there may be elements of security, belongingness, and self-esteem involved, a sense of self-actualization does seem to be met. There is the feeling that the organization is providing an important vehicle for fulfilling one's own purpose in life. Although it may not be explicitly stated in such philosophical terms, many people who experience this form of reward can acknowledge its self-fulfilling nature.

Given the wide range of needs it taps into, it is not surprising that identification with the organizational mission tends to serve *all* the purposes of a reward system. By itself, it may not be enough to sustain long-term performance, especially if inadequacies in other rewards frustrate some basic needs. Even the most dedicated physician or teacher will find it difficult to keep up maximum performance and initiative if the pay scale is grossly out of line or the working conditions are very poor. However, when the other sources of reward are present, this one tends to complete the picture in an ideal way. What more could you ask for than to work in a context that not only satisfies your survival and growth needs but also reflects your own personal identity?

6. Social Satisfaction

People are certainly social beings. Place two or more people in close proximity and they are almost certain to interact. The interaction might or might not be related to work, but it will occur. When jobs require interaction, that process is normally expected to enhance productivity. This may generate a sense of accomplishment. A secondary benefit is often that people find the interaction *itself* to be rewarding, since it meets interpersonal and social needs and provides some sense of membership and belonging in the organization, at least with respect to the immediate group of people.

Social satisfactions have for so long been associated with nonwork activities that they have tended to be considered more of a hindrance than a help to productivity. The more modern view, however, recognizes the inevitability of social factors and appreciates that the social norms of a work group can enhance productivity. It has also been recognized that social rewards can compensate for the lack of intrinsic rewards in routine, dull work.

In Herzberg's theory, social needs are grouped with hygiene factors and, consequently, are not stressed as important for sustaining motivation. Maslow's model takes a different view, treating interpersonal and social needs as powerful elements of most situations. Whichever view you adopt, there is no doubt that organizations are social systems with social rewards. An appreciation of this fact can help a manager to enrich his or her reward system and, when necessary, legitimize the social rewards where no others will suffice.

Social rewards serve limited purposes. They might draw people into the job market, but they rarely attract them to specific jobs initially. However, they do *retain* employees, since personal attachments are hard to break. Social rewards may help to keep performance up to at least a minimal level, but they infrequently serve as an incentive to performance beyond that or to initiative and creative efforts. By themselves, social rewards do not promote task-related collaboration, but coupled with other rewards (e.g., intrinsic satisfaction), they reinforce the collaborative process. Overall, social rewards are important as part of a total reward system, but they serve very limited purposes, especially in comparison with individual rewards, intrinsic satisfactions, and identification with organizational mission.

In addition to the points already covered, we wish to mention one other purpose of a reward system—that is, to foster *loyalty* among employees. Loyalty implies a commitment to the organization, a willingness to give of oneself, a willingness to go along with changes the organization seeks to make, and even a willingness to accept some short-term personal loss to facilitate organizational well-being.

Internalization of organizational values and identification with the organization's mission tend to build loyalty as well as hold people in the organization. To a lesser extent, general system awards, insofar as they generate a positive attitude toward the organization, tend to build loyalty. Social satisfactions may also; although generally whatever loyalty is so generated tends to be to a department or primary work group rather than to the total organization.

The other types of rewards do little to foster loyalty. Although intrinsic satisfaction may tend to hold people in the organization, they will not stay out of loyalty. As with individual rewards, given a better opportunity elsewhere, the individual is likely to leave one situation providing intrinsic satisfaction for another. The classic example of this is the scientist who doesn't care where he works so long as he can "do his thing." His loyalty is to his profession rather than to the organization.

The Entrepreneur—A Special Case

The entrepreneur is an interesting example of someone in a situation that contains multiple rewards. He or she is usually motivated by a strong need to achieve combined with an enjoyment of high-risk ventures. The organization created by the entrepreneur (which might be anything from a one-person operation to a medium-sized, complex system) normally reflects his or her interests and abilities, produces rewards that are directly related to personal effort, and poses constant challenges to one's creative talents. Thus, identification with the organization is high, as are intrinsic satisfactions and individual rewards. Although rewards related to rule compliance and basic security (general system rewards) are not likely to be part of an entrepreneurial venture, members of an organization of this type normally find the other rewards to be more than adequate and usually also experience a kind of social camaraderie frequently missing in more "secure" organizations.

As long as the rewards continue, commitment and loyalty remain high. Over the long run, however, most organizations that are successful and grow (especially in numbers of employees) tend to change in character and stabilize around ongoing functions and activities that do not reflect the entrepreneurial spirit that built the organization in the first place.

One irony of organizational life is that very often when an entrepreneurial approach (i.e., high risk) is most needed, the organization focuses on consolidation and security. In today's world, where environmental changes constantly plague modern organizations, the freewheeling inventive mentality of the entrepreneur is often needed. Unfortunately, the tensions created by environmental uncertainty push managers toward control and conservatism. The entrepreneur thinks in the opposite direction and, consequently, is not likely to carry much influence.

OVERVIEW

1. To the extent that organizational policies or rules of behavior are reasonable and not arbitrary, *compliance* with them tends to serve as a reward for many members of the organization. Being a "member in good standing" can be an incentive for energetic and productive activity. Although not everyone finds rule compliance to be an attractive reward (apart from its being a means to the attainment of some other reward, such as job security), the fact that many find it so makes it important to consider when linking performance to organizational rewards.

2. To the extent that organizational rewards connect to the *basic and most general needs*—survival and security—they serve as incentives to large numbers of people. Most organizations, for example, include among their rewards such things as the establishment and improvement of benefit plans, retirement packages, health benefits, and cost-of-living increases. Success in the attainment of these kinds of rewards directly benefits all members of the system. Consequently, their existence is an almost built-in guarantee of some minimal level of performance.

3. To the extent that an organizational reward system can be translated into specific and varied *individual* incentives, it enhances the performance of a wide range of people. For example, organizational rewards for employee development can be an incentive to individual efforts to learn and grow. Two important features of such rewards are that they be attainable and realistic.

4. To the extent that organizational rewards are attached to activities that are *intrinsically satisfying*, they (the rewards) serve as natural incentives to performance for its own sake. For example, a hospital might include among its rewards the opportunity for a person to learn about new aspects of medical care. For a member of its nursing department, such a reward would probably be intrinsically satisfying, apart from whatever other benefits might accrue.

5. To the extent that organizational members can *identify* with and internalize the organizational goals (i.e., their own personal goals are consistent with those of the organization), they tend to find the

organization a rewarding place to work. Often it is the most general mission or purpose of the organization with which people identify, as might be the case with people who work for a church or some humanitarian institution. Sometimes only a few of the goals provide a basis for identification. Working for a bank, for example, might offer the opportunity to provide financial help to people who are struggling to make ends meet.

6. To the extent that an organization includes among its rewards a supportive and stimulating *social environment,* it is likely to retain and enhance the commitment of its members. When people feel that they *belong* to a social system or to a primary group, they feel commitment to its survival and growth. The social system of an organization includes both its formal departments and its informal natural groupings of people. As social beings, most people have social and interpersonal goals, many of which are attained directly in organizational life.

7. When all is said and done, organizations develop different degrees of loyalty among their employees.

Think about some of the organizations for which you have worked or with which you are familiar. List the organizational rewards that reflect each of the six categories. Can you assess their adequacy insofar as they are broadly or narrowly based? Where do your own needs lie, and what should you look for in the reward system of your prospective or present employer?

REWARDS AND THE INDIVIDUAL

The next portion of this chapter will look at reward systems through the eyes of the individual as he or she might experience them. The more general view covered so far can help a manager to understand and plan rewards for organizational members collectively, but to understand and predict the performance of an individual, it is necessary to adopt a more personal frame of reference. This section should be especially useful as a way to look at your current performance in school, at work, or in other contexts, as well as in relation to future career and employment choices.

Our focus is on individual performance, which, as shown in Figure 5–2, leads to the attainment of rewards for the individual and goals for the organization. We will show how effort and, in turn, performance are determined by the *attractiveness* of the rewards to the individual and by his or her *expectancies* about the connection between effort and perform-

FIGURE 5-2

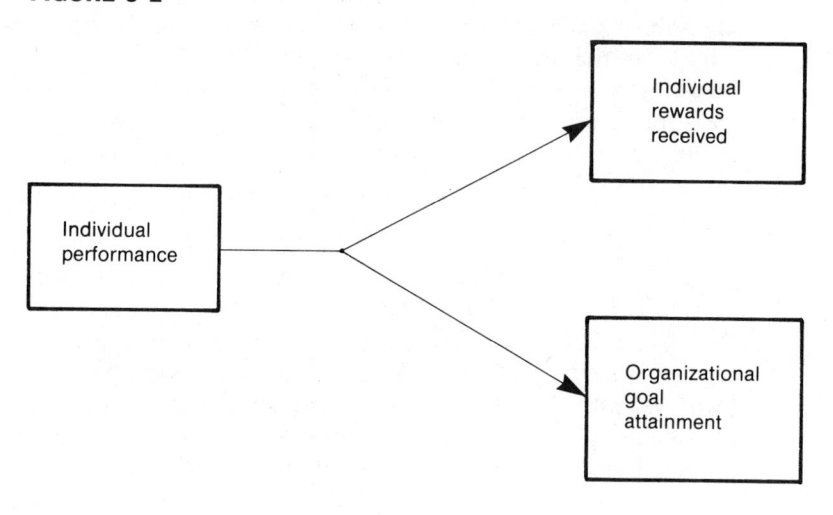

```
                                    ┌──────────────┐
                                    │ Individual   │
                                    │ rewards      │
                                    │ received     │
                                    └──────────────┘
                                         ▲
                                        /
                    ┌──────────────┐   /
                    │ Individual   │──<
                    │ performance  │   \
                    └──────────────┘    \
                                         ▼
                                    ┌──────────────┐
                                    │ Organizational│
                                    │ goal          │
                                    │ attainment    │
                                    └──────────────┘
```

ance and between performance and rewards. Then we will show how attraction and expectancies are determined by the individual's *perceptions* of the organization's reward system and his or her *needs and abilities*. Finally, we will show how all these factors are influenced by the organizational context—that is, goals, structure, and climate. First we will look at performance itself.

Determinants of Effort and Performance: Attraction and Expectancy

As reflected in Figure 5-3, an *individual's effort/performance on the job is directly related to (1) the degree to which he or she finds the rewards for performance to be attractive, (2) the degree to which he or she expects efforts to result in performance that meets established standards, and (3) the degree to which he or she expects that performance to result in the attainment of rewards.* This proposition is simple and straightforward, but very basic. If you think about your own behavior, what you want, and what you believe will get you what you want, you will see that this model applies. Obviously many other factors can prevent you from acting where you might choose to act or push you to do something you would not normally find attractive. However, the combination of attraction and expectancy seems to be a powerful force that affects individual behavior, especially performance on the job.

If the rewards are seen by the individual as of little worth and ones

FIGURE 5-3

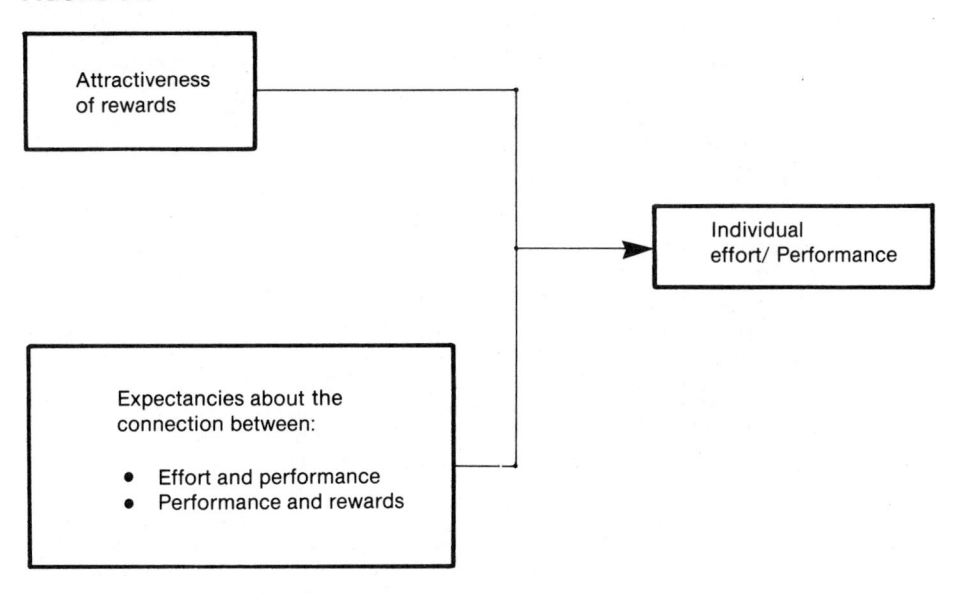

```
┌─────────────────────┐
│ Attractiveness      │
│ of rewards          │────────────────┐
└─────────────────────┘                │
                                       ▼
                              ┌─────────────────────┐
                              │ Individual          │
                              │ effort/ Performance │
                              └─────────────────────┘
                                       ▲
┌─────────────────────────┐            │
│ Expectancies about the  │            │
│ connection between:     │────────────┘
│                         │
│ • Effort and performance│
│ • Performance and rewards│
└─────────────────────────┘
```

that will not satisfy his or her needs, there will be little incentive to perform. Even if the rewards are seen as worthwhile, if the person sees little connection between performance and obtaining the rewards, he or she will have little reason to put forth much effort. For example, you might find that in a family-owned business, entrance into top management is limited to family members. Nonmembers would probably not feel much incentive to perform to reach a high position even if such a position were seen as attractive. Similarly, in organizations where promotion is strongly based on seniority, junior members who are seeking advancement would undoubtedly feel that efforts in that direction were relatively useless. (See Box 5–2.)

Your behavior will also be affected by your expectation regarding how *much* effort is required to obtain an adequate level of performance, even when you know with complete certainty that the reward will follow performance. Consider how many times you have asked yourself: Is it worth it? Often the attractiveness of the reward provides the critical balance for the amount of effort required to achieve it. In summary, you put forth effort to obtain rewards if you expect that the rewards will, in fact, follow from your efforts and that they are valuable. Doubts about those connections are likely to reduce your level of effort; negative expectations in most cases will eliminate effort altogether.

BOX 5-2

EXPECTANCY THEORY: THE CONTRIBUTION OF VICTOR VROOM

Expectancy theory says that the likelihood that you will engage in a particular behavior is related to your belief that it will lead to a particular outcome. That belief can range from 0 to 1 (absolute certainty) and is purely subjective. The theory also says that you normally have a preference for a particular outcome, and the strength of that preference, which Vroom calls its *valence*, is related to the extent to which you perceive it to be *instrumental* to other outcomes. Also, a valence may be *positive* or *negative*, again in degree, which means that some outcomes will be perceived as attractive and others unattractive. In essence, then, you are most likely to engage in an act that you believe strongly will result in a highly valued outcome, and you are least likely to engage in behavior that you have little belief will lead to a desired outcome or that you believe will lead to an undesired outcome.

Suppose, for example, you want to predict the probability that your boss will support some innovations you want to make in the work of your department. If your boss believes that supporting you will result in the increased cooperation and effort of other members of the department, which will, in turn, make him or her more successful as a manager, then he or she is likely to support you. However, if your boss's boss tends to oppose innovation, then your boss might perceive support for you to be a potential threat (negative valence) to his or her own success. Then the probability of support for you will go down.

As you can see, it is possible for a given behavior to be related to conflicting outcomes and, consequently, pull you in opposite directions. According to Vroom, the final choice you make will be a function of the aggregate relationship among all the factors. If, for example, your belief relative to an expected positive outcome is stronger than your belief relative to a negative outcome, you are more likely to engage in the act. Also, if the valence of the positive outcome is stronger than the valence of the negative outcome, you are likely to engage in the behavior.

Vroom offers systematic procedures and quantitative methods for translating all the variables into manageable predictions. If you are interested in pursuing Vroom's pioneering work in expectancy theory, see his 1964 book entitled *Work and Motivation* (New York: John Wiley & Sons).

Determinants of Attraction and Expectancy (Figure 5-4)

Needs and Abilities   Earlier in the chapter we discussed individual needs (motivation) and how a reward system is effective only to the extent that it addresses those needs as they exist in large numbers of people. You bring your personal needs and abilities into the work situation; they are not given to you by the organization. *To the extent that you perceive your needs to be congruent with the rewards of the organization, you find the rewards attractive.* Furthermore, *to the extent that you perceive yourself to be capable of and willing to perform those behaviors that are necessary to fulfill performance standards, you are likely to increase your expectations about obtaining those rewards.*

Assume you are a talented dancer who has joined a well-known ballet

FIGURE 5-4

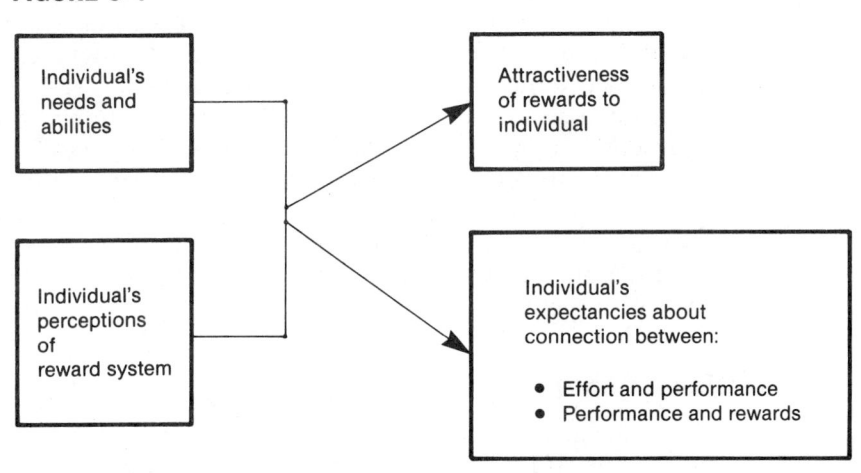

```
┌─────────────┐
│ Individual's│                    ┌──────────────┐
│ needs and   │─────────┐          │Attractiveness│
│ abilities   │         │      ┌──▶│of rewards to │
└─────────────┘         │      │   │individual    │
                        │      │   └──────────────┘
                        │      │
                        │      │   ┌──────────────────────────┐
┌─────────────┐         │      │   │Individual's              │
│Individual's │         │      │   │expectancies about        │
│perceptions  │─────────┘      │   │connection between:       │
│of           │────────────────┘   │                          │
│reward system│                    │ • Effort and performance │
└─────────────┘                    │ • Performance and rewards│
                                   └──────────────────────────┘
```

company. And suppose that you would like nothing better than to play a starring role. Will you put forth the effort in the hopes of eventually being rewarded? That's likely to depend on a number of things, but perhaps most importantly on an assessment of your basic ability. Whether or not you feel that you have the ability, the reward will certainly remain attractive. However, whether or not you *expect* to ever attain your goal will depend on your perception of your ability relative to the level of skill required to become a star. The greater the discrepancy, the lower will be your expectancy. Your actual effort and even performance will, in turn, be affected by that expectancy.

Can you think of real examples where your effort/performance on a job, at school, in a sport, or at any activity has been similarly affected? It might give you useful insight into your behavior to trace the various determinants of what you did and how you did it. Also, it could be a valuable exercise to examine your work and career choices to see whether you can anticipate your level of effort/performance based on your analysis of the attractiveness of rewards, your expectancies relative to performance, and your own needs and abilities as they affect the picture.

Perceptions of the Reward System Your perception of the rewards available are based on information you receive from the organization and the subsequent experience you have as a member of it. Your instructor may inform you of his or her grading system, but your perceptions of it will be strongly affected by the actual grades you receive. Your experience might confirm your expectation that hard work will lead to adequate performance and, in turn, a good grade, or it might indicate that some other kind of behavior gets the high grade.

How attractive the rewards appear to the individual depends not so much on any objective statements or pieces of information provided by management, but more on what that individual *perceives* to be the reward system. Those perceptions are based on a number of factors, including the information available and the person's subsequent experience, as already indicated. Often overlooked is the *total context* in which the reward system exists, especially the effects of goals, structure, and climate. (Also see Box 5–3.)

Organizational Context

While managers can and do determine directly the nature of rewards, much of the reward system is determined both directly and indirectly by goals, structure, and climate.

BOX 5–3

EQUITY THEORY

Sometimes, perhaps most of the time, how you judge the reward you receive for a given effort depends on your perceptions of what other people receive for their efforts. Did you ever work very hard on a term paper and receive a grade that was lower than your friend's grade when he or she put in much less effort? Or did you ever work in a job where you were paid less than people who were less competent or less hardworking than you? Any situation like these will affect your subsequent effort; it is hard to ignore inequity when you are the victim of it.

Equity theory, initially propounded by J. S. Adams, explains and predicts work behavior using the reasoning process reflected above. His theory states that a worker's productivity will be affected by his or her perceptions of what he or she receives for a given effort in comparison with what others receive for comparable effort. If you experience inequity, you will, according to the theory, make an effort to correct it. You might reduce your effort, ask for a greater reward, complain to your boss, or just live with the discomfort until you can change jobs. If the inequity is the other way around—that is *you* are getting more for your efforts than someone else who is working just as hard—you are still likely to want to correct the inequity. You might do it by convincing yourself that you really deserve more (for some reason), you might try to help the other person get an increase in reward, or, as seems to be fairly common, you might just work harder to justify the greater reward, thereby reducing the inequity, at least in your own mind.

When added to expectancy theory, equity theory provides a very useful model for understanding people's work behavior. It recognizes the influence of social system dynamics on individual perceptions of a reward system.

Source: J. S. Adams, "Toward an Understanding of Inequity," *Journal of Abnormal and Social Psychology* 67 (1963), pp. 422–36; also, with P. R. Jacobsen, "Effects of Wage Inequities on Work Quality," *Journal of Abnormal and Social Psychology* 69 (1964), pp. 19–25.

Using Figure 5–5 as a reference point, imagine yourself entering an organization and learning about its goals, structure, and climate without knowing anything about its reward system. Your perceptions of how rewarding it will be to work there will be strongly affected by the attractiveness of the organizational goals to you as an individual, by the position you will occupy within the overall division of labor, and by the "feel of the place" as it affects your energy and commitment. Although organizational goals play a major, perhaps dominant, role in determining a reward system, the connection is modified by both the formal and informal aspects of the organization.

For example, an organization might translate a goal of improving the competencies of its employees into such rewards as paying for courses and providing time off for educational pursuits. How *effective* such rewards are as incentives to performance, however, depends on such things as access to information about educational opportunities and the connection between current position and freedom to take advantage of the opportunities, which are related to one's position in the formal structure. In addition, the rewards are likely to be effective only to the extent that the climate and norms support learning and growth. Where they don't, the rewards become meaningless and fail to serve as incentives.

Goals, structure, and climate jointly determine the *information* about rewards that flows to any given member of the system. The information is not the same for everyone, since it tends to reflect the particular goals and sub-goals relevant to the individual's function, to that individual's place in the system, and to what the individual is "allowed" or "allows himself or herself" to hear.

Suppose, for example, you are working on something that has high priority for the organization, you are relatively isolated in your job (as might be the case for a research person), and the climate has high task

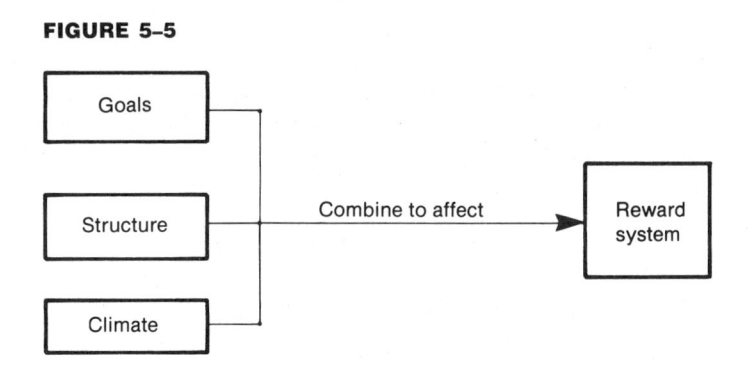

FIGURE 5–5

Goals, Structure, Climate → Combine to affect → Reward system orientation. That combination of factors may limit the amount and kind of information you have pertaining to certain aspects of the organization's reward system—for example, opportunities for other positions, chances for personal development, and informal contacts with colleagues. Furthermore, if the setting is highly competitive with fewer opportunities than people seeking them, information is very likely to be guarded and not easily accessible. The rewards you can and do choose to work for are always a function of your perceptions about your role in the organization. And certainly these perceptions are determined by the goals of your work, the position you hold, and the atmosphere surrounding you. The closer you perceive your role to be to the high-priority goals of the organization, the more likely you will perform to achieve those goals, providing you expect relevant rewards to follow.

In a more subtle way, the surrounding climate exerts a powerful influence on how you see the rewards. For example, organizational claims that certain rewards will follow from individual performance can be cast into a shadow in a climate of mistrust or fear. Rewards appear more credible and attractive in a climate of positive excitement where the norms support behavior relative to those rewards. In fact, a positive climate often adds intrinsic satisfaction to one's efforts, especially when those efforts reinforce that climate.

The norms of your most immediate work group can play an especially important role in determining your attitude and behavior relative to rewards. What you *permit* yourself to work toward and its value as a reward reflect both your own needs and the pressure exerted upon you by your peers. This can cause stress, sometimes forcing you to choose between two conflicting rewards—for example, outstanding achievement versus peer approval. In addition, goals, structure, and climate combine to generate what *alternatives* are even possible for an individual. Some rewards, for example, become available to members only after they have achieved a certain status or level in the system, or only after they have established themselves as "acceptable" in the normative sense. In many ways, an organization requires that an individual *earn* the right (formally and informally) to the full benefits of its reward system. In short, the rewards exist relative to both one's position and one's informal status in the system.

Figure 5–6 portrays the overall picture, showing the general effect that organizational context has on the more specific factors that determine individual effort and performance. It shows how, within the context of the organization's goals, structure, and climate:

1. Individual needs and abilities combine with
2. Individual perceptions of the reward system to determine
3. The attractiveness of the rewards and
4. The individual's expectancies about the connection between effort

FIGURE 5-6

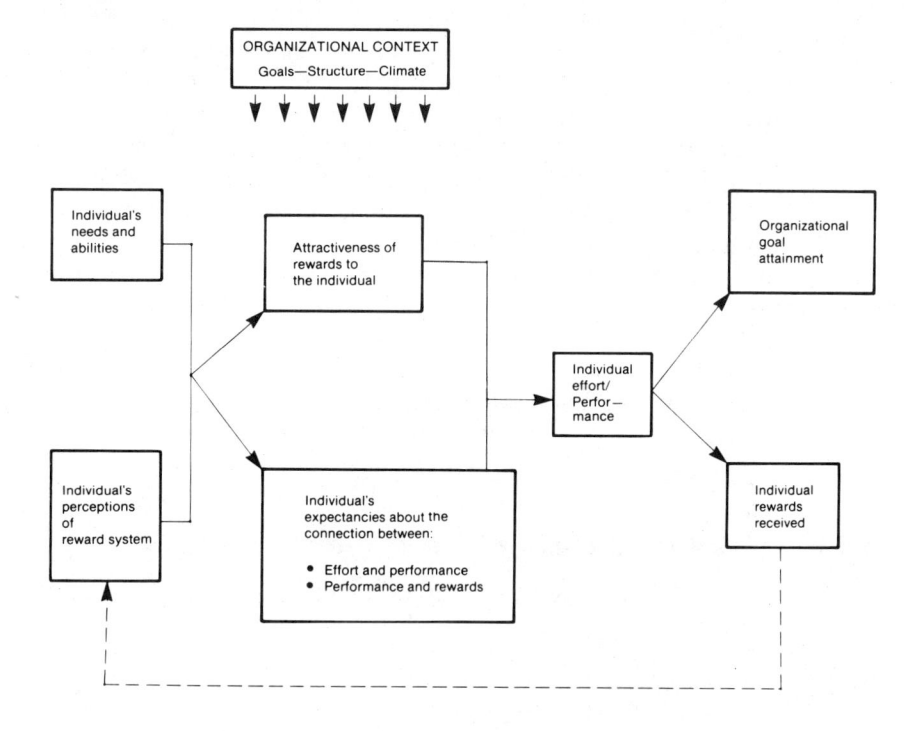

```
                    ORGANIZATIONAL CONTEXT
                    Goals—Structure—Climate
                    ↓ ↓ ↓ ↓ ↓ ↓
```

[Diagram: Individual's needs and abilities → Attractiveness of rewards to the individual; Individual's perceptions of reward system → Attractiveness of rewards to the individual and Individual's expectancies about the connection between: Effort and performance, Performance and rewards → Individual effort/Performance → Organizational goal attainment and Individual rewards received (with feedback loop to Individual's perceptions of reward system)]

and performance and between performance and reward attainment, which combine to affect
5. Individual effort and performance leading to
6. Organizational goal attainment and
7. Individual rewards.

The loop is completed by the feedback effect that the attainment of rewards has on the individual's perceptions of the reward system.

You can see how important it is to be aware of organizational rewards as reflections of the goals, structure, and climate. If you decide to join an organization because you are attracted to the rewards, be sure to look at them in the broader context of structure and climate. Pay attention to the assigned position or role you will have, especially as it does or does not give you easy access to the rewards you seek. Also, pay attention to the "feel of the place" and what seems to be ok or not ok to do, again as it might affect the availability of rewards. And finally, don't underestimate your formal position and the overall atmosphere of an organization as rewards in and of themselves. Sometimes it can be very satisfying just to be in a certain role in the right kind of setting, and sometimes it can be pure agony to be in the wrong position in a cold climate.

Experience with an organization's reward system necessarily affects subsequent performance. It does this by modifying the individual's information about the reward system in general, and it also affects the individual's attraction to and expectancies about the rewards as related to performance. Informational feedback helps you to form a broader and more credible picture of the reward system, which in turn helps you to see it more clearly in relation to your needs, abilities, perceptions, and alternatives.

Apart from the informational aspects, a person experiences rewards in a very immediate and often emotional sense. Attractiveness increases or decreases almost immediately following outcomes, and expectancies are confirmed or disconfirmed in varying degrees, all combining to affect subsequent performances.

An Imaginary Experience with a Reward System

You've just started working for a large hotel chain; you are in one of the more plush hotels in a wealthy resort town on the East Coast. The *organizational goals* toward which you are working emphasize high-quality service, personal attention to the needs of the clientele, and maintaining a first-class reputation, to name just a few. You are in charge of all special activities and room services, which includes arranging parties or events that customers request as well as providing food and drinks to rooms as ordered.

The hotel has a fairly tight *hierarchy;* your position is at the *third level from the top,* reporting to the hotel's assistant manager for client services. You have half a dozen people reporting directly to you; each, in turn, supervises 8 or 10 others. Your position carries a great deal of authority and responsibility for which you are held strictly accountable. Your formal position gives you access to much information about the personnel who work for you, the general operations of the hotel, and the kinds of people served by the organization. Thus, you are in an excellent position to plan for the active season and to anticipate most of the needs and problems of the clientele.

The *atmosphere* is "controlled casualness"; that is, from the customer's point of view, everything seems related and homey, but from the hotel's perspective, it is all very carefully managed. In addition, there is a feeling of wealth and exclusivity in the air; people dress informally, but one *knows* that every pair of slacks costs at least $90.

Given the hotel's goals, structure, and climate, its management has created a reward system that (1) emphasizes strict compliance with the rules of operation, (2) pays its employees well and provides them with excellent accommodations and benefits, (3) supports individual initiative and opportunities to advance in the overall organization, (4) tries to match employee interests and abilities with assignments, (5) hires only people who have a career interest in the hotel industry, and (6) permits free interaction and socializing among employees during nonworking hours, thus allowing for a group identity.

You were told all these things before you took the job; every aspect of the setting and its rewards, as *you* perceived them, appealed to you. You like having things clear-cut, so that abiding by carefully prescribed rules and being in a formal position of authority are relevant rewards for you in working there. Although not a primary consideration, you like the high salary and fringe benefits. Opportunities to take initiative and advance in the system are major attractions of the job. You enjoy managing people and you like the challenge of having to respond to special requests; this you find intrinsically rewarding. You identify with the industry, since you seek a long-term career in the hotel field. Finally, being a very social person, you enjoy the opportunities to interact with other employees outside of work.

Your perception of your role and the expectations attached to it, given the information you have about the rewards and your own needs and abilities, makes the reward system highly attractive. The rewards fit your needs and the performance standards fit your abilities. You have every reason to expect that your performance will, in fact, lead to the attainment of those rewards, along with the attainment of the organizational goals. Since you have had no prior experience in the setting, you have little reason to question the information you have received. Subsequent experience, as you know, will affect the attraction of the rewards positively or negatively.

This is a very idealized picture, as well as an oversimplified one. However, it illustrates how the various elements related to a reward system combine to affect performance. In the example, your effort and performance would undoubtedly be maximized by the reward system. Imagine, however, what would happen if some of the elements were changed. Suppose the management did not allow employee socializing. This might dampen your enthusiasm for the job, depending on the strength of your social needs. Moreover, if initiative were not rewarded or if there were little opportunity for advancement, your performance might drop off considerably. Or if your real interests were not in the hotel industry, you would probably not identify very strongly with the mission of the organization.

In short, each of the six aspects of the reward system contributes to the attractiveness of the total package, some aspects more than others, depending on both the person and the situation. Ideally, all the pieces fit together additively, but rarely does this happen. More often deficiencies in one element of a reward system are offset by strengths in other elements. If this is not the case, then the organization's reward system will be seriously deficient overall.

Even the best reward system cannot always meet everyone's expectations. Most people at one time or another have found that the pot of gold at the end of the rainbow was not as large as imagined; such an experience can dampen one's performance the next time around. The proper design of a reward system, however, not only reinforces present behavior, but also helps to build future expectations that one's overall efforts will be appropriately recognized and justly rewarded.

DESIGN OF A REWARD SYSTEM

So far we discussed the nature of human needs as a basis for understanding why people work and the range of needs they seek to meet on the job. We also presented a way to categorize the rewards an organization can offer in response to those needs as it seeks to encourage the behaviors it requires to reach the organization's goals. Finally, we sought to connect the two at the level of the individual, showing how the relationship between the individual's needs and the organization's reward system is complicated by differences in individual capabilities, wants, and perceptions. This latter discussion has given you a basis for assessing your own job opportunities and planning your way through a career in an organizational setting. Now we want to explore how you, as a manager, might design a reward system, or at least evaluate and modify an existing one.

In evaluating and designing a reward system, a manager needs to consider three questions:

1. What are the organization's current goals and what behaviors will help it reach those goals?
2. What is the nature of the employee group? What rewards will appeal to them and encourage the behaviors identified in question 1?
3. What are the organization's long-run development plans?

1. Organizational Goals and Related Behavior

Consider first the rational goals (refer to Chapter 1) of an organization. Most manufacturing organizations face some kind of trade-off between cost (price), quality (technical excellence), and service (delivery, etc.). Although all are important, typically one predominates depending on market conditions. For example, in the space program and in weapons manufacture, product performance (quality) is typically number one, with delivery often a close second, and cost a distant third. Under such circumstances, it would be inappropriate to have a reward system that encourages such close attention to budgets that special expenditures to test products or requests for overtime work to meet schedules are automatically rejected. On the other hand, if the market is highly competitive with respect to price, then a reward system that encourages close attention to costs and even leads to an occasional cutting of corners on quality would be appropriate.

Similarly, if the tasks that must be carried out to reach the goals of the organization are highly interdependent, then a reward system that encourages cooperation, even at some cost of individual effort, would be best. Consider, for example, an engineering department where the design of one part of the product is significantly affected by the design of another part. If such a department is set up so that the engineer is rewarded only for his/her individual effort regardless of the other engineers' endeavors, the ultimate results are not likely to be satisfactory. Or consider a job shop where market conditions are such that it realistically makes sense to interrupt an ongoing production run to satisfy some customer's emergency needs. If the shop foreman is rewarded only for the cost-efficiency of his shop, marketing is likely to complain bitterly about the lack of cooperation on the part of manufacturing, and the company will undoubtedly suffer.

One complaint about government agencies is that the bureaucrats are too bound by rules and are never willing to try something new and different. If this is valid, part of the problem probably lies in a reward system that does little to encourage risk taking and may actively encourage playing it safe. If the goals of an organization require creative risk taking, then rewards that encourage it are essential.

The same principles apply to the attainment of both natural and open system goals. If an organization's goals include manpower training and development, then the reward system should encourage managers to spend time coaching their subordinates and include opportunities for advancement for those subordinates. If an organization's goals include promoting affirmative action, then it is likely to get better results if managers are rewarded for making the program work rather than just subjected to policing by a watchdog office.

2. Nature of the Employee Group

The foregoing discussion is based on the assumption that the rewards offered are seen as attainable and desirable (attractive) by the employee group. But, as previously discussed, this depends on the nature of those employed. It accomplishes little to offer high wages and dull work to highly trained specialists whose reward is intrinsic interest in the work itself. An intelligent management will seek to know its people and what will have meaning for and attraction to them.

As pointed out, managers too often assume that blue-collar workers have no higher-level needs and are motivated only by hygiene factors. Although the form of the motivators and the rewards that will satisfy those higher-level needs may differ from blue-collar to professionally trained employees, both groups have a full range of needs for which fulfillment can be sought on the job. The trick for management is to find the particular rewards that will appeal to its employees or to the type of employee it seeks to attract, hold, and stimulate to productive effort.

Changing an existing reward system, even when necessary, can pose serious problems. For example, if, over the years, an organization has attracted and retained employees who enjoy social interaction in a climate of friendly cooperation, it ought to think twice before it changes the reward system to emphasize individual effort in an internally competitive environment. Such employees are not likely to be very responsive to, or even productive in, an environment that pits one person against another. While such a move may be appropriate, the management should anticipate resistance and turnover and should determine whether the ultimate results will in fact be better.

3. Long-Run Development

In addition to designing a reward system to fit the current situation, management must consider the future. As implied above, a change in the reward system could generate turnover and attract a different type of employee. Less drastically, the reward system can be designed to encourage individuals to grow and develop in ways that will build the organization's human resources toward what will be needed in the future.

In designing a reward system or modifying an existing one, the management of an organization should address itself to the three questions posed earlier, considering which purposes of a reward system need emphasis to promote organizational goals and which rewards will appeal to employees for both the present and the future. This is particularly important in light of recent concerns about the quality of work life. Employees at all levels of organizations seem to be looking for ways to balance or integrate their work lives with their personal lives. Modified workweeks, flexible working hours, job sharing, and part-time work are some of the ways people are achieving this balance.[4] These

---

[4] See A. Cohen and H. Gadon, *Alternative Work Schedules: Integrating Individual and Organizational Needs* (Reading, Mass.: Addison-Wesley Publishing, 1978).

trends are opening up the job market to more women with schoolchildren and to people who are going to school part time. Add to this the fact that the average level of education has been increasing and more people over age 35 are returning to school to advance or change their careers, and you can see how the design of a reward system is an increasingly complex challenge.

SUMMARY

A reward system represents the way an organization links the needs of employees to the goals of the system. A reward system serves the following purposes:

1. Attracts and holds employees.
2. Guarantees at least minimal performance.
3. Encourages performance beyond the minimum.
4. Encourages initiative and creativity.
5. Promotes collaborative behavior.

To understand human needs (or motivation), several theories are particularly useful. The two presented in detail were Maslow's Hierarchy of Needs and Herzberg's Two-Factor Theory. These two were selected because they have had a major impact on the thinking of managers, and each provides a simple but very practical framework for understanding motivation.

Rewards were classified (using a schema developed by Robert Katz) under the following headings:

1. Rule compliance.
2. General system rewards.
3. Individual rewards.
4. Intrinsic rewards.
5. Internalized organizational values.
6. Social rewards.

At one extreme, rewards related to rule compliance, general system benefits, and social factors tend to have limited overall value. They may attract and retain employees, and they may foster at least minimal performance, but they normally do not stimulate higher levels of performance, initiative, or collaboration. In contrast, individual rewards and intrinsic rewards tend to promote performance beyond the minimum as well as initiative and creativity. Internalized organizational values as a reward seem to serve all five purposes, including collaborative behavior. Similarly, rule compliance, general system rewards, and social rewards are less related to higher-level needs (esteem and self-actualization) or motivators than are individual rewards, intrinsic rewards, and internalized values.

In addition to understanding rewards in a very general sense—that is, as they apply to the organization as a whole—it is equally important to understand rewards from the perspective of the individual employee. Within the context of an organization's goals, structure, and climate:

1. Individual needs and abilities combine with
2. Individual perceptions of the reward system to determine
3. The attractiveness of the rewards and
4. The individual's expectations about the connection between effort and performance and between performance and reward attainment, which combine to affect
5. Individual effort and performance leading to
6. Organizational goals attainment and
7. Individual rewards

The final two steps (6 and 7) provide feedback to the individual, which then affects subsequent perceptions of the reward system and the expectancies regarding effort and performance.

In designing or evaluating a reward system, a manager needs to consider:

1. The organization's current goals and related behaviors.
2. The nature of its employees and what kinds of rewards fit them.
3. The long-run development plans of the organization and the kinds of rewards that will be relevant in the future.

A reward system exists to increase individual job performance in the service of organizational goals. This chapter has shown how complicated the process is, since the connection between individual performance and rewards is affected by interrelated factors that are constantly changing. It may not be possible to understand exactly how these factors play out in the mind of any one individual, much less in the minds of the great variety of people who constitute an organization. Perhaps the best a manager can hope for is periodically to reevaluate the overall impact of the reward system and only occasionally attempt to understand all the nuances of the more personal frame of reference. However, one should not forget that in the final analysis an effective reward system enhances the value of the organization to the individual and the value of the individual to the organization.

ANNOTATED BIBLIOGRAPHY

Arnold, H. J. "Effects of Performance Feedback and Extrinsic Reward upon High Intrinsic Motivation." *Organizational Behavior and Human Performance* 17 (1976), pp. 275–88.

The authors examined the effects of feedback and extrinsic rewards on feelings of competence and degree of intrinsic motivation. The study focused on undergraduates playing a complex computer game that simulates conditions aboard the Starship Enterprise. The authors measured the subjects' rate of volunteering to return to play, feelings of competency, satisfaction, and enjoyment. Results of the study indicate that in instances of high internal motivation, external rewards neither enhance nor affect intrinsic motivation.

Atkinson, J. W., and W. R. Reitman   "Performance as a Function of Motive Strength and Expectancy of Goal-Attainment." *Journal of Abnormal and Social Psychology* 53 (1956), pp. 361–66.

The authors assert that "the missing link among studies already accomplished is a demonstration that the relationship between achievement and performance can be substantially reduced even *when the achievement expectancy is explicitly aroused* by systematic arousal of other motives to perform the same act . . . Our experimental task, then, is to engage the achievement motive in two different situations by instructions that are known to arouse it." Experimental method, results, genotype and phenotype, and role of the situation are discussed. The authors conclude that "the total *motivation* to perform the act is conceived as a summation of strengths of all the *motives* that have been aroused by appropriate expectancies of goal-attainment cued-off by the situation."

Bartol, K. M.   "Expectancy Theory as a Predictor of Female Occupational Choice and Attitude toward Business." *Academy of Management Journal* 19 (1976), pp. 669–75.

The author discusses research that examines the validity of the Mitchell and Knudsen expectancy model as an indicator of occupational choice and attitude for female psychology and business majors. The validity of the model is supported by Bartol's research. The author suggests that further research should be conducted to determine the extent to which the study's results are applicable to other groups of women.

Deci, E. L.   "The Effects of Contingent and Noncontingent Rewards and Controls on Extrinsic Motivation." *Organizational Behavior and Human Performance* 8 (1972), pp. 217–29.

Deci discusses the effect of intrinsic and extrinsic rewards on a worker's behavior. Theories concerning job enrichment and participative management are reviewed. Deci details research testing the assumption that the effects of intrinsic and extrinsic rewards are additive. He concludes that the assumption is false and discusses managerial implications.

Dunnette, M. D.; J. P. Campbell; and M. D. Hakel   "Factors Contributing to Job Satisfaction and Job Dissatisfaction in Six Occupational Groups." *Organizational Behavior and Human Performance* 2 (1967), pp. 143–74.

"The taxonomy of job situations suggested by Herzberg et al. [*Personnel Psychology* 18 (1959), pp. 393–402] was used to develop two Q-sort decks of 36 statements each, one describing satisfying job situations, the other describing dissatisfying job situations." This article details the use of this Q-sort deck by subjects in six occupational groups. Method, scores, and results are discussed.

Ford, R. N.   "Job Enrichment Lessons from AT&T." *Harvard Business Review* 51, No. 1 (1973), pp. 96–106.

The author, who has been responsible for a number of job enrichment programs at AT&T, describes job enrichment at the company in terms of improving work by changing the module or "slice" of work, giving the employee more control of this module and considerable feedback in regard to work accomplished. Ford also discusses job "nesting"—a technique that goes beyond enrichment strategies by grouping related and dependent positions together to facilitate interaction and improve morale and performance.

Freedman, S. M., and J. R. Montanari "An Integrative Model of Managerial Reward Allocation." *Academy of Management Review,* July 1980, pp. 381–90.

The authors present an integrative model of the reward allocation process in organizations. Four general categories of variables affecting reward allocation decisions—environmental, organizational, managerial, and subordinate—are investigated in terms of their influence on organizational reward strategy. The authors suggest that managers need to be aware of both the effects of rewards on employee performance *and* the effects of the variables on their own decision making in allocating rewards.

Hackman, J. R., and G. R. Oldham "Motivation through the Design of Work." In *Work Redesign,* ed. J. R. Hackman and G. R. Oldham. Reading, Mass.: Addison-Wesley Publishing, 1980, pp. 71–94.

The authors present an approach to the design of a work situation that enhances productivity and, at the same time, makes the work personally rewarding and satisfying. Their model describes the "core job characteristics" that produce the "critical psychological states" (in workers) that ultimately result in "high internal work motivation." The core job characteristics include: skill variety, task identity, task significance, autonomy, and feedback from job. The critical psychological states include experienced responsibility for the outcome of the work and knowledge of the actual results of the work activities. In addition, the authors include in their model certain moderating factors: a worker's knowledge and skill, the strength of his/her growth needs, and the satisfactions associated with the work "context."

Klein, S. M. "Pay Factors as Predictors of Satisfaction: A Comparison of Reinforcement, Equity and Expectancy." *Academy of Management Journal* 16 (1973), pp. 598–610.

The article presents research that compares three theories—reinforcement, equity, and expectancy—in regard to their ability as predictors of satisfaction for various kinds of pay variables for blue-collar workers. While both equity and expectancy variables were predictors, equity was the most powerful. The research indicates that (1) salary administrators should design pay systems where merit is rewarded; (2) employees engaged in similar jobs should receive similar wages; (3) differences between skill levels among similar jobs should be made explicit to employees; and (4) employees should be made aware of and understand an organization's pay structure.

Korman, A. K. "Expectancies as Determinants of Performance." *Journal of Applied Psychology* 55, no. 3. (1971), pp. 218–22.

"This research reports five studies which all support the general proposition that high expectancies of competence by others are positively related to performance." Korman details methods and results and then considers theoretical and practical implications. Research limitations and suggestions for further study are also discussed.

Lawler, E. E., and J. L. Suttle "A Causal Correlational Test of the Need Hierarchy Concept." *Organizational Behavior and Human Performance* 7 (1972), pp. 265 87.

The authors examine the validity of Maslow's need hierarchy concept. Questionnaires that measured need importance and satisfaction were given to 187 managers in two organizations. While the authors contend that the results offer little support for the need hierarchy concept, they warn against rejecting Maslow's theory until it is examined in broader situations. The authors do, however, suggest that needs may be arranged in a two-level hierarchy as opposed to Maslow's five-level hierarchy.

Pinder, C. C. "Concerning the Application of Human Motivation Theories in Organizational Settings." *Academy of Management Review* 2 (1977), pp. 384–97.

The author begins by assessing the validity of a number of theories of motivation. Pinder then raises the question of premature application of motivational theories in regard to ethical, organizational, and academic considerations. The author concludes that in the application of organizational theories, practitioners must respect the differences among organizations and individuals, and should be aware of the limitations of theories.

Schneider, B., and C. P. Alderfer "Three Studies of Measures of Need Satisfaction in Organizations." *Administrative Science Quarterly* 18 (1973), pp. 489–505.

The authors present three studies exploring relationships between motivational concepts developed by Maslow, Alderfer, and others as applied in organizational settings. The authors found little convergence between the theories of Maslow and others, and they suggest that this may be due to the fact that Maslow's theories were not oriented toward organizational settings.

Schwab, D. P.; H. W. DeVitt,; and L. L. Cummings "A Test of Adequacy of the Two-Factor Theory as a Predictor of Self-Report Performance Effects." *Personnel Psychology* 4 (1971), pp. 293–303.

This article investigates Herzberg's two-factor theory through a study of 124 male managerial personnel from a public accounting/consulting firm. Although some support was found for Herzberg's model, the authors state that no evidence was found indicating that motivators are usually associated with positive performance effects while hygiene factors are associated with negative performance.

Stedry, A. C., and E. Kay "The Effects of Goal Difficulty on Performance." *Behavioral Science* 11 (1966), pp. 459–70.

The authors discuss relevant theory involving goal difficulty, and develop three hypotheses. A field experiment involving foremen is described in terms of performance measures, experimental design, results, and ex-post analysis. The need for future theoretical work is detailed concerning "models which incorporate 'total challenge'" and "long-run effects of different kinds of stable goal-setting procedures."

Telly, C. S.; W. L. French; and W. G. Scott "The Relationship of Inequity of Turnover among Hourly Workers." *Administrative Science Quarterly,* June 1971, pp. 164–72.

This article presents a research study to determine whether perceptions of inequity are associated with turnover among hourly employees. Inquiries were made using a questionnaire distributed to a random sample of employees from high-turnover and low-turnover shops in an attempt to identify the differences in the perceptions of inequity. The findings support the theory that inequity perceptions are among the reasons for turnover, and they indicate some of the inequitable treatment perceived in the particular environment studied.

Wanous, J. P., and A. Zwany "A Cross Section Test of Need Hierarchy Theory." *Organizational Behavior and Human Performance* 18 (1977), pp. 78–97.

The authors discuss the results of a study that examined the effects different jobs within one organization have on an individual's need satisfaction. The study was based, in part, on a previous investigation by C. P. Alderfer that examined the effects dissimilar organizations have on need satisfaction. The research was conducted on 208 telephone company employees in 13 different job classifications. Results indicate that need fulfillment by job type is moderated much the same way it is moderated by organizational differences.

SUGGESTED READINGS

Alderfer, Clayton P. "An Empirical Test for a New Theory of Human Needs." *Organizational Behavior and Human Performance* 4 (1969), pp. 142–75.

Andrews, John D. W. "The Achievement Motive and Advancement in Two Types of Organizations." *Journal of Personality and Social Psychology* 6 (1967), pp. 163–69.

Campbell, John P.; Marvin D. Dunnette; Edward E. Lawler; and Karl E. Weick *Managerial Behavior, Performance, and Effectiveness*. New York: McGraw-Hill, 1970.

Deci, Edward L. *Intrinsic Motivation*. New York: Plenum Press, 1975.

Dowling, William F. "Job Redesign on the Assembly Line: Farewell to Blue-Collar Blues?" *Organizational Dynamics*, Autumn 1973, pp. 51–67.

Ford, Robert "Job Enrichment Lessons from AT&T." *Harvard Business Review*, January–February 1973, pp. 96–104.

Ford, R. N. *Motivation Through the Work Itself*. New York: American Management Association, 1969.

Hackman, J. Richard "Work Design." In *Improving Life at Work: Behavioral Science Approaches to Organizational Change,* ed. J. Richard Hackman and J. Lloyd Suttle. Santa Monica, Calif.: Goodyear Publishing, 1977.

Hackman, J. Richard; Greg Oldham; Robert Janson; and Kenneth Purdy "A New Strategy for Job Enrichment." *California Management Review* 17, no. 4 (1975), pp. 57–71.

Herzberg, Frederick *Work and the Nature of Man*. New York: World, 1966.

Herzberg, Frederick; Bernard Mausner; and Barbara B. Synderman *The Motivation to Work*. 2d ed. New York: John Wiley & Sons, 1959.

Lawler, Edward E. III *Motivation in Work Organizations*. Monterey, Calif.: Brooks/Cole Publishing, 1973.

Lawler, Edward E. III, and J. Lloyd Suttle "Expectancy Theory and Job Behavior." *Organizational Behavior and Human Performance* 9 (1973), pp. 482–503.

Locke, Edwin A. "Personnel Attitudes and Motivation." *Annual Review of Psychology* 26 (1975), pp. 457–80.

Luthans, Fred, and William E. Reif "Job Enrichment: Long on Theory, Short on Practice." *Organizational Dynamics* 2, no. 3 (Winter 1974), pp. 30–43.

Maslow, Abraham H. *Motivation and Personality*. New York: Harper & Row, 1970.

Maslow, Abraham H. *The Farther Reaches of Human Nature*. New York: Viking Press, 1971.

McClelland, David C. *The Achieving Society*. New York: Free Press, 1961.

McClelland, David C. *Motivational Trends in Society*. Morristown, N.J.: General Learning Press, 1971.

McClelland, David C.; John W. Atkinson; R. A. Clark; and E. L. Lowell *The Achievement Motive*. New York: Appleton-Century-Crofts, 1953.

McGregor, Douglas *The Human Side of Enterprise*. New York: McGraw-Hill, 1960.

Mitchell, Terrance R. "Expectancy Models of Job Satisfaction, Occupational Preference and Effort: A Theoretical, Methodological, and Empirical Appraisal." *Psychological Bulletin* 81 (1974), pp. 1053–77.

Morse, John J., and Jay W. Lorsch "Beyond Theory Y." *Harvard Business Review* May–June 1970, pp. 61–68.

Nebeker, Delbert M., and Terrance R. Mitchell "Leader Behavior: An Expectancy Theory Approach." *Organizational Behavior and Human Performance* 11 (1974), pp. 355–67.

Ouchi, W *Theory Z*. New York: Avon Books, 1981.

Roethlisberger, Fritz J., and William J. Dickson *Management and the Worker*. New York: John Wiley & Sons, 1964.

Ronen, Simcha "Personal Values: A Basis for Work Motivational Set and Work Attitudes." *Organizational Behavior and Human Performance* 21 (1978), pp. 80–107.

Schrank, Robert "On Ending Worker Alienation: The Gaines Pet Food Plant." In *Humanizing the Workplace,* ed. Roy P. Fairfield. Buffalo, N.Y.: Prometheus Books, 1974, pp. 119–40.

Strauss, George "Job Satisfaction, Motivation, and Job Redesign." In *Organizational Behavior: Research and Issues,* ed. G. Strauss, R. E. Miles, C. C. Snow, and A. S. Tannenbaum. Madison, Wis.: Industrial Relations Research Association, 1974, pp. 19–49.

Wahba, Mahmoud A., and Lawrence G. Bridwell "A Review of Research on the Need Hierarchy Theory." In *Organizational Behavior and Industrial Psychology: Readings with Commentary,* ed. Kenneth N. Wexley and Gary A. Yukl. New York: Oxford University Press, 1975, pp. 5–11.

Wahba, Mahmoud A., and Lawrence G. Bridwell "Maslow Reconsidered: A Review of Research on the Need Hierarchy Theory." *Organizational Behavior and Human Performance* 15 (1976), pp. 212–40.

CHAPTER 6

Control Systems

INTRODUCTION

HAVING CONTROL over one's life is important for most people. How much control one needs, by what means it is exercised, its source (e.g., yourself or others), and what purposes it serves vary from person to person. As you enter organizational life as an employee or prospective manager, it will be important for you to understand your own attitude about control as it relates to the requirements of your job. You will encounter a great variety of control systems—that is, more or less explicit guidelines, rules, and procedures that are designed to keep things "on track." These systems are intended to allow you, as a manager, to guide your own actions and the actions of those for whom you are responsible toward organizational goals, but they also can have powerful effects on your own personal goals.

From a manager's standpoint, control systems are essential. They are the means by which managers can feel confident that the work flow is moving in the desired direction, that important decisions are being implemented, and that the organization's resources (money, material, people) are being used wisely. In a way, management *is* a process of control.

In this chapter, we will discuss the kinds of devices or mechanisms that can be used to exercise organizational control, when controls are most effectively applied, for what purposes, the various sources of control, the effects of different kinds of control systems, and finally a set of guidelines for designing a control system. We begin with some definitions.

WHAT IS CONTROL?

Control is a way of making sure that something happens the way it's supposed to happen. If you're driving a car, you want to make sure that you get to your destination, stay on the road, avoid hitting other cars (or people), turn the corners safely, and so on. All this takes control. And to exercise this control you need to have certain *devices* or *mechanisms* (these terms are interchangeable)—namely, brakes, steering wheel, and accelerator—and you need to know *methods* or *procedures* (also interchangeable)—for example, how to shift, how to coordinate speed and turning, and when to put on your brakes.

Control in an organization is gained through the mechanisms and procedures managers use to make sure that things happen the way they're supposed to. A budget is a control device; what a manager does with it is a control method. An instrument that checks material defects is a quality control device; how it is used is a quality control procedure. We stress the distinction because it is easy to fall into the trap of thinking that a control mechanism is enough to provide the needed control, without fully appreciating the *behavioral* element—namely, that *how* the device is used is a key element in control. For example, quizzes and tests are control devices intended in part to encourage you to study. But consider the difference between a test announced ahead of time and one "sprung" on you as you enter the classroom. The two have quite different effects on feelings and behavior. Furthermore, the control process may pertain to operations that can be mechanized and, consequently, controlled by means of computers or other types of equipment, or it may pertain to the behavior of people, in which case the procedures are not likely to be simple and easily predetermined.

Control is also associated with "keeping things moving." In this sense, controls manage the *flow* of activities, a major problem for some organizations, especially those subject to the demands of the outside world. Hospital emergency rooms, university registration procedures, and checkout counters in markets and department stores are common examples. Let's look at one familiar example: a line at the teller's window in a bank.

The Bank Line Example

A problem faced by most banks is the flow of customers to teller windows. During peak hours a customer may face long delays that interfere with other important business or cut into already tight lunch hours. In many banks the control process is left to the customers, who are forced to guess which line will move fastest. If a bank takes seriously its goal of providing efficient service to its customers, it may institute more formal methods, such as separate lines for fast check cashing as opposed to lengthy payroll transactions. And some banks use a single line from which customers move to the first available teller. If a small bank in a nonurban area values an informal climate, it may have to trade off some informality for the sake of efficiency. On the other hand, such a bank may feel that the trade-off should work the other way. Its customers may prefer to choose their favorite tellers, even if it means some additional waiting time. Whatever mechanisms are used, there are always trade-offs; the best choices will tend to favor the organization's highest priorities.

This example illustrates how the choice a manager makes with respect to the mechanism or method of control is related to other organizational considerations. Although most controls are intended to increase *efficiency* in the flow of work activities, how *effective* these are in relation to important organizational goals should not be overlooked. If efficiency experts had their way, control that eliminated human judgment might be the ideal; whether or not the final product or service would be ideal is a different matter. Too often the increased mechanization or automation of the work process has led to dehumanization of the work environment. In some instances that might actually be desirable—for example, the monitoring of radiation in a nuclear plant—but in those cases where the output of the company is dependent on the commitment of the employees, efficiency through mechanized control might have deleterious effects.

WHAT IS A CONTROL SYSTEM?

We have been talking about control systems on a relatively small scale, at least implicitly. The complex combination of devices that control the movements of a car is a control *system*. Class hours, assignments, grading, and classroom rules constitute a control *system* in a course. We generally associate the concept of a control system with organizational life, however, involving many people engaged in many activities related to many objectives. In that context a *control system can be defined as a constellation of devices and procedures established and organized to make sure that the activities of the organization achieve the intended results.*

In the next section, we will explore a variety of devices and procedures that make up control systems. We will first consider the *timing* of controls, since some are implemented in advance, some serve in an ongoing manner, and others rely on outcome data as feedback. We will then discuss how control systems serve different purposes.

TIMING OF CONTROLS: PRE, CONCURRENT, AND POST

Returning to the driving example, most of the time you have some idea where you're headed and how you plan to get there. You have a mental "map" (if not an actual map) in advance of your trip, you consciously or unconsciously use checkpoints (signs, buildings, distances, and streets) as ongoing guides to your progress, and your arrival at the correct destination serves as the final confirmation that you were, in fact, in control all the way. In other words, you have a *precontrol* device in the map (mental or otherwise), a *concurrent control* method in your checkpoints, and *postcontrol* data in your arrival. An additional element might be the time it takes to get there; the map supposedly gives you the shortest route, the checkpoints tell you whether to speed up or slow down, and the arrival time confirms or disconfirms the effectiveness of your control efforts.

All three time periods of control are important in exercising effective control, but the third one really measures your success and, subsequently, helps you to improve performance in the future. In other words, your success is measured in terms of achieved *consequences*. When you receive feedback on how well you did on a task, you can then judge how effectively you controlled the work process. This also gives you a basis for evaluating the control system itself and for initiating improvements. In fact, feedback, whether through direct information, as might be provided by a computer or radar scanner, or through more complex information, like product quality or worker output, is undoubtedly the essence of the control process.

Postcontrol Consequences

Control can be viewed as a way of making sure that you achieve intended consequences. Exercising control relative to the intended consequences requires *planning;* assessing the effectiveness of control requires *standards* for measuring performance. When we teach a course, for example, we develop a syllabus and a set of more or less specific planned activities *in advance* of the course. We exercise some degree of control throughout the course to achieve the objectives we intend, and we compare student performance with our past experiences to judge how well we are achieving those objectives. In a similar manner, students exercise control over their behavior relative to the course by planning study time, establishing some desired goal (e.g., a grade), and comparing their performance with that goal. An important element of this situation, especially as it affects student performance, is the way students' own controls do or don't match those of the instructor. In the final analysis, the student can control the planning and ongoing use of his or her own time but may feel less control over the outcomes that the instructor determines—namely, the evaluation of the work.

PURPOSES OF CONTROL SYSTEMS

Control systems serve a variety of purposes, which we have categorized into three general areas:

1. Maintaining behavior related to the required task roles in the organization.
2. Maintaining the organization as an institution—i.e., its traditions, customs, norms, and culture.
3. Minimizing and/or correcting deviations from standards relative to:
    a. *Quantity* of work.
    b. *Quality* of work.
    c. *Flow* of work.
    d. *Costs.*
    e. *Safety.*

As we address the main issues inherent in each area, we will also suggest ways of handling these issues from a managerial perspective.

1. Required Task Roles

Any role that you play in life (worker, parent, friend, supervisor) is defined by a set of expectations. When you are hired on a job, you are expected to perform certain duties, report to certain people, and manage your time. Some of these expectations may be spelled out in a written job description determined by the division of labor established by the organization, while others may be outlined by your immediate supervisor. There may even be some that are related to the expectations of those whose work is interdependent with yours. The latter expectations are not always very clear at first, and all expectations are likely to require some clarification of detail as time goes on. Insofar as you are able to live up to the expectations of a given role, you are likely to succeed in your work.

Obviously, however, things change, demands change, and, consequently, expectations change. These changes often make it difficult for you to live up to the role you are in. Suppose, for example, you are suddenly faced with a more complex task or greater responsibility than you bargained for. What do you do? If your work slips, what would your boss do?

As stated, one purpose of a control system is to ensure performance in required roles. By looking at the expectations associated with any given role as a matter to be *negotiated* between employer and employee, supervisor and worker, we can see how to establish a control mechanism that, if managed properly, can ensure performance in required task roles.

Role Negotiation and Renegotiation[1]   The foundation for satisfactory performance lie in well understood and accepted role expectations. If you don't understand what you're supposed to do, you cannot really be expected to do it very well. If your instructor gives you a confusing assignment, his or her expectations regarding satisfactory performance on your part are not likely to be realized. Furthermore, even if you do understand the assignment, if you have little interest in carrying it out, the performance expectations again may be greater than the likely outcomes.

In short, the control process in relation to task roles begins with *mutually understood and agreed upon expectations*. Once established, these serve as the basis for *commitment* to carrying them out and normally for some *period of stability* during which "the work goes on." If the foundation is well established, the control process, in effect, takes care of itself, barring unanticipated disturbances that affect an individual's

---

[1] The ideas in this section are based on John Sherwood and John Glidewell, "Planned Renegotiation: A Norm-Setting OD Intervention," in *Contemporary Organization Development*, ed. W. W. Burke (La Jolla, Calif.: NTL Learning Resources Corp., 1972).

ability to live up to the role. Unfortunately, however, there *are* usually disturbances, requiring that role expectations be renegotiated from time to time.

There are very few jobs, it seems, that do *not* over time require a modification of role expectations. Wise managers *never* take the task roles of employees for granted or view them as permanently established. How many times have you found yourself so overloaded or overcommitted that it seemed impossible to live up to task requirements in the way you would like to? One irony of this world is that competent people attract work, perform it well, raise others' expectations, and attract even more work, often until they burn out. Those who have sense enough to "blow the whistle" and renegotiate expectations usually find that they can maintain satisfactory control over their own work output and, consequently, honor the expectations associated with their jobs.

Therefore, to maintain behavior related to required task roles, a manager would do well to:

a. Establish job expectations, both written and unwritten, that are realistic but subject to revision. Things that might typically warrant discussion and clarification are:
   1. Job duties and responsibilities.
   2. Authority for different types of decisions.
   3. Priorities among different responsibilities and job objectives.
   4. Frequency and form of feedback to the boss.
   5. Nature of interaction with and degree of cooperation with other individuals.
   6. Political sensitivities, including identification of topics not for public consumption.
b. Spend enough time initially with an employee to make sure that the role expectations associated with the job are understood and agreed to.
c. Establish regular review meetings with employees to check on possible revisions of job requirements and to renegotiate expectations as necessary.
d. Remain open to and actively watch for indications that role renegotiations may be necessary.

These steps, though no guarantee that all will go well, can help considerably to control the quantity, quality, and flow of work. They also serve to move the source of control away from the exclusive province of the manager and more in the direction of delegating it to the employee. Many managers who are afraid to let go of unilateral control are often victims of the assumption that the role expectations of a job can be firmly established in advance and will not need changing later on. Obviously there are many jobs for which this is a valid assumption, particularly work associated with relatively unchanging systems; however, in this day of rapid change, it is unlikely that many jobs will remain static for very long.

It is also important for the employee to keep in mind the importance of intiating action for role renegotiation. Too often the boss is too busy to see what is happening to each person. Waiting too long can make it more difficult, since tension increases and things can get disruptively out of control.

The methods of control related to task roles touch on all three time periods (pre, concurrent, and post). The precontrol methods (initial job descriptions and role negotiations) are worth considerable time and effort, but the key to making the control process work is the early and effective use of both concurrent data and postcontrol consequences as bases for renegotiation. The control methods are akin to the process of recycling information and using it to improve the appropriateness of task roles.

2. Organizations as Institutions

It is obvious that the survival of an organization depends on the attainment of ultimate goals, but it usually is not so obvious that survival is affected by the maintenance of the organization's *identity*. That identity consists of the traditions, customs, memories of past triumphs and crises, norms governing behavior, and collective beliefs that have evolved during its history. It gives the organization the *character* that distinguishes it from other organizations.

Maintaining its identity becomes an ultimate goal of the organization because it represents the members' collective self-image, and that is something people typically wish to preserve. But it also provides a degree of stability and a sense of unity for the organization, which are important for survival.

Learning to understand the informal control system can be difficult and, on occasion, painful (if you learn by error). But becoming a "member in good standing" of an organization that has its unique character requires that you pay attention to much more than the formal job requirements or role expectations; it requires that you observe, ask about, and check out the unwritten "rules of the game." In many organizations it is important for a manager to convey to new employees the rules of the institution, not just the requirements of the job. In some ways, you feel more controlled by the informal rules when you don't understand them and have to play guessing games than when you understand them in ways that help you to appreciate them in their proper perspective. Furthermore, your understanding enables you to challenge outdated and inappropriate institutional customs from an informed position.

When the informal norms are related to task, they can support a manager's objectives, provided he or she is willing to trust them. A newly hired manager of a group of proposal-writing specialists in a large consulting firm had such a strong need to exercise control in the new job that she took a highly committed group of people and turned them into a mob of malcontents. For years the group had operated in a fairly loose but responsible manner, governed by strong norms supporting productivity. The new manager did not understand, much less trust, the informal norms to serve as control. Rather, she began to require people to keep a strict accounting of their time and work output. You can imagine what followed. Resentment and malevolent resistance became rampant. As it turned out, the overall organization's customs as an institution were consistent with the group's control system and not with the new manager's. She felt the pressure to change and learned quickly and painfully how powerful the informal rules can be.

When informal norms are related to task and supportive of a manager's objectives, the manager can be tempted to formalize them as rules. It appears logical to formalize and make explicit what is functional, and making it formal can give the manager a sense of greater control and security. Yet formalizing the informal is not always the best thing to do. People sometimes resent and rebel against a custom that is taken over as a rule, even though the required behavior is unchanged.

Perhaps the best advice we can offer in this regard is for managers to learn to understand and appreciate the value of the institutional aspects of their organization but be willing to challenge outdated customs or rules that are obstacles to growth and development. Some of the old customs may no longer be germane to the central thrust of the organization, yet it can be important to retain and nurture those that help to give the system its special character and still be careful about formalizing customs that are working effectively.

If you are familiar with the growth of family businesses into larger, more externally (relative to family) managed firms, you can probably bear witness to some dilemmas caused by giving up the informal controls based on common goals and commitment in favor of more formal controls, which often get little more than compliance from employees. One such company in the Northeast is at a critical juncture where the majority of employees are recent hirees and have little or no sense of the history of the firm. The company's character as a family institution could disappear unless top management can build the mechanisms for retaining it. How important it will be for such a firm to retain or give up (to any degree) its historical character depends partly on the kinds of people it needs or desires to have in its employ. Does it want and need people who thrive best in an informal system, or does it seek those who prefer formality?

Effective managers in any organization, whatever its stage of development, can convey to employees the importance of the informal control system, its legitimacy as a mechanism of control relative to both task and social behavior, and a responsibility to inquire about and even challenge informal rules or customs that are confusing or dysfunctional. Finally, it behooves a manager to provide feedback to employees when informal rules are being violated and at a time when corrective action can be taken.

You can see how informal controls pervade all three control times. They are in place when you arrive on the scene (precontrol); they look over your shoulder as you do your work, walk the halls, and eat your lunch; and they leap out at you with an accusing finger when you fail to pay proper attention. Do not underestimate the power of these informal controls; the most technically competent employee can be unemployed overnight as a result of breaking an "institutional law." However, try also to maintain a sense of your own integrity so that you know how large a price (if any) you are willing to pay in going along with these kinds of controls when they conflict with your own preferences.

3. Deviations from Standards

Organizations typically need to produce a certain volume of goods or services in a given time. In addition, they need to obtain an appropriate level of quality; they need to make certain that a new supply of raw materials will arrive before the old supply has run out yet not be overstocked, and they need to keep costs down to a reasonable figure and not incur unnecessary expenses. They also want to avoid accidents and protect their trade secrets. For all these activities and a host of other ones, organizations generally follow a basic model of control, involving:

a. Setting a target level or objective for a future period.
b. Measuring progress during the period.
c. Taking corrective action as indicated by any deviations, hopefully soon enough to get back on target.

While this model, which basically amounts to a feedback loop that provides information to compare actual with intended results, sounds fairly straightforward, in practice the process can be quite complex. It is not always easy to set clear, let alone measurable, targets or standards. It is easy for an instructor to say that "quality or depth of analysis" is the grading criterion for a written assignment but quite another matter for the student to gain a clear understanding of what that means and how it will be measured in determining a grade. Similarly, how would you measure "good employee relations" in a factory or "good quality of care" in a hospital? Both are important goals that require effective control, but the meaning of each is imprecise and does not lend itself to concrete measurement.

Furthermore, organizational activities are subject to predictable and unpredictable variations. Consequently, when deviations occur, it can be difficult to determine whether they represent natural expected variation or a process gone out of control. And it can be difficult to figure out an appropriate corrective action.

Despite such difficulties, the concept of a feedback loop has widespread application to organizational life. Let us now see how it applies to the control of the quantity, quality, flow, cost, and safety-security aspects of organized activities.

Quantity Have you ever found yourself thinking: I really ought to review 20 pages of the text each night for the next 10 days if I'm going to be ready by the day of the examination. Have you ever been hired as a house painter only to discover that what you believe ought to take four days, your boss or the owner of the house expects you to do in three days? Both reflect standards of quantity—that is, how much should be accomplished within some period of time.

Thus, organizations establish standards for the following:

- Number of pieces to be produced per hour.
- Number of products to be shipped each week.
- Number of hotel rooms to be cleaned each day.
- Number of inquiries to be handled per day by an airlines reservation agent.
- Dollar volume of sales to be made by a retail salesclerk each day.

Such standards are established by organizations to ensure meeting commitments (getting the job done on time) and to assess individual and department performance.

Two issues are relevant to setting quantity standards. One concerns how much the individuals and organizational units are *capable* of producing. The other is what level of output is *needed* to meet customer demand, fulfill commitments, or reach desired levels of productivity.

You may have good reason to believe that four days were reasonable to finish the painting referred to above given the area to be covered and the care required to do a quality job. But your boss may be of a different opinion, expecting you to work harder or more efficiently (fewer wasted motions) than you believe is physically possible. Unions and management often disagree over this kind of question. The union may accuse management of wanting to run a "sweat shop" that requires people to work at a rate that is inhuman. Management may believe that the union wants to turn the organization into a "country club" where people give less than a fair day's work.

Various techniques have been developed for establishing standards. Time and motion studies have been used historically for repetitive factory operations. Individual operations are timed with a stopwatch over and over again, and a standard time is arrived at on the basis of carefully studying the actual time taken. Standards can also be based on prior *experience* with identical or similar operations. This is the basis used by commercial painters and job shops. Though less scientific than a time and motion study and, therefore, subject to more disagreement, it is an approach that is widely used. Finally, standards can be based on early experience with a new process and negotiation between supervisor and subordinate. Whatever technique is used, whether subjective (such as past experience) or not, any standard-setting process requires judgment in determining what constitutes reasonable effort.

Finally, it is important to know when and how to correct deviations from quantity standards. Appropriate action requires two steps:

a. Investigate to determine why the deviation occurred. It could be normal variation requiring no action. It could be due to faulty material, inadequate effort by employees, or a decline in demand warranting a reassessment of one's expectations.
b. Initiate steps to correct the deviation. Whether this requires correcting problems, providing more resources, exhorting people to work harder, or modifying standards, the goal is always to get back on target in a timely manner.

Quality   All of us have had experience with the quality of a product or a service rendered. Perhaps our first concern relative to a product is for *functionality*; does it work as it is supposed to do? A can of bug spray that won't operate is of little use in the battle to remain unbitten; a can that operates only intermittently may be even more frustrating. A second concern is that a product be *durable,* that it last as long as it is supposed to. Of course, the length of time a product is supposed to last varies with market tradition and personal experience, but for most products there is some standard. Product *appearance* is a third criterion of quality. At times, it appears to be more important than durability, particularly where changes in fashion can make an item obsolete before it's worn out.

Quality of service involves both *content* and *manner*. We all want good advice from a lawyer, accurate information from an airlines reservation clerk, and appropriate and skillful treatment from our doctor. We want the service to meet our needs. Yet we are also likely to be concerned that the service be provided in a prompt and courteous manner. Few of us enjoy being waited on by a slow and grumpy ticket agent at the bus terminal or salesperson at the discount store.

As organizations seek to establish quality standards for the goods and services they provide, it is often as important to avoid establishing standards that are unnecessarily good as it is to avoid standards that are insufficient. One of the authors knows of an engineering department of a large company that designed a built-in ashtray for an airport control tower radar console that was of such high quality that it cost taxpayers $50! The ashtray was made of stainless steel and mounted in such a way that it could withstand the forces of space travel, but it was totally unnecessary to have such high quality. This is an extreme example, but it makes the point that higher quality is not necessarily better.

The ashtray case is also an example of the fact that quality can be designed in; that is, it can rest upon product design as well as upon care and attention during manufacture. Quality control can come through precontrol as well as through concurrent control.

A primary issue relative to quality is accuracy of measurement. Many devices are available for measuring the physical properties of a product, ranging from simple micrometer calipers to sophisticated test gear. Their accuracy is dependent on the care taken by the person making the measurement. When it comes to judging the physical appearance of a product or the courtesy of the service rendered, the measurement is much more subjective and the door opens wider to variation in judgment and disagreement. The umpire's "measurement" of the quality of a tag at home plate is an example of the problem; however, such subjective measures are used and play a role in the control of quality.

In our present state of technology and knowledge, problems of quantity are minimal; that is, we know how to produce as much as we want of any given product. Few industries compete with respect to the number of items they can produce in a given period of time. The problems faced and the areas for competition seem to be more related to *quality*. When you consider the success of Japanese products in this country compared with our own products, you can understand the major emphasis the consumer places on quality. Consequently, American business and industry have finally awakened and started to push hard to improve the quality of items heretofore released into the marketplace with less than adequate attention to quality. The day of planned obsolescence may be waning.

Several methods are used to control quality, but the one with the longest history is *inspection*. Product parts, partially assembled units, and finished items are, in most companies looked at carefully by quality control experts—that is, people trained to spot defects and select out parts of products that fall short of standards. The two key elements in the process of inspection are the *level of standards* used and the *competence/care of the person applying them*.

With the aid of computers, x-ray scanning devices, and other advanced instruments, quality controllers have been able to advance the art to a high degree of perfection. Therefore, it is not so much the quality control device that actually produces the improved quality, but it is more often the level of standards against which measurements and judgments are made that account for the outcomes, along with the commitment of employees to the maintenance of those standards.

In recent years, the concept of "quality circles" has emerged as a powerful method of maintaining quality (see Box 6–1). Although the term may be new, the essential elements of quality circles are probably as old as the concept of a worker group. Did you ever play in a team sport in which, after a game or during the half, the members evaluated the team's effectiveness and used that evaluation as the basis for improvement? Extrapolate that idea to a work group (or team) that takes "time out" every once in a while to share observations and ideas about how to improve the quality of their work effort. That is, in essence, what quality circles in industry are all about.

The concept is associated with Japanese management, which institutionalized it with a label, but, as suggested above, it truly has been around for a long time. What *is* new from Japan (although its developer is American) is the use of statistical data in combination with quality circles.[2] Members of work teams are trained in how to use basic statistics (averages, expected values, standard deviations, correlations, etc.) as a tool for identifying and correcting deviations from standards. The

BOX 6–1

QUALITY CIRCLES

Quality circles, as a formalized control method, emerged in Japan in the 1960s. The circles are composed of approximately 10 workers, usually led by a supervisor, and they meet regularly to analyze and solve production (at the shop level) problems. In theory, the circles are voluntary and autonomous groups, although company policies and norms generally put some pressure on workers to participate. At Toyota, almost all employees participate in the quality circle program. In 1980, Toyota reported that it received more than 17 suggestions per worker, of which it adopted around 90 percent. Not only do employees in quality circles come up with more suggestions for improvements than employees not in such programs, but the quality of these suggestions, a reflection of group resources, has been superior.

For an interesting article on quality control in Japanese companies, see: R. E. Cole, "The Japanese Lesson in Quality," *Technology Review*, July 1981, pp. 29–40.

---

[2] See W. E. Deming's article, "On Some Statistical Aids toward Economic Production," *Interfaces* 5 (1975), pp. 1–15.

combination of these statistical techniques and the shared thinking of group members provides a powerful method of quality control.

An interesting and important point of contrast between the former quality control inspector and quality circles is the shift from supervisory to self and social control. The results, at least so far, indicate improvement in the bottom line via reduced waste and better products. If sales are an indication, consumers of automobiles feel that the Japanese methods are quite successful.

Quality control is not just an issue for industry alone. Organizations that provide a service may be even *more* concerned about quality control. Their very survival may be highly dependent on the quality of service, not just on the numbers of people served.

People seek high-quality medical care, education, financial counseling, repair service, entertainment, and so on. Managers seek high-quality (at least well-informed) decisions, information, and guidance. Here again many organizations are discovering that the complexities and uncertainties of management may require managerial quality circles. A group of executives that takes the time to evalute the effectiveness of its meetings may find that time well spent in minimizing wasted effort and improving the quality of both the discussions and the decisions that result.

By gathering postcontrol information, feeding that back into discussions and planning, and comparing that information to agreed upon objectives and standards, managers can reduce some of the uncertainties that often affect quality. Although the underlying model is a simple feedback loop, the social process that makes it work is not simple. This may be especially true for quality control, where human judgment plays a dominant role.

One final issue deserves mention. Quality and quantity objectives often conflict. There are times when one can be gained only at the expense of the other. In an effort to get something out the door on time, quality may suffer; in an effort to check and double check quality, there may be a decrease in quantity. In some ways this problem is reminiscent of one discussed in Chapter 2: the issue of inherent goal conflicts. A failure of management to establish priorities with respect to quantity versus quality, where these factors do conflict, can produce confusion and low standards in both respects.

As indicated, standards of quality in this country are on the rise. Perhaps this will slow down production somewhat, perhaps a great deal. Will people wait longer for a quality automobile? Or perhaps if demand is high enough, manufacturers will develop the resources to attain *both* quantity and quality. If you want things to move faster, then you need the resources to make it happen. If you stretch existing resources to meet excessive quantity demands by increasing the rate of flow, then something suffers, usually quality. Imagine, for example, a university moving students through undergraduate education in three years instead of four. This would produce more graduates but with mediocre qualifications. In some circumstances it is not possible to maximize both quantity and quality without incurring considerable costs.

Flow (scheduling) The basic components of any system are inputs, throughputs, and outputs. Flow is concerned with having the necessary thing in the right place at the right time and not losing track of where something is at any moment. Thus, flow is concerned with coordinating the movement of inputs into the system with the various throughputs so that the outputs leave as planned or needed. It is concerned with integrating these various elements in both time and location.

There are many flow control mechanisms. Appointment books are a common device that many people use to schedule their time. Airplane schedules allow people to plan trips so that they don't have to waste time waiting for a connecting flight. Factories use production schedules to plan and control when jobs will be run and how the work will be assigned to different machines and work stations. Factories also use work tickets to identify boxes of parts and products so that they are not lost. Such tickets may also contain routing instructions so that each station knows where to deliver the box after it completes its task. These and other devices establish precontrol through integrated planning, and then allow for concurrent control by providing a picture of how things are supposed to be moving through the system.

One major device for controlling flow is an *inventory control system*. Since most markets for manufactured goods tend to fluctuate, few firms can expect their products to flow out the door in a steady stream. Seasonal fluctuations produce demand peaks that could tax the resources of a company beyond its capacity. Consequently, by creating inventories—sometimes of raw materials and parts, sometimes of finished goods—a company can use its resources (money, materials, technology, people) in efficient and effective ways.

The field of operations management (OM) has developed models for managing inventory control. These models help managers to decide on how much raw material (or parts from suppliers) to order, when to order, and how to balance the cost of "holding" against the cost of ordering in varying amounts (discounts, delivery, etc.). The models provide guidance in determining the *optimum* inventory control system —that is, one that possesses the best balance of costs of goods ordered versus costs of goods held in inventory.

One valuable inventory control method is called material requirements planning (MRP); it uses a combination of human effort and computer information (see Box 6–2). In essence, MRP allows a manager to use a wide range of interrelated information—customer orders, forecasts, engineering changes, and raw material availability—to make decisions on ordering and inventory. Although it was developed for manufacturing problems, MRP as a concept has also found uses in relation to other kinds of problems, including cost control, medical care, and the food service industry.

One very effective control device used by managers is PERT[3] (program evaluation and review technique), which was devised for controlling the flow of projects of various kinds. Its basic principles and underlying thought process work well in managing the sequential relationships among ongoing work activities. In some respects, PERT is an elaborate feedback model covering a network of interrelated tasks, each with an expected time for completion. Through frequent periodic progress review, PERT enables one to correct, speed up, slow down, or redirect any element of the system to maintain the appropriate interdependency, thus keeping events as close to schedule as possible.

Whether or not you choose a particular technique (such as PERT) to help with scheduling and flow management is less important than being conscious of the underlying process (checking, reviewing, and correct-

BOX 6–2

MRP

Material requirements planning (MRP) is a method for planning inventories and scheduling operations using those inventories in a way that meets end product demands. The essential elements of MRP are:

1. *A master production schedule*, which links forecasted product demand to present and expected inventory levels.
2. *A product structure record*, which identifies all the parts and sub-parts required for assembly of the final product, as well as the hierarchical relationship among the parts.
3. *Inventory status records*, which show exactly how many items (and which) are on order or in stock, how long it takes to obtain new items, and the most cost-efficient way to do it.

Most MRP systems are computerized, which maximizes both the effectiveness and efficiency of the system. Computerized information permits immediate access to accurate data throughout the production process, which allows for constant updating and correcting. Consequently, MRP serves both as a precontrol (planning) method and as a concurrent control system.

---

[3] A similar and related technique is CPM (critical path method). Both techniques are described in Box 6–3.

BOX 6-3

CPM AND PERT

The critical path method (CPM) is a way of analyzing and planning the *network* of activities necessary for accomplishing a large-scale task. As shown in the diagram below, each activity is represented by a circle, with the arrows indicating the sequencing of the activities.

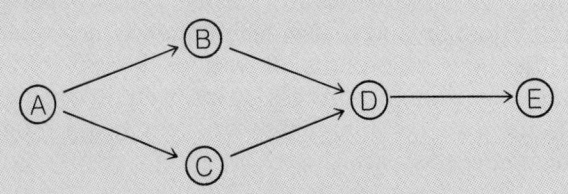

```
        B
      ↗   ↘
    A       D ——→ E
      ↘   ↗
        C
```

You can see that the final step (E) cannot be completed until D is, and D is dependent on the completion of B and C, which follow A. Note that the paths to D are by way of both B and C; whichever takes longer is called the *critical path* because it is the one that determines the time it will take to reach D. If you can envision this diagram multiplied many times over, you would be representing a CPM chart for the kind of large-scale task for which the method is most suited. By identifying all the critical paths in a project, one can see where special effort or control might be needed to complete the total project on time.

Program evaluation and review technique (PERT) is a method of analysis and planning similar in concept and purpose to CPM. There are two differences between PERT and CPM worth noting. In PERT, the arrows (in the above diagram) represent the activities, while the circles represent starting and finishing points for those activities. The second and most important difference lies in the assumptions each model makes about the time it will take to complete an activity. CPM treats time as a certainty; it assumes that an activity will take a given amount of time and, consequently, builds an overall CPM plan around a relatively fixed total time. PERT, on the other hand, uses probabilistic times, which provide ranges from optimistic to pessimistic relative to project completion.

Conceptually, CPM and PERT are the same, and even the differences noted may not be all that important, since there is no reason a user of CPM couldn't use probable times instead of fixed times.

ing) and the objectives that require juggling (such as quantity and quality).

Flowcharts, critical path models, and various forms of work schedules are at best devices for control. They don't do the work or make the decisions. They are maps that enable a manager to exercise control unilaterally, in consultation with employees, through consensus, or through outright delegation. In many cases, they also can be of use to the employee, as well as the manager, in controlling the flow of work.

Costs   If the quantity produced each day is within standards, if the quality is neither too good nor inadequate, and if the various flows are on schedule and therefore coordinated, costs will be controlled to an appreciable extent. Yet attention to costs and methods of controlling costs other than these accomplished by control of quantity, quality, and flow is essential.

Raw materials (input) need to be secured at prices that are competitive. Some amount of shopping around to get the best price, with due consideration for service, reliability, and the maintenance of good vendor relations, is warranted. Sometimes an organization's purchasing function can even bring the supplier and its own engineering people together to discover ways that the input can be redesigned for lower cost of manufacture (precontrol). Certainly knowledge of market prices can allow a purchasing agent to evaluate a supplier's current prices to be sure they are still in line (concurrent control).

Throughput costs are directly affected by quantity, quality, and flow. But even when these are under control, excessive use of overtime, high turnover rates, and excessive defects or waste can all contribute to overall cost inflation. Sometimes outputs shipped on schedule hold an opportunity for cost reduction through choice of the least expensive method of shipping and packaging to reduce the incidence of product damage during transit.

Finally, a host of other expenditures warrant attention if costs are to be kept in line. Supplies, such as writing paper, soap and other cleaners, light bulbs, and lubricating oils, can cost an appreciable amount. Furniture and office equipment as well as hand tools and machinery must be bought, maintained, and replaced. Costs for travel, entertainment, and fringe benefits can easily get out of hand and require careful control.

Thus, even with quantity, quality, and flow under control, other matters need attention if overall costs are to be kept in line. One major means of gaining such control is through an accounting system and the use of budgets, in which actual costs are recorded and compared with planned or expected costs.

Do you keep an account of the money you spend each day, week, or month? Your checking account record may be one way to do this. Every business has to maintain a strict accounting system for a variety of reasons. For one thing, a company needs to know how well it's doing relative to profit. If costs exceed income, the future survival of the company would not be promising. For another thing, the government requires such records for tax purposes. Also, stockholders require them as a basis for determining dividends.

Cost accounting is a postcontrol device. It is useful insofar as it provides information that can be used for future decisions, such as to step up production, minimize waste, push the product, or improve advertising. For financial data to serve as a precontrol device, they must be used as part of financial *planning,* and a key element of financial planning is *budgetary control.* If you are worried about your personal expenditures, you might decide to put yourself on a budget to control what you spend. Of course, your budget is only a device and is no more effective than your willingness and ability to stay within it.

Budgeting and planning are vital parts of an organization's control system. With appropriate and frequent checkpoints (concurrent control), the organization is in a better position to control its destiny. In this context, accounting serves as a concurrent control device that helps managers to correct for deviations from standards in an ongoing way rather than when it is too late to make changes. In short, with a budget one can establish an objective or standard; with cost accounting one can measure financial performance; and with the comparison one can obtain the necessary feedback to reduce any discrepancy between budgeted and actual amounts.

With spiraling and never-ending increases in the costs of raw materials and labor, most industries are particularly concerned about minimizing waste of both material and human resources. In areas of high technology and rapid growth, it is very difficult to identify and assess the cost of waste, especially since the high profit margins characteristic of these industries often overshadow the extent of the wasted material and human effort. But as these margins level off and return to normal, the problem of waste and inefficiency will become the proverbial chicken coming home to roost. Most managers do not like to see wasted effort or wasted material, but until managers recognize it and make efforts to deal with it, waste in either form occurs.

Can you think of examples where you have wasted time? I think we can all answer that in the affirmative. Do you pay attention and learn from the experience? Probably when it costs you dearly. It is the same in management; waste control is part of cost control. Cost control is an accounting device that tells you whether or not you are getting "your money's worth" out of the work effort (output compared with input). And waste is a by-product of that evaluation. You pay attention to it when it contributes significantly to a reduction in the desired profit margin—that is, when it affects the degree to which you fall short of attaining desired objectives or standards.

Safety and Security Organizations not only need to control operating processes (quantity, quality, and flow) along with costs, but they also need to look out for the security and the safety of their resources: human, physical, and informational.

People are subject to accidents. We cut ourselves, we slip on wet floors, we get our hands caught in equipment, we inhale toxic fumes, we put our fingers into electrical sockets, we catch pieces of flying glass or metal in our eyes, we strain our backs lifting heavy objects improperly, we fall down stairs and off chairs, we hit our thumbs with hammers—the list is endless.

Physical resources are subject to damage by corrosion, fire, theft, and ordinary deterioration ("shelf life"). Machines can be overloaded. Tools can be used improperly. Forklift trucks and other vehicles can crash into walls and into each other. Whole buildings burn. Even large items that one would think were too big to be removed from a plant have a way of disappearing. Theft by employees and customers as well as middle-of-the-night burglars is a significant problem for many organizations. For some items, inventory control is not just a matter of having the right quantity on hand but also seeing to it that the oldest items are used first before their normal shelf life is exceeded.

Many organizations have "trade secrets" and information that they prefer to keep private and not fall into the hands of competitors. This is particularly true of defense contractors but also of many other organizations. Whatever the type of information, it can be subject to industrial espionage or merely gossip-seeking individuals—hence, the need to maintain control over records, files, engineering drawings, and the like.

In this area of control, the establishment of standards is not as clear-cut as standards of quantity and cost. One general approach is simply to recognize the risks and take steps to reduce the probabilities of accidents, damage, and security violations. In some areas, numerical standards can be developed. Thus, many organizations keep track of accidents and strive to keep the accident rate down to a reasonable level.

This is an area where precontrol is vitally important. By anticipating what accidents might happen, steps can often be taken to prevent them. Machinery can be equipped with guard rails and other devices so that they cannot be operated unless the operator's hands are out of the way. Employees can be provided with safety glasses and instructed not to wear clothing that may catch in machinery. Instrument panels, such as aboard aircraft or in the control room of nuclear plants, can be designed so that pilots and controllers are less likely to push the wrong button or pull the wrong lever. Air control systems are now commonplace in hospitals and factories; these remove germs and lung-clogging lint from the air and, thereby, protect patients' and employees' health.

Concurrent safety control is gained through the adoption of safe operating practices by employees. Education or training is a vital part of this. But success in getting people to wear safety glasses or not smoke in fire-risk areas is often no easier than it was to get many of us to brush our teeth as kids. Concurrent control rests in the hands of employees but also depends on training and reinforcement by supervisors and management.

In the area of safety, postcontrol is a common practice and has been the means by which society has learned about necessary safety measures. We study accidents to determine cause, not just for purposes of assigning legal responsibilities; as we gain understanding of the reasons for accidents, we develop prevention methods. Release bindings for skiers, deadman switches on power vehicles, and restaurant doors that open outward rather than inward are three examples of preventive measures that have grown out of the analysis of accidents. By studying individual events (accidents, fires, thefts) and patterns of events, organizations are able to learn from experience and apply postcontrol data to the safety and security of human, physical, and informational resources.

SOURCES OF CONTROL

Suppose, as a manager, you must see to it that one of your employees carries out a task in a way that ensures specific minimum levels of quantity and quality as well as coordinates with the efforts of others in your area. You could, as many managers do, adopt a watchdog attitude and check on every action of your employee; however, that may be entirely unnecessary.

Your employee may already have some internalized standards of quantity and quality that meet the job requirements and may also feel some commitment to working cooperatively with others. If this is the case, your efforts at formal or authoritative control would be unnecessary at best and disruptive at worst (as in the example of the proposal writers).

It also may be that the group of which the employee is a member has a norm that stresses performance and cooperation. This kind of social pressure can be at least as effective in controlling behavior as more formal and impersonal approaches.

Furthermore, built-in organizational mechanisms often exercise control over an employee's performance, including the organization's system of rules or policies and its established goals, structure, climate, and rewards. An individual's own awareness of these system devices and willingness to operate within them provide ongoing control over his or her work effort.

In short, we can categorize the sources of control into four general groupings:

1. Supervisory control.
2. Self-control.
3. Social control.
4. System control.

In most situations, some element of each source affects performance, but usually there is a particular emphasis on one or another, depending on a manager's style, situational pressures, and other factors. It is important for *any* manager to keep in mind that there *are* different sources of control and, consequently, different options available for matching the type of control with the nature of the situation.

Let's examine these options by combining the four sources of control with the timing of the control. Figure 6–1 shows the kinds of controls that one can exercise relative to the combined variables (source and timing), many of which depend on power (see Box 6–4, page 188).

1. Supervisory Control

When you think of control in an organization, you probably associate it with the behavior of a manager or boss in relation to a subordinate. This is supervisory control. It is the source of control most obvious in

FIGURE 6–1
Controls as a Function of Source and Timing

Source	Precontrol	Concurrent Control	Postcontrol
Supervisory	Orders or instructions Expectations of employee	Guiding Watching Checking Disciplining Supporting	Assessing results by application of standards regarding intended and expected outcomes Feedback to employee
Self	Motivation Commitment Expectations of self Competencies	Self-checking Attention to task Attention to interdependence	Rewards Individual performance results Comparison to own standards and expectations Self-enhancement
Social	Norms regarding expected performance of group Interpersonal expectations	Group pressure Peer support Stability of relationships	Success/failure of expectations regarding group output Success/failure of group goals Enhancement of group's identity
System	Rules/SOPs/policies Goals Structure Reward system Job description Plans	Enforcement Information flow Climate Movement Boundaries Momentum	Sanctions Costs Income Profit Growth and development as system

traditional organizations. The church, the army, and, after the Industrial Revolution, the factory all exhibited a pattern of control built upon a hierarchy of authority. Control was maintained through the surveillance of behavior by someone in authority. Whether the authority figure was a priest, officer, boss, or even a parent, his or her primary function was to oversee another's behavior, giving direction and guidance and monitoring obedience.

Although this source of control is a key part of any control system, it is by no means the only source. It can often be more effective to rely on another source of control or some mixture of sources. An important question here is when and where to rely primarily on supervisory control to ensure desired results.

By reading across all three time periods in Figure 6–1, you can see that supervisory control demands greater knowledge, competence, awareness, physical presence, communication skills, and performance evaluation skills on the part of the supervisor relative to the subordinate. Furthermore, to be effective it also requires that the subordinate recognize and accept this differential relationship. Can you think of examples in your own experience where this form of control was exercised appropriately over you? Perhaps you've worked as an apprentice to someone, have taken a tutorial course, or worked as a lab assistant. In all these cases supervisory control is exercised and probably required by the very nature of the situation.

However, you can see how these kinds of working relationships can and often should change over time. As a subordinate becomes more knowledgeable, the value of supervisory control tends to diminish. In fact, if this source of control fails to change, it can become an obstacle to the continued growth and development of the subordinate and, in turn, undercut the subordinate's satisfaction and morale. Eventually, the subordinate's performance can suffer. Since the purpose here is usually to maintain the required task role, renegotiation is needed to shift the source from supervisory to self-control.

2. Self-Control

Some degree of self-control is essential. An organization cannot function without it. A supervisor cannot be in all places at all times overseeing everyone's behavior. Even the best plans cannot anticipate every contingency. Their success often requires that those most directly involved in carrying them out exercise some judgment in adapting the plan to fit developments. An organization built entirely on slave labor, perhaps the quintessence of low self-control, will hardly be efficient and creative in reaching organizational goals.

Furthermore, the more a manager can rely on employees to control their own work effort, the more freedom he or she has to attend to larger issues, such as planning, creative problem solving, and assessing the overall picture.

Not all managers find it easy to delegate; many fear losing direct control over the work for which they are held responsible, whereas others seem to be worried that they won't be of any worth to the organization. Therefore, even though you might agree with the principle of encouraging self-control, you might not find it that easy to implement.

As you look across the columns in Figure 6–1 related to self, you can see that this source of control works best when employees bring to the job the right motivation, commitment, competencies, and expectations of themselves to serve as a background (precontrol) for performance. (This is one reason employee selection and training and the clarification of job expectations are important managerial functions.) Furthermore, they need to be willing to devote attention to their own behavior, the task, and their relationships to others with whom they work (as concurrent controls). Finally, for postcontrol, they must be able to see the results of their efforts, be able to compare these results to standards and expectations, and be rewarded both materially and through self-enhancement.

As you can see, for self-control, the individual must have access to data. An organization that discourages participation and limits the flow of information by emphasizing secrecy is not likely to be conducive to a high degree of self-control.

To the extent that jobs have built-in opportunities for employees to govern their own work activities, and to the extent that the people hired for those jobs bring the necessary attributes for self-management, the organization will find little need for managers to exercise direct, frequent control over their employees.

Think about the jobs you have held. As a teenager, you were probably given little responsibility for making decisions; you were told what to do and how to do it and were probably checked on fairly often. Did you ever feel that you could have done the work better if the boss had just stayed off your back? Or perhaps you experienced the opposite—that is, a situation in which you were left too much on your own, where the boss didn't provide enough control by way of instructions or checking or telling you whether you were on the right track. Deciding the proper balance between supervisory and self-control is not easy. It can become especially difficult when the shift needs to occur from self-control *to* supervisory control.

An insurance company introduced desk computers into its record offices to improve and speed up the recordkeeping procedures. The office manager was given a training course in how to use the new equipment. When the clerks were learning to use the computers, it was necessary for the manager to check constantly on the work of all her employees. They understood the importance of her watchdogging, but they also resented being placed in such a position. Prior to the change, they had been allowed to control their own work, using the supervisor as a resource when needed. Fortunately, it was only temporary. The employees were willing to put up with the increased supervisory control while they learned, both because they recognized its necessity and because the supervisor did not extend her watchdogging any longer than necessary. However, such a situation can create more serious and long-lasting problems if, for example, a group of employees who are used to a manager who encouraged self-control is suddenly assigned a new manager who overuses supervisory control. This is not unusual, especially because many new managers are concerned about establishing their influence. What better (or worse) way to do so than through the control of subordinates?

The situation becomes more complex as we add social controls. Ever since the original Hawthorne studies (see Chapter 3), it has been obvious that workers are affected by peer pressures or group standards just as strongly (or even more so) as by the formal requirements of the job.

3. Social Control

One of the authors once had a summer job as a plumber's assistant at a large commercial construction project. He was eager to please the boss and also had certain standards of his own regarding "a fair day's work for a fair day's pay." The other members of the plumbing team had other ideas about how much work ought to be done, standards that were far lower than the author's. As he continued to outproduce the others, the team made snide remarks and then more forceful demands that he slow down and produce at a reasonable rate. The threat of verbal abuse and isolation, if not more, was clear. Because of his need to survive the summer job without constant harassment, the individual gave in to the group. It was *social* control that ruled that summer.

The group is a powerful force in any social system. Task groups, departments, and committees all develop norms for expected member performance. These norms exercise control over the individual group members, and they (the norms) may or may not be congruent with the expectations of the organization or individual. Figure 6–1 identifies norms and interpersonal expectations as the precontrol forces that affect performance. These are translated into concurrent controls by ongoing group pressure, peer support, and the stability of interpersonal relationships. Finally, postcontrol data reinforce social control through the group's output relative to its expectations, the attainment of the group's goals, the enhancement of its identity, and the sanctions it imposes on its members. The more these outcomes reinforce the norms of the group, the stronger a source of control the group becomes.

Social control can affect a manager of a group as well as its members. For example, when conflicts occur among groups in an organization, there is always a battle for control over what or how things will be done. Managers who are required to negotiate with each other can get caught in the bind of loyalty to their respective departments versus loyalty to other managers and to the organization as a whole. When tensions increase, people tend to seek more control. Therefore, the pressures exerted by the group on its manager can increase to the point where the manager, if he or she feels dominated by the pressures, might put aside all other considerations and act on behalf of the group at all costs, thereby contributing to suboptimization.

Social control, as indicated earlier, helps to maintain behavior related to the organization's informal system. We can see from the preceding example, however, that the informal system has many components, not all of which exert the same kind of pressures. Membership in a complex social system subjects you to informal social controls from a number of sources, some more immediate and direct than others. When tension is highest, people tend to respond more strongly to immediate pressures than to remote ones. The paradox in this for many organizations lies in the fact that when an organization as a whole is faced with stressful external demands, it often needs to exert greater overall control over its operations. Instead of trusting self-control, it resorts to more formal procedures and to tighter supervisory control. In turn, employees, feeling threatened, close ranks and increase the social (normative) controls that, in turn, may work against the overall system's need to coordinate the total work effort.

4. System Control

Some system controls have already been discussed (including budgeting, planning, and scheduling) as methods of minimizing and correcting deviations from standards. Others, including goals, structure, climate, and rewards, were presented in previous chapters but require some discussion as elements in an organization's control system. Before doing that, we want to devote some attention to the topic of rules, standard operating procedures (SOPs), and policies (guidelines) for employee behavior.

Rules, SOPs, and Policies When you entered college, you probably received a booklet on student rights and rules. These are usually intended to give the student a set of guidelines established by the institution to protect freedom, property, and the general welfare of all concerned. Because roughly 25 percent of the student body is freshmen, the institution makes a concerted effort to indoctrinate them in regard to rules, SOPs, and policies that will affect them for the four or more years of their lives in college. How carefully these rules and SOPs are enforced varies from setting to setting; how effective and reasonable they are also varies. What does not vary, however, is that every college or university has them and that they control the behavior of all students.

All organizations establish rules, procedures, and policies that govern members' behavior in ways that are not covered by other controls but are usually related to them. For example, if it is company policy that employees start work at 8 A.M., it may fall to a supervisor to police it, employees themselves to control it, or social pressure to ensure it. The basic source of the control is the system, but the implementation depends on one or more other sources of control. Looking back at the previous example, who enforces the university's rules: the student, the administration, peers, or some combination?

The effectiveness of SOPs and rules in controlling people's behavior is often related to the manner in which they were established in the first place. SOPs that are imposed on you tend to be less palatable than those you created or had a part in creating. Therefore, as a manager you might keep in mind that SOPs and rules are no more effective than the willingness of employees to abide by them. Certainly, the fear of punishment can keep people within "the law," but if it is only fear that does the job, you might find yourself investing great energy just in law enforcement.

In general, an organization that has rules and policies that are broad, flexible, and subject to change provides managers with the freedom to involve employees (where appropriate) in the process of establishing the ones that will be functional to their jobs and to the overall work effort. And it allows managers to modify and update rules and policies in response to changing demands both inside and outside the organization.

Furthermore, in some instances, managers have been known to use lack of rule enforcement as a reward. By bending the rules laid on the department from above or by not enforcing them closely, a manager can obligate employees to follow directions in other matters. This may not be a very effective form of control in the long run; it hardly builds a sense of trust in a manager's intentions.

In Figure 6–1, as you look across the three time periods, you can see that the ongoing rule enforcement process is dependent on the use of *sanctions* for making sure that the rules, procedures, and policies remain in force. While the tone of this discussion sounds heavy and almost legalistic, try to keep in mind that this will be strongly affected by the other sources of control that come into play. A supervisor who calls a worker to task for coming in late and docking his or her pay has a qualitatively different tone than an employee who accepts full responsibility for abiding by organizational policies and rules. When all sources of control are in accord, then the control system as a whole works most effectively; when any one source is in conflict with any other, then the total control system is negatively affected.

Goals, Structure, Climate, and Rewards If the goals and subgoals of the organization are clearly understood and accepted by its members, if each person's place in the structure is well matched to his or her talents, if the climate is conducive to organizational success, and if the reward system provides a suitable link between organizational purposes and individual needs, you might think there would be little need for a formal control system, especially supervisory and system controls. And you would be correct—up to a point. Certainly effective goals, structure, climate, and reward systems provide guidance for people's behavior, in the same way that the detailed programming of a space launch provides advanced control for the vehicle. But there are always uncertainties, even with the space vehicle; therefore, there is always some need for *guidance, corrective action,* and subsequent *revision* of the mechanisms and methods of control.

GOALS   In general, *the more closely the rational or official goals of the organization match the natural goals of its members, the less need there is for formal controls.* The sources of control, where the match is close, tend to be self (individual) and social (group). This is especially important in regard to the *selection* of employees. If you, as a manager, hire people whose personal goals are congruent with those of the organization, or at least with that part of the system in which they work, then you are likely to save yourself some formal control headaches later on. Furthermore, if you can combine people in departments or work groups in ways that encourage norm pressures that support the system's goals, you can further capitalize on employee commitment rather than their compliance to more formal pressures. For example, care in assigning new employees to groups that are effective and have norms that contribute to organizational effectiveness will enhance the chances that the new employee's early socialization is compatible with organizational goals.

Establishing a clear and realistic hierarchy of goals provides an important precontrol framework; reviewing the progress and movement of the organization relative to these goals provides concurrent control; and evaluating goal attainment (e.g., profit, income, costs, growth, etc.) may be the most important postcontrol data the organization obtains—it's the *bottom line.* In essence, you might say that the overarching control system of an organization is its network of goals, from ultimate long-range ones to the most immediate specific ones. All the other vehicles of control already discussed, along with the other dimensions of an organization (structure, climate, and rewards), exist to serve the overall goals of the system.

STRUCTURE   As soon as you are hired into an organization and become part of its division of labor, a set of boundaries is placed around you that, in effect, controls what you do. The job description, the physical location, your rank, to whom you report, and your sources of information all direct your behavior. An organization's structure is a constellation of boundaries with varying degrees of interconnectedness. In some very formal organizations, the boundaries are so fixed that you dare not cross them; you're supposed to "know your place." In other settings where more informal controls (self and social) are emphasized, the structural arrangements tend to be more ambiguous and boundaries are more easily crossed.

In comparison with classical bureaucracies, where structure exercises very tight control, some modern matrix organizations tend to be rather chaotic and seemingly out of control. There are vague boundaries, and control seems to reside with individuals, groups, and the technology of the organization. Which type of structure best fits your own needs for control may be an important consideration for your future career.

CLIMATE   The climate of a setting exerts a subtle but powerful effect on people, as discussed in Chapter 5. In this sense, climate is a source of control over people's behavior. Compare how people behave in a library, in a bank, at a sports event, or in a high-technology company. Each setting has its own characteristic tempo, noise level, and pressure. Normally, people do not charge noisily through the executive offices of an insurance company, nor do they operate in a slow, relaxed manner in a department store during the peak hours of a discount sale.

Think about your own behavior in various places. In the final analysis, you exercise self-control in varying ways and degrees, but you probably find that the atmosphere surrounding you is a major factor controlling your behavior.

A climate of suspicion and fear makes you cautious and tense. You tend to withhold information and not take very much initiative. By contrast, a climate of excitement, trust, and high energy tends to push you to your limits, support openness, and encourage you to take risks.

To the extent that an organization's climate moves employees to behave in goal-related directions, managers find it unnecessary to use more formal methods of control to attain their ends.

REWARDS   You've heard the expression "the carrot and the stick." Does it refer to rewards or controls? In its most common usage, the expression is connected with motivating people through incentives (carrots) on the one hand and fear (sticks) on the other. It probably doesn't matter whether you classify this idea as part of a reward system or a control system; the effect is the same.

If the rewards you expect are the ones you receive, if these are meaningful relative to your needs, and if the effort you have to put forth is reasonable (in your mind), then you are likely to continue to put forth that effort. In turn, if what you do fits with what the organization requires, then the reward system encourages people to work in ways that contribute to organizational goals. Would any additional controls be needed in such a case? Relative to your *behavior*, probably not; the reward system itself serves as an effective control system. However, for you to correct or improve your work behavior, you would still need information on the outcomes of your efforts relative to the objectives or standards. In other words, the reward system may minimize the necessity for formal supervisory control, but it has little, if any, bearing on those aspects of control used to correct deviations from standards.

To the extent that a reward system is broad based with respect to employee needs and organizational purposes, few additional behavioral controls are necessary. Furthermore, such control devices as information feedback, statistical data, and quality circles tend to be most effective when supported by a reward system that encourages employees to use these methods. For example, the effectiveness of quality circles depends directly on the degree to which cooperative interpersonal behavior is rewarded by the organization. A system that encourages interpersonal competition will hardly support successful quality control circles.

One final point about control needs to be made. As an open system, an organization is subject to control by the wider system of which it is a part. Thus, an organization is influenced by its environment. Pressure from other organizations, the government, and society at large constrains (controls) organizations and influences their internal characteristics. We will discuss this in greater detail in Chapter 9.

ASSESSING AND DESIGNING A CONTROL SYSTEM

As we indicated, one important managerial function is to evaluate the control system's effectiveness, which means evaluating the postcontrol consequences. The question is: How does one assess the suitability of a control system? At first blush, the answer would seem to be by determining whether the control system yielded control, whether the organization or a unit stayed on target and reached its objectives. Were the operations in control? Was the plan accomplished?

These are the basic questions, but the issue is more complex. A control system can fail to yield exact control and yet be judged satisfactory. Conversely, a control system can yield great control and yet be judged unsatisfactory.

A first question to be asked in assessing or designing a control system is: What *degree of control* is physically possible? Attempts to obtain tighter control than is realistically possible, given the technology of an opera-

BOX 6-4

THE BASES OF POWER

The more power you have in an organization, the more control you can exert over people and events. In the same way that it is important to understand the various sources of control, it is valuable to understand the different sources of power.

In a classic article entitled "The Bases of Social Power" [in *Studies in Social Power*, ed. D. Cartwright (Ann Arbor: University of Michigan Press, 1959)], J. R. French and B. H. Raven identified five bases of power:

1. *Reward power*—Based on the perception of the follower or subordinate that the leader or superior has the capacity to administer (or withhold) valued rewards.
2. *Coercive power*—Based on the perception of the follower or subordinate that the leader or superior has the capacity to inflict punishment or threaten one's well-being.
3. *Legitimate power*—Based on the belief of the follower or subordinate that the leader or superior has the right to exert influence (control).
4. *Referent power*—Based on the follower's or subordinate's identification and desire for association with the leader or superior.
5. *Expert power*—Based on the perception of the follower or subordinate that the leader or superior possesses valued knowledge and expertise.

Other bases of organizational power—and, thereby, sources of control—are related to such factors as:

1. One's ability to reduce uncertainty.
2. How close one's job is to the highest priorities of the organization.
3. How unique and/or critical one is as a resource in the organization.
4. How important the information is that one has access to and control over.
5. The social network and personal associations one has or is perceived to have.

You can probably think of other bases of power that operate in organizational life, but the above lists cover most of the critical ones. If you are interested in pursuing the topic further, we recommend reading *The External Control of Organizations: A Resource Dependence Perspective* by J. Pfeffer and G. Salancik (New York: Harper & Row, 1978).

---

tion, can be as dysfunctional as insufficient control. Most operating systems have some natural variation. A drill will never drill two holes exactly the same size. You never sign your name exactly the same way each time you sign a letter or a check. The output of an assembly operation that is subject to frequent interruptions to handle rush orders will vary from week to week. To attempt to control an operation to limits more restrictive than its natural variation, such as expecting the assembly operation to produce a fixed dollar output each week, is to seek *overcontrol*. The energy expended to reach the targets could better be spent elsewhere, and anyone judged by the results would soon view the system with disrespect and resentment.

The system must be evaluated in relation to the degree of control that is realistically possible. As long as the results fall within the range of natural variation, even though that variation is significant, the system may, in effect, be a satisfactory control system.

A second question to be asked in assessing a control system is: What is it *costing* to gain the degree of control obtained and are the results cost-efficient? Do the gains from close control exceed the cost of obtaining that control? It is technically possible to drill holes that vary in diameter by no more than a hundredth of an inch. Yet if the holes are to be used for mounting picture frames on a living room wall, there is no need for such close control. To operate to such close tolerances is to incur unnecessary costs. Similarly, the cost of paying for additional supervisory personnel in an attempt to ensure that people are under full surveillance and working all the time may cost more than is saved in idle time, especially if the employees are responsible and likely to exercise self-control. A control system that results in a high degree of control is not effective if the costs outweigh the benefits.

The example just cited pertaining to excessive supervisory costs suggests a third question. Is the *source of control* relied upon the most suitable? If employees are reliable and have reason to support organizational goals, then reliance on self-control rather than on supervisory control may be most appropriate even though there may be little cost savings involved. People appreciate autonomy. Self-control can contribute to personal growth as well as to job satisfaction. Reliance on self-control can free the supervisor for other work, including training and coaching. Even when the balance between supervisory and self-control is appropriate, results may suffer from inadequate system controls. Employees may need more data if their efforts at self-control are to be effective. The installation of a recordkeeping system or a similar system control device may allow individuals to exert concurrent control not otherwise possible. Thus, whether a control system is working or not, the question of what sources of control are relied upon remains important.

A fourth question in assessing a control system concerns the *intangible costs* of the system. In other words, what are the consequences of the control system aspects of the organization's functioning other than those directly controlled by the system in question? We have hinted at some of these. A control system can affect employee job satisfaction, morale, attitudes toward management, and loyalty to the organization. There can also be an impact on employee cooperativeness with other functions and on the care with which work is done.

To a great extent, these corollary consequences of a control system depend on whether the control system is seen as *legitimate* by the employees affected by the system. Three aspects are subject to questions of legitimacy:

1. Degree of control.
2. Domain of control.
3. Manner of control.

Attempts to control an operation more closely than its natural variation suggests will be seen as unreasonable and will result in a loss of respect for the control system. In addition, people have beliefs about what is reasonable. Professors usually like to start class on time; we know of one who locked the door at the starting hour and would not tolerate a student being even a minute late. In many schools that would be seen as attempting to exercise more than a legitimate amount of control. Furthermore, people have ideas about what activities are within the organization's right to control. Today, in most undergraduate universities, attempts to require students to wear a necktie to class would not be seen as legitimate. Similarly, a company's efforts to limit an employee's right to "moonlight" (hold a second job) may or may not be viewed as legitimate. Finally, some ways of exerting control, such as spying, may be viewed as illegitimate, although the use of closed-circuit television has become more accepted. Thus, a key element in evaluating a control system is the employee's acceptance of the system as legitimate.

Finally, an evaluation of a control system can usefully include the question: Does the control system fit the organization's *goal priorities and values?* A control system that focused on only the quantity produced could easily distort the balance between an organizational goal of cost-efficiency and a goal of product quality. Similarly, a control system that focused on short-term, tangible results could easily inhibit progress toward longer-term goals, particularly goals related to less tangible objectives such as human resource development. For example, it has happened that individuals are seen as indispensible in a particular position and lose an opportunity for transfer to a different job that in the long run would enhance their growth and ultimate value to the organization. Such a situation would not only distort goal priority but could also violate organizational values if the organization emphasized respect for the personal goals of its members and had a commitment to respect the dignity and rights of each person in the organization.

SUMMARY

Controls are devices and methods that are used to make sure that things happen the way they are supposed to. A control system is a constellation of devices and methods established by an organization to ensure that intended outcomes are achieved. Some controls are applied in advance of an activity (precontrol), some during an activity (concurrent control) and others following an activity to provide feedback (postcontrol).

The purposes for which control systems are used include:

1. Maintaining required task roles.
2. Maintaining institutional character.
3. Minimizing and/or correcting deviations from established standards relative to quantity, quality, flow, cost, and safety.

The sources of control fall into four categories:

1. Supervisory control.
2. Self-control.
3. Social control.
4. System control.

Each source can be applied at any of the three time periods. Figure 6–1 gave examples of various methods of control that are related to each source at each time.

Finally, in assessing a control system or designing one from the start, the factors that ought to be considered include:

1. The degree of control physically possible.
2. The degree of control one can afford (e.g., the cost benefit).
3. The appropriate sources of control, particularly given the nature of the people employed and the values of the organization.
4. The impact of the control system on intangible costs or other aspects of the organization's activities.
5. What degree, domain, and manner of control will be viewed as legitimate by the employee group.
6. The congruence between the control system and the organization's goal priorities and values.

ANNOTATED BIBLIOGRAPHY

Cammann, C., and D. Nadler "Fit Control Systems to Your Managerial Style." *Harvard Business Review*, January–February 1976, pp. 65–72.

This article deals with the problems managers have in designing and utilizing control systems that help the organization and its people be most productive and effective. It suggests that consequences must be considered in terms of the kind of behavior motivated in subordinates, as the control system is a powerful tool in influencing behavior. The authors discuss "process" of control versus "technology" of control and assert that information must be used well to have the control system perform well.

Clegg, S. "Organization and Control." *Administrative Science Quarterly,* December 1981, pp. 545–62.

This is a paper examining the concept of control and the important implications this concept has for organizational theory. The author draws upon extensive literature from many research areas, showing that organizations have been constructed on the basis of differential modes of control of the overall labor process. The author further states that different modes of control become specialized at different structural levels in the organization. The paper concludes by outlining some of the empirical research possibilities that perspective has in organizational analysis.

Jasinski, F. "Use and Misuse of Efficiency Controls." *Harvard Business Review,* July–August 1956, pp. 105–12.

The author argues that managers must recognize limitations of "efficiency reports" that are derived from the concept: "operator efficiency = actual time versus standard time." People may behave in such a way as to impair efficiency. For example, as they try to produce more against the clock, quality will drop, morale will drop, figures will be "fudged," unit costs will rise, maintenance costs will rise, recruitment will be impaired, and management/labor relations will be strained. Efficiency reports are dangerous if not supplemented by other information sources.

Koontz, H., and Bradspies "Managing through Feedforward Control." *Business Horizons,* June 1972.

This article centers on the need for future-directed control systems for cash planning, inventories, and new product development. Systems that rely solely on feedback do indeed signal error, but often as a postmortem, after planning targets have been missed. "Feedforward" systems (such as PERT) monitor critical inputs, detecting and measuring disturbances *and* making corrections before system output change occurs. Managers have access to quickly available data on input variables, enabling them to see problems as they develop, make accurate analyses, and effect timely solutions. It is up to the manager to choose the input variables after careful analysis and goal setting, to develop a model, and to make the system adjustable to change.

McMahon, T., and G. W. Perritt "The Control Structures of Organizations: An Empirical Examination." *Academy of Management Journal,* September 1971, pp. 327–39.

This study demonstrates (1) the importance of agreement on perceptions of different management levels and (2) the need to develop a contingency model of organizational control. Primary analytical tools of "Control Graph," "Mean Level of Control," and "Slope of the Curve," used independently to measure organizational effectiveness on the basis of production indicators and member's satisfactions, are proven to be insufficient measures of control. The authors develop, as a contingency model, the use of *sets* of control curves to provide a clear picture of complex situations of organizational control.

O'Reilly, C. A. III, and B. A. Weitz "Managing Marginal Employees: The Use of Warnings and Dismissals." *Administrative Science Quarterly,* September 1980, pp. 467–84.

A study is presented that examines how supervisors manage marginal employees. Results indicate a positive correlation between a supervisor's use of negative sanctions with ratings on performance by higher-level managers. The researchers suggest that appropriate use of sanctions by supervisors may be perceived by employees as legitimate and may be conducive to the development of productive group norms.

Ouchi, W. G. and Maguire, M. A. "Organizational Control: Two Functions," *Admin. Sci. Quarterly,* 1975, vol. *20,* pp. 559–569.

The authors present the results of a study showing that two forms of control, behavioral and output, are not substitutes for each other; each serves a different purpose. Their research suggests that behavioral controls serve to monitor immediate behavior of subordinates and tend to be used where direction and guidance are needed. Such control also tends to be used when the supervisor has greater knowledge of a subordinate's task requirements. Output controls pertain to overall output, but provide little data on subordinate performance. They tend to become more important and increase in use as one goes higher in the organization's hierarchy. The less familiar a manager is with a subordinate's task performance, the greater will be the emphasis on output controls.

Payne, S. L. "Organization Ethics and Antecedents to Social Control Processes." *Academy of Management Review,* July 1980, pp. 409–14.

The author suggests that certain ethical problems facing organizations are more accessible from behavioral science approaches than from the existing descriptions of ethics in previous organization research. The author believes that further research must include a broader input from the social sciences.

Sasser, W. E. Jr., and F. S. Leonard "Let First-Level Supervisors Do Their Job." *Harvard Business Review,* March–April 1980, pp. 113–21.

This article discusses the difficulties first-level supervisors face in balancing the demands of management, the demands of the collective work force, and those of the individual workers. Although supervisors often have responsibility for implementing goals of upper management, the authors show how they often lack the authority to implement necessary actions. The authors suggest that by allowing supervisors to use the levers of influence of their position, an overall performance for the entire organization will be attained.

Schoderbek, P. "A Study of the Applications of PERT." *Academy of Management Journal,* September 1967, pp. 199–210

This article reports the findings of a survey of PERT (program evaluation and review techniques) systems based on the extent of their industrial use, modes of application, and criteria for employment. These integrated systems of forced planning and evaluation provide useful qualitative and quantitative date for comparing on-the-spot progress with scheduled goals (creating time and cost savings), but Schoderbek notes disadvantages: (1) excessive amount of work involved, (2) specialized training of personnel required, and (3) excessive detail tending to obscure problems.

Schonberger R. "Custom-Tailored PERT/CPM Systems." *Business Horizons,* December 1972, pp. 64–66.

Schonberger is concerned that companies too often use PERT/CPM systems in too broad a manner. Most benefits derive from only a minimal use of PERT or CPM. Graduated levels of applicability should be determined for critical segments—that is to define managerial needs and then custom-tailor systems based on time criticality. Simple systems based on critical networks should be the norm; the expensive control-oriented systems should be the exception.

SUGGESTED READINGS

Beer, Stafford   *Cybernetics and Management.* New York: John Wiley & Sons, 1959.

Beer, Stafford   *Decision and Control.* New York: John Wiley & Sons, 1966.

Burck, C. G.   "What Happens When Workers Manage Themselves?" *Fortune,* July 1981, p. 62.

Burck, C. G.   "Working Smarter." *Fortune,* June 15, 1981, p. 68.

Child, John   "Organization Structure and Strategies of Control: A Replication of the Aston Study." *Administrative Science Quarterly* 17 (1972), pp. 163–77.

Cole, R. E.   "Learning from the Japanese—Prospects and Pitfalls." *Management Review,* September 1980, p. 22.

Cole, R. E.   "Will Quality Circles Work in the U.S.?" *Quality Progress,* July 1980, p. 30.

Haberstroh, Chadwick J.   "Control as an Organization Process." *Management Science* 6 (1960), pp. 165–71.

Hayes, R. H.   "Why Japanese Factories Work." *Harvard Business Review,* July–August 1981, p. 57.

Hofstede, G.   "The Poverty of Management Control Philosophy." *Academy of Management Review,* July 1978, pp. 450–61.

Jackson, J. H., and Susan Adams   "The Life Cycle of Rules." *Academy of Management Review* 4 (1979), pp. 269–73.

Janson, R. L.   "Graphic Indicators of Operations." *Harvard Business Review,* November–December 1980, pp. 164–70.

Lawler, Edward E., and John G. Rhode   *Information and Control in Organizations.* Santa Monica, Calif.: Goodyear, 1976.

Lubar, R.   "Rediscovering the Factory." *Fortune,* July 13, 1981, p. 52.

Lyons, Thomas F.   "Role Clarity, Need for Clarity, Satisfaction, Tension, and Withdrawal." *Organizational Behavior and Human Performance* 6 (1971), pp. 99–110.

Main, J.   "The Battle for Quality Begins." *Fortune,* December 29, 1980, p. 28.

Miller, J. G., and Linda Sprague   "Behind the Growth in Materials Requirements Planning." *Harvard Business Review,* September–October 1975, pp. 83–91.

Newman, W. H.   *"Constructive Control: Design and Use of Control Systems."* Englewood Cliffs, N.J.: Prentice-Hall, 1975.

Ouchi, William G., and Mary Ann McGuire   "Organizational Control: Two Functions." *Administrative Science Quarterly* 20 (1975), pp. 559–69.

Pfeffer, Jeffrey, and Gerald R. Salancik   *"The External Control of Organizations."* New York: Harper & Row, 1978.

Reeves and Woodward   "The Study of Managerial Control." In *Industrial Organization: Behaviour and Control,* ed. Woodward J. New York: Oxford University Press, 1970.

Tannenbaum, Arnold S.   *Control in Organizations.* New York: McGraw-Hill, 1968.

CHAPTER 7

Decision Making

INTRODUCTION

THE JOB OF A MANAGER is to make decisions: how much to spend on something; whom to hire, promote, or fire; how to structure a department, how much to pay people; what to do about a particular problem; which meeting to cancel; where to take a client for lunch; whom to assign to what job; and so on. The range and levels of importance of these decisions are endless.

The *content* of the decisions is normally related to the *kinds* of issues covered in the previous chapters—that is, the organization's goals, structure, rewards, and controls. In this chapter, we will examine the *process* by which decisions are made—that is, the phases or steps involved in the *thought process*. In doing so, we will look at decision making primarily from the perspective of the individual decision maker. However, since most decisions in organizations involve and affect individuals other than just the decision maker, we will also discuss *when* and *how* to use participative decision making.

Furthermore, we want to stress that decisions are often not completely rational processes. In fact, most experienced managers acknowledge that they make many decisions from emotions or intuition. Although we don't know a great deal about the nonrational processes as they affect the way people make decisions, we do know that managers can become more effective decision makers if they learn to use and trust some of their so-called irrational hunches or inclinations. Sometimes feelings, fears, or tensions get in the way of effective decision making; sometimes these factors actually facilitate the process. It is a combination of experience and education that will help one to make positive use of emotional factors and minimize their adverse effects.

Many nonrational aspects of decision making are related not so much to the nature of the decision but more to those involved in it. The more people involved and the more opinions to deal with, the greater are the variation in attitudes and the potential for conflict. You can undoubtedly recall many occasions when what seemed like a simple decision (e.g., what movie to see, television program to watch, or restaurant to eat at) mushroomed into a major negotiation. Managers face such dilemmas every day. In fact, many managers, to avoid these complications, tend to make unilateral decisions that ought to be made through consultation with others.

This chapter begins with a detailed presentation of a rational approach to decision making, followed by a discussion of nonrational factors that affect the process, and finally a discussion of decision making as an organizational phenomenon involving many groups, levels, and individuals in the system.

Figure 7–1 reflects the framework for this chapter. It shows that the various phases or steps in rational decision making (vertical dimension)

FIGURE 7-1
Phases of Decision Making in Relation to Alternatives for Participation

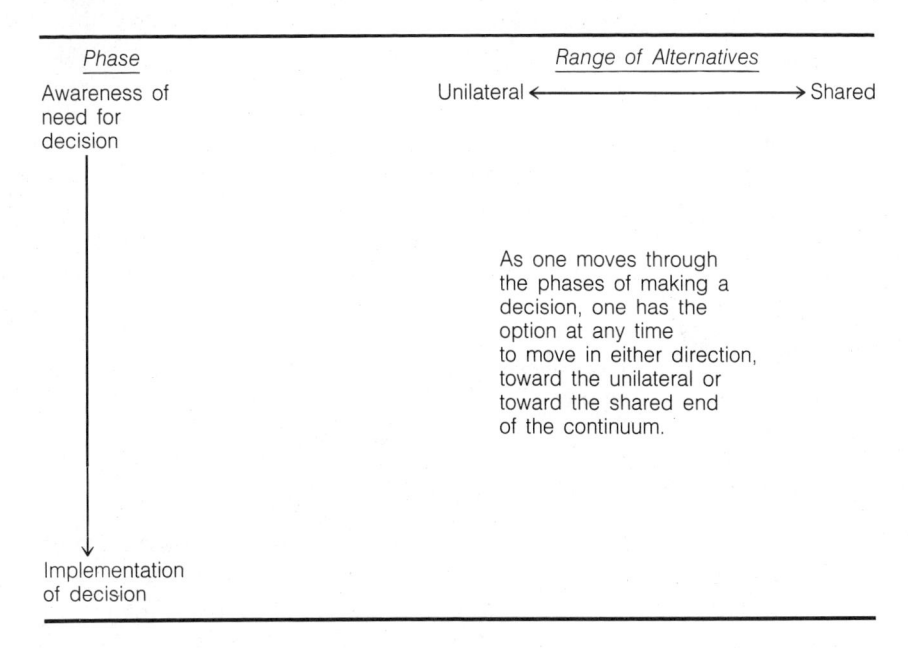

Phase	Range of Alternatives
Awareness of need for decision ↓ Implementation of decision	Unilateral ←————————→ Shared As one moves through the phases of making a decision, one has the option at any time to move in either direction, toward the unilateral or toward the shared end of the continuum.

bear an important relationship to the alternatives that managers have for involving others in the process (horizontal dimension). It shows that a manager has the option at any phase of decision making to act unilaterally or to share the task with others. At the end of the chapter, we will present this same figure with a specific example showing these two dimensions interacting.

One thing that is important to keep in mind is that the sequential steps in the process of making a decision are not, in practice, as orderly as they appear. Some phases occur several times before a decision is made, sometimes a step may be skipped, and often it will be difficult for you to know just where you are in the process. As presented, the approach is linear and simple; in practice, it can better be described as cyclical and complex.

Before proceeding, we want to mention that over the past few years one of the authors interviewed a large number of practicing managers to see how closely their decision making matched the picture presented here. Most, if not all, did follow rational steps in making what they considered major decisions; minor ones tended to be more of a seat-of-the-pants operation. We will draw on the experience (through quotes) of these managers to illustrate the phases of the process. Our objective is not to advocate the slavish use of this approach but to offer it as a generic framework that can help you place boundaries around what otherwise could be a haphazard (and perhaps hazardous) way of doing things.

In our presentation, we view decision making in broad terms, as more than just a particular choice. We view decision making as including activities both preceding and following the choice of a particular course of action. Thus, decision making is akin to *problem solving*, since it includes situation analysis, data gathering, and implementation, as well as choice. We did not use the term *problem solving* in the chapter title because it implies the existence of something wrong; although it is the job of a manager to make decisions in response to a problem, it is also an objective of management to take action (make decisions) to improve existing practices, to forestall potential problems, and to take advantage of opportunities. Decision making, therefore, connotes both a *proactive* and a *reactive* stance.

PHASES OF DECISION MAKING

Figure 7–2 outlines the specific phases of decision making. This approach, which is typical of several in the literature on decision making,[1] portrays a way of reaching a decision that is systematic, rational, and analytical. It identifies a series of steps that you might logically go through in making a thorough analysis of an issue.

The process begins when you first discover (A) the existence of a problem or an opportunity to make an improvement. This is followed by an effort to define the nature and causes (B) of the issue. Your objective would be to identify the "real" problem and avoid "treating the symptoms instead of the illness." Then you would spell out (even write down) a set of objectives (C) to be met in resolving the matter, expressing those objectives in terms as measurable as possible. Next, you would identify a number of alternative solutions (D) and then, after carefully listing the costs and benefits (E) of each, you would choose (F) the one you expect to yield the best results. While all this might require a substantial amount of data gathering, your goal is to develop a thorough assessment and pick the optimal solution. Thereafter, the approach recommends that you spend additional effort to develop a detailed plan of implementation (G). After carrying out that plan (H), the final step is to see what you can learn (I) from the experience by assessing the process used.

Suppose, for example, your grades for a given semester fell far below their expected level. You know you have a problem, but it may take

---

[1] One widely known model is presented in *The Rational Manager* by C. Kepner and B. Tregoe (New York: McGraw-Hill, 1965).

FIGURE 7-2
Specific Phases Of Decision Making

A. Discovery of the existence of a problem or the need to make a decision.
   Proactive search.
   Reactive discovery.
B. Definition of the problem or situation requiring a decision.
   Multiple causes.
   Real problems versus symptoms.
C. Identification of objectives (goal setting).
   Targets.
   Constraints.
D. Development of alternative solutions.
   Brainstorming.
E. Evaluation of alternatives.
   Determine consequences.
      Degree of target attainment.
      Degree of constraint violation.
      Other advantages and disadvantages.
   Determine costs.
   Calculate expected values.
   Develop ways to minimize costs or limit magnitude of negative consequences.
F. Choice.
G. Implementation planning.
   Acceptance.
   Controls.
   Preplan reaction to anticipated contingencies.
H. Implementation.
   Monitor results.
   Adapt as necessary and possible.
I. Evaluation of outcomes and the process used.

---

considerable thought and analysis to determine the causes. They could stem from a combination of difficult courses, low motivation, taking on too much extra work, poor planning of study time, and other factors. The decision you ultimately reach to deal with your problem will depend for its success on the accuracy of your definition and analysis of the problem. You know that your objective is to bring your grades back up, but it could also include other things such as finding ways to relax or have fun. The solutions you consider may have to satisfy these different objectives, and you may need to spend some time and effort planning how you are going to implement the solutions before actually carrying them out. Finally, if you are to learn from the experience, it will be important that you evaluate how well your decision worked. Although you may not normally go through all these steps, you can probably see the merits of engaging in a deliberate and systematic approach to making a decision.

In the next section, we will go over each step in greater detail, pointing out how to approach decision making systematically and rationally. We shall also indicate ways in which you might simultaneously draw on intuitive and nonrational aspects of thinking and creativity.

A. Problem Discovery

Problems, opportunities for improvement, and issues requiring action can present themselves and demand attention. They may be brought to the manager by subordinates, show up in complaints from other departments, result from criticisms and demands made by higher management, or be discovered directly by the manager. Whatever their source, these problems place a manager in a reactive mode; initiative rests with the problem, not with the manager.

At the other extreme, opportunities for improvement and potential problems can be discovered through a proactive search by the manager. Some organizations conduct formal attitude surveys periodically and review the results for evidence that some kind of change is desirable. Individual managers can adopt such a practice at a departmental level or, in some organizations, draw upon the services of staff personnel to conduct such studies. Suggestion systems for tapping employee attitudes and scheduled meetings with groups of employees are additional examples of formal methods used by organizations to discover problems and opportunities before they demand attention. Whatever the mechanism, periodic survey or ongoing efforts, such endeavors put the organization and the manager in a proactive mode; then initiative lies with management, not with the problem.

The personnel manager of one moderate-sized company makes it a practice to sit down occasionally with the department heads individually and ask how things are going. Although this is not as formalized and regularly scheduled a problem search as an annual attitude survey, it is an effort on his part to step away from the press of daily activities and learn what is going on at the management level in the organization. Another manager found it necessary to set aside a two-hour period on his calendar each week for "reflection time"—that is, time to think about the current state of affairs in his organization and to consider where it was headed. Both managers' actions led to problem identification and subsequent efforts to make improvements.

Finally, managers can cultivate the ability to recognize even subtle cues of a problem in day-to-day events. They train themselves to see themes or patterns and, thus, deviations in daily activities. This might be as simple as realizing that whenever two subordinates interact during staff meetings, they constantly needle each other, which may indicate interpersonal friction that could warrant the manager's attention. Or it might be as subtle as sensing a gradual change in the climate when walking through the factory, possibly indicating a deterioration in overall management-employee relations. Whatever the pattern, the manager who can develop the capacity to recognize patterns and be aware of those that depart from expectations or are out of the ordinary can spot trouble before it goes too far.

B. Problem Definition

After a problem or opportunity for improvement has surfaced, you should not be too quick to start thinking about possible solutions but instead define the problem in depth. This may require gathering an appreciable amount of additional information about the situation. The purpose, though, is to clarify the issue, identify the factors that are causing it, and, above all, distinguish the real problem from mere symptoms or secondary problems.

One department of a large organization found that the few women managers it had were not being promoted beyond an intermediate level. Women seemed to reach a plateau and get no further. Initially, the department manager stated, "The women we have do not have the aggressiveness, the competitiveness, and the commitment to results at all costs that are necessary for a manager to be successful in our kind of high-pressure jobs." Although his conclusion may seem logical at first glance, further investigation revealed that:

1. Some of the male managers were uncomfortable with women as peers.
2. Most of the male managers enjoyed the competition and the sparks it generated, even when they were not actually necessary to get the job done. They tended to perceive any other style of interacting as weak and ineffective.
3. The women managers, while apparently assertive and competent, tended to generate fewer sparks. They were seen as better collaborators than the men but more emotionally vulnerable and less effective in getting results.

The way the situation was originally defined indicated that the solution was probably to hire only women who were as competitive as the existing managers. The new data opened up other possibilities, including redefining the range of interaction styles seen as effective and working to help male managers relate to and compete with women as colleagues. The effort to clarify and define the situation provided the basis for a better decision.

In researching an issue, it is important to look for a number of causes. Most situations are not caused by just one factor. For example, poor performance on the part of a small work group could be due in large part to insufficient training. But this factor may be reinforced significantly by a pay system that is seen as unfair and by a leadership style that generates resentment and a lack of commitment to the job. In this situation, simply to deal with the lack of sufficient training is not likely to fully resolve the performance problem.

A thorough exploration of a situation can ensure that you are dealing with the whole problem and the real problem. One manager compared the process to that of examining a precious gem: "What I do is to take what I think I want to do and think about almost every dimension of it, like holding a diamond up and turning the facets, looking at it from all sides, thinking it through over and over again. If I need more information, I go and get it as best I can."

Some models of decision making also recommend that you write a formal problem statement, defining the problem and identifying the causes. Figure 7–3 presents one set of guidelines for writing such a statement. Writing a problem statement can help to clarify the issues, but, whether written or not, it is important to define a problem in a way that doesn't prematurely dictate a particular solution.

The extent to which the situation is researched and the care with which the problem is evaluated and defined can vary. Some managers rely on their past experience with similar types of situations to alert them to the extent and seriousness of a problem. They may move through the problem definition step rather quickly, making a somewhat intuitive judgment that they know enough to proceed without extensive research and analysis. Sometimes they will be wrong and overlook the real issue or significant factors. Nonetheless, some selectivity at this step may be appropriate, particularly as the manager gains experience, although simply asking "What is the real problem here?" is a valuable mental exercise for anyone.

C. Goal Setting

Your ultimate objective, of course, is to solve the problem or to capitalize on an opportunity to improve your organization's operating efficiency or effectiveness. However, to accomplish these very general

FIGURE 7-3
Guidelines for Writing a Problem Statement

1. *Who is affected?* Consider these possibilities before deciding what you want to say about this. Is it you? Is it one other person? Is it a small group of people? Is it an entire organization? Is it the community or society at large?

2. *Who is causing it?* We frequently speak of problems as though they were caused by circumstances that didn't relate directly to people. This is almost never the case. There is almost always some person or persons who could influence things being different. Consider the same possibilities as above. Is it you? Is it one other person? Is it a small group of people? Is it an entire organization? Is it the community or society at large?

3. *What kind of a problem is it?* There are many ways to classify problems. The following considerations may prove helpful:
   There is lack of clarity or disagreement about *goals*.
   There is lack of clarity or disagreement about the *means* of achieving goals.
   There is a *lack* of skills needed to carry out a particular means.
   There is lack of *material resources*.
   There is *inaccurate communication*.
   There is *too little* or *too much communication*.
   People have a *different understanding* of the same thing.
   There is *insufficient time* or *schedules* don't coincide.
   Roles are lacking or inappropriate.
   Norms are restrictive, unclear, or misinterpreted.
   There are conflicts of ideology.
   There is a lack of clarity or a conflict about *decision making*—e.g., power struggles.
   Expression of *feelings* is inappropriate or inadequate.
   There is conflict related to *individual differences*.

4. *What is the goal for improvement?* Ideally, this should be stated so clearly that anyone reading your statement would know how to determine when the goal had been reached. It would tell exactly who would be doing what, where, how, and to what extent. Until you know where you are going, it's very difficult to make and carry out plans to get there. The more clear you are about your intended target at any given time, the more likely you will be to recognize that it is an incorrect target should this prove to be the case.

Source: C. Jung, R. Pino, and R. Emory, *RUPS: Research Utilizing Problem Solving* (classroom version, participant materials) (Portland, Ore.: Northwest Regional Educational Laboratory, 1973).

ends, you need specific objectives that establish measurable criteria for success and define any limits on the means you use to gain those ends. This can best be accomplished through a statement that identifies *target* goals (where you hope to be) and *constraint* goals (reflecting personal limits and finite resources). For example, a manager might need to develop a method for producing a new product that did not entail purchasing additional equipment in the face of budgetary constraints.

Sometimes a manager clarifies objectives later in the decision-making process or even throughout the process. One manager said, "Whenever I find myself either being swept up by a tide or unable to do something, I stop, I slow the world down inside myself, I say wait a minute—what am I trying to do, what do I really want to accomplish?" Another manager, after becoming aware of an alcohol problem in one of his supervisors, spent several months just living with the situation while he verified its existence and explored legal and organizational constraints. After he determined what he could and could not do legally, he informed his superior of the situation and got his backing for any decision he might have to make, including firing the supervisor. Throughout his exploration of possible courses of action, the manager hoped to salvage the supervisor as well as protect the organization. He was prepared to fire the man if necessary, but, as a matter of personal values, he wanted to help him overcome the problem and remain with the organization. He specified his goals in his own mind from the beginning and then clarified them in the process of exploring possible courses of action.

A sense of what one wants to accomplish is usually tied in with department and longer-range organizational goals. One manager's long-range goal was to reduce the personnel department from 30 to 10 people by fostering a greater concern for personnel matters among line managers. Consequently, he moved more and more responsibility for employee training and development away from the personnel staff and directly to line managers, eventually accomplishing his stated goal.

Similarly, departmental decision making needs to be clearly related to overall organizational goals. This was put succinctly by one company president, who said, "One thing I would like to see in decision making (and something I find lacking) is someone making a decision knowing what he's *trying to do*. You start with the organization: What is the organization trying to do? How does this decision fit in? Where do we want to end up after this decision? For example, one of our objectives is to have steady earnings growth. If you start with that, certain deals don't make any sense, because as fast as they come, they can go away. Considered in a vacuum such deals look good, but against that overall goal they would be wrong." Thus, clear organizational goals, a vision of where the department should be headed, and clarity on what one wants

7 / Decision Making

to accomplish with the decision are all important for effective decision making.

D. Developing Solutions

Solutions or alternate courses of action can grow out of thoughtful problem definition and clear goal setting, so that developing solutions is a logical next step. However, developing solutions requires creativity, which does not usually proceed in a straight line from start to finish. In other words, you probably cannot just sit down and develop all the possible solutions to a problem one after another. You might need to work on developing solutions in a way that lets your mind work freely, stopping from time to time, doing something else, or just letting things simmer for a while. Sometimes it is helpful to discuss the issue with someone who is not involved in it and see what ideas a fresh mind can offer. Often shifting attention away from solutions and reviewing all that has been considered previously (problem definition, causes, and goals) may suddenly yield an idea that would not come from working directly to develop solutions. Similarly, you may often find that turning to some other work to allow your subconscious mind to work on the issue will lead to fresh insights when you do return to the task. Sometimes you get your most creative ideas when you are not working at it or pushing for them.

While developing solutions, a "brainstorming" approach may be appropriate. This technique was developed for groups of people meeting together to generate action steps and solutions. The key ground rule for brainstorming is to withhold judgment about the worth of any idea until after the most ideas possible have been generated. An immediate judgment (evaluation) about the worth of an idea tends to inhibit the overall flow of ideas in a group. By adopting a brainstorming orientation and establishing the norm that the group's objective is to generate as many ideas as possible, the inhibiting effect of a judgmental attitude is reduced and the flow of ideas is encouraged. An individual can also adopt a brainstorming orientation and withhold judgment while developing solutions. This approach tends to be especially useful in making decisions under high levels of uncertainty (lack of data, limited expertise, etc.).

E. Evaluating Solutions

In evaluating solutions, you need to determine the probable consequences of each alternative. In part, this will mean estimating the extent to which your objectives, as spelled out in a problem statement, are met or not met or are even violated. It will also mean identifying any other advantages and disadvantages not reflected by a stated objective but recognizable as you reflect on the implications of each alternative. It will mean determining the costs of carrying out the alternatives—costs primarily in terms of time, money, inconvenience, damage to relationships, and other intangible factors. Finally, it may be appropriate to identify problems that might surface later and will need to be dealt with.

Determination of the consequences and calculation of costs may require considerable thought and often involve predicting how employees, other departments, and customers or clients will react. However it is done, a useful step is literally to prepare two columns, listing the advantages on one side and the disadvantages on the other. This document then becomes the basis for selecting one alternative over all others, as will be discussed in the following section on choice.

Keep in mind that identifying advantages and disadvantages requires imagination and creativity, like developing alternative solutions. Under the best of conditions, it may not be possible to state for certain what the full consequences of a course of action may be. You normally have to think in terms of probabilities, and you are likely to have to make decisions under conditions of some risk and uncertainty. Each condition involves a different choice strategy, but part of effective decision making entails working to increase the degree of certainty by gathering more and more data on the problem itself and on the possible consequences of solutions to it.

F. Choice

Once an array of alternative courses of action has been generated with an assessment of each item, you are in a position to make the decision. The choice seems simple: Pick the best one. But the determination of which is best, or which is right for you, is not always obvious. None of the solutions is likely to be perfect. Most will involve some trade-off between positive and negative aspects.

For example, it is unlikely that any college truly fills 100 percent of a student's goals of reasonable tuition, suitable academic quality, enjoyable location, satisfactory reputation in the chosen field (or fields), attractive social environment, professors who are effective teachers and care about students, decent living accommodations, and a record of graduating students directly into secure jobs. Chances are that in some respect every school is less than ideal and, if not unsatisfactory, at least questionable. More than that, chances are that among the schools a student is admitted to, different objectives are met and the mix of satisfactory, questionable, and less than satisfactory varies from school to school. How should a student compare one school that is especially satisfactory on location, questionable on faculty effectiveness, but adequate on all other criteria with one that is questionable on social environment and living accommodations but clearly satisfactory in all other respects? There is some sense of comparing apples with oranges, yet somehow the student has to arrive at an *overall* evaluation of each school.

One approach is to develop a composite index. For example, where there are multiple criteria, it is possible to rate the degree to which each criterion is attained in numerical terms (say, on a scale of 1 to 10) and then sum the scores into a composite score. However, typically some criteria are more important to you than others, so you need a way to construct a composite index that reflects both criteria attainment and criteria importance. This can be done by also rating each criterion's importance on a 1-to-10 scale and then multiplying that number by the attainment score, thereby arriving at an "importance attained" score. Summing across all criteria yields a composite importance attained index for the particular alternative.

Calculating such a numerical index can yield a variety of results. One alternative could score appreciably higher than all others and give you a clear basis for your choice. But you could also have an intuitive feeling that the alternative that scores the highest is not in fact the best choice for you. If this happens, it may be an indication that you have not accurately recognized the importance of some criteria or that other criteria have been overlooked. Although the composite index may not by itself determine your choice, it may help you recognize the need to recycle through the process of goal setting, data gathering, and solution evaluation.

Composite scores can also be so close that they yield no clear indication of which is best. This may also be an indication that you need more data or that you need to reappraise the ratings of both attainment and importance. Or it may indicate that you face a choice between equally acceptable alternatives. In this situation, you can feel comfortable letting fairly extraneous factors influence the choice. For example, a choice among equally acceptable alternatives could rest on which is most expedient (e.g., I can put the decision behind me sooner by choosing alternative A instead of B).

In short, composite indices are useful but may not tell the whole story or necessarily make up your mind for you. Decision makers must balance the disadvantages with the advantages and somehow integrate their competing preferences and concerns into an assessment of the overall effect. Numerical ratings and composite indices can help you do this in a systematic and rational way. But, as suggested, the results may be sterile if they are not accompanied by personal belief that the indicated choice is the right one.

In our experience, effective decision makers spend a great deal of time gathering data and analyzing a situation, but they also test the results of that rational process against their intuitive sense of what is right. In their terms, they pay attention to hunches and feelings. We shall return to the issue of how to *clarify* one's hunches and feelings in the next section of this chapter.

G and H. Implementation: Planning and Execution

Making up your mind can easily loom so large that once you have done it, you feel finished. However, the *manner* in which a decision is *implemented* can be as important for success as making the right choice. An excellent choice can fall apart if the specific steps for carrying it out are so vague that they lead to confusion and inappropriate sequencing. An adequate choice that everyone supports can work out better than an ideal choice that is resisted because people are caught by surprise. Developing a plan for implementing the decision is an important step in the overall decision-making process. The purposes of an implementation plan are several:

1. To identify the steps that may be necessary to carry out the decision, so as to avoid confusion, ensure the coordination and proper sequencing of all aspects involved, and minimize delays.
2. To develop ways to minimize the costs anticipated in the solution evaluation step. For example, if one of the anticipated costs of the chosen course of action is some delay in the production schedule, one may want to implement the decision at a time when the schedule is under the least pressure.
3. To develop ways to avoid or at least minimize potential resistance to the change generated by the decision. Decisions often mean change. People who understand why some change is being introduced, who are consulted and have some influence on the decision, who are given appropriate reassurances that the change will not affect their lives detrimentally, and who are not caught by surprise are less likely to be resistant to change than those who are dealt with in opposite ways. Plans need to be developed for announcing and explaining the decision to those affected.
4. To develop ways to deal with efforts to block the decision. Some decisions will be resisted by some people despite one's efforts to deal with them in a way that avoids that problem. Power politics is a reality of organizational life. One may need to build alliances, solidify one's power base, and plan ways to deal with opposing forces before actually implementing a decision.
5. To develop methods to monitor decision results. Many action plans require a certain amount of "shaping and fitting" to work out properly. Few decisions or action plans are perfect; events occur during implementation that require adapting the initial plan to changing circumstances. Consequently, the decision maker needs

some way to monitor results so that corrective steps can be taken as the need becomes apparent. (This might involve minor adjustments or the initiation of elaborate contingency plans.)

I. Outcome and Process Evaluation

Every decision provides an opportunity to learn; to learn about the organization and about the decision-making process. As one company president stated, "I don't believe in agonizing over decisions that have been wrong, but the worst thing you can do is to not admit them to yourself. If you won't admit them to others, that is your affair, but if you won't admit them to yourself, you're in trouble."

We think of managers as action oriented, and they are. But effective managers also reflect on what is happening to them and what they are experiencing. Thus, they are both doers and observers. It is this quality of being able to take risks, make decisions, and act, yet also be reflective about that process as it is happening and afterward, that contributes to a manager's ability to learn from experience and continue to develop and grow. Therefore, the decision-making process can usefully be thought of as ending only after you reflect back on your approach to each step and your overall decision-making process.

Data Gathering as a Repeated Step

Throughout all the phases of decision making, gathering relevant data is vital to the effectiveness of the process; it repeats itself at almost every step. Several valuable sources of data are available to a manager.

One source of data is *personal experience*. The more a manager has worked on a certain type of problem and "been down the road before," the more easily he or she can rely on his or her own thought process to identify consequences and estimate their probabilities of occurrence.

A second source of information, also closely related to experience, is *knowledge gained through study or general reading*. Concepts and theory are applicable to decision making. Someone who had studied organization literature would be more likely to think about the consequences of a decision in relation to an organization's goals than someone who hadn't. Thus, one's theoretical knowledge about the nature of things, and particularly about how one factor affects another, is an important data source.

A third source of data is *the ideas and opinions of others*. In talking with practicing managers, it was apparent that most use other people as "sounding boards" and sources of ideas, opinions, and facts. A manager's peers and subordinates as well as superiors represent an important reservoir of experience, knowledge, and creativity. Similarly, in making a decision about a job following graduation, a student may find that talking things over with faculty, friends, and family is a time-consuming, but nonetheless important, step, whether these others describe their own experiences in job hunting or suggest specific factors for the student to consider. (This source of data will be discussed further when we go into the issue of participative decision making.)

A fourth method of data gathering is to conduct *some kind of experiment or survey*. Engineering departments run all kinds of experiments to discover the consequences of various designs. Organizations sometimes implement programs on a limited basis as a way of testing an idea. Surveys of employee attitudes and market surveys of consumer preferences are useful tools for developing data relevant to decision making. While each of these three examples may seem far removed from something you might do in selecting a college or picking a job, and even unlikely for an individual manager to do in his or her day-to-day decision making, setting up an experiment or undertaking a structured data-gathering effort can be the most effective approach for making decisions that involve long-term major resource commitments.

Whatever means are used to develop insights into the possible consequences of a course of action and, thereby, provide the basis for listing advantages and disadvantages and evaluating that course of action, the process requires you to be creative in reflecting on your experience and knowledge as well as energetic in "picking another's brain" and generating new data.

APPLICABILITY OF THE RATIONAL APPROACH

Our interviews and experience suggest that practicing managers do follow a process that approximates this textbook model of decision making. They do think about what they want to accomplish, they do generate a number of alternatives, they do consider disadvantages as well as advantages and seek to evaluate each alternative, they do give attention to how the decision is to be implemented, and their choice does rest to a great extent on rational thought and analysis. But also they are selective in how they use such an approach, often shortcutting the full process as circumstances dictate. Furthermore, they typically bring to the process intuitive elements not indicated in the rational model.

For most day-to-day decisions, a manager reaches a decision with less than a rigorous working through of each step. Goals may be less than explicit and not written down. Only one or two alternative solutions may be identified, so it may appear that the manager settled for the first idea that came to mind. There may be little apparent spelling out of the advantages and disadvantages. The choice may seem to be almost an intuitive "knowing what to do," with little systematic analysis. But for other decisions, managers work through a process, like that presented here, with exactness and care. In other words, effective managers seem to have such an approach in their minds and decide how thoroughly and systematically to use it in any given instance. That decision will depend on several factors:

1. The perceived importance and magnitude of the issue.
2. The decision maker's prior experience with the type of problem under consideration.
3. The costs involved in being systematic (cost of gathering data or spending time on the decision).
4. The time available.
5. Political considerations.

The more important the issue and the greater the potential cost if a wrong choice is made, the more important it is to be systematic and thorough—that is, to fully use a rational model. The less familiar a decision maker is with the type of situation in question, the more necessary it is to proceed carefully, following each step explicitly. This means that early in a manager's career, or later when he or she moves into a new position and encounters new problems, the manager should follow some systematic model more closely than otherwise. Taking the time to work through all the steps costs time and sometimes money. Consequently, a manager may have to make a decision before she or he has a chance to work through the process completely and thoroughly. Even where time is available, a manager would like to invest only as much time and money in the decision as will be saved by spending more to make a better choice. Consequently, a manager needs to consider the cost of making the decision as well as the decision itself.

Finally, there may be political considerations. If the norm of the organization is to minimize risk and to be as thorough as possible, or if you anticipate appreciable opposition, you may need to take the time to be fully prepared and, therefore, use the steps in the model to their fullest. On the other hand, if the norm of the organization is to act quickly and stay one jump ahead of the next person, the use of an approach as outlined here will seem cumbersome and not worth the effort.

Thus, a rational step-by-step approach can serve as an "ideal" against which you, as a decision maker, can and should assess your actions, an ideal to be used in greater or lesser degree depending on circumstances. The question to be asked is: How much should I invest in this decision? The effective decision maker will adapt her or his behavior in accordance with the answer.

Finally, we emphasize that decision making even at its most rational level is not always systematic and linear (step by step). As suggested, working through the phases probably will involve a lot of starting and stopping, with frequent recycling to redo an earlier step. Furthermore, various steps may be done out of sequence. Exploring solutions can help to clarify objectives; thinking about implementation may clarify the full costs of an alternative and allow one to get a better feeling for that alternative.

Managers will also tell you that intuition, or a "feeling for what is right," is an accepted and integral part of their decision process. This does not mean that they do whatever they feel like doing; it means that in assessing the meaning of the data, in arriving at the subjective probabilities for the likelihood of some possible outcome happening, in evaluating the overall worth of a particular course of action, managers do pay attention to what intuition and subjective perceptions indicate to be important, plausible, and probable. In essence, the effective decision maker draws on both analytical and intuitive processes. The former paves the way for the latter, and the latter illuminates and guides the former. And, in the final analysis, any given decision is likely to fall short of the ideal. As Herbert A. Simon's research has shown, managers are more likely to "satisfice" than to "maximize" their decisions. (See Box 7–1 for more detail on Simon's work.)

BEHAVIORAL AND EMOTIONAL ASPECTS OF DECISION MAKING

Behavioral Barriers

Even with the best of rational intentions, you are always subject to habits and attitudes that can get in your way and become barriers to arriving at a suitable choice. Some of the typical behavioral barriers are:

1. Being too action oriented.
2. Not being systematic enough.
3. Procrastinating and avoiding.
4. Working too concentratedly.
5. Ignoring intuition.
6. Dealing in single causality and simplistic analysis.

1. Inexperienced managers often respond to a problem by asking themselves: What should I do? In effect, they leap to the choice step and then feel indecisive because they don't have data and have not analyzed the situation. Such action orientation, which may stem from an underlying desire to put the problem behind them, can be very dysfunctional. Effective managers have learned to control the urge to act, while they allow themselves time to analyze the problem, gather data, brainstorm possible solutions, and assess the pros and cons of each possibility. They ask the question: What is going on here? or What does this

BOX 7-1

"SATISFICING"

Herbert Simon is a multidisciplinary scholar, having worked in the areas of psychology, computer science, social science, operations research, philosophy of science, and economics. His professional career, according to Simon's colleague, James C. March of Stanford, can be divided into two stages: (1) 1947–58, when Simon focused on decision-making, particularly in organizations, but also wrote on a variety of problems in the modeling of behavior; and (2) 1958–present, when his concerns shifted to human problem solving and artificial intelligence. The two periods show a common effort to connect the study of intentional action with the engineering design of intelligent systems.

In 1978, Simon received the Nobel Prize for economics for his contribution to our understanding of decision making, particularly in organizations, and for numerous other contributions to social science. It was clear that in awarding the Nobel to Simon, the committee broadened the basis for the prize, for Simon is hardly an orthodox economist.

Much of Simon's work over the 30 years prior to his receiving the Nobel Prize dealt with ways in which economic theories of rational choice might be revised. (It is this work that he was cited for.) Like most economists, Simon assumes human choice behavior is intendedly rational. However, he feels there is a significant informational limit on rationality within organizations. Simon suggests that instead of basing decisions on known consequences of a vast array of alternatives, decisions are based on a limited knowledge of the outcome of only a few alternatives. Thus, the classical economist's theories on "maximizing" in decision making are erroneous, according to Simon; in reality, decisions are not based on a thorough knowledge of all alternatives. Instead, decisions are "satisficed," as the first alternative that is "good enough" tends to be selected.

Simon does acknowledge that the level of satisficing can be raised if the organization decision makers acquire a better and more thorough understanding of historical data and their relevance to the future, and if the organization raises its members' levels of aspirations.

Herbert A. Simon is now the Richard King Mellon Professor of Psychology and Computer Science at Carnegie-Mellon University. His major works are: *Administrative Behavior* (1947), *Models of Man* (1957), *Organizations* (1958), and *The New Science of Management Decision* (1977).

situation involve? before they ask: What should I do? The climate of many modern organizations fosters a tendency for premature action. It is a real dilemma for a manager in such a setting to find a way to think through a problem before leaping to action.

2. Not being sufficiently systematic or thorough often leads to reaching the choice step prematurely, but entails some different behaviors than just rushing to make a choice. It involves not gathering enough data, not exploring a range of factors, not writing things down and so forgetting analysis already done, not making objectives explicit, being judgmental about alternatives before developing a sufficient number,

and sometimes even flitting from issue to issue. It often represents a failure to ask the question: How much do I want to invest in this decision?

3. Analysis is hard work; consequently, it can be tempting to avoid the issue by concentrating your efforts on other simpler matters. How often have you allowed yourself to work on less important tasks that are easily completed and give you a sense of accomplishment, while avoiding or delaying work on the more difficult tasks? We easily fill our schedules with repetitive day-to-day activities and never get time to work on the big issues. Some managers deal with this by scheduling time for reflection and then honor that scheduled commitment just as they would a scheduled meeting or conference.

4. After discussing not being systematic, flitting from topic to topic, being too action oriented, and not getting to the task, our fourth barrier—working too concentratedly—may appear to contradict all that has been said. But the fact is that when you concentrate on using an approach systematically, you can easily slide into the habit of becoming *too* focused or narrow, thus losing a creative perspective. There are times, as suggested, when you need to step away from the task to let the issue ferment and allow your "unconscious" to develop insights. This is not avoidance, since such stepping away from a problem generally follows a period of concentration, whereas avoidance means never approaching it in the first place. Working too concentratedly may mean working too many hours at a stretch, beyond the point where your creativity can function. There are even times when it is inappropriate to work on an issue at all. If you are physically tired, if you are distracted by some immediate crisis, or even, on occasion, if you are just not in a mood to concentrate, it may be wise to turn to other activities. Resting, dealing with a crisis only enough to take care of it temporarily, and working on other tasks you are more in the mood for may all be appropriate activities. These comments can become a handy excuse to procrastinate, which is not our intent. Our purpose is to suggest that managers can usefully cultivate the kind of *self-awareness* that allows them to recognize when they have temporarily run dry or need to work on other matters.

5. The fifth barrier refers to the importance of things you can sense intuitively, and these impressions are worth paying attention to. Typically, they may indicate the need to get more data, to recycle and reevaluate the pros and cons of a particular alternative, or even to wait for events to unfold further before taking action. Ignoring such signals or pushing them aside can cut you off from valuable internal inputs and reduce your decision-making effectiveness.

6. Perhaps we need to say little about the sixth barrier, since it is virtually a truism to say that a simplistic and superficial analysis will lead to ineffective decision making. But it is so easy to think in terms of

simple causes and to consider only obvious factors that we believe it is worth noting. Most situations result from multiple rather than single causes. In Chapter 6, we discussed people's tendency to require greater control in times of stress. They often need to resolve problems rapidly (to relieve tension) during such periods. In an environment of high stress, there is a tendency for managers to reduce problems to single causes, ones that are most easily acted upon; you can readily see the inherent dangers in such behavior.

Emotional Barriers

A variety of emotional states can underlie the behavioral barriers or make it difficult for one to make a choice. These include:

1. Impatience with the process.
2. Panic.
3. Perfectionism and fear of failure or fear of appearing indecisive.
4. Desire to be liked and to avoid hostility.
5. Reluctance to exhibit ignorance.
6. Pride.

1. It is easy to feel impatient and want to get the job done. Such impatience may reflect an underlying discomfort with the uncertainty involved in holding off a decision while you gather data and analyze the situation. Not knowing what to do can be uncomfortable and make you want to rush the process and get it over with. Also, it isn't easy to invest time and energy in gathering data and thinking about an issue if the resulting benefits are uncertain. It is natural to be reluctant to spend time in the library looking for data that may not be there. It's natural to be reluctant to intrude on people to ask questions if you are not sure you need the data. It can be hard to invest yourself in a process where the payoff is not apparent, yet such reluctance can get in the way of doing as thorough a job as necessary.

2. Sometimes a problem or decision can loom so significant that you tend to panic. This can lead to flitting from topic to topic, not being systematic, or not concentrating. This emotional reaction can occur particularly when a deadline is approaching and you find yourself with no clear choice. Instead of reassessing the data or taking some other constructive step to reach closure, you become overwhelmed with a sense of panic and immobilized. Here is a situation where stepping away from the problem, taking some breathing time or space (as discussed earlier), can make a difference. It permits the tension to drop and enables you to adopt a more constructive stance.

3. Perfectionism, a belief that one must be right all the time, acts as another emotional barrier to decision making, along with its companion, fear of failure or fear of appearing indecisive. Managers need to work

hard to make the right decision, but an overly strong concern to "never be wrong" can be counterproductive. As one manager said, "I have learned through bitter experience that the general practice of making a decision, whether it be right or wrong, is far better than delaying. If I don't make the decision, then time, events, or other people will make it for me, and generally that is a less acceptable alternative." And as another manager said, ". . . paranoia about the risk is far more of a problem than the actual risk. My fantasies about what is going to happen are much more debilitating and immobilizing than the actual fact."

4. Many decisions, including giving a failing grade, firing an employee who is not performing, or saying no to someone's idea or request, can generate feelings of dislike and hostility in the other person. Managers can be tempted to soften a decision to avoid such hostility and retain a sense of being liked. Yet this can lose respect and in the long run lead to a loss of liking anyway. A manager needs to be aware of such a personal tendency. Just being aware of the temptation to avoid the tough choice can help you deal with this barrier.

5. Good decision making requires good data. Yet asking questions requires that you expose the fact that you do not know something. Any reluctance to ask a question that may make you appear "stupid" can be a real barrier to getting the data you need for making a decision. However, although you may feel possible momentary embarrassment, the price of a bad decision can make you feel the fool for a much longer time.

6. Similarly, pride or a rigid belief that you should do it all alone can get in the way of making effective decisions. Capable managers try not to allow pride to prevent them from talking things over with others. Instead, they make extensive use of others, not necessarily to make the decision for them, but as sounding boards, consultants, and sources of ideas. The way to learning is through inquiry. Here again, a reluctance to risk asking a "stupid" question or an unwillingness to turn to others can be a powerful barrier to being effective. Sometimes an organization's norms can push managers to make their own decisions even when they could benefit from the involvement of others. This only adds to the problem of a manager who tends already to go it alone.

DEALING WITH INDECISION AND BARRIERS TO DECISION MAKING

At times even effective decision makers, after working through a thoughtful analysis of some situation, are uncertain about what course of action to take. Similarly, we all can fall victim to the barriers just covered. While discussing the model itself and the barriers, we indicated some steps you can take to deal with these matters, such as developing an awareness of your own tendencies, allowing your creative and intuitive abilities to operate, writing things down, and talking with others. In addition, there are two more methods we want to describe, since they are ones that management consultants have found to be effective in dealing with emotional barriers.

Developing Scenarios

One difficulty you may experience is not being able to know what some course of action will really *feel* like before trying it and, therefore, not being able to properly evaluate that choice. Have you ever said you would do something and then later realized that you really didn't want to? Unfortunately, that can happen if you are unable to anticipate the nature of future events. For example, suppose you are considering taking a job in some isolated part of the country. You recognize the location as a disadvantage but cannot really sense how much it may bother you. What can you do to know what it might feel like? The best approach is to visit the location. But another is to do that in your head, by developing a scenario of the experience. You can imagine yourself in the situation and draw on your capacity to experience in fantasy what it would be like. Such a "fantasy trip" can often help you sense the importance of various aspects of a situation and thereby experience the feelings that will actually occur.

Exaggerating the Issues

Psychotherapists have a technique that is often helpful to people who are emotionally conflicted about some issue. Part of their concept is that people can be of two minds about an issue and feel stuck in the middle. One way to break such a deadlock is to explore each extreme of the dilemma by exaggerating it. The objective is to experience personally each part as fully as possible. To do this, the therapist may actually have an individual place two chairs opposite each other and then sit in one chair to present one point of view and in the other to present the other point of view. Physically shifting from chair to chair symbolically helps one to experience each position fully. Although the idea of conducting a debate with yourself out loud while shifting from chair to chair may sound a bit odd, it can help you get in touch with your real feelings. If you discover that you argue for one position more forcefully than for the other, you may have a better indication of which choice would be right for you. Whether or not you literally use chairs, the important element of this approach is that you push yourself to make explicit the horns of the dilemma, which, in turn, helps you to resolve it.

Perhaps you have developed your own techniques to help you deal with difficulties in decision making. We offer this in recognition that decision making is a process with both rational and intuitive elements.

Emotions can be barriers to effective decision making, but they can also be facilitators. A sense of what fits the situation and a strong belief in your choice can facilitate effective decision making.

INDIVIDUAL VERSUS GROUP DECISION MAKING

As a manager you not only have to make a decision regarding a particular problem, but you also need to decide *who else* ought to be involved, *when* that ought to occur (early or later in the process), and *how* that should be done. If, for example, you bring knowledgeable subordinates into the process at a stage when you are close to implementing a choice, you may find that they bring up points that you failed to consider earlier, ideas that pertain, for example, to the definition of the problem. Given the time pressures characteristic of today's organizations, it is a constant dilemma for managers to "decide how to decide." It often seems like a waste of time to involve several people in what *seems* to be a fairly straightforward decision. But it is often easy to fool yourself. Very few decisions are really simple or straightforward when you consider various side effects and implications. Often the extra time spent at the front end of the process saves aggravation at the back end.

There are several reasons a manager might use some form of group decision making rather than acting alone. First, many issues require the resources of many specialties and expertise that no single individual has. Although a manager might consult with several experts, gather data from them, and make the decision alone, it often can be helpful to have a number of points of view interacting. Allowing those with detailed knowledge of each functional area to "bounce off" one another may be more effective in striking a balance among all factors than sequentially consulting with each alone; more ideas may come out of the interaction than will occur in separate consultations. In pulling together a group of specialists, the manager's role changes from being a data gatherer and decision maker to being a manager of the decision-making *process* used by the group. He or she can encourage an open discussion, foster a brainstorming attitude, and prevent the group from rushing to a premature choice. Whether the manager retains the power to make the ultimate choice or shares that power and seeks a true consensus, managing the meeting and the process becomes an important aspect of his or her role.

Concern about acceptance and commitment to the decision are other reasons for group decision making. People typically understand and feel greater acceptance and commitment to a decision in which they have participated and for which they feel some ownership. Where the success of a decision is dependent on those affected making it work, their acceptance and commitment become important and reason to include them in the decision process. How early in the process (i.e., which stage) to involve people can vary, but early involvement usually tends to increase commitment.

Training and job enrichment are reasons for including subordinates in the decision process. Involving people in decisions that affect them can make their work more satisfying and also broaden subordinates' knowledge and awareness. In other words, involving your staff in group decision making can contribute to their development and pave the way for eventual delegation.

Finally, a manager may appropriately involve others when he or she feels a lack of adequate personal expertise or information, particularly if he or she is uncertain about what information is needed (e.g., what factors to consider, what information to get, and where to get it). In such a situation, the manager may consult at the earliest stages with those individuals who have expertise and then make a decision, or he or she may prefer to use joint (group) decision making to gain the advantages of the interaction process of a group.

Victor Vroom developed a useful model for relating the involvement of others in one's decision process with the factors that dictate the degree of involvement that is appropriate.[2] Figure 7–4 lists five options a manager has, as suggested by Vroom, in making a decision. We modified the original concept to include the possibility that a manager

FIGURE 7–4
Alternative Ways of Making Decisions

Unilateral
1. You make the decision yourself, using information you have.
2. You obtain whatever information you need from others, including subordinates, and then make the decision yourself.
3. You share the situation with others individually, including subordinates, to get their ideas. Then you make the decision yourself.
4. You share the situation with others as a group, including subordinates, to obtain their collective ideas through discussion. Then you make the decision yourself.
5. You share the situation with others as a group and also share equally the responsibility with them for making the decision through consensus.

Shared

---

[2] See a "New Look at Managerial Decision Making," *Organizational Dynamics*, Spring 1975. See also Vroom and Yetton (1973) in Suggested Readings.

might choose to share the process with others who are *not* his or her subordinates. (Vroom's wording refers only to subordinates.) As you move from alternative 1 to alternative 5, the process shifts from unilateral to more shared decision making. Certainly there is room for gradations between the five listed, but the ones shown provide a useful framework. Furthermore, there is an obvious sixth alternative—namely, *delegation*. A manager always has that option and, if he or she has done an effective job of employee development, can find it a major help in preventing decision overload.

Figure 7–5 lists seven conditions, or characteristics of a situation, that Vroom found to be important for determining the appropriate decision-

FIGURE 7–5
Conditions Affecting the Choice of Decision-Making Alternatives

1. Importance of quality in the decision.

    The more important the quality, the greater the need for complete information, which is likely to require the participation of others.

2. Extent to which manager possesses needed information.

    The more information the manager already possesses, the less the need to involve others.

3. How clearly structured or defined the problem is.

    The more clearly structured the problem is, the less the need to involve others.

4. The importance of acceptance and commitment of others.

    The more important is the acceptance/commitment of others, the greater the need to involve them in the process.

5. Prior probability that a unilateral decision will be accepted by others.

    The greater the prior probability of others' acceptance, the less the need to involve them in the process.

6. Others' commitment to those organizational goals that are reflected in the decision.

    The greater the commitment of others to the organizational goals reflected in the decision, the more appropriate it is to involve them in the process.

7. Potential for disruptive conflict among others with respect to decision alternatives.

    The greater the potential for disruptive conflict among others relative to the decision, the less appropriate it is to involve them in the process.

making alternative. In his article, Vroom offers a detailed and systematic way for using these characteristics in combination; however, we prefer only to list them along with general propositions reflecting how each relates to the five alternatives. You can see from the list that the conditions are more or less independent of one another, and, therefore, for any given decision, some may favor the unilateral end of the continuum and others the shared end. Let's look at a few examples of how the factors in Figure 7–5 can help you to choose the appropriate option as shown in Figure 7–4.

Suppose you are the manager of a large independent supermarket and you have to decide from which wholesaler to buy your produce. This decision is very important to the sales and reputation of your market, which suggests that you might want to gather some information or even obtain the opinions of the people who manage your produce department. However, if you have been in the business for a long time and are thoroughly familiar with the different wholesalers' produce, you might just make the decision yourself, particularly if your employees already have confidence in your judgment.

By way of contrast, suppose you are a hospital administrator who is faced with deciding whether to purchase the latest computerized blood analysis equipment. Such a decision not only involves a considerable capital outlay, but it will also affect everyone who is concerned with the quality, as well as the turnaround time, of blood analyses. These include lab technicians, physicians, nurses, and certainly patients. The situation may not be a clearly structured one; that is, the decision maker may not know fully the information he or she needs to make a sensible decision. Furthermore, the successful implementation of the decision will be less dependent on you than on others. Assuming that you have their commitment to good medical care and that they are not likely to fight over the issues, you would most appropriately involve those affected directly in the process, probably well toward the group consensus end of the continuum.

One additional factor Vroom discusses is time pressure. The greater the pressure to make a quick decision, the less appropriate or at least the more difficult it is to move toward the participative end of the spectrum. For example, the hospital administrator might find it desirable to have a consensus decision, but time pressure might force him or her to settle for a more limited group or individual consultation. How well that works would depend on his or her previous history of decision making and level of credibility with those affected. As a manager, you can earn the right (in relation to others) to make unilateral decisions that affect others in important ways by demonstrating a willingness to involve them most of the time when appropriate. Certainly you could just assume that right by virtue of your position, but your long-run effectiveness in making decisions will inevitably depend on the commitment of others to carrying them out, rather than their less-than-enthusiastic compliance.

We won't take the time or space to consider each separate phase of decision making in relation to each of the Vroom categories, but you might find it useful to explore some of the relationships yourself. For example, you might consider how a manager could use the resources of subordinates or others during the very early stages (e.g., problem definition) of the process. Does he or she gather some opinions, test out some definitions on others, hold a meeting, and have the group define the problem or just handle it unilaterally? In making such choices, does the manager consider the *importance* of the decision, whether he or she has sufficient *information,* or the potential for subordinate *acceptance* or *rejection?* It would be difficult, if not impossible, for a manager to involve others fully at *all* stages of decision making. But a wise manager is sensitive to his or her own limitations, the risks of too little data, and the possible adverse consequences of failing to involve people early enough for them to have real influence (not just token) on the process.

Figure 7–6 takes the example of the hospital administrator and carries it through the nine phases, showing how you can move back and forth along the continuum of participation as you progress from one phase to the next. The example is built upon certain assumptions; for example, step B assumes that the administrator and lab head can define or structure the problem clearly. If they cannot, then a move toward the shared end of the scale at step B would be called for to obtain the needed information.

You might find it useful to introduce different assumptions relative to each phase and see what the implications are for moving the process one way or the other. Or, you might take an example of your own and plug it into the model to see whether it helps you understand the options you have throughout the process of decision making.

GROUP AS DECISION MAKER

When a group is the decision-making unit, it may have just as much need to define the problem, set clear objectives, identify alternatives, gather data, thoroughly evaluate each alternative before making a choice, and develop a plan of implementation as does an individual. With a group, data gathering and other steps may be delegated to sub-groups, but the process is basically similar to that which an individual might follow, including periods of recycling and decisions about how much time and money to invest in gathering data and carrying out a thorough, systematic process. Although a group will encounter some of the barriers to decision making already identified and need to walk away from the process to let things ferment, individuals in

7 / Decision Making

FIGURE 7-6
Decision-Making Example Using Vroom's Alternatives Relative to The Phases of the Process

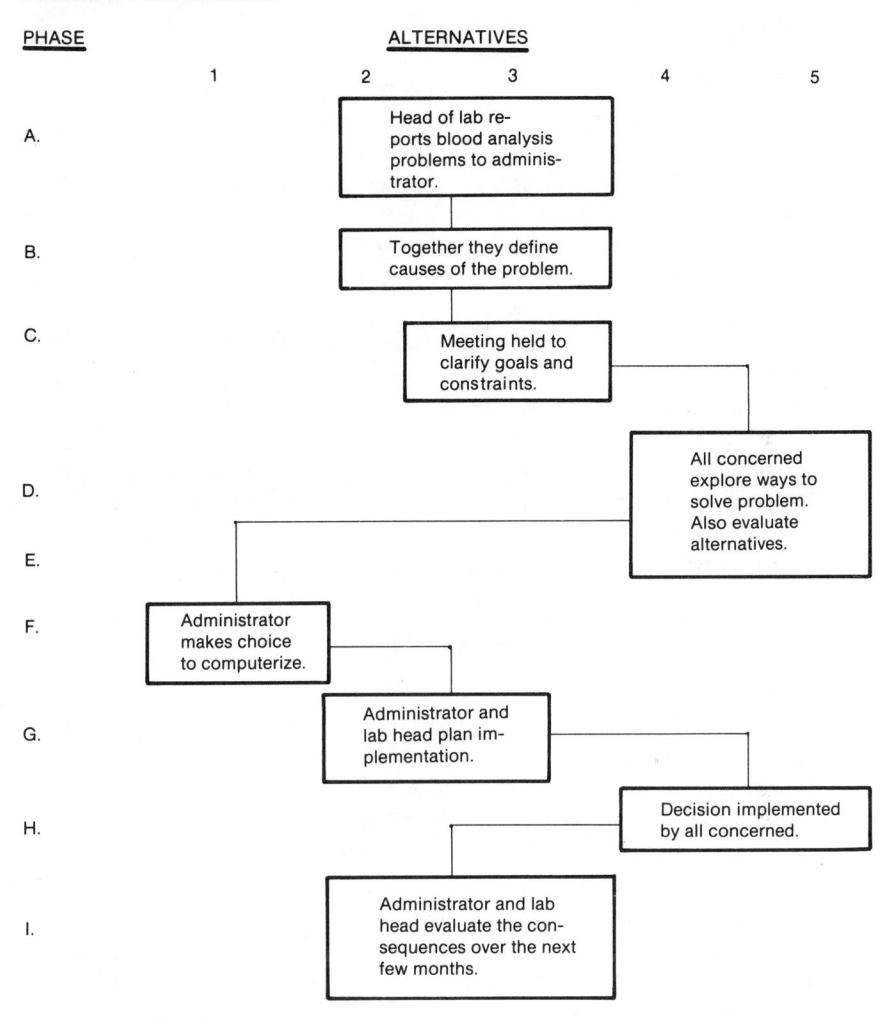

PHASE	ALTERNATIVES
	1 2 3 4 5
A.	Head of lab reports blood analysis problems to administrator. (2)
B.	Together they define causes of the problem. (2)
C.	Meeting held to clarify goals and constraints. (3)
D.	All concerned explore ways to solve problem. Also evaluate alternatives. (4)
E.	
F.	Administrator makes choice to computerize. (1)
G.	Administrator and lab head plan implementation. (2)
H.	Decision implemented by all concerned. (4)
I.	Administrator and lab head evaluate the consequences over the next few months. (2)

a group stimulate one another's thinking and more easily pass through periods of creative dryness. Groups often can use time efficiently because multiple resources can be brought to bear simultaneously and the data-gathering process can be cut short. (See also Box 7–2.)

At the same time, groups need to guard against what Irving Janis has called "groupthink."[3] Groups can become so enamored of their own ideas that they pressure any member who dares to challenge those ideas, and, thus, they can effectively guard against receiving any data that disconfirm their views. By setting up norms that foster harmony in the group or by ridiculing any member who questions an established idea, a group can fall into the trap of groupthink. If this happens early in a decision process, a group can become locked into a commitment to a particular course of action long before it has fully explored alternatives and even before it has fully identified the disadvantages of the favored alternative. Brainstorming is one technique to help a group keep an open mind and not inhibit its members' creativity.

A manager can use group decision making but must remain attentive to its process and take steps to ensure that the potential advantages of group decisions are not lost to emergent tendencies toward groupthink. As a member of a work group, you can contribute to its effectiveness by paying attention to its process and its approach to decision making.

ORGANIZATION AS DECISION MAKER

As social systems, organizations have a tendency to hire individuals whose values and interests are similar to those of current members; they also tend to train or "socialize" new members to act in accordance with the organization's existing ways of doing things. This phenomenon is true not only for new members; all members of any organization are under social pressure to maintain established ways of behaving (see Chapter 6). As a consequence, decision makers in an organization are likely to exhibit some commonalities in the approach they follow, in what criteria they use to evaluate alternatives, and in how much risk they take when faced with uncertainty. It is thus appropriate to think of an organization as having characteristic ways of making decisions that are reflected to some degree in nearly all managers' behavior. We shall end this chapter by looking at how certain characteristics of an organization influence its patterns of decision making.

An organization's *climate* influences the ways decisions are made. Its values, customs, and especially norms generate powerful expectations about how decisions *should* be made and what criteria should be considered. There are likely to be norms that provide answers to each of the following questions:

---

[3] See *Victims of Groupthink* (Boston: Houghton Mifflin, 1972).

BOX 7-2

> ### NOMINAL GROUP AND DELPHI TECHNIQUES
>
> When you think about a group making a decision, you normally associate it with an interaction process, in particular when the decision is intended to reflect the collective thoughts of the members. However, two relatively recent approaches to group decision making represent important departures from the usual process; they both actually limit considerably the interaction of group members but, despite that constraint, have proved to be effective techniques for making decisions that do, in fact, reflect the collective intelligence of the group.
>
> In the nominal group technique (called that because the group exists in name only), participants sit around a table in view of one another, write their ideas on paper without discussion, record the ideas or opinions on a chart, and conduct a very limited discussion to clarify the ideas and to express support or nonsupport for them. Then each member silently ranks his or her preferences and a final decision is made by averaging member rankings. The advantages of this approach over an interactive one seems to be that it equalizes participation; that is, it prevents undue influence or domination of discussion by the more assertive or vocal members. Interestingly enough, the nominal group technique has been found to be highly effective, especially when it comes to generating information and new ideas, as well as in efficiency in the use of time.
>
> The Delphi technique differs from nominal group in that members of the group remain anonymous and the sources of communication, all of which are written, also remain anonymous. All information and ideas are communicated in writing to all members, and all changes of opinion must be explained in writing. Through repetition of this process, the group eventually arrives at a decision. There is some evidence that the Delphi technique can produce better decisions than face-to-face groups, presumably because status and personality are eliminated from the process.
>
> For additional material on nominal groups, see the work of Green and of Gustafson in the annotated bibliography. For material on the Delphi technique, look into the work of Van de Verr and Delbecq and of Gustafson in the annotated bibliography.

1. How much is decision making to be a team responsibility rather than an individual responsibility?
2. Is there a payoff for collaboration or is individual initiative valued above all else?
3. To what extent is a manager expected to think it through on his own rather than use others as "consultants" when decision making is basically an individual responsibility?
4. To what extent is it expected that the process will emphasize minimal risk and, therefore, be deliberate and thorough (closer to the traditional model) rather than venturesome and, therefore, quicker and more intuitive?
5. To what extent are feelings, as opposed to rational reasons, accepted as legitimate?

6. To what extent can humanistic criteria be treated as important for choice even at some cost to "bottom-line" criteria? To what extent will a manager who considers humanistic criteria be seen as weak and not sufficiently hard-nosed?
7. What problems can and cannot be addressed? What are the "sacred cows" of the organization?

Talking things over with others, even to the point of sharing influence, may constitute intelligent behavior that serves to maintain good interdepartmental relations, but this practice may also be an expected and socially necessary step. Individuals who have come from industry to become deans in universities have been known to run afoul of this expectation and, as a result, unnecessarily alienate their faculty and fellow deans by failing to consult with them. As a young industrial engineer, one author worked in a department that insisted that one consider at least 6, and preferably 10, alternatives before suggesting a course of action to line management; the individual who could outline only one or two alternatives was viewed in a negative light. Norms similar to these exist in all organizations and are powerful determinants of the decision process every manager will use.

The *structure* of the organization is a second characteristic that influences decision making, particularly in terms of where certain types of decisions will be made. If the organization is highly centralized with limited delegation, then even small issues tend to be referred upward. Time to get a decision on individual issues is likely to be long, and the organization's decision process is likely to be characterized as cumbersome rather than responsive and quick. In contrast, in a matrix structure there is a conscious effort to push the process lower in the organization and make general decision makers out of those who would be concerned with only one function under a more traditional structure.

Organizations also differ in terms of *where decisions are made*. In some highly technical organizations, technical personnel have considerable contact with the customer, discussing customer needs and product applications. In such situations, a significant amount of the marketing function is in fact done by engineering personnel. In effect, the job descriptions (a structural element) of engineering, whether formalized or not, differ from those in an organization with a more traditional marketing function. This is also a way of saying that the goal balance struck by the organization influences the respective decision power of the various departments and their managers.

Thus, organizations can be contrasted on the loci of decision making, both vertically and horizontally. Where decisions are made and which departments have power over what issues influence organizational effectiveness as well as the individual manager's job satisfaction. An organization that seeks to establish standardized ways of doing things and, therefore, has an extensive array of standard operating procedures reduces the degrees of freedom available to the individual decision maker. Such an organization's decision making, with many decisions preprogrammed, is characterized by consistency and efficiency but risks having rigidity and limited creativity in responding to new circumstances. In other words, a system control can limit a manager's range of options. Similarly, powerful groups or individuals can also pose obstacles if not reckoned with. For example, a decision to automate in a unionized plant had better have worker representation if it is to be implemented effectively.

Finally, organizational decision making is influenced by the *flow of information* throughout the organization. Procedurally, it is a matter of getting the necessary information to the appropriate decision maker at the right time. This, in turn, can be influenced by the organization's climate. A climate of secrecy, as opposed to openness, limits influence in decisions to those in the know and restricts the number of people who have any sense of influencing the process.

In concluding this discussion of the organization as decision maker, we emphasize that an organization will exhibit a characteristic approach to decision making and that the nature of that approach and its suitability for organizational effectiveness constitute another dimension on which to analyze and contrast organizations. Organizations differ in terms of the process followed, the loci of decision making, the criteria used in evaluating possible courses of action, and the information and autonomy available to each individual manager.

SUMMARY

An important part of a manager's job is to make decisions. Ideally these decisions will be rational and well thought out from beginning (awareness of the need to make a decision) to end (implementation and subsequent evaluation of the decision). A nine-phase rational model has been presented as a guideline for decision making. The phases of this approach are:

a. Awareness of the need for a decision.
b. Definition of the problems faced.
c. Identification of the objectives in a decision.
d. Development of alternatives.
e. Evaluation of alternatives.
f. Choice.
g. Planning implementation of the decision.
h. Implementation.
i. Evaluation of outcomes and process.

While these steps are sequential, it is common for the process at any time to involve some recycling to previous steps. In addition, most decisions are not completely rational but are often based on one's intuition or feelings of the moment.

As human beings we are subject to a variety of behavioral and emotional forces that may at times facilitate our decision making but at other times may serve as barriers to effective decisions. The behavioral barriers include:

1. Being too action oriented.
2. Not being systematic enough.
3. Procrastinating and avoiding.
4. Working too concentratedly.
5. Ignoring intuition.
6. Dealing in single causality and simplistic solutions.

The emotional barriers include:

1. Impatience with the process.
2. Panic.
3. Perfectionism and fear of failure.
4. Desire to be liked and to avoid hostility.
5. Reluctance to exhibit ignorance.
6. Pride.

In discussing individual versus group decision making, we used the Vroom model, which offers five options on a continuum ranging from unilateral to fully shared decisions (these are shown in Figure 7–4). The choice of option is related to a number of possible factors present in the situation (these are shown in Figure 7–5). Over and above the issues that might affect a manager's choice of options in making a decision, organizational pressures and limitations also affect a decision maker's freedom. These are related to the organization's norms, structure, loci of decision making, and flow of information. Every organization has its own style of decision making, some more effective than others, but all tend to have a powerful impact on the decision processes of its managers.

ANNOTATED BIBLIOGRAPHY

Bobbitt, H. R. Jr., and J. D. Ford   "Decision-Maker Choice as a Determinant of Organizational Structure." *Academy of Management Review*, January 1980, pp. 13–23.

The article reviews the conceptual-theoretical issues raised by the neglect of decision-maker choice in structure-contingency models. The authors suggest an expansion of the structure-contingency framework to include the analysis of decision-maker choice in explaining organization structure. A proposal is made suggesting that an organization's structure is the result of an interaction of the decision maker's cognitive and motivational orientations and the context in which the organization finds itself. Finally, the implications of the framework are discussed.

Brown, R.V. "Do Managers Find Decision Theory Useful?" *Harvard Business Review,* May–June 1970, pp. 78–89.

The author summarizes the findings of a survey that sought to identify benefits and problems various companies have had using decision theory analysis (DTA). The article discusses the potential of DTA and examines ways to make it effective.

Cummings, L. L.; G. P. Huber; and E. Arendt "Effects of Size and Spatial Arrangements on Group Decision Making." *Academy of Management Journal,* September 1974, pp. 460–75.

A review is made of the literature on the effects of group size and spatial arrangements on decision-making performance, member satisfaction and consensus, and leadership emergence. The study also examines the effects on decision quality and speed. Implications for administrative procedures are drawn.

Dillard, J. F. "Applicability of an Occupational Goal-Expectancy Model in Professional Accounting Organizations." *Decision Sciences,* April 1979, pp. 161–76.

This article presents a detailed study that investigates the characteristics of the occupation-position choice decision process. A goal-expectancy model is presented and tested on a sample population of 136 public accountants employed by two large CPA firms. The findings suggest that the model is useful in explaining and predicting professional accountants' goal choice behavior.

Dion, K. L.; R. S. Baron; and N. Miller "Why Do Groups Make Riskier Decisions than Individuals?" In *Advances in Experimental Social Psychology,* ed. Leonard Berkowitz. New York: Academic Press, 1970, pp. 305–77.

This is a review of much of the research that has sought to analyze why groups make riskier decisions than individuals. The authors examine in detail the major alternative interpretations that attempt to explain group risk taking, focusing on: (1) diffusion of responsibility, (2) persuasion, (3) familiarization, and (4) cultural values. Although the authors acknowledge that the understanding of the group decision-making process remains modest, it appears that the best explanation for risk taking lies in cultural-value interpretations.

Green, T. B. "An Empirical Analysis of Nominal and Interacting Groups." *Academy of Management Journal,* March 1975, pp. 63–73.

The study examines the belief that nominal grouping is superior to interacting groups for the problem identification phase of the decision-making process. Results indicate that there are no significant differences between the quantity and quality of performance between the two groups. The authors present their conclusion cautiously, indicating further experimentation is necessary in examining nominal versus interacting group effectiveness.

Grenier, L. E.; D. P. Leitch; and L. B. Barnes "Putting Judgment Back into Decisions." *Harvard Business Review,* March–April 1970, pp. 59–66.

This article describes an extensive study that investigated the importance of quantified information in enabling managers to arrive at sound judgments in decision making. The authors conducted their study on the Internal Revenue Service and focused on various types of performance criteria used by managers. Although there is a trend to use more quantified data in the decision-making process, the study presents evidence that informed managers rely more on qualitative criteria in evaluating performance, even in the presence of significant quantified data. The authors suggest that management should seek methods of assisting and restoring confidence in the performance judgments of their managers.

Gustafson, D. H. "A Comparative Study of Differences in Subjective Likelihood Estimates Made by Individuals, Interacting Groups, Delphi Groups, and Nominal Groups." *Organizational Behavior and Human Performance* 9 (1973), pp. 280–91.

The study evaluated four methods of eliciting subjective estimation responses from individuals. The methods differed in terms of amount and structure of interaction permitted among the individual estimators. The four processes were individual approach, interacting group approach, and the nominal and Delphi group approaches. The study found that the nominal group process was superior in approaching correct estimates to posed questions.

Hall, J. "Decisions, Decisions, Decisions." *Psychology Today,* November 1971, pp. 51–54 and 88.

This article explores the group decision-making process through the analysis of decisions made by several groups. It discusses several guidelines to use in achieving consensus and illustrates how the group process in decision making is often superior to individual decision making.

Ives, B. D. "Decision Theory and the Practicing Manager." *Business Horizons,* June 1973, pp. 38–40.

Ives defines decision theory as a method of rationally and systematically outlining the selection of alternate courses of action. There are several reasons to recommend its use. It provides an organized approach to problem solving that allows explicit consideration of many variables. Decision theory simplifies the nature of the problem, highlighting key components to be solved and consequently saving time, effort, and money. It also provides a standard framework for problem solving applicable to all problem areas.

Kaufmann, F. "Decision Making—Eastern and Western Style." *Business Horizons,* December 1970, pp. 81–86.

This article contrasts the decision-making process of Western organizations with that of the Japanese. The basic difference is an individual approach in the West as opposed to the collective approach exhibited by the Japanese. A review of the advantages and disadvantages of each style is presented and steps are suggested by which a favorable synthesis may be made possible.

Marks, B. A. "Decision under Uncertainty: A Poet's View." *Business Horizons,* February 1971, pp. 57–61.

This author discusses decision making under uncertainty through an analysis of Robert Frost's poem, "The Road Not Taken."

Padgett, J. P. "Managing Garbage Can Hierarchies." *Administrative Science Quarterly,* December 1980, pp. 583–604.

The article examines garbage can theory (organizations characterized by severe ambiguity) to illustrate how ambiguity impinges on decision making. Also, the managerial implications of garbage can theory are discussed. From the discussion, a number of managerial recommendations are presented for the president or chief executive officer (CEO) interested in controlling a confused (garbage can) hierarchy.

Pollay, R. W. "The Structure of Executive Decisions and Decision Times." *Administrative Science Quarterly,* December 1970, pp. 459–71.

Pollay presents a study of the relationship between the difficulty of a decision and decision time. A theory is presented that decision makers take longer to choose from four alternatives when two are easily rejected than when all four alternatives are equal. The study suggests that decision behavior is correlated with certain personality characteristics.

Shell, R. L., and D. F. Seltzer "Systems Analysis: Aid to Decision Making." *Business Horizons,* December 1971, pp. 67–72.

The article describes the systems analysis approach to decision making and why it should be implemented. The approach involves nine basic steps and, finally, identification of the best solution in consideration of the facts, assumptions, and uncertainties contained in the problem.

Ulvila, J. W. and R. V. Brown "Decision Analysis Comes of Age." *Harvard Business Review,* September–October 1982, p. 130.

The authors argue that decision analysis is passing beyond the stage of being an experimental management technique and has begun to gain acceptance in large corporations for practical applications. This is happening in part because decision analysis techniques have been developed that "can better take into account the people, the politics, the time pressures, and all the messy but critical factors that managers have to contend with." The authors seek to document the claim by showing how three major forms of decision analysis, decision tree analysis, probabilistic forecasting, and multivariate analysis, have been used to solve actual problems.

Van de Verr, A. H., and A. L. Delbecq "The Effectiveness of Nominal, Delphi, and Interacting Group Decision Making Process." *Academy of Management Journal,* December 1974, pp. 605–21.

The study compares the conventional interacting group with nominal and Delphi groups in terms of the quantity of ideas generated and the perceived satisfaction of group members. Recent literature on group process is reviewed and an experiment is described that investigated group effectiveness on an applied fact-finding problem with no known solution. Results indicate that nominal and Delphi approaches are equally effective and both more effective than conventional interacting groups.

SUGGESTED READINGS

Allison, Graham T. *Essence of Decision: Explaining the Cuban Missile Crisis.* Boston: Little, Brown, 1971.

Conrath, D. W. "Organizational Decision-Making Behavior under Varying Conditions of Uncertainty." *Management Science* 13 (1967), pp. 487–500.

Duncan, Robert B. "Modifications in Decision Structure in Adapting to the Environment:

Some Implications for Organizational Learning." *Decision Sciences* 5 (1974), pp. 705–25.

———— "Multiple Decision-Making Structures in Adapting to Environmental Uncertainty: The Impact on Organizational Effectiveness." *Human Relations* 26 (1973), pp. 273–91.

Janis, I. L., and L. Mann "Coping with Decisional Conflict." *American Scientist* 64 (1976), pp. 657–67.

Mintzberg, Henry; Dury Rasinghani; and Andre Theoret "The Structure of 'Unstructured' Decision Processes." *Administrative Science Quarterly* 21 (1976), pp. 246–75.

Patchen, Martin "The Locus and Basis of Influence on Organizational Decisions." *Organizational Behavior and Human Performance*. New York: Academic Press, 1974, pp. 195–221.

Pounds, William F. "The Process of Problem Finding." *Industrial Management Review* 11 (1969), pp. 1–19.

Simon, Herbert A. *Administrative Behavior*. 3d ed. New York: Free Press, 1976.

Smith, Clagett G. "Consultation and Decision Processes in a Research and Development Laboratory." *Administrative Science Quarterly* 15 (1970), pp. 203–15.

Soelberg, P. O. "Unprogrammed Decision Making." *Industrial Management Review* Spring 1967, pp. 19–29.

Stagner, Ross "Corporate Decision Making: An Empirical Study." *Journal of Applied Psychology* 53 (1969), pp. 1–13.

Vroom, Victor H., and Philip W. Yetton. *Leadership and Decisionmaking*. Pittsburgh: University of Pittsburgh Press, 1973.

CHAPTER 8

Human Resources Development

INTRODUCTION

HUMAN RESOURCES DEVELOPMENT (HRD) is rooted in the goals of the organization, which determine the types of skills, attitudes, and values needed now and in the future. Given the goals of the organization, it is possible to develop a long-range plan concerning such matters as sales volume, product mix, new product development, return on investment, improvements in quality and services, additions to and improvement of plant and equipment, and improvement in external relations. These matters determine the types and numbers of people needed by the organization to meet its objectives over any given period of time. Human resources development is the process by which the organization makes sure that it has the people it needs when it needs them. It also enables management to anticipate if it cannot secure or train the necessary personnel in the time available and, therefore, must modify its plans in the light of such realities.

Human resources development involves two sets of goals; on the one hand are the goals of the organization, and on the other hand are the goals of the individual employees. These two sets of goals are neither necessarily in conflict nor necessarily congruent. HRD, therefore, represents an effort to *match* the goals of the organization with the goals of *all* its employees, from the president down to hourly workers.

The first part of this chapter will look at HRD from a *planning* perspective; that is, it takes the view that the basic activities of HRD—recruiting, training, career development, and performance review—are best understood in the context of an organization's long-range plans. Since Chapter 9 will discuss overall organizational planning (in the context of the external environment), we will limit our focus in this chapter to human resources dimensions. After we have established this perspective, we will look at each area of activity normally associated with HRD.

HUMAN RESOURCES PLANNING

Just as managers in organizations must plan for their capital and material resources, they must also plan for their human resources. Nowhere is this more evident than in sports. Owners and managers who plan carefully for their future needs and then recruit against that plan can often achieve dramatic results. The methods used can vary a great deal, but planning is a common element. For example, Chuck Noll built the Pittsburgh Steelers to a dominant position in the National Football League by recruiting rookies and carefully developing them over the years. Exxon, General Electric, IBM, and many other firms have used the same strategy to find and develop future managers. A nondevelopmental approach was used by George Steinbrenner when he bought the New York Yankees. He hired already proven talent from other clubs and built a championship team. This strategy is also followed by some corporations, which hire executives with wide experience and a record of achievement to build their own management teams quickly. Many sports teams and other organizations try to use a number of approaches as their situations warrant. The important point is that there should be *human resources planning* as a basis for finding people to hire, train, and promote.

The key elements in human resources planning are:

1. A strategic plan for the organization's overall growth and development.
2. A work-force plan that is based on the strategic plan and specifies the kinds and numbers of positions that will be necessary to carry out the plan.
3. Job plans (or job designs) that identify the knowledge and skills needed for positions specified in the work force plan.

In the past, activities of this kind were called "manpower planning" and consisted largely of projecting the numbers of people that would be needed by the organization over time. Manpower planning included anticipated upturns and downturns in business and, therefore, included planning for hiring and laying off people as conditions warranted. As organizations became more complex, simple manpower planning became inadequate. To follow our sports analogy, it's not just that five players are retiring after the current season and will need to be replaced by five new players; there are questions of balance between specialty teams (offense and defense), whether to promote from within or hire from the outside, veterans versus rookies, free-agent players, and players playing out their options. Therefore, a more comprehensive plan is necessary, one that takes many factors into account. The field of human resource planning has emerged because most organizations today require some kind of long-range view for managing human resources. Furthermore, many changes in the nature of our country's work force have forced organizations to consider new approaches to human resources planning. Some of the highlights follow:

1. There are more two (career) wage-earner households than ever before and the number is increasing.
2. There are more single-parent households than ever before and the number is increasing.
3. The average educational level is increasing.
4. Professionals seem to have become more loyal to their professions than to organizations.
5. More people are seeking mid-career changes than ever before.

6. There is increasing concern about the overall quality of work life at all levels of society.

As a consequence of these changes, people have higher expectations concerning their careers and the satisfactions they can get from their jobs. Companies can no longer assume that they can hire people who will be content to "stay put" in the same job. People expect to grow and develop through their work. If they cannot climb the organizational ladder, at least they want to have their jobs evolve and expand as they learn more.

Because of the increase or changes in the complexity of jobs in most organizations, coupled with the changes in people's expectations about careers and jobs, human resources planning and development has become a high-order concern for today's manager. Managers have only three kinds of resources to manage: financial, material (equipment, raw materials, finished goods), and human. Over the last 30 years or so, the techniques available to managers to aid them in managing those resources have changed dramatically. The widespread use of computers has had an impact in all three areas, particularly the first two. In some large organizations, like the army, human resource planning has been highly automated. Most computer systems attempt to match the organization's work force needs with the knowledge, skills, and interests of its members. Some systems work better than others. Figure 8-1 depicts this matching process. The center column represents much of what human resources planning and development systems try to do.

1. Strategic Planning[1]

Effective human resources planning and development takes into account the organization's overall strategic plan as the starting point for human resource planning. With the sports team analogy, it can be seen that the kinds of people a team tries to recruit will depend on whether the strategy is more like Chuck Noll's or George Steinbrenner's. In business organizations, some strategies are very different from others. Consider a paving contractor whose work is highly seasonal and requires little technical expertise. An appropriate strategy for staffing might be to have a skeleton crew on the payroll year-round and hire large numbers of college students during the summer months. That way, the skeleton crew could provide continuity from year-to-year, could act as first-line supervisors, and could be well paid, and the owners could afford to train these people in a wide range of skills in anticipation of having them around as ongoing resources. In fact, many

---

[1] In Chapter 9, we will discuss this concept as part of an even broader notion called open systems planning.

8 / Human Resources Development 241

FIGURE 8–1
Human Resource Planning and Development

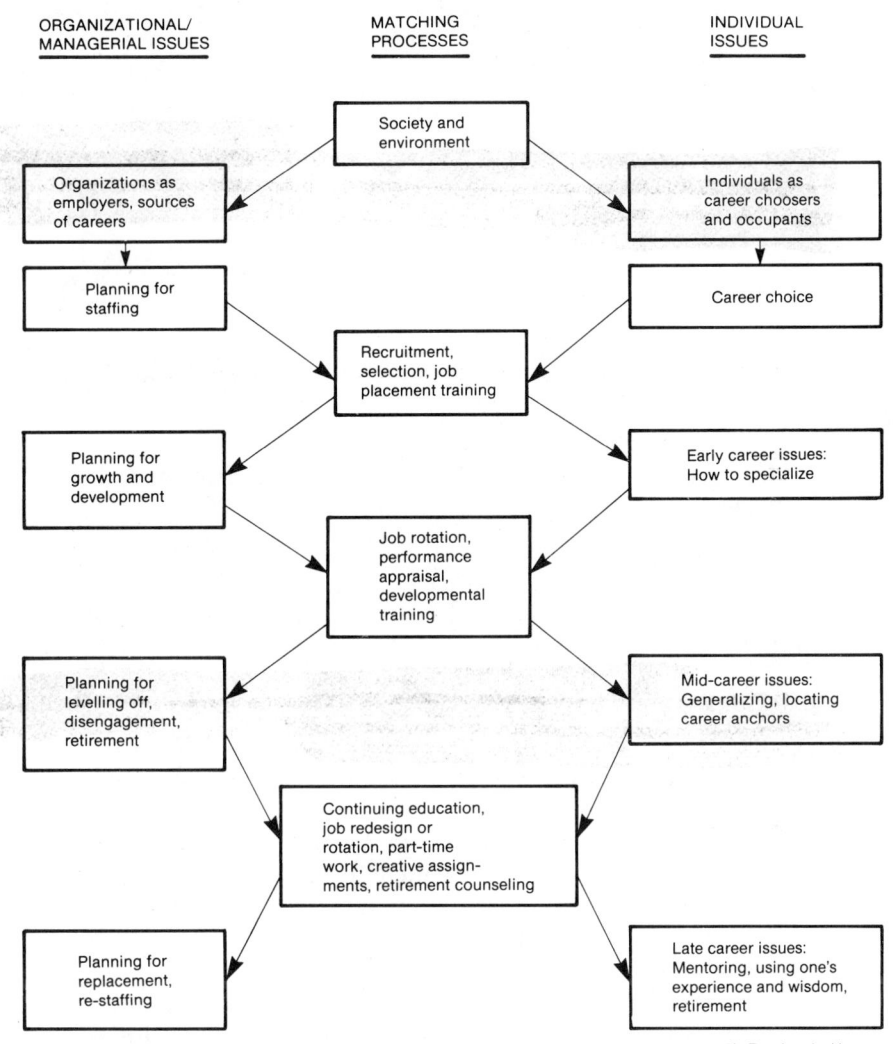

ORGANIZATIONAL/ MANAGERIAL ISSUES	MATCHING PROCESSES	INDIVIDUAL ISSUES
Organizations as employers, sources of careers	Society and environment	Individuals as career choosers and occupants
Planning for staffing	Recruitment, selection, job placement training	Career choice
Planning for growth and development	Job rotation, performance appraisal, developmental training	Early career issues: How to specialize
Planning for levelling off, disengagement, retirement	Continuing education, job redesign or rotation, part-time work, creative assignments, retirement counseling	Mid-career issues: Generalizing, locating career anchors
Planning for replacement, re-staffing		Late career issues: Mentoring, using one's experience and wisdom, retirement

Source: E. Schein, *Career Dynamics* (Reading, Mass.: Addison-Wesley Publishing, 1978). Reprinted with permission of author.

seasonal businesses follow exactly this strategy. By way of contrast, think of the problem faced by NASA with regard to launch and recovery crews. Their work also is irregular, yet it is so complex and technically sophisticated that it was impossible to lay off the crews between the Apollo program and the Columbia launches. NASA's strategy for staffing, training, rewarding, and retaining their crews is necessarily different from that of the paving contractor. Therefore, the first step in building a human resources plan is to look carefully at the overall strategic plan of the organization and to link the two by answering the following questions:

What is our overall mission for this organization?
By what means do we intend to achieve that mission?
What kinds of people will be required to achieve the mission (skills, experience, attitudes, etc.)?
At what rate will we need various kinds of skills?
How are we planning for the organization's growth and development?

Different managerial skills are needed to carry out different business strategies. *Business Week* recently gave some clear examples from companies as diverse as the Chase Manhattan Bank, Heublein, Corning Glass Co., Texas Instruments, General Electric, and Prime Computer. It reported, "Some companies do recognize the link between manpower and strategic planning and are striving to match a manager's personal orientation or style with operating strategy. All too often, however, chief executives speak of manpower and strategic planning as though they were separate functions. Management experts warn that corporations failing to link the two concepts may be sounding the death knell for both."[2] Particular attention was paid to the differences in businesses that were growing, stable, or declining (i.e., at different phases of the product life cycle) and the associated differences needed in managing each kind of situation.

The development of new product lines, market expansions, and acquisitions is normally the result of strategic planning. Information is collected from both the internal and external environments. From an analysis of this information, top management decides on a direction and develops action plans specifically outlining how and when those objectives will be achieved. Inherent in this process is the frequent assumption by top management that there will be enough people who have the necessary competencies when the organization will need them. Not infrequently there is a high potential for this assumption to be incorrect

---

[2] *Business Week*, February 25, 1980, p. 166.

8 / Human Resources Development 243

and costly. Not having the necessary human resources can be a major constraint in achieving the objectives of a business plan.

Managers must plan for necessary human resources as they would for other assets and aspects of the business they are responsible for, such as financial and physical resources. It is amazing to hear so many companies say, "People are our most important asset," and yet pay much less attention to planning for and managing that asset than they do to planning and managing budgets. One reason is that things like budgets often are more concrete, more tangible, and less likely to change. Another reason is that stockholders are interested in product plans, market plans, and financial plans. Seldom are questions asked about "people" plans. What forces organizations to pay attention to people planning is usually a dramatic event in the human dimension: absenteeism, increased turnover, a strike, or difficulties in recruiting the needed skills. At that point, it is difficult to stop reacting to the immediate crisis and make a strategic human resource plan! Figure 8–2 shows some forces that inhibit and some that encourage managers to do human resources planning.

2. Work Force Planning (structure)

After establishing a strategic plan, the next step is to devise the particular configuration of the workforce (structure) that fits the plan. Small or new organizations seldom have sharply defined organization structures; everyone pretty much does everything. As the organization grows or gets older, some kind of structure (role differentiation) gets imposed or evolves because certain people tend to do certain tasks. The process of defining the tasks to be done and arranging the people in the organization so that the tasks can be accomplished efficiently may be a planned effort or a natural evolution, or may not happen at all. Most people like to work for an organization in which they know what their job is and what is expected of them. Without some structural planning, it is difficult to communicate clear job definitions or performance expectations.

Few organizations are static. Most are changing in response to changes in their environment and in their people. Strategic planning tries to anticipate changes in an organization's environment and position the organization to be maximally effective in response to those changes. Work force planning tries to structure the tasks to be done and the people to do them in a sensible manner. It also provides a framework to guide the direction in which the organization is headed structurally. For example, work force planning helps to determine whether an organization will become more centralized or more decentralized. It also helps to focus attention on function or product or geography within the

FIGURE 8–2

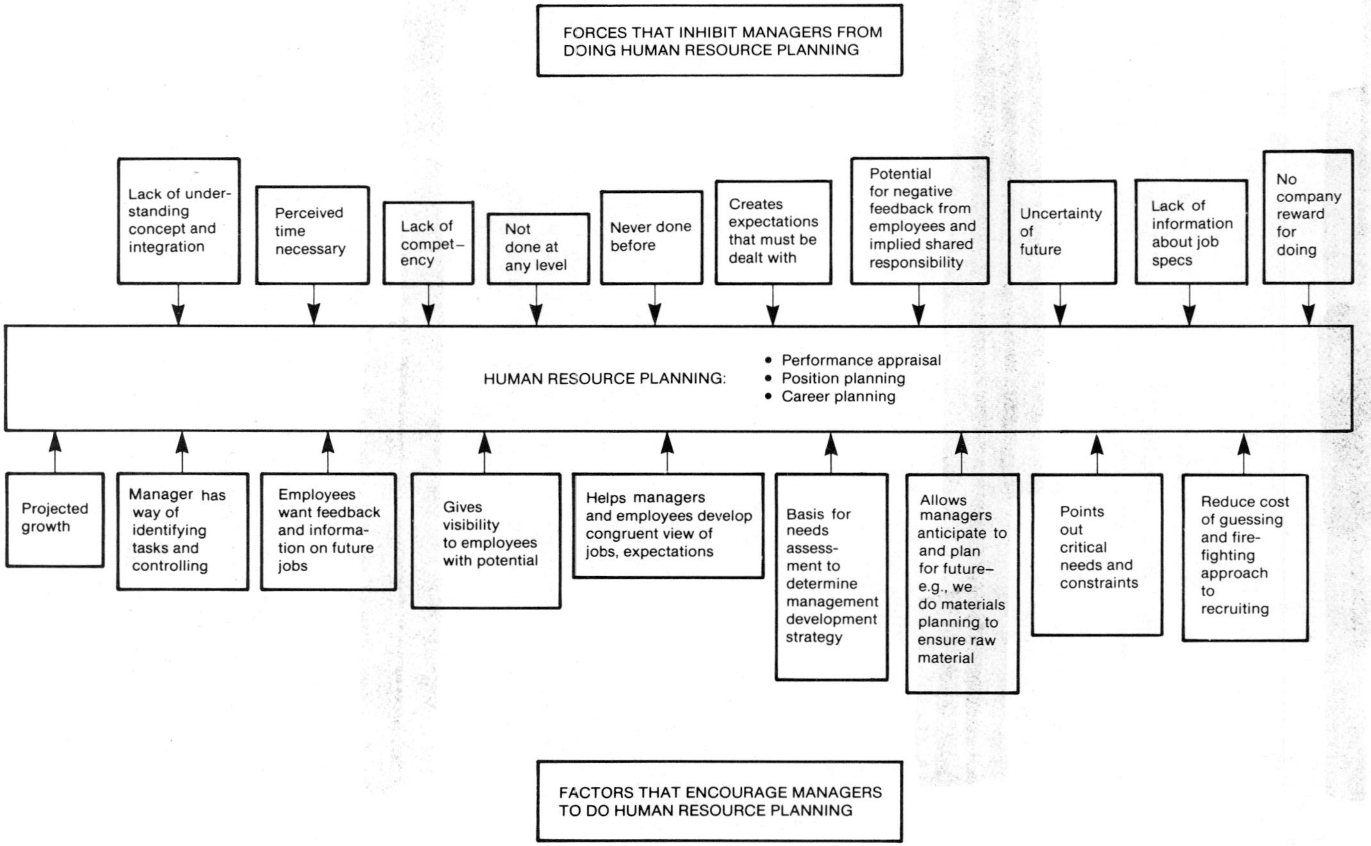

FORCES THAT INHIBIT MANAGERS FROM DOING HUMAN RESOURCE PLANNING

- Lack of understanding concept and integration
- Perceived time necessary
- Lack of competency
- Not done at any level
- Never done before
- Creates expectations that must be dealt with
- Potential for negative feedback from employees and implied shared responsibility
- Uncertainty of future
- Lack of information about job specs
- No company reward for doing

HUMAN RESOURCE PLANNING:
- Performance appraisal
- Position planning
- Career planning

FACTORS THAT ENCOURAGE MANAGERS TO DO HUMAN RESOURCE PLANNING

- Projected growth
- Manager has way of identifying tasks and controlling
- Employees want feedback and information on future jobs
- Gives visibility to employees with potential
- Helps managers and employees develop congruent view of jobs, expectations
- Basis for needs assessment to determine management development strategy
- Allows managers anticipate to and plan for future—e.g., we do materials planning to ensure raw material
- Points out critical needs and constraints
- Reduce cost of guessing and fire-fighting approach to recruiting

Developed at Digital Equipment Corporation by P. Mapps and S. Lotz. Used with permission.

organization. Most smaller organizations are structured functionally. People are recruited to fill particular functional positions in areas such as finance, engineering, manufacturing, or sales. Often, larger organizations (or parts of organizations) get organized on a different basis, such as product lines: industrial product group, consumer product group, military product group. Sometimes there is further differentiation by geography: northeast region, southwest region, Chicago district. Many of these organizational changes can be planned for as an organization gets older, grows, shrinks, introduces new products or services, or enters new markets.

Human resource professionals can help to ensure that the organization is properly staffed and will continue to be properly staffed by working with line managers on strategic and organizational plans that answer the following questions:

How will managerial work change?
What kinds of special expertise will be needed?
What kinds of organization structures may be envisioned?
What kinds of people will be needed to function effectively in those structures?[3]

3. Job Planning

Once there is a plan for how the work force is to be structured and how it is expected to evolve over time, *individual* jobs can be designed and planned. In any organization, each job needs to fit into the overall structure and cannot be designed independently. Therefore, effective job design depends on effective work force planning. The design of a single job will change over time as the organization changes. Consider the job of controller. In a small company, that task might consist of overseeing a bookkeeper and doing all the accounting work. As the organization grows, the role of controller may become more managerial in nature; it may now encompass accounts payable, accounts receivable, and cost accounting. The title remains the same, but the nature of the job has changed. The clearer one is about the work force plan, the easier it is to design jobs that fit together within that plan. People usually work more productively when they know what is expected of them, what they are responsible and accountable for, how they will be measured and rewarded, and what they can look forward to. Job planning encompasses all these elements. The last element—possible future jobs—goes beyond job planning and into career paths. Career paths are clusters of jobs sequenced so that as a person masters one job, he or she

---
[3] From Edgar H. Schein, *Career Dynamics* (Reading, Mass.: Addison-Wesley Publishing, 1978), p. 207.

can look forward to moving to a more challenging and responsible job that draws on the skills and experience gained in previous positions. Job planning helps to locate individual jobs in one or more career paths.

INDIVIDUAL RESPONSIBILITY AND DEVELOPMENT

So far we have looked at only one side of the human resource planning formula—the company side. We have seen that the organization is responsible for defining its strategy, its organizational structure, and the kinds of jobs necessary to achieve its goals. In this section, we will look at the other side of human resource planning—the individual. No matter how effectively the organization defines its human resource needs, management should pay an equal amount of attention to individuals' needs, preferences, and career goals.

The first and probably most important aspect of the individual's responsibility is a *personal plan* with a realistic self-assessment of interests and goals. What are you interested in doing, what would you find challenging and worthwhile? What kind of skills, training, and experience do you bring to the job? How do you envision your career progressing? The answers to these questions lie within the individual, not the organization. Matching the organization's needs and the individual's desires works best when people have self-awareness and are willing to take initiative in managing their own careers. The ideal employment and staffing process is one that matches self-aware people with well-planned and designed jobs.

No organization can meet all of a person's needs. At best, organizational goals and personal goals can approximate each other. The individual's responsibility is to be as clear as possible about his or her own likes, desires, and career goals, as well as to make a realistic assessment of capabilities and limitations.

What you are willing, interested, and able to do will change as you go through life. Therefore, those things at work that you find rewarding will change as well. A great deal has been written about the stages people generally experience throughout their adult lives, and most of it has been supported by research.[4] As you start your career, the kinds of things you look for in a job are very different from some job choices later on. For example, if you've never traveled or been on your own much, you might find a job that requires travel to distant cities or countries exciting and challenging. Usually such jobs become tiring after the excitement of all the new places wears off. Perhaps you've found a partner and want to be at home more, or you've started a family and want to spend time with them. Now the very characteristic of your job

---

[4] See Suggested Readings at the end of the chapter.

that was so attractive—the travel—is the most frustrating aspect of the job. The job hasn't changed; *you* have changed. And so it is throughout your career: a constant matching of the requirements or characteristics of a job with your own desires and the circumstances of your life.

Another aspect of matching yourself to your job has to do with work activities and nonwork activities. Some people want to keep their work-related activities well bounded; that is, they work hard to separate work and nonwork. A production control supervisor who knows his job well, works hard at work, and spends all his free time pursuing his two most important nonwork activities, sailing and skiing, is one example. A salesman who is selling while he's with a customer on the golf course each week has much less desire to separate work from play. In fact, he enjoys his golf game less when he's not also selling. Most entrepreneurs cannot separate work from nonwork, so to others they appear always to be working.

The more compatible the match between you and your job at any time in your career, the more productive you will be on the job. When you are expending energy trying to make a bad match work, frustration is the usual result. And frustrated people seldom are productive people.

No organization can focus totally on the development of the system without considering the individuals who make up that system. Nor can it focus totally on the development of the individuals within the system without considering what makes *overall* sense and allows the system to function effectively. Therefore, the challenge to those who manage human resource planning and development activities is to maintain an appropriate balance between these two somewhat incompatible demands, as well as to maintain a planning perspective (i.e., an awareness of the future, not just the present) in the course of carrying out HRD functions.

RECRUITING, SELECTING, AND HIRING

It's one thing to hire people to fit existing needs, but it's quite another to accomplish that *and* match them to future needs. The planning process we've been talking about requires that you do just that. Organizational and job demands change and often render today's skills obsolete for tomorrow. This is why modern organizations not only assess present capabilities when matching people to jobs, but also assess potential for learning and development, so that employees can, with training and coaching, grow with the changes required of them.

Returning to our sports analogy, suppose you're managing a professional football team and you lose your star quarterback because of injury. Do you try to find another star quarterback, which could be extremely difficult and expensive? Or do you write off the season, look to the long run, and recruit a new, young, up-and-coming talent? If you can find both in the same package, you have it made. But if you can't, which is likely, your choice will be difficult.

Organizations that are large, have been around for many years, and have growth rates slow enough to permit a stable planning process usually recruit into the bottom levels of the system and move people up into higher and higher levels as their experience and training allow. This enables the organization to have a well-planned management succession process. At Liberty Mutual Insurance Co., for example, all entry-level jobs are at the bottom of the hierarchy. People advance as they demonstrate their competence as well as their ability to perpetuate the institutional character of the company, which that particular company deems desirable.

Organizations that are characterized by fast growth, usually accompanied by high technology, often do not have the luxury of a planned succession process. People may enter the system at almost any level; entry is determined by the immediate technological requirements. Since such industries are based on knowledge, the entry-level jobs have less to do with such things as age or number of years of previous experience than with the particular knowledge and expertise possessed by the individual. New college graduates from programs in computer technology may find job openings that entail surprisingly high levels of responsibility. This tends to be especially characteristic of project-oriented organizations in which people move in and out of work activities in relation to demands for expertise.

The process of hiring and matching people to the proper jobs can be usefully looked at in relation to each dimension of organizational life. In Chapter 1, we introduced these dimensions by having you consider a list of questions that have important implications for *your* future employment choices, especially if you expect to work for a large, established organization. Now we will look at these dimensions as they might affect the way an organization would view prospective employees.

Goals

If you go to the personnel office of a company to be interviewed for a job, you will certainly be asked, among the multitude of questions about your skills and training, what your goals are. As discussed in Chapter 2 and earlier in this chapter, an effective organization successfully matches the goals of the people it hires with those of the organization. A match promotes commitment, which tends to minimize problems of control, discipline, absenteeism, and turnover. As pointed out in Chapter 1, however, it is also a choice made by *you*, not just the prospective employer.

Structure

Here again the job of the personnel staff is to find the right place for you within the organization's division of labor. The task is to match skills with job requirements. In this context, decisions are based on your existing abilities as well as on your potential for learning the requisite skills, especially where the organization has training programs in place. *Your* awareness of the structure will help you to see the overall scheme into which you will be hired; the employer's knowledge of the structural interconnections of jobs will help him or her to make a choice based on a broader perspective than just the job itself. Managers are becoming increasingly sensitive to problems of job interdependence and tend no longer to match people to positions out of the context of that broader perspective.

Climate

This is a subtle, yet very powerful, determinant of a good fit between a person and a job. Did you ever come away from a first conversation with someone and describe your reaction in such colloquial language as "good vibes" or "bad vibes"? This can and does happen during the recruiting and selection stages and, consequently, affects a company's hiring decisions as well as your own decision about accepting or rejecting a given job offer. From the employer's perspective, you may or may not have the right "style" or "look" or "mannerisms." From your side of it, the setting may bring out the worst in you, make you tense, and elicit a lack of confidence. Although such elements of climate are not rational or easily justified as bases for making decisions, they are legitimate, since they certainly affect one's ultimate success on the job.

Rewards

Organizations that have successful recruiting efforts, or by reputation are attractive places to work, usually have reached that position because of the rewards they offer to employees. They are perceived by job applicants as places that pay well, offer opportunities for advancement, and have good benefits, an attractive environment, and modern management practices in a growing field. When you walk through the personnel door for an interview, if you have inaccurate perceptions and expectations about the reward system, these *ought* to be brought out and corrected early. Unfortunately, this does not always happen. An overeager employer may want you to see only the most positive aspects of the organization; an overeager applicant may also want to see only the best side of a prospective employer. If you haven't experienced it, you certainly can imagine the mutual disappointment that can result when the bubble bursts. Effective hiring practices take considerable care to prevent such misconceptions; however, only you can take precautions to prevent your eagerness (or possibly your desperation) from distorting your judgments. It can often be wise to check out your perceptions with those of others.

Controls

Remember the section of Chapter 6 that discussed role negotiation? When you take a job, part of the process is to establish expectations for future performance. Even though you and your employer try to be explicit about the job expectations, many things can happen that need correcting: lack of clarity about who is responsible for what, finding yourself in over your head, sudden changes in job requirements, and many other factors that neither you nor your employer considered. An effective control system allows for correction through renegotiation.

An additional aspect of controls that is important in the hiring process pertains to the source of control. An organization that stresses formal supervisory and system control may be a bad fit for someone who thrives on self-control or social control. Even though as a new employee you may require close supervisory control, a relevant question for you to ask is whether or not the system will allow you to exercise increasing self-control as you demonstrate your competence and your ability to assume responsibility. If not, you could end up in the classic dilemma—responsibility without authority.

Decision Making

A rapidly changing aspect of modern organizational life is decision making. Such influences as rapidly changing technology, pressures for fast decisions, and the influence of the Japanese consensus approach have combined to push decisions to lower and lower levels of the system. This is not so much the case with more stable, traditional organizations, although the influx of computers has tended to locate special expertise at all levels of an organization, thus making it necessary for many highly expertise-based decisions to be delegated downward. In staffing even entry-level jobs, most organizations recognize that the ability of an individual to make decisions (minor at first, major later on) has become an important asset, as well it should be. As you consider your own strengths and weaknesses, where do you place your decision-making ability? Do you have a preferred style or specific tendencies either in a unilateral direction or toward the participative end of the continuum? It may be that you have a hard time envisioning yourself as a "decision maker," but you may find yourself in that role a lot sooner than you ever realized. And the organization that is considering you for employment may be assessing that potential carefully.

By using these organizational dimensions as a framework for bringing people into the organization, those responsible for hiring can maintain a broad system perspective, looking at the job as part of an interconnected network of jobs all related to the strategic plan of the organization. In the last section of this chapter—performance appraisal—we will return to these same dimensions as a basis for generating important questions that place the evaluation process into a total system perspective as well as a planning and development frame of reference.

TRAINING AND DEVELOPMENT

Most large organizations have programs for employee training and development. Training activities deal with skill areas and may occur at any level of the organization. They tend to focus on technical skills, supervisory skills, and relatively specific areas of management activity, like communications, financial and accounting methods, materials management, and planning techniques. Development programs are more directed at the *whole* person and, consequently, are most appropriate for individuals who are moving toward assuming more responsibility for more people in a wider range of work. The skill areas covered in the training programs are relevant, but more as sets of integrated abilities that foster effective management. Figure 8–3 shows the relationship between training and development.

Entry-level jobs usually demand more specific skills than broad managerial ability. As you progress in your career in the organization world, more and more *general* managerial competence is required of you. Effective organizations recognize this and plan for the necessary training and development activities to bring people along in their careers. A typical dilemma faced by college students is the pressure to develop specific skills that will help to guarantee an entry position versus the need to have a broad education and to develop an ability to problem solve in a general sense. You can see how each emphasis is important, but each seems to be relevant to a different stage of one's career. Add to this the tension of an uncertain economy with a shortage of jobs, and it is not easy to know which emphasis will make you more or less attractive to prospective employers. Our experience in recent years suggests that most students find greater security in opting for specific technical skill development and leaving the more general managerial orientation to their future work experience. However, when we talk to students 10 years out of school, we find that they need the broader managerial perspective and expertise more than the specific technical skills.

One final issue we want to mention with respect to training and

FIGURE 8–3
Relationship between Training and Management Development

	Managers
Training Areas (Skills)	A	B	C	D	...Z
1. Communication skills					
2. Supervision					
3. Performance evaluation					
4. Leadership					
5. Group process					
6. Decision making					
7. Other					

Training normally involves bringing together a group of managers or supervisors and devoting a block of time to teaching them some particular skill or technique (as shown in the different rows of the matrix).

Management development emphasizes the learning and growth of a given manager or supervisor with respect to the overall range of skills required to be effective. While the learning may take place in groups or classes, as well as through individual consultation, the focus is on the development of manager A, B, or C as a *total person* using various skills shown in the matrix simultaneously.

---

development concerns *where* the programs take place, inside or outside the organization. Many large corporations have extensive in-house programs for supervisors and managers at all levels. These programs are normally designed to address the very specific needs of the company, and they also very naturally reinforce the management philosophy and practices already in place, as well as the norms and culture of the informal system. One danger in this approach is that it can easily reinforce and perpetuate the *least* effective and desirable aspects of the organization, thus perpetuating an unhealthy situation. Sometimes as an alternative and sometimes in addition to in-house programs, organizations send people (in particular upper-level managers) to outside seminars offered most often by universities. These programs bring together people from a variety of settings and tend, therefore, to deal with general concepts and management methods that are applicable to the settings represented. Participants usually report that such experiences enrich and broaden their perspectives as managers and help them bring fresh ideas and energy back to their own settings. You can easily see how *both* internal and external programs are important vehicles for management training and development; the choice of which type is most appropriate for any given manager depends on the specific development objectives being served, especially in relation to the need for new ideas or changes in management practices.

Career Paths

An important source of training is on-the-job learning, which means learning from one's experience. Consequently, as an individual (employee) taking responsibility for your own growth and development, it would pay you to think about *career paths*, each involving a series of positions (job experiences) that would not only get you the rewards and satisfactions you desire but also further your personal development. Thus, sometimes it might be appropriate to seek a *lateral move* to broaden your experience, rather than thinking only of a step up the hierarchy. Similarly, it could even make sense to accept a position with less extrinsic reward in the short run to maximize your long-term development and possibilities for future intrinsic as well as extrinsic rewards.

As a manager you have a responsibility and an opportunity to develop (train) your people through calculated job and task assignments. We know of one manager of quality control who rotated each of his sub-department managers one position as a way of adding to their experience and knowledge. The sub-departments were incoming inspection, final testing, standards engineering, and quality assurance. The manager of incoming inspection was made manager of final testing, who in turn was made manager of standards engineering, and so on. A short-term impact of this action was a drop in departmental effectiveness and a consequent decline in relations with other departments, whose activities were affected by the conduct of the quality control function. However, the quality control manager's action did broaden his staff's knowledge, add to their job interest, and increase the probability that his own chances of promotion would not be constrained because no one was available to replace him.

In career path planning, the organization has an overall opportunity to develop its human resources through on-the-job training. That is to say, it is useful if someone in the organization, typically in a personnel department, takes an *overview of* the organization and thinks about career paths and *planned* job rotation in relation to developing individuals and providing for the organization's future human resource needs.

As a final note, let us suggest that when you are looking for a job, one attribute of an organization that is worth staying alert to is its orientation to human resources development and particularly whether its orientation is largely short range at the expense of long range. An organization that is so concerned with *immediate* results and current effectiveness, because of underlying attitudes or economic conditions, that it will not allow individuals to try something new and take some risks may be a poor choice.

---

[5] We discuss this concept in the context of an organization. You might want to think about the broader implications, such as career moves that lead to self-employment and more entrepreneurial ventures.

Nonprogrammatic Methods: Mentoring

As a new employee, you will need guidance and coaching by someone in a more senior position. In fact, a relationship of this kind—sometimes called *mentoring*—can be important throughout your career.[6] Furthermore, at some time *you* will be in the senior position relative to someone who requires guidance and coaching. This type of relationship is currently recognized as a major part of a manager's job, certainly when the manager is viewed as a developer of human resources.

The role of mentor is not an easy one; it requires interpersonal sensitivity, some knowledge of the kinds of issues people struggle with in their careers, as well as an ability to appraise the skills and potential of another person. If you think about the kinds of people who have been your mentors—friends, parents, teachers, employers—very likely they have had some of these traits. These characteristics can be developed; you may some day need them to be effective as a *total* manager.

MANAGEMENT SUCCESSION PLANNING

One of the most critical decisions top management can make is deciding who will succeed them. These decisions can affect an organization as profoundly as a major financial decision with respect to future directions. In many organizations, however, this decision is made on the basis of very biased and unsystematic information, often becoming extremely political, such as choosing successors from the "old boy network." Top management in most organizations has a tendency to perpetuate what exists by replacing itself in kind, which often leads to organizational rigidity. This tendency is one reason why women and minorities are scarce at the top of the management ladder, and why much of our most creative talent stays far away from many organizations that need it most.

The challenge today is not necessarily to *replace* managers but instead to *attract and develop* the best possible talents to meet the changing requirements of the organization. The organization's decision makers again need to anticipate future managerial staffing requirements and develop talented employees as managers to satisfy these needs. The replacement methods should be as systematic as possible to overcome obstacles to management development, but should also allow for the inevitable subjectivity that enters into the process, as well as be open to people and ideas that do *not* fit the status quo.

---

[6] Here again you could think about a mentoring relationship apart from an organizational setting. It can be a valuable support for someone struggling to sort out overall life choices.

Effective succession planning typically starts at the highest level where it can have the most visible impact. Ultimately, however, this type of planning must include all levels of management. If managers can become effective at their own succession planning, they will be able to staff their own departments more effectively. To the extent that succession planning at the top is open to and encourages a diversity of philosophies and practices, this will be reflected at all levels of the system.

PERFORMANCE APPRAISAL

You may have at one time or another taken a course that was very interesting and rewarding until the first grades were handed out. Suddenly, because the grades either had no apparent relation to the course material or seemed arbitrary and unfair, you became disillusioned with the course and the instructor. This happens in many organizations, especially when employees *think* they are doing well, only to find out (often when it's too late) that the boss didn't think the same way.

Few people like to be evaluated and not many like to evaluate others, but people do it all the time in one form or another. Unfortunately, the forms are usually vague, ineffective, based on poor data, full of preconceived ideas, and badly managed. What kind of performance appraisal system could you live with comfortably? Our guess is that it would have to be one with few surprises, clear acceptable criteria, and a way of allowing (even encouraging) people to *learn and grow* from the process. It isn't easy, especially because we live in a competitive society in which performance evaluation tends to be comparative and somewhat threatening. If you remember the times when you were least threatened by evaluation and the times when you were most threatened, you would probably find sharp contrasts in the circumstances. We would guess that in the former instance, the evaluation tended to be positive, came from someone you respected and trusted, was based on information you knew about, and allowed some self-evaluation as part of the procedure. The latter (threatening situation) was not likely to contain the same ingredients.

When you choose to work for an organization, you should learn as much as you can about its approach to performance appraisal. Everything else you do can be colored by the impact of that approach.

An *effective* performance review system can serve two very general purposes. First, it can provide valid information to the organization from line managers concerning how employees perform in their jobs and even what their jobs are. This will help them plan for future needs, emphasizing information about people that reflects the realities of the work the organization will be doing in the future. Second, it can provide employees with constructive feedback on how they are performing in their jobs as viewed by their managers, thus aiding the employees in their own development.

Appraisal systems are more effective if they are based on a mutual agreement between the manager and employee as to performance expectations and job requirements. Then, as discussed in Chapter 6, they provide a basis for control. Similarly, as in management by objectives, a manager and employee have a joint responsibility to play a major role in how those expectations are set and to manage related performance. Thus, effective performance appraisal systems have the potential to provide an opportunity for managers and employees to *communicate* and agree upon what is expected of each, and to plan for performance based on the overall objectives of the organization.

It is difficult to be objective and systematic in this process, because many other factors influence performance and how people are reviewed. These may include the interaction of the personalities of the manager and employee, the level of challenge on the job, and the self-concept of the employee. Factors that influence the manager's perspective include his or her own personal bias, level of expectation, and skill in giving constructive feedback concerning job performance.

Legal implications often dictate the need for jobs to be defined explicitly, for objectives to be set and agreed upon by manager and employee, and for performance appraisal to be based on criteria that include more than just the judgments of the manager. While performance appraisal cannot be completely objective, it can be clear, understood, fair, and open. However, managers often need training to be able to provide feedback to the employee and to make the appraisals as explicit and as helpful to the individual as possible.

Specific Purposes of Performance Appraisal

For the Manager For a manager who can be expected to conduct performance appraisals, there are several purposes:

1. To give feedback—This provides recognition for what the person is doing and lets the individual know where he or she stands.
2. To influence current job behavior—This is a control purpose, seeking to correct inappropriate actions and reinforce appropriate ones.
3. To encourage future appropriate effort.
4. To clarify duties and responsibilities—The performance appraisal process provides the manager with an opportunity to clarify job duties and responsibilities.
5. To provide a basis for granting rewards—Insofar as an organization uses instrumental individual rewards (e.g., merit raises), perform-

ance appraisal identifies who should receive such rewards. It can also provide a basis for giving praise and other nonmonetary rewards.

6. To provide a basis for job change—Good performance may lead to a promotion and poor performance to demotion or firing. In addition, performance appraisals normally contribute to decisions about lateral transfers.
7. To train and develop—A performance appraisal can often be a time for coaching and training. As implied in point 6, it can also lead to working out a plan for on-the-job training through job rotation and task assignment, as well as attendance at formal training programs.
8. To gain a greater understanding of the employee—In systematically reviewing another's actions and performance, one is likely to gain knowledge of the other, but here our emphasis is on the act of discussing performance and the job situation with the individual. Out of this, if treated as a mutual exploration of the situation and not just as the boss passing judgment, you as a manager can better understand how the situation appears through the eyes of the employee, what his or her aspirations and expectations are, and what his or her needs (for support, guidance, or freedom) are.
9. To set goals for the next period—Anticipating the future and establishing goals are important parts of performance appraisal and can help ensure a "good" appraisal next time.
10. To gain feedback on your actions and performance as a supervisor—This will not occur automatically. People do not easily give the boss open feedback, but the opportunity exists, and with receptivity on your part, it can happen.
11. To provide input to the organization's human resources development program—The data generated through thoughtful and systematic appraisal can yield useful information on potential skills, training needs, and probable future recruiting requirements.

For the Employee For you, as an employee being appraised, performance appraisal also serves several purposes, some of which are implicit in the above:

1. To know where you stand—While you may well have some idea of how you are doing in the eyes of your supervisor from daily interaction, the performance appraisal provides a vehicle for this to happen systematically and officially.
2. To get guidance, assistance, and clarification—This can range from gaining clarification on what is expected of you in terms of duties, responsibilities, and effort to getting coaching and training on how to carry out your duties more effectively.
3. To express your needs, wants, and expectations—The performance

appraisal provides an opportunity for the individual to "make demands" on the supervisor and the organization for that which he or she needs in order to be more effective or more satisfied. There may be steps your supervisor can take that you recognize as contributing to your effectiveness but of which he or she is unaware; and there may be experiences and training opportunities you desire that might be overlooked unless you bring them out. Thus, performance appraisal constitutes a structured opportunity for you and your supervisor to engage in an *exchange*, perhaps the most important element of the process.
4. To give feedback to your supervisor on his or her actions and on the organization in general.
5. To set goals for the next period.

For the Organization   When we discussed the process of hiring people, we emphasized the importance of viewing that process in the context of all the dimensions of organizational life. It follows that performance appraisal, as the link between hiring and development activities, should also be viewed in light of the purposes reflected in these organizational dimensions. Below are listed the kinds of questions (certainly not a necessary or exhaustive list) that can usefully be asked about an individual's performance relative to the organization as a total system.

1. *Goals*—Do the individual's goals match those of the organization? Are these understood? Has he or she been successful in achieving or at least moving toward attainment of the goals?
2. *Structure*—Is this person in the right job? Is he or she growing in that job? What other positions should the individual be viewing as future jobs? What is the potential for upward mobility?
3. *Climate*—Is this person working well within the informal system? Does he or she reflect or deviate greatly from the established norms and character of the place? Is that functional or not?
4. *Rewards*—Are the individual's expectations about the reward system realistic? Are the expected rewards forthcoming? Are they resulting in appropriate effort and performance?
5. *Controls*—With what kinds of controls does this person function best? Does that fit with the organization's control system? Is a renegotiation of job expectations called for?
6. *Decision making*—Is the individual able to make the necessary decisions to be effective in his or her job? How is his or her *way* of making decisions affecting the work of others—superiors, subordinates, peers?

In applying questions like these to the performance appraisal process, there is always the danger of creating a philosophy of conformity. This will happen if the appraisal is one-sided, if it is not open to seeing these questions as an opportunity to evaluate the organization itself. In a healthy system, management remains just as open to changing its practices to suit the changing needs of employees as it is to attempting to get employees to adopt existing practices. For example, if you find that one of your employees shows little potential for upward mobility, you might want to evaluate the organization's *opportunities* for upward mobility and not just pass judgment on the employee.

Performance Appraisal Process

As a final point concerning performance appraisal, we want to emphasize that apart from all the formalities, paperwork, emphasis on results, concern for spelling out specific purposes, and so on, the performance appraisal process almost always requires two people—a manager and his or her subordinate—to sit down and discuss how well one of them is doing on the job. Figure 8–4 lists 10 guidelines for effective performance appraisal, but we caution that you not use them prescriptively or dogmatically. They are guidelines that are consistent with what we know in *general* about people's reactions to feedback and that our own experience with line managers has confirmed as valid. Never forget, however, that what actually happens in a performance appraisal session is strongly affected by such factors as the history of such activities in the organization, the previous experiences of the

FIGURE 8–4
Guidelines for Effective Performance Appraisal

1. Have an *interactive process*, not just one-way communication.
2. Start with *self-appraisal* to find out what the person is already aware of.
3. Focus on *both strengths* (+'s) and weaknesses (−'s).
4. Focus on *specific behavior and attitudes* where possible.
5. Deal with things that are *within the control of the person*.
6. Look for places *where you can provide guidance in the future*.
7. Link appraisal to *specific goals*, both organizational and personal.
8. Be sure that the *reward system supports the behavior that is desired*.
9. Negotiate *frequency of appraisal* in terms of job demands and the individual's needs.
10. Work toward *commitment* rather than compliance.

parties involved, external pressures, and a variety of other factors that may not be under anyone's control. There is no magic formula that will make the process easy.

SUMMARY

Human resources development (HRD) is an outgrowth of the more traditional personnel and manpower planning functions that have been part of organizations for many years. In the more recent HRD approaches, a strong emphasis is given to the planning process; all the functions and activities are carried out within that perspective.

There are three basic elements to HRD planning: (1) the creation of a strategic plan, (2) the development of an overall work force plan, and (3) the creation of specific job plans. The strategic plan is designed to meet the overall mission and goals of the organization and is developed in the context of external environmental demands and opportunities (to be covered in the next chapter). The work force plan amounts to the division of labor necessary to accomplish the strategic plan. Job plans include specifications for individual tasks as well as the interactions required among the various jobs.

At an operational level, the functions of HRD encompass the following:

1. *Recruiting, selecting, and hiring.* These activities require attention to both present staffing needs and future job requirements. Furthermore, they are most effectively accomplished with all the basic organizational dimensions in mind (goals, structure, climate, rewards, controls, and decision making).

2. *Training and development.* As job requirements change, employees usually require training in specific skill areas. As people move into higher and broader levels of responsibility, programs are needed to develop managers beyond the specific technical skills they needed for more narrowly circumscribed jobs (e.g., entry-level jobs). In addition to these formal training and development programs, organizations create career ladders, encourage coaching and mentoring by senior managers, and frequently support individual career advancement in external programs leading to advanced degrees and personal growth. Many firms build on all these activities in their approaches to management succession planning.

3. *Performance appraisal.* This aspect of HRD is a vital link in completing the loop. Both the individual and the organization need to know how well actual job performance is contributing to the accomplishment of the job plans, the staffing plan, and, ultimately, the overall

strategic plan. In addition, the individual employee requires feedback relative to his or her own goals and development and relative to management's expectations. Here again it is suggested that effective performance evaluation encompasses performance relative to all the basic organizational dimensions, an approach that will help to maintain a total system perspective.

ANNOTATED BIBLIOGRAPHY

Beer, M., and R. A. Ruh. "Employee Growth through Performance Management." *Harvard Business Review,* July–August 1976, pp. 59–66.

The authors discuss the performance management system (PMS) they helped install at Corning Glass Works. PMS is the formal process used by management at Corning to "manage, measure and improve the performance and potential for advancement" of the company's managers. The authors analyze the system and discuss strategies that could be used to introduce a similar program in other organizations. The strengths and weaknesses of PMS are also discussed.

Bright, W. E. "How One Company Manages Its Human Resources." *Harvard Business Review,* January–February 1976, pp. 81–93.

The author, head of management development at Union Oil Company of California, discusses the human resource planning system at Union Oil. Bright begins by describing the five major aspects of the system: gathering necessary information; formation and adoption of a simulation model permitting the system to adapt to change; establishment of forecasting procedures for manpower needs; procedures for filling managerial openings; and finally, relating employee output to organizational goals. The author then discusses how the system is integrated with overall corporate planning.

Foulkes, F. R. "How Top Nonunion Companies Manage Employees." *Harvard Business Review,* September–October, 1981, pp. 90–106.

The author discusses his findings in a study of 26 large corporations and their personnel management strategies. The study illustrates how creative approaches to human resource management can be conducive to organizational climate, aiding both growth and profitability. The study identified nine common attributes against which managers can measure the effectiveness of their own personnel practices.

Haynes, M. G. "Developing an Appraisal Program." *Personnel Journal,* February 1978, pp. 66–67.

The author outlines the important points that must be considered in developing an appraisal system. Areas such as selecting factors to be appraised, selecting a base from which to make comparison, selecting appraisers, timing, designing forms, and establishing procedures are discussed. Finally, the author describes a three-step approach for implementing and maintaining an appraisal program.

Louis, M. R., "Surprise and Sense Making: What Newcomers Experience in Entering Unfamiliar Organizational Settings." *Administrative Science Quarterly,* June 1980, pp. 226–51.

The author traces the inadequacies in approaches to organizational entry from the growing disillusionment of new members of organizations. He describes directions and limitations of current research on the subject and proposes a new perspective that identifies key features of newcomers' entry experiences, including surprise, contrast, and change. He also describes the processes by which individuals cope with their entry experiences.

Mitchell, T. R., and B. W. Knudsen. "Instrumentality Theory Predictions of Students' Attitudes towards Business and Their Choice of Business as an Occupation." *Academy of Management Journal,* March 1973, pp. 41–52.

Because of the decreasing interest in business careers by college students during the early 1970s, the authors designed a study to investigate why many students avoided business as a career. The study was based on questionnaires sent to randomly selected male business and psychology majors at a large western university. Results suggest that students shun business primarily because they perceive business as a poor means for achieving the goals they aspire to. The implications of the study, as suggested by the authors, are that business is "out of step" with the values held by students, and/or business has done a poor job of publicizing its methods of contributing to society and to one's intrinsic needs.

Morgan, M. A.; D. T. Hall; and A. Martier. "Career Development Strategies in Industry—Where Are We and Where Should We Be?" *Personnel,* March–April 1979, pp. 13–30.

To learn about the present state of career development programs, the authors conducted a telephone survey of 56 organizations, finding that programs were being conducted in career counseling and planning, organizational human resources planning, management development, and training. A discussion of these activities follows, after which the authors discuss several additional methods that should be pursued by human resources planners, the primary focus of these methods being that career development should come from an employee's immediate supervisor.

Sands, W. A. "A Method for Evaluating Alternative Recruiting-Selection Strategies: The CAPER Model." *Journal of Applied Psychology,* 57 (1973), pp. 222–227.

The article describes the Cost of Attaining Personnel Requirements (CAPER) model. The model provides the information necessary to minimize recruitment, selection, and training costs when meeting specified personnel quotas. The author describes the model and illustrates the application of CAPER to a specific problem. Finally, advantages and limitations of the model are discussed.

Schnier, D.B. "The Impact of EEO Legislation on Performance Appraisals." *Personnel,* July–August 1978, pp. 24–34.

This article is a discussion of the importance of accurate, objective, and appropriate performance appraisals in giving promotions, merit raises, job transfers, etc. Inaccurate appraisals may result in charges of discrimination against the employer. The author discusses the legal requirements for appraisal systems and reviews several cases where employers failed to meet these requirements.

Skinner, W. "Big Hat, Not Cattle: Managing Human Resources." *Harvard Business Review,* September–October 1981, pp. 106–11.

Ever since the Hawthorne experiments on motivation 60 years ago, managers have sought the answer to the problem of human motivation. For the majority the problem remains as apparent today as it was then despite the tremendous research in human behavior in organizations. The author of the article presents four reasons why managers have difficulty in managing human resources, and he discusses five processes that should be used in the management of a firm's personnel in order to improve human resource management. These processes include: doing "the basics" better, establishing a seven-year time horizon for human resources planning and operation, developing an appropriate strategy, and obtaining and developing human resource personnel with adequate skills and experience.

Thornton, G. C. "The Relationship between Supervisory and Self-Appraisals of Executive Performance." *Personnel Psychology,* Winter 1960, pp. 441–55.

The author discusses a study that investigated the relationship between supervisory perception and self-perception of executive performance. The study was conducted on 27 executives of a large manufacturing organization. The criterion used for appraisal was an executive's promotability. The author concludes that individuals tend to rate themselves higher than do their supervisors. Also, executives who overrate themselves tend to be considered the least promotable. The author states that an organization must understand this characteristic of performance appraisal programs to enable such programs to attain their objectives.

Wanous, J. P. "Organizational Entry: Newcomers Moving from Outside to Inside." *Psychological Bulletin,* July 1977, pp. 601–18.

The author reviews a number of studies dealing with organizational entry from the individual's perspective. Three areas of research are investigated by the author: (1) how individuals choose organizations; (2) how accurate the information possessed by outsiders prior to entry is; and (3) what the impact of recruitment activities is on individual choice.

SUGGESTED READINGS

Bailyn, Lotte "Involvement and Accommodation in Technical Careers: An Inquiry into the Relation to Work at Mid-career." In *Organizational Careers: Some New Perspectives* ed. J. Van Maanen. London: John Wiley & Sons, 1977.

Barker, R., and P. Gump *Big School Small School.* Stanford, Calif.: Stanford University Press, 1964.

Byham, W. C. "The Assessment Center as an Aid in Management Development." In *Contemporary Problems in Personnel,* rev. ed., ed. Hamner and Schmidt. Chicago: St. Clair Press, 1977.

Chew, W. B., and R. L. Justice "EEO Modeling for Large, Complex Organizations." *Human Resource Planning* 2(1979), pp. 57–70.

Cummings, L. L., and D. P. Schwab *Performance in Organizations: Determinants and Appraisal.* Glenview, Ill.: Scott, Foresman, 1973.

Dunham, R. B. "The Measurement and Dimensionality of Job Characteristics." *Journal of Applied Psychology* 61(1976), pp. 404–409.

Dyer, L., and E. C. Wesman "Affirmative Action Planning at AT&T: An Applied Model." *Human Resource Planning* 2(1979), pp. 81–90.

French, John R. P. Jr. "Person Role Fit." In *Occupational Stress,* ed. A. McLean. Springfield, Ill.: Charles C Thomas, 1974, pp. 70–79.

French, W. L., and C. H. Bell *Organization Development.* 2d ed. Englewood Cliffs, N.J.: Prentice-Hall, 1978.

Glaser, Edward M. *Productivity Gains through Worklife Improvements.* New York: Harcourt Brace Jovanovich, 1976.

Goldstein, I. L. *Training: Program Development and Evaluation.* Belmont, Calif.: Wadsworth, 1974.

Gyllenhammar, Pehr G. "How Volvo Adapts Work to People." *Harvard Business Review,* July–August 1977, pp. 105–13.

Hackman, J. R, and G. R. Oldham "Developing the Job Diagnostic Survey." *Journal of Applied Psychology* 60(1975), pp. 159–70.

Hall, Douglas T. *Careers in Organizations.* Santa Monica, Calif.: Goodyear Publishing, 1976.

Hand, H., and J. Slocum "A Longitudinal Study of the Effects of a Human Relations Training Program on Managerial Effectiveness." *Journal of Applied Psychology* 56(1972), pp. 412–17.

Heneman, H. G.; D. P. Schwab; J. A. Fossum; and L. D. Dyer *Personnel/Human Resource Management.* Homewood, Ill.: Richard D. Irwin, 1980.

Janger, A. R. *The Personnel Function: Changing Objectives and Organization.* New York: Conference Board, 1977.

Kanter, Rosabeth Moss *Men and Women of the Corporation.* New York: Basic Books, 1977.

Kanter, Rosabeth Moss *Work and Family in the United States: A Critical Review and Agenda for Research and Policy.* New York: Russell Sage, 1977.

Levinson, D. *The Seasons of a Man's Life.* New York: Alfred A. Knopf, 1978.

McGregor, D. "An Uneasy Look at Performance Appraisal." *Harvard Business Review* 35(1957), pp. 89–94.

Pfeffer, Jeffrey, and Huseyin Leblebici "Executive Recruitment and the Development of Interfirm Organizations." *Administrative Science Quarterly* 18(1973), pp. 449–61.

Ridgway, V. F. "Dysfunctional Consequences of Performance Measurements." *Administrative Science Quarterly* 1(1956), pp. 240–47.

Schwab, D. P., and L. L. Cummings "A Theoretical Analysis of the Impact of Task Scope on Employee Performance." *Academy of Management Review* 1(1976), pp. 23–35.

Sheehy, G. *Passages: Predictable Crises of Adult Life.* New York: E. P. Dutton, 1976.

Stone, T. H. "An Examination of Six Prevalent Assumptions Concerning Performance Appraisal." *Public Personnel Management* 2(1973), pp. 408–17.

Wanous, J. *Organizational Entry.* Reading, Mass.: Addison-Wesley Publishing, 1980.

Weathersby, Rita. "Developmental Perspectives on Adult Uses of Education." Ph.D. dissertation, Harvard University, 1977.

CHAPTER 9

The Organization and Its Environment

INTRODUCTION

A HIGH-LEVEL UNIVERSITY ADMINISTRATOR sits in her office pondering the seemingly infinite variety of problems she faces. She remembers the time when the main business of a college or university was to educate young people and prepare them for the tasks of living and growing. Administration was primarily a matter of making sure that there were faculty to provide the education, students to receive it, facilities to support it, and money to pay for it. The outside world was the source of students and financial resources, as well as the recipient of the university's "products." And that world was reasonably stable and predictable, which clearly, in the mind of our administrator, is no longer the case. The world is changing so rapidly and unpredictably that yesterday's decisions seem obsolete today. The university has become a dinosaur that cannot seem to keep up with the changes, and it is too large to get rid of in favor of some other institutional form, presuming a better one could be invented.

Our administrator considers such questions as: Has the world changed so much that we need to redefine our mission and goals? Our university structure seems to be outdated; how can we change it when it is so firmly cast in concrete? How do we hang on to a climate of collegiality in the face of financial crises and threats to long-standing traditions? What will be the rewards for teaching in the coming years? Will benefits and tenure mean very much in an economy such as ours? Do we need to find better ways to make decisions so that we are more responsive to the demands of the outside world? As faculty mobility becomes more limited and as programs need to change, should we think about reeducating some of our faculty members, possibly in their own fields and possibly in new fields? These questions weigh heavily on our administrator; "If only," she thinks, "we could exist as a nice little separate island!" But no individual, family, institution, community, corporation, or government is an island unto itself. Each affects and is affected by its surrounding environment. Sometimes the effects are immediate and direct; sometimes they are delayed and subtle. But they are, nevertheless, important in the lives of these entities, sometimes so important that it becomes difficult to separate what is outside from what is inside the organization.

In previous chapters we alluded to a variety of environmental factors as they relate to different dimensions of organizational life. When we discussed goals, we introduced the concept of open system goals—that is, those that are imposed, more or less, on an organization by the outside world. In Chapter 3 we discussed the importance of such forces as changing technology and rapid growth as they affect the structure of an organization. Chapter 4 made a special point of considering an organization's surrounding culture and its impact on the climate and customs of the organization itself. In short, we have brought to your attention the fact that "no organization is an island" but is, in fact, *an open system that engages in a constant exchange of goods, services, and information with a changing and often turbulent world.*

The topic of the organization and its environment can and does take up volumes of space, given the research and concepts that have proliferated over the past 30 to 40 years (if not longer). A single chapter in a book like this can do no more than give you a taste of the issues, and a rather superficial one at that. Therefore, what we have set out to accomplish in this chapter is to provide you with a way of thinking about the issues, a framework for organizing your approach to understanding and managing them from the perspective of an organizational member and a prospective manager. The annotated bibliography and suggested readings at the end of the chapter will help you to delve further into any topics of special interest to you. In addition, the boxes in the chapter provide you with glimpses of some recent major developments that organizational planners would do well to consider as they look to the future.

The final chapter in the book is designed to serve the special purpose of helping you pull together some key elements of previous chapters. We emphasize how an adequate consideration of goals, structure, climate, rewards, controls, decision making, and human resource development must include changes and developments in the world at large. This is not to suggest that organizations are necessarily passive victims of the outside environment; very often an organization is itself the vehicle for changing the external world in very important ways. Bear witness to the entire history of the Industrial Revolution, with the automobile, television, space technology, nuclear energy, and the computer, to name only a few. What is outside one organization at any given time is also inside another. And what is outside an organization at any given time might later be inside that same organization, and vice versa.

At the end of the chapter, we will provide you with a way of looking at the organizational planning process from an open systems perspective. We will show you how it is possible for a manager to view the future as a set of opportunities, as well as constraints, that can be influenced and controlled by an organization, not just accommodated to passively. Although environmental forces can be powerful and, in many cases, well beyond the control of any single organization, it is possible for any organization, with the proper imagination and lead time, to shape much of its own destiny. But this is a matter for discussion later in the chapter.

Your Personal System

Before going further with our discussion of the organization and its environment, we'd like you to draw a parallel between yourself and an organization. Think of yourself as a system—that is, a network of interrelated parts and functions designed to perform certain activities. You have several sub-systems: your respiratory system, circulatory system, central nervous system, autonomic nervous system, musculature, and so forth. Each of these has a structure and processes, but none can function for very long, if at all, without the others. And these sub-systems depend for survival on exchanges with the external world —air, water, food. As a total integrated personal system, which includes your mental processes as well as the physical ones, you cope with, adapt to, and attempt to control the environment to ensure your survival and growth. In its most fundamental sense, that is what life is all about.

In one environment—for example, your home—you behave in certain ways, exercise certain choices, and eat certain foods that are in part influenced by that environment and that may be quite different from the behaviors you exercise at school, with friends, or wherever you spend time outside your home. At the same time, as you grow and change in your own ideas and habits, you bring these changes into each setting, including your home, and thus produce an impact on those environments.

If you have experienced the effects of moving from one neighborhood to another or from one part of the country to another, or even to a foreign culture, you can probably identify ways in which the external environment—local opinion and customs, political climate, and numbers of people—has had visible effects on your own behavior and that of others in your family. Often we cannot appreciate the power of those effects until we have lived in a foreign environment and then returned home. Think about some ways in which your style of speaking, dressing, and relating to others are affected by the environmental context. (Chapter 4 showed you the power of organizational norms.) Indeed, you are an open system and not an island. As we return to a discussion of organizations, keep in mind the personal parallels. The very same variables that affect organizations of every size also affect individuals of every variety. The concepts are not very remote from your own experience.

MULTIPLE ENVIRONMENTS

So far we have referred to the environment of an organization as though it were a single entity. In fact, most, if not all, organizations deal with more than one environment—economic, political/legal, technological, social/cultural, and physical. And each of these has relatively static (stable or unchanging) attributes as well as dynamic (changing or unstable) attributes. Let us look at each of these environments and then at their static and dynamic attributes.

Economic Environment

At one time it was possible to anticipate (within reasonable limits) economic fluctuations to a degree that made financial decisions something less than earthshaking. At a general level, if you are looking ahead to full-time employment after graduation, you need to have some idea of the probable state of the economy at the time you hit the employment market. If it looks like jobs will be in short supply, you may want to start looking earlier than if it looks like jobs will be plentiful.

Most organizations have to anticipate future economic forces in exactly the same way, but obviously on a much broader scale. While you may be affected primarily by local economic considerations, most organizations are affected by regional, national, and international factors. Furthermore, if the particular kind of job you seek is in a context where economic forces tend to be relatively stable (e.g., the nearby supermarket), you are in a less uncertain position than if you seek employment in a setting that tends to be affected by sudden increases in the cost of gasoline (e.g., a lake resort in the mountains of upstate New York). (See Box 9–1.)

Although we know that economic forces in remote areas of the world have always had the potential to produce significant effects on our own economy, it took the oil crisis of the 1970s to bring home the full meaning of that fact. In some respects, the United States has always considered itself large enough to absorb or adapt to sudden economic

BOX 9–1

UNDERSTANDING THE PAST CAN HELP US SHAPE THE FUTURE

The nation is clearly in a state of transition that challenges assumptions about the organization and the goals of economic activity. The process of change itself and the outcome are tinged with a high degree of uncertainty not only for individuals but also for the business practices and institutions that have so strongly shaped American life over the past two centuries. It may well be that we are entering one of those periods of great discontinuities of change comparable in the history of Western civilization to the Renaissance and Reformation. Many Americans are questioning whether the business of Americans is business as we have known it. It is particularly fitting therefore in the year of our national bicentennial to look to the past to understand what we have become and even more important to ponder the significance of this experience in terms of our future.

Source: *The National Observer*, February 28, 1976.

fluctuations overseas. But in recent decades, our country, like the lion that was bitten by the flea, has found itself flinching at some economic bites of smaller countries.

Technological Environment

In a recent (June 18, 1981) issue of *Public Utilities Fortnightly*, Irwin and Ela stated, "Technology is erasing distinctions between telephone switching equipment and the digital computer. Both can receive, process, store and route." The implications of that single technological development could be staggering, not just in terms of organizational territories, but also in relation to government regulations, interstate information flow, and international control over information ownership. When you consider the simultaneous advancements in microprocessing, fiber optics, and telecommunications, you cannot help wondering how anyone—individuals, companies, governments—will be able to keep track of, much less control, the amount and kind of information that will pass across national and international borders. (See Box 9–2.)

Similarly, revolutionary changes are occurring *inside* organizations as a result of developments in computer technology. The amount, kind, and rate of information flow across departments and divisions of a company offer obvious advantages to management, but also pose problems of protecting confidential data. In many offices you will find microprocessors on every desk, word processors in place of conventional typewriters, and central data banks for information storage and retrieval. The implications of such developments are enormous: the purchase and maintenance of state-of-the-art equipment, training of personnel, and storage and protection of critical data. We have entered a whole new era of management as a result of rapid changes in computer technology alone; what about the added impact of other related areas of

BOX 9–2

THE IMPACT OF TECHNOLOGY CAN BE MANAGED

Technological changes in the 1980s "will undoubtedly affect working environments massively, powerfully, often unpredictably, often perniciously," warns Wickham Skinner, a Harvard business professor. However, there is a trend among companies toward controlling the technological impact that has historically been an enormous influence in shaping work place tasks and environments. Equipment and process technologies will proliferate, but the choices will be shaped by consideration about people and their potential, including the better development of human resources. Skinner predicts that U.S. managers "are no longer going to let the working environment just happen."

Source: *The Futurist*, April 1980.

technological growth? For example, developments in fiber optics in the last five years may eventually make the use of cable obsolete, which is an obvious advantage to the communications industry, but perhaps not so for cable manufacturers. You can imagine the implications for organizational planning and the redefinition of long-range goals for many companies. (Public policy also affects technology—Box 9–3.)

Political/Legal Environment

For about 10 years (the 1970s) political and legal forces exerted major pressures on public and many private organizations to abide by affirmative action guidelines. The university administrator discussed at the beginning of this chapter is an example of someone who would have been faced with such pressures and often without the wherewithal to meet them. Competition for qualified minority group and women faculty was (and may still be) quite fierce. The threat of losing grant money from the Department of Health, Education, and Welfare, the Department of Labor, and the National Science Foundation, among others, made the task a matter of survival for many valuable programs and research projects based at universities. Additional informal political pressures from volunteer groups, women's organizations, student groups, and the surrounding community added to the tensions faced by university officials.

In the private sector, the legal pressures were not as clear-cut, at least in regard to direct sanctions that could be imposed on any large corporation. Depending on the turnover rate in the company, many firms found it nearly impossible to bring minorities and women into jobs previously dominated by white men at a rate that would satisfy the desires of the government, the interested organizations and associations, or the prospective employees themselves. In addition, the counterpressures that developed—most from a need to protect vested

BOX 9–3

CAN PUBLIC POLICY RESPOND TO TECHNOLOGICAL CHANGE?
To say that technology exhibits change, dynamism, and opportunity borders on the cliché. There can be little doubt that the strategic option pursued by the U.S. economy will be profound and far reaching. If public policy anticipates the future, broadens its portfolio, unleashes energy, rewards risk taking, and abolishes regulation, then the U.S. information economy will at least have an opportunity to flourish and prosper in the decade of the 1980s. If, on the other hand, policy continues its jurisdictional creep, stifles creative entry, regulates risks, and penalizes entrepreneurship, then our information economy risks forfeiting its future upon the altar of yesterday.

Source: M. R. Irwin, "Information Technology and U.S. Policy," *Computer Networks* 5 (1981).

BOX 9-4

GOVERNMENT REGULATORY AGENCIES

Below are some familiar examples of the agencies used by the federal government to regulate business and industrial practices. We show two examples in each of several areas; for a more complete and detailed listing, see the April 4, 1977, issue of *Business Week*.

Banking and finance: Federal Reserve Board (1913)	Sets federal money and credit policy; regulates banks that are members of the Federal Reserve System.
Securities and Exchange Commission (1934)	Regulates all publicly traded securities; polices laws preventing fraud.
Competition and trade: Federal Communications Commission (1934)	Regulates and licenses all broadcast communications media; regulates telephone and telegraph rates and service.
Federal Trade Commission (1914)	Prevents unfair trade practices; protects consumer rights and maintains fair competition.
Employment and discrimination: Equal Employment Opportunity Commission (1964)	Deals with matters of employment discrimination based on sex, race, and religion.
National Labor Relations Board (1935)	Regulates the practices of unions and employers relative to labor.
Energy and the environment: Corps of Engineers (1824)	Has some control in construction along navigable waterways.
Environmental Protection Agency (1970)	Develops and maintains standards for clean air and water; controls pollution from all sources.
Safety and health: Food and Drug Administration (1931)	Controls the safety and purity of drugs, medical devices, and food.
Occupational Safety and Health Administration (1971)	Regulates safety and health conditions for all nongovernmental work settings.

interests or fear of being pushed out of secure jobs—often placed employers in great dilemmas. (See Box 9-4.)

With a change in the national political picture, with the recent defeat of the Equal Rights Amendment, and with increasing fears of economic depression, it appears that the pendulum will swing back to a point where many organizations, both public and private, will face less external pressure or at least less severe sanctions for failures to comply to federal laws. You might find it important to consider how these events affect your own future both positively and negatively.

Social/Cultural Environment

In the early 1970s an oil tycoon attempted to buy a considerable area of land in a small town near the seacoast of New England. He wanted to build a large oil refinery in a location that was easily accessible to tankers and had the economic advantage of low taxes. Although his appeal to the local residents made some sense economically (tax revenues, job opportunities, etc.), the prospects of such an operation in the midst of a relatively quiet, rural, and, as it happens, university town represented an enormous threat to the lifestyle of the residents. It was a violation of all the aspects of life that drew people to the area in the first place. To make a long story short, the collective reactions and actions of the residents produced such powerful opposition to the idea of the refinery that the company finally backed down and decided to seek another location.

Many companies are growing and expanding into new geographic locations all over the country and, for that matter, all over the globe. We have all heard tales of unfortunate incidents where "aggressive Yankees" were not very well received in more passive cultures or societies. The stereotype of the ugly American grew out of a combination of zealous enthusiasm and social insensitivity to the feelings of others, particularly people whose values and customs were unlike those in the United States. And even within the continental United States, wide variations in lifestyles and social customs need to be considered carefully by any organization seeking to establish "residence" in a given region. (Individuals also face re-location decisions. See Box 9-5.)

Not only are organizations affected by social forces around them, but organizations also can and do affect those forces in powerful ways. If a high-growth company were to move into a semirural area, this would certainly have an impact on job opportunities, work patterns, the attractiveness of the area as a place to live, the school system, and housing. Organizations interact with their environments; the effects are mutual, hopefully beneficial, but not always. Suppose the oil refinery had actually been built in the small New England town. Imagine the

BOX 9-5

> THE SOCIAL ENVIRONMENT IS IMPORTANT TO A MANAGER'S OVERALL SATISFACTION
>
> With companies opening and closing offices all the time, the unwanted transfer is an occupational hazard for a lot of employees. But the problem is especially vexing for small-town executives, who often grow roots in a community that are deeper than their ties to a corporation. The roots such managers put down can make the transfer problem equally vexing for their employers.

Source: *The Wall Street Journal*, May 22, 1981.

probable industrialization of the entire region as a consequence of spin-off industries. Is it beneficial? It depends on whom you ask.

On a large scale, such social phenomena as consumerism, the quality of life movement, and various other forces that pressure business and industry to be more socially responsible have, in recent years, combined with politics and the law to make the voice of the public loud and powerful. Whether or not some of the economic and political pressures of the 1980s will reverse that trend remains to be seen (at least at this writing). But whatever happens, it is clear that organizations are neither immune to these external forces, nor passive victims of them.

External Physical Environment

If you lived in New England or Colorado during the winters of 1979–1980 and 1980–81, you were painfully aware of the agonies of the ski industry. A resort can manufacture just so much artifical snow to compensate for a lack of natural snowfall.

Any business that depends on nature for its basic resources is highly subject to the vicissitudes of the physical environment. Farming, sports, and leisure industries are familiar examples of areas directly affected by climate and weather conditions. It's interesting to note how some professional sports have chosen to eliminate weather as a factor by constructing enclosed arenas. It's also interesting to compare how some sports, like football, are played in any weather, whereas others (probably most) are played only when the weather is suitable.

Geographic location is an obvious physical factor affecting an organization. One would hardly locate a hydroelectric plant in the desert. This is an example of an industry that is highly dependent on nature for its power; but nature, in this case, is very predictable. Nothing in nature should be taken for granted. It was once believed that the United States had access to an endless supply of inexpensive oil!

Apart from the direct effects of the external physical environment on an organization, there are some important indirect ones. The setting—

rural, urban, near main roads—can make a place more or less attractive to employees. A company that needs to employ large numbers of unskilled workers would be wise to locate in an urban area where there is public transportation and large numbers of potential employees. In contrast, a knowledge-based industry might want to be in an area that is attractive to college graduates whose upward mobility draws them into the suburbs. Although some of these choices seem obvious, there is rarely a simple relationship between the needs of the organization and the character of the surrounding environment. Large companies have multiple and often conflicting needs, not all of which can be satisfied by any one physical setting. In the final analysis, it is management's job to balance the choices to find ones that are optimal and then find ways to cope with environmental factors that pose problems. For example, some companies establish their own busing systems for employees who need transportation to and from work.

With regard to the visual physical environment, many creative organizations really capitalize on their surroundings architecturally. Enhancing the attractiveness of the physical plant by blending buildings and geography can often instill pride on the part of employees, as well as make a job a little more inviting at 8:00 in the morning.

Finally, we cannot overlook the impact of the physical environment on the economics of the organization. Fuel costs for companies in northern climates have forced many to near bankruptcy, if not actual closing. At the opposite extreme are the enormous costs of air conditioning during the summer in temperate areas and year-round in very hot areas. An ironic aspect of all this is that technology provided the wherewithal to control the effects of the outside temperature; then the costs of the technology (i.e., the fuel it required) became a problem to manage.

In summary, we want to emphasize again that organizations exist in a number of external environments—economic, technological, political/legal, social/cultural, and physical—and must learn to live with, adapt to, influence, and actively manage those environments. To do so effectively, managers of organizations need to understand the interplay of forces in these various environments and to what degree these forces are controllable. A failure to do so, along with a failure to plan ways to cope with these forces, can lead to a major crisis in an industry.

Furthermore, sometimes an effort to deal with one set of environmental forces can generate problems with other forces. For example, during the 1950s and 1960s the electric utilities were able to use a "build and grow" strategy. Rates could be lowered as expansion resulted in greater efficiency, which in turn produced a higher return on investment. Everyone was happy; customers got more for their money, inexpensive fuel was available to more and more homes and businesses, and the utilities had no problem raising capital and, therefore, continuing their growth. Then came the 1970s; technology in that industry reached its limit with respect to reducing costs, inflation escalated with a sharp rise in construction costs, environmental concerns put constraints on alternative fuels and created a furor over the use of nuclear energy, and the oil crisis pushed the costs of that fuel up by billions of dollars a year. The planned effort to shift to nuclear power ultimately ended up costing the utilities and the public more than anyone anticipated. The electric companies could not seem to manage all the different environments at the same time.

In the next section of the chapter, we will discuss a number of qualitative attributes that apply to each of the environments, and then we will show how these attributes can guide a manager's efforts to deal with the internal workings of his or her organization, from goal setting to human resources planning.

STATIC VERSUS DYNAMIC ATTRIBUTES OF THE ENVIRONMENT[1]

We use the terms *static* and *dynamic* in a relative sense; the former refers to aspects of the environment that show relatively little, if any, change, while the latter refers to the changing aspects of the environment. The static attributes include four factors: *complexity, routineness, interconnectedness,* and *remoteness.* The dynamic factors include *rate of change* and *predictability of change.* In this section, we will show that organizations that deal with environmental demands that are *simple, routine, from a single source,* and *local* are faced with easier management decisions than are those that deal with demands that are *complex, nonroutine, from several interconnected sources,* and *sociogeographically remote.* Furthermore, you will see how *rapidly changing, unpredictable* environments place incredibly stressful demands on organizations, in contrast to *slowly and predictably changing* environments.

We will first look at each of the static and dynamic attributes briefly and then discuss their impact on the organizational dimensions covered in previous chapters.

STATIC ATTRIBUTES

Environmental Complexity

Environmental complexity refers to the number and variety of constituencies that make demands on an organization's resources. Highly

---

[1] The framework presented here comes from Robert Miles's chapters on the environment in *Macro Organizational Behavior* (Santa Monica, Calif.: Goodyear Publishing, 1980).

diversified manufacturing companies have to deal with customer-supplier complexity; hospitals in densely populated areas usually have to deal with a greater variety of medical problems than do hospitals in rural areas; and public universities have to be responsive even more than private universities to a widely diverse set of outside social and political demands in addition to the normal educational pressures.

Although environmental complexity adds to the demands made on an organization, it also can provide a base of stability or security. Many large corporations are finding that one way to deal with economic uncertainties is to diversify—in some cases by adding new product lines (e.g., Exxon moving into the computer business) and in others by merging with or acquiring other companies (e.g., Sohio's purchase of Kennecott Copper). Very shortly we will discuss the effects of environmental complexity on the internal workings of an organization. You will then be able to appreciate some of the trade-offs involved when a company, agency, or institution considers the costs and benefits of having a highly complex external environment. For now, we just want you to keep in mind that while a simple environment (e.g., a few major customers, a few product lines, a limited clientele) can be more easily managed and adapted to, an organization can also become too dependent for its survival on that simple outside environment. A manufacturer of coal mining equipment in England nearly went bankrupt when its principal customer, the Coal Board, cancelled orders for new equipment following the discovery of North Sea gas. The ultimate survival of the company came as a result ultimately of diversification, which, in turn, meant dealing with a more complex environment.

There is a firm in this country that deals in rare coins. Because its market is so simple and segmented, it is often at the mercy of external forces. The company has been known to go from hundreds of thousands of dollars in the red to millions of dollars in the black over a time as short as a year. And there is little the company can do to control that phenomenon; it is an inherent attribute of the simple external environment with which it must deal.

Environmental Routineness

Some organizations establish "bread and butter" customers, outlets, or clientele as a way of establishing a secure base of operation. Part of that security is the routineness of the relationship—that is, the fact that the organization can establish in advance a schedule for sales, services, delivery, and so forth that simplifies the planning and control functions. Furthermore, in the case of a manufacturing firm, this permits large production runs that may cut costs, permit automation, lower overhead on inventory storage, and, in general, increase efficiency throughout the stages of production. Or in a public agency that provides services on a regular basis to a given known clientele, the scheduling of visits and overall service hours tends to be a relatively simple task, which is not true, for example, for an emergency room in a city hospital.

With the kind of competition and market forces that affect today's large manufacturers and service institutions, *nonroutinenes* is undoubtedly more typical of external environments. Even where it is possible to limit the number of product lines to routinize the manufacturing process, very often the sales and service functions are more dependent on the particular needs of customers at any given time.

Whereas surgery or medical treatments can be established according to advanced schedules that foster routine, many activities in a hospital have to be "on call" at all times. We've all been awakened at 6 A.M. to have our temperature taken; is that in response to a sudden fever? Hardly. It is clearly a reflection of the institution's need to maintain routines that meet medical requirements in a manner that maximizes efficiency. Hospitals attempt to carry that concern into relations with the outside world by establishing routine admitting, discharging, and visiting hours, to cite a few examples. By doing so, the hospital can also increase the availability of resources to respond to the nonroutine external demands—for example, emergencies or unexpected influxes of patients in normally routine areas.

How routine the course registration process in a university can be depends on the extent to which the managers of that process can know in advance the demands of the students who are registering. Preregistration helps to establish a routine, but there are far too many uncertainties to ever expect the total process to be anything except full of nonroutine demands.

Most organizations make every effort to establish contractual relationships with the outside world that help to make the management process predictable and controllable. There are obvious limits faced by every organization in its efforts to minimize nonroutineness; organizational effectiveness requires learning how to operate within those limits.

Environmental Interconnectedness

When the United Auto Workers Union (UAW) negotiates contracts with General Motors, Ford, and Chrysler, it can treat each corporation as a separate entity as opposed to a set of interconnected bodies. The similarity among the separate contracts is more a reflection of the union demands than it is a common posture taken by the respective companies operating jointly. Successes or failures to conclude agreements with Chrysler do not preclude outcomes with either of the other big three, although there is certainly some carryover psychologically. From the other side of the fence, there is no way in which General Motors, for example, can negotiate with local UAW officials without being affected by the interconnectedness of the entire network of locals as part of the total entity of the UAW.

In the public sector, government agencies are often interconnected in ways that make it difficult for organizations to cope with the demands of any one. For example, a university's failure to comply with federal affirmative action guidelines can result in the loss of federal grants from agencies that have no *obvious* connection with the Department of Labor. The interconnectedness of organizations can and does constrain their separate freedom to enter contractual arrangements with organizations outside their network. While the legality of some connections may be questioned (questions of collusion, price fixing, and the like), there is no denying the reality of their effects. The Tucker automobile never went into production because Mr. Tucker could not get the steel companies to sell him the necessary steel. Their interconnectedness with the powerful big three automobile manufacturers proved to be an insurmountable obstacle. This often happens when the inventor of any product that might undercut the markets of a major corporation attempts to develop and manufacture that product. All kinds of external environmental opposition appear to protect the market from "invasion." Recently the Japanese auto manufacturers have had to deal with increasing interconnectedness among the various organizations that collectively could block their growth in the United States. Conceivably, the auto manufacturers, the unions, and the federal government could all join ranks to make it *impossible* for Japanese cars to be sold here. There would be little the Japanese firms could do to cope with that *combination* of forces.[2]

In general, organizations find it easier to deal with noninterconnected external environments; at least the freedom to negotiate is greater. Interconnected external environments usually represent more formidable forces with which to cope, as well as a more intricate, complicated, and often subtle combination of factors to understand.

Environmental Remoteness

It is one thing for a manufacturer to deal with the local government's restrictions on land usage and quite another for it to deal with the federal regulations on air pollution. The former is geographically and socially immediate; the latter is remote. The differences in the opportunities and, very likely, the ability of the company to influence one or the other are obvious. The uncertainties of coping with remote environmental forces may lead an organization to do no more than protect itself from the possibility of outside pressures, rather than make any attempt to influence them at a distance.

---

[2] The *Fortune* article described in Box 9–6 is a recent example of the success just such a coalition can have.

BOX 9-6

> AMERICA, INC.
>
> In a system of open competitive bidding, a company normally assumes that the lowest bidder on a contract will be the recipient of that contract. However, sometimes the interconnectedness of business, labor, and government interests can result in a situation that violates the true spirit of this type of free competition. This happened recently to a Japanese company that came in as low bidder to build a major portion of the fiber-optics telephone network being installed by AT&T to link Boston, New York, and Washington.
>
> As reported in the March 22, 1982, *Fortune* magazine article entitled "Japan Runs into America Inc.," "A coalition of Congressmen and bureaucrats, inspired by a corporate lobbyist and abetted by a labor leader, has apparently locked a major Japanese corporation, Fujitsu, Ltd., out of an important and potentially lucrative American project for which it was the undisputed low bidder." Although the action protected some American business interests, *Fortune* points out that it "could cost consumers many millions more as the benefits of competition are weakened in the developing fiber-optics market."

As an organization grows and expands beyond just a few locations, the once remote forces become more immediate in the sense that they are present in many locations and tend to be exerted more forcefully. As a consequence, large corporations establish offices in Washington or join in lobbies that are designed to increase their influence over the external pressures; an important part of this effort is the reduction of remoteness by placing representatives close to the sources of external pressure.

It often happens that small local agencies, institutions, or companies fail to perceive the impact of remote environmental demands until these strike them at the least opportune time. Federal health standards have resulted in the closing of many nursing and convalescent homes across the country. The administrators of many of these homes claimed ignorance of the standards; many had simply failed to take them seriously enough, since they seemed so remote, to generate immediate corrective action. Remoteness obviously affects one's perceptions of the *realities* of environmental factors, and it also affects the extent to which one feels compelled to deal with them.

Remoteness also occurs along the dimension of time. Legislation that is pending or regulations that will be implemented "next year" tend to be viewed less seriously than already enacted legislation or regulations that require appropriate actions now. For years the Army Corps of Engineers, acting in accordance with federal regulations, planned to take over coastal management and control of thousands of inland waterways, including lakes and rivers that serve only recreational purposes. The prospect of such a seemingly absurd action was not taken seriously by the local governments and communities affected until the corps actually began to implement the policy. The backlash was enormous, producing countereactions that ultimately reverberated through the halls of Congress. In a large number of cases, the Army Corp of Engineers was forced to back down and stay away from the more popular recreational bodies of water. This is an example of how the tables can turn on an external agency, making it subject to its own outside pressures.

DYNAMIC ATTRIBUTES

Rate of Change

The more rapidly things change in the external environment, the more stress there is on an organization to maintain a constant state of readiness to adapt or cope. A computer firm that commits itself to manufacturing units with 64K chips may find itself in trouble when a 256K chip appears on the scene. Preplanning for sudden and rapid shifts in design, production, and marketing is essential to the survival of any high-technology company. This aspect of such an industry makes it challenging and exciting, but you can easily see the stress it tends to create at the same time.

In contrast, advances in medicine and medical technology, while often dramatic, tend to occur at a slower pace than those in most industries. These changes can have powerful implications for diagnosis and treatment, as well as for the management of patient care both in and out of a hospital, but normally the medical and allied professions have adequate lead time to plan for such changes. A university is an interesting example of an organization in which some divisions (programs, departments) experience rapid growth and change, at least for a time, while others remain relatively the same for many years. Business administration and computer science programs are growing and changing much more rapidly than are programs in philosophy or history. Even within administrative operations, some areas have been making rapid changes in data processing (e.g., registration, financial accounting procedures), while others continue to rely on more historically tried and true human-based methods (e.g., admissions, advising, financial aid).

As we will see in the next section, the rate of change of the external environment does not normally pose as difficult a problem as does the *predictability* of that change.

Predictability of Change

Our current state of the art in data gathering, data processing, and forecasting has enabled us to predict trends and changes on a number of important fronts. We have reasonably valid pictures of population composition, migration patterns, and educational needs for at least the next 10 years, for example. Partly because these kinds of changes are relatively slow, but also because they are normally not directly affected by sudden dramatic shifts in other environmental forces, we are able to manage internal organizational life in ways that adapt to or handle these outside influences.

Other areas of our environment are much more turbulent, and even where the change is not rapid, it comes in unexpected bursts. There can be a sudden breakthrough in the computer field, the discovery of a vaccine that eliminates a particular disease, an oil embargo, a skirmish in the Middle East, a sudden upsurge in the price of gold, or the discovery of North Sea gas (see the example discussed earlier). Events like these in and of themselves can have powerful effects on the operations and even the survival of organizations; when they occur "out of the blue" (or seem to), many of the consequences are difficult to manage and may generate organizational crises.

Most organizations make every effort to predict the unpredictable but usually end up learning to live with some degree—and often a high degree—of unpredictability in the external environment. Companies that learn from their own experiences tend not to repeat their mistakes; they use the experience of being caught unaware as a basis for structural and policy changes that help maintain a more acute state of awareness and readiness in the future. In a world like ours, there are severe limits in our ability to reduce unpredictability. In the next section of the chapter, we will provide examples of ways in which organizations use various dimensions of their infrastructure to cope with the demands generated by the outside world, both predictable and unpredictable.

IMPACT OF EXTERNAL ATTRIBUTES ON INTERNAL OPERATIONS

Static Attributes

Although the ways in which external forces are managed internally by organizations are varied and, in many respects, unique to each setting, there are also many common features. Without going into great detail, we want to provide you with examples of the kinds of effects each enviromental attribute can have on the dimensions of an organization covered by the previous chapters.

Figure 9–1 juxtaposes the static attributes with the organizational dimensions. You can best appreciate the relationship by reading down each column as it cuts across the rows (dimensions). This approach generates a set of working propositions as follows:*

---

*It should be noted that all these propositions can be stated in reverse and still reflect the same relationship between the external environment and internal system.

S_1: The more *complex* the external environment,

The greater the possible diversity of goals (products or services).
The greater the degree of differentiation needed.
The higher the sense of external pressure.
The wider the variety of possible incentives.
The greater the amount and variety of control data needed.
The wider the variety of information and expertise required for decisions.
The broader the range of talents needed to be trained and developed.

S_2: The more *routine* the external environment,

The more stable the means-ends chain.
The more effective will be an established division of labor.
The less tension in the system.
The lower the potential for intrinsic challenge.
The greater the ability to rely on precontrol devices.
The more unilateral decisions can be.
The more limited will be career opportunities.

S_3: The more *interconnected* the external environments,

The greater the influence of open system goals.
The more integration is necessary among units that interface with the environments.
The more important becomes an atomosphere of internal cohesiveness.
The more internal rewards will be influenced by outside pressures.
The more important it will be to match internal with external control standards.
The greater the need to consider multiple external consequences of internal decisions.
The more varied needs to be the nature of internal training programs for those managing external relations.

S_4: The more *remote* a relevant external environment,

The more difficult it is to influence related open system goals.
The more necessary are special external liaison roles.
The less directly aware members are of the pressures from the environment.
The less clearly perceived are the connections between external pressures and internal rewards.
The more difficult it is to monitor externally imposed control standards.
The more difficult it is to anticipate and control external consequences of decisions.
The more important is the quality of training for external liaison roles.

FIGURE 9–1
Ways in Which Static Environmental Attributes May Affect Organizational Dimensions

	Static Environmental Attributes			
Organizational Dimensions	S_1 Complexity	S_2 Routineness	S_3 Inter-connectedness	S_4 Remoteness
Goals	Diversity of possible products or services	Stability of means-end chain of goals	Impact of open system goals	Ability to influence open system goals
Structure	Degree of differentiation necessary	Effectiveness of established division of labor	Degree of integration of interfaces with external environment	Need for special external liaison roles
Climate	Sense of pressure from outside demands	Level of tension in system	Importance of internal cohesion and loyalty	Awareness of external pressure
Rewards	Variety of incentives and opportunities	Potential for job challenge	Degree of external influence over internal rewards	Perceived clarity of connection between external pressures and organizational rewards
Controls	Amount and type of control data needed	Ability to rely on precontrol system devices	Need to match internal and external standards for control	Difficulty in monitoring externally imposed standards
Decision making	Variety of information, expertise required	Ability to use unilateral decisions	Need to consider multiple consequences of decisions	Ability to anticipate consequences of decisions
HRD	Range of talents requiring training	Kinds of career ladder opportunities	Range and nature of training programs	Importance of training for external liaison roles

Rather than discussing the propositions in the abstract, we prefer to offer some examples that will illustrate the phenomena they describe. S_1 (at the high-complexity end of the continuum) is reflected in large, highly diversified organizations (sometimes conglomerates) that have many product and service lines dealing with a large number of markets in different regions across the globe. Such an organization's *choice* to grow in that fashion is inherently a choice to be influenced by a highly complex external environment. It is usually a market-oriented enterprise that responds internally as external forces demand.

Although routineness and complexity are not necessarily mutually exclusive, they are rarely characteristics of the same organization. A shoe manufacturer in a small midwestern town catering to a narrow market and offering a limited range of styles will very likely show the characteristics suggested in proposition S_2. If that company were to expand its markets (i.e., increase external complexity), chances are the environment would become less routine, which would have the effect of changing the organizational characteristics as stated in S_2 toward the other end of the continuum.

An example of S_3 (in the case of high interconnectedness) is a company that depends heavily on government contracts for its survival. Most branches of the federal government are interconnected in some way—through operating policies, pricing standards, salary grades, policies on fair practices in dealing with the private sector, enforcement of standards related to hiring, pollution, safety, health, and so on. A company that must deal with these highly interconnected branches of the federal government is faced with major management tasks and problems over and above those that deal directly with the principal tasks of the organization. The boundary lines that separate internal from external become fuzzy; it may even become unclear just who is running the company. The organization creates lobbies, task forces, and special external roles to maintain constant touch with the network of outside pressures. Failure to maintain internal consistency and cohesiveness can make the system vulnerable to "attack." Internal decisions have external consequences, often not perceived at the time they are made. For example, B.F. Goodrich made a decision to manufacture a brake for air force planes despite test data that indicated a faulty product. The ultimate role played by the FBI was not foreseen by the decision makers at Goodrich. When you deal with one branch of an interconnected environment, you may ultimately find yourself dealing with others.

When any two entities are required to deal with each other, how well they do so depends on their mutual accessibility. Distance in such a relationship tends to breed misunderstanding and conflict. Although modern communications technology helps to reduce distance, there are still many external environmental influences whose impacts are measurably affected by this variable. An important element of remoteness is that although it is difficult to influence from a distance, it is also easier to ignore the pressures that are exerted from remote sources. The pressures from a local community on a manufacturer whose by-products represent potential health hazards (e.g., air or water pollution) are impossible to ignore, are obvious to all members of the system, and usually demand responses from top-line management, not just from specially assigned liaison people. However, the opportunities for direct contact enable both parties to negotiate agreements that can be mutually satisfying. The community perceives the importance of the company to its own survival, and the company recognizes the importance of maintaining good relationships with its surrounding neighbors. Federal controls imposed at a distance (an example of S_4 at the remote end of the continuum) require special liaisons to deal with people who have little appreciation of the needs and problems of a given company and its local community.

Dynamic Attributes

Figure 9–2 shows the relationship between the dynamic environmental attributes and the organizational dimensions. Again we offer a set of propositions to describe the relationships.

D_1: The more *rapid the rate of change* in the external environment,
 The more difficult it is to retain commitment to long-range goals.
 The greater the need for structural flexibility.
 The greater the need for entrepreneurial spirit.
 The more important become rewards for individual learning and growth.
 The more frequently should controls and standards be reviewed.
 The more appropriate it becomes to base decisions on expertise, rather than hierarchical position.
 The more important become training and development activities.

D_2: The more *unpredictable are environmental changes,*
 The greater the need for frequent review and modification of goal priorities.
 The greater the need for rapid generation of temporary sub-systems.
 The higher the sense of uncertainty, tension, and perceived risk.
 The more important become rewards for creativity, risk taking, and collaboration.
 The greater the dependence on postcontol data and concurrent self-control procedures.
 The more appropriate are decentralized decision making and delegation.
 The more valuable become support systems and employee assistance to prevent burnout.

Rapidly growing high-technology organizations exemplify both sets of propositions at one end of the continuum. Although it may be less true today than it was 30 years ago, the other end of the continuum (i.e., slow and predictable change) may be exemplified by a large life insurance company or a national food chain. In the former (high-tech), the competition for technological breakthroughs, market expansion, attraction of talent, and physical expansion make it all but impossible to count on the viability of any aspect of an organization's infrastructure. Mixtures of product lines, functional activities, and market-related opportunities keep goals and structures in constant flux. These change

FIGURE 9-2
Ways in Which Dynamic Environmental Attributes May Affect Organizational Dimensions

Organizational Dimensions	Dynamic Environmental Attributes D_1 Rate of Change	D_2 Predictability of Change
Goals	Ability to retain commitment to long-range goals	Need to review and modify priorities frequently
Structure	Need for flexible structure	Need to generate temporary sub-systems rapidly
Climate	Need for entrepreneurial spirit regarding opportunities	Felt level of uncertainty and tension; perceived risk
Rewards	Importance of rewarding efforts at self-development	Importance of rewards for creativity, risktaking, and collaboration
Controls	Frequency with which control data are checked and standards reviewed	Dependence on postcontrol data and concurrent self-controls
Decision making	Necessity for expert-based versus position-based processes	Degree to which decisions must be decentralized and delegated
HRD	Need for ongoing training and development	Need for support systems and counseling to minimize burnout

rapidly and very often in unanticipated ways, requiring constant attention to the management of rewards, controls, decisions, and human resource development.

Organizations that deal with slow change (or growth) in ways that can be predicted for some reasonable period of time do not face internal demands of the kind described above. However, with the types of changes that are occurring in computer technology, telecommunications, demographic and social patterning, and economic needs, even "slow-change" organizations may have to respond and adapt to external pressure that heretofore did not seem to affect them. We may not be very far from the day when we can buy a life insurance policy from an automated booth next to the local supermarket. Who knows, one may even receive a physical examination from a robot in the adjacent booth!

PLANNING FOR THE FUTURE

Desirable versus Undesirable Aspects of the Environment

Suppose you are choosing a place (city, region, or state) to live. You will probably weigh various aspects of the different environments in your decision. One setting may be attractive because of its physical surroundings, but unattractive socially. Another may offer the opposite. Furthermore, some aspects of the environment that are attractive may be changing, while other aspects may be static. The physical geography of a place usually does not change (at least not very much over time), whereas the population density, with all the accompanying economic, social, and political changes of an area, might very well change significantly in 8 to 10 years (e.g., Silicon Valley, Southern New Hampshire, and Houston).

Therefore, as you look at the various environments in a given location, you can sort out their futures along two dimensions simultaneously: *desirable versus undesirable* and *static versus dynamic*. The picture that this procedure generates can help you to assess the *overall* impact or significance of the external environment on the situation you are considering.

Imagine that you are considering opening a sporting goods outlet in northern Minnesota. You have the capital and the expertise, you have sufficient connections to manufacturers to feel confident about obtaining merchandise, and you have an option to lease 1,000 square feet of space in an ideal location along one of the main north-south arteries. Before going ahead, however, you want to examine the various environmental factors that will affect your business and you more personally. Figure 9–3 shows what this picture might look like.

FIGURE 9–3
Evaluating the Environment: Example of Sporting Goods Outlet

	Static	Dynamic
Desirable environmental features	Close to recreational areas (resorts) Low taxes Roads well maintained Accessibility of mountains and lakes	People spending more on recreation Society becoming more health conscious Young people placing high priority on "fun" Improvements in quality of equipment
Undesirable environmental features	Residents tend not to accept strangers Seasonal market Dependence on the weather Conservatism with respect to change	Rising fuel costs Competition from discount outlets Economic uncertainty Increasing emphasis on saving money

Now you would have to decide for yourself, perhaps by giving different subjective weights to the various factors, whether the overall balance of environmental factors favors the location or not. Any decision about what is or is not desirable is in part a matter of values, but you can also evaluate the various factors in terms of your ability and willingness to live with them or manage them; both require planning.

You may, for example, simply have to live with the attitudes of residents toward strangers for some time, and you certainly cannot control the weather. However, you could capitalize on the changing technology (equipment improvements) in your advertising, and you could offset discount competition by offering personalized services and consultation on the use and care of expensive equipment.

In the next section, we will discuss the concept of *open systems planning* for large organizations. You will see how the procedure just described can be applied to long-range corporate planning and that the process and steps involved are not very different (though much more complex) from the ones you might use at a more individual or small-business level.

Open Systems Planning

An organization's ultimate survival in a world of change and uncertainty depends on its ability to look ahead, to plan for the future. Effective long-range planning requires a balance between what is possible for the organization, given its potential resources, and what the external world will demand and allow. Thus, long-range planning begins with the recognition that it is an *open systems* process. Although recent organizational literature offers a variety of models of open systems planning, our purpose here is not to look at specific procedures but rather to expose you to the general thought process and phases of this type of planning. At the same time we will show how the process touches on each of the organizational dimensions covered in the book.

We begin by presenting the steps or phases of open systems planning:

A. Defining the organizational mission.
B. Envisioning the future with respect to:
   1. Environmental opportunities, demands, and constraints.
   2. Internal ideal organizational life.
C. Operationalizing the organizational mission in the light of B.
D. Creating a strategic plan for developing the necessary organization structure, climate, rewards, controls, etc., that will achieve the mission.
E. Identifying critical key results and checkpoints to serve as indicators of the degree of success in achieving the mission.

A. Defining the Mission Since we discussed this concept in Chapter 2, there is no need to go into detail here. Let us reiterate that every organization exists for some ultimate purpose; that purpose (apart from survival) constitutes its mission. Without a stated mission, it can be difficult to build a system of lasting coherence, an organizational identity that members can internalize. However, not all organizations have a stated mission, and many may find it difficult to state one beyond making a profit or providing income for the employees.

In the example of the sporting goods outlet, the mission might be something like "the establishment of a profitable enterprise that will enhance the quality of life in northern Minnesota through recreational sports." That very broad notion then becomes the backdrop against which subsequent planning is carried out.

B. Envisioning the Future To create an organization, you need to look ahead to what the world will be like and what you ideally want to build. The world offers opportunities, but it also makes demands and holds constraints. Sometimes as you think about the external forces, you can feel overwhelmed and at their mercy. Therefore, it is important to establish as clearly as possible some vision of the kind of organization you want to strive for.

Envisioning the future can often best be done through a brainstorming process involving a number of people. It has been demonstrated that the collective unrestrained thinking of a highly motivated group of people can produce surprisingly useful and reasonably valid pictures of the future, sometimes even 5 or 10 years down the road.[3] By addressing separately each external issue—opportunities, demands, and constraints—and then examining the combined picture this generates, you are in a better position to evaluate where your future efforts need to be directed. By sorting the external factors into the categories suggested earlier (see Figure 9–3)—static versus dynamic and desirable versus undesirable—you can begin to think *strategically*, in terms of ways to capitalize on the advantages and work around the disadvantages of the outside environment.

A brainstorming procedure might also be used for envisioning the qualities of the organization itself. A relevant question might be: What would be going on inside our organization—activities, interactions, atmosphere, etc.—if it were operating ideally? Groups that engage in such a process usually find it energizing and enlightening, particularly with respect to the kinds of shared "dreams" that emerge. Most important, this approach tends to produce a proactive stance, which counterbalances the more reactive one generated by the previous process of envisioning the environment. Consequently, the organization that eventually emerges reflects not only what the external world allows but also what the members of the organization desire.

C. Operationalizing the Mission   Once defined and then viewed within the framework of the future as envisioned, the organizational mission has to be translated into goals that can be operationalized. This is where a means-end chain becomes most useful. Working down from the mission statement to the most general goals and then to the more and more specific sub-goals enables you to envision how and where all the pieces fit together. Remember, this breakdown refers to all the things that will have to be going on in your organization for it to achieve its mission. In step D, we will discuss developing a strategic plan to create and develop the kind of organization you will need to accomplish the goals effectively.

Returning again to the sporting goods example, the most general goals might include establishing a certain profit margin, building a stable clientele, providing quality reliable service and help to customers, and building a good reputation in the region. The more specific goals might translate into actual sales of specific items, numbers of customers served in a given period, and gathering of data on the needs of clientele. Although it is on a much larger scale, corporate planning requires a similar procedure—namely, establishing a more or less clear connection between corporate mission and operational goals, from the most general to the most specific.

---

[3] See Box 7–2 on the Delphi technique.

D. Creating a Strategic Plan In Chapter 8 we presented the concept of strategic planning in relation to human resources development. What we discussed there also applies here; however, we now want you to broaden your perspective to the total organization and all its dimensions. In that context, strategic planning amounts to the process of identifying the most effective ways for an organization to achieve its long-term goals (usually in a four- to five-year period). It is a two-stage process beginning with (1) a clear conceptualization of what the various dimensions of the organization will need to look like in the future, followed by (2) a set of predetermined steps that will ultimately result in the creation of the organization as conceptualized.

Just as we described the need for a work force plan as part of human resources development, organizational strategic planning requires an overall *organization design,* which can be accomplished by addressing the following questions:

1. What division of labor will facilitate the accomplishment of the goals?
2. What kind of climate (norms, attitudes) will energize employee efforts?
3. What kinds of rewards will keep employees most productive?
4. What should be the nature and sources of control?
5. What is the most effective way to make organizational decisions?
6. What human resources will need to be recruited and developed?

You see that we have returned to the topics covered in the chapters of this book. However, we are now discussing them relative to the *future,* which means that you need a plan to translate the design into reality. Furthermore, if you are applying the process to an existing organization, you are faced with a *change* task and not one of creating something totally new. Dismantling old forms and practices requires more complex, if not more difficult, steps; as we pointed out in Chapter 7, decisions related to change almost always produce some resistance.

Once you have answered the six questions listed above, you need to plan *how* you are going to translate the design into reality. This requires that you address parallel questions, such as:

1. How can I best go about deploying existing and new human resources into the most effective division of labor? For a large complex organization, this can mean a very careful systematic approach to job reassignments, dismantling of some departments, adding or subtracting layers of the organization, and sometimes even wholesale elimination of parts of the system.
2. What efforts will help to maintain the desirable elements of the existing climate and what will help to change the undesirable elements in a positive direction?

3. How do I go about changing the reward system to one that will reinforce behavior related to the organization's future goals?
4. How do I educate members of the organization to understand and embrace the kind of control system that will help us survive and grow in the world as envisioned in our plans?
5. How can we get managers to learn how to make decisions in ways that may be very different in the future as compared with the present?
6. How do I put in place the human resources development program that will provide the necessary recruiting and training needed for meeting the challenges four to five years down the road?

In addition to addressing these questions, a strategic plan has to cover such matters as capital funding, geographic location, physical plant size, needed technological changes, and other issues related to financial, physical, and human resources. Finally, all these matters must be projected onto a timetable that enables you to anticipate the *sequencing* of activities necessary to achieve the overall plan and, consequently, the organization's mission.

In essence, then, a strategic plan is a way to get you from where you are to where you want to be. It requires a *time horizon,*—that is, a point in the future that represents "arrival," if you will. If you have a personal career goal, you probably have some kind of strategic plan to accomplish it and you know approximately how long it will take you to accomplish your "mission." For an organization, it is a way of conceptualizing and then creating the kind of entity that will be prepared for the future opportunities, demands, and constraints of the outside world, as well as realize its own inner potential as a human and technical system.

E. Identifying Critical Key Results and Checkpoints The only way to know whether your strategy is working is to define certain critical outcomes that will serve as indicators of progress and make sure that you check these out systematically and regularly. For example, if part of the plan is to decentralize decision making, then it would be important to make regular assessments of how decisions are made and who is making them. Then you can judge whether or not progress is being made in implementing the plan. Another example might be in relation to changing from a system of supervisory control to one of self-control. In this instance, a critical indicator of progress would be a reduction in the number of supervisory positions or the amount of time spent in supervisory activities. Key results for a new organization that is implementing a strategic plan might include anything from physical facilities being in place to the successful filling of key jobs in the firm. In any event, identifying key results *in advance* is a vital part of strategic planning, which is part of a total open systems planning process. That process must be judged by its ability to help the organization meet its internal needs and cope with the external environment on the way to achieving its future mission.

SUMMARY

An organization is an open system that engages in a constant exchange of goods, services, and information with a changing and often turbulent world. An organization must deal with multiple environments: economic, technological, political/legal, social/cultural, and physical (geographic). These environments have static and dynamic attributes. The static attributes are:

1. Complexity.
2. Routineness.
3. Interconnectedness.
4. Remoteness.

The dynamic attributes are:

1. Rate of change.
2. Predictability of change.

These attributes of the environment combine in ways that have important consequences for the internal workings of any organization.

For an organization to manage its external environment effectively, it can usefully engage in a process of open systems planning with the following essential elements:

A. Defining the mission of the organization.
B. Envisioning the future.
C. Operationalizing the mission (goal definition).
D. Creating a strategic plan to accomplish the mission and goals.
E. Identifying key results to evaluate the process.

In the course of conducting open systems planning, it is necessary for the management of an organization to address issues related to all the dimensions covered by the chapters of this book.

AND IN CLOSING . . .

We want to encourage you as managers of the future to maintain an open systems perspective on the world of organizational life. At the risk of repeating ourselves, we want to emphasize that you as a manager will never be an island inside your organization any more than your organization will ever be an island in a constantly changing world. We hope that what we have offered in this book will help you in some way to build more effective organizations in the future.

ANNOTATED BIBLIOGRAPHY

Aaher, D. A., and G. S. Day   "Corporate Responses to Consumerism Pressures." *Harvard Business Review,* November–December 1972, pp. 114–124.

This article identifies some of the consequences that the pressures created by consumerism have on corporations. Corporate responses to these pressures are discussed, as are specific barriers to developing effective response programs. Finally, a strategy focusing on underlying consumer problems and values is recommended as an effective response to consumerism.

Andrews, K. R.   "Replaying the Board's Role in Formulating Strategy." *Harvard Business Review,* May–June 1981, pp. 18–26.

An illuminating discussion on corporate strategy, this article centers primarily around the issue of to what extent strategy should be implicit or explicit. In discussing the former, the author cites a study that investigated strategic mechanisms used by nine large multinational corporations. The study revealed that due to reasons of decentralization, flexibility, and security, implicit methods are more desirable. On the other hand, the author suggests that, in order to pursue and identify the proper goals of an organization, strategy should be explicit, as open discussion of strategy has the virtue of making the best use of an organization's resources and of obtaining goal commitment from these resources.

Bourgeois, L. J. III.   "Strategy and Environment: A Conceptual Integration." *Academy of Management Review,* January, 1980, pp. 25–39.

This article is a discussion of the concepts of strategy and environment and their relationship. The author categorizes environment into its objective and perceived states, and subdivides strategy according to content or process. Finally, the author presents a synthesis of the concepts by relating them at their hierarchial levels.

Burgen, Carl   "How Companies React to the Ethics Crisis." *Business Week,* February 9, 1976, pp. 78–79.

The author discusses some of the steps that the business community is taking to ensure that corporate policy and a corporation's employees follow ethical standards. Specific cases are examined and areas where business can improve its credibility are put forth.

Fahey, L., and W. R. King   "Environmental Scanning for Corporate Planning." *Business Horizons,* August 1977, pp. 61–71.

This article is a descriptive analysis of a survey of 12 large corporations. It examines environmental scanning techniques for seeking information about events and relationships which are external to an organization but important in planning activities. Three scanning models are identified. The study demonstrates that while the importance of environmental scanning is acknowledged, the corporations surveyed have not succeeded in developing sophisticated environmental scanning practices, nor have they integrated findings into their planning process adequately.

Gluck, F.W.; S. P. Kaufman; and A. S. Walleck. "Strategic Management for Competitive Advantage." *Harvard Business Review,* July–August 1980, pp. 154–161.

An examination of the relation between formal planning and strategic performance across a broad spectrum of companies revealed to the authors a progression of strategic planning. From the review, a four-phase model revealing the evolution of strategic planning is developed. The article describes this model and how it can be useful in evaluating and improving corporate planning systems.

Hall, W. K. "Survival Strategies in a Hostile Environment." *Harvard Business Review,* September–October 1980, pp. 75–85.

The author discusses an ongoing research project that is involved with analyzing how 64 industrial organizations in mature markets are evolving in the face of adverse external pressures, and how they are reacting to these pressures. Successes and failures are found in common industries. Uniformly, successes come to those companies that achieve either the lowest cost or most differentiated position.

Leone, R. A. "The Real Costs of Regulation." *Harvard Business Review,* November–December 1977, pp. 57–67.

This article examines the forces that have precipitated the recent expansion of government regulations. The author supports the view that this expansion reflects fundamental changes in environmental and social expectations and are a legitimate expression of society's interests. The costs of the "regulatory boom" are examined, as are its consequences.

Loudal, M. L.; R. A. Bauer; and N. H. Treverton "Public Responsibility Committees of the Board." *Harvard Business Review,* May–June 1977, pp. 40–64, 178–181.

The authors report the findings of a research project that examined the impact of public responsibility committees that corporations have established to deal with social issues. The experiences of 30 corporations that have established such committees are discussed, and the findings indicate that, although there is a lack of clear information about such committees' functions and potential value, it is felt that they can make a major contribution to a corporation's public responsibility.

Magill, R. F. "A Prescription for Survival in a Regulated World." *Business Horizons,* February 1980, pp. 75–81.

Magill discusses the costs of government regulation to the business community and ultimately to the consumer. He also examines methods to make regulations more effective in serving society's and the business community's interests and emphasizes that business should increase its involvement in formulating regulatory policy in order to reduce or eliminate unneeded regulation.

Reich, R. B. "Regulations by Confrontation or Negotiation?" *Harvard Business Review,* May–June 1981, pp. 82–93.

Although there are numerous explanations for why business and government are unable to cooperate in the regulatory process, the author identifies the growth in the role of intermediaries in dealing with the regulatory process as being a central reason. Because intermediaries (lawyers, lobbyists, trade association groups, etc.) thrive on government-business conflict, they continuously encourage and cultivate it. To arrive at the most positive atmosphere of negotiation, the author suggests that business and regulatory agencies must meet directly to discuss problems, must alter incentives of intermediaries, should establish public dialogue proceedings on controversial issues, and should communicate problematic areas as early as possible to all concerned groups so that resources can be assigned to assist in arriving at sound solutions.

Rummel, R. J., and D. A. Heenan "How Multinationals Analyze Political Risk." *Harvard Business Review,* January–February 1978, pp. 67–76.

The article examines several approaches multinational corporations can take in analyzing political risk factors relative to foreign investments. To illustrate, the authors focus on the experiences of one country, Indonesia. The analysis is based on discussions with senior executives and on research conducted in several leading private and public enterprises.

Sethi, S. P. "Grassroots Lobbying and the Corporation." *Business and Society Review,* Spring 1979, pp. 8–14.

The author discusses the topic of corporate advocacy advertising as an approach corporations are following to publicize their viewpoints in controversial public policy areas where their vital interests are at stake. The proper and improper uses of advocacy advertising and their consequences are investigated. To advance the corporation viewpoint and expand the free flow of ideas, the author suggests that a National Council of Public Information be established to fund the dissemination of ideas on important social issues.

"The SEC vs. Gulf & Western: Nagging Questions." *Business Week,* January 21, 1980, pp. 98–102.

This article discusses the (then) impending legal clash between the Securities and Exchange Commission and Gulf & Western Industries, Inc. Gulf & Western's charges of abuses of power by a regulatory agency are identified, as are the SEC's charges against Gulf & Western of improper disclosure and reporting practices.

SUGGESTED READINGS

Ansoff, H. Igor; Roger P. Declérck; and Robert L. Hayes. "From Strategic Planning to Strategic Management." In *From Strategic Planning to Strategic Management,* eds. H. Igor Ansoff, Roger P. Declérck, and Robert L. Hayes. London: John Wiley & Sons, 1976, pp. 39–78.

Ayres, Robert U. *Technological Forecasting and Long-range Planning.* New York: McGraw-Hill, 1969.

Bell, Daniel *The Coming of Post-industrial society: A Venture in Social Forecasting.* New York: Basic Books, 1973.

Bell, Daniel *The Cultural Contradictions of Capitalism.* New York: Basic Books, 1976.

Chamberlain, Neil W. *Enterprise and Environment: The Firm in Time and Place.* New York: McGraw-Hill, 1968.

Chamberlain, Neil W. *The Place of Business in America's Future/A Study in Social Values.* New York: Basic Books, 1978.

Chandler, Alfred D., Jr. *Strategy and Structure.* New York: Doubleday, 1962.

Child, John "Organizational Structure, Environment and Performance: The Role of Strategic Choice." *Sociology,* 6(1972), pp. 2–22.

Duncan, Robert B. "Characteristics of Organizational Environments and Perceived Environmental Uncertainty." *Administrative Science Quarterly* 17(1972), pp. 313–27.

Emery, Fred E., and Eric L. Trist "The Causal Texture of Organizational Environments." *Human Relations* 18(1965), pp. 21–32.

Forrester, Jay W. "A Great Economic Depression Ahead? Changing Economic Patterns." *The Futurist* 12(1978), pp. 379–85.

Foy, Nancy, and Herman Gadon "Worker Participation: Contrasts in Three Countries." *Harvard Business Review,* May–June 1976, pp. 358–73.

Gallese, Liz Roman "The Soothsayers: More Companies Use 'Futurists' to Discern What Is Lying Ahead." *The Wall Street Journal,* March 31, 1975.

Gerstner, Louis V. Jr. "Can Strategic Planning Pay Off?" *Business Horizons* 15(1972), pp. 5–16.

Guth, William D., and Renato Tagiuri "Personal Values and Corporate Strategy. *Harvard Business Review,* September–October 1965, pp. 123–32.

Hake, Barry "Values, Technology and the Future." *Futures Conditional,* June 1973, pp. 6–7.

Hirsch, Fred *Social Limits to Growth.* Cambridge, Mass.: Harvard University Press, 1976.

Jurkovich, Ray "A Core Typology of Organizational Environments." *Administrative Science Quarterly* 19(1974), pp. 380–94.

Kahn, Herman; William Brown; and Leon Martel *The Next 200 Years: A Scenario for America and the World.* New York: William Morrow, 1976.

Kimberly, John R. "Environmental Constraints and Organizational Structure: A Comparative Analysis of Rehabilitation Organizations." *Administrative Science Quarterly* 20(1975), pp. 1–9.

Lodge, George Cabot *The New American Ideology.* New York: Alfred A. Knopf, 1975.

Mahoney, Thomas A., and Peter J. Frost "The Role of Technology in Models of Organizational Effectiveness." *Organizational Behavior and Human Performance* 11(1974), pp. 122–38.

Mattill, John I. "The Coming of Automatic Factories." *Technology Review,* February 1975, p. 60

Mattill, John I. "Are We Ready for the Computerized Factory?" *Technology Review,* November 1978, p. 21.

Miles, R., and C. Snow *Organizational Strategy, Structure, and Process.* New York: McGraw-Hill, 1978.

Miles, Raymond E.; Charles C. Snow; and Jeffrey Pfeffer "Organization-Environment: Concepts and Issues." *Industrial Relations* 13(1974), pp. 244–64.

Newman, William H. "Strategy and Management Structure." *Journal of Business Policy* 2(1971), pp. 56–66.

Organ, Dennis W. "Linking Pins between Organizations and Environment." *Business Horizons,* December 1971, pp. 73–80.

Osborn, Richard N., and James G. Hunt "Environment and Organizational Effectiveness." *Administrative Science Quarterly* 19(1974), pp. 231–46.

Ouchi, William G., and Reuben T. Harris "Structure, Technology, and Environment." In *Organizational Behavior: Research and Issues,* ed. George Strauss, Raymond E. Miles, and Charles C. Snow. Madison, Wis.: Industrial Relations Research Association, 1974, pp. 107–40.

Pfeffer, Jeffrey "Size and Composition of Corporate Boards of Directors: The Organization and Its Environment. *Administrative Science Quarterly* 17(1972), pp. 218–28.

Pfeffer, Jeffrey. "Size, Composition, and Function of Hospital Boards of Directors: A Study of Organization-Environment Linkage." *Administrative Science Quarterly* 18(1973), pp. 349–64.

Pfeffer, Jeffrey, and G. Salancik *The External Control of Organizations.* New York: Harper & Row, 1978.

Ringbakk, K. A. "Long-Range Planning in Major U.S. Companies." *Long-Range Planning,* December 1969, pp. 46–57.

Roeber, Richard J. C. *The Organization in a Changing Environment.* Reading, Mass.: Addison-Wesley Publishing, 1973.

Rosener, Marvin M. "Economic Determinants of Organizational Innovation. *Administrative Science Quarterly* 12(1967), pp. 614–25.

Rue, Leslie W., and Robert M. Fulmer "Is Long-range Planning Profitable?" Proceedings, Academy of Management, 33d Annual Meeting, Boston, August 1973, pp. 66–73.

Sarason, Seymour B. *The Creation of Settings and the Future Societies.* San Francisco: Jossey-Bass, 1972.

Schoeffler, Sidney; Robert D. Buzzell; and Donald F. Heany "Impact of Strategic Planning on Profit Performance." *Harvard Business Review,* March–April 1974, pp. 137–45.

Thune, Stanley S., and Robert J. House "Where Long-Range Planning Pays Off." *Business Horizons,* August 1970, pp. 81–87.

Toffler, Alvin *Future Shock.* New York: Random House, 1970.

Vancil, Richard F. "The Accuracy of Long-Range Planning. *Harvard Business Review,* October–November 1970, pp. 98–101.

Cases in this book not otherwise noted were prepared by various individuals with the guidance of the authors. We are grateful to these individuals and organizations for their assistance. For reasons of preserving the anonymity of the organizations involved in the cases, we list the individuals' names below and gratefully acknowledge their contribution in this manner.

>Charles F. Battista
>Steven R. Bouchard
>Stephen P. Day
>Andrea de Anguera
>Deborah Downs
>Pamela J. Fuhrer
>Deborah J. Kilgus
>Robert V. O'Brien
>Evelyn B. Pearson
>Tetsuo Saitoh
>Carl F. Spang
>Judith Thomas Spang
>James C. Van Fleet
>George R. Whitehead
>L. Wickremarachchi

Cases

An Administrative Decision*

YOU ARE ERIK TOY, the manager of a highly regarded budget division of one plant in a multiplant organization. The work of your office involves all aspects of the budgeting process for your plant, including the budget preparation, its dissemination, the development of control procedures, the monitoring of budget performance, and recommendations for changes in the budgeting process.

These activities involve the processing of a large amount of data and the preparation of detailed reports, which are then sent to different divisions within the plant and to the headquarters office. While some of the work is routine, much of it requires technical expertise and some of it requires high personal skills to handle conflict situations with other organizational units over budget allocations and the control of expenditures.

You have just returned from a meeting at the home office of the various heads of the budgeting departments in the company. At that meeting you were given the assignment by your boss to choose one person to fill a vacancy caused by the death of the head of the budget office in a smaller plant. The vice president in charge of budgeting for the corporation has asked that you recommend a person from your office because of some of the excellent results that your division has produced both in developing new budget techniques and in getting them successfully implemented within the plant.

While your initial reaction was one of pleasure (because the assignment to pick a person for the vacancy reflected credit on your organization), you are now having some second thoughts about what this responsibility might entail—you must think not only of the person being promoted but also of the effect which his leaving may have on your organization. As you consider the people in your organization, the possible candidates can be very quickly reduced to two—Sissel and Tom—each of whom heads up one of the two main sections in your department.

Sissel is a 29-year-old college graduate with a master's degree in accounting who has been with the organization for four years. While she is fairly young for the responsibility required in her present assignment, she has done an outstanding job. One of her characteristics is her ability to get people to work with her and for her. She does an excellent job of planning the work and delegating it. She has also been one of the people who has been instrumental in getting often recalcitrant department heads in other parts of the organization to go along with new and different budgeting ideas. The fact that she is attractive has opened

---

*Excerpted and modified from I. R. Knudson, R. T. Woodworth, and C. H. Bell, *Management: An Experimental Approach* (New York: McGraw-Hill, 1973).

doors for her, and her ability to work with other people in the organization has meant that the number of enemies that a budget department normally accumulates has been reduced significantly.

While Sissel is single, she has mentioned several times that she is very career minded and plans to keep on working whether or not she marries.

As you further mull over the situation, you also remember the recent meeting in which the word was passed to all executives in the organization to pay special attention to assure that women got an equal opportunity as far as promotion opportunities were concerned.

On the other hand, Tom has also done an outstanding job. He has worked for the department for 15 years and is now 45 years of age. He has an undergraduate degree in mathematics and philosophy. His progress in the organization has been slow and steady, but for the last six years he has been a very effective head of the other section in the department. As you look back on the work that he has done, you see that almost all the creative innovations in the budgeting processes in your plant have come as a result of his suggestions. He is not only creative, but technically is extremely sound. He has been able to devise a number of very effective yet simple procedures to carry out his plans.

You feel that there is probably no one who works harder in the organization than he does. He is often at work an hour before everybody else, leaves an hour or so after everybody else, and it is not surprising to find out on a Monday morning that he has been in on the weekends.

When he is in the office, he is all business and expects the people working for him to be the same. As a result he seems somewhat abrupt in his contact with employees working for him and with other people in the organization. He is married, has two children, and has talked with you before, indicating that if an opportunity for promotion came up he would certainly like to have a shot at it. The workers in his section tend to respond to his "lead-horse" style of management by working hard themselves. Sometimes there are some conflicts due to missed communication signals, but overall the output of his group has been of extremely high quality.

You are aware of the following information regarding the small plant to which the person you select would go to head up its budget department. Located about 50 miles away, it has about 40 people in the department—about half as many employees as are in your department. The department has had problems in the past getting new budgeting ideas developed and implemented, and as a result the plant it serves is one of the plants with a somewhat obsolete budgeting system. The plant manager has given assurances to you that he is very interested in getting someone to modernize his budget system and that he would give that person his full support. However, you know from many talks with the former budgeting manager of that plant that there are many line managers there who see no reason to change the present budgeting procedures and who would resist any changes.

The new job would require both technical and personal skills. As you think back on this, Tom has been more involved in creating new ideas, and Sissel has been more involved in the process of getting them implemented. You recognize that, in general, you have less technical skill than Tom does and probably on balance are not as good a leader as Sissel has shown herself to be. In fact, you have counted on these strengths in the past and used them to build what you think is an exceptionally fine and smooth running department. At the moment you see no one else in your department who could easily replace either one of them. However, you remember a comment from Sissel saying that one or two of her people were showing great promise and developing quickly.

Finally, there is the nagging recognition that whatever decision you make, you would have to tell the person not promoted that he or she has not been promoted. It would be nice if the organization has enough flexibility so that you could give the one not promoted a raise or some other sort of reward. However, you know that the circumstances under which the organization is operating would not permit this kind of action.

*Associated Insurance Services, Inc.**

MIKE JANSEN could hardly keep his anger from welling up inside of him. His eyes stung as the vice president of personnel told him that he was being relieved of his duties as director of employee development for the Associated Insurance Services, Inc. (AIS). Mike could not believe his ears as the vice president told him that he no longer fit into the needs of the company. Mike knew that there were some problems, but he had no idea that the situation had deteriorated this far. As he left the vice president's office, all he could ask himself was—why?

Two years ago when Mike accepted the position of director of employee development, he thought that he was entering the opportunity of a lifetime. AIS was a growing company and in need of developing its human resources, particularly in supervisory and management personnel. Mike was given a carte blanche for budget, as well as free rein to develop a staff and implement a program of human resource development and management training. Reporting directly to the vice president of personnel, Mike was made responsible for all employee development throughout AIS. With ample money and management

---

*Prepared by Charles Battista under the supervision of Professor Robin Willits.

support, he thought that the job would run smoothly, but how wrong he was.

COMPANY HISTORY

Shortly after World War II, three young friends (Al, George, and John) decided that their liberal arts education best prepared them for jobs in a service-type industry. Consequently, all took jobs in sales for different well-established insurance companies. All were reasonably successful, but after a few years they were ready to admit to one another that they yearned for something better than waiting their turn for real responsibility and advancement in their respective firms. In discussing their career prospects, they conceived of a new marketing approach for automobile insurance and decided to start their own business. With increasing national interest in leisure and recreational activities, it appeared obvious to them that there was a natural, rapidly growing market for insurance of a special kind that could be offered on both an individual and group basis. Recreational clubs and associations were growing and provided a ready-made basis for offering reasonably priced comprehensive insurance packages that could be easily serviced. They also anticipated that the various associations would find such packages attractive as a way of expanding their membership.

In order to reach the large numbers of potential individuals who would find it attractive to have their policies handled by "specialists," there were mailing lists available from subscriptions and association memberships.

Each of the three founders had had some specialized experience which enabled him to bring valuable expertise to the newly formed company; Al had handled marine insurance for his former employer, George was familiar with the area of recreational vehicles and camping equipment, and John had spent the past couple of years handling insurance for the AAA.

Their contacts and personal track records in the insurance field enabled them to receive the necessary backing from underwriters and the needed capital to get started. The fact that the economy was in a period of stability and steady growth made a venture like this one attractive to capital investors.

Each founder took full responsibility for the particular type of service with which he was most familiar. By forming together, the founders were able to share the costs of processing the mail and keeping the records. Also, they were able to benefit from their common name, once some consumer recognition was established, even though each line of service was relatively independent.

The company's main activities were (1) marketing: the design of appropriate service packages and the development of relations with the staffs of outside associations and (2) office work: recordkeeping and the processing of accounts. The founders concentrated on the former and hired clerical personnel for the latter.

During its early years the company exhibited steady, though unspectacular, growth and provided the founders with a good income and a sense of independence and satisfaction.

Then with the increase in leisure-time activities in the United States and the general growth in the service sector of the economy, AIS found itself in the right place at the right time. During the second decade of its existence, sales mounted dramatically.

Following a strategy of riding the wave of expansion as rapidly as possible by responding to any association that expressed an interest in an adaptation of the basic service packages, the founders were kept busy designing new packages, meeting with association officials, and hiring personnel to run the AIS office activities. Sales doubled, tripled, and then quadrupled, and by 1980 the company had grown to 8,000 employees.

THE STATE OF THE ORGANIZATION PRIOR TO MIKE'S HIRING

While the company had seen a number of structural additions and changes during its 20-year history, the position of the founders, as heads of the major operating divisions, had remained a constant, and each division provided a type of service that was independent of the others.

As growth occurred, each division expanded as space became available, so that by 1980, each division had space throughout the company's quarters, which were spread through several buildings in the downtown area of a large Midwestern city. The growth rate being what it was, and the subsequent movement of offices, a standard company joke was that AIS published a new telephone directory and management listing with every full moon.

The managerial and supervisory staff of AIS was comparatively young. The top executives, vice presidents and directors, just below the founders' level, were people in their late 40s that had been hired away from the older companies in the field.

Members of middle management, managers and assistant managers, were largely in their 30s, while lower-level management, supervisors, and even some assistant managers, were often only around 25 years of age.

In fact, AIS had gained a reputation as a place where a young person could go to put his or her career on a fast track. AIS hired young people away from older firms, individuals who might normally would have had to wait 20 years to gain real managerial status. For an individual with 5 to 10 years experience in an older, more staid and conservative company, it was a heady experience to move into a position where you were dealing with real problems and had to make decisions without constant direction from above.

Through hard work, AIS gave managers the chance to earn an annual bonus based on profits (almost guaranteed by the expanding market) and the chance to establish one's reputation as a problem solver. This was true even if the problems were of one's own doing because of inexperience. Many would depart after 3 to 5 years, having moved from one position to another every 9 to 12 months, rising through the ranks from assistant manager to manager and even director. It was an expectation, if not a norm, within middle management ranks, that if you weren't promoted within a year, it was time to move on; and if you were, after a few years you could return to your old company or a similar one with a much better salary and higher status. Some, of course, moved on because they could not handle the pace or they experienced frustration and burnout with never-ending problems that were being solved, but never prevented.

One 32-year-old manager's description of AIS was typical. "AIS is one happy madhouse. You can get any amount of money you need to try anything without having to go through a lot of red tape. Nor do you need to worry if it should fail, as long as you continue to get the day-to-day work done so that the accounts are serviced on a regular basis and profits assured. The motto is, 'If you've got an idea—go! Don't stand around waiting to see a boss.'"

Also typical were the remarks of another manager. "One never gets bored at AIS. There's always another fire to put out, and there's always something new to deal with. We start programs and then drop them before they're fully launched. We move departments around on the organization chart and then back again. We adopt a new method of handling some process and then decide to reverse our field when spring arrives. I'm not sure where the company is headed, but it's going there in a hurry, profitably, with never a dull moment."

A similar situation existed at the lower management levels. Many were high school graduates who had started as office workers processing mail, etc., and then had been promoted from the ranks. Some were promoted after only six months experience. Those that had more education were typically liberal arts graduates who started directly as supervisors with the expectation of moving up into middle management or higher.

One attribute of AIS's *organization style* that did not seem to fit its youthful, nonconservative, action-oriented orientation was a strong degree of *stratification*. The executive level kept to itself. The president talked to vice presidents, vice presidents to other vice presidents and directors, directors to directors and managers, and so on. In part, this reflected a *vertical division of labor*, in part a "hands-off" policy of expecting people to do their jobs without constant supervision, and in part, a carryover from the *status-conscious* organizations that most managers had come from (and would probably return to).

THE CEO ATTENDS A CONFERENCE

Of all the founders, the chief executive officer was the most attentive to operating conditions within the organization, particularly the high turnover rate (25+ percent) and the resultant lack of continuity in customer relations. He had become increasingly aware that it was not unusual for customers to call in, discuss a problem with one person and when it was not resolved or came up again, call later only to get another person who had no background on the situation. He also knew that the managerial, supervisory, and even worker groups were not only young, but inexperienced.

While attending an American Management Association Conference, the CEO was very impressed with a speaker who discussed the merits of a planned program in human resources development (HRD). He returned from the conference excited about the idea of launching an HRD program at AIS, seeing it as a way to reduce turnover, build continuity, and enhance operating efficiency through improved managerial skills. His excitement soon translated itself into a decision to establish the Employee Development Department as a subunit of the Corporate Personnel Department.

At the AMA conference the CEO had met Mike Jansen and been impressed with his general competency as a person as well as his philosophy of management and proven expertise in management training. Mike soon became his choice to head up the new department. In their final meeting to discuss the opening, the CEO introduced Mike to the vice president of personnel, who gave Mike (once he was hired) a free rein to spend whatever was necessary to build an effective HRD program for the company.

MIKE'S INITIAL ACTIONS

After being hired Mike's first action was to spell out a set of objectives for his new department. One obvious objective was to develop a training program for managers and supervisors at all levels. As Mike saw the situation, the company's obvious lack of experienced personnel meant that there was a need for training in basic management skills, such as decision making, handling people, delegation, performance appraisals, and conflict management. At the same time, recognizing the company's pattern of fire fighting and dealing with one problem after another, Mike believed that the training program should examine the role of manager as organizer and planner. A primary component should be to train people in long-range planning for problem prevention rather than just problem solving. Finally, believing that self-knowledge and self-awareness were important ingredients of any successful manager, Mike felt that personal growth should be an important component of the training endeavor. Knowledge of one's strengths and limitations, knowledge of one's characteristic ways of reacting to situations, and heightened awareness of how one was affecting others and being affected by them were all desired outcomes of the training program.

A second objective was to assemble a staff capable of designing and carrying out such a training program. While, as Mike knew, there were several individuals with training responsibilities scattered throughout the various divisions of the company that he could probably utilize as the nucleus of a staff, he believed that basically he would need to look outside the company for the type of people he needed. He wanted energetic and assertive individuals, with a good grounding in human interaction and basic psychology.

A third objective was to establish a corporate training facility. Recognizing the fact that the various divisions of the company often went their separate ways and acted more like independent companies than divisions of one company, Mike believed that it was important to have a place where groups from all over the company could meet together and be removed from the pressure of daily activities. He saw such a facility as symbolizing the company's commitment to employee development and a common identity as AIS. Also, Mike wanted a facility that would allow large groups to work in small clusters and be equipped with closed-circuit television, one-way mirrors, etc., so that there could be greater flexibility in the approach to training than possible in any of the training areas available in the separate divisions.

Mike's fourth objective was to manage his own department in a manner that would provide a model of the style of management taught in the training program. Mike saw his development of clear objectives and the evolution of a plan for reaching them as a part of such modeling. Also, he intended that his own actions as a manager would emphasize delegation and development of his staff, with his role more that of adviser and coach than designer of training programs and sole spokesperson for the department.

Finally, Mike had a personal objective of responding to the CEO's confidence in him, by taking the initiative to build his department and the program without bothering the CEO and making demands on his time. He knew that the CEO was extremely busy with a variety of company, civic, and personal activities, so Mike believed that it would be appropriate not to intrude anymore than essential. He felt that much the same posture should apply to the vice presidents and even the directors who were equally involved in activities in and out of the company.

With these objectives, within the next six months Mike accomplished the following:

1. He built a $2 million training facility that became known around the company as the "Parthenon."
2. He hired seven dynamic young people for his training staff. All were well trained in up-to-date techniques, some as counselors and most in interpersonal relations and management. All had some prior experience on the training staffs of other companies; except for one or two Mike drew from within AIS.
3. He developed a personal modus operandi that modeled the style of management which he hoped his department would cultivate throughout the organization. For example, when Mike got a request from another director to discuss a management problem or training need, he would typically send the staff member whose background seemed most relevant to discuss the division's needs.
4. He had his staff making contact with the management of the different divisions and hard at work designing and running workshops in response to the problems and training needs identified by these managers, whom the staff found responsive to their efforts to identify potential projects.

Some of the workshops offered covered such topics as:

- Performance appraisals.
- Selection interviewing.
- Finance for nonfinancial managers.
- Business communications.
- Effective meetings.
- Time management.
- Conflict management and problem solving.
- Effective public speaking.

A ONE-YEAR REVIEW OF PROGRESS

While there was no objective measure of results available to Mike, such as direct testing of the learning or data on turnover, morale, or profits, that could be attributed to the training programs at the end of the first year, Mike was able to look at what he had created and, by an intuitive measure, know that the department was offering workshops of high professional quality. He had good reason to believe that his staff was eminently qualified to provide training in the latest concepts of modern management with a solid focus on the long-range development of people as well as short-term administrative techniques.

He had been successful in demonstrating a different style of management than had historically been characteristic of AIS. His department clearly was a model of a style that emphasized planning, delegation, and individual development through autonomy, support, and coaching.

It was clear that his staff of seven was growing in capability and breadth under his approach. Morale was high. In the words of one 30-year-old staff member: "Mike was modeling the kind of management style he was trying to infiltrate into the organization, and it worked. We loved it. We were able to take off and do a job. We worked hard, and learned and grew in the process."

More than that, the members of AIS's middle management and supervisory group had responded enthusiastically to the opportunity for management training. Many had expressed a genuine interest in attending the programs which they felt would help them to deal with the sense of overload and disorganization that was their daily life. While enrollment in the workshops was strictly voluntary, new workshops were soon filled. Mike's staff felt they had good rapport with the managers and supervisors with whom they interacted, and knew that they were respected for their ability to make learning interesting. Mike's department was dubbed "AIS University."

True, there were some rough edges, and Mike did not ignore them in his assessment. He had not been able to get any directors, let alone vice presidents, to attend any training sessions. Also, they seemed to exhibit less interest in the program than Mike deemed desirable. There certainly was a noticeable lack of inquiry from the top level about what was being done, and Mike had little feedback from them on their assessment of the program, pro or con.

Second, each division continued to believe that its needs were unique and to resist having its people attend workshops designed for corporate-wide attendance. This feeling led to the development of divisional training departments offering similar programs as the corporate department.

Of greatest concern to Mike was the pattern of attendance. Typically more individuals started a workshop than completed it, and hardly any one made every session. Attendees were constantly being called away from sessions, or failing to attend, to deal with some crisis. When asked to block out the time and honor it as they would a scheduled meeting, the inevitable reply was that their bosses expected them to be available on call and to get all their work done (without overtime in the case of working supervisors). This pattern was true of supervisors whose bosses (assistant managers) were attending other workshops, and of the managers themselves. Even when not pressured by a boss, attendees were reluctant to allow work to pile up, particularly near the end of a period as they became more aware of insuring profits and the bonuses that were tied thereto. Managers wanted to be trained in the shortest amount of time, making it difficult to design good, solid programs.

Finally, Mike had to admit that the training didn't stick as much as appropriate. Individuals would complete a workshop with high enthusiasm to alter their managerial or supervisory style, such as to delegate more, keep subordinates better informed, or listen before they judged, but subsequently complained that things didn't work out in practice. Usually they said time was too short to practice the lessons, or they got too busy to remember them, or their boss's expectations (such as having instant answers) prevented them from applying the lessons as much as they had initially hoped.

In view of this, particularly the last "rough edge," Mike resolved to increase his efforts to develop that part of the program designed to allow managers to become more aware of their own style and patterns of behavior. Also, the picture confirmed his belief in the value of more emphasis on long-range planning to prevent problems.

YEAR TWO DEVELOPMENTS

The Employee Development Department continued to expand its activities throughout the second year. Mike increased the staff to 10 and the department added additional workshops to its repertory, particularly in the area of manager personal growth.

The staff continued to work hard and expand its skills as a training staff, but the demand for programs did not reach a level that fully utilized the training center and the "rough edges" remained. Then, toward the latter part of the year, individual staff members began to experience more and more frustration.

They experienced a growing awareness that the skills and concepts they were teaching were not being reflected in any change in day-to-day behavior. All of them itched to get some members of top management in their workshops, but top management continued to seem to see training as something that was "good for the troops" but not for them. Many began to feel the lack of coordination among the various workshops and realize that the creation of the individual workshops had followed a laissez-faire pattern based on what each division or department manager wanted. This, combined with the fact that they were being used as trainers, and not as much as counselors to individuals and management consultants to departments, was putting some constraints on their own sense of accomplishment and growth.

Finally, the staff was confused by some of the teasing remarks they were beginning to receive. "The touchy-feeling boys are here again." "Management by theory rides again." "Have you put in shuffle board yet to utilize the excess space down at the Parthenon?" They knew that they were providing good programs but were feeling increasing frustration that the departments were viewing them increasingly as an expensive luxury. The staff was hard put to provide a fully satisfactory reply that could document the tangible benefits of their training activities.

Late in the second year, the vice president of personnel brought in an organization development (OD) specialist from a multinational company with a strong reputation in the OD field. He took one look at the training programs and was heard to remark, "They were doing it all wrong." Two weeks later Mike was fired, and the Employee Development Department started to dissolve.

*Blair, Inc. (1)**

THE INFORMATION FOR THIS CASE was obtained from Mr. Burton L. Davis, a recent employee of Blair, Inc.

Burton Davis started work last September as a mechanical engineer in the Engine and Motor Division of the Blair Company, a large multiple-industry corporation. The division, with 400 employees, was the principal employer in Midland. Formed four years ago, the division designed and manufactured small gasoline-combustion engines used in lawnmowers, motor scooters, snow throwers, portable saws, and power plants. Recently, the division had begun to turn out small electric motors. Division sales were currently $6 million.

Davis, seven years out of Purdue, had previously worked as an automotive engineer for two major automobile manufacturers and had excellent references from both. His salary at Blair was $950 per month.

He found that the engineering offices were new, of modern design, and air conditioned. Supporting personnel in drafting, machine shop, and laboratory were adequate, and excellent physical facilities were available. Fringe benefits were at or above the industry level. For instance, Davis was promised a two-week vacation before completing a full year of service. His moving expenses were paid in full, in addition to $500 for an earlier trip to locate suitable housing. His travel expenses had also been covered when he came to Midland to interview the division chief engineer, Charles Lyons, and the corporate executive personnel director.

Burton Davis was assigned to the Design and Development Department (see Exhibit 1 for partial organization chart). Four of the six other engineers had no work experience with other employers (which was

---

*This case was published in Garret L. Bergen and William V. Haney, *Organizational Relations and Management Action* (New York: McGraw-Hill, 1966). Copyright (case) © Northwestern University. Reprinted with permission.

EXHIBIT 1
Partial Organization Chart for Engine and Motor Division

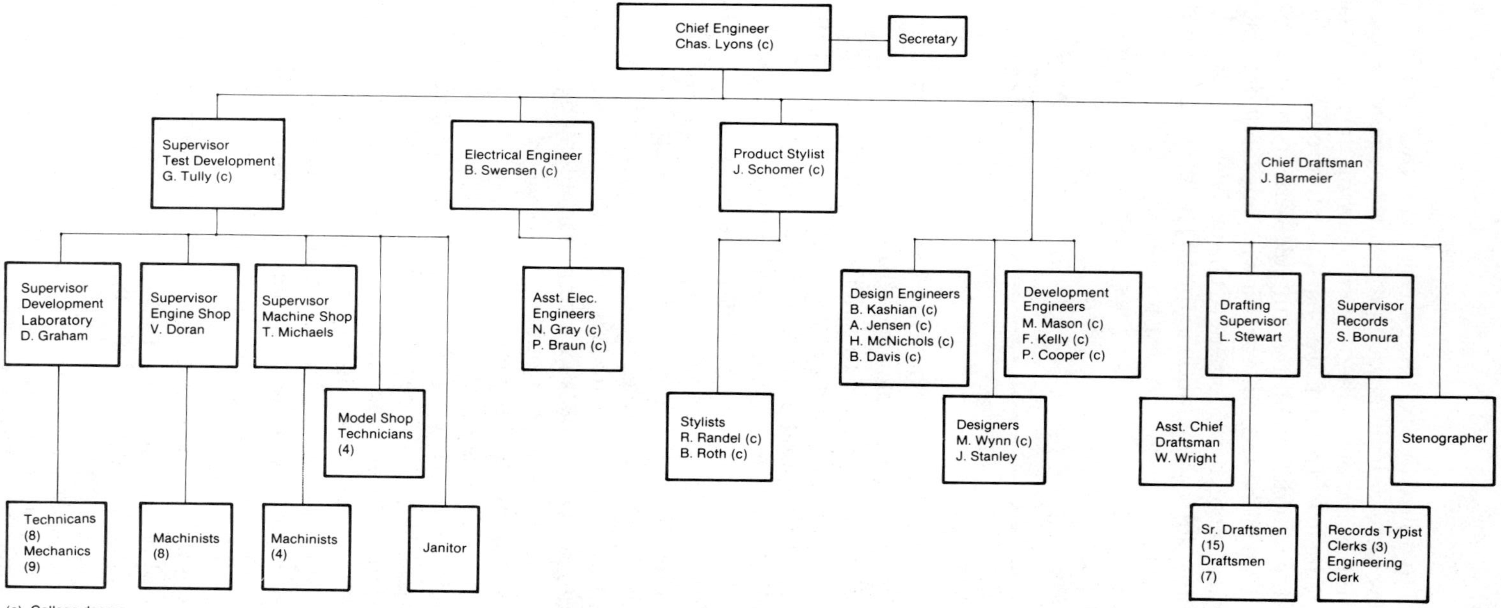

- Chief Engineer — Chas. Lyons (c)
  - Secretary
  - Supervisor Test Development — G. Tully (c)
    - Supervisor Development Laboratory — D. Graham
      - Technicans (8)
      - Mechanics (9)
    - Supervisor Engine Shop — V. Doran
      - Machinists (8)
    - Supervisor Machine Shop — T. Michaels
      - Model Shop Technicians (4)
      - Machinists (4)
      - Janitor
  - Electrical Engineer — B. Swensen (c)
    - Asst. Elec. Engineers — N. Gray (c), P. Braun (c)
  - Product Stylist — J. Schomer (c)
    - Design Engineers — B. Kashian (c), A. Jensen (c), H. McNichols (c), B. Davis (c)
    - Development Engineers — M. Mason (c), F. Kelly (c), P. Cooper (c)
    - Designers — M. Wynn (c), J. Stanley
    - Stylists — R. Randel (c), B. Roth (c)
  - Chief Draftsman — J. Barmeier
    - Supervisor Records — S. Bonura
      - Stenographer
      - Records Typist Clerks (3), Engineering Clerk
    - Drafting Supervisor — L. Stewart
      - Asst. Chief Draftsman — W. Wright
      - Sr. Draftsmen (15), Draftsmen (7)

(c) College degree

also true of the chief engineer) and had been with the company from 2 to 13 years.

Davis was assigned a numbered space in the main parking lot and was given a decal for his car window. Only the first three rows in this lot were reserved by number. Employment was high at the time, and the only space available was one vacated by a draftsman who had just resigned. (See Exhibits 2 and 3.)

Davis soon noticed that more than half of those who parked in the two parking areas adjacent to the engineering offices were people he would not have expected to have more favorable parking locations than the engineers (see locations 6A and 6B in Exhibit 3). Talking with his fellow engineers, he found they also thought it strange and had been irritated about it for some time.

The following personnel parked in these areas where space was reserved by name: C. Lyons, B. Swensen, J. Schomer, G. Tully, J. Barmeier, W. Wright, L. Stewart, S. Bonura, T. Michaels, V. Doran, and H. O'Brien. O'Brien was a disabled draftsman who used crutches—all agreed he deserved this location. Most engineers also agreed that Barmeier should park there; although his title was chief draftsman, he functioned almost as an assistant chief engineer and had been with the company for 20 years.

The engineering group felt strongly that Wright, Stewart, Bonura, Michaels, and Doran should not have parking privileges in a more desirable area than their own. Wright, assistant chief draftsman, supervised three drafting checkers and was seen constantly at Barmeier's elbow. The engineers called them "the Bobbsey twins." Stewart supervised some 20 draftsmen. In the engineers' view, his job consisted mainly of handing out timecards and paychecks. Draftsmen were allocated among the engineers and rarely changed assignments. Stewart usually asked the engineers to fill out job-rating sheets for the draftsmen since he had no basis for appraising their performance. Bonura supervised several office clericals. Michaels, of the machine shop, and Doran, of the engine shop, were called supervisors, but the engineering group felt that "foremen" was a more accurate term.

Arnold Jensen (eight years with the company) and Paul Cooper (two years with Blair and two with Ellington Electronics) told Davis they were glad to find someone else concerned about this situation. Other engineers agreed but were reluctant to make an issue of it. One of them told Davis he might be considered a "rabble-rouser" if he talked too much about it.

From what Davis could determine, everyone had parked in the main lot until a few years back. Then two sections of grass were removed to make the small parking areas (6A and 6B in Exhibit 3).

Since there wasn't room to include Lyons, Swensen, Schomer, Tully, Barmeier, and all the engineers, Lyons said that, rather than draw a line

EXHIBIT 2
Index to Plant Layout (Exhibit 3)

---

1. Main office door—visitors only.
2. Division administration.
3. Entrance—all administrative and engineering employees.
4. Entrance—factory employees.
5. Entrance—engineering labs (not an employee entrance).
6. Parking—engineering personnel, reserved by name.
7. Parking—administration personnel, reserved by number.
8. Parking—most of the engineers, reserved by number.
9. Parking—most of the draftsmen, reserved by number.
10. Parking—Burton Davis, reserved by number.
11. Engineering gate—open all day.
12. Truck loading dock.
13. Paved empty space (could park eight cars).
14. Storage area (could park 10 cars).
15. Storage area (could park 5 cars).
16. Storage area (could park 10 cars).
17. Parking—supervisor of development lab, later supervisor of test and development also.
18. Parking—engineering station wagon and pickup truck.

---

among them, he would not have any of the engineers park there. Instead, all "direct" supervisors were given reserved slots, which just filled the space in the new area. Some engineers felt that Barmeier may have influenced this decision. Technically, the engineers were not "direct" supervisors, although they might have as many as 10 people (draftsmen, typists, etc.) working under their control at one time.

Davis knew that every company had irritations with which one learned to live. However, as the weather grew worse, he walked through the unpaved gravel lot (which developed many holes in winter), plodded along the street (there was no sidewalk), and, still halfway from the entrance, watched others drive in, park near the engineering offices, and enter before he reached the door.

Other things began to disturb him about his position. He found that Barmeier and Wright, without his approval, changed drawings he had released from Engineering.

There were three blank boxes on each engineering drawing. The draftsman would initial the "drawn by" space; the checker, the "checked by"; and the engineer, the "approved by." Lyons usually also initialed the last box, which provided room for two sets of initials. A few

Blair, Inc. (1)

EXHIBIT 3

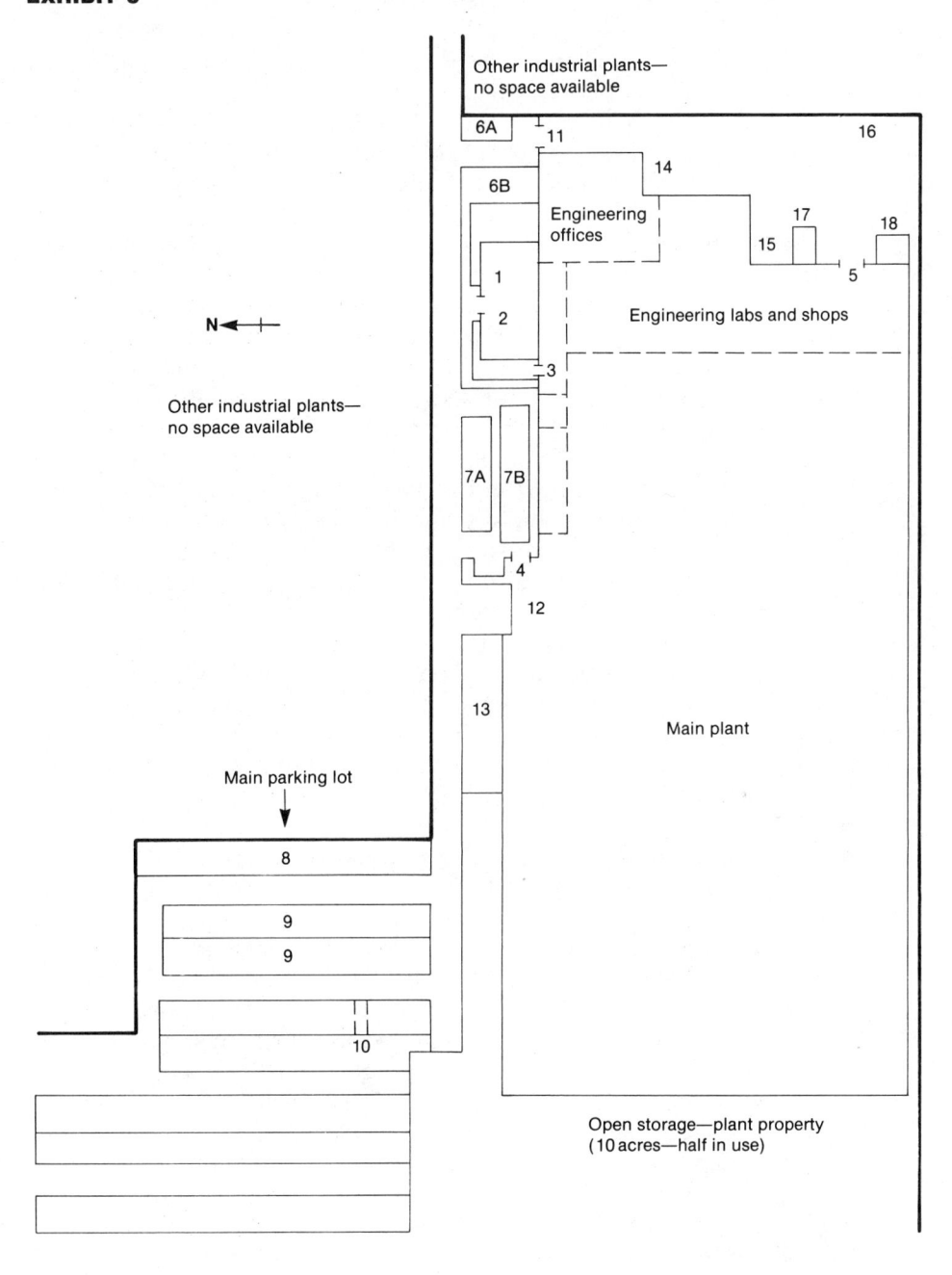

Other industrial plants—
no space available

6A	11	14		16
6B	Engineering offices		17	18
1		15	5
2	Engineering labs and shops
3
7A	7B
4
12
13	Main plant

Other industrial plants—
no space available

N ←

Main parking lot

8

9
9

10

Open storage—plant property
(10 acres—half in use)

months after Davis had started work, Wright started erasing the engineers' initials from the "approved" box, entered his own, and told the engineers to initial after the checker's in the middle box. Jensen and Davis immediately told Wright that he could put his own initials after the checker's, since he was supposed to be the checkers' supervisor and they were the engineers in charge of the project. Davis told Wright, "If you feel otherwise about it, let's go to Lyons right now." Wright immediately agreed to initial after the checker.

Some time after this incident, a sign reading "Authorized Personnel Only" appeared on the door to the blueprint records storage room where Bonura and the clerks worked. Barmeier told the engineering group that the purpose of this was to avoid disturbing the overworked print girls and that the sign applied to all draftsmen and engineers. Although the engineers protested, Barmeier refused to change his stand. Lyons came by during the argument and moved the group into the conference room. The engineers explained that they often needed information from a tracing; a quick glance was enough before returning it to the file. Under the new system, they would have to order a print and wait to get the information. Lyons agreed with the engineers. Davis, Jensen, and Cooper were particularly pleased. Jensen said later, "At last *we* won something around here."

It gradually became apparent to Davis that Lyons planned most of the engineering for his engineers. When assigning a new project he would suggest the handling of it in such detail that all chance of creative or original work was eliminated. He frequently went out in the drafting room and told layout draftsmen how he wanted things done. Sometimes he even failed to bring the responsible engineer in on the discussion.

No engineering meetings were held. The only regular meeting was a "production" meeting for which the division manager and his plant manager came to Lyons' office. Lyons was the only engineer in the meetings, although he often stepped out to get a drawing or to get a question answered from a design or developmental engineer whose project was under discussion at the time. On the rare occasions when an engineer *was* called into the meeting, it was without any advance warning, so that he was frequently unable to furnish the desired information on the spot. Barmeier, Wright, and Bonura sat in on all meetings. Since these were the only regular conferences, discussions inevitably went beyond production problems and dealt with new products and plans as well. The sales manager and the corporate director of engineering attended some of the meetings. To find out what was going on, the engineers relied on the grapevine or were forced to ask Barmeier, Wright, or Bonura. They rarely talked with Lyons except when he was giving them ideas on how he thought they should do their jobs.

Dissatisfaction grew among the engineers, although several still felt there was nothing to be gained by "stirring things up." Davis felt that if Lyons realized the extent of the developing morale problem he would try to do something about it.

One evening, he had an opportunity to talk to Lyons alone. He made it clear that he thought the situation was becoming critical. He told Lyons what he thought were the main points: The generally low status of the engineers and the feeling they had that they were not given enough responsibility. Davis pointed out that the parking situation was one of the main symbols of the engineers' status since it was a visible method of ranking. Lyons seemed uncomfortable throughout the discussion but said that he would think about it. Davis told Lyons that he was speaking only for himself but that he was sure his feelings were shared by most of the others. On leaving, Davis gave Lyons a reprint of an article on morale and suggested it might be of value.[1]

As months passed, no perceptible changes were made.[2] George Dunlop was hired to supervise the engineers, with the title of "Chief, Design and Development" and with the design and development engineers and the designers reporting to him. They had formerly reported directly to Lyons. (Dunlop parked in the engineering lot; Tully was moved to the rear with Graham, area 17 on Exhibit 3—actually a more desirable spot, only 10 feet from a door.) Before Dunlop arrived, Lyons held a meeting with all salaried personnel to explain the decision to bring in a man from outside. He said that he thought the position could have been filled from within the company but that Edward King, the corporate director of engineering, thought that a man with considerable experience was needed. Davis considered it interesting that Lyons was only 34.

Dunlop was 48 years old and had worked as an executive engineer for National Motors, for Burling Aircraft, and for Duvall Manufacturing. Lyons mentioned that people might wonder why a man with this background would come here. He explained that Dunlop liked small towns and enjoyed this type of work and that money was not that important to him. Davis commented later to Jensen that "executive engineer" at National Motors meant a big job and that Dunlop must have had a real setback somewhere along the way. The engineers considered it significant that Dunlop was placed in charge of seven engineers, with the draftsmen and technicians still reporting to others. Moreover, Barmeier was still next to Lyons, with no intermediary. They

---

[1] A portion of the article is reproduced in Exhibit 4.

[2] During this period, Burton Davis typed a memo and circulated it informally among individuals in the division (see Exhibit 5).

EXHIBIT 4

Indicator Area	High Morale Exists When—	Low Morale Exists When—
1. The company	Lines of responsibility and authority are clear; coordination good; line staff teamwork generally productive; organization structure is flexible; managers can get to right official when necessary.	Authority overlaps; organizational structure is too complex; company has too many layers of review; communication breakdowns are frequent; reorganizations don't add up; committees interfere.
2. Company division practices	Good rapport exists among managers; agreements are honored; men know where they stand and how they are doing; policies are clearly and quickly communicated; reward system is fair and current.	There's too much paperwork; managers have to beat the system; excessive rivalry exists among the departments; deadlines don't mean a thing; it is hard to get needed information; ideas die on vine.
3. Decisions	Decisions are tied in well to policies and plans; managers get chance to participate in decision making; delegation is adequate; bad decisions are withdrawn when necessary; accountability is clear.	Decisions are too slow, poorly timed; subordinate has little chance to participate in the making of decisions; delegation is meager; decisions unduly influenced by tradition; real issues are evaded.
4. Leadership	Staff meetings are well run and produce results; boss keeps subordinates informed of policies and plans affecting them; men know the scope of their responsibilities; boss shows dignity and fairness.	Assignments and orders of boss are unclear; men have to work without knowing policy limitations; boss sets unreasonable deadlines; too many attempts are made at regimentation; standards fall.
5. Group climate	Team takes pride in its performance; men will go to bat for each other; professional aims, standards are high; grievances of a member	Too many cliques exist; favoritism is shown some; work output is inadequate; one man dominates the group; bickering is common;

EXHIBIT 4 (concluded)

		are heard; overall quality of group output is high-grade.	there are recurrent rule violations; professional standards are low.
6.	Job conditions	Managers find sufficient challenge in their jobs; abilities of men are utilized well; employees able to express their views; performance standards are realistic; workers get recognition when deserved.	It's difficult to get a job done; ideas put aside too often, too fast; men have to break rules to get action; boredom and restlessness are prevalent; pay scales lag behind the rates in other firms.
7.	Status	Job privileges are modest but good; management is receptive to a man's views; talents are utilized; employees enjoy higher status in community because of their association with the company.	Favored few get recognition; opportunities for development are restricted; criticisms far exceed compliments; men must look out for themselves; firm has too many dead-end jobs.

Source: From Nathaniel Stewart, "You Can Keep Morale High," *Nation's Business,* March 1963. Reprinted by permission.

**EXHIBIT 5
Office Memo**

ENGINE AND MOTOR ENGINEERING SECTION

To: "Supervisory" Personnel

Subject: Fitness Program

Going along with the present Washington administration's emphasis on hiking as a means of improving the fitness of the American people, it is suggested that those Blair employees now parking near the building exchange parking places with the Engine and Motor Section *engineers*. The engineers are in splendid shape from their long hikes and feel that it is only fair to share this conditioning. After a suitable "building up" period, a rotation system will be worked out to insure the retention of all the fitness benefits.

The Personnel Department

also noted that Dunlop had not been given the title of assistant chief engineer.

Several engineers with long experience with the firm believed they should have been candidates for the job. Other engineers thought Dunlop might become a useful go-between for them. They saw that Barmeier took care of *his* people and Tully took care of *this*. Perhaps the engineers now had someone to put in a few good words for them. Dunlop seemed, at first, to be a much better administrator than Lyons. At least, the engineers felt he "talked a good game." They began to tell him about things they felt needed improvement or correction, but, after two months, it became apparent that Dunlop had not recommended any changes to Lyons. It appeared to Davis and others that he was loath to tell Lyons anything that might be disturbing. The engineers felt that he was "running scared."

Davis suggested to Jensen and Cooper that talking to Dunlop was not unlike a session with a psychiatrist. You talked about your problems and felt better even though nothing really changed. Whenever anyone returned from a talk with Dunlop, a colleague would ask, "Did you have a nice couch session?"

As the small group talked about their problems, the situation became almost unbearable to Davis. There was considerable talk of other jobs, and occasionally one of the men would have an interview with another firm. Finally, Davis, Jensen, and Cooper decided to approach Lyons in a group. They had decided that they would all leave anyway unless changes were made. This "group action" was distasteful to them, but they felt that it was the only way to get Lyons to realize he had a real problem to face. There seemed to be little to lose.

Following are some of the comments made by the engineers and Lyons as they talked in the chief engineer's office one evening after work:

ENGINEER: We feel a little silly talking about this, but since it does bother us and affects our morale, we feel you should know.

ENGINEER: The parking position ranks everyone, whether or not you believe it does.

LYONS: Where you park doesn't have anything to do with the way I rank you.

ENGINEER: We feel that as highly paid college graduates who actually do the creative work, we should rank above "assistant chief draftsmen" and "foremen."

ENGINEER: Specifically, we feel that we should rank ahead of Wright, Stewart, Bonura, Doran, and Michaels.

LYONS: Do you feel you are better than those people?

ENGINEER: In terms of working for this company, yes. We would certainly be harder to replace. In any case, ranking is inevitable; we would like to think that you agree with us on where we rank.

Lyons: You know that you make much more money than those people, don't you?

Engineer: Yes, which is another reason for keeping the other symbols of rank in the same order.

Engineer: Salary is not a problem. We do not feel overpaid or underpaid in our present jobs.

Engineer: Whether or not *you* feel this is a problem, the fact that *we* feel it is a problem *makes* it a problem, by definition.

Engineer: The fact that parking ranks us in status actually affects our job efficiency as it relates to others. We have more trouble "getting things done" if we don't have the status to back it up.

Engineer: Saying that status symbols are unimportant doesn't make them go away. We live with status symbols all the time; unless they are distorted from the way most people expect to see them, they go unnoticed. Only when the symbol system gets out of line does it become a problem. This means that to have a smoothly functioning organization, an administrator has to consider status symbols and make every attempt to allocate them as his subordinates expect him to.

Engineer: Doran and Michaels are foremen, no matter what fancy names they are called. Stewart is the drafting supervisor and should rank under us, but Barmeier and Wright are doing engineering work. If you want to rank them above us that is your decision, but their titles should be changed. A chief draftsman and his assistant should never rank above any engineer. The situation is similar to the army, where a master sergeant may have many years of experience and be valuable, but he does not outrank the greenest second lieutenant.

Engineer: We note that you have the closest space to the door in the lots near engineering, and the division manager has the space closest to the door in the administration lot. Isn't it logical that the no. 2 ranking people have the next spaces, and so on down the line? That's the way almost everyone looks at it.

Engineer: We don't care *where* we actually park. The question is *who* parks where. If everyone had the same long walk, there would be no problem.

Engineer: Locating our parking spaces more conveniently without changing the relative status of the spaces will be no solution at all.

Lyons: But where can I find more parking space?

Engineer: We think there are a number of areas that could be used, but some effort would be required. There is unused space in front of the plant (13 in Exhibit 3), or space could be made available by moving some of the stored materials from the area east of Engineering (14, 15, and 16 in Exhibit 3). Even if you can't find space for improved parking for everyone, engineers should park in that lot. Not necessarily the three of us, but *engineers*.

Engineer: The fact that you don't or can't trust us with more responsibility affects our morale and job interest also.

Lyons: But I do give as much responsibility as possible.

Engineer: But you act as if you don't really trust us.

Lyons: It's not that I don't trust you, it's just that I want to see the job done right.

As the talk ended, Lyons appeared to be disturbed and concerned. He said that he would think about what had been said and would see if there was anything that he could do.

Nevertheless, the three engineers were sure that Lyons had not really understood them. In spite of their emphasis on "not where, but *who*," they sensed that the chief engineer believed that all they wanted was better, closer parking places. They felt he didn't understand their desire for more responsibility, either; he seemed to think they had all the responsibility they had a right to expect. They agreed that his comment on "doing the job right" demonstrated how little effect they had had.

They predicted that any solution that Lyons might devise would be unsatisfactory. They wondered if they should take any other steps or just wait and hope that Lyons had more understanding than they suspected. They realized that if the solution was unsatisfactory, it was the end of the road. They could hardly start the process all over again.

*The Case of the Missing Time**

AT APPROXIMATELY 7:30 A.M. on Tuesday, June 23, 1959, Chet Craig, manager of the Norris Company's central plant, swung his car out of the driveway of his suburban home and headed toward the plant located some six miles away just inside the Midvale city limits. It was a beautiful day. The sun was shining brightly and a cool, fresh breeze was blowing. The trip to the plant took about 20 minutes and sometimes gave Chet an opportunity to think about plant problems without interruption.

The Norris Company owned and operated three quality printing plants. Norris enjoyed a nationwide commercial business, specializing in quality color work. It was a closely held company with some 350 employees, nearly half of whom were employed at the central plant, the largest of the three Norris production operations. The company's main offices were also located in the central plant building.

Chet had started with the Norris Company as an expediter in its eastern plant in 1948 just after he graduated from Ohio State. After three years Chet was promoted to production supervisor and two years later was made assistant to the manager of the eastern plant. Early in 1957 he was transferred to the central plant as assistant to the plant manager and

---

*All names and organizational designations have been disguised.
 Northwestern University cases are reports of concrete events and behavior prepared for class discussion. They are not intended as examples of good or bad administrative or technical practices.
 Copyright 1960, Northwestern University.

The Case of the Missing Time

one month later was promoted to plant manager, when the former manager retired.

Chet was in fine spirits as he relaxed behind the wheel. As his car picked up speed, the hum of the tires on the newly paved highway faded into the background. Various thoughts occurred to him and he said to himself, "This is going to be the day to really get things done."

He began to run through the day's work, first one project, then another, trying to establish priorities. After a few minutes he decided that the open-end unit scheduling was probably the most important; certainly the most urgent. He frowned for a moment as he recalled that on Friday the vice president and general manager had casually asked him if he had given the project any further thought. Chet realized that he had not been giving it much thought lately. He had been meaning to get to work on this idea for over three months, but something else always seemed to crop up. "I haven't had much time to sit down and really work it out," he said to himself. "I'd better get going and hit this one today for sure." With that he began to break down the objectives, procedures, and installation steps of the project. He grinned as he reviewed the principles involved and calculated roughly the anticipated savings. "It's about time," he told himself. "This idea should have been followed up long ago." Chet remembered that he had first conceived of the open-end unit scheduling idea nearly a year and a half ago just prior to his leaving Norris's eastern plant. He had spoken to his boss, Jim Quince, manager of the eastern plant, about it then and both agreed that it was worth looking into. The idea was temporarily shelved when he was transferred to the central plant a month later.

A blast from a passing horn startled him but his thoughts quickly returned to other plant projects he was determined to get under way. He started to think through a procedure for simpler transport of dies to and from the eastern plant. Visualizing the notes on his desk, he thought about the inventory analysis he needed to identify and eliminate some of the slow-moving stock items; the packing controls which needed revision; and the need to design a new special-order form. He also decided that this was the day to settle on a job printer to do the simple outside printing of office forms. There were a few other projects he couldn't recall offhand but he could tend to them after lunch if not before. "Yes, sir," he said to himself, "this is the day to really get rolling."

Chet's thoughts were interrupted as he pulled into the company parking lot. When he entered the plant Chet knew something was wrong as he met Al Noren, the stockroom foreman, who appeared troubled. "A great morning, Al," Chet greeted him cheerfully.

"Not so good, Chet; my new man isn't in this morning," Noren growled.

"Have you heard from him?" asked Chet.

"No, I haven't," replied Al.

Chet frowned as he commented, "These stock handlers assume you take it for granted that if they're not here, they're not here, and they don't have to call in and verify it. Better ask personnel to call him."

Al hesitated for a moment before replying. "Okay, Chet, but can you find me a man? I have two cars to unload today."

As Chet turned to leave he said, "I'll call you in half an hour, Al, and let you know."

Making a mental note of the situation, Chet headed for his office. He greeted the group of workers huddled around Marilyn, the office manager, who was discussing the day's work schedule with them. As the meeting broke up Marilyn picked up a few samples from the clasper, showed them to Chet, and asked if they should be shipped that way or if it would be necessary to inspect them. Before he could answer, Marilyn went on to ask if he could suggest another clerical operator for the sealing machine to replace the regular operator who was home ill. She also told him that Gene, the industrial engineer, had called and was waiting to hear from Chet.

After telling Marilyn to go ahead and ship the samples, he made a note of the need for a sealer operator for the office and then called Gene. He agreed to stop by Gene's office before lunch and started on his routine morning tour of the plant. He asked each foreman the types and volumes of orders they were running, the number of people present, how the schedules were coming along, and the orders to be run next; helped the folding-room foreman find temporary storage space for consolidating a carload shipment; discussed quality control with a pressman who had been running poor work; arranged to transfer four people temporarily to different departments, including two for Al in the stockroom, talked to the shipping foreman about pickups and special orders to be delivered that day. As he continued through the plant, he saw to it that reserve stock was moved out of the forward stock area; talked to another pressman about his requested change of vacation schedule; had a "heart-to-heart" talk with a press helper who seemed to need frequent reassurance; approved two type and one color order okays for different pressmen.

Returning to his office, Chet reviewed the production reports on the larger orders against his initial productions and found that the plant was running behind schedule. He called in the folding-room foreman and together they went over the lineup of machines and made several necessary changes.

During this discussion, the composing-room foreman stopped in to cover several type changes and the routing foreman telephoned for approval of a revised printing schedule. The stockroom foreman called twice, first to inform him that two standard, fast-moving stock items were dangerously low; later to advise him that the paper stock for the urgent Dillion job had finally arrived. Chet made the necessary subsequent calls to inform those concerned.

He then began to put delivery dates on important and difficult inquiries received from customers and salesmen. (The routine inquiries were handled by Marilyn.) While he was doing this he was interrupted twice, once by a sales correspondent calling from the West Coast to ask for a better delivery date than originally scheduled; once by the personnel vice president asking him to set a time when he could hold an initial training and induction interview with a new employee.

After dating the customer and salesmen inquiries, Chet headed for his morning conference in the executive offices. At this meeting he answered the sales vice president's questions in connection with "hot" orders, complaints, the status of large-volume orders and potential new orders. He then met with the general manager to discuss a few ticklish policy matters and to answer "the old man's" questions on several specific production and personnel problems. Before leaving the executive offices, he stopped at the office of the secretary-treasurer to inquire about delivery of cartons, paper, and boxes, and to place a new order for paper.

On the way back to his own office, Chet conferred with Gene about two current engineering projects concerning which he had called earlier. When he reached his desk, he lit a cigarette, and looked at his watch. It was 10 minutes before lunch, just time enough to make a few notes of the details he needed to check in order to answer knotty questions raised by the sales manager that morning.

After lunch Chet started again. He began by checking the previous day's production reports; did some rescheduling to get out urgent orders; placed appropriate delivery dates on new orders and inquiries received that morning; consulted with a foreman on a personal problem. He spent some 20 minutes at the TWX[1] going over mutual problems with the eastern plant.

By midafternoon Chet had made another tour of the plant, after which he met with the personnel director to review with him a touchy personal problem raised by one of the clerical employees, the vacation schedules submitted by his foremen, and the pending job evaluation program. Following this conference, Chet hurried back to his office to complete the special statistical report for Universal Waxing Corporation, one of Norris's best customers. As he finished the report he discovered that it was 10 minutes after six and he was the only one left in the office. Chet was tired. He put on his coat and headed through the plant toward the parking lot; on the way he was stopped by both the night supervisor and night layout foreman for approval of type and layout changes.

With both eyes on the traffic, Chet reviewed the day he had just

---

[1] Leased private telegram communication system using a teletypewriter.

completed. "Busy?" he asked himself. "Too much so—but did I accomplish anything?" His mind raced over the day's activities. "Yes and no" seemed to be the answer. "There was the usual routine, the same as any other day. The plant kept going and I think it must have been a good production day. Any creative or special project-work done?" Chet grimaced as he reluctantly answered, "No."

With a feeling of guilt, he probed further. "Am I an executive? I'm paid like one, respected like one, and have a responsible assignment with the necessary authority to carry it out. Yet one of the greatest values a company derives from an executive is his creative thinking and accomplishments. What have I done about it? An executive needs some time for thinking. Today was a typical day, just like most other days, and I did little, if any, creative work. The projects that I so enthusiastically planned to work on this morning are exactly as they were yesterday. What's more, I have no guarantee that tomorrow night or the next night will bring me any closer to their completion. This is a real problem and there must be an answer."

Chet continued, "Night work? Yes, occasionally. This is understood. But I've been doing too much of this lately. I owe my wife and family some of my time. When you come down to it, they are the people for whom I'm really working. If I am forced to spend much more time away from them, I'm not meeting my own personal objectives. What about church work? Should I eliminate that? I spend a lot of time on this, but I feel I owe God some time too. Besides, I believe I'm making a worthwhile contribution in this work. Perhaps I can squeeze a little time from my fraternal activities. But where does recreation fit in?"

Chet groped for the solution. "Maybe I'm just rationalizing because I schedule my own work poorly. But I don't think so. I've studied my work habits carefully and I think I plan intelligently and delegate authority. Do I need an assistant? Possibly, but that's a long-time project and I don't believe I could justify the additional overhead expenditure. Anyway, I doubt whether it would solve the problem."

By this time Chet had turned off the highway onto the side street leading to his home—the problem still uppermost in his mind. "I guess I really don't know the answer," he told himself as he pulled into his driveway. "This morning everything seemed so simple but now. . . ." His thoughts were interrupted as he saw his son running toward the car calling out, "Mommy, Daddy's home."

EXHIBIT 1
Organization Chart

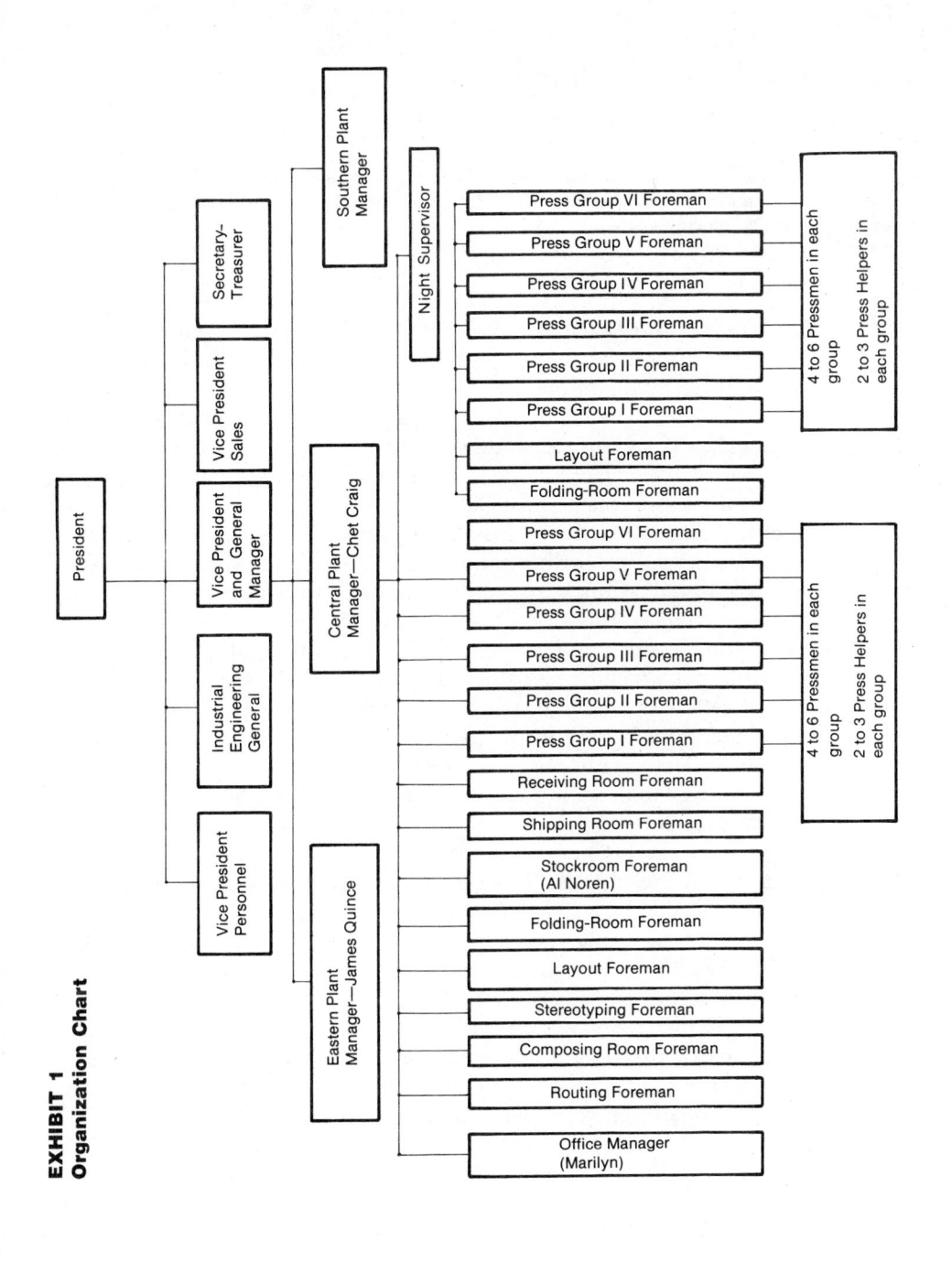

- President
  - Vice President and General Manager
    - Vice President Personnel
    - Industrial Engineering General
    - Vice President Sales
    - Secretary-Treasurer
    - Southern Plant Manager
    - Central Plant Manager—Chet Craig
      - Night Supervisor
        - Press Group VI Foreman
        - Press Group V Foreman
        - Press Group IV Foreman
        - Press Group III Foreman
        - Press Group II Foreman
        - Press Group I Foreman
          - 4 to 6 Pressmen in each group
          - 2 to 3 Press Helpers in each group
      - Layout Foreman
      - Folding-Room Foreman
      - Press Group VI Foreman
      - Press Group V Foreman
      - Press Group IV Foreman
      - Press Group III Foreman
      - Press Group II Foreman
      - Press Group I Foreman
        - 4 to 6 Pressmen in each group
        - 2 to 3 Press Helpers in each group
    - Eastern Plant Manager—James Quince
      - Receiving Room Foreman
      - Shipping Room Foreman
      - Stockroom Foreman (Al Noren)
      - Folding-Room Foreman
      - Layout Foreman
      - Stereotyping Foreman
      - Composing Room Foreman
      - Routing Foreman
      - Office Manager (Marilyn)

Adirondack Preservation Council
("Help, what do I do now")*

NOTE: Do not read this case until directed to do so by your instructor. It has been set up as a prediction case so that you can test your analysis by answering questions before reading the entire case.

PART I

CHARLES GRAINGER had seldom experienced such uncertainty as he now felt, wondering what he should do with the information he had about the financial affairs of the Adirondack Preservation Council. Should he say nothing and avoid trouble, should he "blow the whistle," or what?

Chuck was a graduate student at the state university in upstate New York seeking a master's degree in management and finance. Following graduation from college, Chuck had gone into factory management, but after three years of satisfying experience and progress he had decided to return to school for further professional training. Now nearing the end of his program, Chuck had undertaken an internship as his major (12 out of 16 credits) academic activity for the final semester.[1] Chuck saw the internship as a way to further his training through direct application of the concepts which he had studied. Also, he hoped to learn more about the upstate region, an area with which both he and his wife had fallen in love since moving there for graduate study. Furthermore, he looked forward to working under the general guidance of Professor Hartcote, a new, young, and exciting faculty member who taught finance.

Through some work during the fall on local election campaigns, Chuck had met Charles Knowlton, the president emeritus of the Adirondack Preservation Council (APC) board of directors. Both had a common interest in environmental questions, and both had a common concern for the problems associated with managing a nonprofit organization. When Mr. Knowlton learned of Chuck's desire to undertake an internship, he asked Chuck to study APC. Specifically, he wanted Chuck to make a general review of the financial and administrative functions of the organization, to make specific recommendations for modifications, and then to organize and implement those changes the staff and board felt were necessary.

APC was a private nonprofit conservation and environmental education organization promoting the wise use of all renewable resources in

---

*Copyright 1979, Whittemore School of Business and Economics, University of New Hampshire. Reproduced with permission.

[1] Under an internship a student is expected to study some aspect of an actual organization, make concrete recommendations to management, and prepare an academic report conceptualizing his learning from the experience.

the Adirondack region of upstate New York. Since early in the century APC had been actively involved in land management, land protection, and general conservation activities, ranging from helping establish wilderness land as state forests to preventing unnecessary spoilage of lakes and streams from the routing of new highways.

Prior to the start of the semester, Knowlton had briefed Chuck enough for him to know that the staff position of manager of finance and administration had been vacant for some six months and that it remained so because the director, Harold Hayes, was not convinced that the position required a full-time professional person. In fact, much to Knowlton's dismay, Hayes, a wood technologist by training, felt that the bookkeeper could handle all but the most difficult financial affairs of the council with the more trying transactions being managed by Hayes or the board. Hayes's attitude had led Knowlton, a former chief financial officer of a large Fortune 500 company, to become even more leary of a situation he thought had at least the potential for trouble, although there were very little hard data on which to base a sound judgment.

Thus, Chuck Grainger found himself "hired" by the president emeritus to perform temporarily a project which might ordinarily be done by a staff member, but one whom the director felt was superfluous. Hayes had accepted the internship concept reluctantly but with the admission that it might be a means for accomplishing several activities and hence eliminate the long-term need for a full-time manager. Knowlton had very different thoughts and had even proposed to Grainger that if his performance met expectations there might be a full-time employment opportunity at the end of the semester, though Hayes would not only have to concur in principle that the position was necessary but would also have final approval of the candidate for the position.

Chuck began by analyzing the recent financial affairs of the council with an eye on future computerization, one of the semester's higher priority projects. He soon recognized that the multifund structure of the council's financial affairs would require more than a perfunctory analysis to determine mechanization needs. A quick and superficial look at the previous three years' audit reports showed consistent surpluses of revenue over expenses for all APC funds. However, the more detailed examination of the audit reports and the council's current accounts led to an unexpected conclusion. By the end of the first month Grainger had identified a severe financial crisis which was evidenced by cash operating deficits, which for more than a year had been covered by the unauthorized use of at least $300,000 of principal endowment monies.

This cash had been available to meet ongoing expenses because the bookkeeper, knowing little about the difference between accounts set up to cover current costs and capital requirements, had deposited monies acquired in a capital fund drive to the General Fund account instead of to a new Capital Fund account.

Once he saw the magnitude of the problem, Chuck was perplexed as to what he should do. Here he had embarked on a fairly routine procedures analysis and study of a potential computer application and now was faced with evidence of what he considered to be at best incompetent, and at worst unethical and illegal, behavior by the director. Help, what should I do now?

The thoughts raced through his mind. Were his dreams of working in a socially useful organization about to be shattered? Could he, a student, expose the director? What would happen to his internship?

Discussion Question

What questions should Chuck seek to answer as a prelude to taking action?

PART II

The first thing that Chuck decided to do after the shock had passed and he felt calmer was to review what he knew about the people involved by posing several questions to himself.

1. Why should *I* do anything at all?

    Under the terms of the internship I can focus on the computer application and avoid the issue entirely. Thus, I can fulfill the academic requirements and avoid the "hot potato." But I know that I'd never be able to live with that. In the first place, I would feel like I was running away from a responsibility and challenge which anyone calling himself a manager should be ready to face up to. Furthermore, the situation which I alone recognize has potentially serious consequences for an organization which I personally care about. If it were allowed to continue, it would eventually come out and threaten the very existence of the organization. Early action could prevent such a disaster and insure that APC could continue its work, which I see as important and vital.

2. What did I know about *Hayes*? Was Hayes competent? Was he approachable? Was he a power to be reckoned with?

    As I perceive Hayes, he is a man of integrity whose dedication to the goals of the organization are unquestioned. In Hayes, I am not dealing with a self-serving dishonest person. But Hayes is a person of strong convictions and a person with power and influence. If he saw himself being presented in an overly unsavory light, particularly by a mere intern, he could make things very uncomfortable for me. Hayes cannot be ignored.

3. What did I know about Charles *Knowlton*?

Knowlton is a retired executive who knows his way around big corporate life. Rather austere in personal style, he can be easily misunderstood as secretive and nit-picky by those who do not know him. He clearly has power in the council through his reputation among environmentalists. Knowlton is not power hungry, so while I'm sure he would fight for what he sees as right, I'm also sure he would only go that route as a last resort.

Also, I sense that his relation with Hayes, while rather formal, is one of mutual respect despite occasional differences of opinion.

I can count on Knowlton as an ally but not as the only person to be reckoned with.

4. What do I know about the *board of directors?*

The board, which meets six times a year, is composed of busy influential people from around the region. They would not tolerate some smart aleck young person stirring up trouble based on academic niceties reflecting some ivory tower theory about how things ought to be. On the other hand, they would not tolerate policies that were proven to be unethical or illegal.

As a group, the board respects Knowlton and would not be quick to ignore his assessment of a situation. The same could be said of its view of Hayes. Given a disagreement between Knowlton and Hayes, the board would probably want to find some mutually acceptable solution and avoid a Knowlton/Hayes split.

5. What about *my personal goals?*

I certainly want to come out of this with my self-esteem intact and the organization whole. But also, I like the idea of a job after graduation with APC. There is need for a manager of finance and administration; the situation proves that! If Hayes doesn't count me as an enemy, I see him as a guy I could work for, even though at times I suspect I'd find his technical orientation to be frustrating. That job possibility has definitely been on my mind.

6. What about *Professor* Hartcote?

He is new to the region and while he can give me good advice he has little political influence. He is not known by members of the organization other than Knowlton, so he does not represent a source of influence. But he does control the internship and the 12 credits I'll need to graduate. I *think* he would accept my diverting my energies from the internship's stated purpose to solving this problem. In fact, dealing with this issue successfully should provide the basis for a report that can fulfill the academic requirements satisfactorily, but Hartcote will have to agree.

7. What do I know about the *APC staff?*

They are something of an unknown since I've not had much contact with them. All seem busy and dedicated. However, any new set of financial policies and procedures, such as would prevent what

has happened from happening again, would affect their work and need their compliance. Also, it seems likely to me that possible steps to restore the $300,000 misused funds would affect them too.
8. Is it possible to develop a solution that satisfies all *constituencies?*

With varying degrees of intensity, all parties have a vested interest in the financial situation. The staff and Hayes will be concerned about job security. The board will want the council to survive and stay strong but will also want to insure that the staff is adequately paid. The general membership will certainly want the organization to remain responsive to them and not become embroiled in bureaucratic financial red tape. Should I try to satisfy everyone's needs?

Discussion Question

Given the above diagnosis, what should Chuck do?

PART III

Needless to say, Grainger was hard pressed to find a source of action that would satisfy everyone. The only real avenue seemed to be complete disclosure, and his judgment was reinforced by a discussion he had with Professor Hartcote.

He felt he had to go to Hayes, partly because ultimate responsibility for the problem rested in Hayes's lap, but also because he wanted the job, and Hayes would have the final say on that score. He needed a strategy that would let Hayes continue to value him.

Before going to Hayes, however, Grainger double checked his information to make certain that he was right. Then, reasoning that he needed to help Hayes save face, he developed a clear rationale for why such a problem could develop under *anyone's* leadership (e.g., Hayes and the staff had been without a financial officer for nearly 11 months) and prepared a proposed plan of action. That way Hayes, and eventually the board, would be presented with a general solution and not just with a problem. And he could be seen as helpful and competent by Hayes, rather than as a hostile spy.

The problem itself, to say nothing of its magnitude, was met with incredulity by Hayes. He could not believe that the "mistake" had happened. After going over the complex financial transactions with Chuck several times, Hayes began to be worried because he saw that responsibility for the pending crisis lay at his doorstep. Thus, he was quite interested in Chuck's ideas about how to proceed, how to deal with the board, and how to go about replacing the misspent funds. Chuck had managed to come off as supportive rather than accusing.

Grainger felt that the next step should be to include Knowlton. He felt an obligation to Knowlton for arranging the internship and saw him as an important constituency. Grainger had good rapport with Knowlton and looked upon him as a helpful resource on financial solutions. Furthermore, Knowlton would lend financial credibility to any plans. Hayes concurred and together they presented the situation to Knowlton and reviewed Grainger's proposed next steps. Knowlton was upset at the news but supportive of the plan of action.

The third step was to inform the staff. Grainger and Hayes discussed the staff and planned the meeting. They were particularly concerned about staff members' lack of knowledge about financial procedures. Knowing that they could not give them a crash course in accounting in the short time available, they decided to cover only enough principles to make the problem clear. With a plan in hand, Hayes called a staff meeting to "review the financial situation of the council." Grainger was in attendance.

Next, the board of directors had to be informed. Time did not permit going to the board with detailed recommendations, but a general framework for a solution was presented, along with the problem. The board's reaction was naturally one of dismay and irate concern. Hayes, now under fire, promised detailed remedial recommendations by the next board meeting, and both he and the board asked Grainger to prepare a specific plan of action—a plan that would simultaneously restore the battered endowment and create a financial control system that would prevent future problems.

As the fiscal year was to come to a close in the near future, it was necessary to have a final budget approved and ready by the next meeting. Grainger decided that although time was short an entirely new program budgeting process was obligatory. It would have to include program and budget goals and objectives which would be cumulatively developed from ground zero to completion by the entire program staff, the director, the board's finance and planning committee, and ultimately the entire board, an unfamiliar process to all. The plan was to include a whole new approach to budgeting, which, when implemented, would allocate (for the first time) controllable direct income and expenses to the appropriate program manager, facilitating the comparison of planned to actual finances on a quarterly, rather than annual, basis. In addition, the new system would allow every participant in the process a chance to contribute to the cumulative prioritization of all program goals and objectives and the allocation of available monies. Grainger felt it would also help restore everyone's confidence in the council, whatever their position. All this was to be approved at the next board meeting but was agreed to in principle beforehand by the staff and by the board through informal discussions.

Funds which had been used for current expenses still had to be returned to the capital account, and cash had to be raised for the purpose. A plan was put together by the staff, ultimately approved by the board, to take advantage of a program the council had developed to encourage donations of land to the council by persons interested in land protection and a tax write-off. After obtaining the concurrence of the donors, gifts of land originally intended for other purposes were earmarked for sale.

As Grainger put it, "The most difficult part of the process was behavioral. The new demands on the staff required by these plans were great. The program managers would not only have to formulate and document future program goals and their associated budgets but would also have to try to prioritize objectively their own and each other's programs for the good of the whole. A good deal of my time was necessarily spent laying the foundation for this change, primarily through preliminary meetings with each program manager in which we discussed the recent past and projected future of the council. Being an intern does not lend itself easily to credibility or leverage, nor is the bearer of not very good tidings welcomed with open arms. This tended to make me particularly cognizant of developing a working rapport with each program manager. On the other hand, I was an agent working for both the president emeritus and the director, which had the effect of increasing my internal influence."

One final outcome was that Hayes reversed his stand on the need for a professional manager of finance and offered the job to Grainger.

Chris Hammond (A)*

SHE IS 26, single, and grew up in Hibbing, Minnesota, "the kind of town where if you dated a boy in high school more than twice you were expected to marry him." A senior market support specialist for a major electronics corporation that has seen tremendous growth in the past 10 years, she currently works in the firm's new office headquarters in southern Vermont and travels frequently. Ultimately she would like to be president of her own company. Right now she is enthused about her present position, the talent of her co-workers, and the matrix organization of the corporation for which she works.

"My family has been involved in the mining steel industry back to the 1890s. This heritage of big business is almost second nature to me.

---

*This case was prepared by Deborah Downs and Pamela Fuhrer under the direction of Professor Allan R. Cohen for the purpose of classroom discussion. Special thanks is given to Anne Jamar for her assistance. Copyright 1979, Whittemore School of Business and Economics, University of New Hampshire. Reproduced with permission.

"When I look back on it, my dad's career path was very similar to mine which means that I'm very similar to him which means that talking about him reveals a lot about myself. He is my role model for how to behave in the business world. My mother is also a role model that I downplay and make fun of, so that some people give me a hard time about not liking my mother. That's not true, but my mother lives vicariously, and I don't. Until last year we were not able to communicate as adults, and she assumed that I was still going through a phase. This year she is beginning to believe in herself as a person and is also treating me like one.

"My father is an engineer and so my brother and I had a more technical childhood than the average child. I remember a number of things from my early childhood, which may sound unusual but really isn't because I've always been cognizant of my environment and the people in it. Right before my fifth birthday we moved into a huge house. My mother painted and carpeted what I considered to be beautiful wooden floors. Ugh! I was so stubborn that I said, 'You aren't going to do anything to my bedroom floor!' She said, 'Well then, you'll just have to do it yourself.' So I did. I sanded and stained the bedroom floor, at age 5! With some help, of course!

"What stands out in my childhood? I learned to play the piano before I could read. At age 9 I read the story of Helen Keller, which became a source of inspiration for me. That same year my goal was to go eventually to Radcliffe College. I knew Hibbing wasn't the place for me.

"My two loves in life from age 9 on were music and science, especially physics. The physics probably came from reading about Madame Curie—I always enjoyed stories about successful women, and I envisioned myself growing up to be one. I never dreamed of being a mother or being married. I thought playing house was dumb, so I played football and sensible things like that instead (laugh).

"Externally I'm a very jovial person, but internally I'm exceedingly serious, which probably explains why I've acquired the storytelling ability I have and why I do some rather cavalier things. When I was young, I was always kidded about my precocious ideas. It was very painful not to be taken seriously. The reason I giggle a lot today is because I used to cry then.

"My dad taught us three things to live by, which I do live by today: first, that you had better like what you see in the mirror when you get up in the morning because you're the only person that has to live with yourself all of your life; second, that one should be honest with oneself and with others; and third, that no one is any better than I am, and I'm no better than anyone else in this world. This last one is what I attribute my success in the business world to. In the microcosm of Hibbing it would have been very easy for me to say that I was the best at most everything. But for me it's not that challenging to be a big fish in a small sea.

"My mother always told me I was a fat ugly slob and a stupid klutz, and she pestered me about why I wore ugly clothes and why I didn't date the president of the senior class. I always felt I was a failure to my mother, and to this day I feel that way when I'm around her. My mother's influence was so strong that I always felt that I was hurting her, that I was a failure as her daughter. And when my dad would reinforce that, I always felt like I was really a failure as a human being because my social life was not too great. It's interesting to me that my mother had such a powerful effect on me regarding these things, since they are so important to her but do not really matter much to me.

"I graduated from college with a B.A. in math and a low GPA—2.8—after having several majors including piano performance and elementary education. I was very active in school, including participation on several committees to improve the teaching of mathematics and social sciences to young people and future teachers, student/faculty affairs, and racial conflicts. I was also a dorm adviser. In general I had a pretty standard college life especially considering that I attended college in an era when nearly everyone was going around blowing their brains out on drugs. The incredible thing was that the only two people in the whole wide world who told me that I was a lousy, screwed-up, crazy, hippy freak who was totally unsuccessful and a total disaster were my parents; so at the ripe old age of 19 I said who needs them? Everyone else in the world has given me fairly positive feedback about my being a nice person, fun to be with, fairly decent looking, pretty smart . . . and I've never really lacked for friends. In fact, I tend to have too many and am often accused of being negligent of them.

"One thing I've never had is what I call the 'victim mentality.' I just assume that no one is going to do anything bad to me and it usually seems to work out well. People tend to fulfill the dreams that you have for them, to live up to your expectations. If I manipulate people at all, it's along these lines. For example, I'll say to my boss, 'You're really terrific . . . you know how to handle women, which is extraordinary. I've worked for seven years and I've never had a boss who could do that.' So he really tried to live up to that expectation. You want him to treat you like a person and not like a sex object or a woman or anybody special. This allows me to say to a manager, 'You are really screwing up, I don't like it,' and not be afraid of what that's going to do to me. Once a vice president at one company I worked for asked me what I thought was the major problem between the field and headquarters. 'You guys are always having meetings,' I replied. 'Don't you ever even go to the bathroom so you could get your messages? Why don't you put a telephone in the bathroom?' What I was actually saying, of course, was that headquarters was not responsive to the field. Since one of the major requisites in the job is responding to all phone calls in a reasonable amount of time, we were really failing at one of the key dictums. Well, he laughed and jokingly brought the comment to the business management committee. Being able to criticize through humor has served me well, and several people have commented on my ability to make pointed but funny, witty remarks.

"Why did I choose the minicomputer industry? Because frankly that's where the action is. Minicomputers can do so much for the world. And the future of the industry meshes perfectly with my goals. I want to change the world of education and it's going to take computers to do it. Audiovisual technology is passé. Someday everyone will have a computer in their home that is going to be tied in to their television sets, and they'll be able to get any information they want and are legally authorized to have access to. My role will be to make sure it's good information. I want to do for computers in education what *Sesame Street* has done for television in education.

"Computex has a charisma all its own. You have to be a special type to work here. If you need to be told what to do, you leave the company. People don't get fired, they just leave because they can't stand not being told what to do. You can virtually make your own world. It's a company filled with prima donnas and entrepreneurs. You have the opportunity to do your own thing. For example, I decided I wanted to learn more about marketing to government. I could have traveled to any government in North America, but I chose Washington, D.C., instead. Even though it wasn't in my territory, I figured that I couldn't obtain the big picture without it. I presented my ideas to my manager and he said, 'Sure, go try it.' After my first visit I found five or six projects developed by agencies who are based in Washington. By servicing these agencies, I built up a rapport that now gives me valuable leads. Now I go down on a weekly basis and it is accepted as part of my job description. I also decided I needed to know COBOL to do my job better. I could register for either a college or an internal course on COBOL and Computex would pay for it. Every month I write down my goals—a person chooses what they feel it takes to do their job as defined by them. If a person doesn't determine their goals, they will have nothing to do. The result of this process for me is that I'm buying myself authority by making myself more and more knowledgeable.

"Personally, I won't be happy until I'm president of my own company. I truly believe that. I established this goal for myself in college, and what I'm doing now is getting experience. First in finance, then in sales, and now in marketing.

"To be successful in business, you have to learn how a company really operates. In my first job out of college I was so incredibly naive. I had no political awareness, I wasn't cognizant of chauvinism, and I was cocky. I even had a Mickey Mouse hat, ears and all, that I wore when I felt that the work they were giving me was of that level!

"When I came to Computex as a sales trainee, I knew what I needed to know and I set up a program to learn it. It's like having an outline for a research paper. The hard part is creating the outline—i.e., setting the goal. The easy part is filling in the body between the headings. For example, I knew nothing about computers, sales, marketing, and Computex's organization. I decided to learn how to learn about these things by setting up meetings with the 10 managers in the group and by asking what projects needed to be done that could be done by a trainee, but were not being done now because of lack of manpower. The 10 managers each mentioned about a dozen projects. Seven were listed by everyone and accomplishing those seven would give me experience in sales and marketing situations, answer my questions about computers, and force me to learn Computex's organization by using it to accomplish my objectives. I wrote up the project plan and presented it to my three supervisors; they approved it and off I went. After completing the projects I had in fact learned a great deal about the four aspects of the business that I felt I needed to know in order to sell their products successfully. Some people never have any goals and never set forth a program for themselves to follow. Goals can change, by the way, but that's irrelevant. It is important to have goals and a program to achieve them. I do.

"I also make decisions. I'm beginning to realize that what made me a leader as a kid was that I made decisions. Most people won't make a decision if they have any way of not making it. If I'm willing to take the heat and think I've done the right thing, my experience is that I'm generally in a good position. So if I decide something, I do so with a series of contingency plans that ensure it's going to work out alright. Also I have no problem falling flat on my face and saying, 'Hey, that was stupid,' and standing up and trying again. I don't expect myself to succeed the first time I try everything, or even the second. I have a longer list of failures than I have successes, but it doesn't matter. If you're doing nothing, then you can't make mistakes. At Computex, the culture is such that you're permitted to fail once at everything you try. You fail once, and the next time you succeed; and then the failure is wiped out completely in everyone's mind. In a fast-growing organization, it's necessary to give people the freedom to make decisions and to try and to learn.

"When I was a sales trainee, I knew that if I didn't make the Computex sales award, my career at Computex would be ended. Although they wouldn't fire me, I would just be a sales rep, twiddling my thumbs for however long I stayed. You have to make your numbers or nothing happens to you. So there I was, with a manager who had 20 items which he needed to make to achieve his budget by the end of the quarter and who was trying to make sure that I didn't make the Computex sales award. Sales trainees aren't supposed to make the sales award; and if I did, then he should have promoted me to a sales representative. So I asked his secretary what budget numbers he needed. I wasn't being devious; I was really trying to support him. I wanted him to succeed because that was the only way I could succeed. But I had to do it with a power play because he wouldn't treat me seriously.

"So I read the numbers and said to myself, 'Okay, he can't make it in these six areas.' As it so happened, I had an account which was going to make the numbers in four of those areas. Then I called up every single lead which we had received in the office over the last four months and on which no one had returned calls, identified the ones which were going to close in a month, and found 15 accounts.

"As a sales trainee, that wasn't what I was paid to do; I was paid to learn. But I was tired of being a sales trainee; I was determined to be a sales rep and sell and make the Computex sales award—and be the only sales trainee to do it that year.

"Another dimension entered into the situation. My manager had a fair-haired boy, a sales rep and the only individual whom he had personally hired; he wanted him to make the sales award. Since I was leaving on July 1, *if* I made the sales award, to take a job at corporate headquarters, my manager reasoned that I should give 50 percent of anything I booked to the sales rep. The motives behind this request were pretty transparent to me, so I told my manager that I didn't think that was fair unless he was willing to give me 50 percent of all the sales rep's bookings, since I had done a considerable amount of the work and could document it on two banking orders he had. In effect, however, I was being asked to give the rep a split so that he would make the sales award, and I was getting nothing for it. That was a key link in my strategy, since exposing my manager would not be advantageous for either the manager or the sales rep.

"So I went to the district manager and asked whether I would make the sales award if I closed such and such accounts. He said yes. So I said that that was not what my manager told me, that he had told me I would have to give 50 percent to the sales representative. The district manager asked why, and when I answered, he looked at me in total disbelief. I explained that I didn't think it was fair that the sales rep should make the award on behalf of my efforts, and if that was the case, the company would not get any of the business I had found. I would leave the company today, take my vacation pay, and go. The district manager said to go back and talk to my manager. What none of them knew was that I had already pulled this off, that the bookings were in my drawer, and this was not idle conversation. I could make good on any deal I worked with them, and I knew what they needed to make their numbers to look good to their bosses.

"So I went in to my manager. There were two weeks left in the quarter and he was scared now because he wasn't going to make his numbers. I said to him, 'I have a problem. I really want to go back to headquarters and I need your help. I need to make the sales award. You know that and I know that. I can't go back to corporate as a turkey who hasn't succeeded in making the sales award. I believe I've put forth the sales effort required to do that. I also believe I should go back as a sales rep. I believe I've earned that. Now I think I can make the following budget numbers for you, and I can bring in these two accounts. All that I need from you is the assurance that I will receive the Computex sales award if I do it. Otherwise I'm not going to work another day.'

"He looked at me and finally said, 'If you get those orders in, you can make the sales award, and yes, if you bring in that business, then you're more than qualified to be a sales rep.' What he was banking on was that I didn't have the orders. I walked into his office with them two days later.

"What motivated me for the most part was realizing that they were not taking me seriously, and not paying attention to what I was doing, to how many accounts in which I was involved were closed as a result of my efforts. I also wanted them to know that I was fully aware of their attempt to use me. That kind of approach is a very strong power play and a high-risk strategy, but if you succeed, you are given much more respect and higher levels of managerial credibility.

"That's one of the reasons why I don't feel that this kind of power play is self-centered or opportunistic. As an individual you have a choice. You can take what the corporation dishes out to you, or you can choose to modify your own career path within a certain amount of reasonableness. I don't mean that you can walk up to a corporation, your first day on the job, and say I'm going to be president of this company tomorrow. They'll probably send you to the loony bin. But as long as it's reasonable and you are performing in accordance with, or better than, the expectations, I think you can succeed and get what you want.

"If you don't take risks, I would say that you're not going to go nearly as far as the person who does. There's an expected behavior of successful individuals that they are risk takers. If someone doesn't have the guts to risk himself, do you really want him risking millions of dollars of the corporation's money?

"Most women in management whom I've observed don't seem to

have the career direction or goal orientation to say, 'Okay, if I'm not at such and such a point within this time period, I'll have to find out why and do something about it.' Most men in management that I know do have a game plan. Several of my business friends, male and female, tell me that I have this kind of direction.

"A uniqueness that I think I bring to my job is the ability to deliver constructive criticism to people in frank conversation, without having it come across as an interpersonal conflict. Another point is that I don't appear to any of my management as a female per se. After a short amount of time they forget that I'm a female and treat me as a person.

"Concerning my social life, I don't have to strain for one. I had a secure relationship with Jeff for five years in Denver a while back, and I have ample opportunity to go for a drink after work or to blow off steam by playing tennis or racquetball or going sailing or skiing.

"I don't make very many sacrifices because I'm only pursuing what I want to do. However, there are some people who would say that I am giving things up. My mother would claim that I'm forfeiting a social life and a normal life with marriage and children. But I have a very active social life even though no one can get hold of me because of the extensive amount of traveling I do. They generally contact my secretary and the result is that my calendar is generally full at least a month in advance. I take time for people who are important to me and I am learning to take more time for myself. I run on my own timetable. For example, I've decided that I will have my first child when I'm 29. It's highly probable that by the time I'm 29 I will be married and pregnant and, of course, working.

"I have had an extremely colorful life. I'll try almost anything once; I find all people interesting and enjoy talking to any kind of person. Generally, I get a big kick out of life. My outside interests are wide-ranging, and there's hardly anything I'm not interested in. Certainly the love of my life is music . . . it can release all types of emotions. I've managed to maintain a childlike curiosity and honesty and integrity throughout. I can concentrate for 24, 36, 48 hours at a time without any sleep or food. I keep going until something is finished. If I get to the point where I feel I'm making a sacrifice, I'll just quit the task, but that rarely, if ever, happens. On those tests that measure your aptitude in different fields, I always scored high in several categories. The psychologists say that they rarely see a score like that.

"From what I have seen in the business world, I have a fairly unique ability to contend with an extremely large amount of pressure. Except when the pressure has negative overtones. I can't cope when people start backbiting or playing 'cover your ass' games. The kind of emotional tension that occurs when people are losing their jobs and trying to befriend the ones who aren't really upsets me. I can't survive that; that's where being sensitive can demolish me. I can't put up a shield for those kinds of hassles. All of my good traits go away. I lose my sense of humor, and my interpersonal skills, which are my strongest asset, degenerate. I become autocratic and begin to manifest all those behaviors which are bad if you are male but can kill you if you're a woman. I'm aware of all this, so I have to spend about 40 percent of my time and energy under this kind of pressure making sure that I'm not displaying these behaviors. My credibility and my productivity drop. I tend to call people up and ask, 'Why did you do such a horse's ass job?' and then I have to call them back and apologize and smooth things over.

"Men have a very strong belief that they are fair and that their decisions are objective. Only women know that they really aren't. It's a game that men appear to play among themselves, and they all support each other in this belief. Now women come along and shatter their belief on a daily basis and that's not cool. So if a woman expects to be promoted by a man in a man's world, she has to establish an identity which allows men to measure her with their set of rules. So if you are competing for a promotion with men on a peer group level and none of them have an MBA but several have three years, five years, seven years more experience than you, your superiors aren't going to be able to find a reason to justify promoting you, even if you're better. They can't do it because they can't explain it to all the other guys who will all go rushing into their office, and they would be risking perhaps seven people quitting even if your promotion was the right thing to do. You as a female have to set the stage with your peer group, while you are in it, that this is what you want, these are the reasons that you want it, and this is what you're doing to get it. That washes out about 80 percent of them, as about 80 percent of them say, yes, I could really work for you, and the other 20 percent are either going to leave or they're the people who emerge as your real competition. The MBA degree gives an objective added value. It also shows a dedication to a career, that you're not planning to get married and have children and therefore abandon your work. You have to dispel this image constantly on a daily basis, and even then you never completely succeed in dispelling it.

"Things that I'm unsure of in my life? I'm not sure I'm lovable. I'm not sure that I'm loved. I believe one has to give love to receive love, and I have no way to measure that. Love is a gift which other people give to you. You just never can tell. Are you familiar with the song from *Mr. Chips:* 'Was I brave and strong and true; did I fill the world with love my whole life through?' This song says a lot about me.

"Let me share a theory with you. I see the human being as five entities: an emotional self, a social self, an intellectual self, a physical self, and a spiritual self. My intellectual, spiritual, and physical selves are pretty solid. My emotional self will probably never be totally put together, because I can be jerked around emotionally very easily. If I have a major fault that may hold me back, that is probably it. I recall in my first job that I once came into the conference room filled with people with all my books and papers, slammed them down, and said to my boss who was also the vice president and treasurer: 'If you're so damn smart, why don't you do it yourself.' Then I left without waiting for any response. Although I didn't get fired, I didn't get the job I wanted. They let me stay on payroll for three months but without any work to do. I was too stubborn to apologize and they said I couldn't handle stress.

"My social self is the least secure part of me because I don't have any social system. I'm like an infant in that area. I'm totally inept but you have to know me really well to tell. Certain things get in the way of my developing a social system. I have a value system which says anything which you do that is selfish is wrong. Being self-centered is wrong, as is being an opportunist. A lot of this can be traced back to my family life. We are a self-sufficient, self-contained, upstanding, do-it-yourself, all-American, pull-yourself-up-by-the-bootstraps, work ethic, go-to-church-on-Sunday family. All this led me to feel that needing other people was wrong and showed that you were weak. I know this isn't true but it's hard to erase all those childhood tapes. I'm going to have to change my value system, to improve my social self.

"The only real conflict that I and many other people at Computex have is that it's easy to become so involved in your work that you're married to it, so occasionally I'll come home from work and collapse and say to myself, 'This is stupid, I'm going to die by the time I'm 30!' But I love my work. . . . It's not work to me, it's fun. As long as I'm aware of what I am doing and what is happening to me, and as long as I am happy and having fun at whatever I do, then I know that life is okay. Whatever happens, happens, and as my grandmother always says in times of trouble, 'Everything works out for the best.'"

Chris Hammond (B)*

COMPUTEX WAS a rare breed of company, Chris Hammond was still discovering after three years with the fast-growing, innovative computer firm. Perhaps its most striking characteristic was its matrix management organization, comprising traditional functional departments on the one hand, and product lines on the other, which overlapped as circumstances required (see Exhibit 1). This organizational setup agreed with what Chris knew about matrix organizations from her general knowledge of the subject; and she considered the following to be the main features:

People have more than one boss.

Project responsibility becomes unclear.

Open and timely communication is a must, as is a high level of trust.

Good collaboration skills are required.

Tasks come and go—an urgent project today may be tabled indefinitely so a high degree of flexibility is required.

Competition among teams and groups is more open than in traditional structures, and is in fact encouraged.

It forces people to think in different ways, in at least *two* dimensions.

Problems occur no less frequently in matrix organizations than in other groups. Computex had only recently encountered problems because of a lack of proper communications and an imbalance between the functional groups and the product lines. For example, the manufacturing department, in an effort to maximize its production, would ignore information from the marketing department, and consequently the mix of the computer products which they produced did not reflect sales trends. This caused inventories to build to an all-time high, and the stock price of the firm plummeted until the president of Computex finally intervened. He called a halt to production in order to lower inventories, but the inventories kept building before ultimately dropping off. "He was standing on the bridge of a supertanker shouting '90 degree turn!' and expecting it to respond with the agility of a motorboat!" one outside analyst commented on the event.

A supertanker it was. In the previous year alone, sales had grown by more than 40 percent to nearly $1 billion. R&D expenditures increased by 40 percent over the preceding year to nearly $80 million, and earnings per share also increased handsomely. Nor was that year atypical.

---

*This case was prepared by Deborah Downs and Pamela Fuhrer under the direction of Professor Allan R. Cohen as a basis for class discussion. Special thanks is given to Anne Jamar for her assistance. Copyright 1979, Whittemore School of Business and Economics, University of New Hampshire. Reproduced with permission.

To make this supertanker more manageable and to focus more closely on customer needs, Computex changed half of its matrix structure—the product lines—into four major market or user segments. The former product line structure, as its name implied, focused on marketing a specific product to all market segments. Product lines were responsible for the engineering, developement, manufacturing, and support for these products. They "managed" the functional departments with respect to their products, and the functional departments were structured in accordance with the product focus. Over time the product lines began marketing their products to very diverse market segments, each of which required specialized knowledge, for example, medical centers, governmental groups, or schools. Several of the product lines were therefore beginning to focus on a small number of market segments and were using a catch-as-catch-can philosophy for others. As it turned out, there was a significant amount of duplication of effort in certain market places, and in addition, several customers were requesting products from multiple product lines. It was at this point that the decision was made to change from a product focus for the marketing organization to a market segment focus and to allow all products needed to service a market segment to be "sold" into that marketplace. Major market segments such as commercial, data communications, and government were organized.

In addition, the market directors were given more influence over the functional departments as a further means of ensuring a balanced organization. One result of the change was that customers were now more likely to be called on by just one salesperson rather than the four or five under the previous product line focus.

If the company appeared to have solved the structural problems of the matrix, it was still having some problems with individual employee adaptation to the system. One former personnel manager described the situation as follows:

> My two bosses, one in a line position, the other a staff executive, didn't always share the same priorities. Consequently, I often got caught in the middle. In a matrix or quasi-matrix company like Computex, the pain is felt by the people lower down. . . . What you have, or had until the recent reorganization which alleviated the problem somewhat, is 30,000 employees around the world each trying to make his or her own decisions. And the reward system which compensates people for doing their own thing compounds the problem.

An outside behavioral consultant commented about Computex and matrix organizations:

> They demand maturity from employees. An immature employee will play one boss off against another. A mature employee will discuss disagreements openly with his boss and if the boss remains intransigent, respond

by acquiescing—but only under the condition that all bosses are apprised of the situation and of the employee's stand on the matter. . . . There are a lot of lost souls at Computex who don't know who their bosses are. The company's response to them has been "Go find out for yourself."

This same consultant had conducted several group sessions among the company's employees regarding norms within the firm. Time and time again, the same norms were revealed. These included:

Be compassionate.
Be a self-starter.
Deal directly with conflicts.
Be responsive.
Treat people informally.
Do your homework—give 120 percent.
Learn to swim fast.
Be yourself.
Be a team player.
Don't mismanage resources.
Don't cover your ass.
Don't listen to your boss if he's wrong.
Spend two years maximum in any one job.
Downplay status.
Work long hours.

This was the Computex that Chris Hammond joined three years ago as a sales trainee. Several things had attracted her to the firm: Sales were growing at such a phenomenal rate that job opportunities not usually found in average-growth firms were being created for those who aspired to them; the company had a reputation for caring about its employees; and it was in an industry that appealed to Chris personally. A math and physics type, she thought that learning about computers would be fun and challenging. Moreover, small computers, for which Computex was renowned, were in her opinion the key to improving education in this country, one of her long-range interests.

Chris progressed to full sales representative within two years at Computex and achieved the respected Computex sales award for making her quota. It was well known that this achievement was a prerequisite for continuing upward in the firm.

Her next position was that of marketing representative for government markets, and as such she was responsible for providing support services, developing marketing plans, generating new business opportunities, and for arranging trade shows for business in the western half of North America.

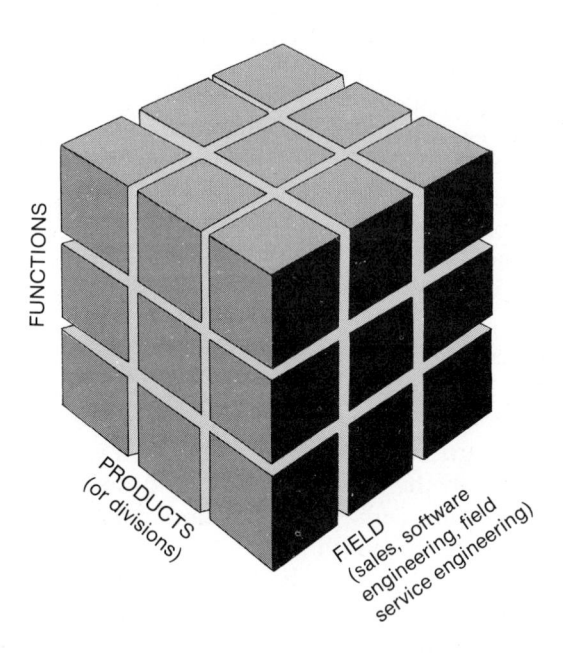

EXHIBIT 1
Simple Representation of Matrix Organization

FUNCTIONS

PRODUCTS (or divisions)

FIELD (sales, software engineering, field service engineering)

As a marketing representative, Chris was brought in to work in Computex's new headquarters, an attractive two-story glass and concrete structure nestled in the New England woods. The interior was decorated in bright colors, and the offices were a maze of three-sided, shoulder-height module units spread around each floor. Offices had no doors. The only way to recognize a top executive was by the greater amount of floor space inside his module. Quite unlike other firms where secretaries never occupy prime space, at Computex they were frequently situated so that they had a view of the exterior enviroment. A further example of the company's egalitarianism was the rule of thumb that transportation on the company helicopter went to employees on a first-come, first-served basis.

The upward job movement had not been as easy for Chris as it appeared on paper. Chris recalled problems because managers had not kept some of their verbal promises and because she had had to resort to power plays in order to extricate herself from situations where individuals were out for the interests of their own department.

Chris was a marketing representative for about 10 months when she began to be disgruntled with the amount of work which she was required to do for what she considered a relatively low salary of $17,000. College graduates with no previous work experience were receiving starting salaries of $17,000 as sales trainees. However, before approaching her manager about the matter, she talked to a number of men (there weren't any women at her level or above in her area) to get advice on how to ask most effectively for a raise. She was well prepared when she entered her manager's office.

"You and I have a problem," she began, "which we've both got to solve or else you'll have a problem. And the decision you make will tell me something about us, our relationship, and Computex." She then listed her major accomplishments—assisting in closing one of the biggest pieces of business the company had ever obtained, a multimillion-dollar contract with the government; becoming the first sales trainee ever to receive the sales award; receiving three promotions in a little less than three years; and receiving outstanding performance appraisals on several occasions.

Next, she explained her discontent with her low salary. "Though I appreciate pats on the back and commendations for my work, those don't buy groceries. When they do, I'll let you know. I know how much I'm worth on the outside market, and how much other employees in similar jobs are being paid. I'm simply asking the company to put its money where its mouth is."

Reclining in his chair, her manager was pensive for a moment and then said, in an attempt at commiseration, "You're right, but there's really very little we can do right now, especially in view of the hiring freeze and management's limit on salary increases to 8 percent." Chris responded that there were several things he could do, some of them even under current constraints: one, give her 100 shares of stock; two, raise her salary by $5,000 to $22,000; three, give her six-month rather than annual reviews so that she would receive three over an 18-month period; four, promote her to senior marketing representative; five, enumerate specific reasons why she shouldn't be considered for any of these.

"So that you won't have to worry about setting a precedent, I can give you the names of others at Computex for whom similar things have been done."

After a moment's silence, her boss remarked that she had certainly done her homework.

To emphasize her seriousness, Chris set a time limit. If she didn't receive at least one of the four items within the next three months, she would leave. One month later, the only point that she had not received was the first; she was given a raise, promise of more frequent reviews, and a promotion.

Chris's job changed with her promotion from market support ("answering the telephone" and "holding hands" with the sales force) to project management. She has recently spent most of her time on a special project in which Computex hopes to install minicomputers for use by local police departments. The system will have the capacity to cross-check files, to retrieve data on past criminal records—in short, to cross-reference almost anything in police records in much the same way that library files are cross-indexed. For example, less than 30 seconds will be required to check an auto registration through city, county, state, and federal files. Since a large percentage of crimes are committed by repeat offenders, the information obtained by cross-checking factors involved in crimes may be used to reach quicker solutions to cases and to ensure a more consistent sentencing of criminals.

The project is a critical one for several reasons. The first is its size. Several million dollars are involved in this, compared with other sales which averaged around $100,000. Second, ultimate responsibility for the success of the project lies with Chris. If it fails, she is accountable. Likewise, if it succeeds, she will get much of the credit and her career prospects may benefit accordingly. Third, the vice president of the division knows about the project and expects it to be completed successfully. This involvement of superiors places extra pressure on Chris to perform. Fourth, the project provides an opportunity for Computex to associate its name further with the idea of serving the public good. The public interest nature of the project makes it a potential source of pride for Chris personally and for the company as an organization. Last, if successful, the project will serve as a model for Computex to go out and seek large government contracts instead of sitting back and waiting for business to come to it. This interest in being more aggressive reflects a recent change in the corporation. The president himself has proclaimed a need for the firm to take more aggressive planned approaches to growth. As Chris sees it:

> This job involves more planning, not a response mode. . . . If we succeed in winning this award, we are proving a prototype for how to go after a big project. Private industry generally will not write specs like that; they generally don't have to do legal bidding like government contracts. . . .

Early on a particular Friday morning midway into the project, Chris, dressed in a maroon knit suit with a cream-colored blouse, no make-up, scarf at her neck, and gold barrette to keep the hair out of her face, visited the computer terminal room, accompanied by the casewriters. There three software engineers, members of the project team, were ironing out final details for a demonstration, or benchmark as it is called, in a few weeks, at which time the prospective client will be shown in detail the project and its capabilities. The three software engineers were responsible for preparing a prototype system that would be demonstrated to prove that Computex could indeed design the special systems required and could make them operational. These individuals were on loan in a sense to Chris for the duration of the project, although they were to return to Kansas shortly to work on other assignments. Jeffrey had been setting up a sample file to ensure that the data could be retrieved accurately, quickly, and easily. JoAnne was programming the system in COBOL language, while Carol was testing the screening of data. Chris's expressed reasons for visiting the three in the terminal room was to show concern and to make it clear that she had worked just as hard and long as they had (they had worked until close to midnight the night before). "It's important—it's a motivator. It lets them know you're interested in what they're doing." Her parting words to the group were "See ya."

Chris's major responsibility, as she perceives it, is to put together the right group of people to get the job done. Her team includes 30 individuals in all, drawn from the functional departments (manufacturing, hardware engineering, and so on), the sales and software departments (the field organization), and from several marketing groups (see Exhibit 2). However, in order to obtain the best talent for this particular project and to tap the corporation's resources, many of the individuals on the team come from outside the normal liaisons which the matrix structure allows—that is, a three-dimensional working relationship bound together by the appropriate marketing personnel. In addition, the geographical dispersion of the team members required that several very high-level managers had to buy in to the support of the project in order to pull resources from one location to the project location.

Such a team makeup "really strained the matrix system," commented Chris and forced her to invest a great deal of time and effort in developing personal relationships and in using the more familiar hierarchical protocols to obtain resources. "I have to go to the level at which the various branches converge and report to a higher-level manager. I have to get the top person's buy-in and then keep all levels informed of the project's progress."

Chris had arranged to take several members of the team to lunch on Friday, since they would be returning to Kansas shortly. Following lunch, she had scheduled a meeting to tie up loose ends and check on the status of team members' work. Although the meeting had been planned for 1:30, at 1:45 people were still filtering into the small conference room and seating themselves around a large oblong table with plump comfortable chairs.

John, the software project co-ordinator from St. Louis, arrived first and settled at one end of the table. Chris arrived, put a pile of papers on the table, and stood by a chair in the middle. "Where's the agenda?" asked John. "It's in my head, John. Would you like to run this meeting?" Silence. Al, a benchmark expert from headquarters whom Chris had previously described as super-brilliant and having a short attention span, sauntered in saying, "What time is this meeting supposed to end?" When 6 of the 10 people expected had arrived, Chris opened the

**EXHIBIT 2
Team Players†**

Name	Role	Level	Organization	Location
*John	Software project co-ordinator	(4)	Field (software)	St. Louis
*Al	Benchmark expert	(4)	Marketing	Headquarters
*Joanne	Software engineering expert	(4)	Functional	Headquarters
*Tim	Data center manager	(4)	Functional	Headquarters
Ted	Demo systems co-ordinator	(1)	Functional	Headquarters
*Dick	Product planning manager	(6)	Marketing	Headquarters
*Tom	Small systems expert	(5)	Marketing	Headquarters
Carol	Software specialist	(2)	Field (software support services)	Florida
*Jeff	Software consultant	(4)	Field	California
*Roger	Account manager	(3)	Field (sales)	St. Louis
*Henry	Regional manager	(8)	Field (sales)	Chicago
Art	Software engineer	(5)	Functional	Headquarters
Walt	Sales manager	(5)	Field (sales)	Minneapolis
*James	Vice president	(10)	Marketing	Headquarters
*Steve	Marketing manager	(4)	Marketing	Headquarters
*Harry	Technician	(1)	Functional	Headquarters
Fred	Engineering expert	(3)	Functional	Headquarters
Jack	Branch manager	(3)	Field (maintenance)	Omaha
Ken	Supervisor	(2)	Field	Kansas City
Sam	Field service engineer	(1)	Field	Kansas City
*Phil	Corporate marketing	(6)	Functional	Headquarters
*Chris	Project manager	(3)	Marketing	Headquarters
Ed	Software expert	(3)	Field	New Jersey
*Kevin	Regional manager	(8)	Field	New Jersey

*Critical team players.
†Names and places are fictitious and used to represent relationships and geographical dispersion.
Note: Levels denote a loose hierarchical structure.

meeting, amidst laughter and friendly banter. She introduced the casewriter as someone present to see that she did her job, then laughed and explained in a more serious vein. Reluctant to admit that the cases were in fact about her, Chris explained that the casewriter and she were working together on them and that the focus was matrix organization. The casewriter indicated that she would be taking notes. One or two people seemed a little surprised, but no one seemed at all bothered. Chris immediately proceeded with her "agenda." She turned to JoAnne, a software engineering expert seated on her left, and said: "How are you coming along?" As JoAnne reported on the status of her tasks, Chris listened intently and jotted notes on a yellow legal pad in front of her. Later she said to the casewriter:

> I'm a pretty effective team member, and now I'm trying to learn to be a team leader. One of the hard things for me in making the transition is that you can't be a team leader and have opinions. You can't switch those two roles in the same meeting; it doesn't work. Everytime I did that I lost the credibility of the group, so what I did in subsequent meetings was to plant all of my ideas with one or two others and then pull those ideas back. That works extremely well.

One of the software specialists, sitting stiffly in her chair, rushed through her report as if she felt that any admission of difficulty would be an admission of inadequacy. Chris listened intently and probed, "What can we do to help you get the time to do this task?"—her efforts to remain patient beginning to show.

> I am very impatient with incompetence and that's one of my faults that I try to shore up. . . . There were two individuals there who don't belong on the project and don't have the skills required to participate in the project, and in order for the project to succeed we have to work around them. One nice thing about the matrix organization is that you can have team members who are not particularly effective members of the team who can also not hurt the team. All you do is neutralize their ability to hurt the team, which is how we succeeded in overcoming this. By the way, it's not inherent incompetence for those two; they have absolutely no training, background, or information that's relevant—so they are extra baggage, so to speak. And we just do not have excess personnel to allow for two slack resources. Ultimately we put those people in positions where they are doing very useful work, but if it never gets done, it doesn't matter, and if it does, then we've got fantastic documentation. All the critical tasks are being done by those people trained to do them. It took some finessing for that to occur.

At no time did Chris relax in her chair, though the others were all sitting back in various positions of comfort. Al leaned back so that his head rested against the blackboard behind him and put his hands behind his head. When Chris came to John, the tone of the meeting became a little strained. An unanticipated problem had cropped up, creating a need for John to ensure that certain personnel would be at Computex the following Monday. John responded vaguely, suggesting that he would see what he could do but that he couldn't guarantee anything. Chris paused and said, "It's clear that we need to have this person here Monday to keep on schedule, John. What can you do?" In the silence which followed, John mumbled yes, he would call. Chris appeared to be exerting a great deal of self-control simply not to be visibly peeved, and she quietly repeated, "John, quite a few things hinge on his being here Monday." Chris's manager commented later on the overall situation:

> Today Chris walked a very thin line. Since marketing has no authority over sales, Chris has to convince the salesman that he will best meet his quota by selling this group. Her job is as a backup, a resource. At Computex the product line has no access to the customer without the salesman taking you in. John has a very parochial view about who controls the benchmark. He's from Kansas and thinks in terms of my customer. As the software manager, his responsibility is to ensure that all sales made are doable on the system being sold. So Chris has to tread extra finely. She must be acutely aware of his sensitivities. Without him feeling driven by her, she has to get him to do things. If he detects this, he won't co-operate.

Al, visibly bored with the meeting, left as soon as he had given his status report, having referred to several solutions offered by team members to current problems as "tacky, tacky." Chris encouraged his participation, however, as he was clearly adept at problem solving. Her style was very participatory, and leadership seemed to shift from John to Al and back again, as both of them assumed the role of sceptics and behaved in a somewhat condescending manner. Chris kept the meeting on track with verbal reminders or questions, kept complete notes of what was said, and clearly appeared to be ticking off agenda items in her head.

At about 2:30, Chris's manager and the corporate contracts negotiator joined the team. A reference was made to another project team's poor communication, and Chris commented: "They make us look as if we have instantaneous communication around here." The other team members laughed, and tension subsided—though John quipped, "They must be really screwed up."

John mentioned that he had a plane to catch and had to leave by three. Chris continued around the table until she was satisfied that everyone was on schedule or had a strategy for getting back on schedule. She did not interrupt; she was more apt to listen until an individual had finished and then push: "What other problems do you have? Where do you go from here? When would it be reasonable to get that information?" JoAnne also commented that she needed to leave as she had an appointment for an automotive repair, so the meeting ended.

> If you succeed in building a matrix team, then you become the manager of that group, and they look to you for the answers to questions and for direction, and if you don't provide it, then nothing occurs. So eventually you build up the ability to be autocratic because first of all, they know that you're not going to ask them to do something unreasonable. You can say I want you to do such and such by Friday, and the decision process goes

very fast. The first day on this project was an eight-hour, totally draining, status meeting that I thought wouldn't take very long. Now it's down to half an hour. I say, "Is everything done?" They'll say yes. I say, "I want this and this and this on my desk tomorrow." "Well, those things aren't quite done." "OK, let's negotiate."

The casewriter remained after the meeting to talk with Chris's manager:

With Chris, you have not chosen the average . . . she is exceptionally good at matrix management . . . adept at getting people to do things for her. She is very good with people . . . can pick out in a person what motivates them, and she can do this quickly. If you don't have interpersonal relationship skills here, you're not going to move at all. It's a self-driving thing. No one comes to you and says "Can I help you?"

Because Chris is adept at interfacing with other parts of the matrix, she gets exposure at every part of the organization. So she can move in a number of directions; and this is encouraged at Computex. Anything holding her back? The only thing would be lack of experience. That's why I have stayed out of this project. This is something she'll be able to hang her hat on.

Chris is also, however, very impatient and not willing to wait. She gets job offers a lot because she has so many contacts. She tends to poke around outside—not actively—but people tend to recognize her strengths. I encourage her to take advantage of the respect she has built up in this part of the organization because everyone sees her on a daily basis. Openings will occur here eventually. In the meanwhile, it's my job to get her exposure.

Chris pondered her future career plans. "One thing I have learned by this time is that, in a matrix organization, power and recognition flow to those who assume it." The next step, some 12 to 15 months off, is marketing manager, the beginning of top-line management. After that, within a decade's grasp, is a corporate VP post. Or, Chris figured, she could start her own firm by then.

Regarding the more immediate future, the marketing manager job a year away is not a sure thing. Computex rarely promotes anyone from within, let alone a woman, to that position. Part of the reason is that Computex doesn't know how to train people, Chris commented, and few people bother to train themselves. That's where Chris sees herself as different.

She has begun to formulate her strategy. First, she must pull off a marketing coup. A well-conceived, well-implemented project which paid off could prove her marketing prowess. She will also have to convince both her manager and his superior that she is in earnest about her career. If she cannot involve them in her plans, she will, she says, have to seek out someone else to help her along—a mentor. Just the fact that people know that she has kept to the timetable she set for herself five years ago is gaining her respect. In a sense, she is a self-fulfilling prophecy.

Third, Chris says that she will have to gain entry into the "boys club," both on and off the job. The latter will involve learning how to play racquetball and probably golf. She'll have to get the men to call her by her last name and have them be able to swear in her presence without blinking. The "boys club" is, she commented, comprised of aspiring young men of the "in group" who know that they are on a fast track. Being known is terribly important.

In addition, Chris observes that she will have to change her mode of dress, to dress more for success, as the saying goes . . . wear tailored gray suits, navy pleated skirts, and white crepe blouses. And everything she does will have to be done in an honest and open way, because that, she says, is her style.

*Conference at Miniatronics**

THE LATE GEORGE APLEY, who was given life and reality by the late J. P. Marquand, once wrote to his children about his grandfather's early business career:

> Moses Apley left the farm at the age of 14 to enter the Derby counting house in Salem. . . . At the age of 15 he sailed as a clerk on the Derby brig *Stella* for the Baltic. At the age of 18 he was master of the Derby brig *Good Hope* bound for Madagascar and China with a cargo valued at $15,000. This, as you see, was the beginning of our commerce with the Orient. At Madagascar, on hearing of the outbreak of war between England and France, this boy—somehow boys in this part of the world matured more quickly then, in spite of there not being a Harvard Business School—contrived to sell his cargo for three times its value and to place the proceeds in currency, which itself doubled its value, before the *Good Hope* left port three months later.

Businessmen in the days of Moses Apley, no doubt, did contrive to mature with nothing in the way of training and little in the way of experience. They did not think about doing business, they did it. And their lack of self-consciousness seems not to have impaired their capacity to do what they did.

Whether our current emphasis on formal business education represents a weakening of our moral fiber or a strengthening of our capacity to teach, may not be possible to answer. We do know that in the last

---

*From Abram Collier, *Management, Men, and Values*, 1960, Harper & Row Publishers, Inc., New York, N.Y. Reproduced by permission of the author.

century or more, the role of the businessman has been drastically changed. While in the past he was typically a trader, today he is typically an administrator in a large organization. While formerly he often traded with his own money, now he almost always uses someone else's. While once the businessman's success was measured by the size of his fortune, now it is measured by the magnitude of his innovations. However it has come about, there is no doubt that one of the striking features of a business life today is the enormous expenditure of time and effort in formal training, both in the universities and in business itself.

Can an executive be trained as one trains a living tree, or is he a machine which is fixed in his major characteristics at an early age? Hoping to approach some answers to the question, Morgan entered the Roger Williams Building in Providence, got off the elevator at the office of Kenneth Eckerman, president of Miniatronics Corporation. It was 9:15 A.M. Through the "squawk box," the girl in the outer office announced that Professor Morgan had arrived. Morgan entered a large but cluttered office.

ECKERMAN: Very good of you to come down to see us, Professor. Delighted to meet you.

MORGAN: The pleasure is mine, Mr. Eckerman. I have wanted to meet you ever since I first heard about your remarkable company. I am indebted to Dean Fay for suggesting my name to you.

ECKERMAN: Great fellow, the dean. Yes, he says you may be able to give a hand in this training business.

We've only a few minutes before the others get here, so let me tell you what our problem seems to be. We're only 11 years old, so it won't take long to give you our history.

MORGAN: I shall try not to interrupt.

ECKERMAN: Good. Professor, we are the victims of our own success. I don't need to tell you what has happened in the field of semiconductors. I still can't believe it. Eleven years ago, I went into business with Fred Andrews, a man who is both a Ph.D. and an authentic genius, two things that don't always go together. We started out to make printed circuits for radios and TV, but Fred was more interested in the small substitute for the vacuum tube that Shockley, Morton, and all the others had worked out at Bell Labs. Before we knew it, Fred developed one of the first processes for making silicon transistors on a commercial scale. By 1955—it now seems like a thousand years ago—we were really in business. I won't bore you with the details, but we got into the big time with diffused-base transistors and last year we really went through the sound barrier when we came out with solid-circuit semi-conductors. I won't dwell on our recent shakeout.

Have you ever seen a semiconductor, Professor? Well, here is our newest one. I wear it on my watch chain. I had it embedded in some lucite. It saves a lot of talk. In this little item, no bigger than the head of a match, we have built an entire circuit on a single-crystal semiconductor slab. This type happens to be an audio amplifier, but we have a dozen others used in military computers, missiles, and rockets. They have not only opened up tremendous possibilities in the field of miniaturization but they provide reliability unknown up to now. In very little time you will see a large computer housed in a package no bigger than a desk drawer.

Now I know you don't want to hear all about our past headaches in learning to build thermoelectric furnaces to make bismuth telluride bars, or how we learned to cut diamond-hard crystals into tiny wafers. These were some of our toughest problems, technically that is. Money at first was hard to come by and our receivables were pledged up to the hilt, but now the banks come through with whatever we need for working capital. Our problem now is neither technical nor financial. Our problem is men. We have grown faster than we can find and hire trained men to run our plants.

We operate by putting full responsibility for each group of products in one man, who must satisfy our customers with his service and satisfy us with his profits. We get semimonthly reports on all operations. If sales or profits are not making the kind of growth we have projected, we want to know why. Long ago we decided not to put up with sloppy operations and if we are not satisfied with an executive's performance after six months—or a year at the outside—we get ourselves a new boy.

MORGAN: Do I take it that you have now reached the point where you are questioning these policies?

ECKERMAN: Yes and no. Turnover *has* been high. Some of the new men we have taken on have seemed to have such fine records that we have gone all out to get them—given them high salaries, large expense accounts, liberal stock options, and so on—but often as not they don't pan out. I guess we have been like a baseball club that has started out by buying a lot of established players. In the process we have bought a few sore arms, ailing backs, and one or two characters that were just over the hill. No, we don't mean to change our basic policy of decentralizing responsibility and holding men to their responsibilities, but we do think we should be doing a better job in training some of our own talent. If we train our own, we ought to know what we are getting.

MORGAN: I see. You feel you would get talent at less expense and with less risk if you establish a training program. Grow your own, so to speak.

ECKERMAN: Right. Let me take just a minute now, before the rest of the executive committee gets here, to tell you who they are. I have already mentioned Fred Andrews; he's the brains behind this outfit; I'm just the promoter. Along with a lot of other longhairs he did a great deal of important work on radar research during the war. As a supply officer in the navy, I became acquainted with him and we became fast friends. Instead of going back to teaching when the war was over, Fred went into TV research with the same company I joined as a salesman. A few years later—it so happened that we got fed up with giant bureaucracy at about the same time—we decided to start out together, with my handling all the sales and business problems and Fred handling research and production. We soon found we needed more help.

The first major addition to our staff was Ralph Bauer. When we started to grow, Fred found that he was spending all of his time on production problems and we knew that it would be disastrous to get behind in research in a fast-moving field like electronics. So we got Bauer, a man we had both known back in the war days. Bauer was also young, but he had had five years of production experience in a good outfit. People don't warm up to Ralph quickly, but they all respect him for his sense of urgency. He always seems to be saying: "Let's get on with the job."

Nick Carbone came next. We thought at first that any bookkeeper could give us the facts and figures that we needed to have about our costs and expenses. We learned better after a sobering experience that I won't go into now. It was then we got hold of Nick to head up all our financial and accounting work. He was a young comer with the firm of public accountants that audited our books. When we went after him, they offered him a partnership to hold him, but he saw potential in the option we gave him to buy 10,000 shares of stock. Today, at 38 he is a millionaire several times over.

Our last top addition is Paul Duncan, head of personnel and public relations. We didn't hire Paul away from anybody. He asked *us* for a job back in 1953 right out of college. He ran errands for all of us until we discovered he wasn't doing what we asked. Better than that, he was using judgment of his own. He seemed to have an unusual capacity for getting close to people and they were always telling him their problems. He also seemed to have an uncanny sense of how to handle reporters; he would tell them everything he reasonably could, but be disarmingly candid when he refused to answer their questions. So we came to rely on him, put him in charge of personnel about two years ago, and last fall we put him on the board and the executive committee.

The average age of our top group is in the low 40s. New industries seem to require young . . . Oh, Fred, come in. I want you to meet Professor Morgan, the man Dean Fay suggested that we talk to.

Messrs. Andrews, Bauer, Carbone, and Duncan enter. After introductions, the men sit down at the conference table at the side of Eckerman's office. Eckerman opens the meeting.

ECKERMAN: I have already given the professor a thumbnail sketch of our history. I haven't given him a chance to ask any questions, but maybe he can do that as we go along. So we won't waste too much time, I'd like to get right into our subject: What should we be doing to develop the executives we need, not for now but for the distant future, say five years from now? In view of our earlier talk, I assume everyone has been giving this a lot of thought. I'd like to ask everyone to express his views. Who would like to start off? Fred, do you want to go first or last?

ANDREWS: I don't care, Ken. I might just as well be the first to confess my ignorance. I just don't *know* how you develop executives. *I'm* not even sure I know what an executive is or what he does. I'll tell you though, what *may* be true:

To my mind an executive is anyone who tries in an organization to get something done through other people. We characterize him by the way he thinks. We can be easily fooled if we pay very much attention to his personality or the way he behaves, or even to his ability to understand and get along with other people. The important thing, that distinguishes one top executive from another, it seems to me, though I could be quite wrong, is a man's capacity to use his head.

What do I mean by "using his head"? There are probably a hundred different ways in which a man can or should use his head, but there are four that stand out for me. For lack of better terms, let me call them will, imagination, reason, and judgment.

An executive, it seems to me, is someone who wants to get something done. Many people can see the "something"; but most fail to feel the "want." A key ingredient, then, is an executive's will, his determination, his stick-to-itiveness, his overall capacity to know instinctively in what direction the organization should be going and his persistence in driving relentlessly toward that goal. This point certainly needs no documentation from me. You cannot name a successful business or any other organization that has not had this sense of purpose. It is what stirs all men to action.

Another essential quality of the organizational leader, as I see it, is imagination. I started out in life as a scientist, and I still like to think that this is my real work. To me the capacity to think thoughts that have not been thought before, to see things that have not yet been created, to foresee the results of acts that have not yet taken place—acts that will not take place unless they are willed to take place—this capacity is at the heart of all creative work.

I should make it clear that I don't consider myself a leader of men, a real executive. That's Ken's job. Whatever ability I have is for applying basic discoveries to practical problems. Both jobs require imagination. Ken has it in large measure and uses it in meeting the extraordinary demands of making executive decisions.

After will and imagination I come to reason. By reason I mean something a bit more restricted than the philosopher's usual definition; I am simply referring to what we call the normal processes of logical thought. Logic and mathematics are not found in the world of nature; they are contrived by the human mind. They may have to do with the relationships of energy and matter in time and space, but they are not *in* time and space. The premises or axioms on which logic is based may perhaps be observed in the external universe, but the reasoning process itself is in the mind.

Lastly, I come to the critical quality of judgment. Here will, imagination, and reason meet at the place where choices must be made. The executive's job achieves its final expression in such choices. On some major problems, and often on minor ones, the executive makes choices where he is guided only by hunch or intuition. In these choices, a subtle sense of value must guide him. Sometimes he deals with the great moral values, but more often with contemporary social values. A problem such as selecting a site for a new plant or expanding into another line of business all require a sense of sound judgment which somehow balances all the many interests that are bound to be involved.

Let me stop. I did not mean to ramble on. It must be the teacher in me coming out.

ECKERMAN: No, go on Fred. Any questions, Professor?

MORGAN: No. I think Dr. Andrews has expressed his views clearly, for me at least. Would you mind going on, Doctor, and say how you believe these capacities can be developed, particularly how they can be developed in the mature men who work in this organization?

ANDREWS: I hoped you might let me stop here, for now the water gets way,

way over my head. I am not sure in a commercial concern, that we should *want* to educate men's minds. It's an awesome responsibility. But even if we assume that we want to, I am not sure how we go about doing it.

Take the question of will, for instance. Old Justice Holmes used to teach at the Harvard Law School. Referring to his teaching days, he once said: "I often told my students they could do anything they wanted to, if only they wanted to hard enough. What I did not tell them was that they must be born wanting to." He was, of course, a great phrasemaker and I am not sure I agree with all his philosophy, but I think he was right in this. He was saying, I think, that the desire to be a leader is inherent in a man and thus leaders are born not made. Qualities of mind and heart which make up the essential characters of great leaders are innate. They stem from something in a man's genes. His immediate forbears may not have these qualities, but it just happens that the particular combination of genes that produced him did.

I do not mean by this that a born leader does not have to fight or that he does not have to learn by experience. From his own point of view, he can take nothing for granted and he must struggle to learn by every means available to him. But he is born with the desire, with the interest, with the will, with the purpose, or whatever you call it.

If I am right about this, then there is really very little that any organization can do about developing its executives, except in a negative sense. We should not block off good men from becoming what they want to become. This sounds simple when I say it, but I believe many organizations fail because they try too hard to perpetuate in the next executive generation the same kind of leadership they happen to have in this. If we relax and let men develop themselves, then it seems to me we have a better chance to discover which men have the desire, imagination, judgment, and all the other qualities which a good leader must have.

I have heard it said that if a company does not have a positive executive-development program, it will encourage politicking, apple-polishing, and all the other schemes by which men advance their own interests. Perhaps so, but is that bad? Certainly we will not be fooled by the more obvious forms, and if a man is clever enough to fool us, may this not be some proof of his ability? Besides, who can prove that there is no politicking in organizations that *do* have development programs?

I realize that we have to find good men to run our divisions and we should get the best we can. But I get a bit angry when I hear talk about making leaders. We cannot make men differently than they are. If anybody makes men it is *the* Creator, or at most, the men themselves, And they're creators, too—with a small "c."

It seems to me that we are doing a first-rate job right now. Good men can learn what they need by watching how we do things now. We have no trouble finding any number of people who want to join us. Why can't we just hire as many good executives as we need and let them learn what they need to know about us as they go along?

Am I way off the reservation, Professor?

Morgan: Not at all, sir. Your viewpoint seems to me quite a valid one. A great teacher once said, "Knowledge of the first rate gives direction, purpose, and drive: direction because it shows what is good as well as bad; purpose because it reveals an ideal to pursue; and drive because an ideal stirs to action." It is fair to argue that since what you are doing here is already "first-rate" management, you need only bring in able men who will gain purpose and drive just from observing what you are already doing.

ECKERMAN: I wish I really knew whether we were doing a "first-rate" job or not, I think it is hard to tell a really good executive job from one that is just fairly good. We can't measure it by profits alone or by productivity or morale alone. And I doubt we could measure it even by some neat combination of these or other elements. When a business organization is sick, it is easy to see the symptoms in losses—poor quality and volume, terrible morale. You know then that the management in charge must be doing a lousy job. It's much harder when the patient is perfectly "normal" and is going through the daily motions.

MORGAN: You are right, of course, Mr. Eckerman. It is impossible to be categorical about these things. But just as I know one student is smarter than others, I know from evidence that Miniatronics is better managed than others.

ECKERMAN: Okay. Well, Fred, let me see if I understand your position. You say that the essential job of management is to provide the organization with purpose, drive, imagination, and a set of values by which sound decisions may be made. With these attributes the organization can then move towards the goals that have been set. You seem to imply that these are characteristics that men either have or they haven't. If they don't have them, they can't be taught, but if they do, then perhaps all we can do is not to interfere with their own development.

ANDREWS: Yes, I guess that's about it, Ken.

ECKERMAN: All right. Let's go on to Ralph. Ralph, what do you think about this business of training our own top men? Can we or can't we?

BAUER: Of course we can, Ken. There's no doubt about it in my mind.

In saying that we can and must train our own managers, I am not disagreeing with most of what Fred says. Purpose, drive, key decisions, and so on are important, all right—that goes without saying. But a business only needs one or two men to make top-level decisions. Mostly we need executives who can make the organization hum, who really know the business from the ground up. But there is only one way to train such men: by practical experience.

Executive action, as I see it, is not so different from any other kind of action. It can be taught and learned. All that a business leader has to do is to pick the most likely men he can find, tell them what he wants them to do and how he wants it done. Then, of course, he watches how they do it, corrects them when they are wrong, and tells them so when they are right. Most important, he uses the authority given him by the owners of the business to back up his directions. The carrot and the stick used to be pretty good incentives; I think they are the only real controls we have today.

Look at it this way: When we were in school, teachers taught us reading, writing, and arithmetic, and we learned the skills well or poorly. If we learned them well, we received good marks—if poorly, we were kept back or expelled. We learned subjects so they would become habitual tools, ready to use without thinking. The same was true when I was in engineering school. I had to learn the formulas and all the rest well enough so they became second nature. Thus I believe that every executive must know his job well enough so that he can teach it to all the men who work for him. Certainly this is true at the level of the foreman; I don't see why it isn't also true in middle and upper management as well.

Please don't think I have gone soft in the head. I obviously don't mean that the president has to be able to do every job in the shop, though ideally, if it were humanly possible, it would be a good thing. All I mean is that each of our executives should be pretty familiar with the job for which he is responsible, and able to do it as well or better than the men under him. Take the control equipment division for example. The boss there must know not only the key problems in the electronic unit, where we make control equipment devices for regulating petroleum and chemical plants; he should also know the key problems and techniques of the infrared unit, where we make control devices for the glass industry, and the ultrasonic unit, where we put together control devices for drillers and welders. To know all this he needs to have worked in these various units.

ECKERMAN: Wait a minute, Ralph. You may be head of operations but don't tell me you could tell our boys how to make the Rube Goldberg installation we put in for the Missouri Plate Glass Company.

BAUER: No, of course not, Ken. Though I believe I could have done the job had it been mine to do. All the men in that division know that at one time I *did* do jobs of the same sort. They know I understand their language and that if a real nasty snag is hit, I can still dig into it with the boys and ask some of the questions that may lead toward the answer. No, all I mean is that I favor the *dirty hands* method of executive training. I say: Learn the job on the job. Certainly that is what all of us have done here. We had no choice; no other way was open.

MORGAN: From what you have said, Mr. Bauer, I take it that you would favor some program for rotating your trainees from job to job so that they could acquire the necessary experience. Is this so?

BAUER: No. Not exactly, Professor. I would object to a job rotation program for trainees on at least two counts. I want to move men from job to job, but not on a "program," and not with "trainees."

I'm afraid of a program that is a capital "P" Program. I am afraid it implies that each job is just a stepping stone, when it should be an end in itself. I think when a man is given a job, he should think of it as the last job he will ever have, or at least as one where he is going to have to live with his own decisions for an indefinite period of time. If he takes on the job as part of a *Program* of rotation, where he knows he will have the job for six months, one year, or whatever time, it is almost as though he were play acting. He goes through the motions, does what is expected of him, hopes to come up with one or two ideas or proposals that will mark him as a bright fellow. But all the time he is playing to the gallery. He is not really living in the job he is in. His eye is on the job ahead.

My other objection is to the idea of trainees, or at least to the practice of designating certain men as "promotable," or as "crown princes." I think every man should be regarded as promotable, *if*—I say *if*—he has the capacity to do the job ahead. By this I do not mean to imply that all men should come up from the ranks. Our business especially depends on our getting trained brains and preferably young ones. But, while we hire as many of these smart, young, technically trained men as we can, and we promote them very rapidly as a rule, we do it only because they have the capacity to do the job that has to be done.

In this business, Professor, we talk a good deal about experience, because you can't do much that is new without having had experience with what has gone before. But never think we make the mistake of equating experience with age. To us, age, or length of service on a job, means absolutely nothing. Whenever anyone says he has had 20 years' experience in something, our standard response is to ask: "Have you had 20 years' experience, or one year's experience 20 times?"

MORGAN: Perhaps if a man has little else to boast about, the *durability* represented by 20 years is still something! But back to your basic position. Mr. Bauer: How far *would* you go in shifting men from one job to another? As I understand it, you have decentralized your organization so far that you place profit responsibility and customer satisfaction on each of the managers who head up each of your units. If this is so, doesn't your line of reasoning lead you to say that your technical men who know what goes on inside a semiconductor and in the little black boxes that house so many instruments, need also to hold sales jobs, financial jobs, and personnel jobs?

BAUER: That is a good question, Professor. I *do* want my budding executives to be real experts in what they are doing technically. I also want them to be skillful in understanding the figures that they use to measure and control costs, in dealing with customers, and in sizing up and handling our own men. But it is not essential for them to hold down all of these special jobs. If we continue in the direction we are now going, I think these men can learn all they need to know in their operating jobs themselves. Most of our customers now want to deal directly with the technical experts who really know the answers. Thus almost without regard to whether or not these men make a good sales impression, we are beginning to send them out on sales calls. And whenever they make a proposal, they are also responsible for their costs, and all of the operating problems of getting the job done. These men are thus using the common tools of business to get their jobs done—and *incidentally* they are learning the habits and skills of the executive's job.

ECKERMAN: Thanks, Ralph. Now let's see if we can get a few more ideas on the table. Who wants to go next? Nick or Paul?

CARBONE: I'd like to try it, Ken. My views may not be any better but at least they are different.

If I understand what has been said so far, Fred believes executives develop themselves while Ralph believes they can be trained by their jobs. Both seem to rely heavily on experience, either self-generated or job-generated. Experience may be the best teacher when there is no other, but in these days to rely on experience is to rely on obsolete information and on obsolete techniques. Exerience is always out of date. It deals with what *has been* rather than with what *will be*. Our real problem is to train men to deal with problems that have not yet arisen. Thus I believe an executive can best be trained by going to the places where people are thinking ahead. One of these places is a top business school.

You don't have to go to business school as I did while you are still young. There is no reason why you can't go after you have been in business and know from all the mistakes you have made how much you might have learned. The army and navy, years ago, learned the necessity for training and retraining their officers at regular intervals throughout their careers. And now, during the last 10 to 15 years, most substantial business schools have offered and most businesses of any consequence have accepted various types of advanced training programs. These programs have provided most of the executive training worthy of the name. My only complaint is that many of them do not go far enough in what they teach and or in what they require their students to learn.

Professor Morgan, you know a great deal more about what the business schools are doing than I do, perhaps you would comment on their importance and what it is they do in executive training?

MORGAN: Thanks, Mr. Carbone. I think I would rather reserve my comments. Besides, I want to hear more what you have to say about us. It's not every day I hear outsiders speaking well of our business schools!

CARBONE: All right. I will go ahead, but I hope you will correct me if I am very wrong on any point.

What I want to say is that universities are not just reservoirs of pedantic scholarship—at least, not the best ones. A good university, whatever it is teaching, will always keep abreast of all the important current developments in its field and it will have on its faculty men who are engaged in creative work. This is obviously so in the case of engineering schools and medical schools. I believe that it is also true of law and business schools, although much of the really creative work in law and business is done by the active judges and lawyers, and by those who are actively promoting new businesses or developing old ones. In any case, if I am right, the business schools are devoting their full time to observing the job of management. And they are experts in communicating that kind of knowledge to others.

ECKERMAN: Let me see if I understand, Nick. You would turn the whole problem, to the extent we try to deal with it consciously anyway, over to one or more of the business schools? I thought you said a moment ago that they did not go far enough in what they taught. How can we tell if these schools can help our men to do a better management job for Miniatronics?

CARBONE: The answer, Ken, is that we cannot tell for sure that the business schools will help us. All I say is that they offer us the best bet. We might hire a management consulting firm. A lot of them would be glad to come in here and tailor-make a training program just for us. But I'm not sure they are any abler than the men in the universities and most of the good consultants ask at least $200 to $300 a day for their time. I won't say they aren't worth it in the proper case—they must be, or they wouldn't have clients waiting in line. But I believe the established schools are able to do our job more effectively at lower cost.

MORGAN *(with a wry smile):* Thank you again, Mr. Carbone. I hope we deserve your confidence. You almost make me think we should raise our fees.

CARBONE *(also with a smile):* Perhaps you should. It might be a good way to test your market acceptance.

ECKERMAN: Let me come back again, Nick, to your criticism of what the schools *are* teaching. What about that?

CARBONE: What they teach now is all right as I see it, but they don't go far enough. Right now most of the executive training programs take men for one to three months and give them a smattering of knowledge in a number of fields. There seems always to be a bit of broad economics and politics, and introduction to problems of accounting and finance, something on labor relations, and a lot of human relations and the "big picture." Handled by lectures and discussion groups, these courses serve to enlarge the perspective of some of the students, but, in my judgment, they barely scratch the surface of what can be done.

MORGAN: What should we be doing, Nick—I mean Mr. Carbone?

CARBONE: Nick is just fine, Professor.

It isn't for me to tell the business schools how they should be doing their jobs. But I have visited a lot of management programs and have attended several. I get the impression that there is a lot of time wasted on inert knowledge and irrelevant talk. Most of the men couldn't care less about a lot of the subjects discussed and a lot of the discussion wanders so far from the point that it wastes the time of the 50 or 75 others in the classes.

What I would like to see is more concentration on pay-dirt subjects and on practical exercises that test a man's executive judgment. Let me give some examples. Accounting should be given real emphasis. I may feel this way because it is my own profession, but I do think it is the only way a business can measure what it is doing and what it has done. Not to know accounting in business is like not knowing how to keep score in a tennis match. What you do depends partly on what the score is at a particular time. Also, you may lose if you place too much reliance on the honesty of the scorekeeper. But when accounting is taught, it should be taught by getting right at the kind of problems a businessman actually faces. It shouldn't be too hard to set up exercises with balance sheets and other reports that demonstrate real situations where a layman might easily be fooled if he is not skillful and alert. Accounting *is* a technical subject, but that is all the more reason for teaching it; it may not be learned otherwise.

I feel the same way about most of the other subjects that are taught in school. When a course in labor relations is taught, I don't think it is enough to discuss the techniques of conflict and cooperation; students should be taught the essentials of the labor law, the economics of "real" wages, the sociology of group behavior. When human relations are taught, it isn't enough to discuss the skills and the blunders of given people in given cases; there ought to be a chance for them to learn about the psychology of personality and group dynamics.

I believe, Professor, that classroom learning should not stop with the acquisition of knowledge. It should also provide training in problem solving and in social skills. In teaching pricing and business policy, for example, students should be given real problems to solve. They might, for example, be given the problem we faced a few years ago. At first, we sold our transistors to the manufacturers of hearing aids. Their price was $16 apiece, and we made darn little profit at that. The market was small, the price was high, and our problem was if and how we could break into the radio field where the market was large but prices were low. That was a good problem then, but I am not sure our solution then will fit our problem now.

MORGAN: I'm sorry to interrupt, but would you explain, for my benefit, how you solved it.

CARBONE: Oh, I think you know the answer, Professor. We took a big gamble and broke the price of transistors from $16 down to $2.50. Luckily, the gamble paid off; the increased volume more than made up for the lower unit return. Our problem now, of course, is whether we should try the same thing again, so as to sell transistors and other semiconductors for use in the manufacture of relays, switches, and transformers. We might have to sell them for, say, 85 cents, but we have no assurance that the gamble would pay off another time.

To get back to my point. In school students can wrestle with problem solving, where a mistake will not bankrupt the company. One common technique, with which the professor is doubtless familiar, is to fill an "in basket" with a lot of memos and letters, phone messages, and the like. Then the student is asked to decide what he should do in each case. The discussion of the why's and wherefore's that follows each decision is most instructive.

When it comes to social skills, one big problem is that many managers do not have any real understanding of their own personalities and how they affect others. A two-week experience in a session of the type sponsored by the National Training Laboratory will in many cases give a man a lasting insight into his own behavior.

Formal school training can also teach through the so-called intergroup competitions methods. As the professor knows, in this exercise, it is customary to take two groups of 8 or 10 people drawn from several different levels of management. Each group is asked to come up with its solution to a big problem, for example, how to improve labor relations. After separate discussion each group presents its solution and the leaders of each group are then asked to agree upon the winner. When the leaders fail to agree on the winner, as they invariably do, the matter is referred to an impartial judge. He then decides, to the great gratification of the winners and the dismay of the losers. What finally happens, of course, is that all the participants in the groups learn by direct experience; they find themselves feeling and showing loyalty to their own group regardless of the merits of the argument. They discover that the leaders cannot concede points to the other side without losing face with their own group. They observe that the groups emphasize their differences rather than the points they have in common. And lastly, they find that the search for creative solutions where both sides agree is almost impossible when conducted in a win-lose orientation. To me, this is *important* knowledge.

I won't go on. I think you see the drift of my thinking. I think executive training needs to be consciously and formally dealt with by those who are experts in the field. Leaders are not born, nor, as I see it, are they made by experience alone.

ECKERMAN: Thanks, Nick. Any questions? No? Well, Paul, I guess you have the floor. This problem of training is really in your jurisdiction anyway, isn't it?

DUNCAN: No, Ken, I really don't think it is my problem alone; developing executives is a responsibility that belongs to all of us.

Before we can talk sensibly about executive training, it seems to me we need to know what we are training for. We need some theory of leadership, some idea of what a leader is. Fred said leaders are born and not made. Whenever this assumption is made, one is committed to the "great man" theory of leadership, where the born leader or great man makes history rather than the other way around. This viewpoint has been accepted by many people for a long time and it is just as easy to see businessmen cast in terms of heroes and great men as it is political leaders.

Nick, on the other hand, put his emphasis on what a leader learns and knows. This leads me to think he would make the reverse assumption: that history makes men. If the leader must rely heavily on knowing the ways of the society and of men, then it is evident that society as a whole—or history—moves the great man into action, in fact makes him possible. In this view, external influences are determinative of events.

To Ralph, I think it matters little whether men make history or the reverse. He stresses the internal aspects of the organization, the strength and the effectiveness of the bonds between leaders and followers. A leader in this view is anyone who, in a particular situation, actually directs and controls the work of others. In a business he receives his authority from the shareholders and the board of directors, and by firm methods of direction and control he sees to it that the rest of the organization gets done what they want done. Am I about right, Ralph?

BAUER: Well, I won't quarrel with it now, Paul.

DUNCAN: Good, because my own point of view is perhaps the converse of yours. I agree with you that the man-history equation is unimportant (events are all the result of the interactions between some men and others). But I do not agree that leadership is a matter of directing and controlling the work of others. Thus, I see authority coming less from above than from below; no one can be a leader unless he has followers who want to follow. I see leadership as the problem of achieving "integration and self-control."

The term *integration and self-control* is not mine. As Professor Morgan knows, it has been used in recent years by Douglas McGregor at MIT. It was used first, I believe, by Mary Parker Follett over 40 years ago. The essential idea is that the principal function of business leadership is to *integrate* the goals of individuals with those of the business itself. This doesn't sound very remarkable until one stops to consider that we usually think business requires people to give up their own interests and adopt those of the organization, because there is a basic antagonism between them. In general we have operated on the assumption that, given a free choice, most people would not work at all; that they *do* work—"give up their own interests"—only because they need the money they earn in business.

It was Miss Follett's idea that while this antagonism between the individual and the organization did exist, it did not need to exist; that most persons really wanted to work, for only by what they contributed to organized efforts could they give meaning to their lives; that it was possible by effective leadership to alter both the individual's and the organization's interests enough so that the genuine interest of both could be served. Thus she preached that individuals should have a chance to "participate" in the decisions that directly affected their work, that the job of the creative leader was to help subordinates plan their own work.

McGregor has added to Miss Follett's insights by pointing out that nearly all of the research findings made by social scientists over the intervening years have supported what she observed. Research in group behavior seems to show that the more effective groups are those where the atmosphere is informal, where everyone enters the discussion in due course and listens in turn to what the others say, where there are open disagreements with respect to the means of tackling the task the group is trying to solve, disagreements which are consciously examined and resolved. Such task-oriented arrangements are a far cry from the traditional hierarchies of authority, where leaders are assumed to have the powers of supermen, where direction and control are imposed from above, where workers are believed to be willing only in response to rewards and punishments.

In a business such as ours it is particularly important that we accept the principles of integration and self-control. I say this because we can survive and grow only by living out at the far frontiers of new knowledge. To do our job the way we want to do it, we have to be first, or among the first, to come up with each new device or each new application of an old device. We cannot afford to miss any ideas, regardless of their source. Under such conditions we cannot expect the "boss" to be a superman; we *do* expect that most of the "boys" will know more in their own special fields than he does. What we expect of the *boss* is that he will be capable of maintaining such a high degree of cooperation in the group for which he is responsible that we will be first in new ideas, first in productions, first in profits, and as a result, first in esprit de corps.

ECKERMAN: This is interesting theory, Paul. How do you think we are doing in the matter of integration? Does your theory have implications for management development?

DUNCAN: You have asked two questions, Ken. As to the first, I think we are doing pretty well. As a matter of fact, I do not believe we could be where we are if you and Fred and Ralph, from the very beginning, hadn't been remarkably adept at achieving "integration and self-control" throughout the organization. You may not have thought of it in these terms, but success in a new and complicated field like semiconductors requires that you actually operate this way.

With respect to management development, however, we obviously haven't done so well or we wouldn't be here. The reason, I believe, is not far to seek. Our business is technical, so we have made most of our promotions on the basis of technical competence. We have neglected to reward men for their capacity to teach others. According to my view, the most important factor in executive development is the relation between the man and his immediate superior. In every new job the boss can make it a genuine learning experience or not, depending on the interest he has in his men and the time he is willing to spend with them. He is probably the only one who can really help a man to comprehend the dimensions of the executive's job. Our problem is that we have been rewarding "bosses" for their know-how and imagination in making semiconductors, and paying too little attention to their know-how and imagination in developing their subordinates.

Our situation is somewhat like that in a university. Faculty members are supposed to be promoted on the basis of their teaching ability *and* their scholarship. Scholarship in the form of research or writing is fairly easy to measure. So what happens? Men who are good teachers, but indifferent scholars, are passed over; good scholars, but indifferent teachers, are rewarded. With this lesson in plain view, most men act accordingly.

What we must do, I believe, is to let our people know that we intend to reward those who are developers of men on the job. Then we must follow through and show them we mean what we say. At present we have *some* men who do a good job with their men, but you do not know them or hear about them. We will have more when the whole organization knows that top management is interested in how well their men come along.

Eckerman: Thanks, Paul.

Well, professor, we have unburdened ourselves so fully, I think you can see why we have called you in. I listen to these different lines of reasoning and they all make good sense to me. But they can't all be right, or can they? Do I have to conclude that there is a bit of truth in each viewpoint? Constitutionally, I resist this kind of solution. It seems like a compromise and I don't like compromise. To me, a compromise is an admission of defeat, of not being able to find a really good answer. I don't like to admit that this problem cannot be licked. What do you think? Can it be?

Morgan: I appreciate your saying the problem is tough. It makes me feel that you will not be disappointed if what I say still sounds like a compromise. Of all the problems philosophers have tackled, education has always seemed to be the most resistant. There has never been any agreement on what it is that education is trying to accomplish, or on the methods that can be effectively employed. But let me divide my comment as the others have done: between ends and means, between theory and practice.

It seems to me that most of the disputes over the theory of leadership, the basic ones anyway, stem from a difference in the frame of reference of the commentator. If he is on the outside of an organization looking in, he has one frame of reference; if he is on the inside looking out, he has quite another. Let me see if I can explain the difference.

If we are on the outside of an organization looking in, we try to observe as carefully as we can what goes on, what actions cause what results, how policies are decided, how they are carried out. We look for uniformities in behavior, things that happen with sufficient regularity to make us feel safe in predicting that, if items X and Y exist, then item Z may be expected to follow. In the field of leadership we are apt to focus on the personal characteristics of the leaders, and we try to say that leaders with certain grades of intelligence, with certain types of personality, with certain kinds of experience are more effective leaders under certain conditions than others. A great deal of work has been done in this field, but up to date the results have been far from satisfying: We just do not seem to be able to predict with a high degree of certainty whether individual A will or will not be successful in job B. (Unless, of course, he happens to be the son of the owner!) For myself, I believe that we have only scratched the surface in these studies.

From this frame of reference we also examine a lot of other factors that seem to bear on leadership. We look at the basic charter of the organization, the lines of authority and communication—*de jure* and *de facto*—the system of incentives, the methods of producing the goods and services which the business sells. We also look at group behavior, at the tendency to polarization and either/or debates in win-lose environments. Both Mr. Carbone and Mr. Duncan commented on a number of these studies.

Also from this frame of reference we examine a business in relation to its environment. In concentrating on this relation, economists and economic historians are thus concerned with the ecology of business organizations. They want to know what kinds of competition, or what levels of taxation, or what policies of regulation will produce what reactions by what businesses. They try to see a business and an industry in the full sweep of history, examine the influences upon it, and its reactions to those influences. These influences have their effect on leadership. In the railroad industry, for example, with its long history of state and federal regulation, it was to be expected that the railroads would have trouble in attracting or keeping leaders of great ability. Able men who want to make imaginative advances as free as possible from outside influences will tend to drift into other types of business where they can use their abilities. In a broad sense, *leadership* is the product of the relation between a *business* and its *environment*; and the basic equation may be written: $L = B \leftrightarrow E$

Now, this frame of reference is common among most teachers and government officials. They look at business from the outside. It is the reason why you do not, and should not, trust them. Their view of business is a partial view in both senses of the words *partial*. A businessman's view is also partial for he is on the inside looking out. The prime question he asks is not what *is* going to happen, rather what *ought* to happen. This is an entirely different frame of reference. It is the difference between the observer and the actor. An observer is not personally involved in what he is observing, except to the extent that he observes accurately and reports accurately. The actor on the other hand, while he is also an observer, is primarily concerned with deciding what he or his business ought to do, what action he ought himself to take.

At my school we teach little economic theory or history as such. The reason for this is that we are trying to give men similar experiences to those which they will get when they become active on the inside of a business. They will be making choices—often on inadequate facts. Thus we place our emphasis on making decisions. The two questions we continually ask are: (1) What additional information ought we to have before deciding this case? (2) What, when we know as much as we are going to know, ought we to decide?

If I were to advise you today from the first frame of reference, I might say: "Don't worry. You are in new industry. It is glamorous and exciting. It will attract some of the nation's brightest young men. Government policies, through defense spending and supports for basic research, will favor your industry for some years to come. I predict that you will, therefore, have an adequate supply of able executives."

But this is no answer for you. It may be reasonable to predict that you are going to be successful, but this does not mean that you can sit back and expect success to come without your doing something about it. Like our friends in Moscow, you want to "encourage" the inevitable. So you may reasonably ask me: What ought we to do as a practical matter from the second frame of reference?

Let me give you my answer in the form of comments on the four positions which have been set forth this morning. (If I may be forgiven a small flattery, let me say also they were set forth quite well.)

Mr. Andrews spoke of the essential qualities of the mind as the essential qualities of leadership. As to the qualities, I agree with him fully; but I do not agree that nothing can be done in a formal way to help men acquire these qualities for themselves. Every time a man exercises his will in self-discipline, he strengthens that will. And when he exercises his imagination, reason, or judgment, he strengthens those powers. I believe that we can provide men in business with the freedom needed to gain this exercise. Good judgment, it has been said, comes from experience, but experience comes from bad judgement! Business *can* provide men more opportunities to make mistakes.

In any event, I believe that men acquire leadership capacities by leading. None do it perfectly, but all *good* leaders *do* learn to do it better. Thus I am inclined to agree that Waterloo *was* won on the playing fields of Eton.

Mr. Bauer also emphasized practical experience, but in a somewhat different sense. He was talking, I believe, about learning the skills and routines of this particular organization, not just the qualities of mind that are required by leaders in all organizations. I agree on the importance of these skills, but I would not let their learning take care of itself. I believe that appropriate experience *can* be planned by the individual *or* by the organization, preferably by both.

The skills of the executive which become habitual are many. And habit, as William James remarked, is the enormous flywheel of society, the most precious conservation agent. Day in and day out the busy executive needs to do most things easily, without conscious thought. He should know his business so well that he responds almost automatically to most of the personal and technical demands made upon him. In all these matters, established routines and the much maligned "company policy" play a highly constructive part. But it is equally or more important that the executive learn to recognize those situations that do not fall into routine, or those cases where routines have outlived their usefulness. Too much emphasis on practical experience can result in failure to make these essential distinctions.

This leads me to Mr. Carbone's views. I appreciate the confidence he displayed in our schools of business administration, even though he would have us attempt more than we do now. We are grateful for all votes of confidence. But we are limited by the time we have available, and even if we had unlimited time I should not want you to rely exclusively on what we or any other school can do. Nevertheless, the notion is gaining ground that businessmen are entitled to have—indeed ought to have—some type of sabbatical leave program. I think these leaves should be encouraged, for they can provide men with new perspectives. Many of these perspectives can be gained in a two-or three-month advanced management program; others can be gained elsewhere. A man might, for example, use his leave to take a trip to Europe to visit concerns engaged in the same lines of business. Or perhaps he would use the time to do some writing or research not directly related to his job. These experiences cannot be translated into measurable additional profits; they may be no more than fringe benefits for the executive concerned; yet on the whole, I believe they are helpful in stimulating the growth of the men you need to run important segments of your business.

Mr. Duncan's views come as close to my own as any, although I recognize more limitations than he does to the principal of integration. To me, integration is of most use in complicated tasks and in upper levels of management. It is of much less use in low-level and routine work. I was, nevertheless, especially pleased to note that these views seem to be broadly shared by your whole organization. This being true, I expect that you will have little difficulty in adopting the suggestion that you place greater emphasis on the teaching or coaching aspects of every executive's job. This is where you will get your greatest results, I am convinced.

ECKERMAN: I have been hoping you might offer to give us some specific recommendations of your own. Do you think you can?

MORGAN: I don't know. You already have before you the basic choices in the field of executive training. Perhaps some suggestions will occur to me. In any case, what I would like to do, with your approval, is to visit with you again in six or eight months, and see how your program—with a small "p," Mr. Bauer—how your program is coming. Meanwhile, if I can offer any further thoughts, I shall be glad to do so.

ECKERMAN: Yes, of course. We should be glad to have you come back to see us. And thank you for coming down this morning. I'm glad you do not think we have been too far off the mark.

Conflict at a Research and Development Laboratory*

THIS CASE IS ABOUT a series of changes made in an engineering services division over a period of some 14 months. This division was one of 14 divisions in a large federal government research laboratory. The 13 other divisions were engaged in basic and applied research, and the Engineering Services Division, as it was called, was actually part of the Administrative Services Division which provided service functions for the research divisions.

Within the Engineering Services Division, there were four branches: the Engineering Design and Drafting Branch, the Production Analysis and Planning Branch, the Mechanical Shop Branch, and the Electronic Services Branch.[1] Primarily we are concerned with the Engineering Design and Drafting Branch.

The Design and Drafting Branch was divided into three design sections—A, B, and C, two drafting sections, and one checking section. Altogether there were some 50 people in this branch.

Within Engineering Services the men knew each other well; many of them played golf together, advised each other not only about technical matters but also about social and personal matters, and frequently did favors for each other.

The work of the division was to design, develop, and build models,

---

*From Robert E. C. Wegner and Leonard Sayles, *Cases in Organizational and Administrative Behavior*, © 1972, pp. 159–167. Reproduced by permission of Prentice Hall, Inc., Englewood Cliffs, New Jersey.

[1]Hereafter, the Production Analysis and Planning Branch will be called the Planning Branch, and the Mechanical Shop and Electronic Branches will be called the Production Branch.

mechanisms, and instruments for use by scientists in their experiments in the research divisions. The devices varied enormously in purpose, from high precision-measuring equipment to large support structures. Most of the devices were constructed only once: however, continuous modifications and refinements were made to many of them as required by the changing needs of the experimenters.

Requests for engineering or production services normally originated in the research divisions. The requests went to the Planning Branch, which sent those needing engineering services to the Design and Drafting Branch. Generally the remaining requests that could be met without engineering services were handled by the Planning Branch.

In acting on the work requests sent to them, the Design and Drafting Branch would contact the Research Division, try to determine the experimental requirements and acceptance boundaries, and then develop working designs and drawings to build the equipment.

However, in the development of a design and working drawings, a great many alterations were made in order to include additional experimental requirements and accessory equipment or to provide better accessibility or easier machinability.

Scientists and designers started many alterations. However, many alterations were also started by people in the production area. They were initiated by different levels and at different times, depending on the nature of the changes. For example, sometimes these alterations involve a different sequence of finishing and coating operations that production thought would be easier to handle, or which would result in a better product; this might have been pointed out by an electroplating worker, or a leadingman.

Many designers went to see particular machinists several times a day to discuss progress on a project. Frequently alterations were made on the spot. It was essential for most designers to be able to do this; otherwise, the amount of work that would be required in going through the official channels—making changes in drawings, sending them through checking, through planning, and then through the master mechanic, chief quarterman, and on down—would have caused a virtual standstill in production. This system of communications was not always embraced wholeheartedly by everyone, but was accepted because it usually worked without conflicts and disagreements.

It was because of this necessity for frequent alterations that much interaction took place, especially between designers, draftsmen, and production. Although no one liked to alter what he thought was complete, almost everyone recognized that constant modification was part of the work.

The checking and drafting people worked within the Engineering Services Division building most of the time, but the design sections had quite different patterns of work from the drafting and checking groups, and also among themselves. One design section (section A) almost always stayed at their desks, or at least within the building. This was attributable to the very strong personality of their supervisor, who watched their work and work habits very closely. In another section (section B) conditions varied. Some men worked for months or years with a research division, and had a room in the other division for themselves; others in that section usually worked at their desks. In the third section, where I worked, the situation again was different. The designers worked at their desks, but they also made frequent trips to the research divisions during the day. This section (section C) also had more contacts with people in the production shops and with planners.

Designers and, to a certain extent, draftsmen and production personnel often identified closely with a project and helped in setting up experiments. They shared with the scientists the tense excitement of throwing on switches, gradually but inexorably bringing a variety of instruments into operation, and intently watching dials and gauges for the first indications that a new device was working. Not infrequently designers would go out on field trips with scientists, attend their meetings, and have lunch with them. In these instances, the relationship was informal and friendly with a mutual exchange about progress and bottlenecks. Many of these designers became familiar with future experiments being planned as well as with the functioning and capabilities of other equipment in use in the laboratories. They often suggested changes and alterations, which many times resulted in additional requests being issued by the research division.

Many projects were expanded in this way, and for the scientists and the designers this insured continuity of relationships. Those divisions that submitted requests only sporadically could not always be assured of fast service. Designers were reluctant to break away from comfortable relationships with scientists they had come to know well; and scientists were reluctant too, since they could not be sure when they could get design services again, or whether they would have to explain their work to an unfamiliar designer.

CHANGES IN THE ENGINEERING SERVICES DIVISION

At this time, and throughout the period covered in this case, there was a great emphasis in the government on cost savings. Posters, leaflets, and stickers with "WOW" (war on waste) were placed in every building, on many doors, on most bulletin boards, and in other conspicuous places. Cost savings permeated discussions and practically all activity. This was especially noticeable in the Engineering Services Division, and coincided with the arrival of a new manager from another federal government activity.

The new manager came to the laboratory to head the Engineering Services Division in July 1968. In contrast to the manager who had just left, the new manager was a cigar-brandishing, aloof fellow who impressed most people as being definitely unfriendly. From the grapevine it was learned that the new manager had been "successful"—nobody knew how successful—in instituting a series of changes in the production operations of another government—but nonresearch—activity. Hence many people were apprehensive when he asked for a report about the status of all work and available manpower. A great flurry of activity took place as people attempted to find out what was to be included or excluded from the report, and what the report was to be used for. Nevertheless, the report was somehow put together and turned in.

THE AUGUST CONFERENCE

In August 1968, the new manager called the Design and Drafting Branch and the Planning and Production Branches (in separate conferences) to discuss a new promotion policy and a new arrangement of personnel. The promotion policy for the Design and Drafting Branch included the establishment of "super" grades for those who "excelled" in their work, and also a sort of journeyman level for other designers and draftsmen. Other positions were to be added in which the personnel were not going to report to the chief engineer but directly to the manager. Specifically, a staff of industrial engineers and a staff of project engineers were to be added.

It was explained that design would now not have to worry about coordinating projects between scientists, planning, and production, but could for the present remain at the board and do what they were "best suited to do," that is, design. The project engineers were to act as "quarterbacks—carrying the ball between scientist and designer, designer and planner, and designer and production problems, and so forth, between groups."

The industrial engineers were to conduct studies—the exact subjects of which were unclear, although everyone "knew for certain" that industrial engineers made work measurements and methods studies. The implications were obvious, and this generated much discussion and anxiety. One very important point should be made: The manager was normally rotated in his assignment to other facilities every two years, so that there was a definite period of time in which the new manager had to act and accomplish things. People were conscious of this, and it affected their degree of cooperativeness although they also knew that in exceptional cases an extension of assignment time was sometimes granted.

At the end of the conference the new manager announced that he would supply details about the promotion policy and related matters in December. But when December arrived he said he had been too busy but that early in the new year he would definitely call a conference. However, it wasn't until April that he called another conference to discuss the promotion policy.

Soon after the (August) conference there were many earnest discussions, and there was unanimous agreement that research and design work was not subject to the kind of work measurement and methods techniques associated in most people's minds with the work of industrial engineers.

The idea that project engineers were going to be brought in was especially rankling, for many designers, particularly among those who worked closely with scientists, planners, and production on their projects, thought that they were already performing their duties, and what's more, relished their position. Furthermore, only a few weeks before the conference was called, a memorandum was sent from the chief engineer to the designers stating that designers were to act as "project engineers"—follow the project through from conception through testing and delivery.

THE INDUSTRIAL ENGINEER

When a group of IEs were hired in early October, they were doubtless bewildered to be met coldly and resentfully by almost everyone except the new manager and a few politically astute and alert types. To make room for these new engineers, desks, equipment, and files were moved out into the design and drafting areas from another room. There was just a little less room in some of the aisles, and design and drafting people subsequently resented the industrial engineers even more.

The industrial engineers began making inquiries about the work soon after arriving. It was obvious that they had direct access to the new manager, so overt uncooperativeness was not practiced. On the other hand, it was immediately clear that the industrial engineers were hardly at all versed in the kind of work that was being done—especially with regard to the technical aspects, not to mention the system by which the work got done. As a result, it was quite easy to confuse the IEs.

THE MEMO SYSTEM

One of the industrial engineers decided that the system of transmitting requests for desired alterations between design and production (by verbal instruction) was far from the way it was "supposed to be done." So one day the designers were called in to a conference with the chief engineer who informed them that alterations were now to be transmitted via written memo, and they were advised to keep a copy of such memos. Not only alterations, but also requests for revised estimates on production scheduling on one's design were to be transmitted via memo. Since no one was monitoring or enforcing the directive, this system broke down almost immediately. Also, production refused to transmit memos to design and drafting for each revision and to commit themselves to anything but a conditional completion date.

TASK SHEETS

About November, after the industrial engineers had been in the Engineering Services Division for some time, the Engineering Design and Drafting Branch was instructed to fill in what were known as "task sheets." Designers and draftsmen were to keep a record of each part designed, giving a short description of the part (like "gear housing") and the number of hours spent on designing the part. This was extremely distasteful to everyone who had to fill in these sheets. The designers felt that the future use of the task sheets was obvious, and that their usefulness was far from evident in view of the fact that no two parts were ever built alike.

The task sheets were filled in, but were accompanied by long and bitter complaints ("I'm not going to get any work done now with all this paperwork," was the most frequent complaint). As soon as it was discovered that not all the sheets were being collected, and that their interpretation was indeed difficult or impossible, they were stopped abruptly. Nevertheless, from time to time the chief engineer would have the designers and draftsmen fill them in for he was requested to ask them to do so. But most designers and draftsmen plunked the sheets into the wastebasket or "lost" them, and nothing happened.

OUTSIDE CONTRACTORS

During this period the chief engineer and his supervisors were continually asking for more men, particularly technicians, to help with the workload which was steadily increasing. Instead of hiring technicians, contract draftsmen were brought in beginning about December. Furthermore, the Design and Drafting and Production Branches were urged to send work out on contract. The head industrial engineer, who had been with the division for some years, was put in charge of contracting; and some of the new industrial engineers were made liaison men between engineering services, the outside contractors, and the research division. There was the same resentment and antagonism to the idea on the part of the Design and Drafting Branch, and also the Production Branch because, as it was generally expressed, this way of doing things would be more expensive (the government was supposed to be trying to save money).

The way the contracting was to work created another source of contention with the designers. The contracts were to be negotiated by the industrial engineers, but the designers had to go along with the IEs and the contract designer to the research division's building and explain what was wanted by the scientists. Since the industrial engineers admittedly were not specialists in the research and design requirements, plans from the contractors were sent by the IEs to the regular design people who had to review the plans. This being the case, the question arose as to what would happen if the design failed to perform as proposed. If the design succeeded, the contractor would get the credit; if it failed, the designers would be blamed.

The designers also envisioned that if the design failed, the industrial engineers could very easily turn around and ask why the plans had not been looked at more closely, calculations made, or mistakes caught, to which the designers could not reply "It was not my job." Also it was not going to be easy to point at the contract manufacturer unless there were obvious defects. Consequently much time had to be taken from in-house design so that the section supervisor and the designer could go over every detail very carefully.

PROJECT ENGINEERS ARRIVE

Since the new manager came, seven industrial engineers had come into the division, but by April 1969 three of them had left. This was a never-ending source of gleeful conversation among almost all personnel in the division. But in May, other changes took place that appeared to show promise of more long-range and lasting impact. This time a small group of three project engineers were brought in with a rank equal to the supervisors' of the design sections (the IEs were one rank below). They were knowledgeable about research work which their former companies were then doing, and this aroused keen interest among several scientists. The head of the Electronics Branch, who was widely respected for his technical knowledge as well as for his administrative ability, was made head of the project engineering group. Also, design section A's supervisor, considered the best engineer in the division was transferred to the project engineering group.

The designers were puzzled as to what to do next. They could hardly ridicule the new group as a whole, since two of their most respected men were now part of the new group. Some decided to cooperate; others held out, reluctant to supply any information about the research division's work with which was not specifically asked for. Little quarrels began to take place among designers. Hints and questioning tones about "betrayal" were aimed at cooperating designers.

The new members in the project engineering group were quickly learning their way around the organization, considerably aided by the two able oldtimers who were transferred to that group. It was interesting to note that as the new project engineers began to get accustomed to the place, the industrial engineers started showing vague expressions of dissatisfaction.

*Decision at Zenith Life**

IF THE GOALS OF A BUSINESS are important to its future success, it becomes important to consider how those goals are chosen. The situation at Wickersham was certainly not usual. Goals are usually chosen by much less obvious means. In some organizations, goals, and the major policy decisions associated with the determination of purpose, are decided by a high-level group of men, while in others the decision is made by an individual. In either case, the way in which the problem is attacked depends in large part upon the personality and character of the chief executive. One kind of chief executive tries to make or control these decisions himself; another will seek to find a basic policy and objective in the diverse judgments of his associates. One will tackle the job formally and concretely; another will rely on informality and intuition. One thing is almost always true: The character of the organization is strongly affected by the character of its chief executive.

What is meant by character? By personality? What are their major variables? How are they to be described? In matters of such importance to the success of the organization, it is more than strange that to sophisticated business executives and directors of great corporations, they are classed with black magic, or at best, with stereotypes of the crudest sort. Questions of character and personality may seem to be complicated and may seem to be understood by psychologists alone, but it would seem that those who must select others for promotion and development would at least investigate their rudimentary aspects.

To Morgan, the confusion in understanding personality seemed compounded by his observation that the personalities of the psychologists themselves often were quite ordinary. A great deal of knowledge did not seem to help them to become more effective themselves. With psychiatrists it was often worse, for the disorders of their patients seemed to rub off on them. Nevertheless, when Morgan was invited to participate in a seminar at Northwestern, he thought it would be a good

---

*From Abram T. Collier, *Management, Men and Values*, 1960, Harper & Row Publishers, Inc., New York, N.Y. Reproduced by permission of the author.

opportunity to renew his acquaintance with Foster Parsons, a psychologist who had once been an assistant director of admissions at the Graduate School of Business and who was now a consulting psychologist in Chicago. Perhaps, he thought, he could discover how far Parsons had progressed in his effort to discover the variables in character and personality assessment and particularly those variables associated with successful leadership.

Parsons, he had heard, had built up a flourishing practice which included Zenith Mutual Life Insurance Company. Arriving at Parsons's floor, Morgan noticed that he could see the Zenith tower on Michigan Avenue. An attractive secretary promptly showed him into Parsons's corner office.

Parsons (*heartily*): Greetings, Will. Great to see you! (*To secretary.*) Would you take my calls, Miss Fox; unless it's very important? (*She leaves. To Morgan.*) Great to see you, Will!

Morgan (*shaking hands vigorously*): Here, too. Wonderful to see you, too, Foster. I've missed you every time you have been back in New England. (*Smiling.*) And I rarely get west of Dedham, you know!

Parsons: Yes, I remember how you travel west. Well, I'm glad the boys up in Evanston have got you out here now for their seminar. You'll be able to stay most of the morning, won't you?

Morgan: Oh, I think so. The show doesn't begin up there until two. I'll be all right, so long as I get away by noon.

Parsons: Fine. (*Settling down.*) How's everybody at the school?

Morgan: Quite well, Foster. A lot of your friends wanted to be remembered when they heard I might see you. Westgate especially wanted me to say hello.

Parsons: Good old Westy. He was a harried admissions director when I knew him; I can't imagine what he is like now.

Morgan: What is it, four years ago you came out here?

Parsons: No, over five. Time goes faster every year, doesn't it? Tell me, Will, what can I do for you? In your letter you said you wanted to know how my appraisal work had been coming. Did you have anything specific in mind?

Morgan: No. At the school I think we are backward in keeping abreast of psychological theory and technique. I suppose that's the reason we spend so much time on matters of decision making and policy.

Parsons (*wryly*): Yes, I've noticed that. I saw in the *Harvard Business Review* that you were involved in that Wickersham Mills case. That seemed to me to be a perfect example of putting the cart before the horse. I can't imagine anything sillier than trying to select a manager of a business by the policies and objectives he says a business ought to pursue. What a man is, is more important than what he says. Lip service to policy means nothing. *Everyone knows men make policies. Policies don't make men.*

Morgan (*with a tolerant grin*): Okay, Foster, maybe you're right. I won't deny that I know very little about the personalities of the men in the Wickersham case; or at least, I knew only what I could infer from what each man said and did. But this is just what I want to ask you. What information about an executive *is* pertinent? *How* do you get it? Is it *possible* for those who must make decisions about top business leadership to get more accurate or more comprehensive information about the men they select?

PARSONS: Yes, Will, I think it is. As a matter of fact, I will let you judge for yourself from a case I have been working on during the last few weeks. One of my most important clients is the Zenith Mutual Life Insurance Company, one of the big companies that has its home office right here *(points out the window)*. You can see its home office right over there. Do you know it?

MORGAN: Yes, I do. Joe Speller, their director of agencies, is a good friend of mine. Had me at a sales meeting in Kentucky just a month or so ago.

PARSONS: Good. You may know then that Zenith has grown rapidly during the last dozen years under the leadership of John Robbins, "Cap" to his navy friends from both wars. Zenith has grown so fast, it is now one of the top 10 companies in the country. Its basic business has been in ordinary and group insurance, but in both lines it has been quite unconventional—both in the wide variety of coverages it has offered to write, and in the special incentives it has given to its agents. The agents, working out of branch offices operated by branch managers, have pushed their average sales well above those of the business. While other companies have complained about Zenith's tactics and apparent willingness to insure people while still in hospital beds, they have come to give the company a measure of respect.

Cap is now 63, and while he feels as hale and hearty as ever, he is confronted with the old problem: Which of the several key men in the company should be selected to succeed him as president two years from now? Each year Cap has put off the decision, hoping something would happen to make the choice clearer than it is. A couple of months ago, however, he called me in along with Stewart Pool, his executive vice president. Stewart is the other top executive at Zenith who is Cap's age and who has always worked closely with him. Apparently, one or two board members had asked such pointed questions, Cap felt he couldn't delay any longer. After some talking around, we decided I would give each of the four principal candidates an "image analysis." We also agreed that Stewart and I would interview each of them and make tape recordings of the interviews. Fortunately, we finished the last one a week ago, and Pool has told me that I could let you listen to the tape recordings (confidentially, of course) and ask your professional advice.

Frankly, this stuff we have collected is terribly exiting to me. After you have been exposed to it, you can tell me what you think—whether it gives you a deep insight into the personalities and characters of these men; whether, if you were on the Zenith board, you would know which one of these men you would want as the top man. How does this sound?

MORGAN: Sounds wonderful, Foster. I'd love it. But what is this analysis thing? What did you call it?

PARSONS: The "image analysis." It's a method I have worked out to allow men to describe their own self-images—their major personality variables. But before we get into that, let me introduce you to the men at Zenith Life.

Come over here; I have the tape recorder all set up ready to roll. Let me explain. I have recordings here of four interviews. The first one is with Clifton

Aaron, who is financial vice president at Zenith, and quite a remarkable fellow. After we have the interview with Aaron, we'll hear one with Blaine, the agency vice president, and then with Close, who is general counsel, and then with Frank Darmody, the actuary.

For all these interviews, we set up our equipment in Stewart Pool's office. When Cliff Arron came in, we weren't sure we wouldn't pull a rock on the very first one. Aaron is a big man, must be 6 feet 3 or 4 inches. Here is his picture. He is 58; gives you the impression of quiet power. His dress is always conservative; plain, dark clothes, a simple necktie. In addition to his size, probably his most striking features are his prominent nose and chin, his slate-gray hair, and deep-set eyes that seem to look right through you.

Around Chicago in financial circles, Cliff is well known. Many people like and admire him. They know him as a football celebrity who had received several awards as an "athlete who has made his letter in life." Others say they don't trust him, think that he is too ruthless in his business dealings, too pushy, too anxious to be accepted as a powerful businessman. Nobody questions his intelligence and capacity, though some think it may be overrated.

But let the recorder give you the rest of the story. I'll interpolate some parenthetical comments on the action as we go along. *(Turns on recorder.)*

Recording

POOL: Thanks for coming down here, Cliff. I believe Cap explained to you the purpose of the interview. I hope you don't mind if we make a recording so we won't be interrupted by my taking notes as we go along.

AARON *(cautiously):* Stewart, I'm sure you know what you're up to, but to me it looks like another one of Cap's stunts. I trust you, Stewart, but I am sure you will understand if I withhold judgment until I know better what is going on.

POOL *(dryly):* Okay, Cliff. I appreciate your trust. I won't try to sell you anything. Let's go ahead. You understand that the same questions we are going to ask you will also be asked of the three other officers as well, and what you say will be reported to the special committee of the board. *(Aaron grunts.)*

First of all, would you tell us about your background and experience? Anything having to do with your education and training that you may think relevant.

AARON: Well, Okay. *(Quickly.)*

I don't need to go farther back than Ohio State. I went through college during the torrid '20s, the years of prohibition when everything went. *(With growing force.)* Wacky years! I even played football against Grange, Friedman, and all the rest. When I got out of college in 1927, I joined the other bond salesmen, first in New York, then in Chicago. By 1931 the bond business folded and I found myself applying for a job at Zenith.

Zenith, of course, was concerned with a whole mess of mortgage foreclosures and corporate reorganizations. I carried the officers' bags, learned a good deal about another side of the investment business. Then came the SEC—someone was needed to work out the procedures for getting exemptions from SEC regulations. I dived in and learned about private placements from the ground up. Without being immodest, I think the way I handled this job was the principal reason I came to the attention of the top financial men in the company.

Pool: Thanks. How about your outside activities, business and social?

Aaron: I am a member of the board of the Second National Bank and of Mississippi Valley Power. I am also on the finance committee of both concerns. These are two of the top boards here. I have refused to get tied up with hospitals, community funds, and so on. They take too much time away from work.

Pool: Can you say anything about your family situation?

Aaron: Not much. My wife and I used to live on the North Shore. Now we have an apartment over on the Outer Drive. I get my exercise walking to work. My boy is 30 now; he's married with two children, works in the data processing unit at Zenith.

Pool: What about your personal financial situation?

Aaron: I think it may be sufficient to say that I have made enough money in the market so I don't *need* a job working in an insurance company. I can be independent if I want, and I can do the things I want.

Pool: What about your health, Cliff? Anything there that would bar your taking on additional responsibilities?

Aaron: Never had a sick day in my life.

Pool: I thought you were out for a month or two, 8 or 10 years ago?

Aaron: Oh, that! It was damned nonsense. One fool doctor thought I had an ulcer. Couldn't prove a thing. Cap made too much out of it.

Pool: Now, let me ask you what you would regard as your greatest accomplishment with this company?

Arron: When I took over the financial operation nine years ago, the earnings on the Zenith portfolio were lower than any other life insurance company in the top 10. Bond yields were improving, but I persuaded the Finance Committee to make a major shift in our entire portfolio. We sold our governments and most utilities and went into mortgages. Our mortgage portfolio was boosted from 20 to 45 percent. Then we risked trouble with New York by putting 6 percent of our assets into common stocks. This took some doing, but our earned rate last year was better than average; as a matter of fact, there are only three companies in the top 10 that did better than ourselves. Right now, we're lightening up on mortgages. While we've taken some profits in the common stocks, they still constitute nearly 10 percent of our portfolio because of the appreciation.

Pool: Yes, that was really something. If you were chief executive, Cliff, what would you consider your greatest asset?

Aaron: My greatest asset, Stewart, is that I'm willing to take responsibility. In fact, I like it. There are too damn many pussyfooters in this company who are not willing to stand up and be counted.

Pool: What then do you think is your greatest liability?

Aaron: The same thing, obviously. I think what I say and say what I think. It's a dangerous practice.

Pool: Now, Cliff, what do you think is the most important job for the president of Zenith Life?

AARON: To take responsibility for results. He's got to see that the company gets where it wants to *go*. He's got to set our targets and make damn sure we get there. The top man has to see to it that everybody does his job.

It's a lonely job if you do it right, for everything ultimately depends on you. If you fail, there are no excuses; only the fact of failure.

I suppose if I were to put management's principal function in technical words, I would call it "control." The top manager of any company has got to have effective control over his own organization if he is going to get results. He's got to hold out the carrot and carry the stick.

POOL: That leads to my next question. What are your views on how executives and others in Zenith Life should be paid?

AARON: This is one of which I have strong feelings. The trouble with too many life insurance companies is that they don't pay their top men enough. If you want good men, you have to pay them. If I were running this company, I would see to it that we had a few top-flight executives and that they were paid as well as anybody in any industry. If they weren't worth the dough, I would see that they were fired and that we got people who were. I would pay the technicians and our clerks what I had to. I believe I would save money in the long run.

POOL: Now let me ask you a few questions of policy. My first question is this: Suppose the company were asked to make a loan, a large loan, to a policyholder which had a substantial group insurance policy with the company. Suppose the company were a second-rate credit, but that it wanted a prime rate on the interest paid. What would you do?

AARON: That's simple. Give them the loan without any fuss. I'm a realist; you can get into trouble if you don't recognize the power realities immediately.

POOL: All right, here's another question. Do you think we should sell group insurance in those cases where the group is competing with our ordinary sales? In other words, should we sell group to so-called fictitious groups and in jumbo amounts?

ARRON: Sure. Give the customer what he wants and stop squirming. If we don't sell the group, somebody else will.

POOL: Good. How about state and federal regulations? Do you favor state or federal regulations?

AARON: The business has been pussyfooting on this for too long. I favor federal regulation, even though I know that the SEC is made up of a bunch of damn bureaucrats. Still, the SEC would be better than the state politics we face now.

POOL: I see. Here's another question. We have a salary continuance plan providing continued salaries for employees according to their length of service. Suppose we had a short-term employee who was very good and who was still sick when his salary payments were to stop. What would you do?

AARON: If I didn't like the rule, I would junk it. If the employee was good and I wanted to keep him, I'd continue to pay him his salary. If he weren't good, I'd drop him.

POOL: What do you think about going into other lines of business, that is, other lines of business in addition to regular ordinary life insurance and group insurance?

AARON: If we were smart, we would be in the equity business today. In my opinion, the mutual fund fellows have had a good thing of it and are going to have an even better thing as the years go by. The public is sold on equities today as it was sold on life insurance a generation ago. We ought to start selling them along with our life insurance. If we can't sell investment fund shares under the present insurance laws, then I say why don't we set up our own mutual fund and let our present agency force sell those mutual fund shares?

POOL *(in the same tone of voice):* And now, Cliff, what is your opinion of Marilyn Monroe?

AARON: I think—hey, what do you think you're doing? What's the joke?

POOL: Excuse me, Cliff, thought I'd have a little fun. Here's another serious question. What do you think about the other men who are being considered for the top spot upon Cap's retirement? How would you rate Blaine, Close, and Darmody—forgetting yourself, of course?

AARON: You really want me to answer that? I like to be fair, but I can't be frank, except by saying I don't believe any of these men are competent to handle the top job in this company.

POOL: I understand, but suppose you *had* to pick one of them?

AARON: Well, I would have to pick Close. He's too young and inexperienced, but at least he has a hard head and a hard nose. I don't think he'd be shoved around too much by the sales people or the actuaries.

POOL: Have you anything else that you would like to say?

AARON: No. You and Cap, and most of the board know me very well and what I can do. If that is not enough, I don't know what else I can do. There are several banks that have made me attractive offers. I know a lot of people think I'm too old to take on a job like this. There is an absurd illusion around that a man is old at 58. The fact is, he's just coming into his prime of life. Cap has asked me to turn down top jobs elsewhere; I don't know, but I think this spells out a kind of commitment.

(Parsons turns off the tape recorder.)

MORGAN: Wow! Quite a fellow!

PARSONS: Yes, we'll come back to him in a moment. Now let's hear the interview with Blaine—F. DuMont Blaine, our agency VP. Here is quite a different type of man. Monty, as we call him, is slight, not over 5 foot 8 and 145 pounds soaking wet. He may not be impressive to look at, but listen to him for five minutes, and you will be so trapped by his charm, you'll forget about his size. Look at this picture here.

Monty bounced into our interview a few weeks back dressed nattily, as usual, a flower in his buttonhole, a starched handkerchief in his pocket, a double-breasted vest, three rows of cording on the sleeve of his jacket. He seems to jump right out of the pages of *Esquire*.

Monty is an ebullient, enthusiastic, colorful person. Aaron is well known, but Monty knows everybody. He is not only on a first-name basis with the presidents and board chairmen of many large businesses; he knows governors and senators quite as well. And what may be equally important, Monty makes a point of knowing the "comers." He'll meet a new man, find out something about him, and then a few days later, send him a personal note recalling their meeting and referrring to something they have in common. Young men don't forget this type of gesture.

The tape picks up the interview at the beginning. Here goes. *(Turns on tape.)*

Recording

BLAINE: Greetings, Stewart. How do you do, Dr. Parsons? I understand you have been doing some wonderful things with our branch offices. Dr. Parsons, if you can tell us what motivates agents and what agents are motivated, you will be doing a wonderful service for our great business.

(Turning to Pool.) Stewart, it's always a pleasure to see you. I understand you have something exciting in store for me.

POOL: Yes, I think Cap told you what he wanted us to do. He wants to get some additional background data and viewpoints for use with the board. If you're all ready, let's get started. First of all, tell us a little about yourself and your background, whatever is important.

BLAINE: I hardly know what to say, Stewart. I try not to talk about myself except when I need a career illustration for *other* men.

I have been with Zenith since 1935, when I joined the Detroit Agency. I was 27 years old then. It seems like yesterday. I felt I was a wise old bird, Stewart, because up to that time I had worked in a great many different jobs. I'd sold everything from vacuum cleaners to Fuller brushes. But when I came to Zenith, a transformation came over me; I realized that I had finally found my real life's work. My zeal for this business has never flagged since.

I am a small-town boy, Stewart. I grew up in Grand Rapids, where my father was a minister. He had come from Maine. I'm proud to say that my great-grandfather was James G. Blaine. When he ran against Cleveland, it was thought he had made a lot of money, but none came down my line, and I have always had to make my own way. I got my college degree studying nights, but I have been blessed with a strong constitution. I've always enjoyed working, so long as I could be with people.

POOL: Yes. Now, tell us something about your outside activities.

BLAINE: That's quite an order. I have to get into so many things. Right now, I'm vice president of the Board of Trade, program chairman for the Rotary, governor at the Tavern Club, director of the Boy Scouts, warden of our Episcopal Church in Winnetka, and I guess there must be some other things, too. I wish I didn't get into so many things, but when they say they always "ask a busy man to get something done"—I end up agreeing that they are absolutely right. A salesman is an easy mark when he is tackled by another salesman.

POOL: Yes, Monty, I know how it is. Tell me a little about your family and your home.

BLAINE: Well, as I said, we live in Winnetka. We have a wonderful new home we built on the shore. It's awfully expensive, I suppose, but I will confess to you, Stewart, I like a few of the finer things in life. We only go this way once, and I like to be able to enjoy my friends. Besides, I think I have earned a few comforts, and so does my present wife.

POOL: Yes. How about your personal financial situation?

BLAINE: Well, I don't know. I sometimes think I should have stayed in the field. I have so much entertainment expense, you know. Home office jobs put a ceiling on what you can earn, and I can't be reimbursed for all the entertaining I do. We do have a superb pension plan, though. As I said, Zenith is a great company, and no one can fairly complain about the great benefits the company provides us.

POOL: How about your medical history? This is pertinent where one takes on greater responsibility.

BLAINE (*with alacrity*): Oh, yes, it's very important. Fortunately, I am strong as an ox. I can go for days with only a little sleep and sometimes I have to. When you are out on the road and talking at agency meetings, at Rotaries, and so on, you know how it is, you can't rest and relax, you just have to keep going. But I have been blessed; really, Stewart, quite the worst thing that has happened to me is that I have occasional attacks of hay fever.

POOL: Thanks, Monty. Now, may I ask what you think your greatest accomplishment has been since you became agency vice president?

BLAINE: Well, Stewart, I guess you'd have to say I have put Zenith Life on the map. Until I took over full responsibility for sales—what was it, about six years ago—Zenith, you know, was not really very well known in this country. Oh, we had a large business and everybody in the business knew what a substantial company we were, but the public didn't know much about us. So we analyzed all the publics Zenith was concerned with. Then we followed with a big advertising campaign and a big public relations program. I think you can safely say today that every important person in Chicago knows who Zenith is and recognizes what an important operation we have here. I believe this has been one of the big factors in our sales results.

POOL: Yes, and what do you think is your greatest asset as an executive of the company?

BLAINE (*without hesitation*): Contacts, Stewart, contacts of all kinds. I serve as the company's ambassador, you know. I make it my business to have important contacts in every other city between New York and San Francisco, and in the city of Chicago, I know everybody who is anybody. Cliff Aaron uses my contacts from time to time in the investment field. They are absolutely indispensable to a good agency vice president.

POOL: And what would you say was your greatest weakness?

BLAINE: My weakness, Stewart? I suppose my greatest weakness is that I try to do too much for other people. I'm not hard-boiled enough when other people need me. And, I'm afraid they don't always appreciate what is done for them, you know.

POOL: And now, Monty, let's talk about management. What do you consider the most important job the president has to do? If you found yourself in the chief executive's spot, what is the single most important management principle you would want to establish?

BLAINE: Good, I'm glad you're getting away from personal questions?

To answer your question, it seems to me that management should be concerned primarily with *communication*. In keeping an organization alive and interested, it is most important that people understand each other and that they talk to each other. This is what I have tried to do throughout my career with Zenith, that is, to tell our people in the field what a wonderful company Zenith is, and what fine people we have working with us. And I've tried to let the home office know what a great job the agents in the field are doing.

You know, if we can *communicate* with each other, everything will always come out well in the end. The executive must be the communications center. Ever since I was in the field myself, I have always laid great stress on the importance of being able to listen as well as talk, to read as well as write. You know, Stewart, you can't sell anything without good two-way communication, and in a big company, you can't talk to everybody, so it's especially important. So I spend a great deal of my time visiting the field or writing newsy letters to all of our people there. When I write, I try to write with a sparkle, so as to express all the excitement I feel for the great missionary job we have to do. If I have done this job well, the company will be the greater for it. The field, Stewart, is the heart of a life company, you know that.

POOL: And would you say something about your philosophy of compensation, Monty? How do you think people, particularly executives in Zenith Life, should be paid for what they do?

BLAINE: I have always believed, Stewart, that people should be paid for what they contribute to the organization. They should have a strong motivation, Stewart, don't you agree? There is nothing like commissions to motivate agents, and nothing like bonuses to motivate executives. I have urged this on Cap Robbins I don't know how many times, but he really has never understood how important it is.

POOL: And now, may I ask you a number of policy questions? Suppose one of our large group policyholders were to want a loan, which we would not ordinarily make at the rate the policyholder is ready to pay? What would you do under these circumstances?

BLAINE: That's not too difficult, Stewart. I would call up the president of the group policyholder immediately and talk to him. I'm sure I could explain how important it was for us not to give any person preference over anyone else. I would try to get him to understand he was asking us to do something we really couldn't do.

POOL: But suppose he insisted?

BLAINE: Well, in that case, perhaps we might have to find some way out of the problem. After all, if it was a really big piece of business, we might have to make some concession.

POOL: All right, here's another question. What do you think about our selling group insurance when it competes with our individual sales? I mean, fictitious groups, jumbo cases, the sort of thing that our ordinary salesmen complain about.

BLAINE: Oh, you have some tough questions, Stewart. I like volume as much as anybody, more than most, I think, but I'm especially sympathetic to our men in the field. I think we have a higher obligation to our men in our own agencies than we do to the brokers who sell us the jumbo group cases we take. It's not an easy question, Stewart, I know.

POOL: And what do you think about the problem of federal regulation as opposed to state regulation?

BLAINE: I don't know much about regulation, Stewart, but I hope we can prevent the federal government from moving into the insurance field. I think we must fight as hard as we can to maintain state regulation. After all, that's all we've had for many years. The great American agency system has grown up in a friendly environment. We shouldn't tamper with it if we're not sure where we're going.

POOL: Now suppose you have an employee with short service, who becomes ill and who, under the company rules, is no longer entitled to salary continuance. Suppose he is a very valuable employee and you want to keep him. What would you do?

BLAINE: It is impossible to answer a question like that. Rules must be upheld, but there is always a way around them. I think rules are important, you understand, but certainly an executive ought to be able to make an exception in the proper case. I don't think it would be necessary to advertise what he does; he ought to be discreet, but I would certainly extend the pay of an employee of mine under these circumstances if it seemed wise. He would become a friend of mine and loyal to the company.

POOL: What do you think, Monty, about the future? What kind of expansion should the company undertake? Should we go into any new lines of business?

BLAINE: Yes, we should, Stewart. I have been urging Cap for quite a long time to do something to get us into the fire and casualty business. The fire and casualty people started it first, and they're all now selling life insurance, so I think the life insurance companies have got to answer back. We should sell fire and casualty. We have to "fight fire with fire"! Right?

POOL: Very good. And what do you think of Marilyn Monroe?

BLAINE: A doll, Stewart; she has fire, all right. I see fire makes *you* think of sex!

POOL: Well, not exactly, Monty. I can't put you off stride.

Now, one last serious question. It's no secret that the principle candidates for the top job here are, in addition to yourself—Cliff Aaron, Irwin Close, and Frank Darmody. Aside from yourself, how would you rate these other men?

BLAINE: That is quite unfair, Stewart. I make it a rule never to say anything critical of others. These men have been my close friends for many years.

POOL: I know, but suppose you had to decide.

BLAINE: Well, in that case, I suppose that I would have to put Cliff Aaron first. I know he is very tactless and blunt; I know he doesn't fully appreciate the importance of the field. But he has the longest service and would have only seven years in the position. By that time, another executive might be trained for the job.

POOL: Have you anything else that you would like to say in connection with this whole matter?

BLAINE: Yes, there are many things but I will limit myself to this: Life insurance is a great business, and Zenith is a great company. It has been my life. There are some wonderful men working for it in the field, in the home office, and on the executive floor. I know a great many of the directors—they are good friends of mine. I think they appreciate what I have done and will do if I should be called to the front office. But I should like to say this for the record: Whoever is selected by the board will be all right with me. Loyalty to the company is the thing most important to me. I have been loyal to it for over 25 years, and I will continue to work just as hard as I have, no matter what happens. I don't believe any man could do more than that, do you?

POOL: No, I guess not, Monty. Thanks very much.

(Parsons turns off recorder.)

PARSONS: Well, there's Monty Blaine. Monty loves people, and people love Monty. They really do. We'll come back to him, too.

Now, let's take up the interview with Irwin Close. Irwin is vice president and general counsel. A brilliant lawyer, though with his round baby face, he doesn't look it. He's a big man—must weigh over 220 pounds, though he's only 5 foot 9 or 10 inches. He looks at you with a benign half-smile with heavy-lidded eyes. His clothes are baggy and unpressed, covered frequently with ashes from his ever-present pipe. Irwin also has a tendency to pull on his ear and to rub the back of his neck. He appears to be thinking and most of the time he is.

Irwin has a charming wife who is the favorite niece of childless Cap Robbins and the mother of Irwin's four little youngsters. There's not much question that these kids mean everything to him. When you get him in the mood, he'll talk about them till all hours. He'll tell you he's sorry they can't grow up on a farm out in Nebraska where the wide open spaces give a child elbow room for his thoughts as well as his person. But let's have Irwin give us the story direct.

(Turns on tape recorder.)

Recording

POOL: Thanks for coming down to my office, Irwin. I suppose Cap has filled you in on the reason for this interview. Did he tell you that we were going to take a tape recording of it, too?

CLOSE *(slowly)*: Yes, Stewart; that he did.

POOL: All right. First of all, Irwin, let me ask you a little about your background history. Why don't you tell us something about it—that is, what you think the directors might regard as interesting and distinctive.

CLOSE: Well, I was born in Broken Bow, Nebraska. You might call that distinctive. That was in 1917. Ah—My father was the judge of the county court. I always thought I'd be a lawyer, too.

I worked my way through the University of Nebraska. Got a scholarship at Yale Law School in '39. Ah—When I got through law school, I thought I might like to teach law, but we were in war so I went off to Washington. During the next four years I must have worked at—ah—five or six different jobs. Fortunately, one of my bosses in Washington was senior partner in a good firm here in Chicago. When the war over, he offered me a job. I snapped it up, because the girl I married came from Chicago, too. Ah—four years later, Cap Robbins persuaded me to come over here as associate general counsel. He was—ah—needed a man to replace the then general counsel who retired in 1953.

POOL: Thanks, Irwin. Now would you tell us something about your outside activities?

CLOSE: Just a moment while I stuff my pipe. Outside activities? A man with four children doesn't have time for any others! I'm a member of the Bar Association, the Life Counsel, and that sort of thing. I get away from Oak Park, where we live, one week in the spring and fall for fishing and hunting, both favorite sports.

POOL: What about your personal financial situation?

CLOSE: A situation, yes; but finances, no. My life insurance is all protection at this stage. The bank is still the major partner in my home.

POOL: What about your health, Irwin? Is there anything in your medical history that is important?

CLOSE: Excuse me. This damn pipe needs lighting again. . . . My health, Stewart? I have a checkup every year. Ah—at the end, the doctor tells me I'm overweight, which I know. He says I ought to take off 25 to 30 pounds, which I don't, and that I ought to cut out smoking, which I plain refuse to do.

POOL: I'm glad I'm not your physician. Now let me ask you a different kind of question. You haven't been with Zenith Life a long time, but what would you consider was your greatest accomplishment during the time you have been here?

CLOSE *(pauses)*: That's difficult to say—in one word. Er—I suppose the most important thing I have tried to do is to make the Law Department—ah—an integral part of the company. When I got here, the general counsel was a man who had already passed normal retirement. He had one assistant who advised the Claim Department and handled a few cases in litigation; another man who reviewed questions on mortgage loans. That was about it.

Since then, I've tightened up our claim procedures; we're now winning about 75 percent of our cases in litigation, instead of 50 percent. I have three top-flight men serving the Finance Department, handling the private placements and the large mortgage loans we now have. I have two fine tax attorneys giving advice to our Agency Department (helping them boost sales, they tell me) and another fellow who has become an expert in premium taxes and the federal income tax. We are now saving—er—well, over a half-million dollars in our tax returns. Ah—does this give you the picture?

POOL: Yes, thanks. Now from your own personal point of view, what do you regard as your greatest asset for the company?

CLOSE *(slowly)*: Er—know-how, Stewart. I've made it my business to learn everything I could about the life insurance business. Lawyers have to learn about their clients' businesses. Fortunately, life insurance is not too difficult.

POOL: You'd better not let the actuaries hear you say that! *(Chuckles.)*

Okay, Irwin, what do you consider your greatest weakness?

CLOSE: I'd be a poor counsel if I made an admission against interest? I'm what Learned Hand called a "jobbist"! My main interest is in *doing* the job at hand, not in *talking* about it.

Pool: Now, let me ask you, if I may, what you consider to be the most important aspect of management's job? To put it another way, if you were president, what would you regard as your principal job?

Close: The principal job of the top executive is easy to state, hard to do. It's to make the organization run. If he succeeds it runs—not with a lot of noise, but quietly, like a Swiss watch. Er—to do this he needs to establish clear lines of authority.

As a lawyer, I know that laws form the outside framework within which the company operates. Similarly, law is needed *within* the company. Thus, our principal job is to make sure that every individual, every executive has a clear understanding of what law governs him, what his authority is, what his responsibilities are. Once these things have been clearly set forth, and clearly understood, once they know the rules will be enforced, then—er—you have a reasonably good chance of success. I don't think you can fly a large company like this by the seat of your pants. Cap Robbins has flown it that way, but I think we need to get the company on instruments. We need more—er—scientific methods.

Pool: I see. How would you compensate the staff, especially your executives?

Close: The same way, Stewart. By establishing a specific policy. We have a salary classification program for lower and middle grade jobs. There is no reason why we can't have job evaluation right up to the top. The president's job, if we are honest about it, can be rated just like any other.

Pool: Thanks, Irwin. Now let's move to a series of policy questions. First of all, take the case where a loan is requested by one of our group policyholders, which we wouldn't normally grant without a high rate of interest. If one were requested at standard rates, what would you do?

Close: This is just another example of what I had just been trying to say. The company needs to have clearer policy on matters of this kind. Each department should be a tub that stands on its own bottom. The Loan Department should make its own decisions independently of their effect on the insurance side. If the facts were as you state, there would be no alternative but to reject the loan. I don't think we'd lose many group cases—not the kind we wanted to keep, anyway.

Pool: Now, what would your view be about group insurance which is sold to the detriment of individual sales? I have reference to the so-called fictitious groups and jumbo cases.

Close: So long as we are in the group insurance business, we should sell any legitimate form of group insurance without regard to its impact on our other lines of business. Er—to mix metaphors, if the Investment Department's tub must stand on its own bottom, the Ordinary and Group Departments should stand on their own feet!

Pool: You're confusing me, Irwin, but I guess it's all right. What is your feeling about state and federal regulation? Do you think that we should support federal regulation instead of state?

Close: No, of course not. We would merely be changing the devil we know for the one we don't know. To gain federal regulation of insurance is not to eliminate state regulation. We would obviously have both systems, dual regulation. The two systems would overlap, with the evils of both.

POOL: Let me now ask you a question of personnel policy. Suppose we have a fine young employee who is disabled and whose salary continuance payments have reached an end under our rules. What would you do under these circumstances?

CLOSE: Ah—if you're going to have rules to control personnel policy, you've got to obey those rules. They mean nothing at all if you don't follow them. You may hate to follow the rule in a particular case, but you must. Hard cases are the quicksand of the law.

POOL: Now let me ask you a question of general policy with respect to the lines of business in which the company should be engaged. Do you think that we ought to embark upon some new lines of business like variable annuities, equity funds, fire and casualty insurance?

CLOSE *(without hesitation):* No, sir. The shoemaker should stick to his last. Companies can't be all things to all people. It's difficult to be the best in any field. It's hard to be the best miler, the best auto maker, the best life insurance company. If we go into equity or the fire field, I think we'll end up being mediocre—or worse—in *all* the lines of business we engage in. Do you see what I mean?

POOL: Yes, Irwin, and what do you think of Marilyn Monroe?

CLOSE *(with a chuckle):* Okay, Stewart, I guess I have been preaching too much. Right?

POOL: No, just a change of pace. Now, one last question. I think you realize that Arron, Blaine, and Darmody are also being seriously considered for the top post. Overlooking your own position for the moment, which of these other men would you regard as most competent for the job?

CLOSE: Er—anyone who is as directly involved as I am is bound to have prejudiced views. Sometimes I can't see the forest for the trees. It seems to me that Cliff is powerful, quick, and extremely able, but is not objective enough about himself. Monty is a fine agency man, he has great charm and more friends than Jim Farley, but I don't see him as staying put long enough to give the company a stable administration. I like to joke about the actuaries as well as the next man—but if I had to choose, I would have to put Frank Darmody first. He's soft, visionary, but at least he thinks before he acts. Of course, I'm fully aware he has personal problems.

POOL: Thanks, Irwin, have you any other comments that you would like to make?

CLOSE: Yes, I have two. My first is I think it is unfortunate Zenith has no man who is really skilled and experienced in the problem of general management other than the president himself. As a lawyer, I claim no broad executive experience which would qualify me as president, but the others are not much better off.

My second comment has to do with this interview. I think it's a good idea for the board to know as much about the men they are considering as they possibly can. The court is entitled to all the relevant facts; I hope in concentrating on particular men it will not fail to examine the needs of this particular organization, and thus uncover "the law of the situation." Shouldn't you consider what the company now needs before you decide what man you want?

Pool: That is a very good question, Irwin. You may be sure we won't overlook it. Thanks very much for joining us. *(Parsons turns off tape recorder.)*

Morgan: I'd like to meet this fellow, too.

Parsons: Well, we'll talk about him again in a minute. Let's go on now to our last fellow, Francis X. Darmody, actuarial vice president, 50 years of age. Frank, I should tell you, is tall, about 6 foot 2 inches, lean, maybe 160 pounds, walks hunched over; sits with his legs twisted into a corkscrew. He wears a puzzled expression, and has a habit of tapping his lips with his forefinger or rattling a pencil between his teeth.

You heard Irwin say Frank had personal problems. He does. His worst problem is that his wife is a neurotic; she has been in and out of various places for years. There is nothing he can seem to do. Frank is loyal to her and won't talk about it, though it might be better if he did.

Frank is an intellectual in business, something that used to be quite rare, but is more common now. He's better known in Chicago than Irwin, but he doesn't try to compete with Monty. While Cliff's friends are mostly businessmen, Frank's are professors and artists. This crowd is attractive to him, because he gets most excited when he comes across new ideas.

But now, let him tell his story. *(Turns on recorder.)*

Recording

Pool *(cordially)*: Glad to see you, Frank. Are you ready for the ordeal?

Darmody *(in a deep voice)*: Ordeal? I've been looking forward to this.

Pool *(doubtfully)*: Looking forward to it?

Darmody: You think I'm crazy? Maybe. But I think when you're trying to pick a man for a responsible position, *you* ought to know all that you possibly can about him. And it's probably just as important that he know just as much about himself. He ought to consider whether he really wants to take on added responsibility. Too often the man who seeks more responsibility is not the one most qualified to handle it.

Pool: A good point, Frank. Let's get on with what is the ordeal for me, if not for you. As you know, we have asked all the candidates the same type of questions and made recordings of all of the interviews.

First of all Frank, will you tell us a bit about your background and history? Whatever you think is important.

Darmody: Well, Stewart, I am one of the few people who live in Chicago who were actually born here. My father was a contractor on the South Side. As Eisenhower once said: "We were poor, but we didn't realize it." We ate well, because six of us kids always worked and added our bit to the cookie jar. Anyway, I finished high school and went off to South Bend for college. Then in 1932 (no, it was 33, after I took my M.A.) I got a job teaching mathematics in the Peoria High School. I'd still be teaching now, if I hadn't married and discovered that eating had become a habit with me! Somebody told me something about actuarial work, so I wrote a letter to Zenith as the most prominent company in the Midwest. I ended up coming here to Zenith in 35, as an actuarial trainee. At first I didn't eat much better, but I have been with the company ever since.

POOL: Thanks, Frank. Now would you say something about your outside activities?

DARMODY: Surely, I have a number of jobs. I'm on the board of the University Hospital and the Chicago YMCA. I'm also interested in modern art. I have a modest collection and serve on the board of the Chicago Art Institute. I'm a member of the Chicago Athletic Club where I play bridge every week or two. We have a duplicate bridge league there. I also like to swim two or three times a week to keep in shape.

POOL: How about your personal financial situation?

DARMODY: Except for high medical expenses, I've had nothing unusual about it. I have one youngster out of college, married, on his own. My girl is in her senior year at college, so in another year, I expect, she will have a teaching job herself. With my family off and most of their obligations out of the way, we have an apartment near the university. We are really quite comfortable.

POOL: You mentioned medical expenses, what about your health?

DARMODY: My expenses haven't been my own. No, for myself I only had an appendectomy a few years ago. I did have a breakdown in 1939, just after I finished my actuarial exams; must have been out for three or four months at that time.

POOL: Now let me ask you a different kind of question. Your career with Zenith extends over a quarter of a century. What would you consider is your greatest accomplishment during this time?

DARMODY: I suppose you mean within the actuarial field. My greatest interest, I think, has been with the problem of equity between policyholders, something I believe is of critical importance especially in a mutual company. Determining scales of surrender values involves questions of equity between old policyholders and recent policyholders. Similar problems are involved in the computation of dividends. Without being immodest, I think I can say the work I did here at Zenith led to our adopting a terminal dividend structure which many other companies now use. This lets terminating policyholders take with them an equitable share of surplus, you know. A mutual company is only in business for the benefit of its policyholders. We have no obligation to grow large or to build a large surplus. In the mad race for volume, these considerations are sometimes overlooked, or worse, deliberately ignored.

POOL: You may be right, Frank. Now let me ask you what do you think is your greatest asset to the company?

DARMODY: That is difficult to say, Stewart. The thing that I try to do most is to bring an open mind to every major problem. In this business the companies that will survive are those that are most alert to new developments, that are most responsive to changes in the requirements of the insuring public. My job, as I see it, requires me not to have so many convictions of what will or won't work that we miss the boat, or miss it often.

POOL: And what would you consider your greatest weakness?

DARMODY: The advantage of a closed mind is that you never have any doubts—if your mind is open, your weaknesses arise from the difficulty you have in dispelling doubt. If you listen to *all* considerations, you may find yourself indecisive, even when you ought to be clear and firm.

POOL: Now, let me ask what you consider the president's most important function? If you were able to determine the key policies of top management, what would you regard as your principle job?

DARMODY: To me the principal job of top management in any organization is to secure the commitment of all members of that organization to the achievement of the company's objectives. We live in a highly complex society; no one can *order* anyone to do anything. Authority stems from below, not from above. Under these circumstances, people do only what they want to. The job of management is to lead each individual member of the organization to *want* to reach company goals.

The best way to secure this personal commitment to the company, I think, is to make every worker a partner in the organization. Our policyholders are partners in an enterprise that is designed to last a lifetime. Our employees, from top management down, are also partners for the same length of time. As partners they are entitled to participate in the decisions that affect them, to voice their attitudes on all matters of company policy on which they have some competence. Now this does not mean that stenographers should be consulted on financial policy; it does mean that top officers in charge of financial policy ought to listen—really listen—to the views of those who work under them and are knowledgeable in their respective fields of expertness. Just as agency officers listen to the views of the men in the field, so all in management need to do a good job of listening. If it does a good job, and if the ideas of the members of the organization are, when appropriate, carried out in fact, then their sense of partnership and participation will be greatly enhanced and their sense of commitment deeply ingrained.

POOL: I understand. Now let me ask how you would compensate persons within the organization, especially management personnel?

DARMODY: I'm glad you asked this because my philosophy of management extends to compensation as well. I think we have to pay competitive salaries in order to attract men and women in all of our various kinds of jobs, but the competitive salaries should be supplemented by a bonus arrangement. The bonus could be based on the ratio between income and expense, so that when income goes up and expenses go down, a pool is created out of which these bonuses can be paid. For example: If our expenses are 10 percent of income, and if by good work we can cut those expenses to 8 percent of income, 2 percent would represent savings which the company had made. Some part of those savings, say 50 to 75 percent, can be used and should be used as bonuses to the staff which made those savings possible. The point of such an arrangement, of course, would be to make concrete the philosophy that members of the organization are partners and participants in that organization. It would show that what individuals do for others affects their own desserts.

POOL: Thanks, Frank. Now let's move to a number of policy questions. First of all, take the case where a loan is requested by one of our group policyholders, a loan which we might normally grant only at a high rate of interest. If you were asked to make the loan at standard rates, what would you do?

DARMODY: You have picked a tough question. Obviously, you don't want to lose the group business, but you don't want to give a group policyholder any benefit not authorized in the policy. This would be a rebate, of course. I can't give you a categorical answer except to say that I would analyze the situation carefully. If it were possible to bend a little in giving a loan to one of our good group policyholders, I might do so, but it would only be a little.

POOL: Now, what is your view of group insurance that seems to cut into individual sales? I speak particularly of so-called fictitious groups and jumbo cases.

DARMODY: I don't believe this is a question on which anyone should be doctrinaire. I am not convinced that fictitious groups and jumbo cases hurt ordinary sales. This may be, but what concerns me most is that we have allowed competitive pressures to influence our underwriting judgment. Jumbo groups are frequently just bad underwriting, and so are the so-called fictitious groups. Where we don't have a cohesive membership, we run up high costs which just don't fit with the low group rates we charge.

POOL: What is your feeling about federal and state regulation? Do you think we should support federal regulation instead of state regulation?

DARMODY: Not right now, but the time will come, perhaps sooner than we think, when federal regulation will be a practical possibility. At that time I would favor it. Right now we are in an impossible situation trying to satisfy the requirements of 50 states with reference to a single policy form. Different requirements with respect to these policies force us to print many special riders with consequent high expenses. We could save a lot of time and trouble if we had one central place in the federal government where policies could be approved for issue in all the states.

POOL: Now let me ask you a question of personnel policy. Suppose we have a fine young employee who is disabled and whose salary continuance payments have reached an end under our rules? What should we do?

DARMODY: I think we have personnel rules of this sort because they give us a track to run on; and so long as we have the rules, I think we should follow them. In the case you put, a circumstance might be created where the rule was inadequate. If so, it should form the occasion to reconsider the rule and perhaps to rewrite it.

POOL: Now, let me ask you a question of policy with respect to lines of business. Do you think we should embark upon any of the new lines of business that have been suggested?

DARMODY: This is another question to which no categorical answer can be given. These are questions of timing and degree. We have some studies under way which may give us the answer for our own company. I don't like to generalize for the business as a whole, but we may well come up with plans for entry into the personal fire insurance field and for insurance that involves a high equity investment.

POOL: And what do you think of Marilyn Monroe?

DARMODY *(with mock seriousness):* Oh, yes, as we were saying; beauty is a matter of taste. *De gustibus est non disputandum.* Now if she is your type, Stewart, I can understand why. . . .

POOL *(interrupting):* Okay, Frank, I give up. Let's get back to our last question. You realize that Aaron, Blaine, and Close are also being seriously considered for Cap Robbins's job. Without considering your own position for the moment, which of these other men whom you all know quite well would you regard as the most competent person for the job?

DARMODY: I've thought a good deal about this, of course. My man would be Blaine. I know a lot of people are inclined to brush off Monty as a nice guy who has made a career out of knowing people, that while you can't help liking him, he doesn't think deeply about the problems of the business. He may not be the ideal administrator of the home office, but he's a lot more observant than you think. He can leave the technical and administrative jobs to other people. What Monty would bring to the presidency is what every life insurance company requires: the capacity to stimulate a sales organization to ever greater effort. Life insurance is not, to the buyer, so much an investment as it is a commitment. The salesman must persuade people to do what they otherwise would not do. Monty is an expert in the art of persuasion. This, above all else, is what we need.

POOL: Thanks, Frank. Do you have any other comment that you would like to make?

DARMODY: Yes. You asked me whom I would support for the presidency if I excluded myself. I do not want to leave the impression that I would not be interested in the job. A person can't work in an organization for 25 years without getting a lot of ideas about what he would like to see done; it gets into his blood. Zenith is basically a sound organization, but it needs to do a great many things if it is going to be more alert to changes in economic circumstances and the needs of the insuring public, if it is going to improve the efficiency with which it operates, and effectiveness of its sales organization. We have a tremendous job to do in all of these areas and I should like to have a big part in doing it.

POOL: Good, Frank. You may be reasonably sure your position won't be misunderstood. *(Parsons turns off tape recorder.)*

MORGAN: Well, I'll be damned. I have never heard anything like this before.

PARSONS: And I don't believe that you're likely to hear again interviews with men whose personalities are quite so plainly differentiated. They fall almost too neatly into the classic personality patterns.

Now, I promised to go into the image analyses and show you the patterns of these men.

MORGAN: That's right, Foster. What is this analysis thing?

PARSONS: First of all, we shall have to make a quick review of personality theory. It goes way back. The Greeks and Romans thought they saw four major types of personalities depending on the humors in the body. Hippocrates and Galen talked about men who were dominated by:

1. Blood (choleric).
2. Yellow bile (sanguine or optimistic).
3. Phlegm (phlegmatic).
4. Black bile (melancholic).

Probably equally old are the personality types that are observed in men under the influence of alcohol. The (1) bellicose, (2) verbose, (3) comatose, and (4) lachrymose types are well known to everyone. If you have any doubt about the kind of person you are, just get drunk. You'll find out if you're a fighter, a talker, a sleeper, or a crier. *In vino veritas.*

Nowadays, I regret to say, many psychologists have not progressed far beyond these ancient insights. Oh, they have analyzed thousands of instincts, traits, or reactions, but when it is all boiled down, a good many have concluded that there are only four independent variables. These are measured roughly by scales of:

1. Aggression-submission.
2. Extroversion-introversion (sociability).
3. Stability-instability.
4. Dependence-independence (cooperativeness).

You can see that these scales are very closely related to the traditional or classic types. One thing that modern theory *has* done has been to demonstrate that these classic types fit into the basic equation of elementary psychology; i.e., the equation that behavior is the result of the interaction of an organism and its environment. Broadly speaking, we say every organism perceives its environment as either hostile or friendly, and its reaction is either positive or negative. Thus it is evident that every organism develops four basic kinds of reactions. These reactions are displayed by every organism to some extent; but they vary widely from one individual to the next. *(Pauses briefly.)*

MORGAN: These are *more comprehensive* dimensions of personality than the older ones? Is that it?

PARSONS: Yes, that's right. The first dimension relates to the degree of positive reaction made by the organism in a situation it perceives as *antagonistic*. This is, of course, the direct attack on whatever threatens. Included in it are the traits of aggressiveness and choler.

The second relates to the degree of positive reaction in a situation perceived as *favorable*. Here we talk of the outgoing behavior with friends, sociability and its related traits of optimism, cheerfulness, and talkativeness.

The third dimension relates to the degree of the organism's negative reaction in a favorable situation, its power to relax and thus its stability or phlegm.

The fourth dimension relates to the degree of negative reaction in an antagonistic situation or the organism's tendency to move away from trouble. Included here is behavior that leads directly to dependence upon someone else or some group to deal with trouble, together with the traits of cooperativeness, anxiety, sensitivity.

You see how modern psychology has thus shown the relationship between the basic types of reactions and how these four basic variables are contained in different degrees in each individual. Ambrose Bierce once put it this way: "In every heart are a tiger, a pig, an ass, and a nightingale. Diversity of character is due to their unequal activity."

MORGAN *(interrupting)*: I have been following along all right until now, Foster, but let me see if I understand. The tiger is obviously the aggressive personality; the pig is phlegmatic; and the nightingale is dependent or melancholic; but what about the ass—surely it is no extrovert!

PARSONS *(smiling)*: Touché. You have put your finger on a good point. Bierce overlooked the extroverted personality. I think he should have included a peacock in his list; it would represent the extroverted personality that expands under a friendly environment. When we speak of major personality elements, we are speaking of them when they are demonstrated by a particular organism in response to relatively strong stimuli. In many cases, however, they are demonstrated only a little, if at all. Thus the ass represents stubbornness or independence which means that it has only a little of the tendency of the nightingale. Similarly, a mouse demonstrates only a little of the tiger's aggressiveness; the mole only a little of the peacock's expansiveness; the chickadee only a little of the pig's calm.

MORGAN: I think I see, but how does this fit in with the men at Zenith. How do you describe their personalities?

PARSONS: Okay, take my analysis of Aaron. Here it is. We can see that he is a tiger. He rates extremely high in aggressiveness, fairly high in sociability also, an average rating, however, in terms of stability and fairly low in cooperativeness. Looking at this part of his pattern, you have the picture of a man who is hard-driving, quick, persuasive, very difficult to move off any course he has selected. His self-esteem depends on the power he has been able to acquire.

MORGAN: How about Blaine?

PARSONS: Okay. Look at Blaine's analysis. Here, you find a man of normal aggressiveness, but a man who has an unusual rating in sociability. Here is the peacock who lives on the opinion in which he is held by others. With all his color, he's reasonably stable, has a good deal of get-up-and-go. He also has a high rating in terms of cooperativeness or sensitivity to hostile situations. This sort of person often finds his way into sales or social work. Some people might call it a pattern for a do-gooder. Clearly, it is a pattern of a person who likes people and who, generally speaking, is liked by others. He is a talker, most impressive, but somewhat superficial.

MORGAN: That seems to fit the picture that I had formed about him. How about Close?

PARSONS: Well, Close's image analysis, I would say also fitted the picture that we saw during the interview. We have a semantic distaste for the pig, but Irwin has all the pig's good traits. He is steady, persistent, calm and happy. He rates fairly high in terms of drive and aggressiveness, very high in terms of stability and deliberateness. He is relatively low in terms of sociability or dependency. This man appears hard to move, but once he moves, he continues in the direction in which he started.

And here is the analysis on Frank Darmody. This is the nightingale, or if you prefer Thoreau's analogy, he marches to a "different drummer." If you look at his pattern, you will see a man who rates high both in aggressiveness and sensitivity. In fact, these two qualities fight with each other under certain circumstances, and may result in conflict and indecision. You can also see that he rates a little less than average in terms of sociability and stability. Not being concerned about being with other people all the time, he tends to think over his experience and to be imaginative and inventive. Not being too deliberate or too stable, he is quick to react and quick to do something about his experience.

MORGAN: This is fascinating; I begin to see how these traits tie together. These characteristics you have been talking about are *animal* in nature. But human beings are *not* just animals.

PARSONS: Right! This is precisely where some psychologists miss the boat—in my view, anyway. If they become overly much concerned with the behavior of mice and monkeys, they may overlook the principal aspects of human behavior which are quite different from those of other animals.

One of the principal aspects of a human being that distinguishes him from other animals is that he has a degree of self-awareness. In the process of maturing, he develops an increasingly clear idea of the kind of person he is. He becomes more self-conscious and more self-aware. The result is he acquires a clear self-concept or a self-image. It doesn't matter too much what you call it, so long as you realize that probably the most important driving force in the lives of every one of us is our desire to maintain and enhance our own self-image, whatever that image may be.

If this is true, one of the greatest concerns each individual has is the possibility that other people will not think of him in the same way that he thinks of himself. Thus everyone develops in his own mind a fairly clear idea not only of what he thinks he is, but also of what he thinks *others* think he is. His self-concept is thus enlarged, and combines what he thinks he is and what he thinks *others* think he is.

MORGAN: Hold on a minute. Let me see if I'm still with you. You spoke of the four major personality elements. Am I to understand that each individual has a picture of what others think of him, *also* in the terms of these four elements?

PARSONS: Yes, that's right, except that it's still more complicated than that. A "normal" human individual—if you will allow me the term—not only has a high degree of self-awareness, but he also has the power to determine his own conduct, to see the difference between what will help or hinder himself and his friends, to choose *certain* courses of action rather than other courses of action. Every individual develops an idea, not only of the kind of reactions he typically has, but of the kind of reactions he thinks he *ought* to have. Therefore, it becomes important in understanding the whole personality also to describe a man in terms of his self-image based on his reactions as he thinks they *ought to be* and as he thinks *others* think they ought to be.

This may sound a little complicated; actually it coincides with common sense. Each of us in a new job becomes reasonably well aware not only of what the boss and our associates think about our mutual behavior, but also about what they think it ought to be. People around us may think, for example, that we *ought* to be more aggressive, or that we *ought* to be more cheerful and outgoing, or that we *ought* to be more sensitive to the needs of others. In assessing the full personality, these dimensions are often overlooked.

MORGAN: Yes, I see. This must be the same thing Alfred North Whitehead had in mind when he said: "The ideals cherished in the soul of men, enter into the character of their actions." But tell me, how do you bring all this to bear on the men at Zenith?

PARSONS: Well, the image analyses I obtained from them showed me a good deal about the differences between the various aspects of their self-images. In Arron, for example, you think you are dealing with a fairly conceited individual. Actually, a study of his different orientations tells us that he believes he really has a good distance to go to bring his self as it is into line with his self as he thinks it ought to be. For a man of his age still to be growing is quite remarkable. He appears to be *trying* to be more sensitive to others.

With Blaine, we have a fellow who is really quite happy with himself. There are only minor differences from the self as perceived by himself and others, and as he thinks it is and as he thinks it ought to be. So also with Close; he likes himself the way he is. He probably won't change—if that is good or bad.

When we come to Darmody, however, we find a fellow whose various selves are widely split apart. He thinks he ought to be quite different than he is, that he is in fact different from the person other people see. This man is capable of great change and growth but, I fear, he is also subject to being torn apart, psychologically, if he is subjected to excessive stress.

MORGAN: I can hardly believe you can see all this in what a man puts down on paper. By the way, how do you actually find out what men think their own self-image is?

PARSONS: This is a $64 or a $64,000 question—but only one of them. Some psychologists have used the projective tests, you know, where the individual is asked to tell stories about ink blots or pictures; others have used incomplete sentences where the individual is asked to finish a sentence already started. Still others have asked questions about the individual's interests, typical behavior, and so on. For my own part, I have developed my image analyses on the basis of simply asking an individual to fill in two forms which consist of lists of adjectives descriptive of personal behavior. My analysis simply asks the individual to say whether he thinks these adjectives are (1) descriptive of him as he would like to be, (2) descriptive of him as he is, (3) descriptive of him as others think he is, and (4) descriptive of him as others think he ought to be. It has taken a great deal of study to work out the statistics of these forms, but within a tolerable degree of error, I think I can prove that the answers which most individuals give to these questions provide a fair picture of the individual's typical reactions as of the time the self-analysis is made.

MORGAN: This sounds quite impressive, Foster. Is there more?

PARSONS: Just a little, Will. I'll stop drilling in a minute. But this second frame of reference is really important, although it is fairly original with me.

You pointed out a moment ago that human beings are not like other animals. All animals have traits, instincts, and so on, things we call *reactions*. If we say a man is aggressive, phlegmatic, or whatever, we are usually talking about his unconscious or instinctive reactions. But in contrast to other organisms a man also is capable of conscious and intentional behavior—what Murray and Allport call "proactions." If we adopt the premise that "all behavior is caused," we speak of *reactive* behavior; but if we adopt the premise that "all behavior is chosen," we speak of *proactive* or intentional behavior. It used to be thought that the two premises were mutually exclusive; now most people agree that both are "partly true."

The reason we get into the field of intentional behavior is because it is obvious that reactive behavior doesn't reasonably describe all the really important things about the way people think and act. Many of the really important things people do, they do as the result of their conscious decisions, as a result of their trying to achieve goals they have deliberately chosen. Perhaps I can best get at what we mean here by asking you to tell me how you would describe great men. What kinds of men are called great?

MORGAN: Do you mean geniuses?
PARSONS: Yes, that is *one* type of great man, but there are others, too.
MORGAN: Yes, I suppose there are. *(Pauses.)* I suppose you're thinking of heroes and saints.
PARSONS: That's right, and there is still a fourth class. For this, the best term seems to be *wise men*.

From time immemorial, Will, men have recognized that there are these four major classifications of conscious intentional behavior:

1. The *hero* is obviously a man who exercises discrimination in his choice of objectives, and demonstrates unusual resolution in pursuing these objectives. Where other men give up, the hero by strength of will carries on. Where other men influence few others, the hero influences many others. In every man, it can be said, there is a touch of the hero, although if that touch appears to be only slight compared to the generality of man, then the individual is regarded as weak-willed, cowardly, or purposeless.

2. The second great class of men may be called *geniuses*. They are the great performers, those who have developed their talent to perform unusual acts of body and mind. It includes not only athletes of every kind, but artists and poets, and musicians. It also includes great intellectual performers who, by feats of memory and calculation, can store in their brains vast quantities of information and make lightning computations. I say everyone has a touch of genius, although if that tough be light, we may regard the individual as undeveloped, clumsy, or stupid.

3. A third class of great men is obviously those who are considered *wise*. A really wise man has to have some of the hero's will power and some of the genius's skill, but the special capacity of the wise man has been his capacity to understand the nature of the world about him, especially his capacity to understand human nature. Wise men have long been thought to be gifted with foresight, for more than others, they have been able to observe and predict the course of events—both physical events and human events. Here, too, all men have a touch of wisdom, but if they have it in small degree, they are considered ignorant, credulous, or dull.

4. The last of the basic types of great men is obviously the *saint*. Men in this category have had the capacity, in unusual degree, to ignore their own selfish feelings and interests and to transcend their own limitations. The saint is filled with wonder at the universe and with sympathy for every creature in it. Again, it can be said that everyone has some capacity for saintliness, but if it is crude and undeveloped, we call that person sinful, selfish, or insensitive.

Much as modern psychology has been able to derive four basic factors of reactive behavior from the stimulus-response equation, so, it seems to me, it is possible for psychologists to derive four dimensions of intentional behavior from a similar equation. The basic equation here is that intentional conscious behavior is the result of the interaction between the will and the world. In this frame of reference, we distinguish between the subjective and objective points of view, and between one's own self and other selves.

MORGAN: Foster, you have certainly put this business into a neat framework. I have been groping for these terms. In attempting to measure a person's capacities in the area of intentional behavior, do I take it that you use the same kind of form you mentioned in connection with reactive behavior?

PARSONS: Yes, I attempt to get at both the reactive behavior and intentional behavior by asking people how they describe themselves. As I said at the beginning, what really counts is a person's self-image and what I have done is simply to develop a method for allowing a person to examine and express his own image.

(There is a knock on the door, as Parsons's secretary peeks in.)

MISS FOX: Excuse me, Mr. Parsons, but Mr. Pool is calling. He says he is coming over this way in a few minutes. He wants to know if he can stop in?

PARSONS: Yes, that would be fine. Tell him Professor Morgan is here, and I'll hold him so he can meet Mr. Pool for a few minutes. Okay?

MISS FOX: Yes, sir.

MORGAN: Yes, I'd like that. *(Miss Fox shuts door.)* What about the so-called intentional behavior of the Zenith men?

PARSONS: Yes, I want to cover that.

All of these men rate fairly high as heroes; they all have a good rating on will power, sense of purpose, and follow-through. Blaine rates particularly high. From his reactive behavior you might think Monty was easily distracted from his goals. These results say no. He may not be as aggressive as Aaron, in an instinctive way; but you should find he will stay "on course" longer than the rest.

In terms of skill, Close comes out on top—though the others are not far behind. He may seem a bit ponderous and slow, but his mind is clear, it works easily. He is heavy set, but he is also able to move fast when he wants. Note that he is a hunter and a fisherman, both sports that require quick subtle movements as well as patience.

When it comes to wisdom, knowing what's going on in the world, and knowing what to do about it, Aaron comes out a fair distance ahead of the others. I'd say he must be a real bear for facts, realistic and objective.

In rating compassion, Darmody is clearly way ahead of all the others. While the others are inclined to be self-centered and quick to take offense, Frank does quite a job of seeing problems from his neighbor's point of view. This is one of the Christian virtues, I guess, but it can be overdone, too.

MORGAN: Now I don't know what to think. Perhaps you can help me if you tell me about their motivation. What *would* be their principal motivation. What kind of leaders would they make?

PARSONS: All of these men are able and intelligent. They are honest according to their own lights, but each has different dominant traits. All are aggressive men, but in Cliff Aaron, aggressiveness outweighs his other traits. This simply means that what *Cliff* does is the important thing to him. He's interested primarily in his own achievement. This isn't so bad because in most cases his ambition and desire for his own advancement lead to achievement for the organization as well, but his underlying motive is personal wealth and personal power. Such a man demands obedience and respect, runs a taut ship along authoritarian lines. He may consult others, but he will reserve decisions to himself. He may be secretive; those who deal with him may hear part of the story, the part he wants them to hear, but not all of it. Because such a man is smart, quick, and a doer, he fills many of the top jobs throughout industry today. His major defect is that he does not trust others. He fears others may be trying to take away his power. Under pressure, he may become somewhat paranoid.

MORGAN: That sounds bad. Is it?

PARSONS: Not necessarily. As I say, it is very common among strong, effective leaders. Up to a point, it is an asset; people don't put things over on them. Cliff knows a lot about the ways of people and the world. He's a real wise apple.

With a man like Monty, however, you have quite a different story. While all of these men are extroverts to some extent, Monty is an extrovert among extroverts. Such a person is rarely genuinely friendly; he's too busy making friends! With him, it's who you know that counts when the chips are down. Head of a large corporation, such a person is primarily interested in the customers, in the general public. He wants them to be happy. He wants everybody to be happy and to think that he and his company are just about the handsomest things to be seen on the beach. This can be very good for business. The difficulty is that this kind of leader often has little time or inclination for the other men who work for the company. In an effort to please everyone, he may make commitments that can't be carried out, issue conflicting orders, and so on. While such a person is sharp and quick, his information is quickly retailed, his learning is superficial. He can be easily identified as the fellow who deals in "hot dope" and "inside information."

MORGAN: I know this kind of fellow well, but you gave him the perseverance of a hero in one of your comments. This makes me think he might be just the man.

PARSONS: He might be. Now with Irwin you have a much more genuinely friendly man, but he doesn't make a friend unless he really likes him. Once a person becomes his friend, he'll stick by him, whatever the weather. This is because Irwin is essentially a very stable person. He is always his own man. So long as his family is getting along all right, so long as everyone in the shop is doing their assigned job, Irwin couldn't care whether school kept or not. In that case you would find him out fishing—with his hat down over his eyes!

Irwin would be extremely conscientious in fulfilling his commitments both to the public and to employees, but he would always get a good night's sleep. His problem would come from the fact that he is slow to react, slow to respond to what other people urge; his imagination and spirit of adventure are limited. He just wouldn't give too much of a damn what people outside of the company thought or did. There would be a serious risk that he wouldn't be aware of the important trends in the community or in the nation and he would not take the steps he should to head off future dangers. He is talented, deft, skillful in his field; dependable but conservative and restrained.

MORGAN: I must say it must be comfortable to work with a fellow who is dependable.

PARSONS: Yes, he's very dependable, but only because he's predictable. The others are much more unpredictable, but far more exciting.

Look at Frank; the trait that stands out is his sensitiveness, his compassion. He's sensitive to other people's feelings, to other people's ideas, to other people's aspirations. He's about as selfless as a practical man can get. As a leader, he would try to fire the organization with a sense of mission, the feeling that it was working in a great cause. Because he's interested in words and ideas, he's able to express things that elude others. He would tend to beat out policy in conference, rather than to assert it from on high. He really means it when he says he would seek the commitments of others to the goals of the company; and, in him, this is a sign of strength not weakness. His great difficulty would be that he might not be single-minded enough, or ruthless enough. There would be times when he would have to hurt others, and this he would try to avoid. He would thus have a hard time making up his mind; he would procrastinate; his feelings would be frequently hurt. If pushed too far, he would become highly neurotic.

MORGAN: How can you be sure of that?

PARSONS: You can't be sure of it or anything, but it's a good guess. *(A knock at the door.)*

MISS FOX: Here's Mr. Pool, Dr. Parsons. *(Stewart Pool enters.)*

PARSONS: Delighted you dropped in, Stewart. Meet my friend, Will Morgan. You remember my saying he was going to visit.

POOL: Yes. Good to see you, Professor. Has Foster been filling you up with his theories? I'm not sure I understand them, but I like to listen. What do you think of Zenith? Has Foster let you hear the tapes?

MORGAN: Yes, and I'm fascinated. I've heard your interviews, but I can't say I envy you the decision Zenith has to make. May I ask *you* a question? *(Pool nods assent.)* Would you mind telling me how these four men fit with the organization? Who would the agents and employees vote for as president, if they had the chance?

POOL: Oh, I guess there's not much doubt about that. Monty is the most popular in the field; Irwin in the home office. Monty has the color agents like, Irwin is the comfortable "old shoe" home office people like. But is popularity a good criterion? Maybe things ought to be stirred up by a fighter like Cliff? Maybe we ought to have an intellectual like Frank to prod us with new ideas?

MORGAN: Yes, popularity may be only one factor. May I ask you another question? How well have these men done in bringing along good men in their own departments? Do they have adequate replacements ready?

POOL: A good question. I'll give you my impression. In the Finance Department, Aaron has brought in a number of bright young men in the 30 to 40 age bracket. He has given them good training and, in many cases, a lot of experience in handling complicated loans; but there is no one in this group who is an obvious choice as his successor. Maybe one could do it. The older men have been good second men to Aaron, but could never compete with his strength.

Monty has been smart in developing a good administrator in Joe Speller, his director of agencies. Monty is away a great deal, and Joe has kept the agency shop running. Joe doesn't have Monty's charm, but I think he would be an acceptable replacement.

Irwin Close has brought in a number of smart lawyers. They are all young and relatively new since they were hired in the last five to seven years. There are several comers, but I can't say Irwin has done anything to promote the men or to bring them to our attention.

Frank Darmody, however, has been working on actuarial training for a good many years and he has filled the pipeline very well. He has two top-flight men in Jim McCurdy and Al Solomon. Either is competent to be top actuary, but I don't think Frank has made a choice between them.

MORGAN: All right, may I really be impertinent and ask whom do *you* favor for the job?

POOL: Well, Professor, that all depends.

MORGAN: Depends?

POOL: Yes, I believe the answer depends on what direction the company wants to go. If Cap Robbins or someone else will tell me what the basic objective should be for the company, then I might be able to say who should get the job.

MORGAN: What sort of objectives do you mean?

POOL: Well, if they think the company ought to expand further, then perhaps the job ought to go to Cliff. He's hard, he's ruthless, he has a fair amount of megalomania. If the company wants to improve its public relations, let everyone know that it's in the business, then the job should go to Monty.

If, on the other hand, the company thinks that it has already expanded enough, that during the next 10 to 20 years or so it ought to digest what it has already acquired, then Irwin would seem to be the fellow.

MORGAN: What about Frank?

POOL: Well, Frank should go in only if the company is prepared to do things differently, tackle novel and nonconforming ways of handling business.

MORGAN: Let me put the question another way. Which one of these men do you think would be more likely to run the business in the interest of the policyholders?

POOL: Well, if you mean the interest of present policyholders, then I think Irwin or Frank, but if you mean in the interest of policyholders that haven't yet been signed up, then I think you'd have to go with Cliff or Monty, because they would certainly put on the pressure to expand. Does this help?

MORGAN: I don't know, Mr. Pool, but I have one more question. What does Mr. Robbins think the company's principal problems will be during the next few years?

POOL: I've heard him mention several. First, he says that while recent investment record has been fairly good, he's quite worried because the staff under Cliff is not well acquainted with the New York banking situation; so we tend to get the "pickings" of the good deals. He also wonders if they are doing an adequate research job to anticipate the big swings in the composition of our portfolio. He's also concerned about our high agency costs. Everyone knows the managerial system of selling life insurance is expensive even though it can produce business in large volume. Competition from other forms of savings is getting so large that we've got to do something about this. Another thing, the company's been having trouble getting converted from simple machine methods to electronic data processing. This takes men with know-how and good judgment. The company started on one conversion and got so mixed up in the middle of it, it had to backtrack and go back to its old methods. Outside, he wonders if we have enough influence in Springfield or in Washington to protect the business from adverse legislation. Inside, he's afraid a lot of people have been allowed to do about as they like and in too many places don't work as hard as they should. He thinks we need to bear down on doing a more efficient job and to buck up morale at the same time.

Now, *you* know as much as the directors will know. Whom would *you* vote for?

MORGAN *(looking at his watch, and turning to Parsons):* I've just discovered what time it was! I've got to rush! Seriously, though, I don't know how to answer.

Mr. Pool, I'm delighted to meet you. And Foster, I can't tell you how much I appreciate your giving me all this time this morning. You've filled me so full, my head is reeling. Perhaps if I sleep on it for a night or two, it will begin to make a bit more sense. I'll let you know if I have an answer and some advice for the board.

PARSONS: Come back, Will, anytime. I'll be waiting for your note.

*Design and Delivery: The Dilemma at Eleanor Roosevelt**

IN THE OFTEN CRITICIZED FIELD of mental health, one of the most important new developments is the concept of "de-institutionalization," a concept which represents a dramatic change in delivering services to those in need.

Since the late 19th century, the concept underlying the care of the mentally ill in state-supported facilities has been primarily custodial (what some critics have termed "warehousing"): The patient is simply locked away in an overcrowded, understaffed, depersonalized institution. Because of the growing countrywide dissatisfaction with such care, in 1955 the Mental Health Study Act was passed at the federal level, and

---

*From John E. Dittrich and Robert A. Zawacki, *People and Organizations*, 1981. Reproduced by permission of Business Publications, Inc., Plano, Texas.

the Joint Commission on Mental Illness and Health was established to investigate the nation's mental health problems.

In 1961 the commission published its findings and recommendations. Citing fragmented service delivery and the custodial concept itself as key problems, the commission recommended the creation of integrated and coordinated community mental health delivery systems and the de-institutionalization of antiquated public hospitals. The essence of the concept advocated by the commission is expressed by an excerpt from its report:

> The objective of modern treatment of persons with major mental illness is to enable the patient to maintain himself in the community in a normal manner. To do so, it is necessary (1) to save the patient from the debilitating effects of institutionalization . . . , (2) if the patient requires hospitalization, to return him to home and community life as soon as possible, and (3) thereafter to maintain him in the community as long as possible. Therefore, aftercare and rehabilitation are essential parts of all service to mental patients, and the various methods of achieving rehabilitation should be integrated in all forms of services, among them day hospitals, night hospitals, aftercare clinics, public health nursing services, foster family care, convalescent nursing homes, rehabilitation centers, work services, and expatient groups[1]

Since the commission's report, various legislative acts at both the federal and state levels have elaborated the de-institutionalization concept and have provided funds for its implementation. Among the most important elements are: the establishment of a geographically defined "catchment" or service area (usually an average population of 150,000); an emphasis on "comprehensive" services that meet all the client's needs; continuity of care as the client moves through stages of development; consumer participation in decision making; and networks of contractual arrangements between public and private service agencies in a community.

THE NEW YORK STATE DEPARTMENT OF MENTAL HYGIENE

New York State has the second largest population of any state, with a total budget now approaching $11 billion. That is not only the second largest amount spent by any state in the union but it also greater than the budgets of most countries. Although the budget supports numerous agencies and programs, by far the largest single portion of the New York State budget for state operations is allocated to the New York State Department of Mental Hygiene.

Charged with the responsibility for the care, treatment, and preven-

---

[1] Joint Commission on Mental Illness and Health, *Action for Mental Health* (New York: Basic Books, 1961), p. 17.

tion of mental disorders, the New York State Department of Mental Hygiene has more than 69,000 employees and spends more than $1 billion per year. The New York State Executive Budget for 1974–75 provides the following official statement of the objectives and strategies of the Department:

1. To reduce the incidence of mental disabilities through the development of unified systems of health care by state and local governments.
2. To develop, through research, methods of treatment and prevention for all mental disabilities.
3. To rehabilitate and support as many as possible of the mentally disabled in their communities.

While the department has a large number and a wide range of facilities scattered throughout the state, the central office of the DMH is located in the capital, Albany. Shortly after his election, Governor Hugh Carey announced the appointment—subject to approval of the state legislature—of Dr. Lawrence Kolb as the new commissioner of the DMH. Dr. Kolb, a 63-year-old psychiatrist, was formerly director of the New York Psychiatric Institute, a DMH research facility located in New York City.

As indicated in the above document, the primary objective of the DMH is "to reduce the incidence of mental disabilities through the development of unified systems of health care by state and local governments." This objective is commonly referred to as the unified services concept. It is New York's approach to de-institutionalization.

Enacted by the state legislature in 1973, the "Unified Mental Health Services Program" took effect on January 1, 1975. The program design calls for individual counties or combinations of counties to submit a five-year plan for the care of the mentally ill, mentally retarded, and alcoholics in the geographic area. Public, private, and state agencies are to be brought together in providing an integrated and coordinated program of health care, including diagnosis, outpatient and inpatient care (both short- and long-term), counseling, aftercare, and social services. If one agency cannot provide the services needed by a client, he is referred to another facility in an area equipped to handle the difficulty. In summary, the concept calls for people to be moved out of institutions and into a community where they will receive integrated rather than fragmented services.

ELEANOR ROOSEVELT DEVELOPMENTAL SERVICES

One nationally noted program within the Department of Mental Hygiene is called Eleanor Roosevelt Developmental Services. ERDS is a program for children with developmental disorders and for the retarded of all ages in a six-county area which includes Albany, Rensselaer, Columbia, Greene, Schnectady, and Schoharie counties. The organization of ERDS includes the Oswald D. Heck Developmental Center and seven "teams" or subsystems which operate in the six counties. It has a staff of over 800 and an operating budget of over $9,047,000.

The ERDS program has been directed since its establishment in 1969 by Dr. Hugh G. LaFave. Dr. LaFave, a psychiatrist nationally noted for his writings and his work in the area of community mental hygiene, is no ordinary administrator. Few of his associates feel indifferent toward him, and though he tends to be either loved or hated, both supporters and critics are in agreement that he is a near-genius in conceptualizing innovative solutions to the problems of service delivery.

Dr. LaFave's past work and writings in community mental hygiene have generated a series of beliefs about the treatment of the mentally disabled which have in effect become the organizational ideology around which ERDS operates. It is called the developmental model, and can be broken down into six elements: (1) developmental perspective; (2) community-based services; (3) consumer involvement; (4) collaborative programs and services; (5) comprehensive assessment; and (6) prevention.

The ERDS Developmental Model

The *developmental perspective* is simply stated as follows: "Whereas the traditional approach labels the disability and on that basis excludes the individual from certain activities, the developmental approach assesses the individual's capacities and then seeks to develop them as fully as possible." The people at ERDS argue that the traditional approach is negative while the developmental approach is positive because it builds on the individual's strengths. The assumption is that, given a recognition of his strengths and needs and given appropriate opportunities, anyone is capable of change and growth. The model diverts professional energies from diagnostic labeling as an end in itself to the development of action programs for growth.

The idea behind *community-based services* is to maximize the individual's participation in the community. As many services as possible are provided by or through the collaboration of the family, schools, state and local hygiene units, and other agencies in the community. It is assumed that the community is responsible for its developmentally disabled, and an effort is made to strengthen the community's ability to accept and serve the individual. The approach is not only more economical than institutional care but also affords the client an opportunity to become integrated with other members of the community.

Consumer involvement ensures parent and community input to the program. Each ERDS team has a consumer board of community representatives who discuss planning, implementation, and evaluation; advise the professional staff on priorities; assist in community education; and assume various responsibilities. A representative from each consumer board is appointed to attend meetings as a nonvoting member of the board of visitors for the entire organization.

A heavy emphasis is placed on *collaboration* between two or more agencies to provide multiple services to the individual or his community. To establish such collaborative relationships, communities are encouraged to assess service needs and to develop plans for implementation. In order to maintain the patterns and rhythm of daily living, planners are encouraged to build needed services around day, evening, and overnight time periods.

Comprehensive assessment means that a child is viewed as a whole being who lives in the context of a family and community. The cooperation of family and specialists is employed to arrive at an individual prescriptive program that maintains and builds on assets and addresses the needs of both family and child.

Finally, the development model emphasizes *prevention*. Programs with parents, consumer groups, and various agencies operate in such areas as prenatal care and counseling for mothers considered as high risks, screening for lead levels, advocacy programs for the implementation of statutes regarding lead-free substances, genetic counseling, and a comprehensive neonatal program for high-risk newborn infants.

As indicated in Exhibit 1, the development model provides the organizational ideology around which ERDS operates. The advocates of the model summarize its unique features as follows: "(1) It recognizes the existence of weaknesses but makes full use of such strengths as the individual has; (2) it enlists the cooperation of a whole range of agencies through voluntary associations to government on all levels from community to state; and (3) it embraces all phases of the problem from prevention to an individualized program for the fullest possible realization of the handicapped person's potential."

ORGANIZATIONAL STRUCTURE

ERDS is composed of seven teams and a support group. Although the teams are relatively autonomous, they follow a common set of guidelines. The leadership of the teams is characterized by a multidisciplinary orientation (social work, child psychiatry, special education, pediatrics, psychology, rehabilitation counseling, etc.) and they are staffed to maintain a balance among at least four areas: social-recreation, psychological, educational-vocational, and health care. For every professional hired, at least one person from the community (with a bachelor's degree or less) also must be hired.

The unique quality of the teams is summarized and symbolized in the

Design and Delivery: The Dilemma at Eleanore Roosevelt

EXHIBIT 1
Orbit of Community-Based Developmental Services

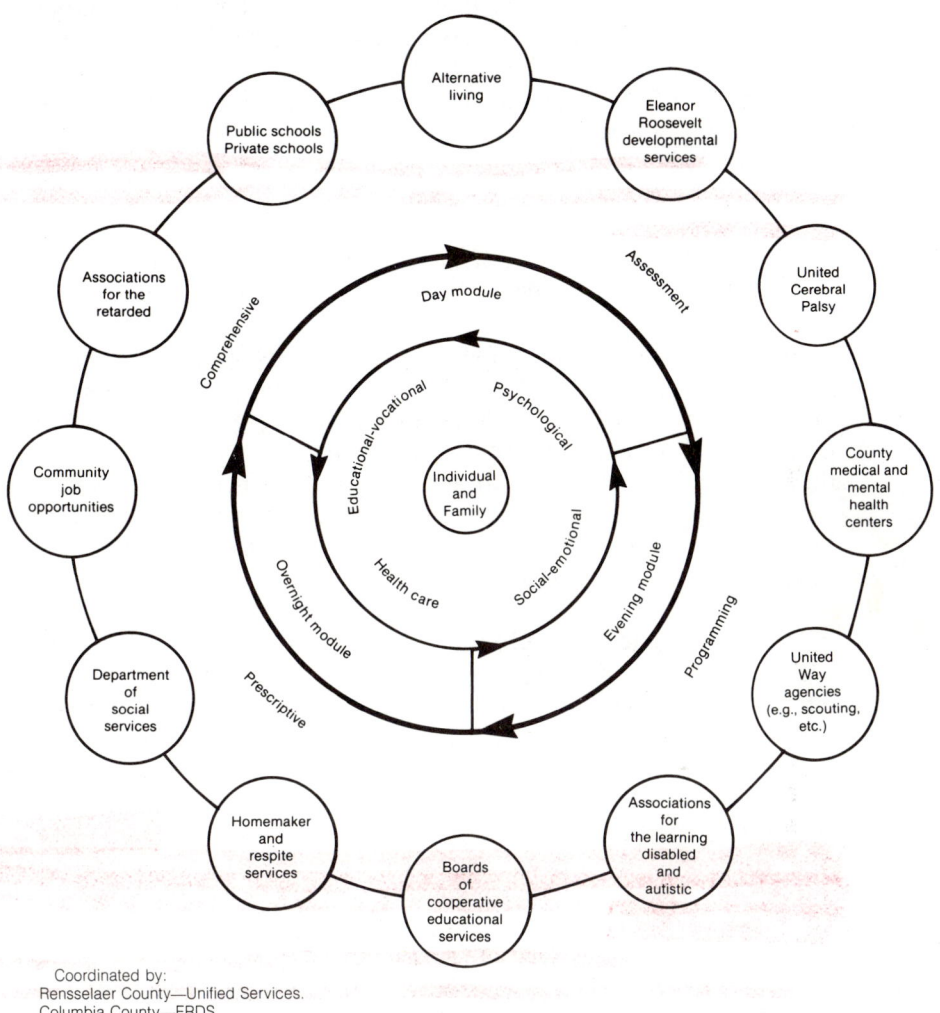

Coordinated by:
Rensselaer County—Unified Services.
Columbia County—ERDS.
Albany County—ERDS.
Green County—ERDS.
Schenectady County—ERDS.
Schoharie County—ERDS.

use of the word *team* to refer to the organizational unit, with its connotations of a highly integrated group of people sharing the same objectives and differentiating themselves from others. The concept of team implies the existence of an opponent who must be fought through cooperative efforts.

At the team's administrative level, a high value is placed on the development of a nonbureaucratic organization to carry out the team's functions. The administrators feel that an unstructured organization is best suited to the tasks of advocacy and the achievement of the ERDS treatment model.

Further, the assumptions of the team leaders regarding the motivation of the team's members are also based on a self-actualizing, nonbureaucratic model. The team members are described as flexible individuals, desirous of working in a flexible environment and willing to experiment with both traditional and innovative ways of organizing. The team leaders take pride in what they feel is high-quality work, and they also feel strongly about being associated with a pioneering effort in the delivery of mental health services. The team leaders seem very aware of their impact on other organizations, and team members place a high value on their power to influence other organizations and to spread their ideology of treatment.

In summarizing the organizational structure of ERDS, each element of the system reflects the philosophy of its director, and as a result the organization is clearly nonbureaucratic. For example, Dr. LaFave has no office but goes where he believes he is needed, establishing a temporary base of operations. Strong emphasis is placed on openness, cooperation, creativity, and innovation. While LaFave reserves a veto power over group decisions, he seldom uses it, and most major decisions are arrived at through participative decision-making techniques. The physical plants of some teams are intentionally too small, as it is felt that overcrowding will encourage members to be out in the community and not in their offices. Dress standards and strict attention to seniority are not in operation. The chain of command is not easily identifiable, and there is a heavy emphasis on face-to-face communication rather than formal written documents. (In fact, there is little emphasis on evaluation of professional performance.) The organic or ambiguous nature of the structure is reflected by the fact that despite attempts to do so, no one has been able to draw up an organizational chart that satisfactorily reflects the functioning of the organization.

GOALS AND PERFORMANCE

The objectives of the ERDS program are explicitly articulated in a series of five-year plans. These objectives are displayed in Exhibit 2.

Design and Delivery: The Dilemma at Eleanore Roosevelt

EXHIBIT 2
Summary of the Goals of Eleanor Roosevelt Developmental Services

First Five-Year Plan Jan. 1970–Jan. 1975	Results of First Five-Year Plan (Jan. 1975)	Second Five-Year Plan Jan. 1975–Jan. 1980	Third Five-Year Plan Jan. 1980–Jan. 1985
1. Reduce admissions to institutions outside the area by development of full range of community based service choices	Zero admissions accomplished by 1973	To maintain zero admissions to facilities outside the area	To maintain zero admissions
2. Develop community-based services for 2,500 clients and families through the collaborative model	2,600 persons and their families served in community program*	To serve 5,000 persons and their families in community settings through collaborative programming (as of March 1, 1976, 3,900 persons were receiving services.)	To serve 2,500 persons and their families in community programs; reduction in numbers due to increased prevention programs and attrition
3. Assimilate the 1,363 persons in institutions outside the catchment area equal to the capacity of O.D. Heck (744-bed capacity)	745 persons assimilated back into the community	To reduce the number of persons in institutions outside the catchment area to zero by resettling remaining 575 (472 remaining as of March 1976)	—0—
4. Utilize only 10 percent of O.D. Heck 744 overnight placements while developing community programs (74.4)	75 persons using O.D. Heck for living arrangement	To utilize fewer than 300 overnight placements at O.D. Heck for living arrangements	To utilize fewer than 100 overnight placements at O.D. Heck for living arrangements

*During the month of April 1975, 14,000 services were provided to 2,500 clients. More than half these services were provided collaboratively between Eleanor Roosevelt Developmental Services and community agencies. This includes services such as:

Day Module:
Education-vocational.
Medical treatment.
Speech and hearing therapy.
Physical therapy.
Family therapy.
Activities for daily living.
Transportation.

Evening Module:
Social-recreational.
Adult educational programs.
Respite service for parents.

Overnight Module:
Homemaker service.
Respite.
Family care homes.
Halfway houses.
Hostels.
Nursing home care.
O.D. Heck.

As indicated in Exhibit 2, the ERDS staff claims a number of impressive accomplishments:

1. 1,373 children and adults were in state schools for the mentally retarded or in children's psychiatric units in other parts of the state in January 1970. This number has been reduced to 472.
2. Reduction in the rate of admissions to state facilities outside the area from an average of 79 people per year to 0. (At the original rate, over 450 people might have been admitted to such facilities in the six-year period.)
3. Assumption of responsibility for 200 people from other parts of the state who had been placed by other state facilities in the area prior to 1970.
4. Provision of services to over 3,900 children and adults in community settings.
5. Establishment of a range of services involving parents and other agencies that, although not yet sufficient in number or uniform in quality, provides a comprehensive coordinated system.
6. Involvement of consumers and parents in work with staff and communities at all levels of the system to develop programs and evaluate program quality.
7. Provision in community settings of services that have reached over 4,000 children and adults with developmental disabilities, or who are at high risk of being so labeled, at less cost than would be required to maintain 650 such people in institutional settings at 1975 levels of cost. At projected levels of cost for institutional care conforming to Willowbrook Consent Decree standards, as few as 300 persons might be served.[2]
8. Establishment of a system of services that makes it possible to envision a decreasing state role in favor of locally sponsored, comprehensive, community-based services. Those services would require state financial assistance, but they would cost less than a system operated and financed primarily by the state.

For further indicators of performance, see Exhibits 3, 4, 5, and 6.

In addition to the above there is still further information on the performance of the ERDS program. In spring of 1975 a team of consultants from the nearby Graduate School of Public Affairs at the State University of New York at Albany completed a three-month analysis of one of the ERDS teams. While the report is intended to

---

[2] The Willowbrook Consent Decree is the result of a suit initiated by families of patients in the Willowbrook Development Center in federal district court to improve standards of care. The governor agreed to support the court's decree.

EXHIBIT 3
Percentage Reduction of Resident/Leave Population at State Developmental Centers: December 1968 to September 1975

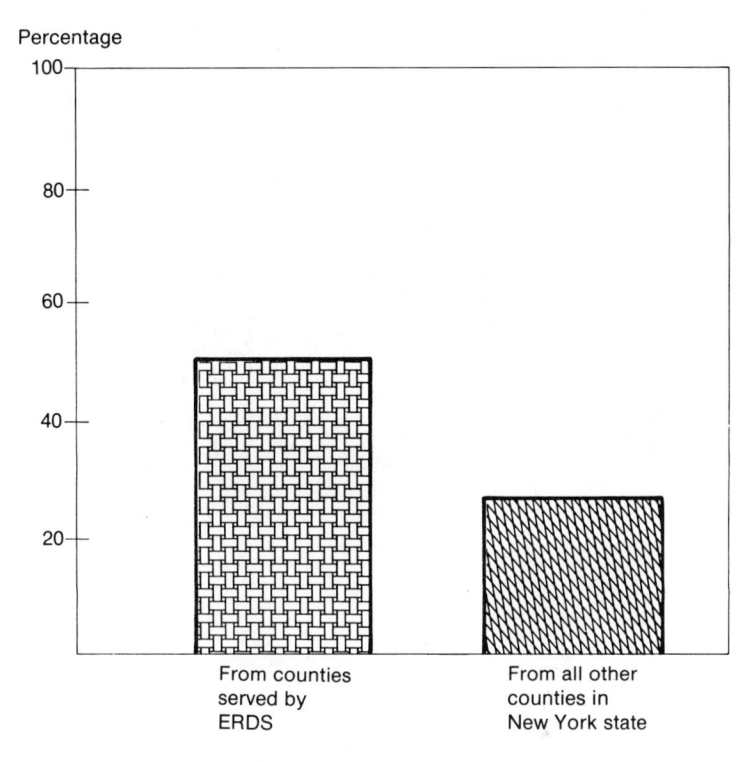

Percentage

```
From counties        From all other
served by            counties in
ERDS                 New York state
```

describe only one of the teams, the conclusions seem to describe adequately the characteristics of the overall ERDS program.[3]

A. Organizational strengths.
 1. Organizational resources.
    The team has been very successful in marshalling the energies of its own workers and those of the community to develop and provide an array of services to the retarded not available heretofore.

---

[3] This material is used with the approval of Dr. LaFave.

EXHIBIT 4
Percentage of People Remaining in State Developmental Centers since December 1969

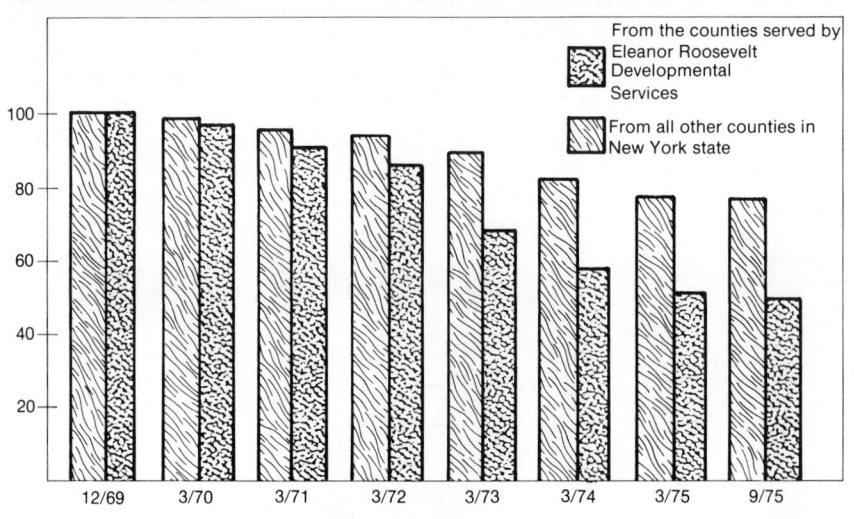

From the counties served by Eleanor Roosevelt Developmental Services

From all other counties in New York state

Source: New York State Department of Mental Hygiene.

Both the staff and the community workers exhibited a high degree of esprit de corps and an intense dedication to the cause of the retarded. It was our observation that a good deal of the community's interest was a result of the zeal of the staff of the team.

As indicated by our survey, the members of the team generally have a level of education that far exceeds the minimum required for their respective jobs, particularly at the worker level. The team has been very successful in identifying and obtaining monies from various sources, including appropriations from the Department of Mental Hygiene, the legislature, grant monies from the federal government, as well as convincing community agencies to redeploy some of their monies to services for the retarded.

A third resource is Unified Services. This concept provides a viable structure and mechanism for joint planning, development, and sharing of resources between all agencies in the county. Unified Services provided the team with a legitimate forum in which to express their philosophy about methods of treatment and it has been a major variable in increasing the

EXHIBIT 5
A Comparison of the Decrease in Number of People in State Developmental Centers (three different upstate catchment areas versus area served by Eleanor Roosevelt Developmental Services)

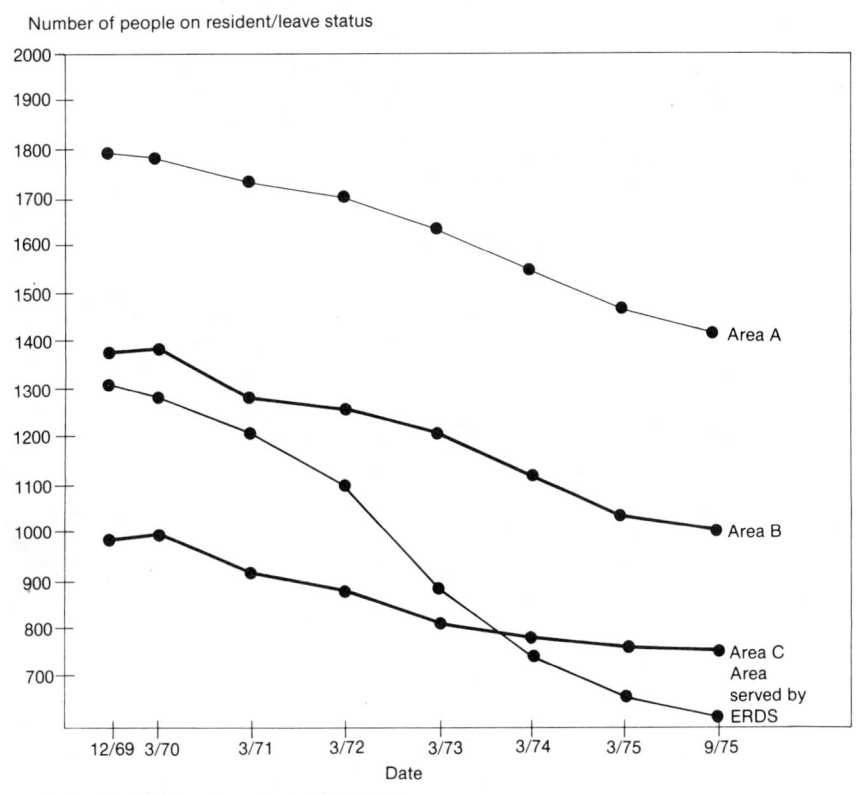

Number of people on resident/leave status

[Graph showing four declining lines from 12/69 to 9/75:
- Area A: declining from ~1800 to ~1400
- Area B: declining from ~1380 to ~1030
- Area C: declining from ~990 to ~750
- Area served by ERDS: declining from ~1310 to ~650]

Source: New York State Department of Mental Hygiene.

team's influence with other agencies and groups in the county (see DMH objectives).

2. Organizational Goals.

The team has a comprehensive and clearly defined set of goals for themselves. This is embodied in the five-year plan. The goals have considerable appeal for community organizations and groups. The goals are well understood and accepted by the administrators of the team who, as indicated above, are highly committed to the stated goals.

3. Leadership.

EXHIBIT 6
Rates of Admission to State Developmental Centers

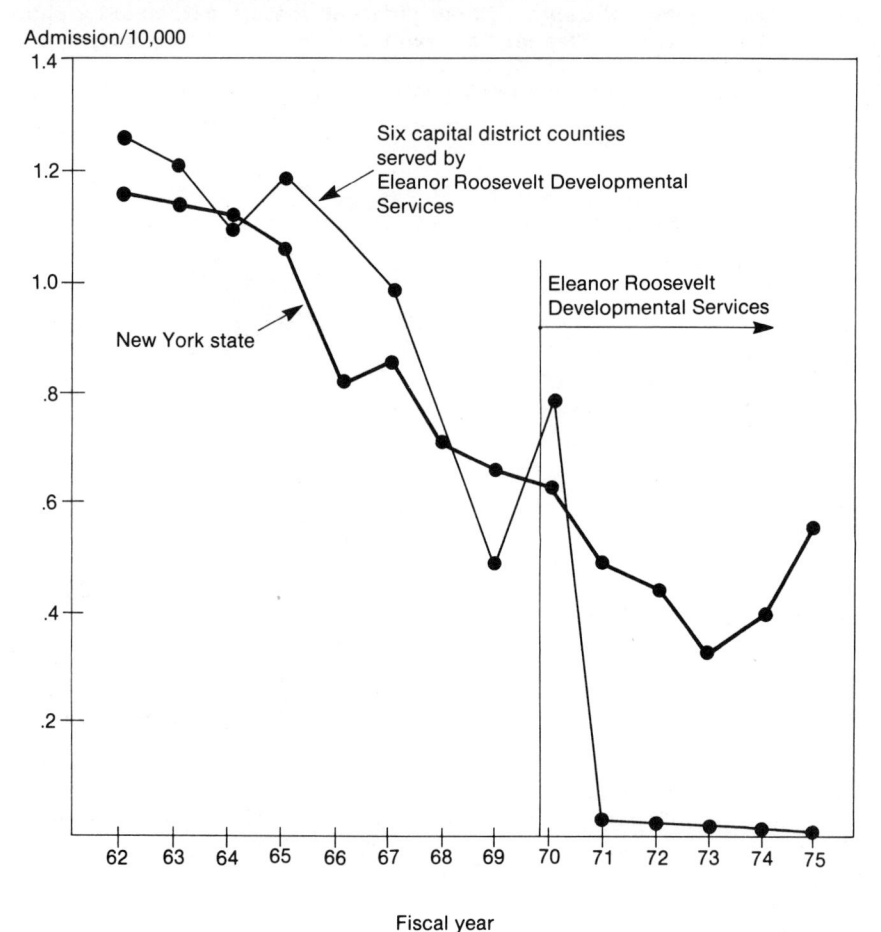

Admission/10,000

Six capital district counties served by Eleanor Roosevelt Developmental Services

New York state

Eleanor Roosevelt Developmental Services →

Fiscal year

Source: New York State Department of Mental Hygiene.

The director of Eleanor Roosevelt Developmental Services is a highly charismatic, hard-driving, and innovative leader. He conceptualized the goals for Eleanor Roosevelt Developmental Services, and his concepts have heavily influenced the development of team goals, as well as the organizational structure and the allocation and utilization of resources to achieve those goals. The organizational design of ERDS is unique in the Department of Mental Hygiene. The leadership of the team is highly motivated, professional, and dedicated. They see their role as more than a job; thus they habitually spend long hours at work, work weekends, carry out multiple organizational roles, and expand or stretch their talents and influences almost beyond a point of reason. This almost missionary dedication and zeal are infectious to other staff and are a valuable tactical tool in their dealings with the community.

4. Organizational flexibility.

The team is a fluid, nonbureaucratic organization. It has a capacity to immediately assign and reassign staff in response to changing organizational needs. Even the use of the administrators is characterized by flexibility since they often have more than one organizational role. The organization appears to have been very successful in identifying needs and reorganizing staff and other resources to meet these needs. This style of organization has been well matched to the characteristics of the environment and the nature of the task. In general, the staff expressed satisfaction with the fluidity and informal nature of the organization and the subsequent freedom, responsibility, and room for creativity which this type of organization facilitates. There appeared to be a real climate for the self-actualization.

B. Potential impairments.

While we judged that the organization has been successful thus far, certain signals were picked up in the external environment and within the organization that revealed potential sources of organization impairment. We have divided these potential impairments into two categories, namely, short-run impairments and long-run impairments. The short-run impairments we identified fall primarily in the area of utilization of team resources and were impairments the team was already experiencing to some degree, and which we feel have the potential of seriously affecting staff attitude and effectiveness, if left unattended. The long-run impairments we identified pertained to the goals of the team and its interaction with the environment and were impairments the team did not appear to be aware of but which we perceive as potentially challenging the viability and adaptability of the team in the next few years.

1. Short-run impairments.

   a. Crisis management.

The organization is characterized by an atmosphere of crisis, disorganization, and overcommitment of resources. Offices double as meeting rooms and diagnostic clinics; people carry out multiple roles and there is a constant demand for staff to work beyond the normal workday. The atmosphere affects the administrator's capacity to perform

the traditional functions of supervision, coordination, and integration.
    b. Integration and communication.

The organization seems to lack unity. Few members have a total view of the organization. Staff members' confusion regarding their roles and their responsibilites is another area causing coordination problems. Staff do not know to whom they are accountable, to whom they are to look for guidance, socialization, and rewards. This problem is particularly acute in the case of the many new employees. Since the organization does not have written job descriptions, role guidelines, or training programs, the new employee depends on informal socialization into the organization. Since lines of authority are unclear and roles are unclear, new employees experience great difficulty integrating themselves into the organization. The strongest evidence for weak integration in the organization lies in the area of communication. There are three types of communication that have to be improved within the organization: information regarding day-to-day activities; information regarding the effectiveness of the organization; and information regarding long-term goals and plans. In our study, we noted a lack of knowledge on the part of staff members of the activities, procedural changes, and personnel changes within the organization. We also noted an absence of concrete information regarding the performance of the organization and its achievements. Furthermore, especially at lower organizational levels, we found a lack of knowledge regarding broader organizational goals and philosophy.

2. Long-run impairments.
    a. Adaptability.

The organization's main way of dealing with its environment is through advocacy. This is a unidimensional way of dealing with the environment, in that the organization is focusing on sending messages rather than receiving them. Hence, we question their ability to realistically sense and interpret the environment. The team came into the county with a set of goals and a philosophy of operation several years ago. We have perceived messages from other agencies in the county for a change in emphasis in the way the team defines its relationship with the county.

    b. Organization direction.

The organization has had a fixed philosophy which

should be reexamined. The dual pressures of changing signals from the environment and internal stress, as outlined under short-run impairments, can undermine the organization and reduce effectiveness if left unattended. It is necessary to examine the degree of fit or lack of fit, between new external and internal goals and the team's philosophy, goals, and style of dealing with the community.

c. Leadership.

The fundamental force behind the philosophy, goals, and design of the team is Dr. LaFave. The organization has been, and we think will continue to be, very dependent upon his thinking for leadership. He appears to be the main authority in the organization.

THE *ALBANY TIMES UNION:* "WASTED DOLLARS, WASTED LIVES"

Almost simultaneously with the completion of the above report, the *Albany Times Union,* one of the two major newspapers serving the area, began to run an extensive exposé of the entire Department of Mental Hygiene.[4] Entitled "Wasted Dollars, Wasted Lives," the series included numerous devastating reports about bureaucratic inefficiency at the central office of the DMH and numerous descriptions about the bleakest aspects of the life in the institutions. Initially, ERDS and its Oswald D. Heck Developmental Center were only mentioned in summary statements criticizing programs and facilities generally. But beginning on May 9, 1975, the ERDS program became one of the primary points of focus in the series.

On May 9 the *Albany Times Union* ran a front-page article entitled "Heck, it's only (your) money," revealing that more than $6,000 in drugs and supplies were purchased by the O.D. Heck Developmental Center directly from local retail pharmacies instead of using the less expensive state contract procedure. The article indicated that the state Department of Audit and Control was not aware of the practice. The story received coverage for several days and included a response from LaFave, who argued that ERDS wanted clients to buy their own drugs so they would have experience in the community, and that the practice was cheaper than if ERDS ran its own pharmacy.

The article foreshadowed what was to come. On May 25, six articles about the ERDS program appeared in the newspaper, raising a number

---

[4] The quotations and excerpts herein are used with permission of the *Albany Times Union.*

of issues about the administration of ERDS. One article appeared next to a picture of Dr. Lawrence Kolb, the commissioner-designate of the Department of Mental Hygiene, quoting him as saying: "I believe that the Heck operation is one of the most innovative and encouraging developmental center operations in the state, as a matter of fact, in the country." He was further quoted as saying that he hoped the Heck operation might be a model for the whole DMH system.

Next to the above article and Dr. Kolb's picture appeared a long article describing the findings of a state Department of Health report on the Oswald D. Heck Developmental Center. In response to federal regulations governing the payment of Medicaid and Medicare monies, the article cited numerous findings of "deficiencies in the area of administration, treatment programs, medical care, food services, record keeping, pharmaceutical and dental operations, and environmental conditions." Some of the findings were:

> A table or organization indicating the major programs and administrative structure has not been made available to the center's staff;
> Specific job descriptions for the staff of the center have not been developed;
> Resident living staff for each unit does not have clearly defined job descriptions, master-staffing plans, or organizational chart stating channels of communication and delegation of responsibility and authority;
> Policy manuals have not been developed by the disciplines providing resident care;
> There is insufficient documentation to show that senior medical personnel, doctors, and psychologists perform the planning and treatment functions they are assigned;
> Policies are not specific for this center in the areas of admission, transfer, and discharge;
> Policy was not available that indicated the criteria and procedure involved in resident transfer;
> Admission criteria was not available for review in order to determine the extent of the center's ability to provide the services required to the residents admitted.

On May 29, three articles appeared, the most potent, "Heck Center accused of neglect," arguing that the parents of many profoundly retarded children were unable to admit their children to the practically empty center. Two local assemblymen were quoted as saying that they had been unable to obtain admission for patients. The refusal to admit the profoundly retarded was an issue that was to continue throughout the summer.

On June 1, five articles appeared, the strongest arguing that there was poor accountability and control at the O.D. Heck Center, and that "some key doctors" were either ineffective or unavailable because they had "second jobs or other outside interests." The issue of second salaries was also to become a major theme in the weeks that followed.

On June 8, an article entitled "State blasts Heck Center on recordkeeping" appeared, quoting parts of a state Department of Audit and Control report which indicated that recordkeeping procedures in the area of payroll and personnel were extremely weak. Audit and Control, it continued:

> . . . recommends a variety of changes, including verification of appointments and terminations by the business office; good recordkeeping and follow-up by the personnel office; distribution of checks by a "responsible employee" of the business office "who is independent of payroll preparation"; close monitoring of employees by their supervisors so that attendance and leave records are kept "properly," and physical separation of the personnel and payroll offices.

The intense pressure on ERDS continued, and on July 19, it was reported that LaFave was asked by commissioner Kolb to take a six-week leave of absence in the midst of a DMH probe. The DMH investigations centered on administrative and personnel practices at the Heck Center and on DMH training contracts held by Albany Medical College. The contracts were a source of additional income to LaFave and other members of the staff.

The results of the probe were made public on September 7. Findings included:

> (LaFave) has not exercised administrative or managerial direction and has not provided an organizational structure which is manageable and provides direct lines of authority, responsibility, and accountability.
>
> Top-level ERDS administrative and clinical staff have not provided direction, role definition, purpose, guidance, review, or control of the total operation.
>
> A lack of adherence of basic laws, rules, and regulations required by the Department of Mental Hygiene and the various (state) control agencies.
>
> The staff is polarized around the issue of Dr. LaFave's continued appointment as director, to the possible point where client services are beginning to suffer.
>
> Uncertainty of staff from the top down, as to their role and obligations and a resulting lack of accountability.
>
> In order to effect the changes we see as necessary and to tighten up the organizational structure, the responsibility, and accountability that is required now that this organization has reached its present size, we have to recommend strongly that top-level administrative staff be relieved of their present duties at ERDS.

The report was met with outrage by LaFave supporters, who accused the DMH of carrying out a vendetta against LaFave. On September 10, it was reported that the governor, lieutenant governor, and several state legislators had expressed a concern to commissioner Kolb that LaFave get a "fair shake." In the meantime it was announced that Commissioner Kolb would soon have a decision on the LaFave case.

The Devon School Case*

CLEAR RIVER, despite its prosaic name, is a bustling manufacturing and mill community of about 65,000 people. As the only large population center in Tonley County, it also serves as the hub of financial, transportation, and governmental services. On the outskirts of Clear River are smaller population clusters in the manner of suburbs. Devon, known locally as "Nob Hill," is one of them. As its nickname implies, it is the most affluent of these "suburbs" and is the home of many of the area's business and civic leaders.

Devon also attracts professional people who choose to live in the community because of its beauty, reputation, and higher-quality public services. The town is not all middle and upper-middle class, however; there is a fairly sizable minority of tradesmen, service people, and other "blue-collar" types. Although less well off financially than the rest of the town, this group is able to exert some influence in local politics and community affairs. The township manager and three fourths of the town council are Republican; indeed, registered Republicans outnumber Democrats two to one.

The following item appeared in the August 15 issue of the Clear River Examiner:

> NEW SCHOOL OPENS IN SEPTEMBER—DEVON: The recently completed Devon Middle-Upper School will open for classes Tuesday, September 6. The school, under construction for the past 16 months, will represent a radical departure, both architecturally and educationally, from the traditional junior and senior high schools. It is the first of its kind in this area.
>
> Mr. Arthur Magnason of Devon has been appointed principal of the new school. A native of New England with a Master's Degree in Education from the University of Vermont, Magnason has 18 years experience in teaching and administrative duties in the school systems of Tonley County. He leaves Clear River Central High after 4 years as its principal.
>
> In discussing the new school, Magnason said, "This is clearly a case where form follows function. The school has been designed and built with the express purpose of using an 'open classroom' concept of teaching and

---

*This case was prepared by Mr. James Chambers under the guidance of professors Allen Cohen and Robin D. Willits. Copyright 1979, Whittemore School of Business and Economics, University of New Hampshire. Reproduced with permission.

learning. Under this system, small 'learning groups' meet in a large common area and in an environment in which students and teachers are much freer to pursue alternative learning concepts than in traditional programs. The curriculum is also more flexible and students are sometimes allowed to move from one 'learning group' to another to undertake a new subject of interest to them.

"The Upper and Middle Schools are housed under separate roofs but a central walkway connects the two both physically and, I think, symbolically."

Enthusiasm for the new school is not confined to its faculty. Mr. Harold Fowles, of Devon, president of the Greater Clear River School Committee, said recently, "This new school is a concrete example of the committee's determination to give the young people of this community the most up-to-date and best education possible. The school will embody all of the latest innovations in learning and has been thoroughly equipped to meet the needs of all the students whether they plan to go on to college or into a trade after graduation.

"We have brought some excellent teachers to Devon from other schools in the district" Fowles continued, "and have hired only the very best new teachers available."

Designed to serve some 600 students in grades 5–12, the school is indeed an impressive example of a community's dedication to the education of its youth.

Not everyone in the town shared Magnason's and Fowles's enthusiasm, however. Due to the unstructured and highly experimental nature of the new school, some members of the school committee had been outvoted by those members whose views reflected the more active and liberal element in the community. Some parents also had objected to the new school on the grounds that their children might not learn enough to get into top-rated universities, while other parents worried that the new school would encourage permissiveness. The active objections were in the minority and most people in the area appeared proud of the new facility and its modern educational concepts.

MEMO

To: All Faculty

From: A. Magnason, Principal

Subject: Workshop Orientation

    All faculty members are to report to the Multipurpose Room (a combination auditorium and gym) at 8:30 A.M., Monday, August 23 for the preterm workshop orientation.

Standing almost 6 feet 4 inches tall, and of solid build despite his 41 years, Mr. Magnason was an imposing figure as he stood at the rostrum on stage addressing the teachers.

"I would like to take this opportunity to welcome all of you to the Devon Middle-High School. We have before us a once-in-a-lifetime opportunity, a chance that most teachers only dream of. We are going to be using the latest innovations in education—open classrooms, flexible schedules and curricula—in buildings designed and equipped for that purpose, and with the active support of the community."

Magnason paused for a moment, then moving to the side of the rostrum, he leaned against it and struck a more casual pose, "Now, a lot of this is going to be new for many of us. This is the primary reason that we have hired Paulette Trottier as vice principal."

He nodded to a smallish, trim woman in her early 40s who was seated in a chair beside him on the stage. She returned a brief smile.

"She's done a lot of work with open-classroom systems and possesses outstanding credentials. As you know she's taught for eight years in similar progressive schools and has, for the past four years, broadened her experience and skills working for the New Jersey Department of Education as an evaluator of programs and policies."

Clearing his throat, he went on, "As I said before I'm not fully familiar with these new concepts and, like the rest of you, feel that there is much to learn. However, I do feel that, in my 18 years of teaching, I have learned a few things about education and about students." He paused briefly for the polite laughter he knew would follow his mild sarcasm.

"A good school is run efficiently, and I think my record speaks for itself in that regard. Everyone, students and teachers, knows where they're supposed to be and what they're supposed to be doing at all times. When I go into a classroom—oops! I guess I should say into a 'learning group' area, I like to see quiet, attentive students and a teacher in control of the situation. If everything's going well, don't expect to see me. But if things are falling through the crack you will see me and I'll be asking questions. I think Mrs. Trottier has assembled a great team and I look forward to the beginning of the term, as I'm sure you do."

Collecting his notes, Magnason turned to Mrs. Trottier, "And now, Mrs. Trottier, would you like to say a few words?"

Thanking Magnason as she approached the podium, Mrs. Trottier spoke to the group in a voice whose power belied her size. "I don't have very much to say today, but I do expect to work with all of you more closely in smaller groups over the next week and a half. I think Mr. Magnason made a good point when he said that all of us will be learning a lot over the next school year. I've started and worked successfully with a number of these programs over the years and each one is different. One thing that I've learned, is that we have to be open, flexible, and cooperative with each other. Only by working together and sharing our successes and failures can we make this thing work. Thank you."

Magnason once more approached the podium and suggested they break for coffee and doughnuts which had been provided in the rear of the room. Then, excusing himself, he left the group to attend to several administrative details concerning the opening of the school.

As the teachers drifted toward the back of the room, three who had sat together during the opening remarks, began to talk with each other. They were Katherine Amster, Florence Dix, and Louis Spinella. Assigned to seventh-grade classes, they had all taught previously at Clear River Central and had applied for positions at Devon. Their seniority and their reputations as good teachers with records of successfully applying new educational concepts in their classes won them their new jobs. Although Magnason knew each personally, the actual interviewing had been done by Mrs. Trottier and the job offer had come from her.

AMSTER: Well, Lou, what do you think?

SPINELLA: He sure spoke well. It doesn't sound like the Magnason I worked for—he would never have admitted having anything to learn.

DIX: Yeah, it kind of surprised me that he even got the job. After all, he's never been exposed to these ideas before and he's not the most liberally minded administrator in the world. Do you think he can handle it? I think maybe the committee hired him cause they didn't want to go all the way.

SPINELLA: Maybe he's supposed to keep an eye on Trottier and make sure things don't get out of hand. Anyway, you can be sure of one thing, he'll—how did he used to express it—yeah, he'll "run a tight ship."

DIX: You know what he told me once? I was having some trouble with discipline and he said that as long as I could "keep the lid on," he would be happy.

AMSTER: He really stays on top of things, though, I think he's a good administrator. But isn't this place great? Do you still think facilities don't make much difference, Lou?

SPINELLA (*smiling ruefully at an old joke*): You know, Kate, I never felt that a school had to be built to order for an educational concept to be effective. I must admit though, this place is beautiful. Are there any plans to have the parents in for a "cook's tour"?

AMSTER: Well, I thought there were some parents who wanted to see where their kids were being transferred to but I don't know of any plans to have an open house. You know Magnason, he's concentrating on getting things ready to open on time.

As the days went by, the teachers got down to the job of assimilating the new program and making final preparations in their lessons. They also renewed old acquaintances and began to make friends among others.

The teachers who had been newly hired were of a uniformly high caliber. John Langford, for instance, was in his mid-30s and had taught for a number of years at an experimental and exclusive private school in New York City. Alice McNair, though only 25, came to the school from

Sacramento, California. She was highly recommended and had had experience in a school like Devon. Westley Perron and Emily Geoffrion had both completed master's degrees in June and would be starting their first full-time teaching job when Devon opened the following week. They were assigned to fifth-grade classes.

There were also a number of teachers who, like Amster, Dix, and Spinella, had transferred to Devon from other schools in the district. Paul Greene, a seventh-grade teacher, came from Southside Junior High and Dave Resca, the physical education coordinator, came from McNelly High in Clear River. Resca, in particular, was ecstatic over Devon's facilities and equipment and exuded enthusiasm as he planned programs for the fall.

Mrs. Trottier worked tirelessly with the teachers in teaching them about the new concepts and how they could be applied to their respective disciplines. Although she was the vice principal and dealt with matters throughout the school, she concentrated her efforts on the Middle School faculty. Amster, Dix, and Spinella warmed to her right from the beginning. They were familiar with most of the new ideas she was trying to introduce. At Clear River Central they had used many of them in their classes and had often worked together implementing their ideas.

Mrs. Trottier spent most of her time, however, with the new teachers. She had personally interviewed and hired each of them over the summer and was certain that they were among the best young teachers available in the area.

Paul Greene was one teacher who seemed unaffected by the generally high level of enthusiasm pervading the faculty. He had come to Devon from Central High like a number of other teachers, but brought with him a reputation as a traditional, procedure-bound teacher. Spinella, a military history buff, called him the "Old Guard." Although his preparation for the coming year evidenced the same quality as that of the other teachers, his lack of participation during meetings and discussion groups led some teachers to doubt the sincerity of his commitment to the new school and its ideas. Once, after such a meeting, Alice McNair mentioned Greene's aloofness to Mrs. Trottier.

"Don't worry about him, Alice," she answered, "he's one of the ones Magnason brought over from Central. We're going to have to put up with him but if he doesn't get with the program damn quick, I'll fire him. That's all there is to it. In the meantime, so long as he stays over in the Upper School building, we won't lock horns. If it had been up to me, I never would have hired him, and I think he knows it."

During most of this time, Magnason worked primarily in the administration area dealing with the logistics of getting the school fully ready for opening day. Problems associated with late delivery of a few pieces of equipment kept him busy for most of two days. Then there were the impromptu tours to be conducted for visiting dignitaries. What contact he did have with the Middle School teachers was limited to an exchange of pleasantries. Although he didn't participate formally in the preparatory workshop sessions, Magnason did seem to know what was going on generally.

By opening day, Tuesday, September 6, Devon School was ready for classes. All the supplies and equipment had finally arrived and, except for a few minor problems with the air conditioning, everything was in perfect condition.

The 600 students who assembled in the multipurpose room at 9:00 A.M. on the 6th for Mr. Magnason's opening address had previously attended junior and senior high schools throughout the Clear River area. A large proportion of the Upper School students had been transferred from Clear River Central. All were about to begin a new educational process for the first time and there was an air of excitement in the room.

Emily Geoffrion was standing at the rear of the room with Kate Amster and Florence Dix when Mr. Magnason entered through a side door and began walking to the stage at the front of the room. As he mounted the stage muted catcalls of "Tigrrr, Tigrrr" began to rise from the area of the older students.

Kate rolled her eyes to the ceiling and murmured, "Here we go."

EMILY: What do you mean?
FLORENCE: Oh, that's what the kids used to call Mr. Magnason at Central.
EMILY: Tigrrr?
KATE: Yeah, Tigrrr, with the emphasis on the "grr."
EMILY: Why?
FLORENCE: Oh, he's big, I guess, always stalking around and really making them toe the line. They don't like him very much.

As he approached the podium, it was obvious that Magnason heard the students. And the color rushing to his face made it equally obvious that he knew that it was not a term of endearment. He began with conventional opening and welcoming remarks and then addressed the subject of the new school and curriculum.

"This fine new school has been built for you, the students. Not only is it brand new, it is also the only school of its kind in the whole state. I think that you will learn a lot of important things and that you will have fun doing it. I expect you to accord your teachers with the respect they deserve and to obey the school's rules and regulations."

As he concluded his remarks and began to walk off the stage, whispered calls of "Tigrrr, Tigrrr" once again were heard. They didn't stop until he left the room through the same side door.

The first week or two of school were characterized by the usual administrative confusion and snafus (confusion) that mark the beginning of any school year. Also, there were a few problems getting used to new equipment. The automatic smoke detector fire alarm set off two false alarms before it was discovered that the detectors in the chemistry lab were too sensitive and would trip the alarm system at the slightest hint of fumes. This was fixed but the air-conditioning system was still giving some problems. The building was designed for "climate control" and the windows, as a result, were sealed. The fact that the heat of summer lingered through September only made this problem more irritating. But this problem was circumvented by the school's open program which encouraged many teachers to hold classes outdoors.

It was on just such a hot day in mid-September that Magnason walked over to Mrs. Trottier's office in the Middle School building and met her in the hallway.

MAGNASON: Mrs. Trottier, you have a minute?

TROTTIER: Yes, what can I do for you?

MAGNASON: I was trying to find McNair's class this morning but couldn't find them anywhere. Do you know where they were?

TROTTIER: No, not really. She'd probably taken them to a shady spot on the grounds somewhere. The damned air conditioning was really screwing up this morning.

MAGNASON (*stiffening noticeably at Mrs. Trottier's choice of words*): Well, I can't control what's going on when I can't even find out where my teachers have taken their students. Come to think of it, the school seemed half empty this morning. I suppose *all* those students were out roaming the countryside, too? Is this what you mean by "open" classrooms?

TROTTIER: Take it easy, Arthur. Giving teachers and students the freedom to make choices is part of the new concept. The teachers have to be able to flow with the direction the class is taking.

MAGNASON: Well, I'm trying to keep an open mind but I ought to be able to find out where the teachers of this school are teaching their students if I want to. It used to be that classes followed the direction the teacher was taking.

The presence in the hallway of some students returning from late lunch period ended the conversation.

The next evening Mr. Magnason received a telephone call at home. Calling was Harold Fowles, school committee president.

FOWLES: How's it going with your new school. Arthur?

MAGNASON: Pretty well, Mr. Fowles, except for that cranky air conditioner, everything's working beautifully. And you know the way that is, they'll probably get it running perfectly about the time of the first snowfall. Other than that, though, no major problems.

FOWLES: You have another one of those false alarms yesterday morning?

MAGNASON: No, why?

The Devon School Case

FOWLES: Well, I was driving by the school yesterday about 10:30 and there were groups of kids all over the place.

MAGNASON: Oh that. Well that's . . . that's part of the concept of "open" classrooms. Teachers can feel free to take a class outdoors if they want to. And since it's been unusually warm this week and the air conditioning's not too reliable, more teachers are going outdoors. I'm sure things will settle down in a few weeks.

FOWLES: You mean those groups of kids were actually classes?

MAGNASON: Yes.

FOWLES: Well I don't know. It seemed to me that a lot of them were just running around playing. In fact, I can't remember seeing teachers with some of those groups, they were just off doing what they wanted.

MAGNASON: It's interesting you should mention that, Mr. Fowles. I just spoke to Paulette Trottier about that very thing yesterday, as a matter of fact. She didn't seem concerned. You get rough spots when you try to put any new program into operation. I do plan to tighten up on that sort of thing, however.

FOWLES: Well, this is just the type of permissiveness I was concerned about when this new school was being discussed. But I guess you're right about new programs. We have the same problem at the plant. (Mr. Fowles was president and principal stockholder of Fowles Electronics, Inc., in Clear River. It employed about 400 people in the manufacture of computer and other electronic components.) It sounds as if you're on top of the problem, though. Got to run, good night.

MAGNASON: Good night, Mr. Fowles.

MEMO

To: All Faculty

From: A. Magnason, Principal

Subject: Guidelines for the conduct of classes out of doors

In an effort to improve control over and the educational value of outdoor class periods the following guidelines will be observed.

1. Teachers wishing to conduct outdoor classes will submit a written request to their department head no later than one day prior to the day they wish to hold such class.
2. The request will contain as a minimum, the following information:
    a. Grade level of class.
    b. Number of students.
    c. Location of class on school grounds.
    d. Subject matter to be taught.
    e. Time and duration of class.
3. All classes must be supervised by a teacher and conducted in such a manner that the teacher retains full control over the class. Under no

circumstances shall unsupervised groups of students be allowed outside the building.

"Just what is this all about, Arthur?" Mrs. Trottier spoke sharply, as she strode into Magnason's office waving brandishing the memo.

"That, Mrs. Trottier, is an attempt to bring some order and control to these wilderness trails some teachers are taking their classes on," answered Magnason in a measured voice, "we can't allow aimless wandering over the school grounds to continue."

Mrs. Trottier closed the door to his office, "I can read, dammit. What are you trying to do, sabotage the whole program? I told you that the teachers have to be flexible enough to respond to the way their class is going! This 'no later than one day prior' stuff is too rigid! You hired me to implement an open-classroom system at this school."

Magnason clasped his hands on his desk and said, "I am responsible to the school committee to see that their educational objectives for students are met. I am also responsible to the parents of our students to see that they are supervised at all times and not exposed to any danger. And don't forget, not everyone in this town was in favor of this new approach. We're still in the implementation phase. It might be a good idea to proceed with caution."

Standing up, he tried to be conciliatory, "Now, we can still do all of the things you want to do. It's just that I want to make sure we meet all our responsibilities to the school committee and the community."

Mrs. Trottier was about to reply when Magnason's phone rang. As he answered it, she left.

Despite the restrictions on outdoor classes, the implementation of the program seemed to be proceeding smoothly over the next few weeks. Besides, autumn had brought cooler weather so that the air conditioning was no longer important.

It was during this period that Mrs. Trottier spent more and more time with the Middle School and its program, while Mr. Magnason concentrated on the Upper School. She maintained an "open door" policy with the teachers and always seemed willing to see one of them in her office whether to talk over problems or hash out new ideas.

The Amster-Dix-Spinella triumvirate (trio) was beginning to work very well. Dedicated teachers all, they worked together as they had at Central High. Pooling ideas and materials, they were imaginative and unstructured in their teaching. They were popular with their students and it was generally agreed that their students were progressing well. One of the new ideas that they tried was teaching with a minimum of supportive materials. They resorted to textbooks and other such resources only when absolutely necessary. This teaching concept was a particular favorite of Mrs. Trottier's and their success at it enhanced their prestige as practitioners of the new educational philosophy.

Some of the other teachers were not as successful in using this technique, however. Wes Perron and Emily Geoffrion, in particular, were having problems. They spoke with Mrs. Trottier in her office about their troubles one day.

TROTTIER: I really can't understand the problems you're having. Look at Kate, Florence, and Lou in seventh grade. They're doing very well, and enjoying it to boot. Perhaps you have not given it enough of a chance yet.

PERRON: Well, we've talked it over and we feel we need more to work with in class. I just can't teach all day without any books or charts or anything.

GEOFFRION: That's right. Maybe some of these other teachers can do it, but they've been at it a lot longer. When I have as much experience as they do, I'll probably be able to talk all day without a lesson plan too. Right now, it's just too much.

TROTTIER: Look, you're both getting too worried about this. I know it's harder on you because of your lack of experience but both of you have the makings of excellent teachers. That's why I hired you. Sure, you'll have to work harder but you'll be better teachers for it.

PERRON: It gets pretty rough down there, you know. You ought to take a look for yourself. These kids can be pretty wild.

TROTTIER: Look, I know all about it. But I've put this program across in tougher schools than this. You'll be all right. You just need to work at it a little more.

After leaving Trottier's office, Emily was sullen, "'You just need to work at it a little longer.' Is that the best she can do? Why doesn't she at least come down and sit in on a class or two so she could offer some suggestions?"

"Yeah," agreed Wes, "she won't even take a look at what's going on. All she ever does is sit in her office talking to people and drinking coffee. We're supposed to mark the kids on effort and all we ever get from her is 'try harder.'"

The Wednesday morning before Thanksgiving Mr. Magnason was in the hall outside his office, having just gotten off the phone after trying to placate another upset committee member—this time regarding the curriculum not being as supportive of the vocational arts as had been intended. As he stood musing about the call, he heard shouts and loud laughter from around the corner. Rounding the corner were three seventh-grade boys who were engaging in general horseplay. When they saw him, they immediately fell silent.

"Where are you going?" he demanded.

After a short pause, one said, "Uh, we're going to the library."

"Why?"

The same boy answered, "We want to get a book."

"About what?"

"Animals."

"You know very well that the library isn't in this part of the building," Magnason boomed. "Return to your classes at once."

MEMO

To: All faculty and staff

From: A. Magnason

Subject: Movement of students throughout building during class time

It is becoming increasingly clear that the unrestricted movement of students within the school building during class time is counterproductive to the educational process.

Therefore, the following means will be used to control student movement:

1. Any student movement will be controlled through the use of passes which will be issued by a teacher.
2. The pass will be issued only for a specific purpose which will be clearly identified on the pass.
3. Teachers will limit the number of passes issued in any one class period to 10 percent of the number of students present in the class.
4. Students found away from their classes without passes will be considered for disciplinary action.

Passes are being printed now. This policy will become effective upon distribution of passes to each teacher.

"Paulette's going to go through the roof when she sees this one," Kate Amster said as she finished reading the latest memo.

"Progressive school, my foot," snorted Langford. "Why, Magnason doesn't have the slightest idea what we're trying to do here. This place will be just another Central High in a few months. I'm going to call my old school in New York."

During the first few months, it had become a ritual among many of the Middle School teachers to meet at the Silver Pony, an English style pub in Devon, every Friday after work. Such a gathering took place in mid-November.

LANGFORD: Today I had the pleasure of the Tigrrr's company in class.

SPINELLA: Hey John, be careful. The guy's difficult but it's not really right to get down to the kid's level.

LANGFORD: Oh, I know, but he watched my history class today. We were role-playing the Constitutional Convention and the kids were really getting into it. They were moving around and yelling but, dammit, they were interested and involved. After the class do you think he said anything about what we had done? Hell no! All he said was that he thought the class was a little unruly and that I should try to control them more.

BETTY SIVILS (*fiftyish; though considered one of the "Old Guard," she was well liked by most of the younger teachers*): I know how you feel, John, but you must admit that some of these kids are getting out of hand. Open classrooms is one thing but to have them disrupting things is another. Paulette is undermining discipline. Do you know the kids feel they can go to her and complain about teachers and that she'll listen to them? I don't think that's proper and I think we can see the damage it's doing to the climate of learning. She doesn't seem to be aware of some of the problems she's creating.

LANGFORD: I still feel that Magnason doesn't care about content as long as our areas are calm and there's no noise coming from them. He's not even trying to understand the new system.

MCNAIR: I agree. He's been an administrator too long. He doesn't care about people, whether they're students or faculty, as long as he can control them. Some of those memos of his. . . .

RESCA: You mean the "Tigrrr Talks"?

MCNAIR (*laughing*): Yeah, the "Tigrrr Talks." They're very condescending. He treats the faculty like children. And how about our staff meetings. If it's not on the agenda, it doesn't get discussed and Magnason controls the agenda.

SPINELLA: Changing the subject, but did you know Paulette and Magnason had it out again Tuesday? I don't know the full story but I guess it was about that latest memo of his.

LANGFORD: You mean the one restricting student movement from class to class?

SPINELLA: Right. Paulette was pretty hot.

MCNAIR: No wonder. That idea's one of the basic premises of the open classroom concept. If you bog kids down in bureaucracy, exploring new learning experiences will be too much of a hassle.

SPINELLA: You know, this is starting to get pretty serious. Those two are at each others' throats more and more. Things just can't go on like this.

On Sunday evening, December 12, Mr. Fowles made another call to Mr. Magnason's home. After exchanging pleasantries, Fowles brought up the school.

FOWLES: Arthur, I'm starting to feel real concern over what's going on down there in the Middle School. We're starting to get an awful lot of adverse reaction from parents. Arthur, it's been over three months since school opened and I'm beginning to hear complaints from parents that the bugs should be worked out by now.

MAGNASON: But you're going to get that anytime a new school opens. And in our case, we're starting a new curriculum, too.

FOWLES: I know, Arthur, I know. But it's getting to the point where feelings among many parents are running pretty high.

MAGNASON: What are the big complaints?

FOWLES: Well, I guess one of the biggest is that parents never see their kids doing any homework. In fact, they say they never see them with any books at all. Those outside classes in the beginning of the year didn't go over too well either. Oh yes, another thing. Parents don't feel their kids are learning anything useful. One mother told me her sixth-grader spends all day learning about Eskimos. Is that true?

MAGNASON: Oh that. That's the Makos concept, one of Trottier's pet projects. Total-immersion learning, where students learn all aspects of a culture and can compare it to their own.

FOWLES: I see. Well, I'm afraid it looks like the committee meeting in January could be stormy. You'd better get your ducks in line because there will be people there who'll be looking for someone's hide. Most of the committee is still not committed totally to the new school and I think we'll be forced to take a closer look at what's going on from now on.

It started snowing late that night and continued through the next morning, Monday, the 13th. Mr. Magnason had to attend a meeting of school administrators in Clear River and didn't get to Devon School until 1:30 in the afternoon. When he drove up he saw about 30 students milling around in front of the school chanting unintelligible slogans. Parking his car, he went to the front entrance where he found Mrs. Trottier just inside the doors. She and a few other teachers were watching the students.

"What the hell's going on here, Mrs. Trottier?" he demanded.

"The students are staging a walk-out," she said in a matter-of-fact tone of voice.

Magnason started, "A what?"

"I said," she answered in a clipped voice, "the students are staging a walk-out."

"Whatever the hell for?"

Sighing audibly, Mrs. Trottier explained, "Some of the eighth graders tried to pull a fast one. One of them called the bus company and said we were closing early because of the snow and to send the buses right over.

"When the caller didn't give the code word, the bus company got suspicious and called back to confirm. That's how I found out. When the buses didn't show they started getting restless. When I made an announcement over the P.A. that the buses would come at the usual time, about 30 of them walked out. They've been out there about a half-hour."

"And you've done nothing?"

"Why bother?" she said. "Let them get it out of their system. Besides, they'll get cold pretty soon and come inside."

"And in the meantime," Magnason shouted, "we let everybody know that we're making a bunch of revolutionaries out of their kids!"

"Well you do something," she snapped, "you're the drill master around here."

"What?"

"You're the one who wants them all quietly in their places like good little robots." Mrs. Trottier was shouting now, too. Pointing her finger at Magnason, she went on, "You people are all the same. Who cares if they learn anything as long as they behave themselves long enough for us to ship them to another grade? It makes me sick."

With that she stalked off down the hall.

Livid, Magnason shouted after her, "Mrs. Trottier, come back here!"

Then he became aware of the circle of teachers, some watching him, some looking after Mrs. Trottier.

Dominion Acceptance Company Limited*

IN MAY 1973 Mr. B. L. Keast, Atlantic regional manager of operations for Dominion Acceptance Company Limited, faced a number of personnel and operating procedures decisions directly affecting the operations of the Moncton, New Brunswick, branch of DAC. Earlier in the year changes in the management staffing of the Moncton branch had been made and after three months the results of these changes were being evaluated in order to make adequate permanent changes in the Moncton operation. As the problems which had led to the changes had been of a particularly serious nature, it was imperative that Mr. Keast thoroughly examine the possible effects of any changes, as well as the causes of the problems arising earlier. In doing so he was compelled to consider the viewpoints of the Moncton branch manager, Mr. Ronald Snell, Snell's current assistant manager, Mr. Alex DeCoste, his previous assistant manager, Mr. Jerry MacDonald, and the rest of the Moncton staff. In addition he recognized the importance of keeping the Moncton operation consistent with the other branches in his region as well as with national DAC policy.

BACKGROUND

DAC was one of the largest finance companies in Canada. Its primary business was the acceptance of conditional sales contracts from customers who had purchased consumer goods. DAC then paid the retailer while the customer paid DAC in monthly installments. In addition to this retail financing, DAC also made loans to firms to either begin or expand existing businesses. The company was entirely Canadian owned and operated on a national basis. Regional offices were located in five

---

*Case material prepared by Mr. William J. MacNeil under the direction of W. H. Cooper, assistant professor of business administration. St. Francis Xavier University, Antigonish, N.S., Canada. All names disguised. Reprinted by permission of Professor Cooper.

major Canadian cities, viz., Halifax, Montreal, Toronto, Winnipeg, and Vancouver. Branch offices were located in most cities and some towns serving as district shopping centers. Atlantic region branch staff sizes varied from 3 to 40 depending on the population of the market being served and the amount of money loaned.

Corporate headquarters were in Toronto and functioned as a central policymaking and administrative center. Head office established specific policies and procedures regarding loans, branch control, and reporting methods, as well as personnel policies and administrative procedures designed to ensure consistent coast-to-coast operations. To obtain consistency, DAC had in 1968 prepared and distributed to each branch a detailed procedures manual, which, in addition to the above policies, prescribed office procedures and provided detailed job descriptions for all branch positions. In the manual the policy of aggressively seeking new profitable accounts was stressed.

The regional manager of operations (RMO) functioned as the intermediary between corporate headquarters and the branches in their respective regions. As with the Halifax RMO, all RMOs had as their primary source of information regarding branch operations the monthly statistics prepared for them by each branch. The format was prescribed by the procedures manual (including the due date of the third of each month covering the previous month's operations) and consisted of statistics on the number and dollar value of accounts, collections made, total branch expenses for the month, and overdue accounts by age. As part of the computer analysis of branch operations, the RMO compiled this data into a regional report comparing all branches in the region and sent copies to each branch as well as to Toronto. Each branch manager could therefore regularly compare his performance against the other individual branches as well as with the region as a whole.

In his evaluation of branch operations and the resulting report, Mr. Keast placed emphasis on the control of payments. The percentage of accounts 30 or more days late was the key evaluation variable and he expected the collection department in each branch to give special attention to such deficient accounts. The Atlantic region's average delinquency rate was 3 percent. Branch managers were generally quite sensitive about their office's delinquency rate and how their rate compared with other branches in the region, as shown in the monthly RMO's report.

In addition to the monthly reports, the RMO conducted a yearly visit to each branch (without prior notice being given) to perform several kinds of inspection and audits. The RMO and his staff inspected the accounts and credit records, performed employee evaluations of the manager and assistant manager, and if time allowed, reviewed the manager's evaluations of the other staff members. As each manager hired his own staff and operated his branch with some autonomy, the results of the monthly and annual evaluations were of particular importance in judging the manager and his staff's ability.

THE FEBRUARY INSPECTION

Mr. Keast's inspection in June 1972 had rated the Moncton branch's overall performance as slightly below average. The July 1972 and subsequent monthly reports began to show a steadily increasing delinquency rate and a decrease in the dollar value as well as in the number of accounts. By January 1973 the delinquency rate stood at 8 percent and the number of customer accounts had fallen from 3,500 in June 1972 to 3,000. This performance decline was significantly poorer than the other branches in southern New Brunswick. After repeated requests for explanations and unsatisfactory responses, Mr. Keast decided to make his 1973 visit much earlier in the year, and hence on February 14 he arrived in Moncton at 7:15 A.M. Upon entering the airport terminal Mr. Keast and his staff assistant were surprised to find Mr. Snell queuing up for a ticket on the 7:35 A.M. departure for Toronto. An embarrassed Snell explained that he had some personal business in Hamilton, but that it was not urgent and could be delayed, particularly in light of the unexpected annual inspection of the branch which was to be conducted that day.

Traveling to the branch from the airport, Snell explained: "I've been finding it tough to do much to control our late accounts. We've a poor clientele, my assistant isn't qualified, and the girls we've been getting to keep our account records up to date have not worked out. I know it makes the branch look poor but you know I've tried. I think in a couple of months we'll have the office turned around and be back among the regional leaders where we belong." Keast listened politely and expressed concern that something must be done soon to improve the Moncton operations. "If your staff is not up to the job, maybe we can fix that, but as far as customers go, you've got as good an economic area here as Scott does in Fredericton and Angus in St. John. Anyhow, you certainly have a lot more snow here than we do down in Halifax. Let's see how things are looking in the office." Arriving downtown, Keast and his assistant spent the next few hours going over the account cards and other financial records.

Things did not look good. Over 20 account cards had been found which were over 90 days past due (the January report had shown a total of 12 such accounts) and no note of contact between the office and the customer could be found for most of them for the past 60 days. The office was in disarray, the filing system in chaos, key records and papers took some time to locate, and the customer account clerks seemed unfamiliar with much of the routine office procedure. Keast finished the morning going over the personnel files and noted that the turnover rates for clerical personnel was high, absenteeism a problem, and a key staff member (the accounts supervisor) had been fired a month ago and had not been replaced. Leaving his assistant to tabulate the results of the morning's inspection, Keast took a, by now, very worried looking Snell to lunch at Cy's. He intended to utilize lunch to do the performance appraisal and to suggest several courses of action that might be taken to remedy the Moncton problems. He was disturbed and somewhat surprised by what they had uncovered in their morning's work.

The bleak view of the Petitcodiac River at low tide which was visible from the restaurant window provided an appropriate backdrop to their luncheon conversation. Keast began: "Look Ron, you're over $5 million outstanding and $400,000 of that is overdue. We can't find half of what we're looking for in your records, and no one seems to know what they're doing. You admit yourself that things are out of hand."

"But Mr. Keast, I've told you that I know we're having problems but I think it is up to me to solve them. I've been the manager here for eight years and I promise that within six months we'll have everything back to normal."

Toying with his lobster thermidor, Keast considered what he should and could do. He had certainly given Snell ample notice of dissatisfaction with the branch's operation, and the prospect for improvement seemed dim. On the other hand, Snell had a long record of satisfactory work with only one year of poor operation. He had been manager of the Moncton branch for eight years and had the longest stay of any branch manager in the region, as well as the longest service of any of the current staff at that branch. Keast thought that this visit had impressed on all the Moncton staff the alarm with which their performance was viewed by him. Weighing this, Keast advised Snell that "the inspection this morning has convinced me that changes have to be made. I think you knew this. You have worked well in the past but it looks to me that you may need some help in bringing the turnaround about." Snell agreed that he needed help. Keast continued: "My assistant worked at the Halifax branch before he became my assistant at regional. You met him this morning. What do you think of him?" Snell responded in a noncommittal fashion, saying, "He certainly seems efficient and gets right to the problem without fooling around. He seems fine. Why?" "Well, Ron, you suggested that Jerry MacDonald isn't doing his job the way you'd like him to. I'll see him this afternoon for his performance appraisal and I propose to offer him a field salesman position in Prince Edward Island. I would like to temporarily replace him with my assistant, Alex DeCoste." Stunned at this suggestion, Snell could only nod. He had half expected to be fired himself.

Before returning to the office, Keast told Snell that this move was only temporary and would last for three months. At the end of that time he would return to Moncton and reinspect the branch. Both expressed the hope that the results would warrant a rerating of the branch from poor to at least satisfactory.

On returning to the office, Keast spent half an hour with Jerry MacDonald, explaining the reasons for the changes and his new responsibilities. Jerry was 40 years old and had once been the branch manager in Edmundston, New Brunswick, before coming to Moncton. His performance in Edmundston had resulted in his becoming assistant manager at the Moncton branch. Since then he had not shown much interest in becoming a branch manager again. He accepted the proposed change calmly. Keast then met with Snell and DeCoste and they discussed the changes that would have to be made in order to eliminate the current operating problems. DeCoste made several suggestions regarding collections, personnel training, and new business, which were greeted with mild interest by Snell. They agreed to explore these ideas more fully when DeCoste returned February 19 to assume his new duties. Keast and DeCoste then left the Moncton branch to catch their return flight to Halifax. On the return flight Keast impressed upon DeCoste the importance of getting the Moncton branch back in shape, not only for the sake of the branch's health, but also because other branch managers in the region were keenly interested in how Keast would handle the situation.

CHANGES

Returning the following Monday, DeCoste and Snell met briefly and exchanged pleasantries. Snell then formally introduced him to the rest of the staff, some of whom DeCoste had met the previous Wednesday. Most of the staff gave DeCoste a warm greeting. The staff consisted of three collection officers, a cashier/cash journal clerk, and three file clerk/typists (a fourth had quit a week earlier). The accounts supervisor position remained unfilled. (See Exhibit 1 for an organization chart of the Moncton branch.) Snell and DeCoste then returned to discuss the changes that needed to be made.

As with all the DAC branches which had both a manager and an assistant manager, the Moncton manager's job description prescribed his primary duties as that of seeking new customers (both consumer and commercial), promoting sales, and performing all public relations duties. These duties called for significant amounts of field work and as a result the daily supervision of office work was assigned to the assistant manager. DeCoste would assume all responsibilities for directing and appraising office personnel, and acting as liaison between the staff and

EXHIBIT 1
Organization Chart: February 19, 1973

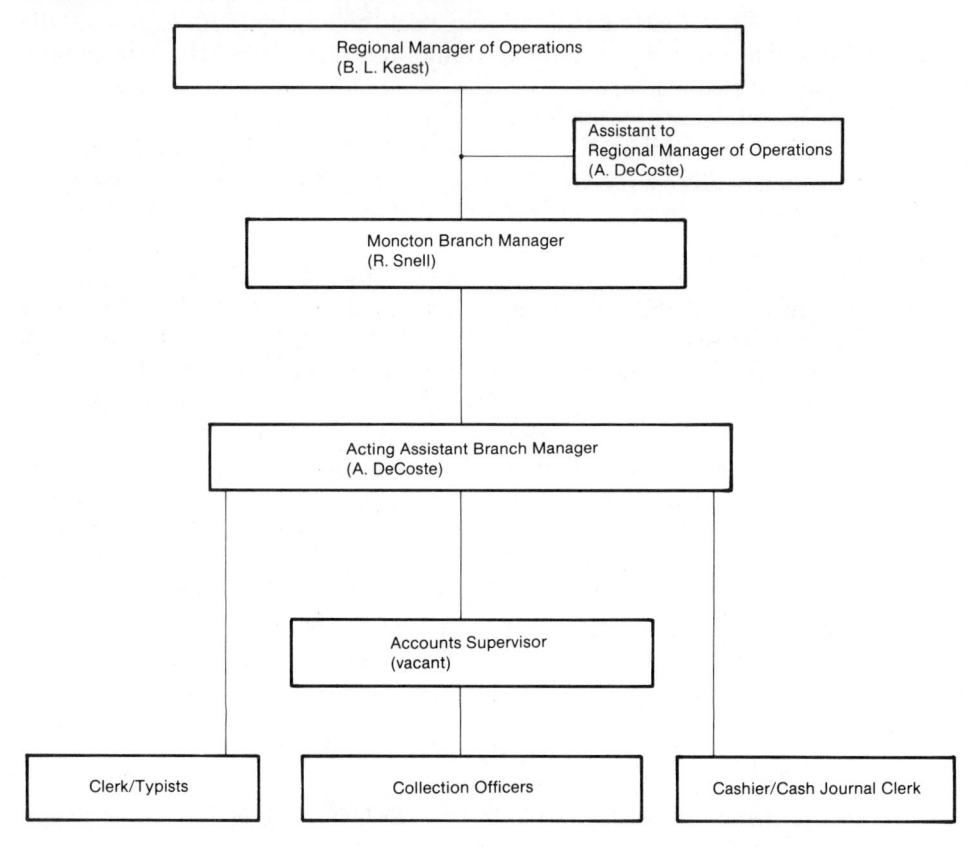

```
                    ┌─────────────────────────────┐
                    │ Regional Manager of Operations │
                    │        (B. L. Keast)          │
                    └─────────────────────────────┘
                              │
                              │        ┌─────────────────────────┐
                              ├────────│ Assistant to            │
                              │        │ Regional Manager of     │
                              │        │ Operations (A. DeCoste) │
                              │        └─────────────────────────┘
                    ┌─────────────────────────┐
                    │ Moncton Branch Manager  │
                    │      (R. Snell)         │
                    └─────────────────────────┘
                              │
                    ┌─────────────────────────────┐
                    │ Acting Assistant Branch Manager │
                    │        (A. DeCoste)             │
                    └─────────────────────────────┘
                         │     │     │
                    ┌─────────────────────┐
                    │ Accounts Supervisor │
                    │      (vacant)       │
                    └─────────────────────┘
         │                    │                         │
   ┌───────────┐      ┌──────────────────┐    ┌──────────────────────────┐
   │ Clerk/    │      │ Collection       │    │ Cashier/Cash Journal     │
   │ Typists   │      │ Officers         │    │ Clerk                    │
   └───────────┘      └──────────────────┘    └──────────────────────────┘
```

the manager where necessary. In the Monday meeting the two men agreed that DeCoste would run the office as his job description indicated, but that any significant changes and decisions that DeCoste might make would be thoroughly discussed with Snell before making them.

On the afternoon of the 19th, DeCoste met with the collections staff and explained the changes to be made in the collection of past due and current accounts. The collection officers were to have all the accounts pulled which were 60 or more days overdue and resolve these accounts according to procedures set forth in the procedures manual. Once these were settled, they would then focus their attention on the next most critical group, the 30 to 60 days overdue accounts. It was agreed that these 250 accounts would be processed in two weeks time. DeCoste promised that a replacement for the previously fired accounts supervisor would be on the job within two weeks. In the meantime he designated the most senior of the officers as the temporary chief of this concerted effort.

That afternoon DeCoste met with the three clerk/typists and spent the rest of the day reorganizing the filing system and instructing them in the standard procedures for keeping account records current. This procedure consisted of the dating of all payments on the reverse of the customer's account card and the daily pulling of all account cards whose payments were due that day. These cards were then placed at the back of the accounts payable file. When accounts were paid, the cashier/journal clerk noted this on the card and placed them in the "to file" box, to be filed by the clerk/typists. Two of the girls claimed to have never been trained in these procedures and made reference to account cards which had been handled somewhat carelessly in the past. It was hoped that this systematic customer accounts method would reduce the number of customer complaints.

By the end of February the office had begun to operate more smoothly than it had for some time. The office now had its full complement of staff, morale had improved, the number of uncollected overdue accounts had been reduced to 100, and DeCoste felt progress was being made. However, new problems were beginning to arise.

MARCH

The first problem arose at the end of the month. The February report was due March 3d, which meant that the actual completion date would be Thursday, the 1st. It was DeCoste's responsibility to complete the task and on Wednesday he asked the staff (exclusive of Mr. Snell) to work overtime compiling data for the report. This request was met with loud disapproval. The staff claimed that this had not been the practice for some time and when it had been, the staff had had to buy their own supper. Mr. Snell had ended the policy of DAC paying for the dinner, claiming that it was too costly, and the evening work at months end ended shortly thereafter. The procedures manual stipulated that agreement to work overtime once a month was a condition of employment and that DAC would pay for any expenses (including meals) incurred as a result.

Another problem related to an informal practice which had existed for some time. Between Keast's inspection visit and DeCoste's arrival as assistant manager, Snell had instructed all the staff that coffee breaks were to be eliminated. Snell continued to take a break twice a day in the coffee shop next door. On two occasions after his arrival, DeCoste accompanied Snell on his coffee break. On both occasions Snell belittled the staff, complaining about their ineptness, criticized his previous assistant manager, and complained that after 18 years of service with the company they had forgotten about him. The staff began to sneak in thermoses of tea and coffee for use during Snell's regular visits to the coffee shop.

A third problem began occurring immediately after DeCoste's arrival. Arguments between staff members began to occur over who was to do what. Snell would hear these disputes, come out of his office, and immediately direct the employees involved to do the tasks in the manner he indicated, all of this before DeCoste could act to resolve the dispute. On these occasions Snell referred to the need to run an efficient office.

An additional problem began during DeCoste's second week at Moncton. One of the collection officers approached him regarding a raise, pointing out that the last raise he had had was 18 months ago and it was for only $3 per week, raising him to $118. Alex checked the employee's personnel file and found he had not been appraised since the time of his last raise, despite the fact that it was DAC policy to perform employee reviews annually on the anniversary of their employment. A raise seemed warranted to Alex as the officer was making $500 below the average for collection officers in the region with similar lengths of service, although there was a considerable range in salaries throughout the region. DeCoste approached Snell but was told that no raises would be granted until the rating of the branch was judged satisfactory by the RMO. He claimed the employee was being overpaid now and referred to the outstanding accounts problem. DeCoste responded "Look, Mr. Snell. I've examined all the personnel files for all our staff and have found the rates of pay to be well below the DAC rates in the Atlantic region and our staff knows this. I think we need to catch up on our raises. I know Jerry MacDonald left this to you but you're too busy as it is and we're way overdue on the annual appraisals. As it is now, none of the staff knows why they have not had raises and that includes Jerry before he left." Snell's response was short and repeated his claim that no raises would be approved until the branch shaped up. DeCoste was sure that Keast had given Snell no directions regarding salary changes. After this conversation of the 27th, Alex informed the employee that he was trying to get a raise of $10 a week approved and that a strong showing on the outstanding collections would improve his case.

Finally, DeCoste noted that he had inherited a staff who had grown accustomed to going to Snell with any operating problems. This practice had been tacitly approved by Jerry MacDonald, who had become used to having Mr. Snell in the office most of the time and left most matters of consequence for Snell to deal with. MacDonald had not, however, refrained from joining in on the jokes made about Snell on the rare occasions when he was out of the office.

THE MAY INSPECTION

During the February–April period the monthly reports showed the branch's improvement in its accounts collections. The delinquency rate for April 1973 was down to 4 percent and only one clerk/typist had quit. Some of the administrative and operations problems had been resolved, but the problems of raises, office supervision by Snell, and the coffee breaks prohibitions remained while the number of accounts had continued to fall. Keast had requested a private report from DeCoste regarding the Moncton operations and had received it at the end of April. In it he made observations regarding the various administrative and operating problems and also noted his own frustration in his current position.

Keast was to arrive on May 7 and the Moncton staff anticipated his arrival with varying mixtures of anxiety, hope, and fascination. Keast's own view of the May visit was one of realizing that there was more involved than the health of the Moncton branch. Keast had tried to carefully consider all the factors regarding the Snell case in light of the current branch control system and the branch manager's job. Keast also had to keep in mind Snell's long service record, his welfare and that of the Moncton staff, as well as the health of the total Moncton operation and its place in the region. On the May 7, 7:30 A.M. flight he reviewed what he intended to say at that meeting. The weather had improved since his last flight to Moncton and he hoped the Moncton operation would continue to similarly improve.

The Eunice MacGillicudy/Marcus Warren Case*

YOU HAVE been the executive director of Big Brothers and Big Sisters of Ecclesville for the past year. The agency is some nine years old, having started as a Big Brother agency and added a Big Sister component approximately two years ago. The professional staff consists of four persons, two men and two women. The two senior workers are Eunice MacGillicudy and Marcus Warren.

A Big Sister/Big Brother agency's historic function has been to recruit adult volunteers and match them with children who have but one parent. The adult volunteer acts as a friend and role model to the child to whom he/she is matched. The agency professional staff worker promotes the adult volunteer with support services and helps the parent with problems when asked.

Eunice, 32, has been with the agency for nearly four years and was

---

*This case was prepared by Lewis Reade and Marsha Klar, Big Brothers/Big Sisters of America. Reproduced with the senior author's permission.

the first additional professional person hired by the previous executive director. She possesses both a BA and an MSW from State University and had some three years' professional experience prior to joining the agency. While her recorded caseload (matches) totals 92, you have much reason to suspect that not all those matches still exist because in reviewing her files at random you have noticed that many matches have not been contacted in nearly one year. There have even been some complaints from mothers about Eunice's "unavailability." However, there is no question regarding Eunice's commitment to the program and especially her skill in developing community relations activities. Indeed, her caseload may be suffering because of both her agency and personal involvement in community affairs. Not only has she worked with groups of mothers, Big Brothers and Big Sisters, and helped form a local council in a minority area (unfortunately unsuccessful), but she is very active in the local chapter of NASW,[1] sits on the Board of Ecclesville's branch of the ACLU,[2] recently ran for the school board (she lost by only a few votes), is a member of the Women's Political Caucus, and undertakes volunteer therapy work with teenagers. Through her efforts a distinguished local citizen joined your board and has arranged for a $10,000 grant from a local trust for the past two years. Chances are that through "the Eunice connection" the $10,000 gift will be forthcoming again this year in November (it is now August) and will constitute approximately one ninth of your yearly income. If Eunice left the agency and went to another social service organization, the $10,000 would probably go with her.

Marcus Warren, 34, a black, joined the agency three years ago as the first minority professional. His background includes an undergraduate degree in journalism, four years in the air force as a personnel officer, and he has completed all the course requirements for an MA in counseling psychology (an analysis of his innovative case work methods will constitute his thesis due next June). Marc is a sensitive and conscientious worker. His ability to develop rapport with the adults, children, and parents he deals with is phenomenal. Treading a fine line, he expertly deals with both middle-class people and the "street wise." He sees his military experience positively as providing him with organizational and administrative skills but has not become rigid because of it. He carries a caseload (matches) of some 70; each match is meticulously recorded, and he had definite proof of personal (phone or visit) contacts at least once a month with each match. He has gladly offered to help the junior workers in learning to do their jobs well. In

---

[1] National Association of Social Workers.

[2] American Civil Liberties Union (an organization devoted to the protection of citizens' civil rights).

spite of all his abilities in working with matches, Marc has some difficulties working with the general public. He is proud of his work and if challenged (or sometimes even questioned) about his methods by the board or an outside group he may get defensive. His knowledge of his real competence sometimes comes across as arrogance, and you have had to smooth over some hurt feelings with United Way personnel as a result of a blowup by Marc at a minority involvement seminar, where his methods were criticized. Then too, Marc is going through a painful separation with his wife, although the situation is eased by the fact that they have no children.

Today you received notice that your LEAA proposal for a juvenile division/court-related program has been funded for the next three years. The program includes the employement of a program supervisor and three workers who will handle referrals of boys and girls from single-parent families at both the police contact and adjudicated level to your service. No similar program exists in Ecclesville, and the entire operation must be developed from the ground up. This includes building relationships with police and courts officials, gaining local support in the center city minority communities from which most of the kids come, and developing the systems and procedures for processing and reporting on the matches made. There had been no secret for the past month that the grant would be made and that Eunice MacGillicudy and Marcus Warren are the two candidates for the program supervisor's job which pays 25–30 percent more than they are presently earning. Word has gotten to you that Eunice has said that she will quit if she doesn't get the job and that Marcus has said he'd seriously consider filing an action with the city human rights commission if he is passed over.

The local criminal justice agency (LEAA) has given you one week to name a program supervisor.

*Evolution in the Mailroom**

ANDERSON FOODS, INC., employs approximately 700 white-collar workers in its administrative headquarters in the Southwest.

The mailroom where I worked performs the function of routing incoming and intraoffice mail throughout the building, and dispatching mail to the local post office twice a day.

Hal Struthers, age 47, is the supervisor of the mailroom and has been with the company in that capacity for nine years. He reports to the office manager, Bert Finnely, who is in charge of all office service departments. In addition to the mailroom, these service departments include the reproduction department, maintenance department, and the stationery and supplies department.

Struthers supervises 11 men who carry out the operations of the mailroom. One of these men, Brian Mancies, is his assistant and officially in charge of the mailroom when Struthers is absent. Mancies is 27 years old and has worked in the mailroom for seven years. The work of the department is divided into two principal functions: the circulation of intraoffice mail, and the routing of outgoing mail. The circulation of intraoffice mail is done by four mailboys, each of whom delivers and picks up mail from a single floor. The routing of outgoing mail is performed by three men. One of the men, Carl Peck, is in charge of this operation and reports to Struthers. Peck is 52 years old.

At 8:15 A.M. incoming mail was sorted into various pigeon holes arranged by floor. At 9 A.M. the four mailboys made their "runs," delivering the mail that was in the pigeon holes to the various offices on their floors. While on their runs, they picked up mail and brought it back to the mailroom. The runs took about 20 minutes. On returning, they sorted the mail into the pigeon holes and placed any outgoing mail on the worktable of the outgoing section. These runs were repeated every hour on the hour until 4 P.M. The intraoffice personnel finished their day at 5 P.M. Struthers also finished work at this hour.

The three outgoing men reported for work at 10:30 A.M. They sorted the outgoing mail into various pigeon holes as it was brought to them by the mailboys. The mail was sealed, weighed, and affixed with postage. They also wrapped cartons and packages for mailing as these were sent down by various departments in the company. The work for the outgoing crew ended at 6:30 P.M., when they "closed up shop" and took the mail to the local post office.

All this work was performed in the same room. Although there was a division in the work performed between the outgoing and intraoffice

---

*From Robert E. C. Wegner and Leonard Sayles, *Cases in Organizational and Administrative Behavior*, © 1972, pp. 111–116. Reproduced by permission of Prentice Hall, Inc., Englewood Cliffs, New Jersey.

personnel, there were no partitions in the room. The outgoing personnel had their work space in one corner of the room, and the rest of it was occupied by the intraoffice personnel. There were only two desks in the rooms, Struther's and Peck's. The remainder of the furniture consisted of worktables, pigeon racks, and postage machines. There were chairs scattered in the room for the personnel to use between runs and during slack periods. The work was usually done while standing, although there were no rules requiring this.

Because of this layout, and the nature of the work performed, there was a lot of conversation and socializing. The work essentially required little attention. The relationship between Struthers and his subordinates was very informal, and usually there was considerable joking and bantering going on throughout the day. Struthers was well liked by his subordinates.

In general, the work situation was characterized by informality and harmony. The two work groups in the mailroom engaged in competition and rivalry both on and off the job. A game that often developed between the outgoing and intraoffice personnel was which group could get ahead of the other in clearing mail off their worktables and into the pigeon holes. The winners had first choice of the most comfortable chairs in the room. A similar game was played within the two groups. In spite of the intensity with which this game was played, there was mutual cooperation and "pitching in" in the instances when the workload became too heavy for one group or one individual.

Off the job, too, there was much socializing. It ranged from eating lunch together and pitching horseshoes during the lunch hour, to occasionally getting together and watching a weekend baseball game. Each summer the employees of the mailroom organized an informal picnic which was held at Struther's home. Generally, all the employees attended the picnics.

In February of my fifth year, a new mailboy was hired to replace one who had been promoted to another department. The new mailboy was Earl Snell. He was 21 years old, and had been employed twice before by other companies in the area. He took over the first-floor mail run.

Two weeks after Snell was hired, a change was introduced into the mailroom's operation. A data processing system was installed to handle customer accounts from the billing department. The system consolidated billing procedures, and was able to print out invoices which showed the amount customers owed Anderson Foods. The bills had previously been handled by secretaries who filled them in, placed them in envelopes, and sent them to the mailroom as they finished them. With the new system this tedious and time-consuming procedure was eliminated, and bills could be processed much more quickly. The bills were sent to the mailroom in stacks, where they were then separated into various regions and inserted into envelopes.

Because of the speed with which the machine processed the invoices, they could be handled efficiently only in large amounts. Hence the billing department ran the accounts off at irregular intervals during the day. The result was that the mailroom often received several hundred bills at a time and at irregular intervals. It was not uncommon to receive over 1,000 invoices in one day. Extra help was not hired in the mailroom because it was planned that the mailboys could help in separating and stuffing the bills into envelopes during their free time between runs.

From the outset of this new operation, I noticed a change in the atmosphere in the mailroom. The joking and bantering were not so prevalent; on several occasions, when some of the mailboys began joking while sorting the mail, Struthers was quick to tell them to "cut it out and keep your minds on your work."

The new mailboy, Snell, was a constant topic of conversation among the other employees. Snell always managed to be somewhere else when there was work to be done. His runs were never made on time, and he often took as long as an hour to get around on the first floor. Struthers was constantly receiving complaints from other department supervisors that Snell was socializing with the secretaries on his mail run and interfering with their work. When Struthers asked him where he had been and why his run had taken so long, Snell inevitably replied, "I had to go to the men's room." Once Snell said to me: "I get a kick out of Struthers. Every time I'm late, I tell him I had to go to the men's room. The number of times I've told him that I've gone to the men's room would have lasted any normal person a lifetime! He is so harmless, though, that even if he didn't believe me he wouldn't do anything about it."

Snell also irritated the other mailroom employees. He often commented that he couldn't wait to get out of the mailroom and into a better job. He couldn't imagine why anyone would settle for a career in such "meaningless" work. One habit of his particularly irritated the other employees. Snell often arrived just after they had cleared off the worktables and dumped another pile of mail on the table. They would complain to him and tell him to clear the table himself. This happened several times, and finally Snell went to Struthers and told him that he was being picked on. Struthers gathered everyone together and gave a "pep talk" about how everyone in the mailroom was expected to cooperate, help each other out. "I like to think of us in this mailroom as a team," said Struthers, "and not as a collection of individuals with individual jobs."

There were several cynical remarks made after Struthers's talk about "team spirit." The favorite expression became "rah, team spirit," when work had to be done. The rest of the employees decided that since Struthers wasn't going to do anything about Snell's lack of cooperation, they would do something about it themselves. The next time Snell arrived late with his mail, all the other employees told Struthers that they had to go to the men's room—and they left. Struthers then took Snell aside and spoke to him privately. After the conversation Snell left the room in a hurry.

Since I was the only one left in the room, Struthers came over to me. "I can't understand that kid. I've tried so hard to reason with him and get him to cooperate. I've gone out of my way to help him out. He only makes trouble for himself the way he acts, and will never get a promotion at this rate. I'm tempted to give him one, just to get him out of my hair! He's making a mess of this whole operation."

Later that afternoon Finnely, Struthers's supervisor, came to the mailroom to find out what was the matter. Snell had gone to him and told him that the employees, including Struthers, were picking on him. Finnely was not ignorant of the situation with Snell, for Struthers had mentioned it to him before. Finnely himself talked to the employees and told them that it was "kid stuff" to do what they had done in the morning. He said that the answer to the whole problem was to concentrate on work and learn to help each other instead of fighting each other.

But the situation didn't improve. Struthers had trouble getting the mailboys to take it on themselves to help with the invoices as they came in. They resented having to stop what they were doing in order to process the invoices when several hundred came in at a time. Often the invoices arrived late in the afternoon, and several employees would have to stay overtime in order to finish them. They couldn't understand why the invoices came in all at once instead of being spread out during the day. Struthers tried to explain to them that the machine could only process several hundred at a time. But this didn't convince them. Struthers himself often commented, "I understand their problems in the data processing, but I wish they would understand mine. There ought to be a better way of doing this. This procedure saves the boys upstairs headaches, but gives a lot of them to me."

The fact that Snell managed to dodge most of the invoice work irritated the other employees. One of them once commented: "Struthers is so gullible. If I were him, I would fire Snell in a second. I can't understand why he doesn't."

About this time Struthers revealed another change. For several months discussion had been going on about integrating some of the activities of the mailroom and the reproduction department, which was adjacent to the mailroom. The reproduction department, like the mailroom, was characterized by periods of intense activity and periods of relative quiet. The initial plan was to have the employees who were not busy in one department assist in the other department if they could be of help. Struthers was very concerned that the mailroom employees should cooperate all they could with the plan.

The cooperation never materialized. The employees suddenly found work which appeared to keep them occupied continuously in the mailroom. One employee was seen to empty the mail out of his pigeon holes and sort it back into them again. The cry was often heard: "Send Snell over to reproduction!" Struthers was upset over the lack of cooperation, and became more and more irritable. He was very concerned because no one was volunteering to help in reproduction, in spite of the fact that on several occasions reproduction had sent men over to the mailroom.

Toward the end of the summer someone mentioned that nothing had been said about the annual picnic. One of the other employees remarked that it was just as well. The lunchtime horseshoe game, a usual summer activity, had never gotten started and nobody ever bothered to play the game of "who could clear the worktables first" any more.

---

*The Fate of the Underwriters**

THE GRANVILLE INSURANCE COMPANY is a very large, nationally known firm with offices and subsidiary companies throughout every state. The company offers a complete line of insurance including life, accident and sickness, fire and theft, automobile, marine, commercial, and so on.

Nationally, Granville is broken down into five major zones; each zone office has under its jurisdiction several district offices to which the numerous branch offices report. The zone offices, of course, report to the headquarters or home office. One such zone office is located in Westchester County, New York. Its office building also accommodates one of the large district offices. It was this district office with which I was associated as a trainee, primarily in the Underwriting Department.

Essentially the underwriter's job is the evaluation of risks. It is the underwriter who must determine whether or not new business forwarded by the company's agents is acceptable, and whether or not the company wishes to continue to insure those persons or companies who have begun to exhibit unfavorable loss patterns. The underwriter's responsibility is therefore considerable, for the company's money is very directly tied to his judgment. In recognition of this, management pays the underwriter more than any of the other nonmanagerial employees. Of course actuaries earn more, given their high level of

---

*From Robert E. C. Wegner and Leonard Sayles, *Cases in Organizational and Administrative Behavior*, © 1972, pp. 137–144. Reproduced by permission of Prentice Hall, Inc., Englewood Cliffs, New Jersey.

professional training, and successful agents can earn more through high commissions. However, aside from managers and actuaries, the underwriter has the greatest prestige.

A life insurance underwriter must study intensely for several years and then pass rigorous examinations in order to become a chartered life underwriter. Factors such as this have increasingly added a professional status to the underwriter's job. Also the underwriters are considerably older than employees in other departments because of the management's belief that older people are more likely to have acquired the wisdom and maturity which are necessary for good judgment.

Granville's Underwriting Department is located on a large, open floor that is shared with other departments. Those underwriters who have served the company longest were given the presumably more desirable desks along the windows as well as the limited number of telephones which were used constantly. Since automobile insurance accounted for the vast majority of Granville's business, the greatest number of underwriters were also involved in this line. The entire Underwriting Department was under the direct supervision of the two assistant underwriter managers, Mr. Jason Coombs and Mr. Neil Russo.

Mr. Russo had been in automobile insurance underwriting for many years and was, therefore, more directly concerned with the supervision of the automobile underwriters. Coombs had previously been in life underwriting and devoted most of his time to this and to the other lines. Both men reported to Mr. Hurst, the underwriting manager.

Because the other lines of insurance (not including automobile) required only two or three underwriters each, we shall be primarily concerned with the automobile underwriters. These were broken down into two formal groups: the in force underwriters and the new business underwriters; each was composed of between 20 and 25 persons. In turn these were again divided into two informal groups. In the past several years, owing to retirements, firings, and growth, the personnel people had recruited quite a few younger people to be trained as underwriters. The result was that both formal groups were now composed of a younger set and an older set of people, with the older outnumbering the younger by about three to one. The disparity in age between the two groups was considerable and it was along these lines of age that the informal groups evolved.

The opportunities for informal interaction were rather limited during the working hours, but very much in evidence during lunch and coffee breaks. There did not at any time appear anything that might have been construed as animosity, jealousy, rivalry, or unfriendliness between the two groups. In fact, interactions which occurred were consistently of a friendly and cooperative nature. Certainly, the younger people had more in common with each other than with the older; they might also have been regarded by the older people—as well as by themselves—as being in a subordinate position (informally) since they were in what might have been regarded as an apprentice relationship to the older set.

INTERACTIONS OF THE UNDERWRITING DEPARTMENT

The underwriters interacted with almost every other department. Personnel was important from the standpoint of training and recruiting. Interaction with the sales force was particularly extensive, with agents constantly trying to "sell" the underwriter on the acceptability of the new business they wanted to put on the books. The claims people supplied vital data concerning the loss records of those whom the company had already insured. The Services Department supported the underwriters with essential clerical procedures, handling, and so forth. Perhaps public relations was the only unit that did not have a directly vital relationship with the Underwriting Department.

New procedures were constantly introduced. Each time a new interaction pattern was developed to accommodate a new procedure, it seemed that a new procedure was introduced which called for a complete revamping of the relevant interaction. Such changes were presented in an arbitrary "you will do this" manner by either of the two assistant underwriting managers or by Mr. Hurst, the underwriting manager. Often there was an attempt to "pass the buck" with comments such as "We're sorry about this, but it can't be helped. Zone wants a more efficient method of expediting new business handling, and this is how we've decided to do it."

Changes of this kind always included an opportunity to ask questions in case one did not completely understand his part in the newest procedure, but one was never to question the need for the procedure or offer an alternative procedure. Needless to say, the management never approached the underwriters with their problem beforehand; management did not solicit suggestions for its solution from those who were actually engaged in the work.

One such change particularly bothered the underwriters. The policy files unit, part of the Services Department, was intimately linked—perhaps more so than with any other area—with the underwriters. Composed of teenage girls (except for their supervisor) this unit had the primary responsibility of locating the file or files for any given insured, delivering these files to the members of any department that needed them, and later returning the files to their correct storage places. Furthermore, these girls were to keep the files in proper order. This meant that each paper within a file was to be fastened, chronologically, by means of a small metal fastening device on the folder of each file.

Simple as this duty appears, it involved no small amount of time. Many files carried over 100 pieces of paper, IBM cards, letters, forms, and the like, often of varying degrees of legibility. If one of those files came apart through handling, age, negligence, or whatever, it might require as much as 15 minutes to properly arrange and fasten it again. Those in charge had allowed these files to become sadly neglected in this respect. It was estimated that approximately 25 percent of the files were badly in need of attention. (The office contained about 800,000 files.)

One day Mr. Coombs and Mr. Russo called a meeting of the underwriters and informed them that henceforth it would be primarily their responsibility to see that no file ever left their desk without being first checked for the required chronology and attachment. If a file was in need of such attention, the underwriter was to provide it. Coombs and Russo admitted that the formal responsibility for such work was still actually the girls' in the policy file unit; but in view of these girls' apparent irresponsibility, disregard, and lack of interest, they felt that the more responsible underwriters ought to perform this duty. There was much resentment because of this change; the underwriters felt that they were not being paid to do "high-school kids'" work.

Another change of some importance concerned the training of the relatively large group of younger people in the department. Formerly a new underwriter trainee was left almost solely to his own devices; his training consisted entirely of on-the-job, catch-as-catch-can experience. However, management now felt that a certain amount of more formalized training was called for to complement the still-existing on-the-job training. With this in mind a few of the older and more experienced underwriters were relieved of their ordinary duties twice a week, and told to conduct a class composed of several trainees.

It is interesting to contrast this training program with those in such major departments as claims and sales. In the case of these two departments, the training program had been conducted solely under the auspices of the Personnel Department. For years, personnel had conducted formal classes—with full-time instructors—in these fields. Class sessions lasted all day for a number of weeks. With the exception of short speeches by various key personnel, claims and sales people were never actively involved in these training programs. The reason offered for the dissimilarity in these two training procedures was that that underwriting unit had never had as great a number of personnel that required training as did the other two departments.

For some inexplicable reason, the entire Underwriting Department was moved to another area on the floor—an area that was considerably more remote from other departments than the original location. Previously the underwriters had been in an area bordered on one side by the claims people, with whom considerable interaction was necessary, and on the other side by the crucial new business units which received work and instructions in a constant stream from the underwriters.

Underwriting now found that the only unit with which it had

face-to-face contact was the touring service unit. But with this unit they had no need for interaction. The result was an increase in misunderstandings in the interactions with claims and new business as well as a need for *more* interactions to straighten out these misunderstandings. Interaction with other units on other floors was also impeded by the fact that there were not as many phones in the new area as there had been in the previous area. Mr. Hurst promised to have this situation corrected; but as of three months later, no action had been taken.

The changes in management which occurred during this period also caused other problems. Originally Mr. Hurst was the underwriting manager; and there was only one assistant manager, Mr. Barry Thorson. When Mr. Thorson was promoted, it was announced that Mr. Russo, who had been in underwriting for many years and who had just completed the company's management training program, would take his place. It was further announced that Coombs, who had been hired from another company and was still in the management training program, would, on completion of the program, join Russo as a second assistant manager. It is worth mentioning that when Russo was selected for management training, most of the other underwriters felt that another underwriter, Mr. Rankin, would have been a better choice. There was a definite stereotype as to what an insurance executive should be in the Underwriting Department, and Mr. Russo did not correspond to this stereotype.

Neil Russo had been with the company for many years, though no longer than Mr. Rankin and for a lesser period than several others. He had never been to college as had most of the underwriters, particularly the younger ones. It was said that his speech was far from "polished," and at times even somewhat crude; and his manner of dress was, in the opinion of many, "flashy" and certainly not in the conservative vein they would have preferred to see. Many held similar reservations concerning the bright red sports car he drove. Coupled with the facts that he was unmarried, not a homeowner, and not a churchgoer, these observations were sufficient to convince the underwriters that Russo presented anything but the proper image. In his favor was the fact that he tried hard, when approached, to be friendly.

Mr. Coombs, when he arrived, turned out to be quite different from Russo. A conservatively dressed, college-educated person, he drove a black sedan, was noted to be more refined of speech, was married, and to complete the antithesis he was also a deacon at a local church. If one observed his interaction with his subordinates, however, quite another facet of the man would have been revealed. Interactions were few and almost always initiated by the subordinate. Coombs's speech was short and to the point, without a display of emotion. Most of the underwriters expressed the opinion that Coombs was "quite difficult to get to know."

Perhaps management itself held certain reservations concerning these two men. So far as was known, the installation of more than one assistant underwriting manager was unprecedented in the history of the zone. Furthermore, at the time the decision was made, it was generally known that certain executives had alleged that the reason for doing so was that both men were "relatively inexperienced."

During the time that these events were taking place, management found that underwriting's production had suffered to a large degree in terms of total output and in terms of output per man-hour. Concurrent with this finding, management was informed by personnel that a recent survey had revealed that morale in the Underwriting Department of the district office was at an extremely low level and was, in fact, lower than any other underwriting department in the country at the time.

Management decided to attack the former dilemma on two fronts, with a third measure to be utilized if necessary. First, the personnel Department was instructed to carry out an extensive recruiting campaign to hire more underwriting trainees. At the same time a former practice—much disliked by the underwriters—was again instituted in the Underwriting Department. At certain times of the year—notably in the late spring and again toward the very end of the year—people in the insurance business are unusually busy with an inordinate amount of paperwork. The underwriters, and particularly those in the in force unit, are especially deluged by the increased burden.

From time to time in the past, during these peak production periods, the underwriters had been "asked" to work overtime to handle this load. Their compensation for doing so amounted to $2.50 for "supper expenses." As salaried employees, they were not entitled to any overtime payments. Most of the trainees, however, were still employed on an hourly basis, and did not as yet enjoy the status of being on salary; consequently they received full remuneration for their overtime work.

Although management was aware that the underwriters deeply resented this practice (many had placed alternative suggestions in the company's suggestion box in the past), it was instituted anyway.

A third line of attack was held in reserve. Other district offices had been contacted to determine if any of these might be able to "loan" our district office some of their underwriting personnel to aid our Under-Writing Department during this period. Those district offices which were reasonably close and had anything even remotely resembling a surplus of underwriters were told by the zone office to stand by. This third alternative was never utilized.

Management did not seem to do anything concrete about trying to alleviate the morale problem. Actually management did not particularly seem to care about the morale of the underwriters. Morale was so low that our turnover rate was one of the highest in the company. Among those who left voluntarily was Mr. Rankin, the underwriter who had not been promoted at the time Russo was selected for management training. About a month after Mr. Rankin left, our manager Mr. Hurst turned in his resignation. It seemed to me that the handwriting was on the wall—the Underwriting Department was simply not a very favored one in the organization—so I quit in order to find employment in a more harmonious atmosphere. From what I hear from some of my old friends who are still working at Granville, things have continued to deteriorate since I left. I am certainly glad that I got out!

Fujiyama Trading Co., Ltd.

IN DECEMBER 1976, Mr. R. Nara, executive vice president of Fujiyama American Corporation (hereafter referred to as FAM), was sitting in his office in New York, recalling the day when he decided to hire an American MBA. It was in January 1976 when FAM first hired an American MBA as a future manager of the company.

FAM's parent company, Fujiyama Trading Co., Ltd. (hereafter referred to as FTC), is one of the Japanese "sogo-shosha," usually translated as "general trading companies," a distinctly Japanese business enterprise. Unlike specialized trading firms which limit their activities to specific types of products on a limited geographic basis, the sogo-shosha handles every kind of product and conducts import, export, and offshore transactions worldwide, as well as trade within Japan.

Characteristics of the sogo-shosha are: a great number of items traded; vast sales with small profit margins; worldwide office and information networks; a large number of highly skilled employees of many nationalities; intimate acquaintance with the law, business practices, trading procedures, customs, and languages of many countries; central position in diversified groups of companies and close ties with many other companies; central roles in the Japanese economy; and growing importance in international trade.

As of March 1977, FTC, one of the leading sogo-shosha in Japan, had a total of 8,400 staff members, including 1,400 employed in foreign countries who devoted themselves to customer service through international trade, development, and processing of natural resources overseas, as well as to distribution, financing, and many other areas.

The company transferred staff members on planned rotation through a variety of jobs to help younger staff members develop into well-rounded employees capable of handling all facets of the company's business. These transfers were made not only within FTC's domestic divisions, but also to overseas offices and subsidiaries.

FAM is FTC's wholly owned (100 percent shares) subsidiary and contributes a growing percentage (currently over 15 percent) to FTC's overall business. FAM, with 12 offices in the United States, has literally become an American sogo-shosha. At any given moment, FAM's divisions are engaged in the import and export of thousands upon thousands of different commodities and products. Simultaneously, they may be working on such diverse ventures as the creation and organization of a consortium of enterprises from different countries to search for and develop new energy or mineral resources. Several may be involved, in unison, in planning and coordinating the construction of ports, plants, or pipelines. Still another division may be guiding an American firm in its first attempt at creating an international market for its products.

FAM's New York head office had 100 Japanese staff members and 200 American staff members. Among the American staff, about 30 were male employees and the remaining were female employees, all of whom were engaged in clerical jobs. In order for the company to meet equal opportunity commitments, some of the top managers of FAM had discussed the hiring of Americans as prospective managers. In other words, in order to avoid trouble and to get government business, it was decided that the company should have a certain percentage of American managers among the total officers of the company.

Mr. Nara, 47 years old, office manager of the New York head office, was in favor of starting and developing this program of hiring prospective American managers. He had spent 25 years with the parent company, including eight years in the United States as office manager in Los Angeles and two years in Argentina. As such, he was interested in management in different cultures and had studied it himself. After one year as an executive vice president, he asked the Personnel Department to find American MBAs suitable as future managers. He commented:

> Through my long experience of working overseas, I have always recognized the differences of managerial cultures. As you are well aware, the American society is based upon individualism, free mobility, and less human-oriented organizations, which has resulted in a very unique and efficient organization. However, it is not necessarily true that this type of organization can function well under any culture and society.
>
> The Japanese organization, of course, is based on the peculiar Japanese value system. In a word, it is often said that America is individual-oriented, while Japan is group-oriented. In America, personal responsibility is always emphasized and one's authority and responsibility are clarified. I think that the job description, for example, comes from this idea. The reason why job descriptions have not been developed in Japan as a basis of personnel or organizational administration is because of differences of culture and social value systems.
>
> In Japanese organizations, authority tends to be a vague concept,

which makes it somewhat hard for each individual to take clear responsibility. Sometimes responsibility is regarded as an ambiguous concept by the Japanese manager. The process of Japanese decision making is very much like consensus building, which makes it harder to determine who should take final responsibility.

The basic principle of Japanese organization is not an authoritarian command, but *wa* (harmony), which is achieved by mutual consideration. The "group-oriented" tendency of Japanese people is related to such Japanese management practices as lifetime employment and seniority systems. These practices reflect the Japanese concept of household, which holds that the high born and powerful have an obligation and a social responsibility to protect the less fortunate and less powerful.

Under such practices, the future of all employees depends upon the performance of the company as a unit. Therefore in Japan, more than in America, management and employees cooperate in working toward the goal of a successful company. We often say "spirit of belonging" or "love for the company" to express our loyalty, which is the outcome of the above-mentioned atmosphere. In short, for the Japanese people, corporate life does not only mean the profit center, but also the social unit where one achieves emotional satisfaction.

As such, the people we want are those who can demonstrate skill at building good personal relationships and performing so-called team work. When we hire college students, for example, observation of their personality takes priority over their special knowledge such as accounting, economics, marketing, and so forth. Therefore, we usually hire college students as soon as they graduate and train them. After joining a company, the college graduates usually find themselves initially spending some time working and learning in two or three departments in the company. This on-the-job training continues for a couple of years during which they gain a wide range of experience in all aspects of the company operation.

Because of such differences about the concept of the business community, I don't believe that American managers would work efficiently or happily if we hired them away from other companies. If we really want an American to manage our organization, we have to train him by on-the-job training and keep him with the company for a long time in order for him to feel loyalty.

I do not deny that in any society organizations must be established on the basis of the value system which prevails in that society for the organization to survive and develop in that society. It is easy to say, but hard to do. I can easily imagine that Japanese staff would not be able to work efficiently here, if they have to work in the type of working environment as in the United States. This will result in unfavorable performance of the company, which I, as a manager, have to avoid. Therefore the very crucial thing is, I believe, how to find the meeting point.

Of course, it is necessary for us to be somewhat Americanized, but at the same time, it is also necessary for the Americans to be Japanized, if they want to work for such a company as ours. In other words, we will preserve our basic Japanese system, which is a very good system, but make the proper adaptations to operating in America.

To begin with, Mr. Nara ordered the establishment of Japanese language classes, opened a library with a lot of books about Japan, and offered flower arrangement classes in the company. These programs were offered for the purpose of raising the American staff's sense of belonging to the company and letting them understand various aspects of Japan. Every program was operated at the company's expense. These programs were very well received by the American employees.

Although these programs were offered mainly for the lower-level staff, Mr. Nara thought of having MBAs join them when they were hired, so as to let them understand Japan. What was in Mr. Nara's mind for after this, was to send MBAs to Japan for several years so that they could learn and experience the Japanese managerial way, business customs, ways of thinking, and so forth; and then to send them back to the United States. By so doing, Mr. Nara believed that MBAs would understand how to bridge the gap between two cultures and function better as international managers.

Upon receiving the order from Mr. Nara, the staff of the Personnel Department, who had just been brought from Japan to establish that department, began to contact several business schools, which were supposed to be interested in Japan, to inform them of the company's desire to hire MBAs. As a result of this, FAM had 15 inquiries and the personnel staff had an interview with each of them. At that time, the company policy was to hire one or two MBAs on a trial basis. The Personnel Department picked five students who seemed to be interested in working for a Japanese company, and left the final decision to Mr. Nara. Through personal interviews, Mr. Nara decided to hire two prospective MBAs.

Mr. Karl Smith was one of the two hired. He had gone to a small college in Maine that reflected and stressed the traditional "Yankee" values of independence, hard work, and self-reliance. After college he continued his education by studying for an MA in international relations at City College of New York. Following this, he took a job with the Savings Bank Life Insurance Company in New York, but continued to study Middle East politics at night. Finally he enrolled full-time in the MBA program and joined FAM at the age of 27. At that time, he described himself as follows:

> My personal goal is to become a top manager in a large corporation. Power, status, luxury, and quick decision making . . . that's the life for me. For this purpose, I'll face up to any difficulties and not run away from them. I don't mind if my whole life revolves around business. I am an aggressive type of person and feel bad if someone gets ahead of me.

The MBA program was a great program that emphasized basic principles of management. I found their emphasis, on such ideas as clear job descriptions and individual accountability, as well as on promotions based on merit, compatible with my philosophy that the rewards of life should go to those who perform the best. The program was just the starting point for my career goals. They gave me some of the skills I will need to be a success!

Mr. Nara made a comment on his decision to hire Karl:

He was more enthusiastic than the others. He personally was interested in Arab countries and he was a member of a study group about Arab politics with other MBA students at the university. Some of them are actually working over there now.

The passion for one, specific thing, which is not necessarily inside the realm of work, is also very important. I remember hiring a guy who was a great college baseball player in Japan, and this led me to feel that he would demonstrate self-discipline, loyalty, and commitment to the company. I have recently seen many young people who don't know what their goals are or even what they would like to do. The person who is vague about these things is useless. If one has devoted himself to a specific thing, it would be possible for him to demonstrate loyalty and commitment to the company for a long time. As a matter of fact, Karl told me that he had a passion for hunting with bow and arrow. I heard that he even makes his own bows and arrows, which is really a specialty.

I also saw another reason for my decision. As you are well aware, Arab countries have a tremendous amount of Eurodollars because of sales of oil and they are trying to industrialize with their earnings. We have technology and knowledge about how to industrialize. There exists a great possibility for us to win big projects in those countries. In such a situation, if we hired Karl, he will be able to provide us with some valuable information. That is why I have come up with the final decision.

Mr. Nara thought that Ferrous Metal Products Division would be best fitted for Mr. Smith and assigned him to this division as the immediate subordinate of Mr. Y. Kato, who was an assistant manager of the division.

As usual with the Japanese trading company, most college graduates find themselves spending time in two or three departments after joining a company so as to develop their general knowledge. Thereafter they begin to specialize. Since the commodities handled vary tremendously, it is necessary for the company to have a specialist in the particular commodity in order to respond to the customer's needs.

Mr. Nara had been dealing with the exporting of steel products since he joined the company. During the 25 years which he had spent in this business, he had brought up many subordinates, a number of whom had become managers of overseas offices themselves. Almost all 120 overseas offices handle steel products. It can be said that Mr. Nara has his subordinates all over the world. One of his subordinates, Mr. Kato had spent his 15 years with the company in the business of selling steel products. During this period, while he had had several trips overseas he had never worked in any of the company's overseas offices. At the beginning of January 1976, he was transferred to the FAM New York office as an assistant manager of the Ferrous Metal Products Division. He recalled the first impression he had when he joined the New York office:

> When I was working in Japan, whenever I was not too busy, I used to take subordinates, sometimes including female employees in section, to the bar to have a talk with them over glass of beer. It was very useful to talk to them in an informal place out of office to get to know them. Sometimes they complained about company policy or customers and sometimes they consulted about personal matters. I believe these relationships were very basis of my management style. I don't think I can manage people without knowing them. Interpersonal relationship between subordinates and myself was that of support and dependence instead of dominance and submission. However, when I first came here, I was really shocked with American people's practical and businesslike way of thinking. I couldn't see any warm human relationships. For example, every female employee leaves office exactly at five o'clock. When one female clerk was working most hard the other day, other female clerk sitting next to her, never helped at all even though she did not have any work to do because of boss's absence. These kinds of things never happen in Japan. If I ask female employee to work overtime, she willingly did it. When someone was very busy, others gave help. I think this is way it's supposed to be.
>
> However, this does not happen here as in Japan and in this way New York office is not comfortable place to work. I am not criticizing company policy about hiring MBAs, because I am loyal and also respect Mr. Nara. But, having American MBA assigned to department is personally unpleasant for me. I've just arrived in this country and I am not good English speaker, so I have hard time dealing with American people. If I cannot communicate well, it's going to be embarrassing to them and me as well.

Mr. Smith joined Mr. Kato's division one month after Mr. Kato was transferred to New York. Mr. Smith quickly learned the steel business through the instruction given him by the other employees and through his inherent aggressiveness and enthusiasm. In the course of teaching the business to him, his peers tried to get him involved in their jobs as well. He had the impression that he was receiving special attention, and he felt pleased that the other managers apparently recognized his knowledge of Arab countries. On the contrary, Mr. Smith's peers were merely trying to make him understand how the Japanese organization works utilizing a group approach.

In October 1976, the company had to send someone to Saudi Arabia for finalizing the business negotiation of exporting steel products to a certain engineering company there. Mr. Kato's boss suggested sending

Mr. Smith to Saudi Arabia, because he thought that this opportunity might give Mr. Smith incentive and motivation. However, Mr. Kato wanted to conclude this business deal without any trouble, and he felt that a Japanese staff member could work more cooperatively with the Japanese staff of Jedda than Mr. Smith could. Furthermore, Mr. Kato thought that Mr. Smith was not yet really ready to represent the company, having observed Mr. Smith's everyday behavior in the office. However, keeping in mind his boss's suggestion, he reluctantly decided to send Mr. Smith, taking into account his abundant knowledge of Arab countries.

At Jedda International Airport, Mr. Smith was welcomed by a staff member of FTC's Jedda office, who had been informed of his arrival beforehand. The staff member spoke to him:

> How do you do, Mr. Smith? How was your trip? If you are not tired, I'd like to have lunch with you and talk about the upcoming business negotiation. Also I can tell you about some of the people you are going to meet, that might be helpful to you. By the way, I used to work as a subordinate of Mr. Nara before and he took very good care of me. How is he doing lately? . . .

Mr. Smith, on the other hand, was surprised with the man's coming to the airport to see him, he thought to himself:

> Gee, I don't understand why he came to the airport to see me. He must have been very busy with his own job. I could go to my hotel or the company office or luncheon meeting without any help. It is a waste of his time, an unnecessary expense, and surely not a professional way to conduct business when time is short.

Karl spoke courteously with the staff member, but kept the conversation on pleasantries and got away from him as soon as he could. This left the staff member feeling very perplexed. He could not understand why Karl asked so few questions of a business nature, nor why he left so abruptly after they reached the Jedda office. He wondered if he had said something that violated American customs, such as mentioning his past association with Mr. Nara (to which Karl had hardly responded). He certainly felt badly that he had been of so little assistance to Mr. Smith.

Besides his original business negotiation, Karl was supposed to meet Mr. Henry Bodwell, his friend from the MBA program, who held an important position in a Saudi Arabian company. When they met, Karl got some confidential information from Mr. Bodwell, which was that Freedman Construction, Inc., of the United States had undertaken a big project for the government of Saudi Arabia. The project was to develop a big outer harbor at Jedda, including construction of berths, highly developed mechanical loaders and unloaders, and many infrastructures. In total, it would amount to about $100 million.

For the steel divisions of FTC and FAM, this type of project was one of the most desirable ones. Since the division earns profit on a commission basis (usually 2.5–3 percent of steel price, which is about $300 per ton) in accordance with the quantity handled, big projects which allow the division to deal with large quantities of steel (15,000–20,000 tons for this project) are always sought by everybody in the division.

Almost all of the people and agencies interested in this project thought that nobody had yet successfully undertaken this project, because the press release was not yet scheduled. Knowing this information, Karl thought there existed the possibility of his selling a large quantity of Japanese steel products to Freedman, Inc., if he approached them before anybody after he got back to New York. On the way back to New York, he was excited about this.

> I'm the one who found out about this project. I can take the initiative and responsibility also. I must finalize this project independently at any cost. This is a damn good opportunity to demonstrate my knowledge about the Arab countries and my confidence in carrying out new business. If I make it, my status in the company will be well established and I will be relied upon by my fellow employees and my bosses as well. The company should appreciate this and my status will rise. Since I was not familiar with the steel business, I have had to be passive in most cases, however from now on, I will be able to be more active and assertive. . . .

After getting back to New York, he reported to Mr. Kato about his original business, and quietly started approaching Freedman, Inc.

When he was asked by Mr. Kato or his fellow workers what he was doing, he used to say that it was not important and he never talked much.

> I'm not going to disclose this opportunity to anyone until I've made real progress. If I do, it will be talk, talk, talk, and more talk. Time will be lost, and more than likely someone outside the company will hear about it. If I carry the ball myself, the company will get the jump on other companies, I'll establish my capability and credibility, and everyone will gain an unexpected dividend. As Professor Chandler used to say, the way to get a job done right, is to assign it to one man and then hold him responsible for results.

In November, Karl succeeded in making contact with a vice president of Engineering for Freedman, Inc. Karl's strategy was to influence the design specifications written by Freedman's Engineering Department. He believed that if he could convince Freedman of the superiority and competitiveness of the quality and price of Japanese steel, then they would write the design specifications in a manner that insured the acceptability, and even favored the use, of Japanese steel. Karl knew that it was important that the specifications not rule out the use of Japanese steel in favor of steel from some other country and he also knew that in Mr. Kato's experience Japanese steel mills would nominate Fujiyama (FTC) as the exclusive negotiator in appreciation for its efforts in attaining "good" specifications.

Karl's discussions with the Freedman vice president were successful; however, there was one condition; namely, the approval of the specifications by the Saudi government. Time was urgent because Freedman had to send the design drawings containing the specifications to the Saudi government in two weeks.

Karl knew that personal connections were very crucial for doing business in Saudi Arabia, therefore he believed that he had to hold direct negotiations with some suitable person in the Saudi government. Keeping in mind the time element involved to prepare the necessary data, Karl believed that he had to fly to Jedda immediately. He felt sure that he could make an appointment with the "key" men of the Saudi government through the cooperation of Mr. Bodwell; and then through "person-to-person" negotiations have them accept the desired specifications.

Therefore he went to Mr. Kato and told him all about the project and the necessity of getting an approval from the government of Saudi Arabia. He asked Mr. Kato for permission to make the trip to Saudi Arabia at once. Mr. Kato was very surprised with this and said:

> Why have you done this all by yourself so far? As you know, we are not manufacturing steel products, therefore, you are supposed to ask about the possibility of getting such a quantity of steel products from Japan first of all. And you have not gotten any approval from the Tokyo office as to this project. Nor have you ever consulted our two offices in Saudi Arabia. If you keep going with this project without cooperation with offices in Saudi Arabia, they will lose face toward Tokyo office, as will others. You are supposed to know that the overseas offices can get commission as a certain percentage of business transactions around the office area. The more the office is involved in the business, the more commission it can get. . . . This time, I think you had better stay in the office and ask the staffs in Saudi Arabia to negotiate with the person in the government. . . .

Mr. Smith was very much disappointed with Mr. Kato's decision and said:

> Maybe you don't know, but personal connections are very important for conducting business over there, and I have that connection. I need no coordinator. This is a project that will be very beneficial to the company; if necessary, I'll ask offices in Saudi Arabia for help myself. I must have permission to go over there.

In order to decide anything, in Japanese business society, people are expected to lay the ground work and get the consensus of everybody involved before taking any action. Mr. Kato was very dissatisfied with Mr. Smith's taking action on his own and finally told Mr. Smith: "As long as you work for Japanese company, you are supposed to understand the Japanese way. . . ."

Very much disappointed with Mr. Kato's words, Mr. Smith went to Mr. Nara's office, told him all about what was going on, and complained:

> I have to leave New York for Jedda at once to get approval from the government of Saudi Arabia. I already have a personal connection, which is a "must" over there for this kind of negotiation. I want to do this even at the risk of losing my job. Since you have influence over the staff of the steel division in Saudi Arabia, you can take care of them. However, I have to go there as soon as possible. Please let me go!

Mr. Nara thought about the impact on everybody and of all the offices which would be affected by his saying yes or no. Whichever his decision, it must be made immediately.

GenRad, Inc.*

INTRODUCTION

For 52 years, management at GenRad steadfastly resisted the growth-ethic, and placidly watched its market leadership position erode, and then vaporize. During this same period of time, GenRad, considered by some economic historians to be the oldest electronics manufacturing firm in the world, slipped into relative obscurity as its competitors caught the world's attention and imagination with their dizzying success. Through it all GenRad had remained loyal to its early values, and had refrained from changing those values while adjusting to a very different reality from the one during which those beliefs had been fashioned.

By 1972, 57 years after its founding, GenRad had nearly become illiquid after having recorded a loss of $2.3 million on sales of $33 million. GenRad's performance since 1972 had been remarkable, and had resulted from the actions taken by a new management team that was installed in 1973. In many respects, GenRad's recent history was an example of a classic management and performance turnaround.

---

*Adapted from the Harvard Business School case authored by J. Stewart Dougherty under the supervision of Assistant Professor Robert G. Eccles. © 1981 by the President and Fellows of Harvard College.

In 1979, GenRad manufactured and marketed electronic test equipment. Fifty-five percent of the company's revenues were generated by sales of highly sophisticated test instruments referred to as automatic test equipment (ATE). ATE products were sold to users and manufacturers of electronic equipment, such as manufacturers of computers, peripherals, office equipment, telecommunications devices, and defense electronics. Twenty-five percent of the company's revenues were derived from sales of less sophisticated and more traditional electronic test instruments. Customers for these less exotic testers were participants in the electronic equipment industry, also. Frequently, purchasers of ATE products would be purchasers of GenRad's more standard testers as well. GenRad had carried many of the standard test products for years, and even decades. The above products were designed and manufactured in the company's Electronic Manufacturing Test (EMT) Division. The remaining 20 percent of GenRad's revenues were derived from the sale of electronic testers to manufacturers of mechanical equipment, such as automobiles, missiles, oil drilling platforms (onshore and offshore), engines, turbines, satellites, airframes, and bridges. The Acoustics and Vibration Analysis (AVA) Division was responsible for this portion of the company's sales. By 1979, 65 percent of the company's sales were made within the United States, 25 percent throughout Europe, and the remaining 10 percent elsewhere around the world.

The ATE market was burgeoning in February 1979 when GenRad's senior officers met to conduct their annual review of the company's operations and affairs. At that meeting, when the participants totaled their strategic projections, it was found that GenRad's 1984 sales level was expected to top $400 million. This figure would represent an increase of 340 percent over GenRad's 1978 sales of $89.3 million and would reflect a 28 percent compound annual growth rate. This projection was a marked increase over the company's former five- and ten-year compound annual growth rates of 14.2 percent and 14.4 percent, respectively. If the projections were correct, it was safe to conclude that the GenRad of 1984 would be vastly different from the GenRad of 1979.

Given GenRad's bright prospects, one might have assumed that a sense of jubilation would have prevailed at the management meeting. There was, instead, a certain anxiety that emanated from deep within GenRad's managers. It was the anxiety that is born of the prospect of fundamental change. For what GenRad's management could not deny was that, for the company to reach the 1984 that they envisioned, drastic changes would have to occur, and promptly.

In July 1979, a special task force was commissioned by President Thurston to examine the firm's organizational and structural situation as of 1979 and to determine if the then-present organization was capable of carrying GenRad into the 1984 of its executives' expectations. The name of this special committee was the Organizational Development Study Group (ODSG).

A HISTORY OF THE COMPANY: 1915–1972

The Eastham Years: Setting the Basic Values

The General Radio Company (renamed GenRad late in 1975) was founded in 1915 by Melville Eastham, a self-taught engineer who became known for his innovative technological devices and for the strong social conscience that guided his actions as an employer and a businessman.

Eastham's interest was in technological excellence and innovative brilliance. From the company's earliest days, management was dedicated to manufacturing high-quality, state-of-the-art, innovative electronic test instruments. GenRad's products were sold at prices that included high margins, and company profits were, therefore, flush. Products were not expected to sell in high quantities, but rather to fill the specific and often unique needs of GenRad's customers. Since engineering innovation was so highly valued at the company, creative engineers found GenRad to be a congenial place at which to work.

GenRad's record in the 1920s and 1930s was impressive. For example, the company manufactured the world's first commercial vacuum tube voltmeter and wave analyzer. In the 1940s it was frequently the recipient of special military commendations for its engineering successes. But as a result of its emphasis on technological innovation, GenRad often fell behind in recognizing the changing dynamics of the electronic test equipment marketplace. Low-priced instruments were meeting the testing needs of a wide array of users and were gaining general market acceptance. GenRad's engineers, on the other hand, were designing exotic instruments which had fewer general applications. Therefore, the company came to cede an increasing amount of business to its more market-oriented competitors.

Somewhat curiously, given the company's commanding technological lead in the field of electronic test equipment and the burgeoning demand for such equipment, Eastham committed the company to policies of slow growth and private ownership. Growth was to be fueled solely by internal earnings and limited borrowings.

The company's style of management was similarly unique. In 1939, top management officially espoused a policy of management by committee. Committees were formed to look after every aspect of the business, including general management, new products, research and development, pricing, and patents. Eastham was strongly opposed to conflict (though not to "brisk, polite debate") and set the direction for the firm by merely intimating his wishes during the various committee meetings. Although an emphasis was placed on management by committee, some thought that Eastham was actually in sole command. Thurston had observed: "Even though Eastham had the various committees fully in place by the early 1940s, he continued to dominate the management of the company. People were too polite, and had too much respect for the founder to challenge him."

Just as the company's engineers developed products that were ahead of their time, so did Eastham establish human resource policies that were extremely advanced for their day. Under Eastham's philosophy, job security was of paramount importance. Therefore, he disallowed plant shutdowns and layoffs. In fact, even during the Great Depression, there were no layoffs despite a steep downturn in business. Rather, production and shift schedules were revised to distribute the existing work evenly among all employees. Eastham was progressive in believing that a company's profits should be shared by stockholders, management, *and* employees, and the firm pioneered in the implementation of employee benefits, profit sharing, and bonus programs. The company maintained a liberal holiday policy and offered a relatively short work-week. Another core practice at GenRad was promoting from within. Virtually all jobs in the managerial and supervisory hierarchy were filled by the advancement of understudies who had years of experience in a subordinate position. When Eastham retired in 1948, his values were firmly established at the company. However, the sense of comprehensive direction he gave the organization departed with him.

The Postwar Years: Emergence of an Industry

After World War II, GenRad faced a dilemma. Many new electronics firms were growing rapidly. Military R&D money was nearly free for the asking and success in the electronics field was becoming the rule, not the exception. As Thurston later remarked, "In the postwar years, you grew in spite of yourself."

But GenRad's top management viewed the postwar environment with concern and skepticism. They believed that a major depression was imminent and, therefore, refused to accept military R&D funds or to develop a growth strategy.

The premium for this policy was exorbitant. Two of the company's prime competitors, Hewlett-Packard and Tektronics (founded in 1939 and 1946, respectively), aggressively met the growing electronics industry's needs for test and measurement instrumentation by committing to rapid growth and massive product development programs. The early 1950s were troubled times for GenRad. During these years the company continued to pioneer in the development of a broad range of technically innovative products, but the percentage of new products that was successful in the marketplace declined.

Indeed, GenRad's product policy may have been outmoded altogether, given the rapid evolution of the electronics industry. Thurston described the company's product approach in this way: "The product policy was to 'skim the cream from the top,' offering only one or a very few products in each instrument category, with each product the best of its type available, and priced accordingly [i.e., at a substantial premium]."

By 1954, when Hewlett-Packard swept by GenRad in sales volume, the market had repudiated that policy. Nonetheless, GenRad's management remained confident that their policies were correct, and were heard to say, "We have seen them pass us on the way up, and we will see them pass us on the way down." Their prophecies were to prove to be unenlightened.

During the first 48 years of GenRad's history, the firm was overseen by only three presidents. Eastham was followed by Erroll H. Locke as president from 1948 to 1955. Charles C. Carey served from 1955 until his death in 1963. Both Locke and Carey had risen through the manufacturing ranks and fully espoused Eastham's management philosophies. GenRad's management was almost religiously dedicated to the company's founder.

Donald B. Sinclair: A Time of Tentative Change

A new era was ushered in at GenRad when Dr. Donald B. Sinclair was chosen to succeed C. C. Carey as president of the company in 1963. After receiving his doctorate in 1936 from MIT, Sinclair joined GenRad full time and rose through the engineering ranks. He served as chief engineer, vice president, engineering, and then executive vice president and technical director, prior to being elected president.

For all of Sinclair's attempts to preserve the harmony that had characterized GenRad's past, significant discontent with the company's traditional management philosophy and policies was being aired by 1967. Several of GenRad's junior executives expressed a consensus that the firm's preoccupation with technological innovation (at the expense of developing coordinated product strategies) and its commitment to slow growth were no longer appropriate strategies given the changes taking place in the industry. Eventually, Sinclair began to agree with the dissenters, and he decided to begin to steer the company on a new course. In 1967, he issued a manifesto entitled, "Company Policies and Objectives," which tentatively outlined the new direction he proposed for the company. He had written the manifesto with the active collaboration of William Thurston. Never before had such a comprehensive statement been issued by the company's management.

The 1967 Statement on Policies and Objectives

It was written in the document that for the first time in GenRad's history, management would espouse a growth policy. Simultaneously (and no less of a dramatic break with the past), the report stated that the company would adopt a focused product strategy and a narrow product line, which would enable the company to build upon its special strengths.

The announcement to pursue growth and narrow the product lines was accompanied by several determined rededications to superannuated company principles. For example, the statement reemphasized the policy of internal, private ownership of the company. Committee management was reinforced. The policy of continuous employment with no layoffs ("fluctuations in business are taken care of by adjustment of inventory and hours of work rather than by the size of the work force") was reaffirmed. The policy of promoting from within was restated. Indeed, despite the fact that the company was dramatically altering its product policy and that the competitive environment had changed drastically, the document stated that the company's traditional premium price structure would remain intact and that head-on competition on a price basis would be avoided.

Acquisitions

As these changes occurred, the company made two acquisitions in 1969, in apparent conflict with the goal to rationalize the product line. The acquired companies were Time/Data of Santa Clara, California, and Grason-Stadler of Concord, Massachusetts.

Management Changes

Throughout 1972, GenRad's board of directors wrestled with the issue of management succession at the company. After a complicated and lengthy internal selection process, it was announced on December 29, 1972, that William R. Thurston had been elected president of GenRad. Sinclair was elevated to the position of chairman/chief executive officer. Steven J. Stadler, a former partner in Grason-Stadler, was named senior vice president and chief financial officer, effective February 1973. Ivan G. Easton (formerly vice president, engineering), the chief financial officer and a 35-year veteran of the company, announced his retirement effective February 1973. Meanwhile, the enthusiasm over the new growth policy collided with the reality of the company's dramatically escalating financial problems in 1972. By January 1973, the company realized that, for the first time since the Great Depression, it had lost money in 1972. The actual loss was a staggering $2.3 million on sales of $33 million. Over $1 million of the total loss was posted by GenRad's 1969 Time/Data acquisition. Other contributors were high R&D spending, inefficient manufacturing processes, and high inventory levels.

The news of the loss was unexpected. Given the state of the firm's financial and accounting systems, there was no sure way that management might have known the state of the company's financial condition prior to the closing of the books at year's end.

In the wake of the company's devastating 1972 financial performance, Sinclair announced in February 1973 that he would resign as chairman effective at the March 1974 annual meeting. Thurston was to become CEO as well as president of the company, effective March 1974. In accepting the position, Thurston had agreed to shepherd the firm through a dire period in its history. Whether or not GenRad would survive as an independent company could not be foretold in 1973.

WILLIAM R. THURSTON: A VOICE FOR CHANGE

Bill Thurston started working at GenRad in 1941 as an MIT Coop student. After receiving his BSEE in 1943, he worked full time doing classified ultrahigh frequency development projects for the defense department. He received a master's from MIT in 1948 and that year moved to sales. As a sales engineer in the early and mid-1950s, Thurston recognized that the company's products were no longer the most respected items of their kind.

By 1967, Thurston and several other "young turks" had persuaded management with the force of their arguments. By continuously challenging management's reasons for adhering to certain inbred policies, he had led them to recognize, for themselves, that the past approaches were no longer appropriate. When Thurston's arguments that the company should follow growth and narrow product line strategies prevailed, his colleagues could not have failed to notice that he was meeting with success in establishing a new set of values at GenRad. When asked why he continued to flout convention by inflicting his opposing views on management, he replied, "Because I was as stubborn as they were" (in attacking the old approaches that they had been defending). In fact, he noted that many of his debates with Sinclair in committee meetings had become "shouting matches," but that they had survived those contests "with genuine mutual respect and warm feelings." While Thurston was experimenting with open conflict, he noted that covert politics thrived beneath the surface with vigorous force.

In 1968 a major part of Sinclair's 1967 statement of mission became reality when the New Products Committee announced that the product portfolio would be decreased from 20 product line areas (containing over

2,000 discrete products) to three. The number of products would likewise be reduced drastically. This announcement marked the company's first actual commitment to fundamental change, and served to open the floodgates of transition upon the firm. This "concentration policy" was to be accomplished by allocating all new product development resources to the three selected product areas, while milking the 17 remaining product lines.

During the period from 1968 through 1972, Thurston pursued his duties as vice president, marketing. When he assumed the role of president of GenRad in 1973, he was faced with the challenge of steering the firm away from disaster.

1973: TURNING AROUND AN AILING COMPANY

Thurston's first action as president of GenRad was to disband all committees, and to thereby place key responsibilities in the hands of individual managers. Next, Thurston took a decisive step to limit the firm's R&D expenditures, which had risen from the historical level of 10 percent of sales to 14 percent of sales in 1972. The reductions meant that entire projects were discontinued.

He also announced plans to shorten the new product development cycle, and to improve the commercial success of future new products by continuing to upgrade the firm's marketing capabilities. He further vowed to equalize the status and influence of the engineering, manufacturing, and marketing functions, thus signalling that the engineering department would no longer be the dominant function at GenRad in terms of status and influence. Thurston expressed a strong commitment to establishing production inventory control, quality control, strategic planning, and project costing systems within the company. Finally, he nominated three additional outside directors to the board. The first outside director in the history of the company had joined the board in 1972. After the election of the nominees to the board, outside members had a controlling voice.

In December 1973, Thurston took the unusual step of recruiting an outsider, Richard Cambria, to head up a new personnel department. Prior to joining GenRad, Cambria had worked in various capacities within the personnel department at Exxon. Thurston had said that by hiring outsiders, he planned to obtain the services of "those who had done it [i.e., performed the respective function] before, at large companies. We didn't want to reinvent the wheel."

Cambria took action promptly. As he studied the company, he and the other senior managers concluded that the work force was too large given the company's business level, and that benefits, in general, were far too liberal. Consequently, the company announced a work force reduction that affected 100 employees, most of whom were located in the Massachusetts facilities. Cambria said that this, the second layoff in the company's entire history, "immediately increased the level of urgency in the company." During 1975, more work force reductions occurred, particularly in the nonexempt ranks. Next, Cambria trimmed employee vacations and increased the standard work week from 37½ to 40 hours. Despite these disruptions, Cambria felt that the employees were pleased with what was happening at the company: "Most of the production people said, 'It's about time. We've been moribund.'"

When asked how long a time he thought that the employees believed GenRad had been moribund, Cambria replied, "It's bizarre, but I would say that they thought GenRad had been moribund for most of its life."

TOWARD RECOVERY: 1975 TO 1978

By 1975 the company's sales and profits were increasing and the strategic wisdom of the decision to push forward in the ATE field was becoming evident. Thurston issued a document in 1975 entitled, "GenRad—Corporate Objectives and Strategy." It was similar in many ways to Sinclair's 1967 statement.

In the 1975 statement, Thurston reaffirmed his commitment to long-range thinking and strategic planning. He rededicated himself to the concept of maintaining a narrow product line. He observed that the company's high inventory levels would have to be reduced. He announced a decision to implement zero-based budgeting and MBO systems within the company. An office for corporate planning was created. A commitment was made to adopt formal personnel and management training procedures. Furthermore, Thurston remained dedicated to the growth policy that had first been enunciated in Sinclair's 1967 statement.

The company became publicly owned in June 1978. The pressure placed on management by the holders of GenRad's old stock, which was illiquid from 1973 through 1978, was relieved. But more, the move helped to change the company's image from that of a slow-moving equipment manufacturer to an advanced electronics technology firm committed to growth.

Many stock analysts were enthusiastic about GenRad's bright prospects. In fact, Thurston had later reflected: "It wasn't until 1978, when the stock analysts told us what they saw that we really began to believe, ourselves, that we were doing things right."

The market was growing at a rapid rate, and GenRad's technology continued to meet the market's needs. Sales in 1978 increased 23 percent over the 1977 figure, to $89.4 million. Profits increased 77 percent to $6.4 million. Return on equity stood at an impressive 22.8 percent. Combined, the figures gave testimony to an impressive recovery from the company's highly unstable 1972 situation and from the 1976 recession.

GENRAD'S STRUCTURE IN 1979
Overview

In July 1979, there were two product line divisions at GenRad: the Electronic Manufacturing Test (EMT) Division, and the Acoustic and Vibration Analysis (AVA) Division. The company's many and disparate product lines were housed in these divisions. Manufacturing at GenRad was essentially centralized, though certain products were manufactured in West Coast plants. All East Coast manufacturing was centralized. Sales and service were centralized, with one exception: Products manufactured by Time/Data were sold by a discrete sales staff. These products were entirely different from the majority of the company's products, and the customer base for Time/Data's instruments was, likewise, different. An advanced development group was engaged in pure and applied research of a sophisticated nature. The finance, personnel, and employee training staff functions were centralized. A more detailed description of the company's 1979 structure follows.

General Organization

The EMT Division was responsible for developing, manufacturing and marketing the company's automatic test equipment (ATE). Additionally, the company's industrial instrument products (older, more traditional test instruments, which were the core product line at GenRad prior to the firm's entry into the ATE market) were handled through EMT. Further, Futuredata, Inc., a recently acquired (February 1979) microprocessor development system manufacturer, reported through the EMT Division, despite the fact that it was a stand-alone product line. Finally, the acoustics test products for AVA East were manufactured by EMT. Eighty percent of GenRad's sales and 100 percent of its profits were generated by the EMT Division in 1978, and these percentages were expected to hold steady in 1979.

The AVA Division directed the marketing and engineering efforts for the company's vibration, shake-test, and machinery health analyzer products [all manufactured on the West Coast by AVA West (formerly, Time/Data)] and its acoustics test products (all manufactured for AVA East by the manufacturing arm of the EMT Division). AVA headquarters were located in Santa Clara, California. AVA Division sales constituted 20 percent of total corporate sales.

Product Line Management

The product line was managed by a product line manager, a product engineering manager, and a product marketing manager. The product marketing manager was responsible for generating product forecasts, developing product marketing programs, maintaining strong communications between the field sales and service forces and the relevant product-line personnel, and coordinating the new product development and market introduction efforts with the engineering group. Consequently, the product marketing manager had to be aware of both the customer's needs and existing technology in order to have a sense of which new products were most worth pursuing. The product engineering manager was responsible for new product development engineering. Product engineering managers were typically promoted from within the engineering ranks, while product marketing managers were generally promoted from the regional sales manager position.

Product line managers were responsible for facilitating the linkage of product engineering and marketing personnel wherever possible. Further, the product line manager was ultimately responsible for overseeing the progress of all new product projects and administered all funds related to new product development.

Manufacturing

As of July 1979, GenRad's products were manufactured in four plants. Three of the plants were under the control of the EMT division: They were located in Concord, Massachusetts; Bolton, Massachusetts; and Los Angeles, California.

Management at GenRad had long been committed to manufacturing the majority of the components for its finished products, as opposed to sourcing components externally. Therefore, GenRad's manufacturing capabilities were extremely broad. Thurston had commented that manufacturing at GenRad was:

> . . . a comprehensive, vertically integrated manufacturing operation capable of producing a wide variety of products, ranging from binding posts and potentiometers selling for dimes to a few dollars, to small and large instruments priced between a few hundred to a few thousand dollars, to complex computer-controlled systems priced at hundreds of thousands of dollars apiece. It also includes a new pilot production facility for new products, material and capital planning and production-control groups, and the company's central purchasing function.

While each product line division contained discrete engineering and marketing functions, manufacturing provided several resources to all product lines. Manufacturing was responsible for production engineering and process engineering services. The process engineers were steering manufacturing toward process automation and away from the old "one-man, one-lot" production technique. Drafting, modeling, test engineering, and quality engineering services were all provided by manufacturing as well. All assemblers and technicians operated from within the manufacturing division. The interface between manufacturing personnel and product line marketing and engineering personnel was achieved by the inclusion of manufacturing personnel in the new product development process.

The effectiveness of manufacturing personnel was measured by their ability to operate within budget and to deliver a quality product on schedule. No systems were in place at the company to enable management to isolate efficiency, product mix, or volume cost variances as of 1979.

Sales and Services

The sales and service division, which sold and serviced all product lines (with the exception of Time/Data's), contained nine United States and six European offices as well as one Canadian office. Manufacturers' representatives and distributors represented the company in other locations around the world. Ninety percent of the company's sales were made through the company's sales offices, with the remaining 10 percent handled by representatives and distributors.

Over the years, many long-standing customer relationships had been established. Therefore, much of the sales effort involved account maintenance activities, as opposed to new account development. National accounts were serviced by national account specialists, who operated in conjunction with a district sales representative.

In 1979, sales and service was said to be functioning smoothly. The major problems facing the sales and service division were related to the recruiting of personnel and the training (in order to update them with the rapidly changing capabilities of GenRad's test equipment) of new and existing sales and service employees.

INVENTORY MANAGEMENT: A PERSISTENT PROBLEM

For most of its history, GenRad's inventory levels had been high relative to its competitors. In the early days of the company, these high inventories were explained by the firm's policy of maintaining steady production levels in order to keep employment levels constant.

The company's excessive inventories created a significant cash drain. In fact, a large portion of GenRad's 1972 loss was attributed to high inventory carrying costs. The problem was further compounded by the fact that by 1978, many managers viewed the situation as being totally uncorrectable. Inventory values could not be isolated by product line, which resulted in product line managers being unable to determine if they were making progress or losing ground in their struggles to control inventory levels. Most managers redirected their attention to other areas and a general sense of defeatism relative to controlling inventories prevailed.

SYSTEMS: A PERSISTENT WEAKNESS

Throughout GenRad's history, its management, while accurately assessing the inadequacy of the company's management information systems, consistently failed to marshall the necessary forces to correct the problem fully. The irony in this was heightened by the fact that management's understanding of the flaws in the company's business systems was generally precise.

During the period from 1967 until 1974, few improvements were made in the company's systems. In fact, not one of the many structural revisions implemented at the company during that time period had been accompanied by the adoption of a new set of systems. Therefore, the company's information systems remained either crude or absent altogether.

By 1979, GenRad's systems were improving, but still fell far short of the needs of its operating managers. The divisions received their first balance sheets in 1979. These reports confirmed the suspicion that the divisions' asset management problems, which had been developing over time, were full-blown by 1979. Individual product costs were still not available in 1979. Rough product cost estimates could be provided, given much effort, if needed.

As a result of the weaknesses in the company's management information systems, management had come to base decisions more upon qualitative, as opposed to quantitative, factors. For example, since product costs could not be generated, direct product profitability figures could not be determined. Hence, decisions relating to specific products were made on the basis of qualitative considerations (such as the importance of carrying a product in order to enhance the company's image as an advanced and innovative manufacturer of test products) and not on the basis of a quantitative determination (such as profitability or ROI). Over time, management had come to rely increasingly on qualitatively informed decisions. However, the company's explosive growth in the late 1970s had made the company's inadequacies in the area of systems more apparent and troublesome, and increased the need for new systems greatly.

THE NEW PRODUCT DEVELOPMENT PROCESS

GenRad had traditionally excelled in technological innovation and new product development. In 1979, the company funded both pure and applied research efforts. The company's pure research and development efforts were conducted by the Advanced Development Division. Pure

R&D was the name given to research efforts designed to yield revolutionary testing methods or testing devices. The company's applied research and development programs were generally directed toward refining the testing capabilities of existing instruments, or toward developing new products that were closely related to existing products. While new products generally took longer than planned to reach full development, they also enjoyed longer product lives than anticipated. Development delays were explained by the fact that engineers attempted to perfect products in the development stage. Delays were increasingly costly, however, and by 1979 many executives were concerned by the skyrocketing costs of new product development.

STRATEGIC PLANNING

Thurston appointed a Strategic Planning Council to coordinate the strategies and financial objectives of the business areas on a companywide basis. Under the plan, each product line manager developed a discrete strategic plan. The product line managers then met with their business area manager, and together they developed a business area plan. The business area plans were compilations of data on competitors' product lines, anticipated strategies, sales and growth rates, changes in product and process technologies, marketing and sales policies, and market shares. Changing environmental factors and their likely effects on the industry were also considered. Finally, based on the strategic data that had been gathered, detailed action plans were developed for each product line in order to maximize the effectiveness of GenRad's product line strategies.

An outside consultant had persuaded the firm to think strategically in terms of "natural businesses." A natural business was roughly defined as one or a group of product lines that claimed similar customers, competitors, process technologies, and functional performance capabilities. A natural business was considered to be akin to an independent business entity and could be liquidated or divested without having an adverse impact on the remainder of a company's product lines. A natural business could therefore function as a stand-alone division. In 1974, there were many fewer natural businesses at GenRad than there were product lines, which implied that the company had not yet been successful in rationalizing its product policy.

In 1976, the corporate-wide formal strategic planning process was discontinued at the company. Strategic planning did continue at the divisional level, however. The discontinuation of centralized planning occurred for a number of reasons. Perhaps most important, the corporate-wide formal planning process did not have the full support of GenRad's managers. Many did not find the process to be valuable, and believed that planning at the division level alone was fully satisfactory.

Therefore, centralized planning expired due to lack of interest. As of mid-1979, formal corporate-wide strategic planning was still not present at GenRad.

FUTUREDATA: BROADENING PRODUCT PORTFOLIO

In February 1979, GenRad enlarged the scope of its operations by acquiring Los Angeles-based Futuredata, Inc. Futuredata was a manufacturer of microprocessor development systems (MDS). These systems were used by product designers to assist them in integrating complex microprocessors into new products. Therefore, these systems shortened the design process considerably. Microprocessor development systems were not similar to GenRad's automatic or other test instruments, since they served a laboratory design, and not a manufacturing test function. Therefore, the acquisition of Futuredata resulted in GenRad's entering an entirely new field.

In explaining the reasoning behind GenRad's entry into the MDS industry, Thurston stated that the microprocessor area was generally considered to hold great promise for future growth. It was thought that GenRad's involvement in the microprocessor field would give the company much-needed exposure to rapidly emerging microprocessor technology. By manufacturing and distributing development systems, GenRad's personnel would have an opportunity to interact directly with the engineers who were pioneers in microprocessor technology. Top personnel at the firm thought that this exposure to the engineers would give GenRad a clear advantage since it would gain an up-to-date understanding of developments in the field. They felt that this competitive advantage would yield future profits. Additionally, several key managers were highly optimistic over Futuredata's growth prospects.

THE ORGANIZATIONAL DEVELOPMENT STUDY GROUP

When the members of the Organizational Development Study Group first convened in July 1979, they faced a paradoxical situation at their firm. GenRad was experiencing the best of times, in the midst of what were, in many respects, the worst of times. In mid-1979, GenRad was reflecting remarkable financial strength. Orders were strong, back orders flush, and profits substantial. The company was expected to generate record sales and profits in 1979, and to set further records in 1980. The automatic test equipment industry was projected to grow at an average annual rate of 21 percent over the next five years. GenRad's technological lead in such areas as functional testing, testing system software, and in-circuit testing gave the company an advantageous position in this high-growth market.

But at the same time, several problems were apparent at the company. Coordination between the functions was not always smooth and this had created interpersonal strains between managers. Decisions were often delayed due to the confusion that often surrounded staff and functional interfaces. Information systems were wholly inadequate and were causing serious disruptions in day-to-day management. Managers feared that these strains would become more pronounced as the firm's sales increased. By July 1979, GenRad's managers were expressing their dissatisfaction over work life at the firm and over the breadth and ambiguity of their responsibilities with increasing fervor. Curiously, the managers expressed their displeasure not to Thurston, but to one another, and primarily to Cambria.

Cambria listened to his peers with increasing concern. He realized that someone would have to fully explain to Thurston the anxiety GenRad's managers were feeling. Cambria decided that a special task force should be commissioned to study the factors causing the problems within the firm, and to generate recommendations aimed at alleviating the problem. He outlined the reasoning behind his decision in this way:

> We were working under a flawed matrix organization in July 1979, and the stress the matrix created was intense. Bill was high above the stress areas, so he didn't feel the pain to the extent that we were feeling it.
>
> Further, we had recently reviewed the divisions' strategic plans. The plans were all highly positive, and indicated a fast-paced future for the company. But, many of us were concerned that the company's internal problems would prohibit us from attaining the goals outlined in the plans. So, I wrote a memo to Bill and requested that we establish a management team to take a broad look at the problems we were facing, and to concentrate on solving those that had the potential of preventing us from reaching the goals enunciated in the divisional plans.
>
> Bill agreed to the formation of the task force, but didn't really share our sense of urgency. He thought it would be a long-term study. At one point he said, "Let the group work for a year or two, and at the end of that period we'll see what conclusions we can draw." Bill was taking a passive view of the task force's mission, but the other members were not, to be sure. After the first meeting, Bill fully understood that we had a problem. That's when he went into action.

The task force was named the Organizational Development Study Group (ODSG). As one of its first actions, the group decided to retain the services of an outside consultant who would monitor the group's proceedings and provide a third-party voice. It was in the context of these viewpoints that the members of the Organizational Development Study Group sat down to work out a plan for GenRad's future.

The Hampton Shipyard*

THE HAMPTON SHIPYARD near Philadelphia, Pennsylvania, was situated on a land-locked harbor which connected with the sea through a channel deep enough to float the largest battleship. Covering an area of 120 acres, the shipyard had 12 building ways, or slips, the biggest of which would accommodate ships up to 1,000 feet in length and 150 feet in beam. Outfitting was carried out on five large piers built on water having an average depth of 30 feet below mean low water level.

Established in 1890, the shipyard was well known for its output of naval and commercial vessels of every type and size. The naval vessels ranged in type and size from small naval vessels to battleships and aircraft carriers. The commercial vessels ranged in type and size from trawlers to luxury liners.

In 1954 the shipyard employed about 3,000 employees and was the largest employer in the surrounding locality. The employees of the shipyard had been unionized first in 1938, and in 1946 they had been organized by a national union. Prior to 1946, industrial relations had been fairly harmonious; there had been a low turnover of labor, and the apprentice school system had led to many sons of old-time employees being employed. In 1946, the national union called a strike on a national issue which was not settled for five months.

The majority of employees of the shipyard were skilled tradesmen. The trades represented included welding, burning, ship fitting, drilling, chipping, pipe fitting, electrical, sheet metal, painting, carpentering, riveting, and rigging. Operations such as riveting and rigging were carried out by gangs, but most of the other operations were performed by individual tradesmen under the supervision of leading men.

In June 1954, Mr. James Ambrose, the general superintendent of the shipyard, was reminded that recently layoffs in manpower, which had been made necessary by the recent decline in the volume of operation of the shipyard, had reduced the numbers of supervisors available for the daily "roving committee." Mr. Ambrose knew that on some days the roving committee had been reduced in number to two or three supervisors. He felt that he would have to rearrange the groups and reassign some supervisors or let the daily patrol of the roving committee expire.

The roving committee at the Hampton Shipyard had first been instituted in August 1949. At the time Mr. Ambrose was dissatisfied with the behavior of employees in that he felt that a number of men were ceasing work before the whistle sounded for lunch at 12 noon and for quitting time at 4 P.M. Mr. Ambrose was particularly dissatisfied with

---

*Copyright © 1955 by the President and Fellows of Harvard College. Reprinted by permission of the Harvard Business School. This case was prepared by Jeanne Deschamps under the supervision of Jay W. Lorsch as a basis for class discussion rather than to illustrate either effective or ineffective handling of an administrative situation.

the lines which formed at the eight banks of timekeepers' clocks prior to the blowing of the whistle. For the plant layout see Exhibit 1. Mr. Ambrose reasoned that the men would have to leave their jobs on the ships being built on the slips and being outfitted at the piers several minutes prior to the time when they lined up at the timekeepers' clocks, and he knew that at some shipyards this practice had ballooned to the point where men stopped work half an hour and more before the whistle sounded. To force the men to work full time, Mr. Ambrose formed a roving committee of divisional superintendents, foremen, and assistant foremen,[1] and required this committee to patrol specific areas of the yard daily at 15 minutes prior to the sounding of the whistle. Mr. Ambrose set up a fixed schedule and required the rotation of assigned areas so that all the areas of the yard were somewhat covered each day by the patrols. To enforce his wishes, Mr. Ambrose instructed the patrol to take badge numbers for subsequent issue of chits wherever offenses warranted such issue. "Chits" in books had been issued to supervisors previously and consisted of a notification in triplicate of the offense, together with the penalty for the offense. Exhibit 3 shows a chit."

The formation of the roving committee was designed to serve as an additional supervision of the men working on the ships. Mr. Ambrose thought that this additional supervision was necessary for a number of reasons. He knew, for instance, that supervisors below the rank of superintendents would never cross the departmental lines in order to question a man about the reason for his presence in any particular locality. Mr. Ambrose thought this questioning of individuals who had left their jobs on the ships without pemission was necessary in order to tighten the discipline of working until the whistle sounded. The daily patrol of the roving committee was instructed to take the badge numbers of men not on jobs and to report these numbers through Mr. Ambrose's office to the foremen of the department concerned. The foremen were instructed to notify action taken on these reports and if a man did not have a good reason for being away from his job, the foremen were to issue chits.

Mr. Ambrose thought that the roving committee was successful in improving conditions at quitting time because he did not observe as many infractions of the rule after the patrol had been instituted. After several weeks, Mr. Ambrose thought that conditions had improved considerably and that the patrol was no longer necessary, so he gave instructions for the patrol to be discontinued.

In June 1950, a few months after the patrol had been discontinued, the work force of the shipyard had increased to 6,000 employees and there were indications that the buildup would continue although Mr. Ambrose did not envisage the buildup reaching the proportions of the

---

[1] For the case writer's concept of the formal relationships at the shipyard, see Exhibit 2.

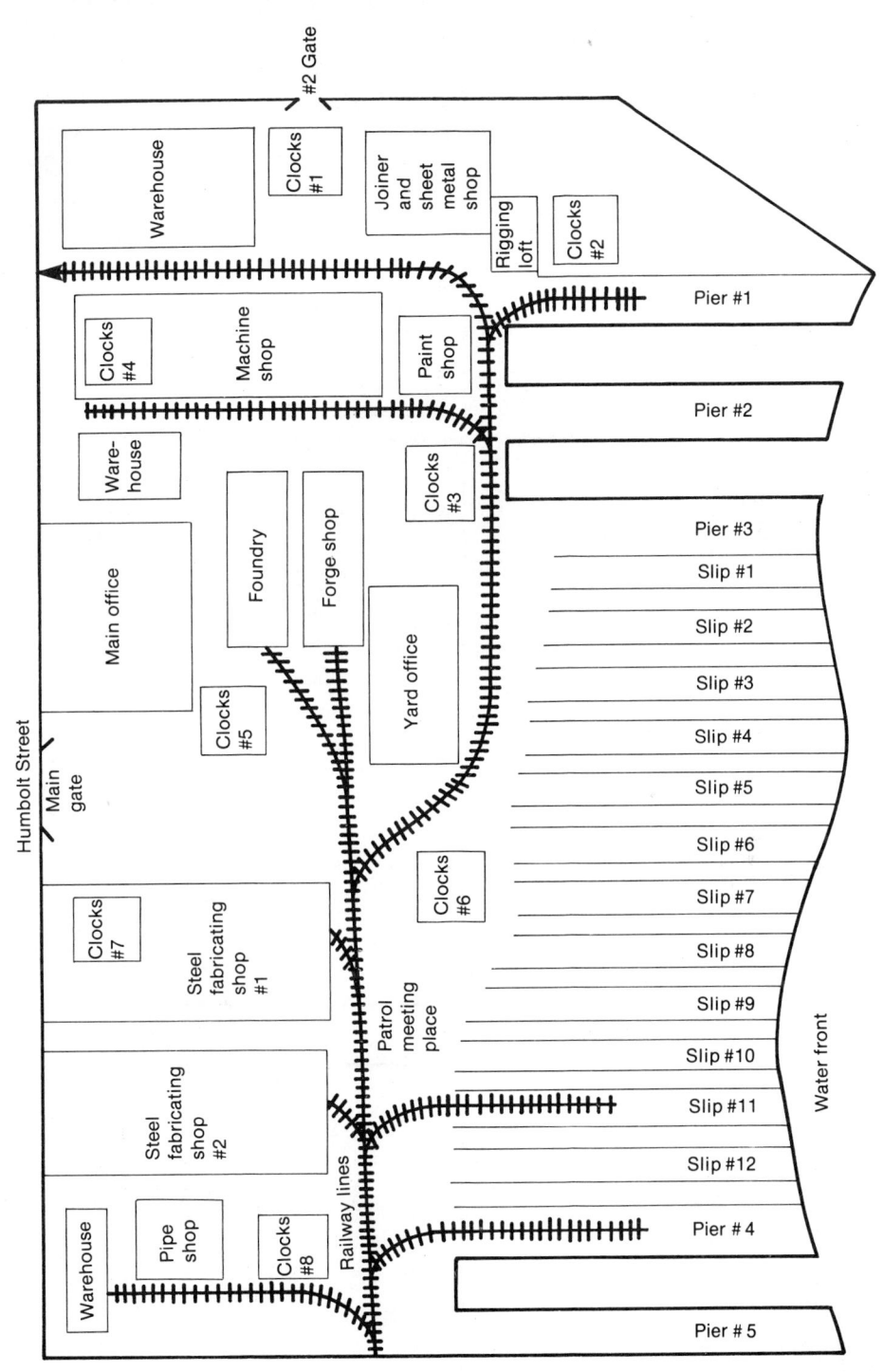

EXHIBIT 1
The Hampton Shipyard Plant Layout

EXHIBIT 2
The Hampton Shipyard Partial Organization Chart*

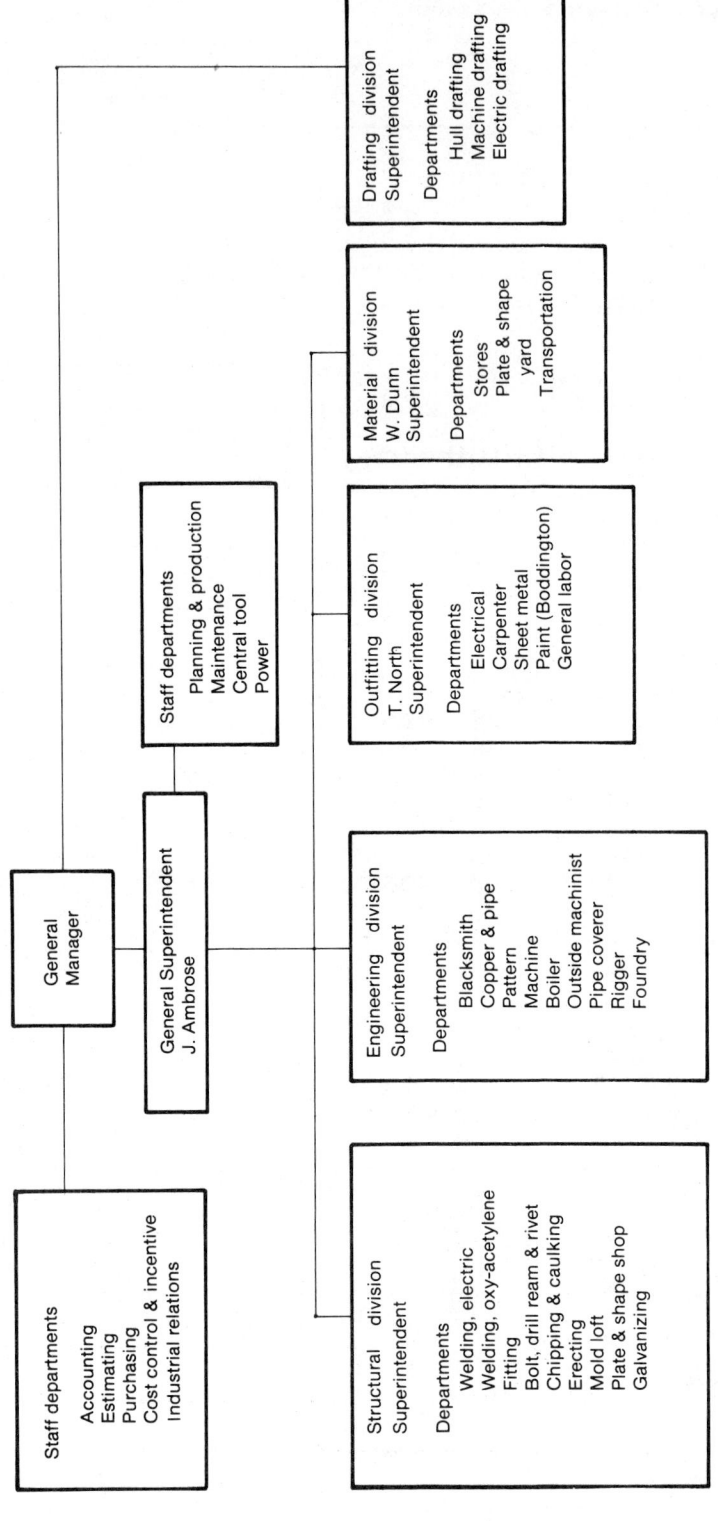

```
                            ┌──────────────────┐
                            │ General          │
                            │ Manager          │
                            └──────────────────┘
                                     │
        ┌────────────────────────────┼────────────────────────────┐
        │                            │                            │
┌───────────────┐           ┌──────────────────┐         ┌──────────────────┐
│ Staff         │           │ General          │         │ Drafting division│
│ departments   │           │ Superintendent   │         │ Superintendent   │
│               │           │ J. Ambrose       │         │                  │
│ Accounting    │           └──────────────────┘         │ Departments      │
│ Estimating    │                                        │  Hull drafting   │
│ Purchasing    │                                        │  Machine drafting│
│ Cost control  │                                        │  Electric drafting│
│  & incentive  │                                        └──────────────────┘
│ Industrial    │
│  relations    │
└───────────────┘
                                     │
                ┌────────────────────┼────────────────────┐
                │                    │                    │
        ┌──────────────┐    ┌──────────────────┐    ┌──────────────────┐
        │ Staff        │    │ Outfitting       │    │ Material division│
        │ departments  │    │  division        │    │ W. Dunn          │
        │              │    │ T. North         │    │ Superintendent   │
        │ Planning &   │    │ Superintendent   │    │                  │
        │  production  │    │                  │    │ Departments      │
        │ Maintenance  │    │ Departments      │    │  Stores          │
        │ Central tool │    │  Electrical      │    │  Plate & shape   │
        │ Power        │    │  Carpenter       │    │   yard           │
        └──────────────┘    │  Sheet metal     │    │  Transportation  │
                            │  Paint (Boddington)│  └──────────────────┘
                            │  General labor   │
                            └──────────────────┘

┌──────────────────┐        ┌──────────────────┐
│ Structural       │        │ Engineering      │
│  division        │        │  division        │
│ Superintendent   │        │ Superintendent   │
│                  │        │                  │
│ Departments      │        │ Departments      │
│  Welding, electric│       │  Blacksmith      │
│  Welding, oxy-acetylene│  │  Copper & pipe   │
│  Fitting         │        │  Pattern         │
│  Bolt, drill ream & rivet│ │ Machine         │
│  Chipping & caulking│     │  Boiler          │
│  Erecting        │        │  Outside machinist│
│  Mold loft       │        │  Pipe coverer    │
│  Plate & shape shop│      │  Rigger          │
│  Galvanizing     │        │  Foundry         │
└──────────────────┘        └──────────────────┘
```

Note: The supervisory force in each department of the five divisions consisted of a foreman, an assistant foreman, quartermen, and leading men. Quartermen supervised from 5 to 10 leading men. Leading men supervised from 10 to 15 men on the ships and as high as 35 in the shops.

*The shipyard did not ordinarily make use of a formal organization chart. This chart is the case writer's concept of the formal relationships.

The Hampton Shipyard

EXHIBIT 3

Chit Stub	*Chit*
Serial no. 23575	Employee's name_____ Serial no. 23575
Badge no.	Employee's badge no._____
Name	1 ☐ Loafing, 2 ☐ Losing time, 3 ☐ Leaving job early, 4 ☐ Arriving on job late without reason,
Hull no.	5 ☐ Off job without permission
Date	1 ☐ 1st offense—*warning*, 2 ☐ 2d offense—*one week off*, 3 ☐ 3d offense—*discharge*
Time	The infraction of some company rules and regulations will result in *immediate discharge*.
Offense Offense no.	Some but not all of these rules are: 6 ☐ Employee found sleeping in the yard, 6a ☐ Intoxicated,
1 ☐ 1 ☐	6b ☐ Gambling, 6c ☐ Stealing, 6d ☐ Defacing or destroying property, 6e ☐ Horseplay, 6f ☐ Other
2 ☐ 2 ☐	
3 ☐ 3 ☐	Hull_____ Date_____ Time_____
4 ☐	
5 ☐	_____
	Supervisor's signature
Immediate discharge offenses	1st copy to industrial relations dept.
	2d copy to employee
6 ☐ 6a ☐ 6b ☐	3d copy to department office
6c ☐ 6d ☐ 6e ☐	
6f ☐	

Note: The local of the national union "went along" with this chit system of issuing written warnings of offense.

---

wartime force of 30,000 unless the United States became involved in another world war. During June, Mr. Ambrose had occasion to visit some other shipyards and during those visits, he noticed a great deal of laxity at the other shipyards regarding the enforcement of the rule of working until the whistle sounded. At his next weekly meeting with the foremen, Mr. Ambrose brought up the problem of men quitting early. He said that if they allowed laxity in enforcing this rule they would soon find the men disregarding all rules. After some discussion wherein the foremen admitted that some men were inclined to quit early, Mr. Ambrose arranged for the timekeeping department to provide him with a list of all employees who punched out at 4:00, 4:01, and 4:02 P.M.

The timekeeping department kept a record of the men who punched out at these times for the next several weeks and each foreman was notified of the badge numbers of the men in his department who appeared on this list of "early birds." Mr. Ambrose noticed that an excessive number of the men listed were employed by the paint department, so he questioned Mr. Boddington, the foreman of the paint department, about the reason for the excessive number of his men listed on the "early bird" list. Mr. Boddington defended his men and attributed the fact that they appeared on this list to the approved practice of allowing painters to leave their jobs on the ships five minutes before the quitting time so that they could return brushes and pails to the paint shop. Mr. Boddington pointed out that this approved practice was the only exception to the rule that all men should stay on the job until the whistle sounded, and he claimed that this accounted for the fact that his men were often first to clock out.

In July 1950, Mr. Ambrose was dissatisfied with the record of "early birds," so he called a meeting with the officers of the Supervisors' Association.[2] At this meeting with the officers of the Supervisors' Association, Mr. Ambrose, the general superintendent, said that it was the responsibility of the immediate supervisors to keep the workmen on the job until quitting time. The officers of the SA immediately agreed that this was the responsibility of the immediate supervisors and they went on to express their view that the supervisors could do a better job of keeping their men working until quitting time if management people of the foremen and superintendent level made it a habit to be present in the slipways and on the piers just before quitting time. They also suggested that the situation was not as bad as the general superintendent had reported and they invited him to take a walk around any part of the yard he chose with representatives from the SA to see for himself that the supervisors were on the job.

After some discussion, it was decided that a roving committee should be set up to patrol the yard daily at 11:45 to 12:00 noon and 3:45 to 4:00 P.M. Mr. Ambrose requested the foremen of departments to assign their supervisors to patrol on different days so that each patrol group contained 10 supervisors from 10 different departments. He decided to leave the assignment of foremen to the patrol at the discretion of the divisional superintendents because he felt that the foremen might have more important things to do around quitting time. When the patrol was first instituted, Mr. Ambrose went with each patrol every day. Subse-

---

[2] The Supervisors' Association was a social organization of the supervisory personnel below the rank of assistant foreman. These supervisors were not organized for bargaining purposes, and the traditional role of the association was social in nature with the specific job of organizing social activities such as yearly picnics. From time to time, the general superintendent had used the officers of the association as a means of conveying information of a general nature concerning all members of the association and in particular the president of the SA often spent considerable time answering questions regarding the group bonus scheme of incentive payment for supervisors.

quently, when he found this assignment interfering with his other work, Mr. Ambrose assigned the divisional superintendents to take charge of the patrol each day with the exception that he retained one day each week when he took charge himself. From that time on, the patrol met each day at the head of slip 9, and fair weather or foul, the patrol patrolled portions of the yard each day. The portion of the yard to be patrolled was selected by the superintendent in charge of the patrol without notice. The supervisors accompanying the superintendent had no prior knowledge of the area to be patrolled on any particular day.

In October 1951, when employment at the shipyard had decreased to approximately 4,000 employees, the groups of supervisors forming the patrols were rearranged to accommodate for some changes which had occurred in personnel. In 1953, when employment at the yard had increased to 6,000 employees, the groups were again rearranged and at that time Mr. Ambrose decided to reduce the patrol from 10 supervisors to 8 supervisors.

During the period in which this regular patrol operated, the supervisors were well aware that the men had set up some countermoves of their own. A very efficient warning system had been organized by the men to alert areas of the yard which were directly in the path of the patrol and conversely areas which did not look like being covered on any one day were informed that they could relax. The men had named the patrol "the Gestapo" and often made unflattering comments to supervisors about the patrol.[3] Most of the supervisors thought that the patrol did assist in keeping men working until the whistle sounded. During this period a number of chits, averaging one per day, were issued. The threat of the issue of a chit, however, was used much more often than the actual issue. From August 1949 to June 1954, 1,601 chits were issued, 1,408 being first offense, 161 second offense, and 32 third offense or immediate discharge chits.

The pay system in force at the shipyard during this period was a complicated one. The company policy was to encourage the achievement of maximum production for the mutual benefit of the employees and the company. In line with this policy the company had established in addition to hourly base rates of pay, an incentive pay system based on standard piecework rates. On the average about 60 percent of the employees were employed from time to time on contract work offering this incentive pay. The contracts for work on the ships varied in size from one day's work to three or four weeks' work. The contracts were written by rate setters employed in the cost control and incentive department. Men working on the ships moved back and forth, sometimes employed on hourly pay and sometimes on incentive contract pay. According to observations of Mr. Ambrose and some other

---

[3] Excerpts from the union flier are shown in Exhibit 4.

supervisors, men on incentive contract pay were just as prone to quit work before the whistle sounded as were men on hourly pay.

During discussions about the patrol the supervisors admitted that they felt they needed some assistance in stopping men from quitting early, because often a supervisor, such as a leading man electrician, would be responsible for men working throughout an entire ship or even for men working on two different ships and he could not possibly maintain a surveillance of his men all at once. The supervisors working on the ships often compared their problem of supervision with the easy task of supervision in the machine and fabricating shops where men were under the immediate eye of their supervisors. Mr. Ambrose had also required his own staff assistants to form and man patrols near the gangways of ships tied up at the piers and to maintain a surveillance of areas near the time clocks, but he felt that these measures and the listing of badge numbers by the guard at the gangways of men leaving the ship 15 minutes before quitting time were not sufficient to enforce the rule of working until the whistle sounded.

The supervisors individually did not like the job of going on the daily patrol, particularly on days when the weather was bad, and they did not like the unflattering comments which were made about the Gestapo.

In June 1954, the employment at the Hampton Shipyard was at the low point of 3,000 employees. Many of the employees who remained were old-timers, and a number of the men in some of the departments had been supervisors at some previous time. Mr. Ambrose, the general superintendent, found some of the patrol groups of the roving committee had been reduced by layoffs and demotions to two or three supervisors.[4] He felt that he would have to rearrange the groups once more or let the roving committee expire. He was not sure whether the patrol was still needed during this period of minimum manpower employed and he knew that some people were critical of the usefulness of the patrol. However, Mr. Ambrose did not consider that the old-timers were immune to the temptation of quitting a few moments before the whistle sounded, though he did wonder whether the patrol served to keep them working on the job, and he was well aware of the unflattering references such as the use of the name Gestapo. One day when he was discussing the patrol with some of his subordinates, Mr. Ambrose said, "I know that conditions at lunch time and quitting time in other shipyards are much worse than this yard. I know also that the patrol is criticized and perhaps it only keeps the fellows out of sight, but can you show me a better system? If anybody comes up with a better answer, I'll certainly give it a try."

On June 15, 1974, Joe Campbell, an engineer in the planning department, had occasion to accompany Mr. North, the superintendent

---

[4]Layoffs and demotions during slack periods were administered in order of seniority.

EXHIBIT 4
Excerpts from Two Union Fliers

GESTAPO

It is to be noted that Ambrose and his roving crew are still hard at work, checking on men off the job. It is my understanding that starting Monday morning that they will check all men off the job at all times. WELL, a word to the wise is sufficient.

AS YOU HAVE NOTICED, LEADING MEN—SUPERVISORS—FOREMEN AND HIGH YARD OFFICIALS ARE CRUISING THE YARD BEFORE THE LUNCH PERIOD AND QUITTING TIME CHECKING UP ON EMPLOYEES THAT ARE NOT ON THEIR JOBS. THIS IS A FUNCTION OF MANAGEMENT AND YOUR UNION HAS NOTHING TO DO WITH IT.
MANY OF THE BOSSES DISLIKE THIS JOB THEY HAVE TO DO—"ACTING AS A POLICE FORCE." BUT THEY TOO HAVE TO TAKE ORDERS. SO BOYS PROTECT YOURSELF AND STAY OUT OF THE TOILETS AND DON'T GIVE THEM A CHANCE TO PASS OUT CHITS.

---

of the outfitting division, on a trip to Trenton to a competing shipyard. Mr. North had noticed and had commented to Mr. Ambrose later, that at Trenton there were at least 1,000 men gathered at the main gate which was 200 to 300 yards from the ships, five minutes before the whistle had sounded. Mr. North remarked that Mr. Welch, the general superintendent of the Trenton shipyard, had been with them when they had encountered this crowd waiting at the main gate and Welch had thought nothing of it. Welch had merely apologized to Mr. North because the crowd of men were blocking Mr. North's car from leaving by the main gate. Mr. North went on to say that in comparison he thought the behavior of their men at the Hampton Shipyard regarding quitting early was remarkably good.

A few days after his visit to the Trenton yard, Campbell happened to stop in at a small stores department shack at the head of slip 10 to get out of the rain. Mr. North was also present sheltering from the rain when the daily patrol under the supervision of Mr. Dunn, the superintendent of the material division, formed at the head of slip 9 and proceeded toward pier 5. As the direction in which the patrol was headed became apparent, Joe Campbell heard Fred Cernot, the store man in charge of the shack, pick up the telephone and call another store man in a shack on slip 11. Campbell distinctly heard Cernot say into the telephone, "Say Ted, Dunn's got the Gestapo today and he's headed your way."

Mr. Dunn was the superintendent of the Material Division, which included the stores department. Campbell was not sure, but he thought that North must have heard Cernot warning Ted, the store man on slip 11 that the Gestapo was headed in that direction. Campbell was sure that Cernot knew North was present, because North, who was well known to the men throughout the yard, was standing right next to the telephone.

The general superintendent's office and those of his divisional superintendents were all situated on the second floor of the yard office. Mr. Ambrose and his divisional superintendents often contacted one another on matters of mutual interest when they were in their offices around about quitting time. About quitting time on the day that North had heard Cernot warning the store man on pier 11, he related the incident to Mr. Ambrose. "I was amused," said North, "to see their efficient warning system in action. That store man at the head of slip 10 lost no time in warning the guy on slip 11 that the Gestapo was headed his way."

Highland College (Student Affairs Division)

As a case researcher, I visited a friend who had been employed for the past three years as an assistant dean and director of housing at a small western college. I approached her with the intention of getting some leads on case possibilities in that educational institution. After a brief discussion about her work experience, it appeared to me that her employment situation would make a good case study. I stayed with her a few days and had an opportunity to talk further with her and some of her colleagues. The following case evolved as a result of my observations and discussions with the members of the student affairs staff of Highland College, located in Woodstown.

Woodstown is a city of approximately 40,000 people which is surrounded by countryside. Located 20 minutes south of Madison, which is the closest large city, Highland occupies a well-landscaped, 100-acre campus. It exists as a self-contained unit within the residential area of Woodstown.

Highland College is a small, private, liberal arts college with an enrollment of approximately 2,000 students. Founded in the early 1900s as an educational institution for men, it remained that way until it began admitting women five years ago. As a result of the somewhat rigorous admission requirements, the majority of the student body comes from the top 10–20 percent of their respective high school classes. Highland College enjoys a respectable reputation in the academic community due to its well-qualified and accomplished faculty and the high caliber of its students. In this small residential college, the majority of the students live on campus. Consistent with other small colleges of its class, such as Hamilton, Oberlin, Lawrence, Reed, and Swarthmore, comprehensive fees at Highland are quite high. Endowment investments presently total approximately $35 million, largely resulting from strong support by graduates and a well-organized Alumni Association.

Woodstown is not a city which one would typically describe as a "college town." Beyond a few local merchants who offer minimal discounts to students, there is not a close, active relationship between the college and the city. The members of the student affairs staff resided in Woodstown or in one of the rural areas surrounding the city, as did the faculty and other staff members. Much of the nonwork lives of the staff members centered on the college, rather than the city, where they had access to the athletic facilities, art facilities, and many cultural events at little or no charge. Staff members were also permitted to take one free course per semester, an opportunity of which many employees took advantage. The college also provided the staff with minimal life insurance coverage and a health insurance and retirement program.

The Student Affairs Division is responsible for non-high academic areas of student life. It reports directly to the Office of the President, but also works closely with academic departments. The dean of students is the director of student affairs and all of the assistant deans and program directors are responsible to him. The dean of students, a Ph.D. in sociology, has been at Highland for the past five years and is also a part-time member of the sociology faculty. He came to Highland from a similar small, liberal arts college where he was the dean of students and a tenured faculty member for 20 years.

Most of the student affairs staff members had been hired by the dean of students following his arrival at Highland. The majority of the program directors and assistant deans were between 25 and 35. Four staff members, the directors of student aid, student activities, health services, and security were over 45 years old and had been in these positions prior to the present dean's employment at Highland. Dawn was hired as the director of housing upon graduating from a similar college in New England and became an assistant dean at the end of her first year of employment. She had a B.A. in psychology and had not planned on a career in student personnel prior to being hired at Highland. Like the other new staff members, Dawn was enthusiastic about getting this job and thought that working with young people would be interesting and challenging. Having been a student at a similar school, she thought it would be fun to work at a college and also a good opportunity to learn about college administration. She considered this job something that would enable her to develop some skills and learn more about her own ability to deal with responsibility. Kirk Evans and

Heidi Johnson (the provost's assistant [Head of faculty], not a formal member of student affairs but in close contact with the staff) had master's degrees in student personnel but, like the other younger and newer staff members, had little previous experience in this field and considered their jobs to be good starting points in their careers.

The day that I accompanied Dawn to work we arrived at the office at 10 A.M. and upon entering I noticed that all of the other desks and offices were occupied, except Dawn's and the office of the director of admissions, Ted Howard. I questioned her about our late arrival, with which she seemed quite comfortable. She explained that she had an early evening meeting with a group of students and didn't have anything urgent scheduled for the early morning hours. When questioned about Ted Howard's absence, she was equally unconcerned about his whereabouts. As if to calm my worries, she said, "Formal policy *does* say that working hours at Highland College are from 8:30 to 5:00, but members of the student affairs staff usually come and go as we please. Our jobs require us to work closely with many groups of people who oftentimes don't have consistent schedules—so we inevitably end up working strange hours and many weekends." This type of policy seemed to me one that would only invite trouble. Since the offices of all but four staff members were located in different parts of the campus, it was obvious that the dean had no way of knowing when and if someone was putting in enough hours. When I asked Dawn if this wouldn't be an easy system to take advantage of, she said that one staff member had been fired by the dean for not putting enough time in on the job and for other reasons: "Our last affirmative action director had been employed in that position for three years and still wasn't 'doing things right.' He didn't put a lot of time in on the job and wasn't on top of his budget. Eventually, students began complaining that he was never in his office and wasn't following up on their requests. He had frequently been spotted by other staff members on the tennis court for three hours at a time and had earned the reputation of someone who was continually slacking off." The other staff members had earned the trust of the dean and respected and valued the freedom they had been given to set their own hours. It all sounded very interesting to me but it sure is a lot different than the way I have to work when I'm in my office.

Soon after our arrival, the dean of students, Bruce Powers (age 50) walked by Dawn's office and took time out to greet both of us. I had met him the previous evening at an informal gathering of the staff at his house. To my amazement he was dressed in the same casual manner that he had been the night before. Had I not met him previously I never would have guessed he was the dean of students. I then realized that everyone else was dressed quite informally, the only exception being the director of admissions who appeared in a sport coat and tie after conducting a tour of the campus for a prospective student and his parents.

When preparing to go to the dean's house the previous evening, Dawn sensed my apprehension since I had never been to my present boss's house, nor had any type of social, informal relationship with him either in the office or outside. Dawn explained that the dean often invited the staff and some of his other colleagues to his house in the evenings. She said that she even felt comfortable just stopping by his house when she needed to talk to him. Expecting to meet a distinguished, easy-going, soft-spoken man, I was surprised to be introduced to someone 6 feet 2 inches tall and very broad shouldered, with a voice as loud as his size who was almost abrasive in his direct and forthright mannerisms. After observing his interactions with his staff members and listening to many conversations about what was going on with specific programs people were working on, I saw another side of the dean. He was very sensitive to the problems people were having and usually could offer helpful advice or insights. He was very direct when giving his opinions but people seemed to accept his comments as valuable information rather than being hurt by his criticism.

The conversation between staff members at this gathering revolved around specific projects people were working on, problems and experiences they wanted to share. It was obvious that everyone didn't have specific knowledge about the details of each other's jobs, but most people were familiar enough with the general nature of other jobs to be able to discuss them and offer suggestions. The atmosphere was comfortable and friendly and everyone seemed to get along well. When I later asked Dawn if she felt obligated to attend these get-togethers because they were at the dean's house, she almost looked shocked. She explained that most of the staff members had become relatively good friends and spent much of their free time together. They looked forward to times when they could get together informally, whether at the dean's house or at someone else's apartment or home. Oftentimes they attended campus functions together, such as lectures, plays, and concerts.

Despite being such good friends, Dawn assured me that disagreements did arise occasionally and were dealt with openly and honestly. Curious as to what constituted a "disagreement" in a group of such friendly people, Dawn told me the following story:

> Last spring at a party at the dean's house I had a run-in with Ted Howard. He was in charge of the "Accepted Candidates Day" program, a type of pre-orientation program. Several members of the Women's Caucus, students and staff, wanted to conduct a special program that day for the incoming women students. They thought the development of such a program was particularly important since there were still rather few

women faculty members (only five) and few women professional staff members. Ted didn't want to do it at all. He thought it was a bad idea and didn't think we should single out women students; but I disagreed with him. I told him I thought he was wrong and that the women were competent and capable of designing a good program. At this point, David Lawrence (another assistant dean), who had heard the conversation, stepped in and said that he thought we were both ignoring the real issue, which was one of control. He proceeded to point out that Ted seemed opposed to my suggestion because it would mean that he would not have control over that aspect of the program, for which he was responsible. For this reason he was not willing to consider the reasoning behind my argument and was ready to reject the suggestion without further conversation. After a lengthy discussion, we arrived at a procedure for planning and carrying out the program which satisfied Ted's control needs and allowed the women to develop a program they believed to be important.

At 10:30 Dawn had a meeting with the members of the Student Housing Committee, which I also attended. Over the past two years she and this committee had been working out a new program for room placement and were now in the final stages of planning before implementation for the next year. The old system, which had been in effect for many years, was a "squatters rights" system where a student could remain in a room for four years if he or she chose to do so. After she became the housing director some students came to her complaining about the unfairness of the present system so she spent some time talking to students to try and assess their attitudes about the issue. It turned out to be quite a controversial issue and after analyzing the situation, Dawn decided that a change needed to be made. She discussed the subject with the dean, who offered some suggestions about possible courses of action she could take, but he left the decision up to her. She decided that since this was such a big issue on campus she would need some student input and support so proceeded to organize a student committee.

This meeting, which I attended, went smoothly and the students seemed to exhibit a great deal of respect for Dawn and her ideas, despite the fact that they didn't hesitate to disagree with her on some issues. When the meeting was over, I asked Dawn if it was always that easy to deal with students, thinking that constantly listening to their complaints must get tiring after a while. She replied,

> I love working with students most of the time. I think partly because of my age, I understand their questions and concerns and I have developed a good rapport with them. Generally students are open-minded and fair, and willing to listen to my point of view as an administrator. Through my dealings with students I think I have made many of them aware of the fact that there is usually more than one side to an issue or problem and that they should at least consider what the people they disagree with are

saying. Listening to complaints does get annoying sometimes but the majority of my interactions with students are stimulating and rewarding.

Then I wondered if she set up student committees for every project she worked on. She said that she used her own discretion in deciding which decisions to make alone and which decisions students should have a part in. She gave the following example:

> After the Student Union was operational I decided that student mailboxes should be moved from the separate dorms to the union. I thought this would be a good way to get many students out of their dorms where many had a tendency to remain for days if they didn't have any classes to attend. Initially some students complained that they didn't like having to walk so far to pick up their mail, but the net result was that students did get out more and it was a much more efficient system.
>
> One great thing about this job is that I can always go to the dean for advice and ideas about problems that arise or programs I am planning, but the final decision is always up to me and my decisions are always supported by the dean and the other staff members.

This fact was soon illustrated to me when an irate parent stormed up to Dawn's desk and demanded to see the dean about a problem with her daughter's room assignment for the following year. It seems that this parent's daughter had one of the better rooms on campus and had mentioned to her mother that she wouldn't be able to keep it for her last two years at Highland. Upon hearing this story, Dawn very politely informed the parent that she was welcome to go in and see the dean but that the dean would probably send her back to speak to Dawn since she was in charge of all housing problems. (In fact, this is exactly what he did.)

Before lunch Dawn had a meeting with the 40 resident advisers, a group she met with regularly to discuss any problems they might be having in the dorms and anything else that was going on. While she was gone she gave me her job description to read. I found out that in addition to meeting with resident advisers and having complete responsibility for student residences and room placement, she was also responsible for planning dorm security programs, for doing a yearly evaluation of the campus food services, and had been involved in planning a large capital budget proposal for housing improvements. Similar to other program directors on the student affairs staff, she was responsible for submitting a yearly budget (all college budgeting was done on a three-year basis) and was required to account for expenses in relation to her budget. I know from previous conversations with her that she was an active member of the President's Commission on the Status of Women and also was working on college budgetary programs with the provost, but those activities were not listed in her job description.

On the way to lunch I asked her about being promoted to assistant dean at the end of her first year of employment and what this promotion involved. She had received a salary increase each year of her employment at Highland based on her job performance as evaluated by the dean of students. Although none of her raises had been very substantial and wages at the college were lower than in area industries, this situation was of little concern to Dawn. The dean was responsible for awarding the "assistant dean of students" title to his staff members, but this promotion didn't automatically include a salary increase. Well, I thought, what is it other than a "title promotion"? When I asked Dawn this question, she explained that assistant deans were given additional responsibilities, such as working on freshman orientation, parents weekend, and special projects, and that they possessed higher status in the eyes of students, faculty, and other staff members. As a result of taking an increased responsibility and getting involved in additional activities, Dawn felt a sense of growing competence and felt she was learning a great deal, a feeling which was shared by most of her colleagues.

We had lunch with Laura Clark, the director of career counseling and assistant dean, and the conversation revolved around the recruiters who were scheduled to be on campus during the next few months to interview graduating seniors. Before Laura had been hired, there had been no formal career counseling and placement program at Highland. At the end of her second year in this position, there was a large increase in the number of companies coming to Highland to recruit and a larger percentage of graduates than ever before were being placed in jobs. Laura had been instrumental in getting alumni involved in helping graduates get jobs and she also had initiated many workshops (interviewing techniques, resume writing, etc.) and organized many women's programs.

At one point in the conversation Dawn asked what the job prospects were like for this year's graduates. Laura replied, "The jobs are there if the students are willing to put out the effort to find them. Even though it's tough to place liberal arts graduates, I still think the educational experience they get here at Highland is invaluable." Dawn was quick to agree.

After lunch we all went back to Dawn's office since she and Laura had a meeting with the dean at 12:30. While I was waiting in Dawn's spacious, comfortably furnished office, Kirk Evans, the director of the student union, stopped in. He had also been at the dean's house the previous evening, so I recognized him immediately. He had a few things that he needed Dawn's secretary to type for him so he left Dawn a note with the message on it. I thought to myself, "Her secretary will probably love that, it looks like Dawn gives her enough work to keep three people busy!" Later that afternoon Dawn politely asked her secretary if she would do the typing for Kirk when she had time and to my surprise the secretary was more than willing. Evidently, only a few of the staff members have their own secretaries and they are always willing to arrange their work accordingly so that everyone's work gets done.

When Dawn and Laura emerged from their meeting in the dean's office, they were talking excitedly about the ideas they had for a parents weekend program. The dean had asked them to be co-directors of the program next fall and they both seemed thrilled with the assignment. After listening to Dawn trying to organize her activities to fit in this new assignment, I was surprised at her eagerness to undertake it. She then explained what effect this project would have on her other duties:

> My workload will not be unique when I start working on this parents weekend project. Almost everyone on the staff is involved in activities beyond the specific requirements of their individual programs; for example, Laura works voluntarily as the women's field hockey coach and Ted has started doing some academic counseling beyond what is required in his position. We are encouraged, by Bruce, to get involved in other areas of the college and partly as a result of this involvement, the student affairs staff has earned a reputation of competence and commitment. Due to this reputation our staff has taken on many new college projects and programs which have previously been done by other departments. If there aren't any qualified people on our staff for a specific project, Bruce will usually hire a new director.

"This must mean that he has unlimited funds at his disposal, is this the case?"

> If a position is transferred to our staff from another department, such as the intramurals program, then additional funds are supplied to student affairs. But Bruce is very capable of using his budget to his advantage and never wastes money. He is able to plan well and has proved himself competent, so when the Planning and Priorities Committee allocates funds, Bruce always gets at least his fair share.

An example of this situation was evident when Dawn told me the story of the creation of the Student Union. Prior to the existence of the union, Highland lacked the "small-college" atmosphere of closeness and familiarity characteristic of other small schools. Students expressed their concern and discontent with this atmosphere and requested the establishment of a place where they could gather. The dean thought this was a good idea and, after speaking with the president and provost, he obtained the necessary funds to convert an old, unused building on campus into the union. He then used the funds he had available in his budget to hire the director and the restaurant/pub manager.

"With such a good reputation, how does your staff avoid taking on projects which really have nothing to do with student affairs?" I asked.

Occasionally the president or provost will ask Bruce to undertake a project which is logically not under the jurisdiction of the student affairs staff or which could be done more efficiently by another group or person. In this event he does not hesitate to face up to whomever is making the request and say no. He usually succeeds in pointing out the inappropriateness of his staff undertaking such projects and makes his opinion stick. They respect and trust him.

On the other hand, there have been times when some staff members have a few projects going at once and are very pressed for time. If this happens to me when we really get involved in organizing parents weekend, I won't have too much to worry about. I have never been directly involved with the parents weekend program but I know that if Laura and I have any problems we can talk to the previous co-chairmen and can get ideas from other staff members. Also, everyone will be aware of the fact that we are working on this project. If we get overwhelmed with work at any point, I am quite confident that any staff member with fewer demands on his or her time will be willing to help us out. Last year when Ted was very busy organizing parents weekend, I went on some recruiting trips to other colleges and other staff members helped him out by conducting some admissions interviews. Working together in this way happens frequently.

This system was all a little confusing to me. "Wouldn't it be a lot easier if everyone just did their own jobs and stayed out of other people's business?" Dawn was adamant in her reply when she said,

> Well, I suppose things might be a little more orderly around here if we each went our own separate ways and had little interaction with each other. But, I don't think it would be worth the price we'd pay in the long run. Where else could we get an opportunity to learn so much about so many different jobs and to develop such satisfying working and social relationships with our colleagues? Some of our jobs would probably be intolerably routine if we weren't able to do all of the additional things we are doing now.

Our conversation was interrupted when the dean stuck his head in to remind Dawn about the staff meeting and to tell me I was welcome to join them. On our way to the meeting, Dawn quickly explained that attendance at monthly staff meetings was mandatory. Everyone arrived at the conference room promptly at 2:00 and took seats around the table. This was the first time I had seen all of the staff members in the same place since many of them have offices in different parts of the campus. The dean ran this meeting according to an agenda which began with brief program reports by each director and a discussion of specific problems people were having. It was obvious to me from his questions and comments to each person that he was well aware of the activities of each director and of the status of each project. From what I had observed, in the office and at his house, he had so many informal conversations with staff members and was constantly being sought out for advice, it would be impossible for him not to know what was going on. Dawn later agreed with my observation, adding that Bruce was very accessible and was continually stressing to them the importance of being open, positive, and solution-oriented. Because he related to his staff in this way, no one was ever apprehensive about approaching him with a problem and no one tried to hide things from him.

Following these reports the dean announced that Dawn and Laura would be organizing the next parents weekend. He also announced that the president had asked him to organize a weekend seminar for student personnel administrators. Bruce was planning to work on this project himself but asked if anyone would like to assist him. David Lawrence eagerly volunteered. He said that the project interested him, he wasn't particularly busy at the present time and he hadn't worked on any projects for quite a while. Bruce accepted David's offer and they set up a later meeting date to further discuss the program.

During the remainder of the meeting the dean talked about other activities on campus and about matters that had come up at the most recent presidential cabinet meeting. Staff members occasionally asked him questions or made comments, but most of the time he talked uninterrupted.

Dawn spent the remainder of the afternoon in her office working on some routine housing matters before her early evening meeting with another group of students. When we returned to her apartment, there was a letter waiting for her from Metropolitan University. The letter contained an invitation to visit Metropolitan about a job.

While at a recent professional conference Dawn had met the vice president for student affairs at Metropolitan and rather casually discussed her job and the nature of student affairs activities at Metropolitan. He had asked her a lot of questions, she realized in retrospect, and must have been checking out her qualifications, because the letter was obviously written to encourage her interest in Metropolitan.

Metropolitan University is located in Culver City (population 300,000) and has a student body of 25,000. The opportunity included a 25 percent salary increase and excellent health insurance and retirement programs. The student affairs function at this school had a reputation of being highly organized and efficiently managed, in addition to being one of the first schools to utilize the computer in housing assignments.

Enclosed in the letter was a lengthy and precise job description which Dawn read many times before showing it to me. I noted that the very clearly spelled out duties were more limited in number than those Dawn had at Highland, but that they involved responsibility for many more students and authority over the expenditure of many more dollars, as well as a clear potential for moving up. After I had read it she asked me if I thought she should take the job, if it were offered, as she thought likely.

The Hillcrest Commercial Bank (A)*

DEVELOPMENT OF THE BANK

THE HILLCREST COMMERCIAL BANK was located in Penn Hills, Pennsylvania, a suburb of Pittsburgh populated by upper-middle class and well-to-do research scientists, engineers, and business executives. Penn Hills' population was well above 50,000 and still increasing as of early 1964.

The bank had been started in 1959 by its president and board chairman, Gerald Adler. Its assets grew rapidly from $2.4 million on December 31, 1959, to $14.1 million on December 31, 1963—a 489 percent increase in four years; deposits rose even more rapidly in the same period, from $1.9 million to $12.9 million, or 577 percent. The dollar increase in assets and in deposits had been about the same each year, or $3 million in each. In early 1964 the bank had one small branch office located in a large shopping center in a small, growing suburb of Pittsburgh. Its manager was John O'Halloran, an assistant treasurer of the bank. Top management planned to open several new branches in 1964 and 1965.

Historically the Hillcrest Bank had been heavily dependent upon the efforts of Mr. Adler and the other directors to attract new business. A large proportion of the new business came from Mr. Adler's contacts in law, business, charitable, and religious organizations, and many of the directors were selected from among his friends and associates. The officers generally gave Mr. Adler the major credit for building the bank's business volume. As was reported in a bankers' trade magazine in 1964, Mr. Adler believed strongly in having the directors actively seek business for the bank. The executive vice president, Arthur Murphy, and the branch manager, John O'Halloran, had also brought in some new business, but the other officers had not been active in attracting new business.

ORGANIZATION AND PERSONNEL

The organization structure of the Hillcrest Bank was not shown on an organization chart, as of February 1964. Some of the officers found it difficult to describe the organization in terms of a formal structure, and there was little agreement as to just how the organization structure would look if projected onto a chart. Exhibit 1, which shows the charts that were drawn individually by the six subordinate officers,[1] illustrates their different ideas.

---

*Copyright Burton A. Scott, Jr. Reproduced by permission of the author.

[1] The "six subordinate officers" refers to all officers under the president: Messrs. Murphy, Hodges, Lento, Jackson, McGrath, and O'Halloran. "Top management" in the bank was considered to be Mr. Adler and Mr. Murphy. "Junior officers" are the four assistant treasurers.

EXHIBIT 1
Officers' Conceptions of Bank Organization as of Late February 1964*

According to Arthur Murphy, Executive Vice President:

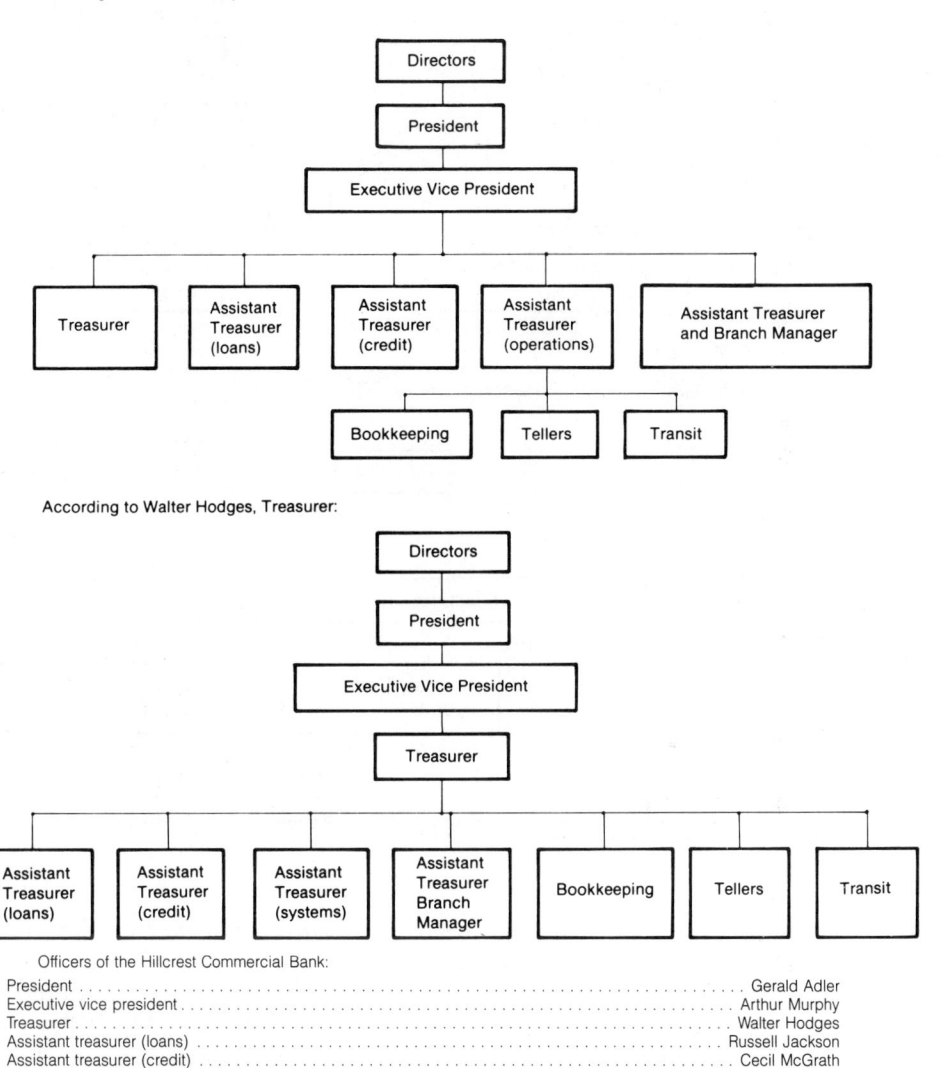

```
                    Directors
                       |
                    President
                       |
             Executive Vice President
    _____|_____
    |         |         |         |         |
Treasurer  Assistant  Assistant  Assistant  Assistant Treasurer
           Treasurer  Treasurer  Treasurer  and Branch Manager
           (loans)    (credit)   (operations)
                                    |
                       _____|_____
                       |            |            |
                   Bookkeeping   Tellers      Transit
```

According to Walter Hodges, Treasurer:

```
                    Directors
                       |
                    President
                       |
             Executive Vice President
                       |
                    Treasurer
    _____|_____
    |         |         |         |         |        |        |
Assistant  Assistant  Assistant  Assistant  Book-  Tellers  Transit
Treasurer  Treasurer  Treasurer  Treasurer  keeping
(loans)    (credit)   (systems)  Branch
                                 Manager
```

Officers of the Hillcrest Commercial Bank:
President .... Gerald Adler
Executive vice president .... Arthur Murphy
Treasurer .... Walter Hodges
Assistant treasurer (loans) .... Russell Jackson
Assistant treasurer (credit) .... Cecil McGrath
Assistant treasurer and branch manager .... John O'Halloran
Assistant treasurer (operations, systems) .... Robert Lento

EXHIBIT 1 *(continued)*

According to Russell Jackson, Assistant Treasurer (loans):

General Banking Functions:

```
                President
                    |
         Executive Vice President
                    |
                Treasurer
                ____|____
               |         |
      Assistant Treasurer   Assistant Treasurer
          (loans)              (credit)
```

Loaning Organization:

```
                President
                    |
         Executive Vice President
                    |
         Assistant Treasurer
              (loans)
                    |
         Assistant Treasurer
              (credit)
```

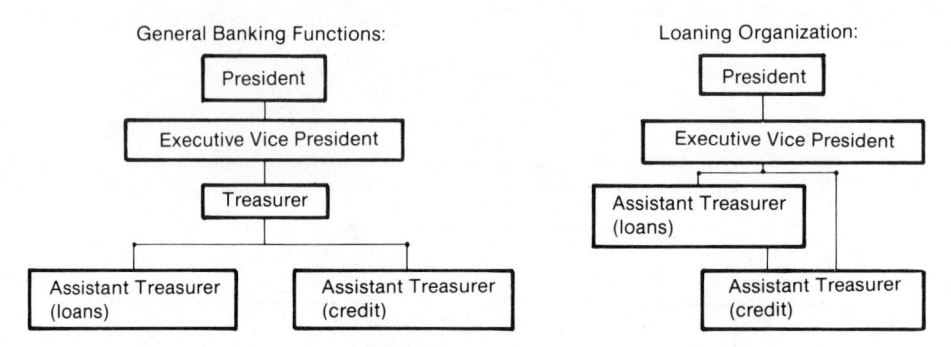

According to Cecil McGrath, Assistant Treasurer (credit):

```
                      Directors
                          |
                      President
                          |
              Executive Vice President
         _____|_____
        |                 |                 |
   Treasurer;      Assistant Treasurer   Assistant Treasurer
   Assistant Treasurer    (credit)           (loans)
   and Branch Manager         |                 |
    _____|_____             Installment Loans
   |      |      |              (2 clerks)
Bookkeeping Tellers Transit
```

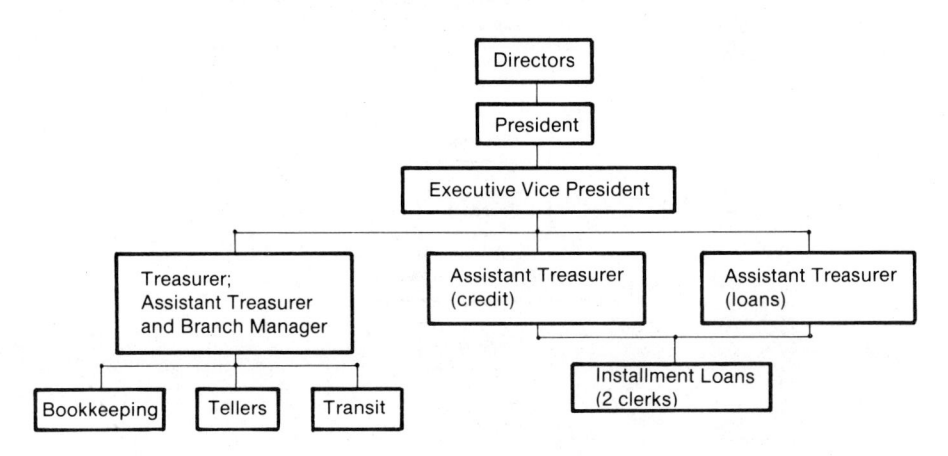

Defenders of this unstructured situation maintained that the informality and flexibility were justified and needed because of the small size of the bank, even though it occasionally meant that different officers gave instructions to the same person at different times. Mr. Adler was the final authority and decision maker, but he delegated responsibility for internal operations almost entirely to Mr. Murphy. Nevertheless, the treasurer, Walter Hodges, and the four assistant treasurers sometimes received assignments directly from Mr. Adler. Employees in the three operating departments (bookkeeping, tellers, and transit) occasionally received instructions directly from one or more of the assistant treasurers, as well as from Mr. Murphy and Mr. Hodges.

According to Mr. Murphy, the bank's rapid growth had necessitated the hiring in early February 1964 of another assistant treasurer, Robert

The Hillcrest Commercial Bank (A)

EXHIBIT 1 *(concluded)*

According to Robert Lento, Assistant Treasurer (operations, systems):

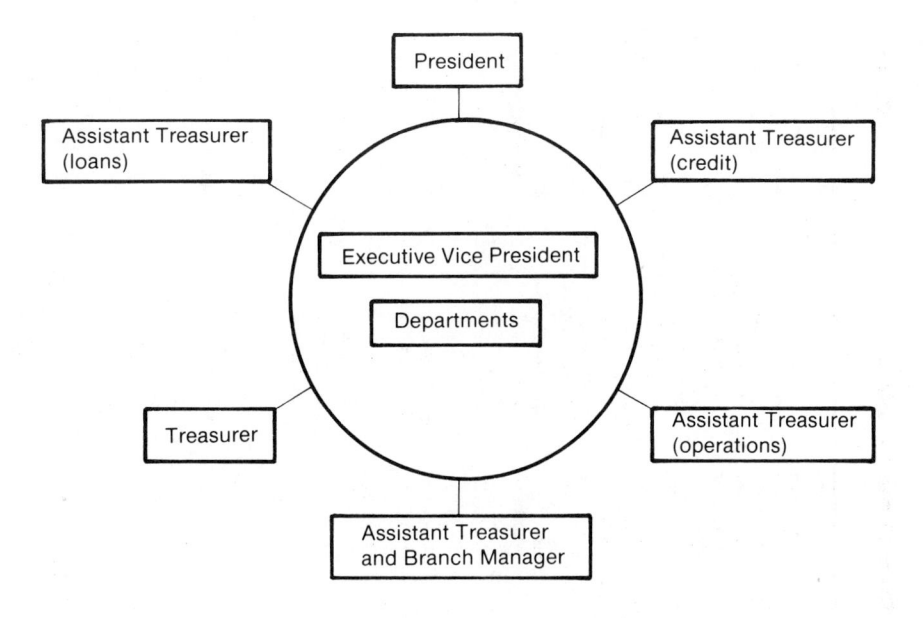

```
                          President
                              |
  Assistant Treasurer         |         Assistant Treasurer
  (loans)                     |         (credit)
         \                    |                    /
          \    Executive Vice President           /
           (              Departments           )
          /                                       \
         /                    |                    \
  Treasurer                   |         Assistant Treasurer
                              |         (operations)
                              |
                    Assistant Treasurer
                    and Branch Manager
```

According to John O'Halloran, Assistant Treasurer and Branch Manager:

```
              Directors
                 |
              President
                 |
        Executive Vice President
                 |
              Treasurer
                 |
        Assistant Treasurers
        and Department Heads
```

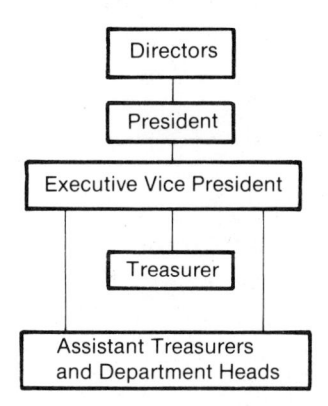

Lento, to work on operations and branch development. Mr. Murphy had known Lento when the latter worked in a large correspondent bank in Pittsburgh, in charge of data processing operations involving 300 employees. On several occasions Mr. Murphy indicated to the case writer his great confidence in Lento's ability. Background information on all seven officers is given in Exhibit 2.

EXHIBIT 2
Personal Data on Bank Officers, as Reported by Them (listed by salary level, from highest to lowest)

Name and Position	Age	Marital Status	Principal Residence	Education	Experience	Memberships	Outside Interests
Gerald Adler, president and chairman of the board	54	Married; four children	Pennsylvania	L.L.B.; banking courses	Law practice; real estate development; finance (12 years)	Member, officer, and benefactor of numerous law, business, banking, religious, educational, and charitable organizations	Education, charities, golf
Arthur Murphy, executive vice president and director	46	Married; four children	Chicago area	B.A.; banking courses	Banking (28 years)	Kiwanis, Chamber of Commerce, Suburban Bankers Assn., a civic assn.	Sports
Walter Hodges, treasurer	47	Married; four children	Pennsylvania	College (3 years); accounting school (2 years)	Bank examiner (8 years); Hillcrest (4 years)	Suburban Bankers Assn., Lions Club, two alumni assns.	Golf, swimming
Robert Lento, assistant treasurer (operations and branches)	35	Married; four children	Pennsylvania	B.S.; banking courses	Banking (11 years in large Pittsburgh bank)	Natl. Assn. of Bank Auditors and Controllers, American Red Cross, Boy Scouts of America	Woodworking, sports
Russell Jackson, assistant treasurer (loans)	36	Single	Pennsylvania	College (3 years); banking courses	Banking (7 years); business (2 years)	American Inst. of Banking, Suburban Bankers Assn.	Sports, cultural events
Cecil McGrath, assistant treasurer (credit)	34	Single	Pennsylvania	B.S.; banking courses	Banking (10½ years)	American Inst. of Banking, Heart Fund-March of Dimes, United Fund, Marsalin Inst. (mental health), and an alumni assn.	Bowling, biking
John O'Halloran, assistant treasurer and branch manager	32	Married; four children	Pennsylvania	College (2 years); religious instruction (5½ years); banking courses	Banking (8 years); business	Rotary Club and a religious organization	Fishing, reading

The Hillcrest Commercial Bank (A)

In addition to the seven officers there were 27 other employees. These included three supervisors, an auditor trainee, three other specialized personnel, four tellers, eight clerks, and three secretaries, all at the main office. At the branch office there were two tellers, a guard, a secretary, and a clerk. Following is a list of the seven supervisory and specialized personnel:

Position	Name
Head teller	Stephen Maggiore
Bookkeeping supervisor	George Martin
Transit supervisor	Conrad Seward
Auditor trainee	James Richards
Installment loans	David Lazarus
Systems and procedures	Edward Heagin
General ledger	Ralph Jervls

BANK OBJECTIVES AND OFFICER DUTIES

The major objectives of Hillcrest, as expressed by the officers, were to continue its sound growth and expansion and to make the highest possible earnings. The bank offered all commercial banking services except trust service, which was to be offered starting late in 1964 in cooperation with a large Pittsburgh bank. (According to Mr. Murphy, the volume of funds in individual and commercial checking accounts was not increasing as fast as was the volume in savings accounts and time deposits; individuals were saving more money, and businessmen were looking increasingly to their bankers for help in investing their extra cash to produce a return rather than let it stand idle in a checking account.)

Among the bank's six subordinate officers, Mr. Murphy and Mr. Hodges thought the six objectives were being achieved "very well" and the other four believed they were being achieved "well." Four officers attributed this successful accomplishment to the bank's rapid growth; the focus of top management had consistently been on increasing business volume during the four years of the bank's existence.

During his periods of observation at the bank, the case writer asked each of six subordinate officers to describe his work in relation to the bank's objectives. Mr. Murphy stated that his function in the bank was "to direct the progress of the bank on the operational and administrative levels." The functions of Hodges as treasurer included, in his words, the following: "To coordinate all internal activities; to supervise the functioning of each individual employee; to supervise the functions of the heads of the various departments; to assist in the formulation of general policies in conjunction with the directors; and to maintain good public relations." The new assistant treasurer, Robert Lento, saw his function as being "to develop the new banking offices being considered, which would involve the preparation and installation of the branches." However, he noted that "the bank is not quite prepared to undertake branch offices immediately; meanwhile I fulfill a necessary function." Russell Jackson, an assistant treasurer, stated that he carried out all functions in regard to loans and that he had in the past done most of the general banking operations, such as opening accounts. Assistant treasurer Cecil McGrath described his work as follows: "One of the most vital functions of banking is the extension of credit. I perform many functions within this area." The assistant treasurer and branch manager, John O'Halloran, described his work in this way: "I'm a branch manager. My job is to build friends for the bank, build up deposits, and develop myself. I am achieving these three objectives . . . *slowly* but surely."

Mr. Adler reported that he spent 60 to 70 hours a week on bank business, while the six subordinate officers generally said they worked about 45 hours a week. Some of the subordinate officers and supervisors didn't leave at any particular time in the afternoon but stayed until their day's work was done, which on some days might be 5:30 or 6:00 P.M. or even later. Mr. Adler was usually in the bank less than half of each working day, since he was often out seeking new business; when he was in, he generally left the bank by 4:00 P.M. He spent most of the time in his office, having interviews and conferences and talking on the telephone. The other officers at the main office (Messrs. Murphy, Hodges, Lento, Jackson, and McGrath) were usually working in the bank.

THE BANK ATMOSPHERE

The first impression that struck the case writer about the bank was that the atmosphere was friendly, relaxed, and even somewhat casual. There was considerable humor shared among subordinate officers, supervisors, and employees. The contacts and relationships among most bank employees seemed informal. Mr. Adler often said of the bank personnel, "We're just one big happy family." The use of humor extended to customers and visitors who had been in the bank a few times and had become friendly with personnel. Mr. Murphy laid much stress on dealing fairly and honestly with one another and with the customers. Officers generally addressed one another by their first names or nicknames, except that they always addressed the president as Mr. Adler. In addition, most supervisors and employees addressed the officers as "Mr.," with the exception of Lento who soon made it known to all employees that he preferred to be called "Bob."

Most of the officers stated that they felt no reluctance at all to express their ideas and suggestions on the bank to other officers. The six subordinate officers rated the atmosphere in the bank's home office on a scale from 1 ("very tense") to 9 ("very relaxed"), with an average rating of 5.5 and a range of 3 to 9.

All the officers at Penn Hills except Jackson said the employees were cooperative, accepting instructions in a good spirit and carrying them out satisfactorily. But Jackson reported that employees frequently did not follow his instructions and/or do a good job, and he complained that sometimes they would "talk back" to him. At the branch office, O'Halloran complimented his employees on their cooperation and good performance; however, he did criticize the lack of cooperation that he had received from the main bookkeeping department.

In the opinions of several supervisory and specialized personnel, there were some indications of employee unrest and uneasiness in the bank. These tendencies were intensified by the arrival of Lento and by his subsequent attempts to tighten up operations and to clarify responsibility and accountability. Maggiore told Lento that the employees were wondering what was going on and that someone had even asked, "Who will be fired?" To Lento, this comment reflected the uncertainty of both employees and supervisors as to just what was expected of them. Since there were no standardized written procedures or written job descriptions, Lento believed that personnel felt a lack of adequate or clear instruction from above, and that this was unsettling to them because they wanted to cooperate and to do good work. Sometimes when an officer or a supervisor became frustrated over the poor performance of his employees he would do the job himself, as when one supervisor started keeping all his records himself after his employees had made some serious errors. Lento felt that bank objectives, plans, and policies sometimes were not formally communicated to employees but reached them as rumors if at all.

Within top management, Mr. Adler reported that he sometimes had to give the same instruction, orally or by memo, several times before it would get done; for example, he waited many months from the first time that he asked Mr. Murphy and Mr. Hodges to have a flagpole installed on the front lawn of the bank before it was finally installed in April 1964. Mr. Adler often expressed concern over his inability, in repeated attempts, to get every officer out of the bank several times a week to call on prospective customers. The "Officer Call Program" was not really under way by March 1964—Mr. Adler was still making most of the calls, with some calls being made by Mr. Murphy and some by Mr. O'Halloran (for the branch). Despite increased pressure by both Mr. Adler and Mr. Murphy, the officers said they could not respond because they were too busy with their regular duties. (In April, Lento did start making some calls on prospective customers.) At the same time some junior officers felt they did not have enough opportunities to demonstrate their ability to top management.

AN EVALUATION OF THE BANK

Shortly after Lento was hired, Mr. Murphy asked him to evaluate the bank's organization and operations and to make recommendations for improvement. Lento made this evaluation over a period of several weeks, while performing his regular duties, and his conclusions and recommendations are reproduced in Exhibit 3.

In late February, at Mr. Murphy's request, Lento drew up a proposed organization chart for the bank (see Exhibit 4). Lento's chart was designed to give the bank a more "conventional" and formalized organization structure. Lento said he drew it after carefully reviewing the bank situation, taking into account the personalities and abilities of the officers and of the supervisory and specialized personnel. He tried to structure the organization to make the best use of the bank's human resources and to clarify responsibility and accountability. Ever since coming to Hillcrest, Lento had felt strongly that it was very important that the organization structure be formalized and that everyone's specific responsibility, authority, and accountability be made clear. Top management had also expressed an apparent interest in this clarification.

Mr. Murphy told Lento to implement right away his fourth recommendation shown in Exhibit 3 (to standardize procedures and tighten up operations), and he assigned the bookkeeping supervisor, Edward Reagin, to work with Lento in the effort to carry this out. Both Mr. Murphy and Mr. Adler had believed for some time that costs were out of line, there was considerable work duplication, operations were relatively inefficient, too many mistakes were being made, and the staff was somewhat too large for the work that had to be done. Thus their concern for greater operating efficiency led to this effort to streamline operations in order to cut costs and increase profits.

Lento first had Reagin write procedures and job descriptions for the bookkeeping department, which had been the most troublesome area. Reagin used two large notebooks of materials that Lento had developed at his former bank as guidelines, and he worked under the close guidance of Lento. When bookkeeping was completed, Lento and Reagin met (jointly and individually) with the new bookkeeping supervisor, George Martin, and his clerks to explain the new procedures and job descriptions and to help them start using them. Then Reagin was assigned to write procedures and job descriptions for the tellers and for the transit department, again working closely with Lento and with the respective supervisors. During March and April these departments were gradually making progress by substantially reducing errors and increasing their operating efficiency.

The implementation of Lento's other five recommendations was less immediate. Lento held several meetings with the supervisors and

EXHIBIT 3
Conclusions and Recommendations of Robert Lento, Assistant Treasurer

The bank is financially sound as a result of wise investment to date and an active board of directors. A steady growth trend is evidenced with sound earnings reflected.

Exposed to Mr. Adler, the president, for only a few hours prior to his vacation leave from the bank, I have had no real opportunity to draw a concrete evaluation, yet because of the many things through which he has reflected his image, I feel I can say he is a deeply dedicated, efficient, humble, and sincere man. The tremendous account activity generated from this man alone is overwhelming, but while not exhaustible, this factor must be evaluated in the light of future growth of this bank. Not enough new business is generated outside of this one man, resulting in a poorly balanced projection for the future.

Organizationally, this bank has grown as a result of the tremendous operational knowledge of its executive vice president, who has developed the official staff personally in each of their functions. The size of the bank dictated the need for versatility in the official staff, but this factor, through growth, has subordinated administrative and functional accountability at all levels.

Accepting the challenge of Mr. Murphy to "explore" the bank and pinpoint any problem areas with recommended solutions, I have concluded as follows:

1. An organizational chart should be drawn up and put into effect immediately. This would serve to clearly define administrative responsibility.
2. Assignments below the official level should be specific and with accountability explained in its fullness and adhered to strictly.
3. Communication is poor. This can be remedied by management's exposing as far as is possible the knowledge of the position of the bank and the direction of the bank to all members of the staff. (This problem would be considerably reduced merely by defining administrative alignment.)
4. Many flaws have been noted in routine procedures. Most of this has crept into the operations as a result of personnel changeover and failure to follow up basic procedures. Procedural manuals must be written as soon as possible to establish policy in this connection. Together with this, proper instruction and education in the application of these procedures must be followed through.
5. Depth must be developed in every function. A minimum of three people should be thoroughly familiar with every function of the bank, regardless of what level it might be.
6. Positive goals must be established and attained.

Expenses in general do not appear to be abnormal. However, compared with income, it appears poor. Income can be considerably improved

EXHIBIT 3 *(concluded)*

through utilization of personnel, i.e., as officials are relieved from burdensome detail which can be readily assumed by other members of the staff. An effective Call Program can be set in motion generating new business, increasing deposits and loan activity which will result in additional income.

It is difficult to come on the scene as a new employee and to draw conclusions early. However, I can justify these conclusions in the light of experience. I believe that a minimum of resistance has been in evidence and this in itself is unusual. This factor only serves to point out more vividly the need to correct the smaller things as described in order to take greater steps toward future development. This is in no way intended as an application of a surgical knife but only as the recommended prescription which will effect a cure for the known ailments.

EXHIBIT 4
Proposed Organization Chart*
(by R. Lento, Feb. 28, 1964)

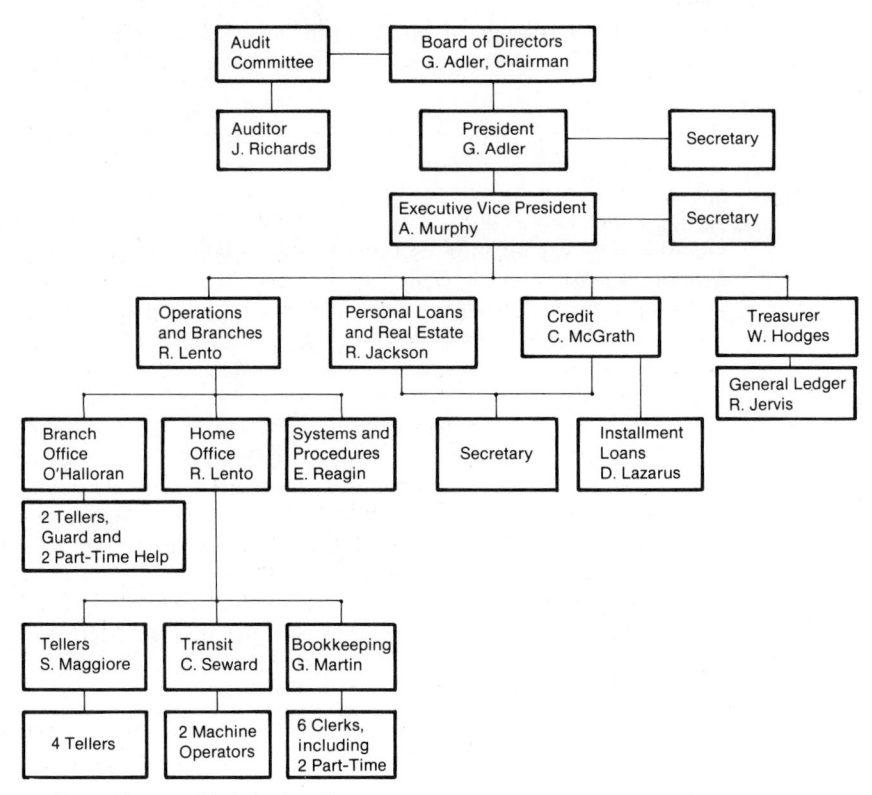

```
                    ┌─────────────┐     ┌──────────────────┐
                    │   Audit     │─────│ Board of Directors│
                    │ Committee   │     │ G. Adler, Chairman│
                    └─────────────┘     └──────────────────┘
                           │                     │
                    ┌─────────────┐     ┌──────────────┐     ┌───────────┐
                    │  Auditor    │     │  President   │─────│ Secretary │
                    │ J. Richards │     │  G. Adler    │     └───────────┘
                    └─────────────┘     └──────────────┘
                                               │
                                   ┌───────────────────────┐     ┌───────────┐
                                   │Executive Vice President│─────│ Secretary │
                                   │      A. Murphy         │     └───────────┘
                                   └───────────────────────┘
                                               │
         ┌───────────────┬──────────────────┬──┴──────────┬───────────────┐
    ┌─────────┐   ┌──────────────┐   ┌──────────┐   ┌──────────┐
    │Operations│   │Personal Loans│   │  Credit  │   │Treasurer │
    │and Branches│ │and Real Estate│  │C. McGrath│   │W. Hodges │
    │ R. Lento │   │  R. Jackson  │   └──────────┘   └──────────┘
    └─────────┘   └──────────────┘                        │
                                                   ┌──────────────┐
                                                   │General Ledger│
                                                   │   R. Jervis  │
                                                   └──────────────┘
```

| Branch Office O'Halloran | Home Office R. Lento | Systems and Procedures E. Reagin | Secretary | Installment Loans D. Lazarus |

2 Tellers, Guard and 2 Part-Time Help

| Tellers S. Maggiore | Transit C. Seward | Bookkeeping G. Martin |

| 4 Tellers | 2 Machine Operators | 6 Clerks, including 2 Part-Time |

*Covers 34 personnel, including 4 part-time.

employees, especially in regard to the procedural changes, but neither formal channels of communication nor regular staff meetings were established as he had suggested. The proposed organization chart (Exhibit 4) that he had drawn up had been seen only by Mr. Murphy and Mr. Adler as of late April. As for developing depth in every bank function, Lento was training Reagin to write procedures and job descriptions for the various departments and Jackson had for some time been training Maggiore, Lazarus, and Jervis in various aspects of the loaning function. As yet there was no coordinated, planned program of job rotation and employee development. Although top management had given thought to long-range goals and objectives, these had not yet been written down and disseminated to all employees or to the officers.

In light of this situation Lento began to wonder if top management really meant to take positive action on these problems, but more gradually than he had recommended, or if they did not intend more than token implementation. He was beginning to wonder whether (1) he should stop pressing for immediate action and wait to see what would happen, or (2) he should change his tactics and seek the changes even more forcefully.

*Hovey and Beard Company**

NOTE: Do not read this case until directed to do so by your instructor. It has been set up as a Prediction Case so that you can test your analysis by answering questions before reading the entire case.

PART I

THE HOVEY and Beard Company manufactured wooden toys of various kinds: wooden animals, pull toys, and the like. One part of the manufacturing process involved spraying paint on the partially assembled toys. This operation was staffed entirely by girls.

The toys were cut, sanded, and partially assembled in the wood room. Then they were dipped into shellac, following which they were painted. The toys were predominantly two colored; a few were made in more than two colors. Each color required an additional trip through the paint room.

---

*Abridged from pp. 90–94, "Group Dynamics and Intergroup Relations" (under the title "Hovey and Beard Company") by Alex Bavelas and George Strauss in *Money and Motivation* by William F. Whyte. Copyright © 1955 by Harper & Row, Publishers, Inc. By permission of the publishers.

For a number of years, production of these toys had been entirely handwork. However, to meet tremendously increased demand, the painting operation had recently been reengineered so that the eight girls who did the painting sat in a line by an endless chain of hooks. These hooks were in continuous motion, past the line of girls and into a long horizontal oven. Each girl sat at her own painting booth so designed as to carry away fumes and to backstop excess paint. The girl would take a toy from the tray beside her, position it in a jig inside the painting cubicle, spray on the color according to a pattern, then release the toy and hang it on the hook passing by. The rate of which the hooks moved had been calculated by the engineers so that each girl, when fully trained, would be able to hang a painted toy on each hook before it passed beyond her reach.

The girls working in the paint room were on a group bonus plan. Since the operation was new to them, they were receiving a learning bonus which decreased by regular amounts each month. The learning bonus was scheduled to vanish in six months, by which time it was expected that they would be on their own—that is, able to meet the standard and to earn a group bonus when they exceeded it.

Prediction Question

What will the new hook line do to productivity and satisfaction?

PART II

By the second month of the training period trouble had developed. The girls learned more slowly than had been anticipated, and it began to look as though their production would stabilize far below what was planned for. Many of the hooks were going by empty. The girls complained that they were going by too fast and that the time study man had set the rates wrong. A few girls quit and had to be replaced with new girls, which further aggravated the learning problem. The team spirit that the management had expected to develop automatically through the group bonus was not in evidence except as an expression of what the engineers called "resistance." One girl whom the group regarded as its leader (and the management regarded as the ringleader) was outspoken in making the various complaints of the group to the foreman: The job was a messy one, the hooks moved too fast, the incentive pay was not being correctly calculated, and it was too hot working so close to the drying oven.

PART III

A consultant who was brought into this picture worked entirely with and through the foreman. After many conversations with him, the foreman felt that the first step should be to get the girls together for a general discussion of the working conditions. He took this step with some hesitation but took it on his own volition.

The first meeting, held immediately after the shift was over at four o'clock in the afternoon, was attended by all eight girls. They voiced the same complaints again: The hooks went by too fast, the job was too dirty, the room was hot and poorly ventilated. For some reason, it was this last item that they complained of most. The foreman promised to discuss the problem of ventilation and temperature with the engineers, and he scheduled a second meeting to report back to the girls. In the next few days the foreman had several talks with the engineers. They and the superintendent felt that this was really a trumped-up complaint and that the expense of any effective corrective measure would be prohibitively high.

The foreman came to the second meeting with some apprehensions. The girls, however, did not seem to be much put out, perhaps because they had a proposal of their own to make. They felt that if several large fans were set up so as to circulate the air around their feet, they would be much more comfortable. After some discussion, the foreman agreed that the idea might be tried out. The foreman and the consultant discussed the question of the fans with the superintendent, and three large propellor-type fans were purchased.

Prediction Question

What will be the impact of the fan decision on morale and relations with the foreman?

PART IV

The fans were brought in. The girls were jubilant. For several days the fans were moved about in various positions until they were placed to the satisfaction of the group. The girls seemed completely satisfied with the results, and relations between them and the foreman improved visibly.

The foreman, after this encouraging episode, decided that further meetings might also be profitable. He asked the girls if they would like to meet and discuss other apsects of the work situation. The girls were eager to do this. The meeting was held, and the discussion quickly centered on the speed of the hooks. The girls maintained that they would never be able to reach the goal of filling enough of them to make a bonus.

The turning point of the discussion came when the group's leader frankly explained that the point wasn't that they couldn't work fast enough to keep up with the hooks but that they couldn't work at that pace all day long. The foreman explored the point. The girls were unanimous in their opinion that they could keep up with the belt for short periods if they wanted to. But they didn't want to because if they showed they could do this for short periods they would be expected to do it all day long. The meeting ended with an unprecedented request: "Let us adjust the speed of the belt faster or slower depending on how we feel." The foreman agreed to discuss this with the superintendent and the engineers.

The reaction of the engineers to the suggestion was negative. However, after several meetings it was granted that there was some latitude within which variations in the speed of the hooks would not affect the finished product. After considerable argument with the engineers, it was agreed to try out the girls' idea.

With misgivings, the foreman had a control with a dial marked "low, medium, fast" installed at the booth of the group leader; she could now adjust the speed of the belt anywhere between the lower and upper limits that the engineers had set.

Prediction Question

What will be the impact of the dial control decision on productivity and satisfaction?

PART V

The girls were delighted and spent many lunch hours deciding how the speed of the belt should be varied from hour to hour throughout the day. Within a week the pattern had settled down to one in which the first half hour of the shift was run on what the girls called a medium speed (a dial setting slightly above the point marked "medium"). The next two and one-half hours were run at high speed; the half-hour before lunch and the half-hour after lunch were run at low speed. The rest of the afternoon was run at high speed with the exception of the last 45 minutes of the shift, which was run at medium.

In view of the girls' reports of satisfaction and ease in their work, it is interesting to note that the constant speed at which the engineers had originally set the belt was slightly below medium on the dial of the control that had been given the girls. The average speed at which the girls were running the belt was on the high side of the dial. Few, if any, empty hooks entered the oven, and inspection showed no increase of rejects from the paint room.

Production increased, and within three weeks (some two months before the scheduled ending of the learning bonus) the girls were operating at 30 to 50 percent above the level that had been expected under the original arrangement. Naturally the girls' earnings were correspondingly higher than anticipated. They were collecting their base pay, a considerable piece rate bonus, and the learning bonus which, it will be remembered, had been set to decrease with time and not as a function of current productivity. The girls were earning more now than many skilled workers in other parts of the plant.

Prediction Question

How will other personnel react and why?

PART VI

Management was besieged by demands that this inequity be taken care of. With growing irritation between superintendent and foreman, engineers and foreman, superintendent and engineers, the situation came to a head when the superintendent revoked the learning bonus and returned the painting operation to its original status: the hooks moved again at their constant time-studied designated speed, production dropped again, and within a month all but two of the eight girls had quit. The foreman himself stayed on for several months but, feeling aggrieved, then left for another job.

Discussion Questions

1. What parallels can you see between the case and this class session.
2. What conclusions can be drawn from this case about leadership, motivation, and change.

Introducing a New Appliance Model*

YOU HAVE RECENTLY TAKEN OVER as division manager of the portable TV Division of the X Electronics Company. Several years earlier this division was a leading contributor to company profits; now it is losing money and can't compete with other domestic companies or imports.

Exhibit 1 is a simplified version of the organization chart of your division.

EXHIBIT 1
Organization Chart for TV Division

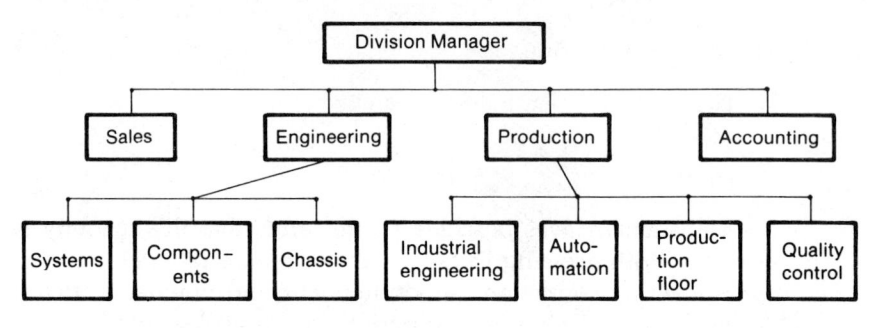

```
                    Division Manager
         ┌──────────┬──────────┬──────────┐
       Sales    Engineering  Production  Accounting
                ┌────┬────┐   ┌────┬────┬────┬────┐
             Systems Compon- Chassis Industrial Auto- Produc- Quality
                     ents            engineering mation tion   control
                                                         floor
```

Your predecessor seemed to have good accounting records which enabled him to know on a biweekly basis when any group exceeded its budgeted expenses. You also have available daily production figures which enable you to spot problems in any area.

The work in your division encompasses the following activities: Sales deals with customers (wholesale appliance dealers) and provides inputs to engineering on what features (and what prices) are desirable from a marketing point of view; and production, of course, manufactures the sets.

New models are introduced annually. This means that the systems group develops the circuitry (the underlying electrical engineering of the new set). The components group converts these specifications and design features into actual component and subsystem specifications (e.g., transistors, tubes, capacitors, etc.). The chassis group designs the cabinetry and frame. Industrial engineering determines the specific production techniques and procedures that will be used. Automation

---

*From Robert E. C. Wegner and Leonard Sayles, *Cases in Organizational and Administrative Behavior*, © 1972, pp. 176-180. Reproduced by permission of Prentice Hall, Inc., Englewood Cliffs, New Jersey.

designs and produces the equipment which makes the printed circuits and assembles components (with the goal of limited human intervention).

In reviewing past history, you note that the greatest problems seem to occur (and is not surprising) during the introduction of the new models. This past year was the worst. Sales noted a new trend toward bright, pastel-colored cabinetry. When the chassis group was consulted on changing its design for the cabinet, it reported that the type of plastics that could be obtained in the desired intense colors could not be molded with the appropriate tolerances into the size and shape cabinet that had been agreed to. More rounding would be required, which would require the components people to relocate one of their subsystems. They, in turn, said that this would have other impacts and they wanted additional time to calculate these and assess their costs.

At the same time production was pushing for final plans, saying that every day's delay meant that their final tooling and training would be off by an extra two weeks. You found a memo from engineering saying that over the years production had stepped up their requirements for lead time (final plans to first models off the line) from two months to four months. Production's response had been that the promised simplifications in design had not materialized, and that budget cutting in various efficiency programs had reduced the number of production specialists they had to guide the work force in making a smooth transition from last year's to this year's model. At the end a number of fruitless meetings were held in which sales, production, and engineering endeavored to resolve their differences.

You found several other memos which indicated that the systems group believed that the company's product was declining in quality; its reputation as the best in the industry was in jeopardy; and that good systems design was being sacrificed for what could be easily manufactured. They noted that the automation group was harassing their design engineers, seeking to get a look at the early plans to see what they were like and to persuade the engineers to make modifications that would allow for greater use of automation, simpler printed circuitry, and more machine-controlled operations. This interfered with the design work and complicated it needlessly, noted the systems manager.

Industrial engineering said that there were a number of improved manufacturing techniques the company could employ if the systems and components people would call on them before introducing major new design features. Often minor changes in the design features would allow for very major manufacturing improvements. The systems and components group argued that industrial engineering sought to dominate these discussions, and that if they employed reasonable effort and ingenuity they could find ways of converting reasonable plans into manufacturing procedures.

It is obvious that as division manager, your predecessor had spent a great deal of time on the production floor during the early part of any new model year, and during the preceding weeks, trying to resolve bottlenecks and speed decisions. During this time there were apparently a number of problems like these:

Inspection shows a badly crimped wire likely to break during shipping and production. The supervisor asks his boss to get the wire shifted, reinforced, or changed in some other way. Production head calls engineering office to see if design can be changed. After locating the man who originally specified that subsystem in components, answer goes back to production that a change can't be made. By the time the answer gets back, a large number of sets are backed up waiting for change or release. Production head then requests that either quality standard (for breakage) be lowered, or that division manager require components to change their specs. Also he requests that accounting modify its costing to take into account that components' delay in responding slows production. (It should be noted that one of the reasons for an almost automatic rejection of production's requests for component changes is that engineers have already been reassigned to new projects, and that redesign would hurt the components' expense budget.)

Another observation you make is that the head of automation is a very forceful personality who managed to influence the work of systems by getting your predecessor to agree that certain aspects of the circuitry would be checked out with automation before being finalized as part of the division's efforts to reduce manufacturing costs. Whenever a problem arose the automation group spoke with a clear, single voice. The head of systems, on the other hand, was a rather mild-mannered, theoretically oriented engineer. He rarely spoke in the name of his group, but answered each charge or request in a very logical, systematic way. Over the past several years the company had lost a good many of its more ambitious circuit designers, and you wondered what was cause and what was effect.

Another problem revolved around the production methods and standards set by industrial engineering. When these seemed too tight to the production workers, the foremen often agreed with their men. Industrial engineering would endeavor to get them accepted, noting that there was a learning curve and what seemed impossible at first, during the new model run, would seem easy after a few weeks. At times the workers would introduce "simplifications" in the job to meet the standard, and when these caused quality problems at inspection time, it was not clear where the problem originated—from incorrect or ambiguous specifications by the industrial engineers, or the changes introduced by the workers or their foremen.

When quality control sought to have the problem investigated and the line stopped, the sales group put pressure on production to ignore this if dealer stocks had not yet been filled. At such times production would argue that the company was dominated by a "sell now and don't worry about the product later" point of view, even though the company's market position had been attained through a combination of quality and technical pioneering. Sales reported that competition became keener each year, and that the end goal of the company was sales and not production.

Is There a Better Way?*

MIKE MILLER was not very fond of personnel rating systems. He had always felt, too keenly perhaps, that the evaluations he made of an individual's performance could dramatically, and sometimes drastically, affect the man's entire career. This was a little too close to omnipotence to suit Mike. Still, it was that time again and, since there wasn't any use in delaying the unpleasant chore past Friday's deadline, Mike got out the 15 rating sheets and started to work.

He had barely gotten started when Pat Parsons, one of the new managers from another department, knocked on his door and asked for a few minutes of time. Noting that Mike was working on the evaluation forms, Pat commented upon the coincidence since this was why he had come to talk. It developed that Pat had no previous experience in rating people and was seeking advice how to proceed.

Mike found himself in a quandary. He knew what he did and how he went about the task, but he was not at all sure that his approach was the best possible. He wanted to help Pat but was reluctant to give advice about a matter in which he truly lacked confidence in his own actions.

As might be expected, Mike temporized, while he gathered his thoughts, by talking about the company's policy statements concerning evaluations. Those written statements expressed the philosophical bases for having personnel evaluations, gave some general guidance regarding completion of the rating forms, and established the reporting and reviewing dates.

Pat listened quietly until Mike finished and then stated that, while this was all well and good, he needed to know specifically how Mike

---

*From John E. Dittrich and Robert A. Zawacki, *People and Organizations*, 1981. Reproduced by permission of Business Publications, Inc., Plano, Texas.

really approached the actual rating of each of his men. Seeing that there was no avoiding the issue, Mike briefly described his procedure as:

1. Comparing the individual's output in terms of what is expected of him.
2. Evaluating the individual's knowledge of his job.
3. Ascertaining how the person relates to his fellow workers and his superior.
4. Estimating his future potential.

Mike stated that this framework permitted him to establish an overall impression of the worker's value to the organization and, from that, he proceeded to record the individual markings required on the form. Mike said that he rarely made any extra written remarks, although it was permissible to do so. Mike concluded his remarks by saying that he mentally ranked his subordinates in an order-of-precedence list and then checked to see that the evaluation ratings came out correctly. If not, he made some adjustments in the ratings.

In response to Pat's question as to whether Mike kept a running record of his subordinates' performance during the rating period, Mike stated that he used to do so but had not found it helped too much, so he stopped. Mike explained that he considered progress, which was best shown by recent performance, to be a better rating basis than trying to "average out" a full rating period's activity.

The next question was really a difficult one for Mike to answer. Specifically, Pat wanted to know whether Mike gave much thought to morale factors in making his markings. After talking about the matter for some minutes, Mike finally admitted that he did consider morale to a great extent.

Mike also was asked if he knew how other supervisors marked, and if he tried to keep in line with the other raters. Mike admitted he had some general idea, but no specific knowledge, of how other people rated their subordinates. Mike expressed the hope that he rated as highly as others did, since he didn't want his good men to suffer because of a difference in raters. Mike admitted that he leaned a little toward the "high side" of the sheet just to be sure of this but defended this action by saying he had some top-notch people in his branch. Mike gave as an example the fact that one of his subordinates, who was the fastest man with figures Mike had ever seen, always received an outstanding rating. After all, as Mike noted, if he was the best "figures man" in the division, no one should be able to get a better rating.

The next question was concerned with the factors Mike considered in assessing a subordinate's potential. Mike said that he considered, basically, the promotability of the employee. If a man was qualified to be promoted—i.e., trained, had sufficient time in grade, and was a good man—then his potential was good. If he wasn't ready for promotion for some reason, then his potential was obviously limited, at this time. Mike stated that he had found it necessary to use this approach in order to be consistent in his rating. He explained that he found it impossible to say that a man had good potential but that he wasn't good enough to be promoted.

Pat's final question was to ask Mike how he handled the counseling interview sessions required by agency policy. Mike said that he had encountered no real problems. You simply told the outstanding employees they were doing a fine job, which they already knew, and advised them to keep up the good work. The few average subordinates were advised that they had done a good job and to keep on improving their performance. Mike did admit that, on two occasions, he had given marginal ratings to employees. In both cases, he told the employees that their work was passable but not as good as they could do if they applied themselves. Both men left the company for other jobs within a few months of the counseling session. Mike was of the opinion that their performance potential was so poor that they and the company were better off for their departure.

Pat thanked Mike for his assistance and advice and returned to his office.

*Lewis Equipment Company**

WHEN WILLIAM CONRAD, a case writer from the Harvard Business School, approached Samuel Coates, the plant manager at Lewis Equipment, about case possibilities, he found that Coates did have a number of concerns that sounded like good case leads. Coates explained that, even though he had been promoted to his present assignment several months earlier, he did not feel that he had as yet made nearly as many improvements in the plant's operations as he believed were possible. In particular, Coates expressed concern about his general foremen (see Exhibit 1 for a partial organization chart of the company).

Sam went on to explain that he personally was under considerable pressure from his superiors to improve factory performance. He did not believe these demands were entirely reasonable, but he believed he could make progress in meeting these demands if only he could find a

---

*Copyright 1963 by the President and Fellows of Harvard College. Reprinted by permission of the Harvard Business School. This case was prepared by Gerald Leader under the supervision of Paul R. Lawrence as a basis for class discussion rather than to illustrate either effective or ineffective handling of an administrative situation.

EXHIBIT 1
Partial Organization Chart

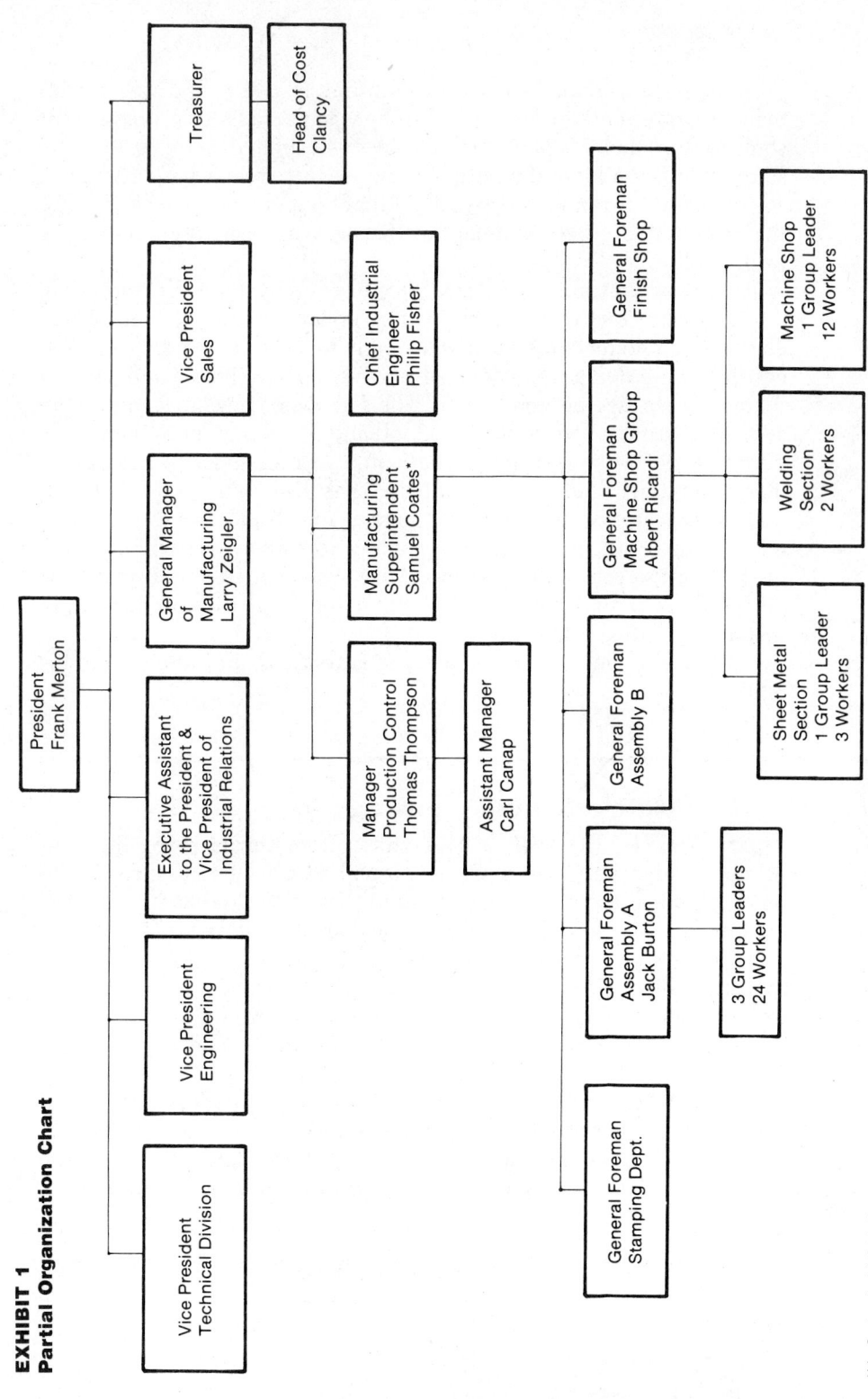

```
                                          President
                                          Frank Merton
         ┌────────────┬──────────────────┬─────────────┬────────────────┐
         │            │                  │             │                │
   Vice President  Vice President  Executive Assistant  General Manager  Vice President
   Technical       Engineering     to the President &   of               Sales
   Division                        Vice President of    Manufacturing
                                   Industrial Relations Larry Zeigler
                                                │                        │
                                                │                     Treasurer
                                                │                        │
                                                │                    Head of Cost
                                                │                    Clancy
                    ┌───────────────┬───────────┴────────┬────────────────┐
                    │               │                    │                │
              Manager          Manufacturing        Chief Industrial
              Production       Superintendent       Engineer
              Control          Samuel Coates*       Philip Fisher
              Thomas Thompson
                    │
              Assistant Manager
              Carl Canap
                                    ┌──────────────┬──────────────┬──────────────┐
                                    │              │              │              │
                              General        General         General         General
                              Foreman        Foreman         Foreman         Foreman
                              Stamping       Assembly A      Assembly B      Machine Shop
                              Dept.          Jack Burton                     Group
                                                                             Albert Ricardi
                                             │                               │
                                      3 Group Leaders              ┌─────────┼──────────┐
                                      24 Workers                   │         │          │
                                                              Sheet Metal  Welding   Machine Shop
                                                              Section      Section   1 Group Leader
                                                              1 Group      2 Workers 12 Workers
                                                              Leader
                                                              3 Workers
```

*Mr. Coates had left his former position as general foreman of the Stamping Department about a year earlier.

way to get better coordination between his formen. Sam also wanted his foremen to spend more of their time and interest on helping their own people overcome the daily problems on the factory floor. He believed his foremen were often too distracted to attend to the practical issues of training and encouraging their employees in getting their work done properly and on time. He wanted his foremen to feel responsible for all aspects of their unit and to fight for the things they felt were necessary to make their unit effective. Sam reported that he was having difficulty in getting his foremen thinking and working along these lines. Starting with this lead, William Conrad decided to spend some time with two of the foremen involved to learn more about the situation.

COMPANY BACKGROUND

The Lewis Equipment Company had been started some 15 years earlier as a science-based company producing an increasing line of equipment and instruments that were used primarily in the oil industry. After a period of early financial success and rapid growth the company had, in recent years, experienced severe competition and had been operating at a loss for about two years. At this time the company employed approximately 900 people, of which a considerable number were engineers and scientists. The factory operated on a job-order basis, and most of the products were produced to customer specifications.

ASSEMBLY DEPARTMENT A

The first department that Conrad chose to study was Assembly Department A under the general foremanship of Jack Burton. During their first conversation, Jack explained about the nature of his work and his problems.

> I have one main final assembly line that makes up 12 different types of equipment that are each produced two to six times a year. There are 10 people in this production line along with a group leader. I also have a subassembly line that makes small quantities of a variety of components and also finishes some assemblies that are produced only once or twice a year. Then I have the wire and harness line—these are the harnesses and cables used in the finished assemblies.
> We're having a lot of trouble with the specifications. The trouble is that we are not given enough time to work out the problems in specifications when they come to us. I have to accept what the engineers give me as the bible, even though there are plenty of errors from the engineers. All the control around here is really in the Engineering Department. The final test is also done by the engineers, but there is a logic in this because we could

develop our own slipshod technique if we did not have the engineers for final tests.

I get a monthly schedule in rough-draft form from production control that tells me what to do and when to do it. It keeps the material flowing. I usually get the report on the first of each month which I don't like, because if I knew in advance what the work would be like for the ensuing months I could go around to the paint foreman, etc., and put pressure on him to get the specific materials that I need for a crash program, so I would be better off.

I get a weekly direct labor utilization report made out by accounting. The Accounting Department makes this report up from the time cards and tells me what percentage of productivity resulted from our past weekly efforts. My yearly percentage of productivity to date is 62 percent, officially, but this note on the side of the sheet shows that actually I should be at 64 percent productivity. Only a small amount of the jobs are actually timed. The standards on about 90 percent of the jobs are estimated. Management is interested in improving the percent of productivity over last year's productivity. For instance we are now at 62 percent while last year this department was at a 45 percent productivity. But that improvement isn't much help, because the selling price and the budget are based on the standard times so that no matter how high the productivity is, if it is anything lower than 100 percent, they always complain.

We would show an even better percentage productivity figure if the rework hours were counted in the proper place. For example, last January we had 21 percent rework. On rework we have to eat it. If a late engineering spec change causes rework, we have to eat it, as far as the productivity figures go.

I think they are hiding their heads in the sand. They don't want to know the true cost picture. If they cross-charged rework costs to the department that caused the trouble, it would be waving a red flag in their faces and showing where the real problem lies.

THE DIRECT LABOR UTILIZATION REPORT

Burton's frequent reference to the direct labor utilization report prompted Conrad to look into this subject. He learned that this particular control system had been initiated by Mr. Merton, the company president, shortly after he had arrived at the company some three years previously. This system, designed to alert management of possible problem areas and to assist in product and inventory control, encompassed all of the company's manufacturing and assembly activities and a somewhat smaller proportion of the remaining hourly paid labor force. Mr. Merton had made every attempt to have all of the manufacturing jobs and assembly operations rated, but with frequent design modifications requested by customers and the frequent introduction of new products, this goal had never quite been achieved. Currently, some 70 percent of the direct labor force in the Manufacturing Division were working on rated jobs.

The control system was primarily aimed at controlling manufacturing labor costs by comparing the total actual time expended in manufacturing work to the accumulated standard times for each part or assembly produced. These standard times for manufacturing the necessary individual parts and for their assembly were determined by industrial engineering.

The Cost Accounting Department distributed weekly on Friday afternoon a direct labor utilization report for each department covered by the system along with a summary for the total factory organization and the total company. (See Exhibit 2 for a guide to the method of calculation of the various items.) The two most significant measures upon which subordinate organizations were evaluated were known as the productivity and efficiency ratings. Of these two ratings, the productivity figure was the more frequently quoted and discussed rating. Conrad asked James Clancy, the head of cost accounting, what the significance was of these weekly reports. The latter commented as follows:

> The reports are of some significance since the president looks at the figures every week. He usually gets the productivity and efficiency for total company and total manufacturing and plots them on a big chart in his office, which goes back several years. Sometimes he asks for reports on individual departments but he never looks at them for more than 10 minutes. I would say Mr. Zeigler[1] better be interested in them, since he knows Merton is going to talk to him every week manufacturing's performance doesn't look good. . . . A lot of the managers say that the system is a bunch of rubbish—Mr. Zeigler always says that he doesn't believe in the system. But I know they're concerned because Merton believes in it. You watch them on Friday pacing up and down, waiting to see what the results are. Their actions show that they are interested in it.

The total factory productivity and efficiency percentages were currently averaging approximately 69 percent and 79 percent respectively, which were slight increases over the previous two years. Exhibit 3 charts the productivity and efficiency percentages for the factory by months for the two preceding years. The company percentages followed closely the total factory figures, owing to the fact that of the total company hours available, 75 percent were made up of hours contributed by the factory.

---

[1] Mr. Zeigler was the general manager of manufacturing.

EXHIBIT 2
Sample Direct Labor Utilization Report with Guide to Method of Calculation

1. Total hours available — The total hours recorded on the time cards of the employees in the department concerned during the reporting period

2. Hours used on indirect labor — Percent of group leader's time spent on supr. plus inspector's and clerical help's time × 8 hours × Number of working days in reporting period

3. Hours available for direct labor — #1 minus #2

4. Hours of direct labor on nonrated jobs — Total hours expended on jobs that industrial engineering hasn't rated and/or on special jobs requested by other departments

5. Hours variance — Hours expended due to "acts of God" (e.g., machine breakdowns, power failures, snow storms) plus total rework hours*

6. Hours of direct labor on rated jobs — #3 minus (#4 plus #5)

7. Standard hours produced — Standard hours allowed for each job × Jobs completed in reporting period

8. Percent efficiency on rated jobs — #7 divided by #6

9. Percent total productivity — #7 plus #4 divided by #1

10. Rework*
    a. Responsible
    b. Not responsible

---

*Work hours expended on rework were broken down into two classifications:
a. The unacceptable workmanship of the particular organization being measured.
b. The rework occasioned by subsequent faulty work in other departments or by revisions in product design made by engineering, necessitating a rework of the job.

Mention was usually made at the bottom of the utilization report of the absolute amounts of rework completed during the reporting period.

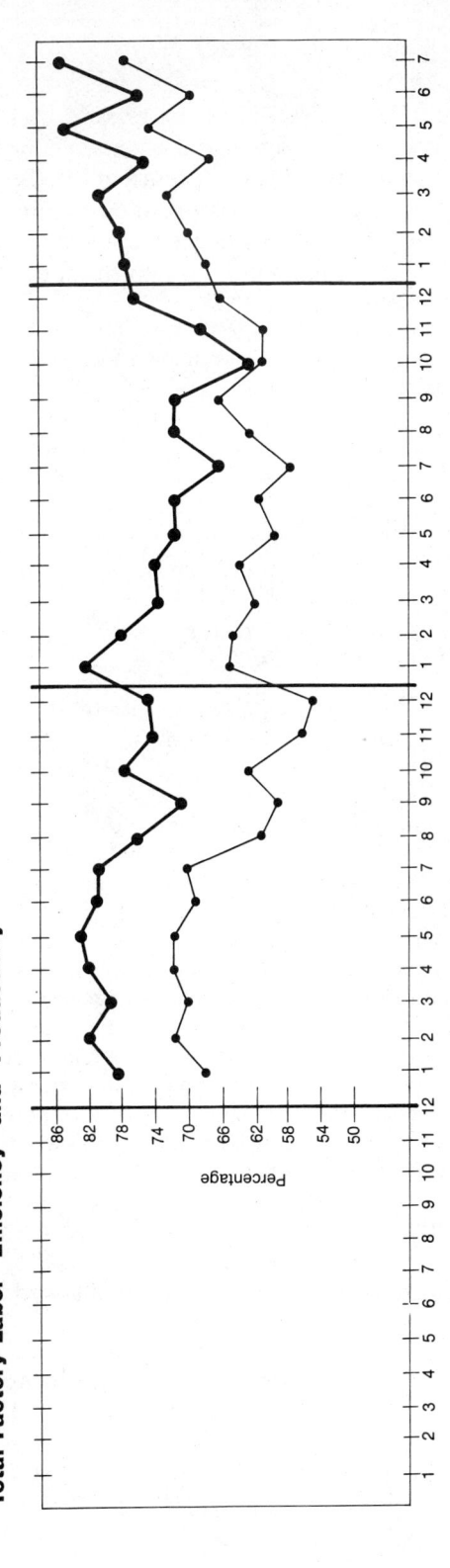

EXHIBIT 3
Total Factory Labor "Efficiency" and "Productivity"

Exhibit 4 is a sample of the actual reports that were distributed on a weekly basis to the managers and foremen concerned.

Conrad also secured direct evidence of Mr. Zeigler's concern with the productivity records. At the end of the first quarter of the current year when labor utilization percentages were dropping in successive weeks, Mr. Zeigler sent the following note to his subordinates:

> Please write up your suggestions on how we are to salvage this situation. Remember, last month's productivity was only 69 percent. By Tuesday I will expect concrete courses of action from each of you, if you are to meet or beat budget.

Conrad learned that Mr. Zeigler had sent similar notes on other occasions.

Fortified with this information, Conrad went back to observing activities in Assembly Department A.

THE PUMP EPISODE

On one of his early trips to the assembly department, Jack Burton started telling Conrad of a problem he was having:

> A little while ago my group leader of the subassembly group brought to my attention a problem concerning this pump unit. He was asking me how we could put them together and be sure they would pass final test. I noticed that there might be a chance of having some brass filings get in the critical parts if we were not careful. My group leader dug up the assembly specs which the engineers had drawn up in order to put this critical subassembly together. It called for cleaning the parts twice so that there would be positive assurance of a positive test. Then the group leader saw that the industrial engineers had not allowed enough time for the double cleaning. My group leader actually timed how long it took him to make the double cleaning, and it was considerably over the allotted time. I had the group leader figure the correct amount it would take so that we could resubmit it and get the actual time put down that we were spending on this cleaning operation.

Later in the afternoon when the case writer was talking to Burton, Phil Fisher, the head of the Industrial Engineering Department, came up and raised the topic of the standard allowed time on the cleaning operation.

FISHER: What's wrong on this pump assembly operation?
BURTON: Come over here and look at this. Our cleaning operation on the pump assembly is taking more time than you people allowed. *(Hands him the engineering assembly sheet which describes the dual cleaning operation.)*
FISHER *(after reading the sheet):* I can't understand why they have duplicate

Lewis Equipment Company

EXHIBIT 4
Direct Labor Utilization Report, Total Machine Shop Group (including the sheet metal and welding shops)

		Week Ending 6/4	Week Ending 6/11	Week Ending 6/12	Week Ending 6/25	Week Ending 7/2	Total Month Ending 7/2
1.	Total hours available	565	892	946	800	812	4,015
2.	Hours used on indirect labor	59	86	85	90	89	409
3.	Hours available for direct labor	506	806	861	710	723	3,606
4.	Hours of direct labor on nonrated jobs	8	26	37	44	17	132
5.	Hours variance	18	19	13	16	5	71
6.	Hours of direct labor on rated jobs	480	761	811	650	701	3,403
7.	Standard hours produced	303	388	508	484	266	1,949
8.	Percent efficiency on rated jobs (standard hours produced/ hours on rated jobs 7/6)	58	51	63	74	38	57
9.	Percent total productivity (standard hours + non-standard hours/ hours available 7+4/1)	55	46	58	66	35	52
10.	Rework						
	a. Responsible	-0-	-0-	-0-	-0-	-0-	-0-
	b. Not responsible	18	19	13	16	5	71

cleaning operations on this. I don't think it's needed. Look, they've got 16 operations for this part. Look, the three sections to this assembly procedure show that parts A and C are almost the same thing. They're exactly alike.

BURTON: I've got to have those chips out of there to get these pumps past final assembly test. We go by the engineering specifications. Look, this is the engineering assembly SOP.[2] It says that we should have two cleaning operations.

FISHER: There's not such a thing as an engineering SOP concerning assembly. I'm going up and see about this. I'm going to see if we can't get one of the duplicate operations for cleaning taken out of the specifications. We've got an ultrasonic cleaner that will do this job perfectly and eliminate one of these operations. That's what we've got the cleaner for anyway, to do jobs like this. This is ridiculous having so many operations. We'll be spending more time cleaning it than it takes to make it. How are we going to make any money doing this? *(Fisher leaves the room.)*

BURTON *(to case writer):* He's worried about the cost of this—claiming that we will never be able to make a profit on the product if we have to have so many

---

[2] Standard operating procedure.

operations. Look at him worried about something like this. That's the chief engineer's job. The chief engineer is the one to worry about whether or not we can make a profit using so many operations with such designs. It's up to the chief engineer to determine whether we can sell a product and make a profit. It's not up to Phil Fisher.

(Jack Burton leaves the room and the case writer talks to Phil Fisher who is coming into Burton's office as the latter leaves.)

FISHER *(to case writer):* Boy, I just can't understand it. If I were to have seen that specification sheet with that many operations on it, I would have blown my top. Some engineer started on this and because he didn't know what he was doing, he just kept applying more operations on operations. I know that if I was a foreman, I wouldn't allow that specification to come into my department without saying anything about it. How is the company going to make any money anyway?

(Jack Burton comes back into his office.)

FISHER: I want to try and clean a couple of pumps, using just one operation. I've got an idea how we can cut this down.

BURTON: Oh no you're not. I want to first check and see what final test has to say about the ones we've already done using two cleaning operations. I'm not going to have you trying to clean them with only one operation when maybe they aren't getting a positive test with two.

(Burton goes out and talks to the final test engineer and returns.)

BURTON *(to Fisher):* The test engineer said that the one we cleaned using the double operation didn't test positively. I'm not going to have you try to make a single operation out of it when we can't even get it with a double. I'm way behind on rework anyway and I can't afford the time messing around with it.

A little later on in the afternoon the case writer had a chance to talk to Jack Burton further about the pump-cleaning incident.

BURTON *(to case writer):* You know what Phil Fisher tried to do? He got my group leader behind my back and asked him to make up two complete units so he could try to test them, using only one cleaning operation. My group leader said definitely no. I'd already warned the group leader of what Phil might do and I told him not to play his game. It's this kind of thing that he does behind my back that really makes me mad. This is no isolated incident. This happens every day around here with him. He's always going off on a different set of directions. He tells me every once in a while that I'm not cooperating with him. I don't know why I have to keep shuffling my people around to try out his ideas when I am so far behind on my work. If they want to test some parts and make a better operation, they can do it themselves. They can set it up. I'm not going to have them disrupting my operation.

A little while later Fisher approached Burton.

FISHER: Hey, Jack. Come on in the test room. I want to show you what we're doing. *(The group moves to the test room.)* Look, we have a valve on the pump in the ultrasonic cleaner. Using this device, we could eliminate the operation "C" *(pointing to the engineering specifications).*

BURTON: I don't care what you do. I just want a final result!

FISHER: I just wanted to show you what we were doing to keep you up to date. This way we can be sure that the top isn't scarred when we put it in the tester.

BURTON (caustically): I don't care if there's any scars on the top!

FISHER: I thought you said it had to pass final test with a good visual inspection?

BURTON: It's the fingerprints and the filings inside the pump that cause the trouble. I'm not interested in the outward appearance. It goes in a shield anyway.

FISHER: Oh. It goes in a shield? I didn't know that.

In a later interview with the case writer, Fisher had a chance to explain some of his motives and methods in running the Industrial Engineering Department.

> This pump-cleaning operation is the type of thing that Jack Burton should be doing and working on. That's the foreman's job. Jack's a good man but he doesn't have enough work to do. When Burton and I get together, it's rather rough between us. He's firm in his opinion and I'm firm in mine.
>
> I guess some people consider me the most hated man in the firm but I'm rather proud of that position if we can get out of our present rut. I just don't have enough men in the Industrial Engineering Department to do any real big work so I have to rely on the foremen doing the job. What I have to do is to create a big stink or something so that we get some reaction from these people. We raise the commotion in the department and let the foremen take over and do the improvements from there. I think we're on the verge of a breakthrough here if we can get these foremen up using a stopwatch and watching these people and seeing if they're using the correct procedures. Why, on this pump-cleaning operation—sure, we're spending. We've got two of our men spending two hours of their time this afternoon in order that we can save a half-hour when we finally go to assembly. But if this works out we'll save the company a lot of money. You've got to spend a dollar in order to make $3.

Later, Jack Burton told the case writer some of his views on Philip Fisher.

> Phil Fisher isn't held in very high esteem because when he came in to the company a little less than a year ago he had too much initiative and tried to do too many things. He got so many projects going that he hasn't had time to finish them up.
>
> I really don't know what the industrial engineers do. It's all I can do to compose myself when I have to talk about them. I get so mad when I think about all their activities. Fisher has them doing so many projects that they don't have time to do the things that they're really supposed to be doing. Take, for instance, the harness board that I showed you earlier this morning. They're supposed to be making those up for us. The boards take about four hours to make up so that we can begin assembly. We're having to make up our own boards, eight hours of nonproductive time that we get

charged with. The last run-through, we had to clear the boards that we already made several weeks before. It took one hour to clear them and then four hours of nonproductive time to build new ones. This is the type of job that they should be doing. They should be working on giving us better standards too. The standards are way off because they are based on methods that haven't been worked out yet. That makes the productivity report an unfair basis for measuring our work. That's my big gripe with industrial engineering.

FINAL ASSEMBLY SHUTDOWN

When William Conrad arrived at the plant on the following day, he found that the main final assembly line had been temporarily shut down. This was necessary because production scheduling was unable to supply some front plates that were essential. The required plates had just been started into the paint shop that morning.

Burton commented, "This shutdown is not unusual because we always have this. It's typical. Tom Thompson[3] works his production schedule from a predicted percentage of productivity figure that Zeigler gives him. I don't know where they get the figure. I know that recently they were talking about an 85 percent productivity. I don't know where they got that. I think it was something about fixing up the line so it would be more efficient, but it certainly has never reached that level of productivity. That 85 percent figure means purchasing has to hurry up and buy some more parts and materials. Then someone gets blamed for high inventories and it swings way over the other way."

THE MACHINE SHOP

Knowing that Sam Coates was also particularly concerned about the machine shop, Conrad decided to spend a few days observing this department and it's foreman, Albert Ricardi.

In one of their early conversations, Ricardi explained, "When I took over this shop last year it was rapidly moving backward. I took over and started instituting some changes. We've made some real progress, but it doesn't show in the figures. Accounting has been cutting us into bits. The standards being used are not real standards. They're guesses—pulled out of the air. Then we get hit with the productivity report and we're bums. All they're interested in is making us look bad. I have to spend about 97 percent of my time just coddling all the people who come down here from other departments."

The case writer came in early the following Monday morning and was

---

[3] Production control manager.

present when Tom Thompson, the production control supervisor for the Manufacturing Division, came into Ricardi's office.

THOMPSON: Al, we really need this job. There's only one operation left on it and it has to be done. Al, I know you're in a bind but we need this by today. Is there anything you can do?

RICARDI: We're really shorthanded today. Well, I could see what we could do about putting it in the process.

THOMPSON: I've talked to Brown over in the model shop and he said he could do it for me, that is, if it's all right with you.

RICARDI: No. We don't get any credit on it that way. We've started the job and I want to finish it.

THOMPSON: Well, Al, I understand how you feel about it and I know it will disrupt your operation.

RICARDI: Well, we'll see what we can do about it, but I'm not guaranteeing anything. Maybe we can get it out this afternoon. *(Thompson leaves.)*

CONRAD: Well, Al, how do you feel on this blue Monday?

RICARDI: Not so good. All my good workers and good machinists are out and I don't know what I'm going to do. My inspector is out and I'm really going to be running around like a chicken with his head cut off. I guess when your luck runs out, it really goes all at once. Saturday we were running around and found that the drill press operator had drilled the counterbore shallow on those plates we were doing. We had to run 84 of those pieces over again. You don't have to be a machinist to see that the men around here leave a lot to be desired. And then there's Tom Thompson coming down here. If they would leave us alone we would get ahead and get something running and we wouldn't have all these rush jobs. Every time they send in and ask us to do something of a rush nature, that cuts out our general efficiency and we just can't get ahead. That's why I ignored Thompson. When the men quit a job in the middle of it, they get confused or forget and make mistakes. It takes them time to get started again. Here's Thompson asking me to do a rush job. I just can't afford to do it.

SCHEDULING PROBLEMS

Several days later Conrad was walking through the shop with Ricardi when he commented on a pile of finished parts.

CONRAD: These castings really look nice, Al. I think Archie did a pretty good job on them.

RICARDI: Yes, they look nice all right, there is no doubt about that. But we have another lot of 50 more coming along right now. I just got the order in today.

CONRAD: What? I thought Archie just finished up this lot.

RICARDI: Yes, I know. They should all have been done at the same time. If we had had the order of 50 that we got today, it would have been a complete gift. As it is now we will have to set up the machines again and run the whole batch through. They really don't know how much it is costing them. That is what is wrong with this company. They are afraid to ask how much something costs. When someone asks them or they try to price a product, they use the standard hours but the standard hours aren't near what we actually spend on making the product. They don't allow us any time for setups or making fixtures or for any unforeseen events. Those are the main times that are involved. I asked the Accounting Department one day how much it really cost to make a product and they gave me the computations from the standard hours; I told them that they were no good. They were left without any answer.

MACHINE SHOP AND PRODUCTION CONTROL

In the course of a number of conversations with Sam Coates, Conrad learned that Coates was well aware of the same signs of trouble in the Assembly Department and the Machine Shop that Conrad had seen. For instance, Coates told Conrad of a recent talk he had had with Ricardi:

> Just today I happened to mention the production control group to Ricardi and he about exploded. He started pacing up and down. He said that Carl Canap, the assistant production control manager, was personally out for him. I was shocked by the vehemence. When he calmed down, I asked him, "Al, what have I been saying to you?" He stopped. "You are running the shop, not Sam Coates or Larry Zeigler or production control. Now why do you feel threatened? Don't you realize that you have forgotten more machine shop operations and the scheduling of machine shop work than Carl Canap will ever learn?" I told him that he had to assert himself in a positive way. I told him that he was running the shop and no one else.

Mr. Coates told the case writer that since this conversation, he was attempting to remedy the conflict between Ricardi and Carl Canap by having the latter's boss, Tom Thompson, temporarily work with Ricardi instead of Mr. Canap. Sam continued, "If Tom can charm Al so that they work well together, then, later, when Al deals with Canap, he'll let all the little things that have been bothering him go by. Just for Al to be with Thompson will help out a lot in smoothing over the relationship between Al and Carl."

In the morning of the day following the Ricardi-Coates conversation, Conrad observed Tom Thompson talking to Ricardi about scheduling problems and procedures. Carl Canap had not made an appearance. Later in the day Coates and Ricardi were sitting in the former's office, when Ricardi's assistant came in and stated that Carl Canap had just requested that the machine shop stop production of an item that was partially completed and substitute a "rush job" which used the same machine. Ricardi immediately commented to Coates.

RICARDI: See, Sam, this is the type of thing that I have been talking about. We lose all our efficiency by breaking down in the middle of an operation.

COATES: Al, what have I been telling you for the last week and a half? You don't stop an order in the middle of production. You clear out the job before you start another.

RICARDI *(after a long pause):* What do I do?

COATES: Al, you're the foreman, not Carl Canap. You're the foreman of this shop, not anyone else.

RICARDI *(turning to face the assistant):* Don't do anything.

Approximately 15 minutes later Coates and Ricardi were interrupted in their conversation by Carl Canap, who burst through the doorway and with an angered tone of voice questioned Mr. Coates.

CANAP: Sam, I understand you and Al won't allow that rush job to be substituted. Is that true?

COATES: Don't look at me, Carl. Al is the foreman of this outfit, you talk to him.

CANAP: What about that, Al?

RICARDI *(pause):* That's right.

CANAP: Do you realize you are hurting the company, losing sales, losing money? What is this company coming to if we can't rearrange the schedule a little just because somebody wants to get a little extra credit on the weekly report. Do you realize what this means?

COATES *(angrily):* Listen here, Carl, Al is right. We're not going to switch and henceforth you'll not be stopping production in the middle of any operation. This is my decision and I want you to stick by it.

CANAP *(walking out of the office):* If that's the way you want it, that's the way it will be.

SAM COATES'S VIEWS

Some few days later Sam Coates was talking to the case writer about the general situation:

> Higher management has become so concerned with the figures that they forget about what we're actually producing, what's finished and what's good quality. The figures get divorced from what they stand for. But if you're going to have the system, you have to play along with it. I'm sure there are a lot of details about the figures that my foremen and particularly Al are overlooking. In fact, I think he's making himself look poor. His desk is in such a disarray and things come so fast that he just gives up and says, "Oh, to hell with it!" Al has got to learn that he can't work on a bunch of long and hard jobs at the same time and expect to get a good productivity rating. He's got to get his work finished up by Saturday so he can get credit for it. He's not making the most of what he's got down there.

Mailorder Merchandise, Inc.

MAILORDER MERCHANDISE, INC. (MMI), is a moderately sized mail-order firm located in the downtown area of a large eastern city. While its success is heavily dependent on its advertising and procurement activities, one of its critical operations is the processing of customer orders received by mail twice daily.

The order processing department at MMI employs about 50 people on each of two shifts. The day shift is composed of full-time employees who work from 8:00 A.M. to 4:30 P.M., taking a ½-hour lunch period. The evening shift are part-time employees who take over at 5:00 and work until 9:00 P.M.

The job itself is rather routine, consisting of typing orders into a computer-based information system. The information thus fed into the computer is automatically transmitted to the warehouse to initiate order packing and shipping, and to the billing department for the processing of checks and bills.

Employees of the department sit at computer terminals. Each receives a batch of orders that have been removed from the mailing envelope. Each batch contains around 25 orders, although the quantity can vary from 20 to 35. The steps required to process each order are fairly straightforward. First, each item number and unit price listed on the order have to be verified for accuracy; in the case of an order for more than one unit of each item, the total price must be recalculated on a calculator. Then a control number has to be assigned, written on the customer's order, and all the information for each item typed into the computer.

Thereafter, the customer's order and check (if a credit card was not used) are attached to the work order produced by the computer, and the order is sent on to the accounting department. Any customer orders with inaccuracies or questionable instructions must be set aside for processing by a working supervisor.

Thus, accuracy, speed, and reliable attendance are the desired attributes of order-processing employees. A knowledge of the company's product line is helpful in spotting errors (erroneous item numbers, items from an outdated catalog, wrong prices, missing zip codes, etc.), and, in time, operators learn item numbers and unit prices of the more popular items and so do not need constantly to refer to the catalog. While anyone with reasonable typing ability and some skill in basic arithmetic can do the job, it usually takes a new employee three to four weeks to get up to speed and do errorless work.

MMI is located in a relatively new and attractive office building. Other organizations in the area include several insurance companies, two electronics assembly plants, two of the city's many educational institutions, as well as retail stores, restaurants, theaters, and various tourist attractions.

The Mayfield Medical Center

PART I

FOR SEVERAL HOURS the quarterly meeting of physicians and board members of the Mayfield Medical Center had been in session. The issue currently in heated debate concerned raising the fees to be charged a patient who is seen by a nurse practitioner; i.e., should the patient be charged the same amount for an office visit with a nurse practitioner as with a physician?

"Yes!" insisted Dr. Harold Bickford, "the NPs perform the same services as most physicians in an office visit situation. Because the patient is receiving health care from a highly trained individual, the fee should be identical especially once the NP has completed her first year of direct physician supervision."

In contention with this viewpoint, Dr. Thomas Hatton retorted, "I see no reason to adjust the fees when the ultimate responsibility for the patient still rests with physician with whom the NP is associated! How do you think the public will react to rising charges?"

As the issue was being forced to an ultimate decision, Dr. Horace Abbott, a young and relatively new member of the medical center staff, sat listening to the debate. His associates appeared to be evenly divided for and against the issue, and heated arguments continued to burst out sporadically among the board members. He alone had not yet voiced an opinion, and he began to realize that his vote would be crucial.

Discussion Question

1. What factors should Dr. Abbott consider in reaching his decision on how to vote?

PART II

The Mayfield Medical Center is located in a relatively small Connecticut community and primarily services this community and adjacent townships. Approximately 30 doctors and 7 nurse practitioners work at the center. Among the services the medical center provides are psychiatry, family practice, pediatrics, internal medicine, obstetrics, and surgery. The center also has an x-ray machine of limited capability for routine x-rays and minor fractures. Because it is in competition with the Mayfield hospital, however, the x-ray machine provides a relatively insignificant income to the center. As a further public service, the center has recently employed a gerontologist and a person in community medicine who does public health education in the local schools and with community groups. Although felt to be a priority function, the employment of someone for public health education has proven an additional source of financial pressure on the already tight financial situation within the medical center. One reason for the tight financial situation is the relatively low patient charges of the center combined with high operating overhead and rising costs. In the past years, the cost of labor and supplies has risen sharply in the medical field. Despite these facts, the center has established a reputation for technically excellent health care as well as for concerned, community-oriented health education. Although the medical center is not an affluent organization and carries a heavy overhead, its charges for medical services are not considered excessive in relation to other clinics.

Normally, the physicians at the center work on a 15-minute office visit or consultation schedule. A patient is charged approximately $30 for an hour-long office visit or $8 per quarter-hour. The medical center's pay system for the physician consists of a set salary with additional salary in proportion to the dollar amount billed to his patients each month. The medical center's charges are on par with those of similar clinics, but the salaries of the doctors themselves are at a fairly moderate level in comparison to what they could make in private practice. "We are not here to get rich," one younger yet highly respected physician at the center had commented, "but this organization is facing a far too serious financial crisis for us to ignore the issue at hand. The fees must be adjusted and the public educated to the necessity. To say that the public won't pay is ridiculous!"

The seven nurses at the medical center, all of whom are female, had been trained as nurse practitioners in an intensive series of six- to eight-week courses. Their evolution in this field had come in response to the needs of the community and the growing number of patients at the center who appeared for routine treatment. Nurses who were trained to meet these needs were utilized in the specific areas of pediatrics, obstetrics, and internal medicine. After completion of a formal nurse-practitioner training course, the NP works under the direct guidance and supervision of a physician for a period of one year. Thereafter, the NP sees patients within a bounded area of responsibility without the presence of a doctor, refering out-of-the-ordinary cases to a designated physician. All of the center's NPs will soon have completed their year of direct physician supervision.

The reactions of the community to the NPs have been varied: "I felt like I had her full attention. Dr. Fisher is always so busy, I hate to bother him with silly questions." "A doctor is a doctor to me; he is not some female who's had a few extra courses!" "It's nice to talk to another woman about delicate matters. I felt more relaxed and was impressed by her competence and knowledge. This is my first baby."

Discussion Questions

1. What factors should the Mayfield Medical Center consider in reaching its decision?
2. What decision would you recommend? Why?

PART III

The debate continued in the board room and Dr. Abbott was beginning to feel the pressure of his silence. As the factions divided, hostility was becoming evident.

"The cost of running this medical center rises every year, gentlemen. Yet we must provide the community with the best medical services we have to offer and at a reasonable price!"

"We have invested time and money in the training of our nurse practitioners. It is common knowledge that other clinics have begun to charge the same office fees for both NPs and physicians. We have every right, morally and legally, to charge equivalent fees."

"The legal aspect of this whole thing overwhelms me. We physicians are still responsible for the medical decisions of the NPs even when we are no longer present during routine consultations, and no longer supervising their every step."

"The reason the center adopted the NP in the first place was to help reduce the cost of health care. To charge the patient the same fee for their services is to defeat our initial purpose!"

"If the patient pays less for consultation with an NP than with one of us doctors, don't you think they'll consider they have received second-class attention?"

"The patient should pay more for a physician because of an MD's ability to see other possible implications in symptoms."

As it appeared to Dr. Abbott, a larger portion of the younger doctors were for raising the center's fee for consultation with an NP. The younger and less experienced physicians often had the most interaction with the NPs and more appreciation of their ability to give good care within a bounded area. He could see some of them looking his way for added support. These were his new friends. Dr. Bickford had helped orient him to the center and in diagnosing that touchy rubella case last week. On the other hand, Dr. Hatton was an old family friend and had initially proposed him to the board of the medical center. He owed him his job and the chance to practice medicine.

The final poll proceeded slowly around the room. Yes, his was to be the decisive vote. In the back of his mind, Abbott recalled a recent Mayfield newspaper editorial by the mayor and chairman of the hospital board harping on the rising cost of medical care. Now all eyes were focused on him. Acceptance by peers or repayment of personal debt? The issue was becoming confused in his mind. How should he vote?

Discussion Questions

1. Given all the information you have, what rate policy would you recommend be adopted by the Mayfield Medical Center? Why?
2. If you were Dr. Abbott, what would you do?

Merger Talks at Canal and Lake*

AS HE OCCASIONALLY FELT outside the mainstream while at the graduate school, it always came to Morgan as a source of wonder how one assignment or contact led to another. The special stockholders meeting at Wickersham Mills led him to become a good friend of Charles Hall of the Massachusetts Bay Bank. Charles, in turn, suggested his name to Gilbert Rhodes, president of Erie Canal National Bank and Trust Company, when the latter was looking for a business school professor who might consult with him for a day or two. Intrigued, Morgan had agreed to visit Rhodes the next week. Entering Rhodes's office, he introduced himself to a stocky bullnecked man in his middle 50s whose thick glasses gave him the appearance of Teddy Roosevelt. Strikingly decorated with scarlet upholstery on divan and chairs, chalk white walls, navy blue drapes, the office was large and impressive.

RHODES *(with a brief handshake):* Won't you have a seat, Professor? I asked Charles to be rather mysterious about my invitation to consult with us because what I have to ask is highly confidential and must be handled with the greatest delicacy.

MORGAN: My curiosity and my patience are boundless!

RHODES: Good. The reason for my caution, Mr. Morgan, is that I am currently engaged in negotiations for the merger of this bank with another highly reputable but somewhat smaller institution. I am not one to beat around

---

*From Abram T. Collier, *Management, Men and Values,* 1960, Harper & Row Publishers, Inc., New York, N.Y. Reproduced by permission of the author.

the bush: The other bank is the Lake Ontario Trust. I must ask you to treat this information with the strictest confidence. If word leaked out before any commitments have been reached, the deal would die a-borning. I am a fair-minded man, Mr. Morgan; I have laid my cards on the table, but every time I think we are making progress, I find there is some new reason for delay.

I have told the men at Lake—Sears and Talbot—that you are doing a research study at the graduate school of business, and that you are interested in the problems associated with mergers. Thus you have expressed interest in talking with the key officers of both banks. I stretch the truth, but am I stretching it too far, Professor?

MORGAN (*doubtfully*): No, I guess not.

RHODES: You still don't sound too sure. I have also told them that I was going to ask you to enter this if everyone would talk freely and fully, that any conclusion you reach would be available to all of us.

MORGAN: Let me see if I have it straight: You want me to try to discover what may be delaying the proposed merger. Any report I file will be available to both parties. Is that it?

RHODES: That's right. Even though they know they may be quoted, I'm betting they will talk more freely with you than they have with us. I may be wrong, but I am ready to take a calculated risk. When you are a banker, Professor, you have to judge people and take risks on people. There would, of course, be a reasonable fee for you.

MORGAN: All right, I go along, Mr. Rhodes—on condition the fee is no secret to the other bank, and that I may be free to withdraw completely if I conclude that I cannot in good conscience file a full report.

RHODES: Agreed. Well, why don't we begin right now? What would you like to know?

MORGAN: You'll have to start from scratch; I am new to banking. What kind of a bank is the Canal Bank?

RHODES: Well, I suppose the first thing you need to know is the pecking order. The Empire State is the largest bank in this city; we are second. We like to think we are a strong second and getting stronger. Empire State is the product of mergers that took place 35 or 40 years ago. We've been gaining during the last 10, partly by mergers and partly by gaining a larger share of new business.

We are known as the bank that is always ready to take a chance on a good man. We've had a rash of new companies formed around here. Other banks feared many would not last, but we made it our policy to go all out with any company that had management that was good, or could learn to be good. We have loaned these companies on inventory, receivables, machinery, anything that had a fair chance to pay out. The result is that we have had to write off a few bad loans, but we have also tied to us several of the fastest-growing companies now in orbit.

We're the kind of bank, Mr. Morgan, that studies account habits. Over the years we have found a depositor shifts his account very rarely. The important thing is to get customers when they are small, so that as they grow, we grow.

MORGAN: What about your staff?

RHODES: It's younger than any other bank in town, and better, too, in my opinion. Most banks are as stodgy as their reputations. They are full of old men—afraid to make decisions if they are in the lower ranks, or afraid to delegate authority if they are in the upper. I had the problem of too many old men when I first became president here. Fortunately, a large number retired just about that time and I helped a few more to take early retirement. Then we went out to recruit the best young fellows we could get. We didn't promise them much money, but we did promise them responsibility. It's amazing what people will do, Professor, simply for the chance to work hard. Now we are well known to young men in the colleges and business schools as the bank that won't make them wait in line for 20 years before they get a chance to show what they can do.

MORGAN: I see. What about the Lake Ontario Trust? Where does it fit in the pecking order?

RHODES: Well, as a commercial bank, the Lake is small. Its assets are less than $100 million, which would make it about sixth in town. But as a trustee and fiduciary, it handles accounts that have a book value of more than $350 million. This is more trust business than we have on our own books, even though our assets are several times larger. The merger with the Lake wouldn't do much to close the asset gap between us and Empire, but it would double our trust business and help us achieve substantial economies in trust handling costs.

What kind of a bank is the Lake? Its fuddy duddies do a marvelous job of dealing with old ladies, and its new business department hardly exists, but it does have a lot of solid trust business.

MORGAN: Who are the key figures at the Lake? Didn't you mention a Mr. Sears?

RHODES: Right—Clinton Sears, chairman of the board, and John Talbot, president. Sears is one of the most charming men you will ever meet. He may be 69, Cornell, the right ancestors, but he's no snob. When you meet him, you will be impressed by his graciousness, his wit, his urbanity. If you resist, you may count yourself among the fortunate few.

MORGAN: What about Mr. Talbot?

RHODES: Quite a different sort of man. John Talbot has been president of the Lake for about six years and he is now about 63. If Clint has charm and wit, old John has none. Not that he's a sourpuss, it is just that John is unruffled, methodical, deeply loyal to the bank. Sears was trained as a lawyer, came into the bank as a trust officer, but old John went into the bank right out of Hamilton over 40 years ago. He married the bank and has never looked at another woman since!

MORGAN: Wonderful! Both of these men are in their 60s; isn't there a younger man to take over?

RHODES: Well, they have Jim Tyler. Bright young chap, but he can't be more than 41 or 42.

MORGAN: Coming back to the Canal Bank, Mr. Rhodes, who do you have here to back you up?

RHODES: George Upham, probably the finest bank officer in the town. George is 48, just about eight years younger than myself. He has the title of executive vice president, but I really delegate to him the running of the bank, just as far as I can. I'm at the age when I feel I am entitled to get away for a week or two every now and then.

MORGAN: What are Mr. Upham's deficiencies?

RHODES: Well, sometimes he bothers people by examining into every little angle of every problem. He's a perfectionist. I like to make up my mind quickly, but George will weigh the pros and cons. I thrive on controversy; George wants harmony. We complement each other, you see.

MORGAN: Good. Now, may I ask how the merger proposal came about?

RHODES: Well, it would be stupid to broach the matter myself. I dropped comments to Sears from time to time from which he might have inferred I would be receptive to an offer to merge. Finally, four months ago, he came to my office and suggested that we ought to get together. But since then he has done nothing but make impossible suggestions: *Tyler*, he says, should be promised the presidency when I move; the main office should be over in the Lake building; the new name should be the Lake Bank and Trust; his directors should constitute half the new board; we should give another half-share of Canal stock for Lake. And, of course, at the age of 69, he demands that he be guaranteed a job as chairman of the executive committee at the same salary he has been getting as chairman of his own board.

MORGAN: Where does your board stand on the merger?

RHODES: My board will be told in due time; a board is no place for secrets. But at Lake, I have convinced three board members that the merger is their only salvation, and I have assured them that I will take them over onto the new board. They won't be just figurehead members of an advisory committee.

Don't waste your time on me, Professor. Try Sears and Talbot. They can tell you more about what the hitches are than I can. Talk to George, too. He'll tell you some of the things I may have forgotten.

MORGAN: Thanks, I will. With luck, I'll talk to all three today or tomorrow. See you later.

That afternoon, Morgan keeps an appointment with Clinton Sears in the chairman's office at the Lake Ontario Trust. Sears is a large man, still impressive at 69. His white hair and pink cheeks combine with a quick smile to put Morgan quickly at ease. The office walls of gold and powder blue are covered with autographed portraits. A table and bookcase are filled with silver cups, gavels, and other tokens of esteem.

SEARS: Professor Morgan? It is a genuine pleasure to make your acquaintance. My very dear friend, Gilbert, has told me of his conversations with you. He presides, you know, over one of the great banks of this city. He was greatly impressed with the speed with which you grasped the essentials of this complicated business. You are most welcome.

MORGAN: Thank you, but I really. . . .

SEARS: You do not need to be modest with me. Dean Fay is one of my very oldest friends and he has told me of his joy when he persuaded you to join his faculty.

MORGAN: Thank you. But tell me, Mr. Sears, what kind of a bank is the Canal Bank?

SEARS: A great institution, sir. A great institution. Fifteen years ago it was nothing, but now by breaking every rule of the business it is the second largest bank in this great city. We used to joke that a fellow could always get a loan at the Canal if only his credit was bad enough. Of course, it does not enjoy the patronage of any of the old established businesses.

MORGAN: How then has it succeeded?

SEARS: By swallowing up every other bank that falters in the race. Gilbert and his crew have an uncanny ability to sense the soft spot in any one. They have my deepest respect.

MORGAN: I see. Lake Ontario Trust, I take it, has a far different reputation.

SEARS: You are joking with me, Professor Morgan. Everyone knows we are the most conservative, the most careful bank west of the Hudson. Long before the Chase Manhattan came out with those cute ads showing how to care for a nest egg, Lake had adopted the nest egg as its trademark and had made the eggs of hundreds of fine families grow to an extent they never dreamed of.

In our offices we have the same green rugs surrounding the desks of our trust officers that were there 25 years ago; we make copies of our correspondence on letter presses; we take pride in our receptionist, a lady who has been here for over 40 years. We are deliberate in wanting our settlors and our beneficiaries to have the feeling we were here yesterday and will be here tomorrow.

Of course, behind the scenes we have one of the most modern installations of electronic equipment, a forward-looking group of investment officers headed up by a young dynamo named Jim Tyler, and a control system that had produced for us a larger profit each year for over 20 years. The result is that our stock has shown a higher percentage increase than Canal Bank itself.

MORGAN: That sounds like a remarkable record. What are Mr. Rhode's motivations for the merger?

SEARS: He is much too smart to allow me to know them, Professor. But if you ask me to guess, I would say that while Gilbert is big, he wants to be bigger. He's like a lot of men who have had to fight all the way: he expects no mercy and he gives none. He has been here many years now, but there is still evidence of the habits he acquired years ago in New York City.

MORGAN: Let me ask about Mr. Talbot, your president here.

SEARS: John? One of nature's noblemen. He's a banker's banker. I came here as a lawyer; John was always here. He did a great job on the investment side. He exudes sincerity.

MORGAN: Are you well acquainted with Mr. Upham in the other bank?

SEARS: George is obviously a brilliant man, he knows banking from A to Z, and he is the fellow who really makes Canal Bank hang together. His problem is that he does not get into things outside the bank. Every good banker must be a salesman for his bank, you know.

MORGAN: I see. Could you tell me how these merger talks came about?

SEARS: All right. Gilbert thinks he teased me into this and it is all his own idea. No harm in his continuing to believe it either. The fact is I have been hoping that we would merge ever since the Niagara and the Mohawk Banks joined the Canal Bank over five years ago. I would have preferred to merge with them directly, but Gilbert moved too fast.

MORGAN: If you are making good progress, why should you feel it necessary to merge at all?

SEARS: Well, a small bank has really no place to go. We are too small to handle the commercial requirements of any businesses that count. And our kind of clientele is too upper register to lead us to the run-of-the-mill small businessman. As far as the trust business goes, from which we derive better than 80 percent of our profits, it has a limited future unless it is tied to a large commercial bank. We have the accounts of most of the fine old families, but they are running out. In competition with big banks for new trust business, it is increasingly difficult to take clients away from them.

MORGAN: If you see it this clearly, why has there been any delay in consummating this deal?

SEARS: Delay? I had not been aware that there had been any delay. We are negotiating an important matter. There is no hurry. I am not yet committed to this deal and I am determined not to play a second fiddle at a concert where Gilbert is calling the tune. After all, there is my reputation and the reputation of this bank. Lake has a proud name to be preserved. It is a name that is synonymous with quality; something the Canal Bank has never really had. They want it; we have it. We will not sell it cheaply.

MORGAN: Thank you, Mr. Sears. May I say it has been an honor to talk with a man who has enjoyed so distinguished a career. Perhaps we will meet again.

SEARS: I truly hope so. Now you want to talk with John. He said he would be waiting for you. I will ask Miss Coleman to take you to his office. *(Presses buzzer.)* Good day.

Following the chairman's secretary, Morgan quickly finds himself in the office of John Talbot. Decorated with Nile-green walls and drapes, the office contains several highly polished pieces of early colonial furniture. From a clear desk, a bland appearing, short and slight man in his early 60s arises to greet his visitor.

TALBOT: Please sit down. Professor. I have been expecting you. Perhaps it would be best if you asked me what you want to know.

MORGAN: Yes, that is kind of you. Perhaps you would be willing to tell me what kind of a bank the Canal Bank is?

TALBOT: The Canal Bank, sir, is a bank that tries to be all things to all people. It's a department store bank; it will do anything that will turn a profit, and some things that are bound to produce a loss.

It has automobile business and loan accounts. It goes in big for construction loans. It trades in municipals and federal bonds. It has a chain of correspondent banks and a foreign department, though there is little foreign business here. In short, I do not know of a large bank that is spread so thinly over so many areas.

MORGAN: By "thinly," I take it you mean it has limited manpower.

TALBOT: Yes, I guess *limited* is the right word. It has mediocrities trying to act like big men.

MORGAN: What about Lake Ontario Trust?

TALBOT: For practical purposes, we have only one type of business: we are fiduciaries. We like to think we are the best in the city. We charge high fees; give top service. What the general public does not realize is that we have pushed our specialities well into the middle-class market. We have the fastest-growing common trust fund in the city—limited, you know, to accounts of less than $100,000. Our appointments as an executor have doubled in the past five years, mostly in moderately sized estates. We have maintained good contacts with the top life insurance underwriters, and through them, have pushed insurance trusts to levels we thought were impossible.

MORGAN: Why then should you want to merge?

TALBOT: I don't. *(Pauses.)*

MORGAN: I am not sure I understand.

TALBOT: I don't wonder. I suppose you have been told this merger talk has come about because of the trends and the times, that it will be good for both banks, etcetera, etcetera. I don't want to disillusion you, but nothing could be farther from the truth. *(Pauses.)*

MORGAN: Oh!

TALBOT: An astute man should begin to suspect the truth, so I suppose I might as well tell you. I have been general manager of this bank for just over 20 years, although I didn't get the title until six years ago. Clinton Sears is about as well connected by family, clubs, charities, as any man in the city. He is on the boards of more than a dozen substantial corporations; he serves as the treasurer of every worthwhile cause. The job of running the bank has fallen to me. And I am about to hit retirement. A team of six white horses couldn't keep me here after I hit 65. Clint likes the idea of being somebody in the city and he will stay until someone pushes him out.

We have been banking on Jim Tyler to take over my spot. He has just about everything: drive, judgment, charm, and sophistication. Unfortunately, he also has imagination and ambition. Our friend, Gilbert, knows this, and he also knows that he cannot deal with me. For me to sell this bank would be like selling my own child.

You want to know what happened? Well, I was double-teamed. First, Gil went after Jim Tyler. He told Jim that he needed a successor; took him up to the top of the mountain and promised him the presidency of the new bank—"in due course"—whatever that means. Jim has his scruples—he said he would think about it, but that he had commitments to us. When I heard the story—how he was to get double his salary and options of 5,000 shares of Canal Bank stock—I said I couldn't advise him. But I did ask him if Gil was the kind of man he wanted to tie his future to.

Gil, meanwhile, went to work on Clint, who along with three other members of our board, owns about 17 percent of our stock. The other three are in their 70s and the bank stock is a large part of their estates. They have never thought they could sell it because of the tax bite, but when Gil comes along with stock having a wide market and offers them Canal Bank stock in a tax-free swap that gives them 30 percent more than current market values call for, all four start to drool.

Now imagine their surprise when Jim, instead of being contrary, says the deal looks good to him. What could be more perfect! Everyone sees, of course, what Gil has been up to, but what could be better—salable Canal Bank stock and cushy jobs for everyone. Who is to complain? No one except me.

MORGAN: And what have you decided to do?

TALBOT: I haven't decided. Clint knows that I'm still not sold and might kick up a fuss. That's why he is hesitating, in my opinion anyway. And my fuss might just cause trouble in Washington.

MORGAN: I see what you mean. The comptroller general, the Department of Justice.

One last question—how does George Upham fit into this picture, or doesn't he?

TALBOT: I can't honestly say. I have known George for a long time, and I like him, but I can't say I really know where he stands. He has to pick up a lot of the chips after Gil. A bit too tense, but he is conscientious and reliable, the type of fellow that every good banker should be.

MORGAN: Well, thank you for the background story.

The following morning, Morgan is back at the Canal Bank in the office of George Upham, executive vice president. Upham, tall, thin, spectacled, seems pleasant, but remote. The gray walls of his office are lined with book cases. A large table which serves as a desk is covered with papers neatly sorted into piles.

UPHAM: . . . Won't you have a cigar while we talk?

MORGAN: No, thanks. I'm trying to cut down on nicotine, if not calories.

As you know, I've been talking to a number of people trying to understand the factors that go into this type of deal. How would you characterize the two banks?

UPHAM: Two vital institutions. Two fine banks with fine people.

MORGAN: You look forward, then, to the merger with the Lake Ontario Trust.

UPHAM: Sorry, I didn't mean to give you that impression. Perhaps I should explain. Just over three years ago, the Canal Bank took over two other banks. We still have not coped with all the strains those mergers created! You must realize that while a merger is easy to talk about, it takes a long time to accomplish.

In both mergers, Gil made it clear that no one would lose his job. Result: confusion compounded—we still have two, and in some cases, three men trying to do many key jobs in the bank. Costs were supposed to drop. Instead they have edged up. Morale that was supposed to soar, has dropped like a duck with a bellyful of shot. Need I say more?

MORGAN: You have a case of indigestion.

UPHAM: Indigestion, Mr. Morgan, is a mild word. I am as loyal to Gil as any man, and Gil knows exactly how I stand on this, but I'm the fellow who has to cope with all the problems these mergers cause. Gil deals only with the "big picture"—and now he wants to take over the sweetest banking operation in town. I have always envied the Lake: clean, tidy, profitable. Everybody there knows what he is doing. I have always thought that working at the Lake would be Heaven, but to take it over: Lord, save us!

MORGAN: You have opposed the merger then?

UPHAM: Of course, but when you deal with a man like Gilbert Rhodes, do you ever change him? No, he smiles as though you never said a word, pats you on the back, and says, "George, I knew you'd think it was a great idea." The trouble is he's almost always right, and he keeps us on our toes.

MORGAN: What are the important things that keep Canal Bank going?

UPHAM: The important thing we do—and I am responsible—is to keep ahead of our customers. Long ago we learned that the men who call on our major accounts rarely find out what they really think. Their relationship is built too much on friendship. To uncover important criticisms of the bank, we have had to employ outside consultants, men who test the market and find out what people *really* think of the job we are doing.

In addition to our customers' opinion on our present job, we also probe to find out what they think we ought to be doing. We're finding that most people do not like easy credit. They rather like the idea that it is hard to get a loan, and they get satisfaction when they qualify for one. Paradoxically, we find there is no real evidence that our customers would think any less well of us if we went into the small loan business and really give the finance companies a run for their money! Excuse the puns, please.

MORGAN: How did the merger talks come about?

UPHAM: Well, last year when we saw that Talbot was within three years of retirement, and knowing that he was looking forward to making reproductions of 17th-century furniture full time, we decided to soften up six of Lake's directors whom we regarded as influential, either because they controlled stock or key accounts. We did this by having our own directors in casual meetings ask Lake directors what their succession plans were when Clint and John retired. Most of them had not given the matter much thought.

Our next step was Clint Sears. Gil told him he and Jim would get key jobs, and that we would pay 20 percent over the market price for Lake stock, paying with Canal Bank stock.

I talked to Jim Tyler myself, invited him to lunch at my club and laid the cards on the table, most of them anyway. I told him if the merger went through, he would probably be elected a senior vice president and get responsibility for the combined trust departments. Nothing guaranteed, but a good bet. Without my saying so, he knew he stood a chance of succeeding Gil—although we have a number of men who are also just as good and in their early 40s. Contrary to the rumors, I did not double his salary, I did not say anything about stock options. I don't see why he would have them when none of the rest of us do.

MORGAN: One last question: Are there any other hitches that may hold this merger up?

UPHAM: Yes, ever since the Philadelphia National–Girard Trust case, and the last-ditch attempts to stop the mergers in Chicago and New York, it has never been possible to tell what the U.S. government will do. The Comptroller of the Currency must approve the merger as in the public interest. Even if we have that approval, we may still get hung up by the Anti-Trust Division on the ground that the merger may tend to create a monopoly. Any idea of a monopoly in banking is silly because all a borrower has to do is to telephone another city and he can obtain his money there just as well. Money rates are so well known that monopoly is inconceivable in the banking field. Much as I hate mergers, Gil thinks size is important, because a larger bank is permitted to make larger loans, and larger loans are essential in a rapidly expanding economy. And the right to make larger loans adds prestige and helps us compete for new business.

MORGAN: Yes, I can see you have turned the government's case around very neatly.

Thank you, Mr. Upham. You have been most helpful.

UPHAM: You're quite welcome. Goodbye.

After a leisurely breakfast on the following Saturday, Morgan enters his study, sits down before his typewriter. With an abstracted air, he shuffles his notes. Then slowly he starts to type a letter addressed to Gilbert Rhodes and Clinton Sears.

Gentlemen:

May I start by thanking you both for all the courtesies which you showed me earlier this week. My talks were most pleasant and they gave me great food for thought. What can I say that you do not already know? Very little, I fear, yet throughout my talks, I observed that each of the key officers had motivations, objectives, and perceptions that differed slightly from the others. Thus, I may be able to add another dimension to your thinking.

Nowhere, I suppose, are the contrasts between individual and company objectives thrown into more evident contrast than in the contemplation of a merger. Whether the motivation for a merger is growth, efficiencies in production or sales, a solution to a problem of management succession, it may be important, in all honesty, to ask whether the objectives are primarily personal or primarily corporate.

For the individual person, doubtless his most powerful motivation is his desire to maintain and enhance his self-concept. Whatever his self-concept may be, however it may have been acquired, it has often been said: "All God's chilluns got self-concepts." What's that, you say? Well, the self-concept is a composite that evolves out of the interaction between what the individual thinks he is, what he thinks he ought to be, what others think he is, and what others think he ought to be.

Let me illustrate, in a broad and general way, how the self-concepts of key individuals in managements contemplating merger may have some bearing on their views. An individual, for example, may see himself as a powerful and "successful" executive, and thus he favors merger because identification with a growing organization is consistent with this image. Another who is advanced in age but still vigorous, may see the merger as a means of satisfying his image as an active businessman. Another who wishes to look with pride and satisfaction at the organization he helped to build, may oppose the merger on the grounds that it would seem to obliterate his life's work. Still another who abhors friction and expense, may oppose a merger on the ground that it would create new organizational costs and dilemmas.

These could be individual motivations, but they are almost inextricably bound up with corporate motivations. For if an individual tries to maintain and enhance his self-concept, the management of a corporation similarly tries to maintain and enhance its self-concept—or what may be more commonly called—its corporate image. If corporate officers see their institution as one that regularly maintains a pattern of growth in size, they may feel justified in pushing for merger even though it may not contribute materially to sales or to efficiency of operation. If their view of the corporate image emphasizes its strength and permanency, they may seek merger as an appropriate means for assuring its continued survival. On the other hand, if management of the corporation perceives the corporate image as based on maneuverability and the agility that goes with smallness, then it will try to avoid merger. Also, if the corporate image of management depends greatly on harmony, cooperation, and efficiency, the desirability of any proposed merger will be judged accordingly.

The foregoing comments are but generalizations on major elements I perceive to be actively at work in the situation you face. Whether two corporations should marry is something that only the principals in each can answer—and I surely cannot play the role of marriage broker. Since both parties will be materially affected by the personality of the other, I can only suggest that you will best be able to reach a decision after you have resumed your conversations, become better acquainted, and explored exhaustively the objectives you think the marriage might reasonably bring about. Just as the goal of human marriage is responsible, healthy, wise, understanding, and creative children, the goal of corporate union, as I see it, should be a child that meets the multiple criteria of stability, growth, adaptability, *and* effective public service.

May I thank you again for the courtesies you afforded me in being able to view at close range so intimate and so significant a development in corporate life.

*McMaster-Barry Communications, Inc. (MBCI)**

WHEN JOHN SHOEMAKER first sat down to talk with Professor Morgan he had not expected to talk about *McMaster-Barry*, the aerospace communications systems company for which he worked as a systems engineer. But as he began to formulate his response to Professor McGrath's inquiry about what steps were involved in designing, manufacturing, and installing a highly sophisticated communications system, he began to realize that he had an even broader awareness of the company than he previously had recognized. While 35 years of age, John was an experienced engineer, having worked for one of the big aircraft companies and now for seven years for MBCI, he'd always seen himself as an engineer concentrating on the task at hand; but as he thought about Professor Morgan's question, he realized how much he knew about the steps involved in developing aerospace communications systems for the Apollo program.

BACKGROUND

McMaster-Barry was in the business of making highly sophisticated and specialized electronic communications devices and systems for the government's space program, and to some extent for commercial

---

*Copyright 1979 Stephen L. Fink and Robin D. Willits.

applications in the transportation industry. It had been founded by J. R. McMaster and S. Barry 15 years ago. One was an inventor and the other an entrepreneur with a technical bent. Between them they had built a successful business that had continued to grow (currently 3,000 employees) and filled an important place in the nation's space and military communications programs. As the president was often inclined to say, "McMaster-Barry's speciality is systems that fit particular needs and 'push the state of the art' technologically. In other words, we're in the business of selling engineering innovativeness and creativity."

Each communications system built by MBCI was unique, designed on a bid-contract basis to meet a customer's specific requirements. Any one system typically consisted of 10 to 30 discrete hardware elements (consoles, antenna, data banks, etc.) and cost $500,000 to $1 million. Ninety percent of the contracts were on a cost-plus-fixed-fee (CPFF) basis where the company received a fixed fee, based on a percentage of *estimated* costs, but the customer paid the total *actual* costs incurred. Most contracts were for from one to five systems and had a life (from contract award to final shipment) of one-and-a-half to two years. At any one time, the company would be working on a dozen contracts, each at various stages of design and manufacture.

MBCI employed a range of technical specialists along with manufacturing and administrative personnel. Of the 700 engineers, there was a range of skills running from those with a very theoretical orientation to those of a quite practical bent. On the former end of the scale there were a few individuals with very specialized training (largely Ph.D.s in esoteric areas of communications theory and mathematics). Every contract seemed to need some of their special expertise now and then during its life, but seldom full time and never throughout the life of the project.

Then there were the research engineers. Less tightly specialized than the first group, they nonetheless had a theoretical orientation, and were a constant source of new ideas and new ways to conceptualize space communications. They conducted some ongoing research and developed the general approach to be followed on each contract.

Every contract needed one or two research engineers, but since they often got impatient if immersed too deeply in the details of a single project for too long, all projects would fail without the mainstream systems engineers and hardware engineers. These were the individuals who carried the main load. The systems engineers worked out the overall parameters. They translated the customers' requirements into overall performance specifications for the system. They're the ones that had to think in systems terms and visualize the system as an operating entity, identifying the major subsystems and their technical interrelationships. Systems engineers were trained in a range of disciplines (electronics, communications, mechanical, etc.) but above all, all had to be able to think in conceptual terms, yet remain connected to the details of the ultimate physical operating characteristics.

The hardware engineers had an even more concrete pragmatic orientation. They too came from many disciplines, but their skill lay in converting the overall performance specifications into a specific design for each main component. Thus they had to have a greater concern for concrete hardware design details than the systems engineer.

Finally, there were technically trained personnel who planned the manufacturing process and dealt with the technical problems that came up during the manufacturing stage. Largely mechanical and industrial engineers by training, they are the least "scientific" and the most "practical" of all.

In addition to this range of engineering personnel, the company had and needed a number of other personnel such as technicians, draftsman, accountants, clerks and production personnel (machine operators, assemblers, foremen).

THE CONVERSATION

PROF. M: It would be very interesting to me, John, if you would walk me through an order from start to finish. How do you get an order in the first place? What happens after it is received? Am I right in assuming that the last step is to pack and ship the material out the door? Just what are the various steps and activities?

JOHN: Well, to answer one question; no, shipping is not the last step. We also get involved in installing the equipment in the customer's control tower, airplane, or submarine. But let me start at the beginning. Most projects that come in are in some way related to projects that have previously been captured by the company. They are in the same line of business and usually come from customers and agencies of the Defense Department (DOD) with whom we've done business before. Generally what happens is that the company is out there in an intelligence role trying to find out what the customers are doing; trying to get a lead on the kinds of procurements they're going to come up with in the next year or two. This tells the organization the kinds of things it ought to be thinking about, including general types of new products, improvements to existing products, and specific procurements that are imminent within a few months.

PROF. M: What kind of people does it require to do such intelligence work?

JOHN: You need people who know their way around government, and who have contacts in DOD. But you also need them to be people with an awareness of technical developments because the company has always taken an active role in trying to influence the government in terms of what it should be doing; suggesting new types of products, as well as suggesting follow-on products to what we are already delivering. The company is a very high-technology organization. It is constantly involved in various research and development activities which are company funded. So the company is constantly at the leading edge of the technology they are involved with, trying to develop new ideas, and also influence the procuring agencies to expand their systems.

PROF. M: How much do you try to take business away from an established competitor?

JOHN: That's another area of attack, trying to unseat the competition, especially those with contracts with other agencies securing similar kinds of equipment. A given contractor, once he becomes ensconced with an agency for a particular system, tends to track that through its various evolutionary stages and procurements. There tends to be an alliance between agencies and major contractors. But any contractor is always a target of competition that does similar things for another agency.

PROF. M: Have you had any success with this?

JOHN: To a degree yes, although we have also had some notable lack of success in proposing against an incumbent. Nonetheless, what you have to do is show that you are interested. In other words, even if you think that there is a high probability of losing, part of the investment is showing your interest by bidding.

PROF. M: If you've been proposing, you would be seen as having knowledge; whereas if you've never proposed, you would be seen as a newcomer?

JOHN: Yes, because part of the process of being invited to bid is establishing your qualifications. The easy way to do that is to actually have delivered hardware, or have a history of bidding in a certain area.

PROF. M: "Being invited to bid," tell me about that.

JOHN: We first have to get on a government agency's "bidders list" so that we will be among those sent a "request for quotation" (RFQ). We get on the bidders list by sending out "qualification descriptions" (QDs) to various agencies. These spell out our areas of technical expertise and explain what we have done and are capable of doing. We also have to reinforce those packages with personal contact and verbal presentations. In addition, we have to keep ourselves informed about what direction government projects are going so we know where to submit QDs and how to focus our research efforts.

If the intelligence is good, we even do some pre-RFQ work, sometimes even going so far as to prepare a mock quotation. Then as soon as the RFQ arrives, we're off and running.

PROF. M: Sounds as if your company is willing to gamble some engineering time for competitive purposes—but tell me what happens when the formal RFQ actually arrives.

JOHN: Upon receipt of a request for quotation, we submit a bid. This, itself, is a long process. The bid or proposal is a lengthy document spelling out a number of technical parameters as well as estimated costs and delivery schedules. Considerable engineering work must go into the preparation of every proposal, even though it may not lead to a contract, and if it does, that contract won't be awarded for another 6 to 12 months.

The bid proposal process entails several steps. First, the RFQ must be analyzed to gain an overview of the technical requirements and to establish an overall technical approach. Then, the design steps themselves must be visualized and a work plan developed that involves partitioning the design effort into separate subtasks. This also serves to identify the many different technical specialists (e.g., mathematicians, logic engineers, analog design engineers, mechanical engineers) that will be needed to carry out the design effort. Thereafter the obtainable performance characteristics, which may vary somewhat from what the RFQ requires, must be established for each subtask area, together with cost estimates and probable schedules for key personnel. Finally, all these data must be assembled into one written package for management review and submission to the customer. There usually is a technical section, a management (including production) section, and a cost section to the proposal.

There is always some adjustment of costs, etc., by management based on its judgment of what the competition might be doing. Costs will sometimes have the highest priority in proposal evaluation, but not usually. The procuring agencies don't want companies to just buy into a job by submitting artificially low costs, so normally costs will not be given the highest priority. Technical creativeness, delivery, and overall quality (performance characteristics) count heavily. Management may make adjustments to the cost estimates, delivery schedules, and even some performance parameter.

PROF. M: How much does it matter who works on the proposal? Are some people better proposal writers than others or doesn't it much matter?

JOHN: It matters! The proposal sets up the work plan. It is often convenient, although shortsighted, to provide whomever is available. But unless the proposal is prepared by competent people, which really means your better engineers, there are likely to be frustrations and problems downstream when the work is under way.

PROF. M: "Whomever is available?"

JOHN: Yes. Proposals must be prepared while work is also going on on firm contracts. So the company has to find a way to staff both activities simultaneously; and there is usually a time crunch in getting a proposal out, you only have four to six weeks. Once done you wait with baited breath for the award.

PROF. M: And that may take as long as 6 to 12 months!

JOHN: Yes, and then the customer usually has changed the statement of work somewhat. So the first step after award of contract is to definitize the contract and negotiate new costs estimates, etc. However, the scheduled starting date is seldom changed so actual work must get started even while the negotiations are still going on. And those negotiations can take time since they can encompass technical issues and legal (contract) issues as well as cost questions.

The first work step is to reassess the planned technical approach and the task partitioning in view of any changes in the customer's statement of work or any new experience we've had with the technology in the interim. It is also done so as to carry the process of structuring and partitioning the work further than was done during the proposal stage. In other words, appropriate individuals and groups of individuals must be assigned to the project and the actual design work begun.

PROF. M: Tell me about what is involved in an actual design endeavor.

JOHN: There are a number of activities. First there is systems design. This involves spelling out a general approach, partitioning that approach into major components, establishing technical parameters for each major component or subsystem. The latter involves establishing written specifications spelling out performance characteristics for each subtask. Obviously the performance characteristics of the major components must be compatible with each other. One component's output is another's input. Systems design entails setting up technical requirments so that these will all fit together, and making trade-offs as appropriate, initially, and also downstream, if equipment design, which I'll discuss shortly, encounters difficulty in satisfying these specifications.

Systems design work may often rest on and require the preparation of highly theoretical analysis of particular technical issues. This is where there is a need for the highly theoretical mathematical and scientific types who will be called upon to perform specific analysis relative to the specific project. They study an issue, prepare a paper, and then go back to doing ongoing research work or switch to another issue.

Now, back to equipment design. The general parameters and specifications developed through a systems focus must then be translated into concrete hardware. Equipment design leads to engineering drawings and specifications covering a "black box" filled with transistors, printed circuits, cables, etc. Developing software (computer programs) may also be involved if the system utilizes computers. Equipment design requires such technical skills as analog circuit design, digital circuit design, integrated circuit design, logic engineers, power supply, etc.

Finally there is packaging. The various components specified by equipment design must be housed in some kind of container—a small black box, a large cabinet, a full-scale console, etc. And this is not a simple job because the customer typically requires that the system be able to withstand punishing environmental conditions of vibration, shock, corrosion, etc.

PROF. M: We're talking about the design process; are there distinct phases or do they merge?

JOHN: Very much merged. Some things have to be done before others; systems design has to precede equipment design; but the total system is big enough so that as soon as part of a system can be specified, the equipment design effort will be started on at least a portion of the project.

PROF. M: What happens if progress on one subtask or black box runs into difficulty and can't meet its output specifications? Or doesn't that happen?

JOHN: Oh yes, that can happen at any time. Someone will say, "We just can't meet those specifications," or "We can do it but its going to cost a heck of a lot of money." Sometimes you even find someone saying, "Heck, I overlooked that requirement and to work it in now will be a real problem." At that point a decision has to be made, to keep working on it, to change the specifications (which will undoubtedly require additional changes elsewhere in the system), or as a last resort to seek relief in the performance requirements from the customer.

Such problems always come up as the design effort goes forward. You have to try and stay on top of what is going on with a systems insight and try to identify problems as early as possible, even before testing.

PROF. M: "Testing?"

JOHN: As the individual black boxes are designed, the engineers will normally rig up some type of bread-board[1] to test our various circuits, or they might end up with a first functional black box which would pretty much look like the final product but if you looked inside it would be kind of messy.

After the equipment engineers test their black boxes by simulating specified inputs and making sure the outputs are as specified, they say, "According to my test it should work to the system requirements." Now if there is a subsystem involved, the black boxes that go in the subsystem must be pulled together and tested as a subsystem to make sure it performs. Finally the subsystems must be put together in the next stage to make sure the system works. Sometimes it is not feasible to test the entire system, but it is feasible and necessary to test some representative group of hardware elements to give a fairly high confidence that the entire system will work when it is put together. That is usually done on an informal, in-house basis first.

Then there is a more formal series of tests that the customer requires. These formal tests require the development of a test plan, then the writing of test procedure statements, and finally the actual testing itself. The customer must approve the test plan and test procedures, and a customer representative must witness the actual testing.

The test report documents the results. When the customer approves the report he validates the fact that the system meets contract specifications.

PROF. M: Are these test procedures developed by the hardware engineers, the system-engineers, or a specialized test engineer?

JOHN: That depends. Testing of bread-boards and black boxes are usually done by the individuals doing the equipment design. When you get to subsystem testing, systems engineers are likely to also be involved. Then there also is some need for highly specialized tests requiring the expertise of specialists who are familar with instrumentation and special test equipment. We also have a small test laboratory for standardized tests, especially environmental testing. For example, they conduct a hammer-blow test for shipboard equipment to simulate depth charge shock waves; a really tremendous shock test on a piece of equipment. We actually have a 400-lb. hammer on a pivot, with the equipment sitting on a heavy base. To test the equipment the hammer comes down and whams the base. It is not unusual for the drawers to fly out and the circuit cards to go up in the air!

PROF. M: After all these tests, how confident can you be that the government will give its stamp of approval?

JOHN: Maybe 80 to 90 percent. The government is likely to want you to do a lot more testing than you initially propose in your test plan. There is another negotiation process involved in getting an approved test plan before you can start. That's part of the game, too.

PROF. M: How close to what would eventually be produced in manufacturing is the physical being that is being tested?

---

[1] *Bread-board* is a term used to describe an operating model of a device that performs the technical functions of the ultimate product but is not in its final form. Thus, certain parts may differ from what will be ultimately used, such as lengths of wire instead of printed circuits, and all of the parts will be spread out on a workbench or tray rather than installed in a chassis or metal container.

JOHN: The formal system test usually involves the next level of maturity beyond the engineering model. An engineering model looks like the final product but is kind of thrown together and there is no environmental requirement imposed on it whatsoever. It is usually mostly built in engineering laboratories. Then there will be a preproduction model, which is usually the model that will be used for the formal government-witnessed tests. That is supposed to be representative of the production version in all respects; although some minor variations will occur, which are themselves individually appraised, or looked at, to make sure that it is close enough so that it shouldn't affect the end product.

PROF. M: So we couldn't use a vacuum tube amplifier if the real thing was going to have a transistor amplifier.

JOHN: That gross difference would not do. It essentially has to be the same design. There are always minor design changes creeping in as test results indicate something has to be modified. Some degree of retesting may be required if the changes are substantial enough.

After the formal test, which is usually called a qualification test or proof of performance test, is witnessed and signed off, the equipment will go into production. Usually it is not permitted to go into production until that formal test has been completed or it goes into production on a very tentative basis at the contractor's risk. This is done to gain time on the schedule.

PROF. M: Does qualification testing complete the design effort and mean that engineers shift to other activities?

JOHN: Well, kind of, yes. There is kind of a switch from design to manufacturing, but in reality now you are starting up a new set of equipment through a manufacturing process. Those nontechnical people who do the work need to be famiarized with what the equipment is all about. Someone must develop manufacturing methods and prepare written assembly instructions and drawings. Sometimes a technical opinion is needed to assess the adequacy of some potential supplier of raw materials or components; should we or should we not purchase components from that source? Also technical problems will merge during manufacturing either in actual assembly or in the testing of each item on a production-line test basis. Oftentimes design changes will be required even at that stage to correct technical deficiencies that suddenly show up. For example, a transistor supplier might give you a transistor that has an unchanged part number, but internally he has modified his transistor production line a little bit and he didn't bother to tell you because it's obviously a little bit better than the unit he was delivering before. Well that little bit better means that it is a little bit different, and a little bit different may cause the system not to do its work.

PROF. M: When that kind of thing happens, what kinds of reactions does it produce?

JOHN: First of all, the red flag comes up on the production line that says there is a problem. Then someone with technical ability must try to figure out what's happening. The company usually tries to get a handle on the problem before it notifies the government. (There usually are some government source inspection people on site who are aware of what is going on, but they won't get involved—they will allow the company some time to handle the situation. They try not to get too excited about it.) But ultimately, if it affects cost and scheduling, or has any major effect on the contract effort, then the customer will be notified and he will want to satisfy himself that the problem indeed has been solved and the solution is at hand.

Prof. M: What is the probability that when this problem shows up the particular individual who did the design has moved off on another project?

John: It's quite likely that the individual would be on another project.

Prof. M: Ideally, when a problem like that occurs you hope that people will take a problem-solving attitude and solve it. Very often, given the kind of invested interest that people have in this kind of thing, it is easy to fall into blame casting. I was wondering if that kind of thing happens?

John: Yes, it does. It really does happen. Those involved in building the equipment will say there is a technical problem. A technical person will look at the problem and often the initial reaction is to blame the manufacturing process: "They are not doing what the drawing says they should do, that's the problem." What happens usually is that after some time agreement is reached. Either the design has to be changed, or the manufacturing process has to be changed. Either way, the problem could either be minor or major.

Prof. M: Give me an example of where the manufacturing process, somehow made it not work, and therefore the answer was not a design change but a change in the manufacturing process.

John: Well, some kinds of problems in electronic equipment, for example, can be caused by the way a cable is routed within the equipment, because signals can cross couple and interfere with each other. But someone will look at the drawing and say, "Gee, I can use less wire," or "I can speed up my manufacturing assembly time, if I just route that a little differently." They may in effect ignore the drawing or the drawing may not be sufficiently explicit. Something can happen if the engineering drawing has been translated into a series of assembly instructions and into an assembly drawing. The essential information might not have reached that level of detail. It is like passing a story around a group . . . it loses its accuracy.

Prof. M: Even if problems don't occur, what is the probability that during the manufacturing process ideas will come up suggesting changes in the design in order to simplify the manufacturing process and reduce costs?

John: That is quite possible. Anybody can propose a design change stating the reason they think it is worthwhile. Then the idea has to be evaluated, with careful consideration given to its impact on operating characteristics and quality standards. There can be different reactions. The technical people can look at the idea and say to themselves, "Gee, we don't want to be bothered with this, we've already been through that." Publically they'll say, "No, it won't work." Or, they may look at it and say, "I don't see any reason why it can't be done, although we might have to look at it a little harder to see if there are any problems." Eventually its impact on quality, schedules, costs, and especially on other subsystems and on testing requirements must be evaluated.

Prof. M: I can see where there might be different priorities for each of these factors.

John: Definitely! Someone is always making choices, choices between quality and cost, cost and schedules, immediate convenience and long-term impacts, etc.

Prof. M: Let me review the sequence a bit. After bidding and receipt of contract, you set up an approach to the design step. Design work produces specifications and drawings and eventually leads to the testing of first a bread-board model and then a prototype. When the formal tests have been completed, production starts after someone plans the production methods; yet even during production further changes in design are likely—and this process requires a lot of ongoing investigation and discussion.

Now did we finish the cycle? We haven't gotten it out of the door yet, have we?

John: Eventually we start shipping equipment. It goes into the government's inventory in its operational environment, whatever that might be—airplanes, ships, ground stations, etc. But as I said in the beginning, shipping is not the end of it. There is a whole bunch of activity related to maintenance support and sparing requirements.

Separate contracts are issued to provide spare parts, manuals for repair, and manuals for instruction. The company can make a heck of a lot more money on the downstream support activities than it does on the basic development and production itself. That stuff goes on for years, kind of bread-and-butter income.

But anyway, after shipment, as they start to install and use the equipment, it will encounter some problems which require field support activities. Sometimes, the company must be involved in the actual installation of the equipment if it is fairly sophisticated and in the initial checkout in, say, a submarine. This has to be done at the submarine bases as the submarines come in for rework and retrofit. Thereafter, the system will be used on a trial basis. The government goes through many stages of working a new system up to full operational status. It will be installed in a lot of submarines or airplanes and be used on a tentative basis until everybody in the operational command satisfy themselves that it will work.

We encounter problems during this period. A lot of them are related to "cockpit-type" problems, because of people who haven't learned how to use the system, or not misuse it. We had one piece of equipment that some guy laid on the runway to stand on so he could reach up and screw the refueling port under the wing of the airplane. The troops out there really have no respect for the sensitivity of our equipment. Also there is sometimes a flurry of communications and activity back and forth about the same kind of problems that had to be solved in manufacturing.

But eventually the bugs get worked out and the cycle is ready to repeat itself as we or the government comes up with new ideas for more flexible and sophisticated equipment. Meanwhile, the spare parts business generates a flow of more certain, profitable business.

Prof. M: I thank you, John! Your comments have given me a much clearer picture of the many steps involved in producing those large communications systems. It's a complex process, involving a number of technical specialties. It must place a lot of demands on the individuals involved. You must live under a lot of time pressure and a lot of uncertainty over quality, cost, and human mistakes. There must be many opportunities for someone to drop the ball, as well as genuine disagreement and even conflict.

The question that is now running through my mind is one of organization.

What is the structure of the company? How is the work divided and activities departmentalized? What formalized procedures exist to control proposal preparation, testing, design changes, etc.? How is time budgeted, and who makes decisions concerning work assignments, design changes, and negotiation issues? Sometime I'd enjoy hearing about these matters.

The Montville Hospital Dietary Department

INTRODUCTION

RENE MARCOTTE BRISKLY WALKED HOME from her part-time job with the Montville Hospital Dietary Department. "Mom," she said as she entered the house, "they may have to close down the hospital! The Montville Department of Health has just found the Dietary Department's sanitary conditions to be substandard. Mrs. DeMambro, our chief supervisor, said that we are really going to have to get to work and clean the place or the hospital is in trouble!"

THE HOSPITAL

As Rene continued to tell her mother about this latest event, she thought about her part-time job at the hospital which she had had now for almost a year. Montville Hospital was a 400-bed community general hospital located in suburban Montville outside of New York City. Montville itself was a racially mixed community of low- and middle-income working families. However, Montville, along with most hospitals, was operating under severe financial pressure and needed to constantly find ways to reduce costs. It offered a range of medical services, but due to the nature of the Montville population, it had an appreciable number of elderly terminal patients. The hospital was well thought of by the community both as a place of treatment and as a source of employment. Through the years it had received strong financial support from the community and had grown as the community had grown. It currently was building a new wing to keep up with expanding demand, and this added to its tight financial situation.

THE DIETARY DEPARTMENT

The Dietary Department, where Rene worked, was located in the wing that had been added during the previous expansion project a little more than 10 years ago. This department employed approximately 100 employees (mostly female) and was under the direction of Mr. Thomas Ellis, food service director. The department employed cooks, dietitians, and "kitchen workers" (of whom Rene was one). The department had two major responsibilities—namely, the planning, preparation, and serving of three meals a day to every patient, and the operation of an employees' cafeteria. Since most of the patients required special diets, such as salt-free diets, the food for each was quite different, although cooked in a common kitchen.

Rene well remembered her initial contact with the department. When applying for a job, she was first "screened" by the hospital personnel office, then sent to be interviewed by Mrs. Kelley, the chief dietary supervisor, and after a second interview by Mrs. Kelley, given a "tour" through the kitchen facilities by one of the supervisors. She never saw Mr. Ellis or Mrs. Johnston, the chief dietitian. As she later learned, Mrs. Kelley did all of the hiring and firing while salary and raises were determined by the payroll department. Rene felt as if Mr. Ellis were some kind of "god," when she eventually heard of his existence two weeks after starting work.

Upon being hired, Rene was put right to work with no formal instructions in standards or procedures. She, as every other new employee, was expected to learn by watching others and asking her peers. Rene, who undertook the job with a deep sense of responsibility, well remembers one of the older kids saying to her, "Hurry up, you're taking too long; don't bother to clean up those spots of spilled soup."

Along with Rene, the majority of the employees were kitchen workers (diet aides, dishwashers, and porters). Ninety-five percent were female. Twenty-five were full-timers working 40 hours per week and 50–60 were part-timers, as was Rene.

Ten years ago the Dietary Department was smaller and under the direction of one of the current dietitians. There were no food service director and no chief dietary supervisor positions. While the kitchen was centralized at that time, tray preparation was not. This was done in a kitchenette located on each floor of the hospital. The workers moved from floor to floor serving food from bulk containers onto individual trays on each floor. The dishroom also was separated physically. When the new wing was built, everything was centralized into one location from which carts of setup trays are sent out to each floor. Now, only the diet aides went to the floors and only for the purpose of distributing and collecting trays from the patients.

The Full-Time Employees

The full-time employees were mostly older women (40–65 years of age) who had been working in the department for a long time; some for 15–20 years. All lived in Montville; most had a high school education;

many were married, and most helping to augment the family income so that their children could be the first in their family to go to college. With few exceptions, they worked a morning shift from either 6:30 A.M. to 3:00 P.M. or 8:00 A.M. to 4:30 P.M.

Most of the women had worked in this organization back in the old days before the hospital expanded and the kitchen was rebuilt. They had many stories to tell about how it used to be and how much easier and less chaotic their jobs had been before the change. One woman, who had recently been re-employed, had worked in the same Dietary Department 20 years ago as a teenager. She was amazed at how different everything was and said how she felt she was in another world from the job she used to know and love 20 years ago. The women, however, took great pride in their work (many had been doing the same job for years). Each woman had her own assigned task which she did every day and there was little shifting around of positions. The dessert- or salad-makers never learned much about the work routine of the tray-coverers, silverware-sorters or juice-setter-uppers. Every woman was set in a specific routine during a day's work. This routine was heavily controlled by the tight time schedule everyone had to follow. There was no fooling around even though the working atmosphere was very congenial and everyone was on a first-name basis, including the supervisors. There was considerable conversation among the women while they worked, but it did not distract them from doing their jobs—perhaps because management required the workers to completely finish their assigned tasks before leaving for home, even if it meant working overtime, without extra pay.

There was a striking cross section of cultural backgrounds among these full-time employees. There were about equal numbers of whites, blacks, and orientals, and many were immigrants. Many spoke Spanish and very little English. Although a language barrier existed between many of the employees, feelings of mutual respect and friendliness were maintained. Malicious gossip due to racial or ethnic differences was uncommon, and the women helped each other when necessary to finish their jobs on time.

The women often expressed their concern about not getting their jobs done on time, especially when they were manning the assembly line. This assembly line consisted of sending a tray down a belt, along which, at certain intervals, each worker put a specific item on the tray as designated by the menu for each patient. After each tray was completed, it was put in an electric cart with each cart containing trays for different floors of the hospital. The carts were then pulled (by men porters) into elevators and transferred to the designated floors. At this time, pairs of diet aides (not working on the line) were sent to the floors to deliver the trays to the patients. Speed and efficiency in delivering trays were very important. If the trays were sent up and then left standing for a long time before delivery to each patient, the food got cold and the Dietary Department received complaints directed at the dietitians. The complaints were relayed to the supervisor, who in turn reprimanded the diet aide(s) responsible for the cold food. This temporarily disrupted the very informal and friendly working relationship between the diet aides and their supervisor, whom they liked and respected, causing uncomfortable guilt feelings for the diet aides. As a result, reprimands were seldom necessary among the full-timers.

At the same time, the diet aides were expected to meet certain established standards governing such matters as size of portion, cleanliness of kitchen facilities, and cleanliness in food handling and preparation. At times, in fact rather often, the standards were overlooked under the pressure of time. For instance, if the line was to be started at exactly 11 A.M. and if by that time the desserts were not wrapped or covered, as required by sanitary regulations, the line might begin anyway, and the desserts went to the patients unwrapped.

The full-time employees received pay raises designated by a set scale based on continuing length of employment. Starting salary was about average for this type of work. They were allowed a certain number of sick days per year as well as paid vacations (the length of which were based on the numbers of years of employment). The uniforms they were required to wear were provided (three per person) by the hospital and could be laundered free of charge at the hospital laundry service. Also the workers paid very little money, if anything at all, for meals eaten at work. Technically they were supposed to pay in full for meals, but seldom did, because of lack of consistent control.

Work performance was evaluated on the basis of group effort. Individual effort usually was not singled out and rewarded in any tangible way. However, supervisors would often compliment an individual on how nice a salad plate looked or how quickly and efficiently a worker delivered the patients' trays. For instance, the woman who prepared fancy salad plates and sandwiches could take pride in the way they looked. Furthermore, the aides recognized that their work could affect a patient's well-being and therefore could be important, and sometimes a patient was a former hospital staff member or neighbor known by the aides. When delivering a tray, a diet aide might chat with a patient and discover particular likes or dislikes which, when reported to the dietitian, sometimes led to a revision in the patient's diet.

Extra care was often taken in arranging food on the tray in an attractive manner to please the patient. Sometimes this dedication produced minor problems such as when a diet aide violated certain rules in order to do something extra for a patient or to promote her own version of efficiency in doing a task. This type of individual initiative (and creativity) was not encouraged. Management set down rigid guidelines for performing all tasks as the only correct way, since they worked out for so many years. Any recommendations for changes in these techniques were approached with caution by management. The equipment also had changed little in the past decade.

The Part-Time Employees

There were 50–60 part-time employees in the Dietary Department whose level of pay was appreciably less than that of the full-timers. They were divided into two teams (team A and team B); each team worked on alternate days of the week and on alternate weekends, a device adopted on the advice of some efficiency experts as a way of avoiding having to pay overtime to anyone. There was no specific supervisor for each team; instead each might have one of two supervisors depending on the day and/or week. Two different shifts exist for the part-timers: 3:30–6:30 and 4:00–8:00 (the kitchen closed at 8 P.M.), but on the average all part-timers including Rene worked a 16-hour week. Their duties were the same as the full-timers; except that part-timers served and cleaned up after dinner instead of after breakfast and lunch. The majority of these workers were young; mostly high school age (16–18 years), working for extra money and because friends were working. Most had not worked in the hospital very long as there was a constant turnover as individuals left to go to college, etc., but other kids were readily available to take their places. There were also several older women working on a part-time basis, who had been with the organization for many years.

The part-timers' situation exhibited a striking contrast to that of full-timers. There were no permanent tasks assignments; each night a part-timer did something different, and the kids often asked to do this or that different task. As a group, the night shift was not as unified in spirit or congeniality as the day shift (full-timers). The younger workers tended to form cliques apart from the older women and gossip and poke fun at non-English-speaking workers.

Most of the teenagers also took their work much less seriously than did the older women (the full-timers), doing only what was required at the most minimal level. As was the case with the full-timers, they worked on a tight schedule and their working behavior was heavily controlled by it. However, they seemed more anxious to get their work done as soon as possible. Once they had finished, they were free to leave no matter what time it was at no loss of pay; that is, if everyone was finished at, say 7:45 P.M., all could leave yet still be paid until 8:00 P.M. It was not uncommon for work areas to become messy, for hands to be left unwashed, and for food to be handled and touched even though it shouldn't be. They also tended to devise their own ways for doing the job, partially to promote efficiency and decrease the time needed for completion. It was not uncommon to hear a more experienced teenage part-timer tell a newcomer, "Oh, come on, we don't have to do it that way. Don't be so eager; relax and enjoy yourself." The supervisor seemed to have little control over the teenagers. They ignored her comments or talked back to her and continued doing things their own way. The working atmosphere was informal and friendly with everyone on a first-name basis except for the supervisor. At times there was a high pitch of excitement among the kids as everyone kidded one another, sang songs, and generally socialized together. At times this led to mistakes being made, which infuriated the supervisor but didn't bother the kids, as they had little respect for her.

Conflict existed between the supervisor and the teenagers about wearing the required hairnets (especially the boys) and aprons and such procedures as not eating during work. They seldom took reprimands seriously, saying that they "hated their job" but needed the money. In general, however, these young diet aides did complete their required tasks in the time allotted, although the quality was often substandard. There was not a total lack of concern for quality because if so, they would have lost their jobs, and they knew this; but quality was maintained most strongly only when "it didn't take too long."

There did exist some conflict between the older and younger workers during the night shift. The older women did not approve of the young people's attitudes even though those older women who worked at night did not exhibit as much pride in their work as did their daytime counterparts. They resented the teenagers' new and different ways of doing jobs, as was especially evident when an older woman was assigned to work with a teenager for the evening.

The Management

With regard to the management staff of the Dietary Department, there were several people involved. Mr. Ellis was the man to whom everyone else was ultimately responsible as the food service director. He was an older man, hired by the hospital about five years perviously. A flashy dresser, he wore no uniform and spent most of the day in his office. He rarely talked to anyone in the department except the chief dietitian and the chief dietary supervisor. He communicated to the rest of the employees by way of memos posted on a bulletin board in the kitchen. His memos usually contained instructions, telling the workers to change or improve some facet of their jobs. He also relayed messages down the ranks via the supervisors to the workers. About once a day he would walk through the kitchen in a very formal manner apparently observing what was going on. The diet aides (and supervisors) became very conscious of their actions as he walked by, hoping they were doing everything right. When questioned about this man, the workers expressed feelings of curiosity mixed with an element of fear. The only time a diet aide came into direct contact with him was on payday, when she entered his office to receive her check after he signed it. One recently hired employee said that she thought that his main job was signing paychecks. There was obviously much confusion by workers concerning who this man really was. He was the mystery man of management to them.

A second management person was the chief dietitian, Mrs. Johnston, a woman in her late 30s. Her job was mainly administrative in nature; acting as a consultant to the dietitians and assisting them when the workload was heavy or someone was out sick. She also helped out in the kitchen once in a while if the kitchen staff was especially shorthanded. In general, however, she tended to remain relatively formal and distant from the workers, although, when she had suggestions to make, she often went directly to the workers instead of using memos. Her relationship with the four dietitians was informal and friendly, and she was highly respected by them for her technical excellence as a dietitian.

The chief dietary supervisor, Mrs. Kelly (about age 44), was in charge of hiring and firing. She was also responsible for making up employee schedules week by week, especially those involving the scheduling of the part-time workers. Workers went to her with gripes and requests for favors and special days off. She was generally sympathetic to employee problems, having been one of them about six years ago before she became the chief supervisor. In general, she was relatively informal with the workers although not on a first-name basis. The employees respected her and her authority was rarely questioned or challenged by any of the workers. She seemed to be regarded as the real boss, rather than the two people who ranked above her.

These three people constituted the main power structure in the Dietary Department. They tended to keep to themselves socially as well as physically. They never ate with the workers and seldom communicated with them except about their work. If any changes, plans, or decisions were to be made, they were made by these three people, the final say being had by the food service director. The supervisors were then told of any new policy and expected to inform the workers and implement the change. The chief dietary supervisor (CDS) seemed to act as a middleman between the director and the workers. When she (or the director) felt that the workers were "sloughing off," a staff meeting would be called and she would exhort everyone to shape up. For instance, a meeting was called after an unusually large number of complaints were received about patients receiving cold food. The CDS said, "We are here to help these patients get well as best we can—they are sick and deserve the best possible care. They won't eat cold food, and that slows down their recovery. Keeping the food warm is more important than whether or not you want to hurry to get the day's work done."

Other members of the management staff included the supervisors, whose main responsibilities involved the diet aides and other kitchen workers. The supervisors, who in all cases were former diet aides, worked in the kitchen. They assigned jobs, made sure they got done, maintained discipline and order (hopefully), and helped out when needed. In general, they saw that everything ran smoothly. Altogether, there were three supervisors, one of whom was part-time. They took turns covering the weekends, and thus had contact with all employees, although they worked with one group most of the time.

The cooks and the dietitians were the other members of the department. The cooks' job was to prepare the food according to standard recipes and to put it on the serving line at meal times. They did their jobs efficiently and effectively. They kept to themselves, eating together and not mingling with the diet aides. The dietitians also kept to themselves both physically and socially. They had their own office and ate together. Little was seen of them by the workers; however, when approached, they seemed quite friendly.

THE CURRENT PROBLEM

The State Board of Health makes periodic, unannounced visits to the Dietary Department to determine whether it meets certain sanitary standards. Although the hospital believes that the Board of Health interprets the regulations too strictly, there is little it can do except make efforts to satisfy any criticisms made by the inspectors.

In the past, the director of the Dietary Department managed to find out when the inspectors were coming and prepared for the visit by a frantic two- to three-day major clean-up campaign. Historically, this has resulted in Montville passing the inspection. However, over the past two to three months, the inspectors have become more successful in making their visits a complete surprise. Frantic efforts to clean up took place the last time during the brief period of time it took the inspectors to get from their car to the kitchen. As a result, the department recently failed the inspection and was given a limited amount of time to correct the situation or else face being shut down. The department did pass a reinspection, but only because of a lot of extra pressure put on workers to do extra cleaning during and after working hours (for overtime pay) for several days. If the organization should fail inspection repeatedly, it will be required to shut down indefinitely. The impact of this would be catastrophic for the hospital as a whole, since it must provide food for both patients and employees! Rene wondered what the hospital would do about the situation and how it might affect her job situation.

Omega Aerospace Corporation*

INTRODUCTION

THE OMEGA AEROSPACE CORPORATION is a multidivisional organization with production facilities throughout the western and southern parts of the United States. Each division is an autonomous organization and is established on a product-orientation basis. Thus, all research, design, engineering, and production for aircraft, for example, are organized in the aircraft division, while all activities relating to space research and space vehicles are organized in the space division. There are four primary divisions—namely, space, aircraft, weapons systems, and commercial products. Each division is functionally independent; that is, each has its own research, engineering, production, marketing, accounting, and personnel departments. Policy determination, however, in terms of corporate policy, is originated and administered by the "headquarters division," which functions as the policymaking and control agency for the corporation. Within the framework of this corporate policy structure, each division operates as an independent "profit center," accountable only to the corporation president and the board of directors.

This particular study is concerned with two department-level organizations which are part of the weapons systems division and are located in a large West Coast city. These two organizations are the Management Analysis Department and the Data Processing Department. To familiarize the reader with the general purpose of these departments, we are offering below a brief description of their functions.

Both organizations are concerned with the analysis, design, and implementation of "management systems." The term *management system*, in this context, refers to any set of activities directed toward achieving improved control of the operations of the corporation in general and the individual division in particular. Closely associated with "control," in this sense, is the notion of improved profitability resulting from more efficient operations, improved communication for management decision making, more timely reporting of financial and operating data, and the ability to predict the results of various operating alternatives (decisions) in a timely and scientific fashion. Thus, the majority of management systems are viewed as requiring "computerization" in order to achieve the quick response time and the ability to manipulate and calculate large quantities of data.

---

*From Rolf E. Rogers, *Organization Theory*, 1975, Allyn & Bacon, Inc., Boston, Mass. Reproduced by permission of the author.

In a more specific sense, the concept of a management system, from a developmental point of view, includes the following general steps:

1. Analysis of management problems and requirements.
2. Evaluation of alternatives for the solution of these problems and requirements.
3. Selection of the "optimum" solution.
4. Design of the appropriate management system based on the "optimum" solution.
5. The implementation of the system—both technically and organizationally.
6. The maintenance of the system (i.e., its continual operation).
7. The evaluation of the system's performance and effectiveness.

The responsibility for developing and operating a management system at the Weapons Systems Division of Omega Aerospace Corporation was divided between two organizations—the Management Analysis Department and the Data Processing Department. The Management Analysis Department reported to the vice president for administration; the Data Processing Department reported to the chief financial officer—the controller. Both executives reported to the president of the division who, in turn, reported to the corporation president and the board of directors. Exhibits 1 and 2 reflect the formal organization of these two departments.

The division of tasks relating to management systems between these two departments was, theoretically, as follows:

An operating or management problem was presented to the Management Analysis Department for study. This could be by executive direction (for example, by the president) or by formal request from an operating or staff manager who felt that he had such a problem. Upon receipt of the request, the director of management analysis would assign the study project to the appropriate manager in his department for scheduling and appointment of an analyst or a team of analysts. The scheduling and appointment were based on the perceived or assigned priority of the problem, the availability of analysts, and the complexity of the required study approach. Upon completion of the study, a formal report would be issued by the Management Analysis Department to the "client" describing the problem, the evaluation of alternative solutions, and the recommended solution. If the solution was a data processing computer system, the system would be described in the report in terms of a conceptual design along with recommended standards, data criteria, input-output specifications, reporting formats, and so on. If the "client" organization accepted this recommended solution, the report would be turned over to the Data Processing Department for detailed computer systems design, programming, implementation, and sustaining operating maintenance responsibility. A coordinator from the Man-

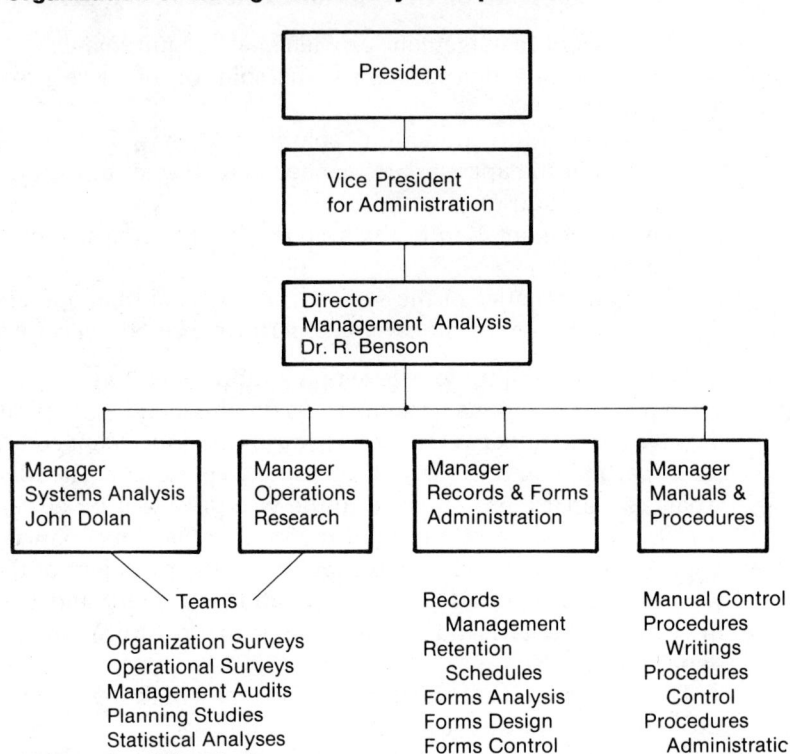

EXHIBIT 1
Organization of Management Analysis Department

```
                    ┌─────────────┐
                    │  President  │
                    └──────┬──────┘
                           │
                  ┌────────┴────────┐
                  │ Vice President  │
                  │ for Administration │
                  └────────┬────────┘
                           │
                  ┌────────┴────────┐
                  │ Director        │
                  │ Management Analysis │
                  │ Dr. R. Benson   │
                  └────────┬────────┘
       ┌──────────┬────────┼────────┬──────────┐
  ┌────┴────┐ ┌───┴────┐ ┌─┴──────┐ ┌┴────────┐
  │ Manager │ │Manager │ │Manager │ │Manager  │
  │ Systems │ │Operations│ │Records │ │Manuals &│
  │ Analysis│ │Research │ │& Forms │ │Procedures│
  │John Dolan│ │        │ │Admin.  │ │         │
  └─────────┘ └────────┘ └────────┘ └─────────┘
```

Teams	Records Management	Manual Control Procedures
Organization Surveys	Retention Schedules	Writings Procedures
Operational Surveys	Forms Analysis	Control Procedures
Management Audits	Forms Design	Administratic
Planning Studies	Forms Control	Organization
Statistical Analyses	Archives	Charts
Feasibility Studies		

agement Analysis Department was assigned to data processing, if requested, for purposes of coordinating the development of the system.

It is apparent that this organization of tasks into specialized activities and into defined areas of responsibility follows the postulates of F. W. Taylor and is inherent in Max Weber's bureaucratic ideal type. As such, this arrangement should, in theory, accomplish an "efficient" solution to the implementation of management systems. The logic of organization design to accomplish this end is demonstrated by first staffing the Management Analysis Department with specialists in various disciplines, which assures the qualification for performing diagnostic analyses of management problems along with the development of conceptual solutions. Secondly, once the solution was identified as being a comput-

Omega Aerospace Corporation

EXHIBIT 2
Organization of Data Processing Department

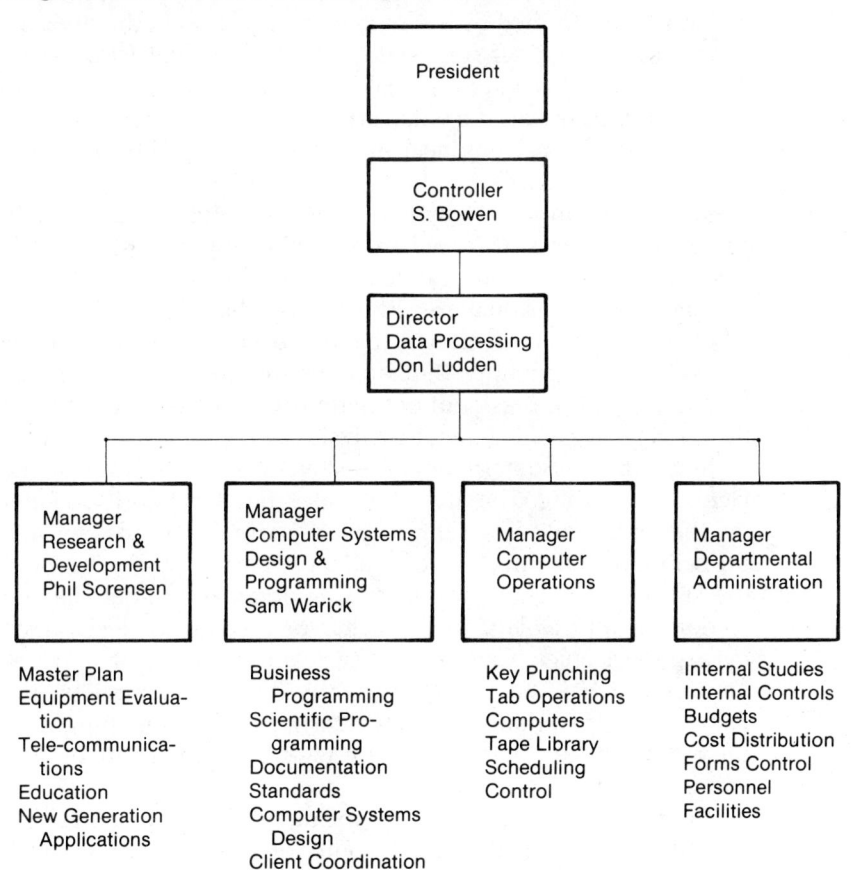

```
                        ┌─────────────┐
                        │  President  │
                        └──────┬──────┘
                               │
                        ┌──────┴──────┐
                        │  Controller │
                        │   S. Bowen  │
                        └──────┬──────┘
                               │
                        ┌──────┴──────┐
                        │  Director   │
                        │Data Processing│
                        │  Don Ludden │
                        └──────┬──────┘
     ┌────────────┬────────────┼────────────┬────────────┐
┌────┴─────┐ ┌────┴─────┐ ┌────┴─────┐ ┌────┴─────┐
│ Manager  │ │ Manager  │ │ Manager  │ │ Manager  │
│Research &│ │Computer  │ │Computer  │ │Departmental│
│Development│ │Systems  │ │Operations│ │Administration│
│Phil      │ │Design &  │ │          │ │          │
│Sorensen  │ │Programming│ │          │ │          │
│          │ │Sam Warick│ │          │ │          │
└──────────┘ └──────────┘ └──────────┘ └──────────┘
```

Master Plan	Business	Key Punching	Internal Studies
Equipment Evaluation	Programming	Tab Operations	Internal Controls
Tele-communications	Scientific Programming	Computers	Budgets
Education	Documentation	Tape Library	Cost Distribution
New Generation Applications	Standards	Scheduling	Forms Control
	Computer Systems Design	Control	Personnel
	Client Coordination		Facilities

er system, the Data Processing Department possessed the expertise to design, program, implement, and operate the system. Unfortunately, as will become apparent later, the practical operation of this process worked quite differently from the intended organization design.

THE CASE

The profitability of the Weapons Systems Division of Omega Aerospace Corporation was solely based on its ability to obtain military contracts for the study, design, and production of weapons systems. The division was one of several enterprises in this field and the award of contracts by the respective government agency was based on competitive bids. The preparation of a bid is an involved, complex process, which was performed by a separate organization in the division known as the Estimating Staff. This staff, headed by a chief estimator, reported directly to the division president. Estimates for bidding were prepared by this staff based on the data furnished by the various departments of the division, such as engineering, production, quality control, accounting, and personnel.

At the beginning of our survey in June 1967, the corporate profit contribution of this division had been showing a substantial decline for some time, which had resulted in considerable concern at both the corporate and divisional executive levels. The division had been unable to obtain any new contracts, having been consistently underbid by competitors. To identify the cause of this problem and to develop a solution to it, the president of the division directed Dr. Robert Benson, the director of management analysis, to conduct a study of the estimating system to determine its effectiveness for providing accurate cost factors for bidding. The project was assigned top priority; a letter signed by the president was sent to all department heads soliciting their cooperation and directing that all possible assistance be provided to the study team. The study team was organized under the general direction of John Dolan, the manager of systems analysis, and headed by a project chief, Carl Abel. The team consisted of four specialists: Vernon Mitchel, an accountant; Bill Ward, a computer expert; Joe Paloze, an operations research analyst; and Ralph Bingham, an industrial engineer. Exhibit 3 depicts the organization of the project team.

The team spent three months examining the estimating system and related procedures and, at the end of that period, wrote a report outlining the problem, various alternative solutions, and recommending the solution considered optimum by the team.

The essence of the conclusions resulting from the survey was that the present procedures of accumulating data relating to labor, material, and overhead costs were cumbersome, inaccurate, and too time-consuming to be of maximum value for estimating purposes. The time factor, especially, was singled out by the team as being a major problem in providing up-to-date cost data to the Estimating Staff when required for preparation of estimates. A second factor, considered equally important, was the inability to efficiently manipulate and integrate the various cost categories (i.e., labor, material, and overhead) to arrive at usable cost figures. To provide these capabilities, the report recommended as the optimum solution, the immediate development of a computer-based estimating system that would utilize the already automated data from the accounting and production systems to integrate these data and produce "estimating cost factors" as a regular output feature of the new computer system. In addition, the new system would furnish "management control reports" reflecting cost and estimate variances, as well as predicted profitability factors for each contract.

The report was presented by Mr. Dolan on September 15, 1967, at the division president's monthly staff meeting (attended by all department heads of the division) and was enthusiastically received by all present—including the chief estimator. The president directed Dr. Benson to submit the report immediately to the Data Processing Department for design, programming, and implementation of the system. He asked Mr. Dolan to express his appreciation to the project team for "a job well done." He further instructed Mr. S. Bowen, the controller, to direct his director of data processing to move with the utmost speed in the implementation of the new system. In addition, the president requested that he be furnished with monthly progress reports by data processing, reflecting the status of the development of the system.

At the president's monthly staff meeting on October 15, the following discussion took place:

PRESIDENT: Mr. Bowen, I have not received a progress report from your organization on the status of the new estimating system. Why not?

MR. BOWEN: I don't know, sir, but I'll check on it immediately.

PRESIDENT: Please do.

(Mr. Bown leaves the room to call Don Ludden, the director of data processing.)

MR. BOWEN *(on the phone)*: Don, where is the progress report to the president on the new estimating system? I told you that this report is due every month in my office on the 10th and in the president's office on the 12th.

DON LUDDEN: We are having problems making sense out of the system proposed by management analysis [department]. I tried to reach Carl Abel but he is out of town.

MR. BOWEN: O.K., but I want action on this project immediately. I'll talk to Dr. Benson about Abel.

(Mr. Bowen returns to the staff meeting.)

PRESIDENT: Well, Mr. Bowen?

MR. BOWEN: My data processing people tell me that they can't make sense out of the management analysis report and they have not been able to reach the project chief, Carl Abel.

PRESIDENT: Dr. Benson?

DR. BENSON: Well, I don't know why there should be any problem in understanding the proposal. Mr. Abel is out of town on another assignment but they could have talked to Mr. Dolan or any one of the team members.

PRESIDENT: I suggest that you two gentlemen get together on this and get the show on the road. I should have been informed immediately of any problems, Mr. Bowen, instead of me bringing the subject to your attention. I suggest that you personally keep track of this project from now on.

MR. BOWEN: Yes, sir.

After the staff meeting, Dr. Benson and Mr. Bowen agreed to schedule a meeting for October 18, in one of the conference rooms, to discuss the apparent problems associated with the proposed system. Dr. Benson agreed to have Carl Abel present at that meeting.

At the October 18 meeting the following were present: Management Analysis Department—Dr. Benson, John Dolan, and Carl Abel; Data Processing Department—Mr. Bowen, Don Ludden, Sam Warick, the manager of computer systems design and programming, and Phillip Sorensen, the manager of research and development.

DR. BENSON: Well, what's the problem in your shop with getting this new system off the ground?

MR. BOWEN: I'll let Sam [Warick] describe some of the initial problems.

SAM WARICK: Well, to begin with, your proposal is too vague for us to do any detail design work. None of my systems people can make sense out of the interface model in the system. Secondly, your proposal calls for the use of the XL2 programming language: we have never used that language here and I don't have anyone who can program in it.

PHILLIP SORENSEN: Yes, that's right. The XL2 is so new that nobody has had any experience with it. I called several computer manufacturers and none of them have used it; they are still testing whether the language can be used at all.

EXHIBIT 3
Organization of Project Team

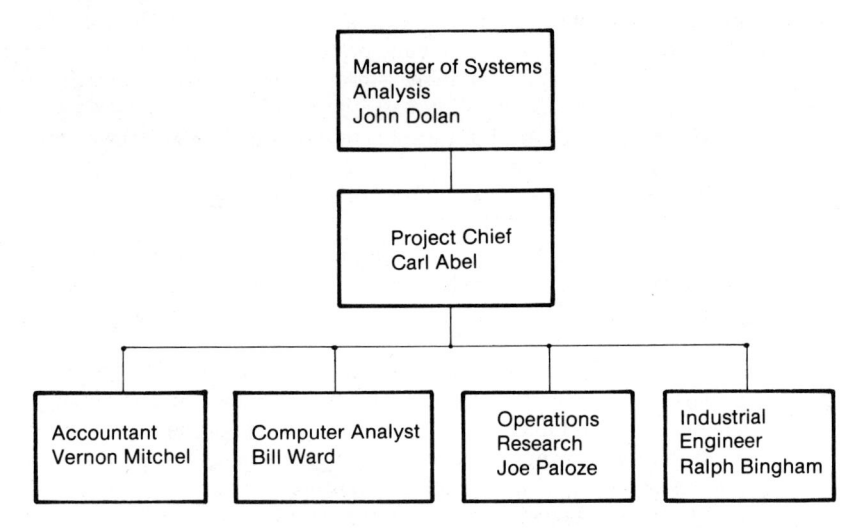

```
        ┌─────────────────────┐
        │ Manager of Systems  │
        │ Analysis            │
        │ John Dolan          │
        └──────────┬──────────┘
                   │
        ┌──────────┴──────────┐
        │ Project Chief       │
        │ Carl Abel           │
        └──────────┬──────────┘
                   │
   ┌───────────┬───┴───┬────────────┐
┌──┴──────┐ ┌──┴────┐ ┌┴────────┐ ┌─┴────────┐
│Accountant│ │Computer│ │Operations│ │Industrial│
│Vernon    │ │Analyst │ │Research  │ │Engineer  │
│Mitchel   │ │Bill Ward│ │Joe Paloze│ │Ralph     │
│          │ │        │ │          │ │Bingham   │
└──────────┘ └────────┘ └──────────┘ └──────────┘
```

JOHN DOLAN: To answer your first point, it is not our responsibility to do detail design work; that is your job and you are supposed to have the people to do it. If you don't, that's your problem not ours. Secondly, on the XL2 language, I'll ask Carl to answer that.

CARL ABEL: I don't know who you have been talking to, Phil, but that language is used by the computer center at the state university and they tell me it's the best approach to the type of computation required in our proposed system.

PHILLIP SORENSEN: That's just great. Who do you think we have for programmers here? Ph.D.'s in computer science? We are lucky if we can get people with bachelor's degrees. If you people would check your high-level solutions with us practical people instead of writing all this theoretical, we wouldn't have half of the problems we have now.

DON LUDDEN: That's right. We are handed the dirty work without being consulted and then told it's our problem.

DR. BENSON: Now let's not get personal. It seems to me that we have two problems. First, there is some problem in understanding the proposed system; second, there is a problem with the programming language. Now I suggest that Carl, Sam, and Phil sit down together and work these problems out. We will meet again, as a group, one week from today at the same time to discuss what solutions you three have come up with. Is that OK with you, Sam [Bowen]?

MR. BOWEN: OK.

During the ensuing week the trio met several times to discuss and attempt to resolve the design and programming language problems, but without apparent success. According to our informants, the relationship between the two factions became progressively more hostile and unyielding; accusations of incompetence and related implications were apparently frequent. As a result of these developments, which were reported by the three participants to their superiors, Mr. Bowen canceled the agreed-upon meeting, and on October 26 scheduled a personal meeting for him and Don Ludden with the division president. According to secondary sources (none of our informants were present at that meeting), the discussion, in essence, went as follows:

PRESIDENT: Well, Sam, you asked for this meeting. What's the problem?

MR. BOWEN: A real problem has developed with Dr. Benson's people over this proposed estimating system. I feel that this is no longer a technical disagreement but a problem of who tells whom what to do. Now my people resent being stuck with the responsibility for developing systems without having had the opportunity to be in from the ground floor. In other words, Benson's people dream up some theoretical system without consulting us and then we are supposed to make the thing work. If it doesn't work, we are the scapegoats while they sit back and call us incompetent.

PRESIDENT: Have they used the term *incompetent?*

MR. BOWEN: Yes, sir. My people feel like second-class citizens around here.

DON LUDDEN: I am beginning to have real morale problems in data processing as a result of the recent meetings between our people and Carl Abel. I feel that my people are the specialists in computer systems and languages, not Dr. Benson's group. His people are diagnostic consultants and primarily trained for identifying problems. But when it comes to computer systems, my people are the experts and they don't care to be told by somebody with less knowledge what's practical or how to do their job.

PRESIDENT: I was not aware of these feelings. What brought all this about?

MR. BOWEN: I think it's primarily the implication that whenever something goes wrong with the development of a new computer system—it's our fault. The management analysis people write a report and sell their proposed solution to the client organization. If the client accepts it, it's turned over to us and they wash their hands of the whole thing. Anything that goes wrong after that is blamed on us—even though the problem lies more often with the proposal which is frequently impractical from an operational standpoint. Yet, if we try to make changes they object immediately and put pressure on us through the client.

DON LUDDEN: In addition to this, they also recommend an implementation time schedule for their proposed systems right in the report. We are never consulted about this and the client organization expects us to comply with it. That simply doesn't make sense. We are the only ones who can and should determine our own work schedules. We have standard operating systems, such as payroll, which must be run at certain times and we certainly object to having some staff outfit telling us how to run our own shop.

PRESIDENT: I was not aware of this situation. There is, apparently, a very undesirable conflict developing between your people and Benson's group. I will think it over and let you know what my decision is.

The next day, Dr. Benson was called into the division president's office. We were not able to obtain any reliable information on what happened in that meeting, however, it is reasonable to assume that the president was attempting to obtain Dr. Benson's point of view on the conflict between the two organizations.

During the next divisional staff meeting on November 15, the president made the following announcement:

PRESIDENT: After due consideration of the current problems between the Management Analysis Department and the Data Processing Department, I have retained the services of an outside consulting firm to advise me of the best solution to the present intolerable situation. I have discussed this problem with members of the corporate staff and they concur in my appointment of an external consultant. I will inform you of my final disposition of the present situation after I have received the consultant's recommendations.

The firm of outside consultants arrived within a few days of this announcement and spent several weeks examining the task structures, organization structures, personnel qualifications, and related aspects of the two organizations. The consultants obtained much of their information through interviews with the various participants involved in the conflict. We were fortunate to obtain a recount from one of our informants who was present in a meeting between the senior consultant and Dr. Benson.

According to this recount, the interview went, essentially, as follows:

Consultant: Dr. Benson, how do you view the differentiation in authority and responsibility between your group and data processing?

Dr. Benson: Well, as you probably know, our primary purpose is to function as internal consultants, so to speak, to the management of this division. Our charter gives us the authority to conduct studies of divisional problems in any and all departments of the division. Of course, our authority is advisory in the sense that we cannot order another department to accept our recommendations. Of course, we can use informal methods if they don't accept them.

In terms of responsibility we are responsible for the accuracy of our analytical methods and the evaluation of alternative solutions. In other words, we have to be able to prove that our proposed solution is the best solution, considering all relevant variables.

Now, as to the differentiation between the two departments, we are responsible to develop a computer-based solution, which is the only time we get involved with data processing, to the conceptual point. This means, that the system's framework must be sufficiently defined for them [data processing] to do the detail work in design, programming, and so forth. We are not responsible for leading them by the hand or doing their work for them.

Consultant: I see. Would you explain what you mean by "informal methods" to assure acceptance of your recommendations?

Dr. Benson: Well, if an organization does not accept our recommendations, I have to explain in the staff meeting to the division president, who receives a copy of all our reports, why the recommendation was rejected. I feel that my people are the experts and therefore are in a superior position, collectively, to solve any problem better than the individual organization. By "informal" I mean, that if our recommendation is not accepted, I make the client prove—right in the staff meeting—why his solution, if he has one, is better than ours.

Consultant: Are there many such cases?

Dr. Benson: There were a couple when I first assumed my present position. After I got through with those people in the staff meetings—well, there have not been any problems since.

Consultant: What about the claim by Mr. Bowen's people that your proposed estimating system is inadequately developed and the programming language technically unacceptable?

Dr. Benson: You, of all people, should realize that the issue here has nothing to do with technical aspects. This is simply a convenient means for Bowen to satisfy his power complex. When the Management Analysis Department was set up, Bowen felt that it should have been placed under his jurisdiction. He wrote memos to everybody in the home office [headquarters corporate staff], using the most infantile arguments. When the group was set up as a separate department and I was appointed director, he became almost paranoid about it. I had been hired from the state university to fill this position, but Bowen would not even talk to me for the first few months after I came here. I think the man needs help.

CONSULTANT: Are you a psychologist, sir?
DR. BENSON: No. My degrees are in statistics.

During the period of the consultants' study little, if any, apparent interaction took place between the personnel of the two organizations. The consultants' report, which was classified "confidential" was presented by the senior consultant to the division president and a select group of corporate executives on January 12, 1968, in a closed meeting. On January 14, the division president called a special meeting of his staff (which included Dr. Benson and Mr. Bowen) at which he made the following announcement:

PRESIDENT: We have received the report from the consulting firm which had been retained to study the recent problems between the Management Analysis and Data Processing Departments. The recommendations have been reviewed by me and members of the corporate staff. Accordingly, the following reorganization will take place, effective February 1.

A new department known as the "Management Systems Department" will be established and will report directly to me. The head of this new department, known as "director of management systems," will be Mr. O'Connel from our corporate management audit staff. The new department will consist of the present Management Analysis Department and the present Data Processing

EXHIBIT 4
Management Systems Department

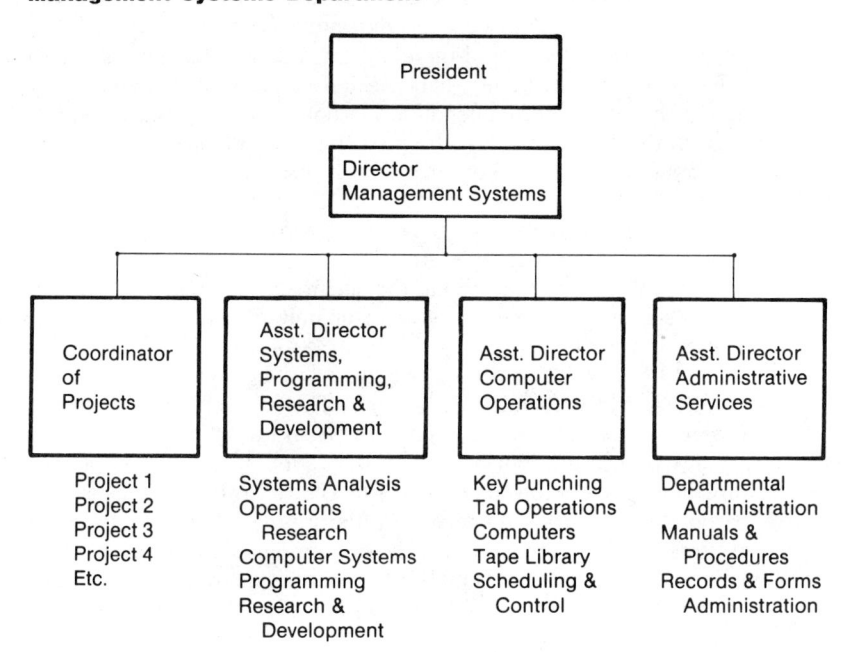

```
                          ┌───────────────┐
                          │   President   │
                          └───────┬───────┘
                                  │
                          ┌───────┴───────┐
                          │   Director    │
                          │ Management    │
                          │   Systems     │
                          └───────┬───────┘
          ┌───────────────┬───────┴───────┬───────────────┐
  ┌───────┴──────┐ ┌──────┴──────┐ ┌──────┴──────┐ ┌──────┴──────┐
  │ Coordinator │ │Asst. Director│ │Asst. Director│ │Asst. Director│
  │      of      │ │   Systems,   │ │   Computer   │ │Administrative│
  │   Projects   │ │ Programming, │ │  Operations  │ │   Services   │
  │              │ │  Research &  │ │              │ │              │
  │              │ │ Development  │ │              │ │              │
  └──────────────┘ └──────────────┘ └──────────────┘ └──────────────┘
```

Coordinator of Projects	Asst. Director Systems, Programming, Research & Development	Asst. Director Computer Operations	Asst. Director Administrative Services
Project 1	Systems Analysis	Key Punching	Departmental
Project 2	Operations	Tab Operations	Administration
Project 3	Research	Computers	Manuals &
Project 4	Computer Systems	Tape Library	Procedures
Etc.	Programming	Scheduling &	Records & Forms
	Research &	Control	Administration
	Development		

Department. Data processing will be removed from the controller's organization. Management analysis will be integrated into the new department and cease to exist as a separate organization. (See Exhibit 4).

The staffing and appointment of managers will be the responsibility of Mr. O'Connel, assisted by the directors of personnel both here and at headquarters. Some recommendations as to personnel are also contained in the consultants' report which will be made available to Mr. O'Connel.

It is my considered expectation that this integration of tasks and responsibilities under one organization will eliminate the present jurisdictional disputes and enable a more efficient performance of systems and data processing activities within the division. To this end, I expect all personnel involved to cooperate fully with Mr. O'Connel in effecting an orderly transition of responsibilities. Any questions of a personal nature should be directed to Mr. Schwenger [the director of personnel for the Weapons Systems Division].

Between the time of this announcement and February 1, the following developments took place:

1. Dr. Benson submitted his resignation on January 15, the day after the announcement.
2. Mr. Bowen, through his "functional" superior—the corporate vice president of finance—requested a transfer to the Commercial Products Division which had an opening for a controller. No action had been taken on his request at the time our own survey ended in February 1968.
3. Messrs. Abel, Ludden, Dolan, and Warick had separate meetings with Mr. O'Connel. Within one week of these meetings, Messrs. Abel and Dolan submitted their resignations. Mr. Sorensen requested a transfer to another division of the company.
4. There was no abnormal turnover reaction in the lower echelons of the two departments.

Opportunities at Mid-State U.

AFTER MY FIRST YEAR of graduate study, I paid a visit to the university where I received my undergraduate education. I dropped in on a few people I had known well as a student and got caught up on how they were doing and what was going on at the school. When I later reflected on the many conversations I'd had that day, I was bothered by the implications of what I had heard.

The first person I ran into was a friend who had graduated with me and had been working in a nonexempt position at the university for four years. I was surprised to hear that she only had one more week of work, having given her notice of resignation three weeks ago.

SYLVIA: I've finally had it with this place. My job was great for a while. I took on a lot of extra responsibilities and really enjoyed what I was doing. When my supervisor requested that my job be upgraded, the Personnel Department told him to have me stop doing the extra work. So when that failed, I applied for some higher grade-level jobs on campus, including one in this department, but I never got one. You know what I found out! They advertised those jobs and had applicants from all across the country! I expected to have to compete with others from within the university for those jobs, but from the whole United States! That doesn't seem fair, especially for the next level job in my own department!

When I was hired all I ever heard about was how committed everyone was to internal advancement. It sure is a different story when you try to get promoted.

The next person I visited with was the director of affirmative action. He had started the affirmative action program at the university during my senior year and I was anxious to see how it was going.

GREGORY: Well, as you can see I'm still here, and I'm happy to say that things are going great. We've been actively seeking women and minority group members for all of our new and vacant positions and we're making real progress toward meeting our targets. Everyone seems to be supporting the goal of equal opportunity at this school. Although, naturally, my staff and I have had to be very alert and firm about insisting that the various departments follow the rules we've set up to carry out the affirmative action policy, such as, advertise all job openings, don't interview anyone before the job is officially advertised, and document the fact that women and members of minority groups have been given equal consideration.

While I was waiting to talk to the director of personnel, I had a brief conversation with a slight acquaintance who was waiting for an interview. She was applying for the job of assistant to the dean in the School of Engineering.

LESLIE: This will be my third interview today for this job, but, judging by the way people treat me (with disinterest), it sure doesn't look good. I've been employed for the past two years as the assistant to the dean of students at a small junior college in the next state, so I have the experience and education required for this position. I never would have known about this job if it hadn't been advertised in the *Journal of Higher Education*. But, I've learned through a friend that they also have a very qualified candidate who has worked in that department for the past few years. I'm beginning to suspect that they've written the job specifications so he's the only person who can qualify and that interviewing me is just a ritual. If that isn't an inside track then I don't know what is!

When I finally got in to see the personnel director, I could see I was lucky he could spare me a few minutes. From the looks of his office he had more than enough work to do and I knew he had squeezed me into his schedule between two interviews. I had been considering applying for an administrative position at the university upon completion of graduate school and was anxious to hear his reaction.

JOSEPH: Well, it certainly would be worthwhile to apply, Dale, but you'll be up against some stiff competition. Now that we advertise job opportunities on the open market, the applicant pools are enormous. It seems like each week I spend more and more time interviewing job candidates, to say nothing about the amount of paperwork. Also, it sure stretches out the process. You can't hire anyone in less than a month these days. We have to thoroughly document our personnel searches to comply with affirmative action regulations. The regulations make sense when you're going outside for someone, but we believe in promoting from within, and when you have a good candidate on the inside, why bother with advertisements, etc.?

I also had lunch with my old faculty adviser who had recently become the associate dean of the School of Social Science.

PATRICIA: Even though I miss teaching full time, I really like this job. The school has been growing rapidly and I've been busy doing a lot of faculty recruiting and recruiting for staff positions. One thing that I've noticed is how much easier it is for women to get faculty positions now, compared to when I was hired 15 years ago. If I hadn't known a few faculty members when I was a candidate, I probably would never have gotten the job. The "old boy" network worked well and smoothly in its day—that is, for those of us who were part of the network. Faculty at one school practically lined up jobs for their graduates with faculty they knew at another school. Unfortunately there were all kinds of assumptions and stereotypes that existed to block people who didn't have the right background or style, or who didn't come from the right schools. The new setup has done a lot to change all that.

The last person I saw that day was the head librarian, whom I had worked for part-time as a student. I had always enjoyed working for him because he took a genuine interest in his subordinates.

RICHARD: Right now I'm up to my neck in interviewing candidates for an assistant librarian position. Do you remember Betty, the woman who works in the technical department? (Betty was a woman about 45 years old who came back to work during my senior year after her children had gone away to school. She didn't have a college education but had worked part-time in libraries over the years and was very competent.) Well, she's the one I want to hire for the position but the rules are that I have to interview every interested candidate. What a waste of time, mine and everyone else's. There are a lot of good people coming in for interviews but I'd like to give the job to Betty. She's reliable, knows our system, and has done a good job for us. Of all my people, she deserves a promotion and would work hard to succeed. I hope the Selection Committee doesn't give me a hard time when I tell them she's my choice.

Other than hassles like this one, everything is going pretty well around here.

Based on what my acquaintances had said about their experiences, I tried to picture what it would be like to work at the university. I then realized that their experiences did not fit together very well. Now I find myself reconsidering my plan to apply for a job at the university as I wonder what the long-run job opportunities are for university employees. I wonder about my chances of being hired and thereafter about my chances of being promoted.

A Promotion in Sri Lanka*

PART I

Introduction

THE YEAR WAS 1978, and Mr. B. Gunawardena of the Ceylon Products Corporation was feeling a great deal of satisfaction as he watched Mr. S. Abeysekara leave his office. It was satisfying to be able to give a promotion to a senior, hardworking employee. It was satisfying to have such a skilled fitter available for the position of supervisor. It was satisfying to be able to fill the position with the man who was his first choice for the job, and who would be seen as a legitimate choice by the union and the workers, given his seniority.

With the more open economy that had come about following the election of the free market-oriented government in 1977, the work load of Mr. Gunawardena's department had been increasing and Mr. Gunawardena believed that in the months ahead it would be important for the new fitting section to have a respected and reliable supervisor.

The Corporation

The Ceylon Products Corporation (CPC) was one of Sri Lanka's important public corporations. It produced a series of basic products needed by other corporations in both the public and private sectors.

---

*Copyright © 1982 Robin D. Willits.

Thus, it did not produce as much for the retail market as it did for the industrial market for use in the production of other products. As a public corporation, CPC was expected to earn a profit and thereby contribute to government revenues, to operate efficiently and thereby keep the price down, to offer a range of products as needed by the nation in its efforts toward development, and to fulfill a social responsibility in providing jobs under safe and decent working conditions.

The corporation was managed by a board of directors who were appointed by and could be removed by the minister of industry and commerce. This meant that the corporation was more subject to political forces in the environment than a corporation in the private sector. Historically, promotion decisions had occasionally been influenced by a call from the secretary to the minister of industry and commerce. More common were calls urging the directors to keep peace with the union[1] and maintain good employee relations, particularly when election time was close at hand.

Corporation policy emphasized promotion from within. Thus, the usual practice was to hire workers into the bottom positions from among individuals who had been trained under the National Apprenticeship Training Program and who had served their apprenticeship period in the CPC. Thereafter, a worker could expect to receive periodic cost-of-living salary increases and be eligible for promotion to higher-skilled jobs as he gained experience and developed additional skills. Eventually, promotion into the supervisory ranks (supervisor, assistant foreman, and foreman) was possible. The Personnel Department was a staff department that maintained employee records. While it made certain that any candidate for promotion met the specified requirements of educational background and years of experience, the ultimate choice was made by the line manager. Personnel also had a training section that administered the awarding of scholarships to all levels for attending training programs conducted by outside organizations, but it had no responsibility for in-service training.

The Department

Mr. Gunawardena held the title of supervising engineer and was the manager in charge of the Mechanical Engineering Department. This department, along with an Electrical Engineering Department, a Stationary Engineering Department, and a Building Engineering Department, constituted the Plant Engineering Division of the CPC. The division's function was to maintain the corporation's production tools, machinery, and equipment in working order.

---

[1] In Sri Lanka every union was generally aligned with one or another political party, and labor negotiations were partly steered by political considerations.

The Mechanical Engineering Department had consisted of two subunits: a forgings unit and a machine shop, with the fitting function residing in the machine shop. In 1978, with the prospect of an expanded workload, the fitting function was organized as a third subunit of the ME Department with Mr. Abeysekara as its supervisor.

The employees in the Plant Engineering Division were paid a salary based on their job, their seniority, and their skill. In addition, the employees, including supervision, shared in a corporation-wide bonus system based on the overall output of the corporation. This bonus scheme reflected the fact that the Plant Engineering Division function was to keep the plant operating by preventing the breakdown of machinery and equipment through preventive maintenance and by repairing any unavoidable breakdowns promptly and expeditiously. The assumption was that if plant engineering did its job well, overall output would be greater, therefore plant engineering should be rewarded along with the production workers.

The Interview

Several years after Mr. Abeysekara's promotion to fitting supervisor, Mr. Gunawardena was talking with a management consultant (MC) about his experiences as a manager. In the course of the conversation, the consultant expressed an interest in hearing the details of Mr. Gunawardena's selection of Mr. Abeysekara as supervisor and its aftermath.

MC: What were your reasons for promoting Mr. A to the position of fitting section supervisor?

Mr. G: Because that was the trend in the organization. Workers who have put in a certain number of years, they are looking for these types of promotion. In Sri Lanka there is a wide difference between a blue-collar job and a supervisory job. Even though the salaries are low, we could not motivate workers to remain workers by giving them a higher salary than a supervisor because all the workers are looking for these promotions. Somehow they want to get to the post of foreman so they can belong to a different class of society entirely. I picked Mr. A because he was the most experienced and the most qualified to become the supervisor among the fitters.

MC: Qualified in what sense?

Mr. G: Qualified in the sense of his amount of experience. Also his personal record does not show any bad marks (absenteeism, disciplinary actions, etc.). In this particular case, the experience gap between Mr. A and the next most experienced fitter was about five years. That was a fairly big gap. We could not overlook that. Also the other workers were not any better than Mr. A, they didn't have any supervisory experience or demonstrated supervisory ability.

MC: What kind of a worker was Mr. A before his promotion?

Mr. G: He was a skilled fitter and was very obliging and attentive to his work. You could give him a difficult job and feel sure that he would do it on his own and stay on it until it was done.

MC: Tell me about his relationship with the other workers before he was made supervisor.

Mr. G: He was more or less friendly with the other workers and attended to business.

MC: Would he have been the social leader of the group or pretty much on his own?

Mr. G: No, not the social leader. Pretty much on his own.

MC: You advertise such openings, I believe. Did any of the other fitters apply for the position?

Mr. G: No, they didn't apply. All the other fitters were very much junior to Mr. A. They knew they wouldn't have gotten this job because of the gap in service and in knowledge about fitting work. For this type of job, if you appoint a person who knows only a little fitting, but who might know a lot about organization, that's going to create some kind of problem.

MC: What kind of problem?

Mr. G: When the subordinate knows better than the supervisor, there may be some problems. We expected the supervisor to attend to the jobs with the help of the other fitters and lead them—advise them how to do the work; handle the organizational aspects and be able to judge time standards. If the time standards are satisfactory, he should be able to convince any worker who might doubt them that they are all right. Also he must assign the right job to each man according to his skill.

MC: If Mr. A had not been available, who would have been your second choice?

Mr. G: Someone from the outside the department but inside the corporation because the next most qualified man from inside didn't have sufficient experience.

MC: If you had had a very skilled machinist in your machine shop with a lot of seniority, wouldn't he have been considered, and been a promotion from within?

Mr. G: No, because a machinist would not be able to discharge the duties of a fitter. A fitter must be a person capable of repairing our machine tools as well as doing bench fitting. He must have the ability to dismantle a lathe, find out the fault, and replace a worn-out bearing or remove a gear wheel from a shaft, etc.

MC: I understand you interviewed Mr. A before you gave him the job. Tell me about that interview.

Mr. G: Of course, we knew his work ability. I made use of the interview to explain to him what additional functions he would have to perform and what we were going to expect from him. After the interview he probably knew that he was going to get the job from the way we conducted the interview. I told him, "You are from the post of fitter, now you are going to be directed to the post of supervisor. The supervisor is the link between the engineering staff and the workers." I told him that there are other supervisors in the department and his function would be similar, as far as the organization of production is concerned. He seemed to understand everything.

MC: What made you think he understood?

Mr. G: The way he responded; he didn't retaliate. He agreed. He said, "I know that I'm going to do those things." He didn't ask any questions. He nodded his head and said, "I understand."

MC: You told him he was to be a supervisor. What did you tell him he was to do, specifically?

Mr. G: I told him that there would be a certain number of fitters working under him and this was what he'd have to do. "You have to establish close relations with machine shop supervisor, since some of the machine shop jobs may also require fitting work. There are machine tools in the department so you have to implement a maintenance scheme for them." I also told him that distributing the work among the fitters was one of his major tasks, and if he had any problems to just come and seek my help.

Further, I told him he would have to see that the substores of consumable supplies in the department were adequate and remind the office staff about the reordering these things. The stores keeper is the one who usually reminds the office, but I told him he can also remind the stores keeper.

MC: Did you discuss anything else with him?

Mr. G: I told him that his supervisory functions were basically similar to those of other supervisors, that there is a certain amount of standard work that supervisors have to perform such as initiating time cards, filling out overtime reports for approval, allocating work, etc., and he would have similar responsibilities.

MC: Did you mention these specifically?

Mr. G: No, I didn't. He presumably knew what supervisors do.

MC: About how long did the interview last?

Mr. G: Oh, about 10 minutes.

MC: So, after the interview he soon went to work as the supervisor?

Mr. G: Yes, and I was involved in giving him advice when I could take time from my other duties.

Before, proceeding to Part II of the case, the reader is invited to answer the following questions:

1. In your opinion, what kind of a supervisor will Mr. Abeysekara be? What will be his strengths and his weaknesses as a supervisor? What are the reasons for your predictions?
2. What additional information would you like to have about Mr. Abeysekara, Mr. Gunawardena, and the situation, so as to have more confidence in your prediction?

PART II

The Interview Continued

MC: After Mr. A was promoted, how did things go?

Mr. G: Initially, I was personally involved in the fitting section, giving him advice and directing him to do this and that. But I was rather busy at that time and couldn't work with him all that much. There were some inherent problems. He did not take responsibility as supervisor. He was not putting other fitters on the job and directing them; he was doing it on his own. In other words, it was like a gang of fitters with Mr. A functioning as the head fitter.

Also, he could not maintain discipline among his subordinates. We have a central time-keeping office. A man can pass the card in there at 7 A.M. but come to the workshop at 9 A.M. I told Mr. A that we could not tolerate this kind of thing, but he couldn't convince people to stop and he thought it was wrong for him to come and complain to me, because he'd come up from the ranks. They were his peers.

MC: During this early period, did you have any talks with him about how he was performing his supervisory work?

Mr. G: Yes, on a number of occasions, I said you have to do this, and you should maintain the shift report in this way. He apparently took some interest, but he couldn't continue it. He didn't have the capacity to discharge supervisory functions.

MC: When you talked to him, how would he respond?

Mr. G: He would agree. He'd convinced me he was going to follow these things. He probably tried his best, but he couldn't.

MC: What makes you think he tried?

Mr. G: Because of his behavior. If he didn't like what I was telling him, he would have retailiated. He would have come out with his problems as to why he couldn't carry out those instructions.

MC: Were there any other problems?

Mr. G: Yes, we came to know that he had a bad habit of doing gambling with his workers. I warned him, "You are a supervisor and gambling is illegal. If you get caught, it could lead to a sacking." Also, he wasn't utilizing the trainees enough. He should have put the trainees with a fitter, but instead there was much idling and wasting of time. Worst of all, he had a bad habit of getting hot-tempered. He wouldn't listen to the workers, and if they disagreed with him, he would get angry.

MC: What about his personality kept him from being able to do it?

Mr. G: He had the mentality of a skilled worker. He found it difficult to change that mentality. Also, because he became a supervisor only for esteem needs.

MC: You told me you eventually decided he'd never be a good supervisor. How soon after he was made supervisor did you decide that?

Mr. G: After about six months.

MC: What made you decide he'd never be a good supervisor?

Mr. G: After severely warning him about gambling a second time, I learned from my peers that in his private life he is a man who is spending whatever he gets; not saving and improving his home, but spending it on gambling and drinking. He's not a man who wants a good living for himself, so he won't listen to us.

MC: How does this pattern of private life connect with his potential to be a supervisor?

Mr. G: I assume that a person who wants to have a good life will want to save money and behave in a responsible manner. One who has some plans for his own life will definitely have plans about his professional life. Then he would work hard and he would want to go up in the ladder of hierarchy: supervisor, assistant foreman, foreman. But Mr. A was not that type of person. He may have been doing this (gambling, drinking, wasting his money) on the sly before his promotion, but it didn't come to the surface as long as he was a fitter.

MC: How do you explain his being reliable and hardworking before his promotion but not after?

Mr. G: After his promotion he was not reliable in his supervisory functions, but he continued to fill the fitter functions reliably. I overestimated his supervisory capabilities.

MC: What were the consequences of his not doing the supervisory and administrative duties?

Mr. G: Delays in the fitting shop. For example, certain jobs have to go through the fitting shop for subsequent machining in the machine shop. Those jobs were getting held up in the fitting shop. Also, the fitters were idling; we were not making use of them fully. Some people were not accountable. They'd come in the morning and quickly vanish, and come again in the afternoon, because there was nobody to check. My staff had to intervene for administrative work. They had to allocate the work, get the work done, and check on people's whereabouts. So I have to make use of my staff, who are supposed to do other functions, to supplement Mr. A's activities.

MC: How was the overall efficiency of the shop?

Mr. G: It was all right because we knew this man's inabilities and we supplemented. He was a hard worker. If one of the people working for him did not do the job, he neither took disciplinary action nor informed me, but he did the job himself. Somehow the results were there, so I was not bothered very much to correct the matters.

MC: How long did this situation continue?

Mr. G: For nearly three years, until Mr. A left the corporation for a job in West Asia.

MC: How has the supervisory work been getting done since?

Mr. G: We appointed an engineering assistant as acting supervisor. He doesn't have the type of experience regarding machine tools, but he has ability in organizing functions and I help him very much, especially in the case of machine tool breakdowns. He is not familiar with machine tools but fortunately I am. I devote some of my time to train him and to tell him the way to get the job done. So he is doing the supervisory function apart from the other activities he's supposed to do.

MC: But he is not officially the supervisor?

Mr. G: No.

MC: Could you make it official?

Mr. G: He would not want to be, because he is an engineering assistant, so appointment as a supervisor would be a step down.

MC: Could this go on permanently?

Mr. G: Yes, or I could appoint a supervisor. But right now I am not thinking of appointing a supervisor, because of the norms of the organization (promotion from within based largely on seniority). If we were to advertise the post, another man will come; maybe someone with political pull, so that's going to create more problems. Mr. A knew fitting but not supervision. We might get a supervisor who knows neither supervision nor fitting!

MC: How does a manager such as you protect himself against hiring someone who is incompetent? Can't you interview him, and if he is unsatisfactory, not hire him?

MR. G: No, not for sure, because there can be a certain amount of politics involved in these things. Right now our corporation chairman is convinced that you cannot give in to politicians' requests and run a state corporation properly. He knows that we need skilled workers. I may be able to get a good man now, but still the time is not good because we are having our elections next year.

MC: How would upcoming elections affect your decision?

MR. G: The members of Parliament will be trying to help people from their electorate, and gain favor during this period. The chairman wants skilled people, but right now he may be under increasing political pressure.

MC: Couldn't you get the process completed before election time?

MR. G: Right now it is not very conducive to hiring a good man. For one thing, most of the skilled people are leaving the country for West Asia and other places where the salaries are very high. Others have been attracted to Free Trade Zone factories. Also, our plans to expand the fitting shop have come to a halt. So I'm going to let the situation stay as it is for some time, and if I ever try to replace Mr. A, I'll try to go outside. That way the man won't be supervising his peers.

MC: I certainly appreciate hearing about this. Your situation is unique yet it has issues and choices of a type that any manager might have to face. It definitely was not a simple situation with an obvious answer.

The Seacoast Mutual Insurance Co.

PART I

AS HE STARED OUT of the window of his spacious office, Peter Shea, vice president and manager of the Accounting Department of the Seacoast Mutual Insurance Company, pondered the alternatives of the decision he was about to make.

Ed Maddix, supervisor of the Data Entry Department, had just left and had urged Peter to move the Data Entry Department from its present location beside a large picture window to a larger location set aside from the normal traffic flow. (See Exhibit 1.) Ed had been unsuccessful in getting the girls in his department to stop staring out the window and talking to other employees; he felt that the move would increase their productivity and stop the dysfunctional behavior.

The Seacoast Mutual Insurance Company, commonly referred to by its employees as "The Seacoast," was a small, conservative New England company located about 30 miles from Boston. Having been in existence for over 100 years, the company was striving to continue its

EXHIBIT 1
Layout of the Third Floor of the Seacoast Mutual Insurance Company

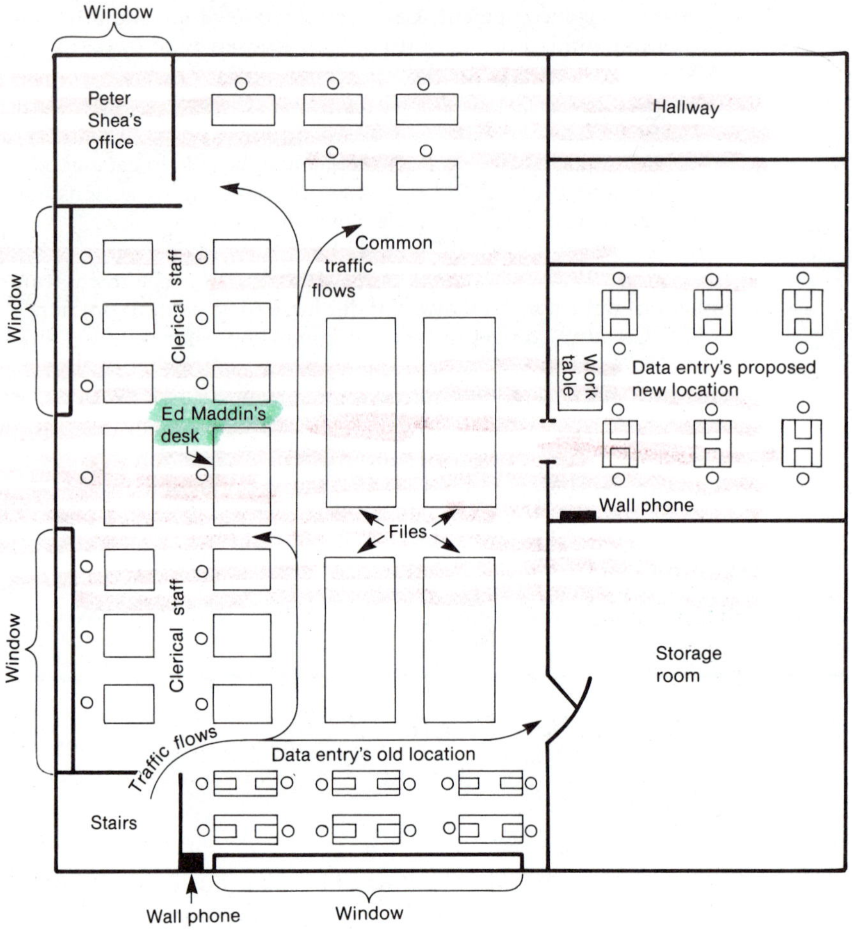

recent growth rate of 10 percent per year and harbored hopes of even increasing its growth rate in the future.

The Seacoast employed over 150 employees, many of whom were lifelong residents of the area. There was little turnover, and few people were ever fired or laid off. Within the community, the Seacoast had the reputation of being a secure, dependable company and a clean, pleasant place to work.

Because of the ample supply of available workers, salaries at the

Seacost were lower than the regional average. Many of the employees could earn more money by commuting to Boston, but they were reluctant to do so; although many employees complained about the low wages, they preferred to remain at the Seacoast with its security, good fringe benefits, suburban setting, and known type of co-workers rather than commuting into Boston.

Close to three fourths of the employees were women, mainly filling clerical and support positions. Many had lived in the area all their lives and had worked at the Seacoast since graduating from high school. The ages of the women ranged from 18 to 65, with the majority being in their 20s and 30s. Most of the women had families and their salaries were needed to supplement their husbands' incomes. Many of the women felt that they were fortunate to have a job, especially one so close to home.

The Data Entry Department consisted of 11 keypunch operators. All of the operators had been employed by the company for at least two years and many had been in the department for five to seven years. Data entry was one of the lower-paying departments and the women were rarely transferred out of the department or promoted.

The job of data entry operator required keyboard skills and involved the keypunching of account information for input into the computer. New operators learned only one type of account at a time, and after they mastered one type, they moved on to another. The operators agreed that it took nearly one year before they had been exposed to and mastered all of the different policies and accounts that the Seacoast handled and could handle them without error. Their supervisor, Ed Maddix, once remarked, "It takes too long to train someone in this department to justify transferring them to another job. The department is most productive when most of the women are trained to process all types of accounts."

The work load was not constant in the department. Once or twice a day, someone from mail and message would leave new work on a table in the middle of the department, and the operators would go and get the work that they knew how to do. The work tended to be heavier at the end of the week when other departments cleared their desks for the weekend. All accounts were computer-run on Saturday, so it was important that the accounts be processed before Saturday. Usually the Data Entry Department was able to work extra hard to clear up the work backlog by Fridays at 4:30 P.M. Oftentimes there was little work to do on Mondays and Tuesdays.

Ed Maddix had worked for the Seacoast for nearly 30 years. Most of the men in management were younger than Ed, who had reached his top position and was waiting for retirement. Ed had other responsibilities in addition to supervising the Data Entry Department, and his desk was located approximately 50 feet away from the Data Entry Department. Although the department was in full view of Ed's desk, he rarely went into the department. Instead, he would call the group's work leader, Jane Smith, to his desk. Ed would relay information through Jane. Because of his actions and attitude toward the operators, Ed was generally disliked by the operators.

Jane Smith was 28 years old and had been an operator with the Data Entry Department for 10 years. Although a group leader, Jane was still required to do the same work as the other women. She was considered "one of the girls" and often remarked that she had trouble controlling the department, especially if it was something that Ed had ordered her to do. As an operator, Jane had shared the department's dislike for Ed, but after being promoted to group leader, she rarely joined in the women's open criticism of him.

The Data Entry Department was located on the third floor and situated beside a very large picture window that overlooked a scenic, tree-lined street. The buildings along the street were colonial and had large well-kept grounds. The window faced south and the sunlight would shine into the department most of the day, adding light and warmth to the atmosphere. The keypunch machines were situated so that each operator had a window view. The building was old and not well insulated, and the department was often hot in the summer and drafty in the winter. The women often complained about the temperature, saying that the condition was the cause of many colds.

The women would remain in the department for coffee and lunch breaks. Often they would stop working for several minutes to watch something out the window. Other employees, especially those who worked on the third floor, often stopped by to enjoy the view. When this happened, the visitors and operators would engage in casual conversation.

Located near the department was a main stairway. Since the stairs were used frequently, there was a steady stream of people walking by the department, and in winter continuous blasts of cold air from the unheated stairwell. Because of the traffic, however, the operators often engaged in conversation with others in the company, and with people always coming and going, the department had a "hustle-bustle" appearance.

The window watching and conversations greatly disturbed Ed Maddix. Maddix felt that conversations while working led to mistakes, lack of efficiency, and an unprofessional tone. From his desk, Ed would often telephone Jane Smith and command her to make the operators stop talking and get back to work. Jane would reluctantly tell the operators to stop. The conversations would stop, but it was not long before the next one would start up again.

Ed had made his feelings known to Peter Shea, his boss. Peter had always let Ed handle the problems of the department and he felt that it was Ed's job to control his workers. However, Peter had become increasingly concerned about the window watching and the conversations and he, too, wanted to see the behavior stopped. Peter realized that Ed's methods were not working and soon something would have to be done.

Peter's conversation with Ed this morning went like this:

ED: Peter, I just can't stand it. These girls just don't want to stop looking out of the window and talking with every single person who wanders by their department.

PETER: I know, Ed. How much has this window watching backlogged the department?

ED: At the moment, not very much. But if we continue to increase our volume of business, someday we are either going to have to hire more girls and buy more equipment, or be backlogged. Of course, if we could find a way to put an end to the window watching, we could probably handle the increased volume of business with our current number of girls.

PETER: Well, you have spoken to them a number of times and that doesn't seem to stop them. What do you suggest we do?

ED: If they are going to ignore me, I think that we should let them know we mean business. I think that we should move the department away from the window and away from the flow of people going past them all day. I think that the old word-processing area that we are now using for storage files would be ideal. It's larger than the present location and well lit with fluorescent lights. It has walls on three sides and six-foot partitions in front screening the room from the rest of the floor. On top of that, it's air conditioned and carpeted. You know how they complain about the fluctuation in temperature near the windows. They should like it a lot.

PETER: Well, Ed, that's a pretty drastic step.

ED: I know it is, but I think that it's about time we did something drastic around here. People have got to realize that we mean business and that they are here to work, not to talk and have a good time.

PETER: You're right, Ed. Let me think about it and I'll get back to you.

PART II

The following morning, Ed telephoned Jane and informed her that the department was being moved across the floor to an area now occupied by the storage files. He told Jane that the reason for the move was because of the great amount of talking and socializing that occurred, and that the new location would not provide them with any distractions.

The data entry operators were very upset over the move. Convinced that they had no choice but to comply, they complained among themselves and to friends but did not talk to Peter Shea or Ed Maddix.

The move was accomplished that weekend, and on Monday the women reported to their new location. Without the sun streaming in the window, the new department seemed darker than the previous location. Although both locations had walls that were painted pale gray, the operators who had never minded the walls before the move, now felt that the walls were dingy and unpleasant. Combined with the dark green partitions, the plainness of the location seemed to stand out. Other employees still stopped by, but the opportunity to do this was greatly reduced. The lack of contact with others in the company further increased their feelings of isolation.

The change had drastic effects on the department. The women no longer remained in the department for breaks and lunch. Since the new location shielded them from Ed's desk, they were able to read paperbacks and magazines at their machines.

The hoped-for increase in productivity did not materialize. Within several months, three operators left the company. Personnel was able to quickly get replacements, but it would be months before they would be as capable as the operators who quit. In addition, there didn't seem to be the drive to complete the work load by the end of the week. Errors increased and it took additional time to correct and re-keypunch the data.

Now, six months after the move, Peter Shea wondered if he had made the correct decision. Since the new location was larger and more comfortable, he could not understand why the women would not accept their new location. Peter could move the department back to the original location, or he could keep it in the present location and "ride the storm." As he wondered what he should do, he continued to look out of the window.

*Southeast Municipal Association**

GEORGE AUSTIN was dismayed. He had just been assigned an article due on Monday for the *SEMA News*, a monthly publication mailed to city and town managers throughout the Southeast. This meant that he would have to drop everything and spend the rest of Friday and Saturday researching and writing to meet the Monday deadline. "Another weekend gone," George said to Bob Pearlman, the assistant director of SEMA, as they left the Friday staff meeting. "You've only been here three months, right?" Bob replied, "Wilbur must have a lot of confidence in you to be asking for an article quite so soon. Do a good job and you have a chance to do others and make a name for yourself with the readers. Got any ideas for what you'll write about?"

"None," said George. "You heard Wilbur. Just 600 words on 'something of interest.' Maybe I'll go through this week's memos for some ideas."

"Not a bad idea. Be sure to let me have a brief bit of autobiographical data so I can work up a new author sketch on you. The city and town managers are always interested in knowing something about the author, particularly a new person," responded Bob.

Wilbur J. Widdlesworth had founded the Southeast Municipal Association (SEMA) in 1970. Having spent several years as a lobbyist for municipal agencies in the Midwest, Widdlesworth had recognized the need for a regional organization that could provide smaller municipalities with access to the millions of dollars being dispersed to nonprofit companies under the New Federalism grants system. This system used organizations classified by the Internal Revenue Service as 501/c/3 as conduits for transferring federal funds to the local level.[1]

Although each state had a municipal league that represented city and town governments in state legislative matters, few agencies existed to represent a regional consortium of municipal leagues to the federal government. Widdlesworth attended a national meeting of city and town managers in 1969, contacted the directors of each state municipal league in the Southeast and explained his concept. SEMA was chartered in the state of Virginia the following year and quickly received 501/c/3 status from the IRS. The primary reason behind this rapid start-up was the fact that southeast municipalities could only tap those federal funds distributed on the basis of population. This policy benefited large urban

---

*Copyright 1980, Whittemore School of Business and Economics, University of New Hampshire. Reproduced with permission.

[1] To obtain the 501/c/3 status, an organization had to meet three criteria: meet state certification as a not-for-profit corporation, be solely engaged in activities "for the public good," and serve a regional constituency as evidenced by a board of directors made up of public officials from each state in a region.

areas, but left the thousands of small towns in the Southeast to compete for a very small portion of the pie. Large cities tended to have their own lobbyists, thus the members of the state leagues tended to be the smaller cities and towns who could not afford a full-time legislative staff. The municipal leagues from the Southeast embraced the concept of SEMA because the organization could dramatically increase the amount of federal funds for their constituents. This meant, among other things, that the municipal leagues could increase their dues, which was often the only source of operating capital for these agencies. Widdlesworth embraced the concept of SEMA because of a standard line item in federal grant budgets entitled "indirect."

The "indirect" line item was typically expressed as a percentage of the operating funds being requested for a specific project. Thus, after developing a budget that included all conceivable project costs (rent, utilities, copying, telephone, etc.), a percentage of these costs would also be added to the budget under "indirect," making the budget very similar to the "cost plus" budgets negotiated between the federal government and for-profit corporations such as defense contractors. The use of "indirect" first appeared in contracts with academic institutions, as various federal agencies used the line item to provide schools with more discretionary funds. The usage soon spread to all 501/c/3 contracts. Each federal agency negotiated a specific indirect rate with each 501/c/3 organization. Rates ranged from 15 percent to 70 percent. Widdlesworth estimated that SEMA could expect to handle approximately $1 million in federal grants annually, with an average of 30 percent indirect funds. Although these indirect funds could not be taken by individuals as "profit," they could be used for salary supplementation, company cars, unrelated travel expenses, and other benefits.

SEMA began with four people: an executive director, two associate directors, and a secretary. An office was established in Collegetown, Virginia, the home of several other regional nonprofit agencies, one university, and two colleges. Its rural setting was favored by the executive director's family.

During the first year of operation, SEMA's financial support consisted of membership dues paid annually by each league ($3,000 per league), a $200,000 annual grant from the Department of Housing and Urban Development's (HUD) Community Development Program, and a $50,000 assistance grant from the Southern Regional Commission. The HUD grant was provided for technical assistance to communities in the region applying for community development funds. These funds, known as CD block grants, were available to all communities throughout the United States in need of infrastructure renewal funds to refurbish municipally owned city center properties. The application process was extremely involved, and many of the smaller cities and towns were unable to tap these grants because the complexities demanded more expertise than was available. The two SEMA associate directors received training from the HUD regional office, then conducted seminars throughout the region. The executive director (Wilbur J. Widdlesworth) was in charge of soliciting new grants from federal agencies. A study commissioned by a private research firm indicated that SEMA could reasonably expect 40 percent of its proposals to be funded. Widdlesworth attempted to maintain a minimum of 20 proposals "in review" at any given time.

During its first 10 years, SEMA was successful in obtaining a large number of grants and grew steadily. By 1980, the staff consisted of 15 full-time staff and 5 secretaries who handled 20 federal programs—$2 million in funds in all. Agencies contracting with SEMA included HUD, HEW, National Science Foundation, Department of Energy, LEAA, National Endowment of the Arts, the Department of Labor, Civil Defense (through the Office of Emergency Preparedness), and the Environmental Protection Agency. Many of the programs had wandered away from the realm of municipal affairs, such as the Arts Program and the Alternative Energy Program, but it was SEMA's policy that as long as it did not compete with its constituent state leagues for federal funds, anything was fair game. The growth in budget and staff size had demanded a change in office space as well, and in 1975 SEMA had moved to a slightly larger office space on the outskirts of town.

As George walked down the long corridor that connected the airy office of the executive director with the staff offices, he stopped by the mailbox area, collected the day's stack of memos—all from Widdlesworth—and then stopped into Marc Barberra's office. Marc was a senior staff member, having been with SEMA since receiving his master's degree in public administration five years ago. He was busy planning the annual city and town managers' meeting to be held next month. "Mind if I sit down, Marc?" asked George. "I was wondering if you might have any ideas for an article?"

Marc's office was like every staff member's office; a tiny cubelike room with a metal office desk and two metal chairs. As none of the staff has windows, each had tried to liven things up with posters, bookcases, and certain varieties of hardy plants. Marc's office was by far the neatest at SEMA due to the two file cabinets he had bought on his own at an office furniture sale. Other offices were cramped and cluttered with stacks of paper. "Let me think," said Marc, "maybe something on the energy project? You're handling that one, right?"

"Yes, that's my project. But as far as the *SEMA News* is concerned, I'm not sure what would be of interest to municipal managers. I've never done any work with them, and I'm up to my ears in work, just trying to get the damn thing off the ground. I not only have to learn the energy field from scratch, with no guidance from anyone, but Wilbur thinks nothing of heaping stuff like this article and other institutional duties on my schedule at the same time. He has no idea what the energy project really is, or what has to go into it. So he loads on this other work, then lectures us every Friday morning on the virtues of working overtime. At these wages? With no extra compensation? And from what I can see, no one can ever get out from under their deadlines long enough to even *take* their crummy two-week vacation. How come you're still here?"

"Easy, George," Marc settled back in his chair. "You, like the rest of us, came here right out of college and already you have sole responsibility for a new and innovative project that is potentially going to be funded to the tune of half a million dollars. It's a project that has the possibility of making a definite contribution to society in this period of rising oil prices."

"Yeah, but Wilbur's never around," began George.

"Furthermore, you're on your way to becoming an expert on energy —writing the article will force you to think about the subject from the standpoint of the local government and get your name out where someone will notice it."

"You've got a point there, Marc, but that's just the problem," said George. "I've got to become an instant expert in a highly specialized field. With SEMA's policy that every staff member is to generate two funding proposals each month, I'll never get the time to really know the area."

"Have faith, George. You can do it," replied Marc. "I've got to finish this report so I'll have to excuse myself. Will you be on the hike up Mt. Baldtop Sunday?"

"That I won't miss," said George as he left the office.

Next George poked his head into Charley Murphy's office, an office similar in size to Marc's but with even more threadbare furniture and clutter. Charley was whistling as he rapidly wrote on a pad of yellow paper.

"Charley, how can you be so cheerful after sitting in on another of Wilbur's Friday morning meetings. You must have heard that complaint about the telephone bills a thousand times by now. Even in my short time here, I've heard his 'if you can get here by 8:30, you can get here by 7:30' too often. I don't think the guy knows the word *overtime*."

"Oh, I'm used to Wilbur's harangues. I guess anybody who has built as successful organization as he has is allowed a few eccentricities. He's quite a guy. Never know it to look at him though, sort of shy and awkward looking. But so prolific a writer—full of energy and ideas. I really have to admire the guy. He built SEMA single-handedly and really knows the business of getting government funding—and not for make-work jobs either. Every contract SEMA gets makes a contribution to the region. SEMA is Wilbur's life. He's here every day from seven to seven and often on Saturday. He's so committed to social betterment that he's even here on Sundays, except when we have an outing like this

Sunday to Baldtop. I hear you are going to write an article for *SEMA News!* Congratulations. You'll be a SEMA alumni before you know it."

"SEMA alumni?"

With that, Charley opened a desk drawer, and pulled out a piece of typing paper. "You'll get a kick out of this. Marc and I were reminiscing the other day about people who have worked here during the last two years. See this list?" He handed the paper to George. "We've seen 10 staff members and 8 secretaries pass through the SEMA portals in the last two years. Pretty astounding, I'd say. This organization began with two associate directors. They left after three years and took jobs with HUD. Others followed. Some to private industry, some to the federal government, and some to the towns and cities we serve. I bet all of them give Wilbur a lot of credit for getting their careers launched."

"But isn't the turnover awfully high?" asked George.

"Sure, the turnover is high," responded Charley. "But each project is so different, I don't think it hurts the organization. It also saves Wilbur from agonizing over raises, and keeps the organization young and growing. Wilbur sets the tone and the staff follows, so why not be cheerful?"

"I understand the pace the guy operates at," said George, "and I admire him for it. In itself, the article wouldn't be that difficult. It's just that I have a report that *must* be mailed to my program manager at the Department of Energy by Monday as well, and he's a real stickler for punctuality. We are supposed to be reviewing those 3,000 applications by now, and I haven't even gotten them sorted yet. I just can't get any secretarial help to do the filing, they're all so busy. I'll just have to request some additional funds to hire some part-time help, or we'll lose track of everything."

Charley stiffened noticeably in his chair. "I wouldn't do that, George. Wilbur believes pretty strongly that we should be able to do everything in-house, with our own staff. As he sees it, it's just a matter of everyone pulling his own weight."

"Well . . . I'm reluctant to ask the secretaries to do this. They're all so hectic all the time."

"Look," said Charley, "you don't have to worry. Just lean on them. That's what everybody does. Their work load is so backlogged that you have to get them to bump someone else's work. So go out to the central office and lean on them."

George started down the long corridor to his office. He wondered what he should be doing with his too-limited time. If he put his DOE work aside, he would alienate the program manager in Washington. It might be difficult for SEMA to get grants from them again—and hadn't Wilbur told him that his project was vital? That he hoped to get an increasing number of grants from DOE in the future? If he had, he'd forgotten it when he piled on these other tasks. Where were SEMA's real priorities? If only Wilbur would send out some constant signals. George wondered if anyone had ever refused an assignment for the *SEMA News*.

As George began to settle at his desk, he heard voices outside his office. He recognized one speaker to be Bonnie Struthers, who had been working on the health care program. She was upset.

"I've had it! During my year here I've developed that program into an effective and worthwhile activity. Now that I've finally gotten Washington to refund it at a higher level—*without* any help from Wilbur—I feel that I've got every right to ask for a raise. And what does Wilbur tell me? He says, 'But Bonnie, you can't get more money than Marc. He's been here longer. You'll upset the whole salary structure.' I think I'll quit."

There was a pause and then George heard Bob Pearlman say, "Now come on, Bonnie. You've always loved that project of yours. You've been interested in health care since you were an undergraduate. I can't see you deserting the ship in midstream. Hang loose and focus on the important things. Look at what you've accomplished on that project without a professional degree."

"Okay, okay, Bob. I get the point," said Bonnie. "You wait, I'll complete that part-time graduate program yet and then I'll tell the turkey what I think of working for peanuts. Let's go to lunch."

*Techni-Cal, Inc.**

As WINTHROP J. GRENFELL, president of Techni-Cal Inc. (TCI), read the management consultant's report (summarized in Exhibit 1) he found his own appraisal of the company's situation confirmed. The company's near-bankruptcy condition was not due to any fundamental weakness. The company had excellent personnel, good physical plant and equipment, and an established reputation in a defined market. While the market was becoming more cost-conscious, it continued to be one with considerable potential. The company's condition was due to its having overextended itself financially on a new product idea, and its having treated costs too casually in its day-to-day operating practices.

BACKGROUND

TCI had been started about 15 years previously by two close friends, Johnson R. Rogers and Richard S. Nelson. Rogers was an entrepreneur with a technical bent and Nelson a technical genius. Acting as a presidential team, the two had built a successful business that had

---

*Copyright 1979 Stephen L. Fink and Robin D. Willits.

Techni-Cal, Inc.

EXHIBIT 1
Summary: Consultant's Report

1. The company has overextended itself financially by investing a huge amount of money in the research and development of a radically new communications technique. This endeavor, which was technically exciting and had engineering management's support, has eaten up all financial reserves and led to heavy borrowing from the banks. While its technical potential is unique, after five years of work, the company does not have a contract and more time is clearly required. In the consultant's judgement the company had bitten off more than it could chew. The project was and is beyond the financial capability of a company of its size.
2. The company has failed to fully exploit existing product lines by failing to push sales of an existing design whenever it came up with an idea for a "new-generation" design. Activity on the old-generation design has too often been curtailed before its market potential was exhausted.
3. The company has not exhibited sufficient concern for costs. Actual costs have consistently exceeded estimated costs on all contracts by an appreciable amount. While this was not a problem in the 1960's when the customer was primarily concerned with performance and delivery, it has become one. In today's market, costs are receiving increasing attention. The company has lost contracts because of its reputation for cost overruns.
4. The company has too readily followed a policy of selling hardware at a loss. This action has been justified due to a need to demonstrate the company's technical capability in a particular applications area, and thereby increase sales of its engineering capability. While such action will sometimes be appropriate, the company has overused this approach.

---

grown (currently 3,000 employees) to occupy an important place in the nation's space and military communications programs. TCI designed and built highly sophisticated and specialized electronic communication equipment for the government, and, to a limited extent, for commercial applications in the transportations industry. As both Nelson and Rogers were often inclined to say, "TCI's speciality is systems that fit particular needs and 'push the state of the art' technologically. In other words, we're in the business of selling engineering innovativeness and creativity."

Each communications system built by TCI was unique, designed on a bid-contract basis to meet a customer's specific requirements. Any one system typically consisted of 10 to 30 discrete hardware elements (consoles, antenna, data banks, etc.) and cost $500,000 to $1 million. Ninety percent of the contracts were on a cost-plus-fixed-fee (CPFF) basis where the company received a fixed fee, based on a percentage of *estimated* costs, but the customer paid the total *actual* costs incurred. Most contracts were for from one to five systems and had a life (from contract award to final shipment) of one and a half to two years. At any one time, the company would be working on a dozen contracts, each at various stages of design and manufacture.

TCI employed a range of technical specialists along with manufacturing and administrative personnel. Of the 700 engineers, there was a range of skills running from those with a very theoretical orientation to those of a quite practical bent.

With salaries that were competitive with other organizations, a good benefit package, interesting work, and an informal, friendly, cooperative, work atmosphere, turnover among personnel was low.

During the early 1970s, TCI had experienced two jolts that led to the hiring of Mr. Grenfell as president. First, the company's financial situation had deteriorated rapidly and drastically to the point where it was on the verge of bankruptcy. Second, Mr. Nelson had died unexpectedly, and since Mr. Rogers, who was much older, had retired a few years previously, the company found itself in trouble without a president.

In response to the situation, the board of directors had decided that an outsider's perspective was desirable and hired Mr. Grenfell as president. Grenfell had considerable experience in the aerospace industry, but although he had begun his career as an engineer, his orientation was to the business aspects of a company rather than the technical, since he had moved from engineering into marketing and eventually into general management.

Following his arrival, Grenfell had initiated the consultant study and spent a month looking over the situation himself. As he reread the consultant's report, he felt that the solution lay in the company's structure and operating procedures.

THE CURRENT STRUCTURE

As shown in Exhibit 1, the company had been organized along functional lines, with departments of marketing, engineering, manufacturing, quality assurance, personnel, and controller, and had adopted a project team approach to administering individual contracts.

Contact with the customer and the intelligence function were assigned to a Marketing Department. Its job was to develop relationships with Department of Defense (DOD) procuring agencies, get the company on all appropriate "bidders lists," and keep the Engineering Department informed of DOD thinking and needs. Consequently, marketing often sought to suggest to engineering new lines for research, ideas for pre-request for quotation (RFQ) efforts, criteria for establishing priorities among current work, etc. At the same time, it sought to "seed" ideas developed by the company into the various procuring agencies.

The department was staffed with individuals who had been around government and had contacts in DOD: typically retired majors, colonels and navy officers. While many of these individuals had had some technical training, as well as experience using or purchasing TCI's type of product and could talk the language of both DOD and TCI technical personnel, they were not practicing engineers. During contract negotiations to "definitize" a new contact, marketing personnel acted as the titular head of the negotiating team, but had to rely heavily on input by representatives from engineering and even manufacturing.

The Engineering Department was perceived by the founders of the company as the central core of the organization. As shown in Exhibit 2, it was divided into two sections: a Systems Engineering Section and an Equipment Engineering Section. This represented a division by technical orientation. Systems engineering's focus was on overall systems performance characteristics, whereas equipment engineering's was on individual components (subsystems). Systems' approach was conceptual, equipment's more pragmatic in terms of specific hardware.

Each section was divided into groups. These groups were loosely organized around technical specialties. Each would be composed of engineers who were specialists in the same technical area, such as ultra high-frequency technology (systems) or printed circuitry (equipment). But the main purpose of the group was to avoid having too many engineers under the supervision of one person. The limit was typically seven or eight. As business expanded, more groups would be added, keeping each group's size small, even if it meant two groups had rather similar technical specialties.

When business fell off, some groups might be closed down, in which case the group manager would return to being a working engineer until such time as overall volume required hiring more engineers and the recreation of additional groups. However, there was little of that. The founders of the company viewed the organization as having the attributes of a family with responsibility for its members' well-being. Thus, company policy was to provide stable employment and avoid hiring and firing with every ebb and flow of business volume. Overtime was used to meet increased demand rather than new hiring. The founders believed this policy to be "good business" as well as responsible and ethical. They believed that creativity flourished in an environment of high performance expectations with underlying job security. They encouraged engineers to build their careers around the company's long-term growth.

EXHIBIT 2

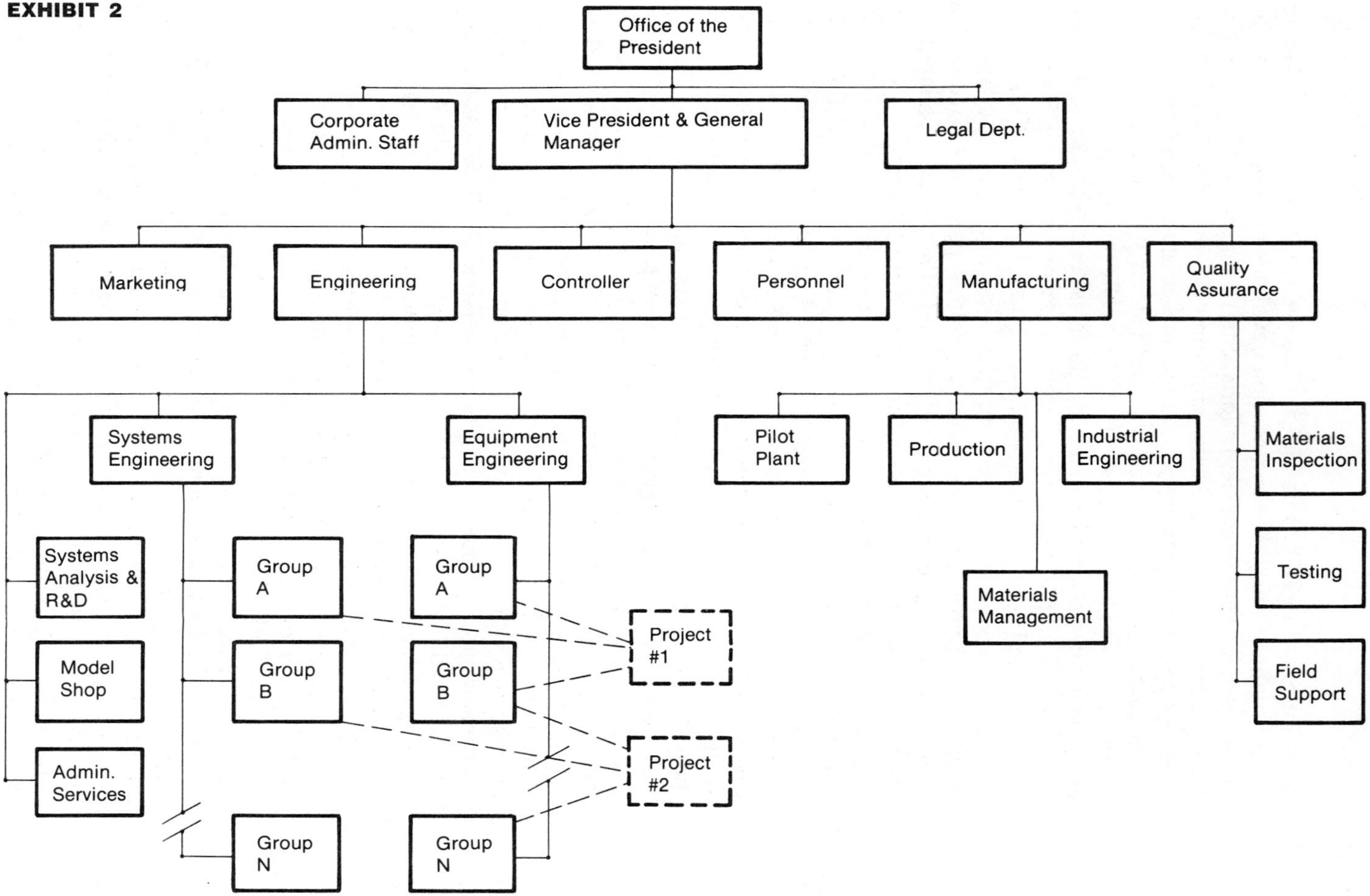
Office of the President
Corporate Admin. Staff
Vice President & General Manager
Legal Dept.
Marketing
Engineering
Controller
Personnel
Manufacturing
Quality Assurance
Systems Engineering
Equipment Engineering
Pilot Plant
Production
Industrial Engineering
Materials Inspection
Testing
Field Support
Materials Management
Systems Analysis & R&D
Model Shop
Admin. Services
Group A
Group B
Group N
Group A
Group B
Group N
Project #1
Project #2

Each group in engineering had a draftsman and technician to assist the engineers. There was also a central model shop within engineering that served all groups. The administrative group in engineering kept personnel files, tallied cost data, and carried out various administrative duties on behalf of the director of engineering and the entire department.

One group did not fit the pattern described above. That was the Systems Analysis Group. This group contained the most highly trained and theoretically oriented personnel, many with Ph.D.s. They worked on long-term research and also on special theoretical studies in support of specific contacts.

When a request for quotation (RFQ) was received, the first step was to put together a proposal team. Marketing would inform the director of engineering of the RFQ's arrival and express its opinion about what types and numbers of engineers were needed to develop the proposal. The director of engineering in consultation with systems engineering section manager, would assign a systems engineer as proposal manager (team leader).

The person chosen was usually someone who not only had good technical ability but also had begun to display administrative and business skills (experience as proposal manager and eventually as project manager could eventually lead to becoming a group manager). The proposal manager first analyzed the work statement in the RFQ, determined what technical skills were in fact needed, and decided what individuals he wanted on the team. His next step was to negotiate with the group managers to have those individuals assigned to the proposal team. This was not an automatic process because every proposal team leader wanted the better people, but their time was also wanted for work on current contracts. The proposal manager needed to have good negotiating skills. He had to fight to get good people. He had no budget with which to buy their services; instead he had to rely on persuasion and his ongoing relationships with the group managers.

Once the proposal team was assembled, including a subteam to work on the manufacturing aspects, the proposal manager organized the effort. He subdivided the work, held coordination meetings, monitored progress, managed the resolution of conflicts between subsystems, and supervised the writing of the final document. He had cradle-to-grave responsibility to see that a proposal was produced, although the final product was subject to review and approval by engineering management (group, section, and department). Once it was done (approximately a four- to six-week process), everyone went back to whatever they were doing and generally ignored the proposal since it might be six months to a year before any contract was awarded.

When a contract was eventually received, a similar process occurred. A systems engineer was chosen as project manager and he in turn pulled together a project team to do the actual design work. Every effort was made to free the individual who had been proposal manager and assign him as project manager. There was less likelihood that other proposal team members would be involved in the actual design effort. They were often too involved in other projects. So the project manager had to negotiate with group managers and other project managers to put together an adequate design team. Once the team was designated, the project manager determined the work breakdown, established a schedule of completion for each subtask, monitored progress, and managed the resolution of problems that might arise (including the modification of design parameters for the various subsystems and black boxes).

He also was simultaneously involved as a member of the company negotiating team, spearheaded by marketing, that worked to "definitize" the contract in response to changes the customer almost inevitably made between the RFQ and the contract.

As shown in Exhibit 2 by the solid and broken lines, project team members physically remained in their groups under the general supervision of their group managers. While the project manager usually worked full-time on one contract, everyone else typically worked on two or three contracts simultaneously. The salaries of each engineer were paid through his group and his performance appraisal, and any salary increases were handled by the group manager (although the group manager certainly would gather data from the project managers about individual contributions).

A record was kept of the time actually spent by each engineer on each project so that project costs could be determined. Procedurally, at the end of each week, every engineer filled out a time card, apportioning the total hours worked to all contracts worked on. Any time not chargeable to a specific contract was charged to an overhead account number. Thereafter, the time cards were sent to the administrative services group in engineering, who tabulated the data and issued a monthly report on total hours and dollars spent on each contract. These reports were sent to the appropriate project managers to let them know how actual expenditures compared with estimated costs.

As the design took form, the engineer, with the aid of his group technicians, made a "bread-board" model[1] and tested his design. Later as subsystems required testing, preproduction models were made either in the Engineering Department model shop or in manufacturing by a

---

[1] *Bread-board* is a term used to describe an operating model of a device that performs the technical functions of the ultimate product but is not in its final physical form. Thus, certain parts may differ from what will be ultimately used, such as lengths of wire instead of printed circuits; and all of the parts will be spread out on a workbench or tray rather than installed in a chassis or metal container.

special group of assemblers set aside as a pilot plant. The formal testing of the preproduction model, which had to be approved by the customer, often required the services of test engineers who were added to the project team as needed. Throughout this later design phase and preproduction test phase, the individual engineer often integrated his work with that of other personnel on his own initiative and sought out the services of model shop personnel as needed. But throughout, the project engineer was the most active, coordinating the interface between subsystem, running meetings to resolve differences and initiate design parameter trade-offs, and negotiating with the customer for relief from unobtainable performance specifications and schedule deadlines. While many people had to have input to the decisions that must be made during the design and testing of a system, the project manager was the "point man" who took responsibility under the supervision of his *group* manager to see that things were adequately coordinated.

Following successful preproduction testing, the project entered manufacturing which, as shown in Exhibit 2, was a separate department on the same level organizationally as engineering. At this point, much of the design effort came to completion, and the systems and equipment engineers shifted to other work, an engineer being deeply involved in his part of the project for six months and much less deeply for another three months as production "bugs" were resolved.

Manufacturing personnel had some exposure to the project before the design was entered into manufacturing through pilot plant activities and through the efforts of the industrial engineers to gather information about the design so as to plan manufacturing techniques and write assembly instructions ahead of time. As manufacturing got under way, there were always problems and suggestions leading to possible changes in the design. The company had a fairly elaborate, formal change control procedure. Anyone could initiate a change, but at this stage each idea had to be investigated by engineering personnel and be approved, eventually, by a change control board which had representatives from engineering, quality assurance, and manufacturing as well as the project manager. Based on established criteria, the board could approve many changes, but some had to be submitted to the customer for approval. The board functioned throughout the life of the contract, which typically required about one year after entering manufacturing.

The inspection of purchased materials and parts, as well as the testing of the actual system produced by manufacturing, was the responsibility of the Quality Assurance Department following the specifications laid down by engineering and the formal test procedures developed during the design phase.

Following shipment, the field support group assisted the customer during installation. This group was often the one to initially investigate and seek to resolve any "cockpit-type" problems[2] that emerged, although the project manager and the designer often got involved.

It was Grenfell's judgment that this structure and operating orientation functioned very much as intended. While some individuals and groups had more influence than their peers, the informal organization was not vastly different from the formal. As indicated to him by the board of directors during the hiring process, the company viewed itself as "in the business of selling its engineering skill and creativity," and emphasized its technical innovativeness in its basic business strategy and operating procedures.

The question facing Mr. Grenfell was how to reorganize the company and its operating practices to deal with the causes of the crisis and return the company to its historic position in the industry.

Why Play Football?

PART I

ALAN LAKE AND FRANK PARKER left the locker room together talking enthusiastically about the coming season and discussing their chances of having a good team. They were both seniors and co-captains of the football team at Woodlawn College. They knew it would be hard to match the 8–1 record of the previous season, especially since so many of their best players had graduated, but nonetheless they looked forward to the challenge.

Woodlawn College is a small, private, liberal arts college with an enrollment of 2,200 students. Located in farming country, it is a small residential college which exists as a self-contained unit in the town of Woodlawn. Having gone co-ed four years ago, the student body consists of both men and women from all 50 states and many foreign countries. The majority of the American students come from the East.

Throughout the years, Woodlawn College has developed the reputation of a prestigious institution known for its academic excellence, and admissions are selective. Combined expenses (tuition and room and board) are quite high, but only 30 percent of the students receive some type of financial aid. The majority of students pay the full expenses on their own; many of them come from upper-income families.

Founded in the early 1800s, Woodlawn had a long football tradition. The college catalog states that the purpose of all athletic programs

---

[2] Engineering colloquialism for problems caused by how the customer treated (used and abused) the product after installation.

(physical education, intramurals, and intercollegiate sports) is to contribute to the development of strong minds, bodies, and character. In reference to intercollegiate sports, it goes on to say that the program is "college-level athletics, sports within the framework of a total education." The intercollegiate athletic program is "based on the principle that people play for the enjoyment of competition and the love of the game."

Athletic scholarships are not awarded, but many athletes do receive financial aid in the form of loans and grants. The financial aid officers are aware of the fact that campus jobs would interfere with varsity practices and games, so they refrain from assigning these jobs to members of intercollegiate teams.

Woodlawn is a member of the small college athletic conference, which includes 11 other schools. The purpose of this conference is very similar to that of sports programs at Woodlawn: to insure that intercollegiate athletics remain within the framework of the educational philosophies for which these schools are renowned. Conference schools, by tradition, play several nonconference schools rather than just conference schools during a season, and the conference consciously avoids naming a "conference champion."

Both Alan and Frank, like almost all of their teammates, had played football since their freshman year. Each year, between 20 and 25 freshmen go out for football, and usually not more than 5 to 10 quit the team. The varsity squad is made up of sophomores, juniors, and seniors; it has approximately 50 members each year. Since the school is so small, there aren't enough players for a junior varsity team. Everyone who completes summer camp before the season begins makes the varsity squad; very rarely is anyone cut.

As they left the locker room they talked about their experiences of the past three years and how they wanted to make their last year on the team different.

ALAN: Remember how awful it was on the freshman team? I didn't think I would last.

FRANK: Yea, it's too bad we couldn't just take that year in stride and realize it was something everyone has to go through. I think we really did benefit from sticking it out together as a class.

ALAN: That's true, at the end of last season I was talking with the coach about how they originally decided to have freshmen on a team by themselves. He said that they thought it was a good way to get a class identity formed so by the time we are seniors, and on the varsity, we'll really feel like a group, like a real team.

FRANK: I'm glad they do it this way. At least when we were freshmen we all got to play a lot, so that it wasn't so bad sitting on the bench a lot during varsity games sophomore year. Can you imagine what it would have been like as a freshman on a freshman/sophomore team?

ALAN: Sure, the freshmen would never get to play and their morale would be pretty low. But at a school this size we really need sophomores on the varsity squad. We couldn't make it without them as second-stringers.

FRANK: Besides being "dummies" for the varsity to practice with when we were freshmen, the attitude toward football around here was really hard for me to take.

ALAN: I know what you mean. I guess we were all so used to being "stars" in high school that it was a rude awakening to come here and be looked down on for being a "jock."

FRANK: I couldn't believe the first varsity game I went to when I was a freshman. Hardly anyone was there to watch except a few fraternity members, and I'm sure banners and posters were unheard of. This was the only college I'd ever heard of that didn't have a band.

ALAN: And, do you remember the varsity guys telling us which professors would never let you miss their class or leave their class early for away games? I guess those guys all went to school when a prerequisite for being an athlete was being stupid.

FRANK: I'm glad that situation is beginning to change. I think one reason it's changing is that the campus unrest of the late 60s, early 70s has died down, and so have a lot of the attitudes that were prevalent then—now it's okay to like sports again. But in a school like this where athletics are always secondary to academic achievement, that attitude will probably always exist to a certain extent, even despite the coaches' efforts to have the team get around campus and mix with people other than our fraternity brothers.

ALAN: That's true, but the lack of strong campus interest may be to the team's benefit in the long run. *(Frank looked quizzical so Alan continued to explain.)* I think almost everyone on the varsity team is here because they really like the sport and want to play football. I can remember a few people who have quit the freshman team through the years because they expected team membership to give them high status on campus.

FRANK: You're right, we do have a bunch of really dedicated guys. I hope it will be a good team. I've been thinking about what we can do to make it a good team. I think we should try to loosen things up a little and see if we can get some real team spirit going.

ALAN: You took the words right out of my mouth! We've won a lot of games these past few years and a lot of records have been set, but I don't think we've worked together very well as a team. For me, it hasn't been much fun being a member of this team. Practices have been a real drag—people were either trying so hard to get a starting position that they didn't care about anyone around them, or so frustrated that they didn't try at all. I even saw some guys deliberately trying to hurt other guys on the field, not to mention some of the things I heard people saying about each other.

FRANK: Yea, the atmosphere has been pretty intense. I guess when you get a bunch of equally talented guys competing for a limited number of positions it gets pretty cut-throat. I've seen a lot more brown nosing and lack of cooperation around here than I ever expected, despite the coaches' saying that they wanted everyone to get some playing time.

ALAN: I think that's one of the problems of a team like this. It's really hard to strike a balance between competition and cooperation, working together as a team. I guess I'm saying that for many of us winning isn't everything if no one enjoys being a team member.

FRANK: I wonder who they chose to be the team managers this year. Since we started having women as team managers two years ago, things haven't been the same.

ALAN: I heard that the two women who got the job are very good. I do think the president is right that having women managers is a good way to help integrate the women students on campus, and to promote the school's affirmative action goals, but I don't think the coaches will ever get used to it. They're always griping about it.

They continued to discuss how they could facilitate the growth of a more relaxed atmosphere and increase teamwork, but at the same time be as successful as possible. They arrived at a team motto: "fun, fair play, and excellence" that summarized all of their feelings about how the team should function. They thought that by fulfilling this motto as students, athletes, and team members, by trying their hardest and doing their best, yet having some fun, the end result would be a winning team.

The first practice started with the distribution of the playbook which stated:

> By electing to become a member of this team, you have acknowledged your responsibility to contribute to the maintenance of the tradition of excellence which has become a part of Woodlawn College. This tradition has grown to the degree that winning is accepted and expected of all Woodlawn football teams.

This playbook was distributed exclusively to the coaches and players and they were instructed (by the head coach) to keep these books in the locker room at all times. He also informed everyone that the playbooks would be collected at the end of the season.

The team members initially started out as in previous years, fiercely competitive for starting positions and showing little intention of cooperating beyond the minimum level necessary to function as a team. But after a few practices, attitudes slowly started changing. Alan and Frank were well liked and respected by the team members and their behavior and attitudes were soon adopted by the other players. Almost everyone was soon joking around a lot and helping each other out during practice, and they soon became a unified team.

The majority of the varsity football players were members of one of the two biggest fraternities on campus. While they socialized primarily with their fraternity brothers, as a team they got along well and their external social allegiances had no disruptive effect on the team's cohesiveness.

The season progressed smoothly and almost all of the team members had adopted the "fun, fair play, and excellence" motto. Most of the team members were good friends and the atmosphere of the team was relaxed. However, during a game against Woodlawn's arch rival, Alan got so caught up in winning that he completely lost sight of the team motto. He was playing opposite the other team's best player, and he had to play extremely well in order for Woodlawn to win. Throughout many practices the coaches got him psyched to play against this guy, and by the third quarter of the game Alan was doing an outstanding job. At this point his emotions got the best of him, and while down on the line he began cussing at his opponent and calling him derogatory racial names. Woodlawn won the game and Alan was carried off the field on the shoulders of his teammates in recognition of his good performance. In the meantime, his teammates playing next to Alan in the line told the coach about his behavior. His reaction was one of disbelief, since it was so out of character for Alan to behave that way, and "dirty play" was not acceptable to the Woodlawn team or any other teams in the league. In the locker room the coach told Alan to write a letter to the coach and player of the other team and apologize for his behavior. Alan felt surprise and shame at the way he had acted and wrote the letter at once.

By mid-season the team's record was 2–2, and a problem had arisen that neither the coaches nor co-captains knew how to deal with. One of the most talented players was not a "team member" in the true sense of the word. Unlike the other players, he was boastful and a loudmouth, always "blowing his own horn." He didn't work hard in practice; instead he tried to impress everyone by making fancy moves which didn't fit in with the plays. On Thursdays and Fridays the team practiced without full uniforms, concentrating on timing and polishing up the plays they had worked out against their upcoming opponents defensive patterns. It was on these days that Jim would come charging through the line and knock someone over when they least expected it, as if everyone was dressed in full pads and hitting their hardest. He wasn't well liked by other players and he didn't associate with team members socially.

In the middle of many close games, during which he had been sitting on the bench, the coach would send him in to play. His presence was often the determining factor in the outcome of the game; the team's chances of winning were much better when he was playing. The following is a typical conversation about this player that occurred during staff meetings attended by coaches and co-captains:

Asst. Coach: I really think we should cut Jim from the team. His attitude is one of the worst I've ever seen—and he has been warned.

Head Coach: Yes, we have discussed this problem with him and he hasn't made any effort to fit in, but I don't think we should cut him. After all, he is a great athlete and he has really helped out in the games we've won this season. He knows he's capable of being in a permanent starting position, but doesn't seem to want it enough to change his attitude.

FRANK: Yea, even though he's against almost everything the team stands for, he sure has helped us out of some tight situations.

ALAN: I know that some players wish he played more to improve our chances of winning, while other players would rather take the chance and let another teammate play, leaving Jim on the bench.

HEAD COACH: Since he doesn't play all of the time it does give the other fullbacks a chance to play, and I do like to get as many guys on the field as possible during a game.

This dilemma was never completely resolved. Jim remained on the team, sometimes starting, sometimes sitting on the bench. The coaches were thankful that he was a senior and were glad that none of the younger team members had adopted Jim's attitude.

The season ended with a 5–4 record and both Alan and Frank had enjoyed the experience of being captains of this team. The coach told them that they had really accomplished something—that it had been a long time since he had seen the varsity football team work so well together and have such a good time doing it. Nevertheless, Alan felt a sense of incompleteness which he discussed with Frank after the awards banquet.

ALAN: I know we had a good team and a lot of student support by the end of the season, but I still feel like something is missing.

FRANK: Well, we didn't win as many games as we did last season, but I think we lived up to our motto as best we could.

ALAN: I guess that's it; it was good to hear the coach say he thought we had accomplished something, but if we had had a winning season I'd feel like we accomplished more. I do feel that we accomplished something; we were a real team, people trusted each other, worked hard, and got along well together.

FRANK: And I can think of a lot of instances where that was really important. How about the time John and Todd [two senior linemen] were competing for the same position? The team divided into cliques made up of their closest friends for a short time, until the coaches decided to rotate them in the starting position. After that the cliques dissolved and there weren't any hard feelings. If that had happened last year, one of them probably would have quit the team and the team would have been split in two for the whole season.

ALAN: We've had a lot better relationships between the offense and defense this year, too. Remember how each group would always complain about how the other group was playing—and say nasty things behind their backs?

FRANK: Sure, but this year the offense and defense were always pulling for each other and helping each other out whenever they could.

ALAN: It always helps to have some guys in more than one group.

FRANK: You're right; our first string offense and defense were the only really distinct groups. Some second-stringers went both ways and our specialty teams were made up of a mixture of first- and second-stringers from the offense and defense.

ALAN: Well, we have been successful in a lot of respects, but too bad the record doesn't show it.

PART II

Each year two members of the varsity football team are chosen by the coaches to act as graduate assistants the following year. These assistants are employed as the coaches of the freshman team and are also members of the varsity coaching staff. The freshman team practiced three days per week with the varsity. The majority of this time was spent running the formations of the upcoming opponents against the varsity to give them practice. The other two practice days were spent learning Woodlawn's formations and getting ready for their own games. The duties of the graduate assistants included supervising the freshmen in their practices with the varsity, coaching them as a team by themselves, counseling them if they were having problems, scouting varsity opponents, analyzing films of varsity opponents, and doing some varsity coaching during games.

Frank and Alan were chosen for these positions, and they were both looking forward to the opportunity of getting some coaching experience. They approached the job with an attitude similar to the one they had as captains. Even though their time to practice together as a team was minimal, Alan and Frank wanted them to work together as a team and do their best.

There were weekly meetings of the varsity coaching staff, and Alan and Frank were immediately accepted as members of the group. They had gotten along well with the coaches as players, the coaches respected them and talked candidly in front of them. After one meeting early in the season, Alan and Frank had dinner together and discussed the meeting.

ALAN: It sure is different being on the other side of the fence. Could you believe the way they were talking about the players? They sure didn't give a damn about Joe's desire to play in front of his parents who will be here for the weekend from California, nor about poor, awkward Harold who never did get into any games. They didn't seem too concerned about how serious Tim's sprained ankle is, as long as they can find someone to take his place who can run as well as he can. They were certainly talking about shuffling personnel around like game pieces. I had no idea that kind of planning went on when we were on the team.

FRANK: I think they're under a lot more pressure than we were ever aware of. I heard the coach talking to John (assistant coach) about how the baseball coach got the word from the president: he's out if he doesn't have a winning season this year.

ALAN: No wonder it was so hard to decide what to do about Jim last year—our record probably would have been worse if he hadn't played at all.

FRANK: I can understand the president's concern; winning teams get more publicity for the school, attract better athletes, and I believe get more alumni support, but I think that our experiences of the past four years showed us that winning isn't everything.

ALAN: Another thing that surprised me is the coach's preoccupation with having the best record on campus.

FRANK: I know what you mean. It sounds like he and the soccer coach have a running battle going to see who can win the most games.

The conversation then switched to the problems they were having coaching the freshman team.

ALAN: That cracked me up when the coach told us that it was our duty to make this experience as good as possible for the freshmen so they won't quit the team. We've only been practicing three weeks and it seems like morale is already slipping.

FRANK: I can really sympathize with them; I think we felt the same way when we were freshmen. It's bad enough going from being a high school "star" to the anonymity of the freshman team, without the added frustration of spending three days a week getting your head bashed in by the varsity.

ALAN: I think they are even more discouraged by the fact that it is next to impossible to get a winning team together with so little practice time to ourselves.

FRANK: That's true, but you know how much we needed those practices with the freshmen when we were on the varsity team. We would have been lost without them.

ALAN: By the way, have you spent much time counseling any of the guys on the freshman team? We are supposed to be helping them out with any problems they're having. I sure haven't had a chance.

FRANK: I haven't either, we really should try to make some time for that sooner or later. Right now we have to work on those plays for the next game.

The day before the freshman team's third game, the head coach of the varsity pulled one of the best freshman players to act as a safety replacement in the varsity's next game, two days away. One of the starting varsity players had been injured in practice and the freshman was needed as a backup player. This incident disrupted the game plans for the freshman team. Alan and Frank tried to reorganize as best they could in the short amount of time available, but they lost the game.

At the next coaches meeting, Alan made a joking remark about how it would be a lot easier to win if his players weren't being snatched away at the last minute and then only to sit on the bench just in case needed. The head coach told him he wasn't fond of doing that, but it was something which couldn't be avoided.

As the season progressed, Alan and Frank did whatever they could to make the experience as tolerable as possible for the freshman team. To break up the monotony of practices with the varsity, they would do things like send in unorthodox plays and formations, which would invariably provide a good laugh and throw off the varsity players. At times Alan and Frank would even run onto the field and play a position, which also added little to the seriousness of practice. On occasion the coach would call one of them over and tell him it was time to "get to work," but most of this behavior was overlooked.

Near the end of the season the freshman players who remained (only four had quit) had adopted an attitude of resigned acceptance of their situation and were glad they would be on the varsity squad next year. After losing three games as a result of players being pulled to serve as varsity replacements, Alan and Frank were more disconcerted than ever.

ALAN: You'd think that they aren't even aware of the fact that we'd like to win a few games too.

FRANK: Yea, it's hard to believe that it matters so much to us this year. We did make it as good an experience as possible for the team, but they're the only ones that know that."

ALAN: The only thing any of my friends ask is "Did you win?"

During the last varsity game, Alan was giving a varsity player advice before an important play. As the player ran into the huddle, Alan turned to Frank and remarked, "This is crazy, just yesterday I was yelling at that guy for blocking too hard against some of the freshmen, and here I am telling him to go out there and do whatever he has to do to block his man!"

Working for the Old Alma Mater

IN THE SUMMER OF 1978 I was a graduate student doing research on reward systems for a class project. I visited my undergraduate campus, a university in the Midwest, and ran into a college friend who was working for the university. She had been working there for four years and had given her notice of leaving at the end of the month. I was surprised to hear that she was leaving because I had heard, through mutual friends, that she liked her job at the school. When she started talking about why she had decided to quit, I realized I might be able to use her story for my class project. We decided to meet again so that she could tell me more about her job experience at the university.

Upon graduating from college, Marcia was employed briefly by an insurance company in a clerical position. It was a large organization which she found much too rigid and impersonal. Dissatisfied with this job, she decided to find out if there were any openings at the university. Having been a student there and still residing in a nearby town (her husband was a graduate student), she had some acquaintances who were employed by the university who seemed to be happy with their jobs. Employment at the university carried a great deal of status with it, not only due to the fact that it is an educational institution, but also because the school was highly regarded in the community. Marcia became increasingly aware of this fact as a result of conversations with friends and neighbors and as a result of statements she heard about Midwestern University while working at the insurance company.

Midwestern University is located in Deerfield, a small town surrounded by countryside. It affords easy access to lakes and some small mountains, and the nearest large city is only 60 miles north of Deerfield.

The campus itself covers 160 acres and contains a student body of 19,000 undergraduates and 5,000 graduate students. Marcia's feelings about the campus are shared by everyone who has spent any time there and are illustrated in her statement that "It is the only place I've known that is just beautiful all four seasons of the year."

After talking to some friends who were employed at Midwestern and contacting some of her previous professors, Marcia found out that there was an opening at the Student Union for the position of information desk attendant. While this job, which was a non-exempt personnel staff (NEPS) position, interested her somewhat, she was more interested in an entry level technical/professional staff position. During her initial interview in the Personnel Department, she found out that there weren't any technical/professional staff openings and was sent on interviews for the Student Union job and two other NEPS positions. She was eventually offered the job at the Student Union, which she accepted.

Nonexempt personnel staff (NEPS), technical/professional staff (TPS) positions, and faculty were the three major job classifications at the university. NEPS employees were nonexempt, and included secretaries, clerks, ground crew, laborers, cooks, and custodians. TPS positions included all professional, administrative, and technical staff, and these employees were exempt. Qualifications for TPS positions involved experience in the specific field and/or the attainment of a specific level of education.

During her orientation Marcia received a nonexempt personnel staff policy and procedures manual, which explained the benefits that Midwestern University offered. (See Exhibit 1.) These also included extensive insurance and retirement plans, in addition to substantial vacation and sick leave allowances. The staff also had access to recreational facilities and the university transportation system. They received bookstore discounts and discounts on many other campus activities. One of these activities was sports events. While MU wasn't primarily an athletically oriented school, all kinds of sports were popular on campus and were strongly supported by students, faculty, and staff members. Another benefit that many employees took advantage of was the opportunity to take two free courses per semester. Marcia knew that this benefit package was one of the major reasons that many people sought employment at MU, which resulted in stiff job competition. Wages were comparable to other businesses in the area and were periodically adjusted so that they remained relatively similar.

EXHIBIT 1
Quotes from the Nonexempt Personnel Staff Policy and Procedures Manual

---

1. Employment practices at this university are designed to provide all qualified applicants with equal employment opportunities.
2. Qualified members of minority groups and qualified women are encouraged to submit applications for job openings before any permanent assignments are made.
3. Employees will be compensated annually for improved performance by the granting of merit increases. Those employees whose work is unsatisfactory will not be granted an annual merit increase.
4. A supervisor may recommend a superior performance bonus for any employee who has a record of outstanding performance on the job and/or has made an outstanding contribution to his/her job.
5. Reclassification of a position occurs in the event that there is a substantial change in the nature of the job. The immediate supervisor of the job under consideration makes a reclassification request to his department head, who reviews it and sends it to the principal administrator. He/she then forwards the request to the Personnel Office who comes in and reviews the position.
6. Employees are transferred and promoted on the basis of skill, ability, diligence, and seniority. Transfer and promotion from within are encouraged at this institution.
7. All employment opportunities are posted for seven days in many visible locations on campus.
8. Any candidate for an open position must meet the minimum requirements of the job. The Personnel Office gives careful attention and initial consideration to university employees.

The board of trustees was responsible for allocating the funds available for university operations and, in addition to designing the benefit package, had developed the system for salary increases. This system included annual merit increases, superior performance bonuses, and area movement (previously described as the method by which university salaries were adjusted to meet area wages). Each NEPS job is pay-graded alphabetically (earlier letters are jobs of less responsibility with lower pay ranges) and each pay grade contains seven merit steps which can be earned by the employee, usually only annually. On the anniversary date of employment in the current job, the employee's past year's performance is evaluated with, and by, the immediate supervisor. If his performance has been good, the supervisor approves a merit increase to the next step in the pay grade, usually amounting to 15 cents per hour, or $260 per year after taxes. Resembling its name, a superior performance bonus is initiated by a supervisor who believes his or her employee has done an outstanding job. The supervisor makes a recommendation to the MU Provost and Personnel Office that a certain employee be given the bonus. Both offices must approve the request before the bonus is awarded.

I conducted the following interview with Marcia during the last week of work.

RESEARCHER: What duties did your job description include when you started working here?

MARCIA: The information desk was part of a small concession area which I was in charge of. My duties included ordering and stocking candy and sundries, keeping track of inventory, and cashing out daily. I was also the assistant supervisor of the work-study students assigned to my area.

RESEARCHER: That sounds like enough to keep anyone busy—how did you handle it?

MARCIA: Well, it didn't take me long to learn how to do these things, and well before the six-month probationary period was over I was looking for other things to do.

RESEARCHER: Do you mean you weren't busy enough?

MARCIA: It really wasn't a question of keeping busy. It just wasn't very challenging after I learned the routine and I felt like I could handle more responsibility.

RESEARCHER: What other kinds of things did you do?

MARCIA: To start with, I did the jobs in a lot more detail than they are stated in my job description. Personnel has to be careful when writing descriptions for NEPS jobs so that they don't sound too much like low-level TPS positions, so they leave a lot of the details out.

RESEARCHER: What would a description for your position include now?

MARCIA: In addition to performing the initially described duties in detail, I have taken over exclusive supervision of the students in my area. I also suggested and subsequently organized the addition of an apparel section to the concession area (sweatshirts, T-shirts, etc.). Since this has been in operation, I have managed it and become the purchasing agent for the clothing, making all the decisions as to supplier and selling price.

RESEARCHER: Well, that certainly sounds like you must have qualified for one of those job reclassifications I was reading about. Has your job been reclassified?

MARCIA: Funny you should ask. About a month ago, soon after I had given my notice of leaving, my supervisor told me that my job was being reclassified, and that the reclassification would be two months retroactive. So I ended up with three months of employment at a higher salary before I leave, when I've been doing pretty much the same things for the past year and a half.

RESEARCHER: I'm not very clear on this reclassification process. Could you explain it to me?

MARCIA: I'd be glad to; in theory it sounds great! Reclassification is usually investigated when an employee has, by his or her skills and efforts, made his or her job expand far beyond its original parameters. The supervisor who notes that this has occurred writes a new job description more closely fitting the job being done, and it is sent to the Personnel Office for approval and assignment to a new title and pay grade. The supervisor can only recommend the change, which can be denied if there is no need for the extra work. Denials have been made on the rare occasions when an individual applies his or her particular talents to a job when these talents aren't necessary for accomplishing the assigned tasks. Special caution is also taken to avoid reclassifications which lead to too close a match with low-level TPS positions. The reason for this caution is the attitude which exists surrounding the difference between NEPS and TPS positions, and the unavailability of funds for higher salaries.

RESEARCHER: It sounds to me like there was a need for the extra work you did. Had you been led to believe that taking on increased responsibility would result in a reclassification?

MARCIA: No, my primary motivation for expanding my job wasn't really in expectation of reclassification or a superior performance bonus. I believe that doing my best, giving 100 percent in any job I have, is important. Having an opportunity to take on additional responsibility and learn new things is very important to me in a job. If I see work that needs doing, I'll do it! I soon learned, through the grapevine and from experiences of friends who worked here, that the attitude of the Personnel Office is that taking on extra work should be discouraged if it is done in the expectation of getting a job reclassification. The university doesn't have enough resources to reclassify all of the jobs that, in reality, have grown far beyond their descriptions.

RESEARCHER: What was your supervisor's reaction to the extra work you were doing?

MARCIA: Oh, he never actually discouraged me from expanding my job, but he probably would have if he thought I did it in expectation of a reclassification. I can sympathize with the position he's in—he can't do much about the way this system is set up.

RESEARCHER: It sounds like very few jobs actually get reclassified, is this true?

MARCIA: My experience is typical in this respect. If a job does get reclassified, it is when they have to hire someone to fill the position. Reclassification at this point is proof that the previous job description is inaccurate and that there is a need for my successor to continue to perform the duties I added to my job.

Of course, it's been nice getting in on a little of the extra money, but I really feel like they've taken advantage of me. Reclassifying my job at this late date signifies a realization on the part of my supervisor and personnel that they won't be able to demand the same level of work for the pay I've been receiving in this job.

RESEARCHER: You mentioned a superior performance bonus and merit increases; you must have received those each year.

MARCIA: Yes, as far as merit increases are concerned; no, if you're talking about a superior performance bonus. I received my 15 cents an hour increase each year, but so did practically every other member of the NEPS at the university. I have seen, and heard of, many NEPS members whose performances are less than meritorious who never worry about whether or not they will receive a merit increase. I was at a meeting of the NEPS caucus once when a trustee addressed this issue by stating that "Any worker who doesn't get the merit increase has to be in *sad* shape!"

RESEARCHER: Well, if your supervisor was aware of the extra work you were doing, why didn't you get a superior performance bonus?

MARCIA: As I said before, I didn't work with the expectation of receiving one because I had heard that they were few and far between. But I was surprised and very discouraged when I didn't get one after my last annual performance review.

RESEARCHER: It sounds like you really expected one at that point; why?

MARCIA: My review had been exceptional and these bonuses usually come out of favorable annual evaluations.

RESEARCHER: Did your supervisor recommend one?

MARCIA: No, he had had bad experiences getting them approved in the past and very rarely recommends them at all any more. The process is so involved that the immediate supervisors have little control over whether the bonus will ever be awarded.

The supervisor submits a bonus request to his or her superior and, if approved by him or her, it goes on to the provost and Personnel Office. Personnel frequently questions the recommendations, and supervisors are aware of the fact that there are limited funds available for the bonuses. Many supervisors fear that bonus requests will be taken out of tight departmental budgets, which makes them reluctant to recommend them at all.

RESEARCHER: Are there separate funds available for these bonuses, or do they actually come out of departmental budgets?

MARCIA: A certain proportion of the university budget is earmarked for superior performance bonuses; they are never taken out of departmental budgets.

RESEARCHER: Then why is there so much confusion about this?

MARCIA: The Personnel Department is responsible for making this fact clear to the supervisors, but they haven't been very successful in their communication efforts. They've been doing a little better recently, ever since the union activity that went on here a year ago.

RESEARCHER: It sounds like personnel has a lot of power over superior performance bonus awards?

MARCIA: They do, and actually it is good in situations where supervisors recommend bonuses for other than superior performance. I know of one instance when a supervisor recommended a bonus for a staff member who was leaving, whose performance had been average, but who had supported him throughout some hard times and controversial situations. For the majority of cases, I believe that the Personnel Office is too far removed from the actual work situations of the NEPS members to provide a legitimate evaluation of bonus recommendations. If personnel was really involved in the whole system, I think they would have questioned the fact that my supervisor didn't recommend a bonus after seeing my excellent evaluation.

RESEARCHER: I get the impression that your opinion of personnel isn't one of complete admiration.

MARCIA: You're right. I've seen a number of cases in which the most qualified person isn't always the one to get the job. I think that people who work here should be at least interested in education, and not just take the job as a "comfortable retirement" or easy second career. And I've seen a lot of this later type.

A good example of personnel's attitude is evident in a statement made to me by a personnel officer last week during my exit interview: "There is tremendous competition to get on campus, even for the lowest NEPS job. We don't have to worry about filling jobs—we have a waiting line a mile deep. It's not pleasant, but people are going to have to stop worrying about getting promotions, and be happy they have a job here at all."

RESEARCHER: That statement makes it sound like promotions are hard to get. Were you ever considered for a promotion?

MARCIA: Since I have worked here, there haven't been any vacancies at pay grades higher than mine in this department. I have applied for a few other NEPS positions on campus but didn't get any of them.

RESEARCHER: With your good record, that surprises me. What was the problem?

MARCIA: Oh, a number of things. First of all, every job opening is posted through the Personnel Office for all on-campus employees to see, and the employer (supervisor or department head) is obligated to interview all qualified applicants. Even when a supervisor has an employee who is qualified to fill a vacancy within the department, policy and procedures dictate that the supervisor must go through the previously described steps before offering the job to his subordinate. The second problem, most applicable to my experience, is being considered a "temporary employee." Any college-educated NEPS member who is taking courses, regardless of one's future employment intentions, is considered to be a temporary employee. I fit perfectly into this category, because I started taking a course here and there to improve my ability to handle this job.

RESEARCHER: But since you are college-trained and are continuing to learn more, couldn't you apply for a TPS position?

MARCIA: That's the third problem. The attitude around here is "once a NEPS member, always a NEPS member." I talked to my supervisor about this attitude and he confirmed it, saying that, "What is really unfortunate is the feeling on the part of nonexempt staff that they cannot hope to get a professional staff job on this campus. Part of the problem here is, I believe, a misinterpretation of affirmative action guidelines that are so rigidly adhered to that no nonexempt staff member can really hope to get the position. By that I mean the practice of advertising not only locally, but nationally, for professional positions —a practice mandated by AA but one that serves to ignore the MU-espoused policy of "promoting from within." NEPS feel they cannot have these jobs, and unfortunately this is the way it is here."

RESEARCHER: Your supervisor sounds pretty understanding. Have you gotten along well with him?

MARCIA: Oh yes, and for that I feel very fortunate. I realize that he has little control over the problems you and I have been discussing and he has done everything he can to help make my work experience here enjoyable and educational. He has chosen me to attend many university training programs, such as workshops and lectures, and on occasion I have received letters of appreciation for efforts beyond those included in my job description. He has always encouraged us to further our educations by taking advantage of the free courses, and he goes out of his way to recognize extra effort on the part of all staff members. Some supervisors don't encourage taking advantage of the educational benefits as much and are less concerned with the well-being of their staffs, beyond granting the annual merit increases.

RESEARCHER: You just referred to "us" and I don't see many people around here. Do you have much contact with other members of the Student Union staff?

MARCIA: In the four years that I've worked here, I've made a lot of good friends, but all of these people have left and that's one reason I've been unhappy these past few months. There always seemed to be nice people working here. Working with people I get along with and having people to talk to are very important to me. There are about 40 people on the Student Union staff and in the past three years 21 staff members have left. Seven of these people were already taking courses and planned to continue, while six more left to return to school full- or part-time. Our jobs were pretty independent and didn't require a lot of contact with each other, but we worked on projects together occasionally and helped each other out whenever we could.

RESEARCHER: What will you miss the most about the job when you leave, besides the great benefits?

MARCIA: The benefits are nice, but I think I'll just miss working at a school like this. I think that a college education is a very valuable experience, and I've been proud to be a part of this institution. I've loved working with students and I wish that things had worked out better so I could have worked my way up.

RESEARCHER: So you would like to continue working here if a better opportunity came up?

MARCIA: Originally I thought I could work my way up to a managerial position, because I was good, I cared about my job, and I care about the university, but it doesn't work that way here. I think the only way I could get a TPS position is to come back in a few years and try again.

RESEARCHER: Do you think you'll ever do that?

MARCIA: Who knows? After I found out that there was a limit to my upward mobility here, I started to think of this job as an opportunity to gain some experience and learn a few things. I'm ready to see what I'm capable of accomplishing outside of an academic environment.

As I drove home from this interview, I thought about Marcia's situation. She seemed typical of many of the NEPS members at the university, and I suddenly realized that many of NEPS whom I had known as a student were no longer working at the university. It sounds like she certainly has done her job well, and it seems a shame that they are losing her.

Williston University*

WILLISTON UNIVERSITY was located in a large city of an East Coast state. It was founded in the year 1931, and its divisions included schools of arts and sciences (graduate and undergraduate), business administration, social work, and nursing. (See Exhibit 1 for a condensed organization chart of the university.) The enrollment of the University in 1959 was about 7,500 students. This enrollment included students in all divisions and in both the day and evening programs of the university. Eighty percent of the students were residents of the city in which Williston University was located. Most of these students lived at home with family or relatives. Seventy percent of the student body worked either part-or full-time to earn their expenses of education and/or living.

Williston, a private and nonsectarian institution, had as its primary aim that of bringing together teachers and students regardless of race, color, or creed who would participate jointly in the formulation and implementation of the university's educational philosophy and policies. The university founders had as a goal the achievement of a high level of excellence in teaching and research, making available the university's facilities to as many qualified students as possible.

In keeping with the institution's aim of democratic procedures in university government, all decisions on fundamental policies of curriculum and academic standards, conditions of university employment, university finance, etc., required the approval of the university assembly, which was elected by voting members of the faculty from the several departments of the university. The university assembly had 95 members who represented the various departments proportionally. According to the university charter, the appointment of the president and the deans of the various schools required a confirmatory vote by the university assembly.

The board of trustees of Williston University comprised 25 members: ten were businessmen, five were local municipal and state government officials, and the rest were miscellaneous professional people of the community. The president, the academic vice president, and the financial vice president were *ex officio* members of the board.

The administration of the university was responsible for initiating action on the yearly budget. A budget committee was made up of the president, the financial vice president, the academic vice president (responsible for all academic budgets), the dean of students, and four members elected by the faculty from the university assembly. The committee worked in formulating the initial budget, which was submitted to the board of trustees whose responsibility it was to give final

---

*Reprinted by permission. Copyright 1964 by the Institute for College and University Administrators.

EXHIBIT 1
Condensed Organization Chart

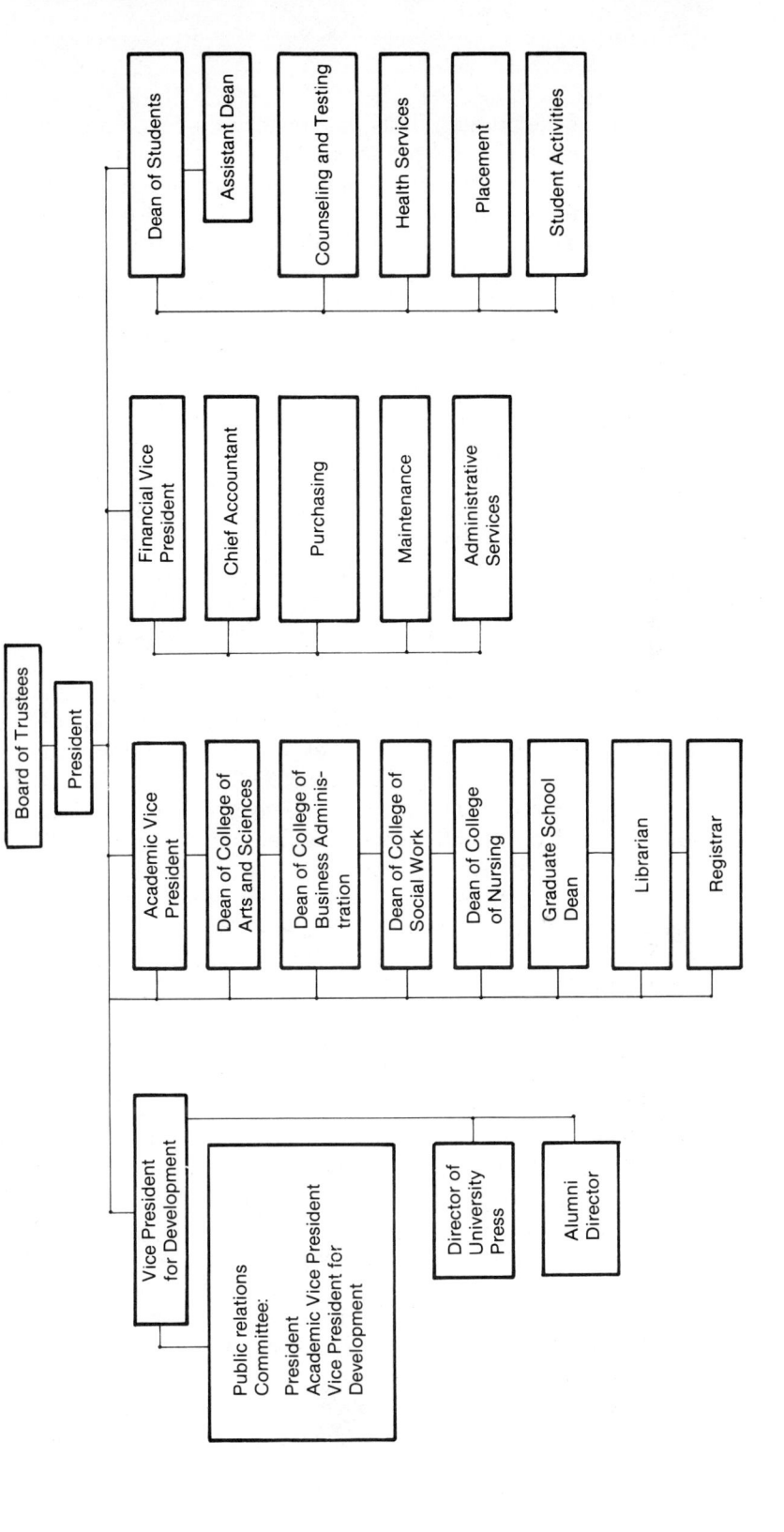

Board of Trustees
President

Vice President for Development
- Public relations Committee:
  President
  Academic Vice President
  Vice President for Development
- Director of University Press
- Alumni Director

Academic Vice President
- Dean of College of Arts and Sciences
- Dean of College of Business Administration
- Dean of College of Social Work
- Dean of College of Nursing
- Graduate School Dean
- Librarian
- Registrar

Financial Vice President
- Chief Accountant
- Purchasing
- Maintenance
- Administrative Services

Dean of Students
- Assistant Dean
- Counseling and Testing
- Health Services
- Placement
- Student Activities

approval of the budget. In its past history the recommendations of the budget committee had been invariably accepted by the board.

The university's financial situation was influenced by the fluctuations of an income whose primary source was the tuition from students. In the recent past, the university had enjoyed its best year in 1949–1950 with an income of almost $3 million. The decrease in enrollment and income in the year 1950–1951 yielded only $2 million. There followed a series of financial hardships. In 1952–1953, the decreased enrollment of students (down to 4,800 from the 1949–1950 high of 9,000 students) produced an income of $2 million; in 1953–1954, the enrollment, then at 4,500 students, produced $2 million; and in 1954–1955, the enrollment of 5,300 students produced an income of $2 million. In these years, annual operating deficits had varied between $7,500 and $90,00 per year. By 1956–1957, the financial position of the university had improved somewhat. Enrollments reached 6,000 students with an annual operating budget of nearly $3 million. The income for these expenditures was provided roughly as follows: 85 percent from tuition and student fees, 3 percent from rental and miscellaneous income, 12 percent from gifts, endowment, and grants.

The assets of the university consisted mainly of 90 percent ownership interest in the university buildings, which were primarily buildings located in the commercial section of the city. In addition, the university had an endowment fund of about $500,000.

The university was founded in the years of the depression's depths, and the faculty at that time had accepted very low salaries. Subsequently, faculty salary increases never fully compensated for this initial low start. By 1946–1947, median salaries were as follows: instructor, $3,600 per year; assistant professor, $4,000; associate professor, $4,500; professor, $5,100. In 1956–1957, the median salaries had risen to: instructor, $5,000; assistant professor, $5,800; associate professor, $6,800; and full professor, $7,800.

The average teaching load for a full-time faculty member was 15 class hours a semester. In practice, for at least half or more of the faculty, this load was increased by at least another three to five class contact hours in "over-load teaching" at the home institution or in one of the extension locations. Teaching these extra hours was necessary to supplement the income of the faculty to meet the necessities of life for themselves and for their families. The need for extra income was aggravated by the high cost of living in the urban area where the university was located. A faculty member was paid from $1,000 to $1,200 a year for this extra work.

In its earliest days, the university had insisted that the faculty establish and maintain relatively high standards for the students in both admissions and academic performance. Owing to subsequent financial pressure, the university had been unable to maintain admissions and probations standards as high as the faculty felt it should. The consensus of the faculty was that too much counseling and faculty time was being spent on the lowest one third of the students who were not equipped by ability or preparation to do college work.

The regional accrediting association had extended accreditation to the new institution in the 1930s on the basis of the qualifications of its faculty and the soundness of its academic programs. Recently, however, the association was disturbed by Williston's weak financial position and had made extended accreditation conditional upon active reporting to the association of the university's financial position. Despite the recurring operating deficits, the regional accrediting association had regularly extended accreditation for several successive years.

In September of 1956 Josiah Martin joined the university as the new academic vice president. His predecessor, who had been on the job for nine years, had left the university to assume an executive position with a large educational foundation. Martin's specific tasks, as he was given to understand them by the president, were to raise academic standards, strengthen the teaching staff, and improve the quality of the teaching program of the university.

The new academic vice president, who had previously served as a professor of English and as an academic dean of a small liberal arts college, arrived on his new job with many hopes and plans for improving education at Williston. He soon saw that few of his ideas had any relevance to the situation with which he was confronted. He recognized almost immediately that there were many basic financial and "housekeeping" problems that had to be solved before even a modest beginning could be made on the schemes he had for faculty development and for improving student-body quality.

In November 1956, at one of his first deans' conferences to which the financial vice president had been invited, Dr. Martin presented and supported the request of the chairman of a science department who wished to approach a national science foundation for aid in securing fundamental scientific equipment. The chairman's proposal stated that this equipment might be the basis for developing more interest in research among the students at the senior and graduate levels. The proposal was opposed by the financial vice president, Herbert Stander, and two of the deans on the ground that Williston University was a teaching and not a research institution. The opponents felt that the encouragement of faculty and student research interests was too expensive for the institution, and that neighboring major graduate institutions would oppose this competitive development when Williston University came up again for regional accrediting. Under the force of these arguments, Mr. Martin felt it prudent to yield at that time to this opposition.

After some months on his new job, the academic vice president concluded that simultaneous efforts for improvement had to be made on several fronts: *(a)* reduction of teaching loads (to give the faculty more time for revision and development of course work, planning of special programs, professional study and research): *(b)* salary increases (to retain good teachers, to obtain qualified replacements for those faculty members who were retiring, and to add to the faculty in a time of increasing competitive conditions); *(c)* raising of student admissions and scholastic standards; and *(d)* promotion of larger scholarship funds (to attract better students on one hand; on the other, to discourage the lower one third of the totally unqualified student body, on whom a disproportionate amount of the university's resources were being spent in largely ineffective counseling and remedial work).

Shortly after, in December 1956, Dr. Martin, at a university assembly meeting, proposed that the standards for entrance examinations should be raised 15 percentiles on the entrance examination scores. In addition, Dr. Martin proposed adding a requirement of a qualifying score on a reading test and refusing applicants from other institutions with D's or low-passing grades in freshman English on transcripts. His proposals were approved in principle by the university assembly after strong opposition from the financial vice president, Mr. Stander, who maintained that they comprised "too large a step at one time" from the financial standpoint, and who urged going only 10 percentiles higher as a minimum for admissions. The authority to set admissions requirements had always rested with the faculty. However, the university assembly gave to the academic vice president the authority to raise, at his discretion, the standards "by stages" to the percentile he desired.

Also, in December, Dr. Martin introduced to the president's council (which was composed of the president, the vice president for development, the financial vice president, the academic vice president, all deans, and the librarian) a proposal to reduce the teaching loads of faculty members to 12 hours for a regular semester, or 24 hours annually.

Prior to making his proposal to the council, Dr. Martin had obtained the approval of his deans in this matter. At the council meeting, he argued that 15 hours of classes per week on a teaching basis was a schedule excessive in terms of national norms. Dr. Martin felt that the university would benefit in terms of improved teaching and that more time would be available for faculty contributions to improvement in curriculum and other university services. Also, he hoped that the free time of the faculty would be applied to research and other projects of a professional nature.

The opposition, headed by the president and Mr. Stander, argued that given the release from class time, the majority of the faculty, in view of the low salaries they received at Williston University, would only devote more time to outside teaching, consultative work, and other activities that would yield them additional income. The majority of the council, however, seemed prepared to grant the reduction in teaching load if the faculty was prepared to take this reduced load in lieu of salary increases. Dr. Martin was not willing to sacrifice the possibility of raising faculty salaries, and in light of the attitude of the members of the council at that time he withdrew his proposal.

During the same month, prior to the opening of the annual sessions of the budget committee (the budget committee sessions usually began in February of the academic year), Dr. Martin encouraged department chairmen to add to their department budgets estimates of the costs of certain specific facilities regarded as necessary for the improvement of their teaching programs. For example, in the Department of Fine Arts, the chairman had described to him the department's need of certain visual-aid equipment and of a library of colored slides. In zoology, the department chairman had proposed the reequipment of a laboratory. In physics and chemistry, the addition of certain fundamental pieces of equipment was requested. In the Sociology Department it was recommended that another teacher be added to the faculty. The Political Science Department chairman had recommended that funds be provided to enable distinguished foreign visitors to give special lecture courses and seminars.

When the budget committee sessions opened in February, Dr. Martin took the opportunity to reopen the question of the reduction of the teaching load of faculty members. The faculty representatives were enthusiastic in their acceptance of the proposal; they insisted, however, that such action should in no way take the place of salary increases, and that these increases should be provided above and beyond the teaching load question and were to be regarded as a long overdue measure to bring the university's salaries into line with those of other comparable schools.

For a period of about five weeks, there were usually one or two sessions a week of the budget committee before the proposed budget was submitted to the trustees. As the budget sessions proceeded, however, Dr. Martin observed that the faculty members of the committee were joining with the financial vice president in a determined effort to reduce the amount of new expenditures for facilities and staff in the academic departments. Dr. Martin surmised, however, that the faculty representatives were not motivated, as was Mr. Stander, by a wish for general economy but rather by a desire to maximize that share of the projected university income that would be available for salary increases. The proposals for funds for fine arts equipment, for science laboratories equipment, for addition of new personnel, and for visiting professors were defeated, one by one.

As the series of budget meetings drew to a close, a surplus of $224,000 of anticipated income over anticipated expenditures developed in the proposed budget for 1957–58. (See Exhibit 2 for the budget of 1956–57 and the proposed budget for 1957–58.) The faculty members of the committee immediately proposed that $200,000 of this surplus be devoted entirely to the improvement of salaries of the teaching and administrative members of the university. This salary increase, they pointed out, would result in an average raise of $1,000 per year for the whole body of the university's faculty and administrative staff. They argued that the faculty and staff had subsidized the university's program and had made the university's survival possible in the early days through their acceptance of abnormally low salaries. Instances were cited of faculty members' mortgaging their homes in depression years to provide needed funds to the university. They stated that the university's finances were somewhat more secure now and that they felt entitled to claim an improvement of their own positions, particularly in light of the high cost of living in their urban community and the relatively low level of the university salary scale in comparison with that of other local educational institutions. They argued, also, that the university would be the loser in the long run if it did not put itself in a position to meet competition for qualified university teachers who were then in short supply, particularly in the sciences, technical areas, psychology, and mathematics.

Dr. Martin strongly supported the faculty stand, although he regretted that the majority of the decisions of the committee precluded a more balanced approach to the the several academic needs confronting the university.

The president and the financial vice president, although expressing the greatest personal sympathy with the needs of the faculty, deplored the "excessive" nature of their demands. Said the president: "No one appreciates better than I the sacrifice you have made in the past, but I feel obliged to point out that the accreditation of this institution is still in jeopardy. The accrediting agency has noted with some concern the operating deficit which resulted from last year's academic operations. I plead with the committee to limit faculty and staff increases so that at least half of the anticipated surplus can be written into the budget as uncommitted surplus funds. This will give the university a better chance of producing a balanced budget for the next year to report to the accrediting agency."

The president and the financial vice president went on to warn that the rise of admissions standards would have effects on enrollments and income that could not be predicted precisely. They cited the estimates of the local board of education showing a leveling off of numbers of high school and junior college graduates in the next three years before the expected nationwide rise of the college student population.

Dr. Martin replied to these arguments by pointing to the fact that

EXHIBIT 2
Budgets ($000)

		Actual 1956–57		Proposed 1957–58
Income				
Student fees and tuition		$2,490.00		$2,823.6
Rental incomes and co-op store		79.05		81.0
Gifts and endowment		387.00		406.5
Total income		$2,956.05		$3,311.1
Expenses:				
University administration		$ 428.40		$ 443.7
Student services		226.05		228.0
Instructional:				
Grading assistants, research, publications		$ 77.55		$ 84.8
College of Arts and Sciences				
Administration	$126.15		$131.4	
Biology	53.40		53.6	
Chemistry	65.55		68.0	
Economics	51.45		41.7	
Education	110.25		120.5	
English	121.35		128.4	
History	42.90		46.4	
Mathematics	37.05		40.2	
Modern languages	59.70		63.3	
Philosophy	43.80		44.9	
Physical Sciences	10.50		11.6	
Physics	22.20		22.5	
Political science	53.10		46.8	
Psychology	68.70		67.1	
Sociology	41.10		41.4	
Total arts and science expense		907.20		927.8
College of Business Administration		197.25		226.7
College of Social Work		324.90		340.8
College of Nursing		43.95		48.1
Total instructional expense		1,550.85*		1,628.2*
Library		178.80		181.6
Buildings, operation and maintenance		372.60		375.8
Development, debt retirement, interest expense		236.40		208.2
Total expenses		2,993.10		3,065.5
Contingency fund		13.80		21.2
Unallocated revenue and surplus		(50.85)†		224.4‡
Total expenses and surplus		$2,956.05		$3,311.1

  *The total expenditures for these colleges included about 1½ percent for supplies and equipment for the various schools and departments.
  †Deficit.
  ‡Includes $200.0 proposed for faculty salary increase fund.

although for the past two or three years the numbers of high school and junior college graduates had remained stationary, college enrollments had shown a general increase, which suggested that a greater proportion of such graduates than ever before were applying for college admissions. In his opinion the estimate in the budget of income from tuition would probably be on the low rather than on the high side. The budget, including the salary increase fund of $200,000, was carried by the committee. Mr. Stander voted no, and the president abstained.

At the April 1957 meeting of the board of trustees, the budget, as approved by the budget committee, was presented. It immediately came under strong attack from members of the board for the extraordinarily large increase in salaries provided for the faculty. Some members of the board felt that there were other needs of the institution equally pressing, such as classroom and laboratory equipment, the redecoration and maintenance of old and deteriorating university buildings, and the improvement of recreation and other facilities for students. Many of the members of the board were sympathetic to the disadvantageous position of the teachers and other members of the university staff, but they felt that on a $3,300,000 budget, and expected surplus of only $24,000, or less than 1 percent, was "quite inadequate." Said one member of the board, "None of us would run our businesses on such a basis."

Mr. Stander made a strong statement in which he employed the arguments already used in the budget committee and ended by referring to the overriding necessity of maintaining the university's good standing with the regional accrediting association. At the end of the meeting, the trustees voted by a majority of three to one to reduce the funds for salary increases by half. The remainder of the excess was to be kept in the surplus account.

At the beginning of the following academic year (1957–58), Dr. Martin, knowing that the chairmen of the departments of physics and mathematics would retire at the end of that year, began investigating the possibilities for replacements. In neither department were there, in his judgment, members of the existing staff sufficiently strong to fill these vacancies. In each case, however, recruiting efforts through attendance at professional meetings, advertising, and personal contacts proved fruitless. No qualified candidates for the jobs as department chairmen were prepared to accept the positions at the highest salary then available on the scale, $9,000, particularly since these departments carried a standard teaching load of 15 class contact hours per week. The candidates thought that the teaching loads of the faculty were too large. A department chairman usually taught 12 hours per term.

In spite of the rise in standards of admissions and scholastic probation, the university's enrollment in 1957–58 exceeded by 450 students the figure anticipated by the budget committee. The public response to the university's appeal for funds improved considerably. At midyear the financial vice president felt safe in predicting a surplus of $180,000, and this was reported to the accrediting agency. The accrediting agency replied that it took note of the university's financial position with satisfaction but again asked for a further report next year. At the end of the academic year Dr. Martin noticed that the financial vice president's report showed an actual surplus of $160,000.

As of the end of the academic year Dr. Martin had no successors for his retiring chairmen in the mathematics and physics departments. The essential facilities that he had proposed for many departmental programs had not been provided. Student enrollment had increased and the enlarged enrollment was exerting further pressure on existing inadequate facilities and staff. The accrediting agency had not given Williston University a complete approval of its financial situation. Dr. Martin, in reviewing his own behavior in these matters, was appraising his actions and raised questions as to what he should do next.

INDEX

A
Achievement needs, 121
Adams, J. S., 140
Adirondack Preservation Council, Case of, 332–38
Administrative Decision, Case of, 304–6
Affiliation needs, 121
Allen, Louis, 101
American Civil Liberties Union (ACLU), 17
Associated Insurance Services, Inc., Case of, 306–15
Attraction, 136–37
 determinants of, 138–40

B
Banks, line control at, 159–60
Behavioral barriers, of decision making, 214–17
Blair, Inc. (1), Case of, 315–26
Body language, role of, in communication, 104
Bottom line, 185
Brainstorming, 207, 226
Bureaucracy, definition of, 50
Bureaucratic model of organization, 50, 52
 authority, 52–53
 departmentation, 58–60
 horizontal divisions of labor in, 57–58
 implications of, 60–61
 line and staff functions, 55–57
 responsibility, 52–53
 span of control, 53–55
 vertical divisions of labor in, 57–58
Burns, Tom, 64, 76

C
Career paths, 253
Carter, Jimmy, 99
Change
 predictability of, as dynamic attribute, 283–84
 rate of, as dynamic attribute, 283
Chase Manhattan Bank, 242
Chris Hammond (A), Case of, 338–47
Chris Hammond (B), Case of, 348–59

Chrysler Corporation, 280
Classical model of organization, basis of, 69
Climate; see Organizational climate
Collaborative behavior, promotion of, 115–7
Colleague organizational model, 69
Collegial model, 78, 79
 of organizational structure, 76
Communication, effect of, on organizational climate, 100–101
Communication style, 104
Composite index, development of, to evaluate decision choices, 209
Computer industry, influences of surrounding culture on, 74–75
Concurrent control, 160
Conference at Miniatronics, Case of, 359–376
Conflict at a Research and Development Laboratory, Case of, 376–383
Control(s), 9
 definition of, 158–59
 effect of dynamic attributes on, 289
 and human resources development, 250
 and performance appraisal, 258
 self, 180–82
 social, 182–83
 sources of, 178–87
 supervisory, 179–80
 system, 183–87
 timing of, 160–61
Control system(s)
 assessment and design of, 187–90
 definition of, 160
 and organizational climate, 186
 and organizational goals, 185–86
 and organizational structure, 186
 purposes of, 9, 161–78
 and rewards, 186
Corning Glass, 242
Corps of Engineers, 274, 282–83
Cost accounting, 175–76
Costs, control over, 175–76
Critical path method (CPM), 173 n, 174
Cross-function communication, 101
Culture, of organization, 73–74

D

Davis, Stanley, 85
Decision making, 9–10, 198–200
　applicability of rational approach, 212–14
　behavioral barriers to, 214–17
　data gathering as repeated step, 211–12
　dealing with indecision and barriers to, 218–20
　　developing scenarios, 219
　　exaggerating the issues, 219-20
　effect of dynamic attributes on, 289
　emotional barriers to, 217–18
　group, 224, 226
　and human resources development, 250–51
　individual versus group, 220–24
　organization in, 226–29
　and performance appraisal, 258
　phases of, 199, 200–2
　　choice, 208–10
　　developing solutions, 207
　　evaluating solutions, 207–8
　　goal setting, 204, 206–7
　　implementation, 210–11
　　outcome and process evaluation, 211
　　problem definition, 203–4
　　problem discovery, 202–3
Decision at Zenith Life, Case of, 383–412
Delegated decision making, 222
Delphi technique, 227
Departmentation, role of, in bureaucratic model of organizational structure, 58–60
Derived goals, 25
Devon School, Case of, 430–43
Differentiation, as basic organizational process, 46–47, 50
Digital Equipment Corporation, 59
Design and Delivery: The Dilemma at Eleanor Roosevelt, Case of, 412–30
Distributive justice, 19 n
Dominion Acceptance Company, Ltd., Case of, 443–51
Dress, as clue to organizational climate, 104
Drucker, Peter, 36
Dynamic attributes of environment, 283–84
　impact of, 288–90

E

Eastman Kodak, 131
Effectiveness, evaluation of, 17, 18
Efficiency, evaluation of, 17, 18
Emotional barriers, of decision making, 217–18
Employee, determinants of effort/performance of, 136–37
Employee demeanor, as clue to organizational climate, 105
Employee group, nature of, and effect on design of reward system, 147–48
Entrepreneur, 133–34
Environment, 270–71

Environment—*Cont.*
　dynamic attributes, 283–84
　　impact of, 288–90
　economic, 271–72
　external physical, 276–78
　political/legal, 273, 275
　social/cultural, 275–76
　static attributes, 278–83
　　impact of, 284–88
　technological, 272–73
Environmental complexity, 278–79
Environmental interconnectedness, 280–81
Environmental Protection Agency, 274
Environmental remoteness, 281–83
Environmental routineness, 279–80
Equal Employment Opportunity Commission, 274
Equal Rights Amendment, 275
Equity theory, 140
Esteem needs, 121–22
Eunice MacGillicudy/Marcus Warren, Case of, 451–53
Evolution in the Mailroom, Case of, 454–58
Expectancy, 136–37
　determinants of, 138–40
Expectancy theory, 138
Explicit goals, 38–39
External context, of departmentation, 59–60
External demands, nature of, on organization, 72–73
External influences, 11–13
Extertise
　levels of, involved in organizational structure, 68–69
　life of, involved in organizational, 69–71
Exxon Oil, 238

F

Fate of the Underwriters, Case of, 458–64
Federal Communications Commission (FCC), 274
Federal Reserve Board, 274
Federal Trade Commission (FTC), 274
Flow scheduling, control of, 172–75
Food and Drug Administration, 274
Ford Motor Company, 280
Free-form organizational model, 69
Fujitsu, Ltd., 282
Fujiyama Trading Co., Ltd., Case of, 464–73

G

Galbraith, Jay, 65–66, 126
General Electric, 59, 238, 242
General goals
　advantages and disadvantages of, 33
　versus specific goals, 31–34
General Motors, 280
General system rewards, 128–29
Genrad, Inc., Case of, 473–88
Geographic location
　effect of, on organization, 276

Geographic location—*Cont.*
  impact of, on organizational climate, 97
Goals; *see* Organizational goals
Goodrich, B. F., Co., 287
Gore, W. L., 69
Group, as decision maker, 224, 226
Groupthink, 226

H

Hampton Shipyard, Case of, 489–98
Hawthorne studies, 65, 182
Herzberg, Frederick, 124–26, 128, 129, 132
Heublein, 242
Hierarchy of needs theory, 118–19
  comparison of with two-factor theory, 125–26
  esteem needs, 121–22
  love and belongingness needs, 120–21
  physiological needs, 119
  safety needs, 119–20
  self-actualization needs, 122–23
  significance of, 123–24
High-disclosing (Hi D) organization, 100
High-priority goals, versus low-priority goals, 36–38
Highland College Student Affairs Division, Case of, 498–507
Hillcrest Commercial Bank, Case of, 508–19
Hiring, 247–51
Horizontal division of labor, role of, in bureaucratic model of organizational structure, 57–58
Hovey and Beard Co., Case of, 519–23
Human motivation
  Harzberg's two-factor theory of, 124–26
  knowledge of human needs and, 117–18
  Maslow's hierarchy of needs, 118–26
Human relations movement, 64, 65, 75–76
Human resources development (HRD), 11, 238
  career paths, 253
  and controls, 250
  and decision making, 250–51
  effect of dynamic attributes on, 289
  hiring, 247–51
  individual responsibility and development, 246–47
  management succession planning, 254–55
  mentoring, 254
  and organizational climate, 249
  and organizational goals, 248
  and organizational structure, 249
  performance appraisal, 255–56
    guidelines for effective, 259
    process of, 259–60
    specific purposes of
      for the employee, 257–58
      for the manager, 256–57
      for the organization, 258–59
  planning for, 238–40

Human resources development (HRD)—*Cont.*
  job, 245–46
  strategic, 240, 242–43
  work force, 243–45
  recruiting, 247–51
  and rewards, 249–50
  selection, 247–51
  training and development, 251–54
Human resources planning, 238–40
  job, 245–46
  key elements in, 239
  strategic, 240, 242–43
  work force, 243, 245
Hygiene factors, 125, 126
  role of, in design of reward system, 148

I

IBM, 59, 238
Ideal bureaucracy, 49, 51, 116
Implicit goals, 38–39
Incentive pay systems, 129
Individual rewards, 129–30, 135–46
Information
  gathering of, for decision making, 211–12
  relevance of, to organizational structure, 67–68
Integration, as basic organizational process, 46–47, 50
Internal departmentation, 59
Internalized organizational values, 131–32
Intrinsic satisfactions, 130
Introducing New Appliance Model, Case of, 524–27
Inventory control system, 172
Is there a Better Way, Case of, 527–29

J-K

Janis, Irving, 226
Japan
  influence of culture of, on organizational structure of, 75
  organizational climate in, 107–8
Job enrichment, and group decision making, 221
Job planning, 245–46
Job security, concern over, 120
Katz, Daniel, 126
Kennecott Copper, 279
Knoll, Chuck, 238, 240

L

Lattice organization, 69
Lawrence, Paul, 47, 50, 64, 85
Lewis Equipment Company, Case of, 529–43
Liberty Mutual Insurance Co., 248
Likert, Rensis, 64, 77
Line and staff functions, role of, in bureaucratic model of organizational structure, 55–57
Linking-pin model, 76, 77
Long-term goals, versus short-term goals, 34

Lorsch, Jay, 47, 50, 64
Love needs, 120–21
Low-disclosing (Low D) organization, 100
Low-priority goals, versus high-priority goals, 36–38

M

Mailorder Merchandise, Inc., Case of, 544–45
Management by objectives (MBO) approach, 35, 36
Management succession planning, 254–55
Manpower planning, 239
March of Dimes, 18
March, James C., 215
Maslow, 128, 129, 132
Maslow, Abraham, 118–26, 128, 129, 132
Material requirements planning (MRP), 172–73
Matrix model, of organizational structure, 76, 77, 78–79, 81–83
Mayfield Medical Center, Case of, 545–48
Mayo, Elton, 65
McClelland, David, 121
McDonald's, 105
McMaster-Barry Communications, Inc. (MBCI), Case of, 558–68
Means-end chain of goals, 22–24, 32, 35, 40
Meetings, communication style of, 104
Memos, as clue to organizational climate, 104
Mentoring, 254
Merger Talks at Canal and Lake, Case of, 548–58
Missing Time, Case of, 326–31
Montville Hospital Dietary Department, Case of, 568–75
Moonlighting, 190
Motivation, as control system, 9
Multinational corporations, influences of surrounding culture on, 74–75

N

NASA, 242
National Football League, 238
National Labor Relations Board, 274
Natural model, of organizational goal setting, 25, 27, 29, 30
Nominal group, 227
Norms
 effect of, on organizational climate, 98–100
 role of, in determining individual behavior, 142
 role of, in determining organizational climate, 100
Norms, census, 104

O

Occupational Safety and Health Administration, 274
Omega Aerospace Corporation, Case of, 576–87
Open system model, of organizational goal setting, 26, 28, 30
Open systems planning, 240 n, 291–92
 creating strategic plan, 294–95
 defining mission, 292
 envisioning future, 292–93
 identifying critical key results and checkpoints, 295-96
 operationalizing mission, 293
Operations management (OM), 172
Opportunities at Mid-State University, Case of, 588–90
Organization(s)
 as decision maker, 226–29
 dynamic attributes of environment
  impact of, 288–90
  predictability of change, 283–84
  rate of change, 283
 environment of; see Environment
 as institutions, 164–66
 planning for future, 290–96
Organizational charts, 62–63
Organizational climate, 7–8
 changing of, 106–8
 consequences of, 105–6
 and control systems, 186
 diagnosis of, 103–5
 dimensions of, 101–3
 effect of communication patterns on, 100–101
 effect of dynamic attributes on, 289
 effect of organization norms on, 98–100
 and geographic location, 97
 and human resources development, 249
 impact of organization size on, 96–97
 impact of rewards on, 95–96
 and organizational goals, 94
 and organizational structure, 73–75, 95
 and performance appraisal, 258
 and physical setting, 97–98
 potential impact of, 7–8
Organizational context, rewards in, 140–44
Organizational goals, 6
 categories of, 24–27
  as aid to diagnosis, 27–31
 conflict in, 27–31, 35
 and control systems, 185–86
 definition of, 16
 dimensions of, 31
  explicit versus implicit, 38–39
  general versus specific, 31–34
  high-priority versus low-priority, 36–38
  long-term versus short-term, 34
  overview of, 39–40
  total-system versus sub-system, 34–36
 effect of dynamic attributes on, 289
 effect of, on organizational climate, 94
 and human resources development, 248
 implication of structure for, 60–61

Organizational goals—Cont.
  importance of, to organization, 16–17
  matching resources to, 65–66
  means-end chain of, 22–24
  overarching social values, 19, 21–22
  and performance appraisal, 258
  relationship of decision making to, 206
  role of, in design of reward system, 146–47
  superordinate goals and values in, 17–19
Organizational life, dimensions of, 4–13
Organizational size, impact of, on organizational climate, 96–97
Organizational structure, 6–7
  bureaucratic model of, 50, 52–61
  classical forms of, 48–50
  contribution of, to organizational climate, 95
  and control systems, 186
  and decision making, 228–29
  definition of, 7, 46
  distinction between organic and mechanistic, 75, 76
  effect of dynamic attributes on, 289
  emergence of modern, 62–75
  formality of, 61–62
  function of, 46–48
  and human resources development, 249
  implication of goals for, 60–61
  and performance appraisal, 258
  variables relevant to, 66–75
Organizational values
  dimensions of, 21
  internalization of, 131–32
Output goals, 25
Overcontrol, 188–89

P

Past, role of, in planning of future, 271
Perfectionism, role of, in decision making, 217–18
Performance, role of reward system in encouraging dependable, 115
Performance appraisal, 11, 255–56
  guidelines for effective, 259
  process of, 259–60
  specific purposes of
    for the employee, 257–58
    for the manager, 256–57
    for the organization, 258–59
Perrow, Charles, 24, 25
PERT (program evaluation and review technique), 173, 174
Physical setting, impact of, on organizational climate, 97–98
Physiological needs, 119
Pittsburgh Steelers, 238
Polaroid, 131
Postcontrol, 160
  consequences of, 161
Power, bases of organizational, 188

Power needs, 121
Precontrol, 160
Prime Computer, 242
Problem statement, guidelines for writing, 205
Proctor & Gamble, 104
Product goals, 25
Project team model, of organizational structure, 76, 78
Promotion in Sri Lanka, Case of, 590–97
Public welfare, 18
Pyramid type of organization, 48

Q-R

Quality
  conflict between quantity and, 27
  control of, 168–70
Quality circles, 170
Quality of work life movement, 70
Quantity
  conflict between quality and, 27
  control of, 167–68
Rational model, 27, 29, 30
  applicability of, to decision making, 212–14
  of organizational goal setting, 25
Recruitment, 247–51
Responsibility, role of, in bureaucratic model of organizational structure, 52–53
Reward system(s)
  changes in, and organizational climate, 108
  definition of, 8, 114
  design of, 146–49
  and human motivation, 117–26
  perceptions of, 139–40
  purposes served by, 114–17
Reward(s)
  and control systems, 186–87
  definition of, 8, 114
  effect of dynamic attributes on, 289
  general system, 128–29
  and human resources development, 249–50
  individual, 129–30
  and internalized organizational values, 131–32
  impact of, on organizational climate, 95–96
  and the individual, 135–46
  intrinsic satisfaction in, 130
  nature of, 126–34
  and performance appraisal, 258
  and rule compliance, 127–28
  and social satisfaction, 132–33
Roles, negotiation and renegotiation of, 162–64
Rule compliance, 127–28

S

Saab, 122
Safety, establishment of standards in, 176–78
Safety needs, 119–20
Sanctions, use of, 184
Scenarios, development of, in decision mak-

Scenarios—*Cont.*
  ing, 219
Scientific management, 49, 51, 116
Scott, Richard, 25
Seacoast Mutual Insurance Co., Case of, 597–602
Securities and Exchange Commission, 274
Security, establishment of standards in, 176–78
Selection, of personnel, 247–51
Self-actualization needs, 122–23
Self-control, 180–82
Sensing, 107 n
Shared decision making, 120, 221, 222
Shartie, C. L., 21
Shelf life, 177
Short-term goals, versus long-term goals, 34
Sierra Club, 94
Simon, Herbert A., 214, 215
Skinner, Wickham, 273
Social control, 182–83
Social satisfaction, 132–33
Social values, overarching, 19, 22–22
Societal goals, 25
Sociotechnical systems (STS), 70
Sohio, 279
Southeast Municipal Association, Case of, 603–8
Span of control, role of, in bureaucratic model of organizational structure, 53–55
Specific goals
  advantages and disadvantages of, 33
  versus general goals, 31–34
Stalker, G. M., 64, 76
Standard operating procedures (SOPs), 183–85
Standards, control of deviations from, 166–78
Static attributes of environment, 278–83
  impact of, 274–88
Steele, F., 100
Steinbrenner, George, 238, 240
Strategic planning, 240, 242–43
Structure; *see* Organizational structure
Suboptimization, 35 n
Sub-system goals, versus total-system goals, 34–36
Superordinate goals/values, 17–19, 20, 21
Supervisory control, 179–80
Survival, as superordinate goal, 17
System control, 183–87
System goals, 25

T

Task differentiation/integration, degree of, as aspect of organizational structure, 71–72
Task groups, 182
Task roles, control of required, 162–64
Task-group development, 120
Tavistock Institute of Human Relations, 70
Taylor, Frederick, 49, 51

Techni-Cal, Inc., Case of, 608–16
Technology
  impact of, on organization, 273
  response of public policy to, 272
Texas Instruments, 242
Thompson, Victor A., 64
Time and motion studies, 168
Time horizon, 295
Time out, concept of, 170
Total-system, versus sub-system goals, 34–36
Training and development, of personnel, 251–54
Tucker automobile, 281
Two-factor theory, 124–25
  comparison of with hierarchy of needs theory, 125–26

U-V

Unilateral decision making, 221, 222
Union(s)
  goals of, versus those of management, 38
  standards of, versus management, 167
United Auto Workers Union (UAW), 38 n, 280
Values, major orientations of, in America, 20
Vertical division of labor, role of, in bureaucratic model of organizational structure, 57–58
Volvo, 122
Vroom, Victor, 138, 221–24, 225

W

Weber, Max, 49, 51
Why Play Football, Case of, 616–24
Williams, Robin M., 20
Williston University, Case of, 632–41
Woodward, Joan, 64
Work force planning, 243, 245
Work teams, 120, 122
Working for the Old Alma Mater, Case of, 624–31